Communications in Computer and Information Science   2862

Series Editors

Gang Li, *School of Information Technology, Deakin University, Burwood, VIC, Australia*

Joaquim Filipe, *Polytechnic Institute of Setúbal, Setúbal, Portugal*

Zhiwei Xu, *Chinese Academy of Sciences, Beijing, China*

Rationale

The CCIS series is devoted to the publication of proceedings of computer science conferences. Its aim is to efficiently disseminate original research results in informatics in printed and electronic form. While the focus is on publication of peer-reviewed full papers presenting mature work, inclusion of reviewed short papers reporting on work in progress is welcome, too. Besides globally relevant meetings with internationally representative program committees guaranteeing a strict peer-reviewing and paper selection process, conferences run by societies or of high regional or national relevance are also considered for publication.

Topics

The topical scope of CCIS spans the entire spectrum of informatics ranging from foundational topics in the theory of computing to information and communications science and technology and a broad variety of interdisciplinary application fields.

Information for Volume Editors and Authors

Publication in CCIS is free of charge. No royalties are paid, however, we offer registered conference participants temporary free access to the online version of the conference proceedings on SpringerLink (http://link.springer.com) by means of an http referrer from the conference website and/or a number of complimentary printed copies, as specified in the official acceptance email of the event.

CCIS proceedings can be published in time for distribution at conferences or as post-proceedings, and delivered in the form of printed books and/or electronically as USBs and/or e-content licenses for accessing proceedings at SpringerLink. Furthermore, CCIS proceedings are included in the CCIS electronic book series hosted in the SpringerLink digital library at http://link.springer.com/bookseries/7899. Conferences publishing in CCIS are allowed to use our online conference service (Meteor) for managing the whole proceedings lifecycle (from submission and reviewing to preparing for publication) free of charge.

Publication process

The language of publication is exclusively English. Authors publishing in CCIS have to sign the Springer CCIS copyright transfer form, however, they are free to use their material published in CCIS for substantially changed, more elaborate subsequent publications elsewhere. For the preparation of the camera-ready papers/files, authors have to strictly adhere to the Springer CCIS Authors' Instructions and are strongly encouraged to use the CCIS LaTeX style files or templates.

Abstracting/Indexing

CCIS is abstracted/indexed in DBLP, Google Scholar, EI-Compendex, Mathematical Reviews, SCImago, Scopus. CCIS volumes are also submitted for the inclusion in ISI Proceedings.

How to start

To start the evaluation of your proposal for inclusion in the CCIS series, please send an e-mail to ccis@springer.com

Kartick Chandra Mondal ·
Munmun Bhattacharya · Parama Bhaumik ·
Somnath Mukhopadhyay · Jyotsna K. Mandal ·
Paramartha Dutta

Editors

Computational Intelligence in Communications and Business Analytics

7th International Conference, CICBA 2025
Kolkata, India, July 4–6, 2025
Revised Selected Papers, Part II

Springer

Editors
Kartick Chandra Mondal
SRM University
Amaravati, Andhra Pradesh, India

Parama Bhaumik
Jadavpur University
Kolkata, West Bengal, India

Jyotsna K. Mandal
University of Kalyani
Kalyani, West Bengal, India

Munmun Bhattacharya
Jadavpur University
Kolkata, West Bengal, India

Somnath Mukhopadhyay
Assam University
Silchar, Assam, India

Paramartha Dutta
Visva-Bharati University
Bolpur, West Bengal, India

ISSN 1865-0929   ISSN 1865-0937 (electronic)
Communications in Computer and Information Science
ISBN 978-3-032-17186-3   ISBN 978-3-032-17187-0 (eBook)
https://doi.org/10.1007/978-3-032-17187-0

This Springer imprint is published by the registered company Springer Nature Switzerland AG
The registered company address is: Gewerbestrasse 11, 6330 Cham, Switzerland

If disposing of this product, please recycle the paper.

Preface

It is our great pleasure to present the proceedings of the Seventh International Conference on Computational Intelligence in Communications and Business Analytics (CICBA 2025), held at the Department of Information Technology, Jadavpur University, India, from 4–6 July 2025 in hybrid mode.

Since its inception, CICBA has established itself as a premier forum at the intersection of computational intelligence, communications, and business analytics, fostering collaboration between academia and industry across the globe. CICBA 2025 continued this tradition by providing a vibrant platform for sharing novel research findings, experiences, and innovations from both theoretical and applied perspectives.

We were honored to host several distinguished keynote speakers, each a noted expert in their respective domains: Dilip Kumar Pratihar (IIT Kharagpur), Narayan C. Debnath (Eastern International University, Vietnam), Anirban Chakraborty (Indian Institute of Science, Bangalore), Ankur Sinha (Indian Institute of Management, Ahmedabad), Niladri Roy (TCS), and Deepankar Choudhury (IIT Bombay). Their insightful talks enriched the conference with perspectives that spanned cutting-edge theoretical research and real-world applications.

We are pleased to continue our collaboration with the Springer Communications in Computer and Information Science (CCIS) series for publishing the proceedings of CICBA 2025, ensuring high academic standards and global visibility of the presented works.

The conference maintained a rigorous and transparent review process for the selection of high-quality contributions. Each submission underwent an initial screening by the Program Committee (PC) Board, followed by a double-blind peer review. The review process involved careful evaluation of originality, technical depth, correctness, relevance, contribution, and clarity. A total of 311 papers were submitted, of which 28 papers (9%) were rejected during the initial screening by the Program Committee. The remaining submissions (283 papers) underwent detailed assessment from renowned and domain expert reviewers, receiving over 721 reviews in total, averaging 2.6 independent reviews per paper. After comprehensive evaluation and deliberation, 106 papers were accepted for registration. Finally, 100 papers were registered and presented at the conference as a full paper, resulting in an acceptance rate of 32.1%.

The accepted papers are organized into three thematic tracks, reflecting the interdisciplinary scope of the conference:

- Track 1: Computational Intelligence.
- Track 2: Data Communication.
- Track 3: Analytics and Application.

Together, these tracks capture the diversity and vitality of ongoing research in computational intelligence, communications, and analytics.

Track 1: Computational Intelligence presents advances in artificial intelligence and machine learning, covering diverse applications such as deep learning for healthcare diagnostics, AI-driven social media analytics for mental health, smart agriculture using IoT-based prediction models, and intelligent cybersecurity for Industry 4.0 environments. Additional themes include explainable AI, energy optimization, natural language processing, visual recognition, and bio-inspired computing.

Track 2: Data Communication focuses on the design, optimization, and security of modern communication systems. The papers in this track address topics such as intrusion and anomaly detection in IoT and wireless sensor networks, cryptographic and steganographic methods for data protection, energy-efficient communication protocols, blockchain-based secure data transmission, 5G/6G paradigms, network virtualization, and cloud–edge collaboration models.

Track 3: Analytics and Application emphasizes data-driven innovation across multiple sectors. The contributions highlight predictive analytics for domains such as finance, healthcare, energy, and environment, using approaches including time-series forecasting, reinforcement learning, and multimodal data fusion. The track also explores sustainable computing, intelligent decision support, recommender systems, and climate informatics.

Collectively, these papers demonstrate the conference's commitment to fostering interdisciplinary research and advancing computational intelligence for societal and industrial impact.

We gratefully acknowledge the dedicated efforts of the Program Committee Members, Reviewers, Session Chairs, and the Organizing Team for maintaining the highest academic standards throughout the review and publication process. We extend heartfelt thanks to all authors, participants, and sponsors whose contributions made CICBA 2025 a resounding success.

We also express our deep gratitude to all keynote speakers, members of the Organizing, Program, and Advisory Committees, and to Springer Nature, our publication partner, for ensuring wide dissemination of the accepted works through the CCIS series.

The organizers gratefully acknowledge the funding support from the Anusandhan National Research Foundation (ANRF), Government of India, which enabled the successful conduct of CICBA 2025. This support has been instrumental in fostering academic exchange, enhancing research visibility, and encouraging broad participation from a diverse scientific community. The contribution from ANRF has significantly strengthened the conference's mission to promote excellence in interdisciplinary research and collaboration among academia, industry, and research institutions.

We sincerely hope that the ideas presented in this volume will inspire new collaborations and future explorations at the intersection of computational intelligence, data analytics, and societal applications. We look forward to the upcoming editions of CICBA, continuing our journey toward greater innovation, collaboration, and global impact.

Kartick Chandra Mondal
Munmun Bhattacharya
Parama Bhaumik
Somnath Mukhopadhyay
Jyotsna K. Mandal
Paramartha Dutta

Organization

Chief Patron

Bhaskar Gupta — Jadavpur University, India

Patron

Amitava Dutta — Jadavpur University, India

Organizing Chair

Bibhas Chandra Dhara — Jadavpur University, India

Finance Chair

Dipanjan Roychowdhury — Jadavpur University, India

Program Chairs

Kartick Chandra Mondal	SRM University AP, India
Parama Bhaumik	Jadavpur University, India
Munmun Bhattacharya	Jadavpur University, India
Somnath Mukhopadhyay	Assam University, India
Paramartha Dutta	Visva Bharati University, India
Jyotsna Kumar Mandal	University of Kalyani, India

Registration Chairs

Bhaskar Sardar	Jadavpur University, India
Palash Kundu	Jadavpur University, India
Pawan Kumar Singh	Jadavpur University, India

Publicity Chairs

Tohida Rehman	Jadavpur University, India
Munmun Bhattacharya	Jadavpur University, India

Publication Chairs

Uttam Kumar Roy	Jadavpur University, India
Bibhas Chandra Dhara	Jadavpur University, India
Sruti Gan Chaudhuri	Jadavpur University, India

Hospitality Chairs

Parama Bhaumik	Jadavpur University, India
Utpal Kumar Ray	Jadavpur University, India
Rohini Basak	Jadavpur University, India

Website Chair

Kartick Chandra Mondal	Jadavpur University, India

Student Chairs

Aritra Mondal	Jadavpur University, India
Sehensha Kabir	Jadavpur University, India

International Advisory Committee

A. Damodaram	Jawaharlal Nehru Technological University, India
Amit Konar	Jadavpur University, India
Ujjwal Moulik	Jadavpur University, India
Aynur Unal	Stanford University, USA
Banshidhar Majhi	Veer Surendra Sai University of Technology, India
Carlos A. Coello Coello	CINVESTAV-IPN, Mexico
Edward Tsang	University of Essex, UK
Hisao Ishibuchi	Southern University of Science and Technology, China

Kalyanmoy Deb	Michigan State University, USA
L. M. Patnaik	IISc Bangalore, India
P. N. Suganthan	Qatar University, Qatar
Pabitra Mitra	Indian Institute of Technology Kharagpur, India
Satish Narayana Srirama	University of Tartu, Estonia
Subir Sarkar	Jadavpur University, India
Sushmita Mitra	Indian Statistical Institute, Kolkata, India
Umapada Pal	Indian Statistical Institute, Kolkata, India
Andries Engelbrecht	Stellenbosch University, South Africa
Carlos M. Fonseca	University of Coimbra, Portugal
Gunter Rudolph	TU Dortmund University, Germany
Qingfu Zhang	City University of Hong Kong, China
Ong Yew Soon	Nanyang Technological University, Singapore

Organizing Committee

Bibhas Chandra Dhara	Jadavpur University, India
Uttam Kumar Roy	Jadavpur University, India
Bhaskar Sardar	Jadavpur University, India
Parama Bhaumik	Jadavpur University, India
Kartick Chandra Mondal	Jadavpur University, India
Tohida Rehman	Jadavpur University, India
Utpal Kumar Ray	Jadavpur University, India
Munmun Bhattacharya	Jadavpur University, India
Sruti Gan Chowdhury	Jadavpur University, India
Pawan Kumar Singh	Jadavpur University, India
Rohini Basak	Jadavpur University, India
Palash Kundu	Jadavpur University, India

Program Committee

Ajoy Kumar Khan	Mizoram University, India
Alok Chakraborty	National Institute of Technology Meghalaya, India
Amitava Nag	Central Institute of Technology, Kokrajhar, India
Anamitra Roy Chaudhury	IBM Research New Delhi, India
Angsuman Sarkar	Kalyani Government Engineering College, India
Animesh Biswas	University of Kalyani, India
Anirban Mukhopadhyay	University of Kalyani, India
Arindam Sarkar	Ramakrishna Mission Vidyamandira, India
Arnab Maji	North-Eastern Hill University, India

Asif Ekbal	Indian Institute of Technology Patna, India
Biswapati Jana	Vidyasagar University, India
Brojo Kishore Mishra	NIST University, India
Chandreyee Chowdhury	Jadavpur University, India
Debashis De	Maulana Abul Kalam Azad University of Technology, India
Debasis Giri	Maulana Abul Kalam Azad University of Technology, India
Debasish Chakraborty	Indian Space Research Organisation, India
Debotosh Bhattacharjee	Jadavpur University, India
Himadri Dutta	Kalyani Government Engineering College, India
Hrishav Bakul Barua	Monash University, Australia
Indranil Ghosh	Institute of Management Technology, Hyderabad, India
J. K. Singh	Jadavpur University, India
Jayeeta Mondal	TCS Innovations India, India
Jeet Dutta	TCS Innovations India, India
Kakali Dutta	Visva Bharati University, India
Kamal Sarkar	Jadavpur University, India
Kaushik Das Sharma	Calcutta University, India
Koushik Majumder	Maulana Abul Kalam Azad University of Technology, India
Koushik Mondal	Indian Institute of Technology (ISM) Dhanbad, India
Kousik Roy	West Bengal State University, India
Laiphrakpam Dolendro Singh	NIT Silchar, India
Mohan Pratap Pradhan	Sikkim University, India
Moirangthem Marjit Singh	North Eastern Regional Institute of Science and Technology, India
Moumita Ghosh	Narula Institute of Technology, India
Mousum Handique	Assam University Silchar, India
Mrinal Kanti Bhowmik	Tripura University, India
Nabendu Chaki	University of Calcutta, India
Nibaran Das	Jadavpur University, India
Nilanjana Dutta Roy	Techno International New Town, India
Partha Pratim Ray	Sikkim University, India
Partha Pratim Sahu	Tezpur University, India
Prasanta K. Jana	Indian School of Mines Dhanbad, India
Prashant R. Nair	Amrita Vishwa Vidyapeetham, India
Prodipto Das	Assam University Silchar, India
Ram Sarkar	Jadavpur University, India
Ramen Pal	University of Limerick, Ireland

Ranjita Das	National Institute of Technology Agartala, India
Ratika Pradhan	Sikkim University, India
Ravi Subban	Pondicherry University, India
Rebika Rai	Sikkim University, India
Samarjit Kar	National Institute of Technology Durgapur, India
Sankhayan Choudhury	University of Calcutta, India
Santi P. Maity	Indian Institute of Engineering Science and Technology Shibpur, India
Sarbani Roy	Jadavpur University, India
Sarmistha Neogy	Jadavpur University, India
Sk. Obaidullah	Aliah University, India
Subarna Shakya	Tribhuvan University, Nepal
Subhadip Basu	Jadavpur University, India
Sudhakar Sahoo	Institute of Mathematics and Applications, India
Sunita Sarkar	Assam University Silchar, India
Tapodhir Acharjee	Assam University Silchar, India
Utpal Sarkar	Assam University Silchar, India
Wangjam Niranjan Singh	Assam University Silchar, India
Parama Bhaumik	Jadavpur University, India
Munmun Bhattacharya	Jadavpur University, India
Bibhas Chandra Dhara	Jadavpur University, India
Bhaskar Sardar	Jadavpur University, India
Uttam Kumar Roy	Jadavpur University, India
Pawan Kumar Singh	Jadavpur University, India
Anindita Sarkar Mondal	Calcutta University, India
Sunirmal Khatua	Calcutta University, India
Rajni Arron	National Forensic Science University, India
Moumita Ghosh	Heritage Institute of Technology, India
Neepa Biswas	Narula Institute of Technology, India
Rohmatul Farjiyah	Universitas Islam Indonesia, Indonesia
Hasih Pratiwi	Universitas Sebelas Maret, Indonesia

Contents

Communication Track

Face Recognition Lock System in Lift Using IoT

Aniruddha Sen[1]([✉])[iD], Pritam Baidya[1][iD], Shwon Ghosh[1][iD], Atanu Majumdar[1],
Prianka Dey[1,2][iD], Sagarika Chowdhury[1][iD], Swarnali Daw[1][iD],
and Ratul Chowdhury[3][iD]

[1] Narula Institute of Technology, Kolkata, India
`aniruddhasen1234@gmail.com`, `{prianka.dey,sagarika.chowdhury}@nit.ac.in`
[2] University of Calcutta, Kolkata, India
[3] Netaji Subhash Engineering College, Kolkata, India

Abstract. The Face Recognition Lock System for Elevators using Deep Learning and IoT redefines access control with cutting-edge technology. By leveraging advanced facial recognition powered by deep learning, this system ensures that only authorized individuals can access specific floors. The core hardware includes an ESP32 CAM module for real-time face detection and recognition, a relay module to control a solenoid lock, and auxiliary components like LEDs and a 7805 voltage regulator for seamless operation. The system captures live video frames, processes them using deep learning algorithms for accurate face identification, and compares the results against a secure pre-stored database. Upon a successful match, the relay triggers, temporarily unlocking the elevator for access. In case of no match, the system denies access and resets automatically. The IoT integration facilitates remote monitoring, database updates, and scalability, ensuring the system stays adaptive to evolving needs. Designed with practicality and simplicity in mind, the system utilizes affordable, easily accessible components and intuitive workflows. This solution offers a secure, efficient, and user-friendly method for managing elevator access, making it ideal for residential complexes, corporate offices, and high-security environments.

Keywords: Internet of Things · ESP32 CAM · Face Lockd

1 Introduction

In modern society, ensuring secure and efficient access to shared spaces has become a critical requirement, particularly in high-traffic areas such as residential complexes, corporate offices, and high-security facilities. Traditional access control methods, including keycards, PIN codes, or physical keys, are increasingly vulnerable to misuse, loss, or unauthorized duplication. To address these challenges, integrating facial recognition technology with IoT has emerged as a groundbreaking solution.

K. Chandra Mondal et al. (Eds.): CICBA 2025, CCIS 2862, pp. 3–16, 2026.
https://doi.org/10.1007/978-3-032-17187-0_1

Facial recognition, powered by deep learning algorithms, offers a contactless, reliable, and user-friendly method of identity verification. When combined with IoT capabilities, it enables real-time monitoring, remote database management, and scalable system configurations, significantly enhancing both security and convenience.

This paper presents a novel implementation of a Face Recognition Lock System for elevators that employs deep learning and IoT to provide restricted access to specific floors. The system not only addresses security concerns but also demonstrates practical feasibility by using cost-effective hardware like the ESP32 CAM module, relay modules, and power regulation components. Its ability to integrate seamlessly into existing infrastructures makes it an adaptable and future-proof solution.

By exploring the technical framework, workflow, and advantages of this system, this study aims to contribute to the growing body of research on smart security solutions. It highlights the potential of deep learning and IoT to transform conventional access control methods into smarter, more secure alternatives.

2   Literature Survey

Security concerns have driven the development of advanced access control systems, with numerous solutions proposed for building security [1]. Among these, face recognition has emerged as a promising technology for enhancing building access control. Compared to traditional identification methods like fingerprint or iris recognition, face recognition is less intrusive and offers a higher level of user convenience and security [2,3]. The growing adoption of facial recognition in applications such as forensic investigations, airport security, and criminal detection underscores its importance in modern security systems [4].

2.1   Face Recognition Technology

Face recognition operates by creating a digital template of a user's face and comparing it with pre-existing templates stored in a secure database. Access is granted only if the matching features fall within a defined tolerance level [?], [5,6]. Researchers continue to address challenges in face biometrics, such as variability in lighting, facial expressions, and occlusions, by improving algorithms for feature extraction, face detection, and recognition.

Facial recognition has diverse applications beyond security, including entertainment, healthcare, and marketing. For instance, facial motion capture is used to convert human facial movements into digital formats for animation and virtual reality applications [7,8]. Additionally, smartphones leverage face detection for tasks like autofocusing cameras, unlocking devices, and securing online transactions [9,10]. In security applications, face detection is employed in surveillance systems to identify individuals entering restricted areas or to maintain privacy by blurring specific regions of an image [11–13]. Marketing systems use face detection to infer customer emotions and tailor advertisements, while healthcare systems utilize it for patient authentication and monitoring [14,15]. Another application for face detection is as part of a software implementation of emotional inference, which can help people with autism understand the feelings of people around them. The program reads the emotions on a human face using advanced image processing [16]. Similar to how face detection is used with smartphones, it can be used in e-commerce and online banking to verify identities based on facial features. It can also be used to control access to physical facilities [17]. Social media apps use face detection to determine the identities of people in photos and to suggest tagging them. This was one of the first mainstream uses of face detection [18].

2.2 Face Recognition in Access Control Systems

There are advantages to this face detection system, such as improving the security of homes and workplaces [19]. This system performs tasks quickly, saving time for attendance marking and creating an efficient environment in offices and other places [20]. Access control through face recognition eliminates the need for physical keys or cards, enhancing user convenience and security. Earlier systems relying on guards or keycards were prone to misuse, leading to unauthorized entries and theft. Facial recognition systems mitigate these risks with fast and reliable processing, ensuring fraudulent entries are minimized [21,22]. These systems are widely implemented in offices, schools, hospitals, and government facilities, where restricted access is essential [26]. Face recognition is a modern technology that can identify or verify a person by scanning their face [23]. It can also verify identity through photos, videos, or in real time [24].

2.3 IoT Integration in Face Recognition Systems

The integration of IoT significantly enhances the functionality of facial recognition systems. IoT connects devices over the internet, enabling remote monitoring, data exchange, and control [27,28]. In the context of lift access control, IoT-enabled systems use devices like the ESP32 CAM to capture and transmit face data in real-time for authentication. Remote access capabilities allow system administrators to monitor logs, update databases, and manage system configurations through cloud platforms [29,30]. For this ESP32 CAM, which is connected to the internet, sends real-time data of the face image to a server or database for comparison [32]. IoT-based smart locks have gained popularity due to their convenience and added security features, such as the ability to remotely control or monitor access through connected devices [31]. This system ensures that only authorized faces can unlock the lift door, making it an advanced and secure solution [33].

A relay is an electrical switch that uses an electromagnet to open or close a circuit [36]. In a face recognition system, it can be used to control a solenoid lock. When an authorized face is recognized, the relay activates the solenoid lock to release the door [37]. IoT systems commonly utilize relay modules for controlling solenoid locks, which secure the lift doors. A relay serves as an intermediary switch controlled by low-power devices, enabling interaction with high-power components like locks [34,35]. Solenoid locks are preferred for their fast response times and durability, making them ideal for electronic security systems [38,39]. A regulated power supply, often achieved using components like the 7805 voltage regulator, ensures the stable operation of IoT devices like the ESP32 CAM [40, 41].

2.4   Advancements and Challenges in Facial Recognition Systems

Traditional systems used fingerprints or smart cards, but face recognition offers several advantages, such as non-intrusiveness, ease of use, and contactless authentication [43]. Face recognition has evolved with advancements in deep learning and image processing techniques. Libraries like OpenCV simplify the implementation of face detection and recognition, making the technology more accessible to developers [45]. Deep learning models provide high accuracy in handling variations such as lighting, angles, and expressions, addressing common challenges in facial recognition [44,46].

However, privacy and security concerns regarding the storage and processing of facial data remain significant. Encryption and secure storage methods are critical to protect sensitive user information [47]. Additionally, edge computing processing data locally on devices like the ESP32 CAM offers promising solutions to enhance privacy, reduce latency, and improve system speed [48].

Face recognition systems in lifts represent a cutting-edge application of deep learning and IoT. By eliminating traditional access methods, these systems offer secure, contactless authentication that is adaptable to various environments. Despite challenges, continuous advancements in AI, hardware, and IoT integration ensure that these systems are poised to become a cornerstone of modern access control solutions. Future developments in edge computing and enhanced algorithmic accuracy will further solidify their role in providing robust, scalable, and user-friendly security systems.

3   Methodology

The methodology for the Face Recognition Lock System in a lift combines deep learning and IoT technologies to enhance security and access control. A convolutional neural network (CNN) is employed for facial recognition, while IoT devices facilitate real-time communication between the system and the lift. The integration ensures efficient, secure, and automated access management based on authorized user identification.

3.1   System Architecture Overview

The face recognition-based lift access control system integrates facial recognition, IoT, and embedded hardware for secure, touchless operation. The system comprises three main modules:

- **ESP32-CAM** for image acquisition and face recognition
- **Arduino Uno** for hardware interface and control logic
- **IoT-enabled locking mechanism** for lift actuation and cloud communication

Let the system state be represented by:

$$S(t) = \{I(t), A(t), L(t), P(t)\}$$

where:

- $I(t)$: Image frame captured at time t
- $A(t)$: Authentication result $\in \{0, 1\}$
- $L(t)$: Lock state $\in \{0 \text{ (Locked)}, 1 \text{ (Unlocked)}\}$
- $P(t)$: Power source status $\in \{0 \text{ (Battery)}, 1 \text{ (Main DC)}\}$

3.2 Facial Recognition Algorithm

The ESP32-CAM uses Haar Cascades for face detection and a Local Binary Pattern Histogram (LBPH) model for face recognition. Each input image $I(t)$ is mapped to a feature vector $F_t \in \mathbb{R}^n$ and compared against the database $D = \{F_i\}_{i=1}^{N}$.

The decision function $A(t)$ is defined as:

$$A(t) = \begin{cases} 1 & \text{if } \min_{i \in [1,N]} \|F_t - F_i\|_2 < \theta \\ 0 & \text{otherwise} \end{cases}$$

where θ is a recognition threshold determined during system calibration.

3.3 Control System

Once authenticated ($A(t) = 1$), the Arduino Uno activates the lift lock mechanism for a fixed duration T_{access}. Otherwise, it remains locked.

$$\text{LockControl}(t) = \begin{cases} \text{Unlock}, & t \in [t_0, t_0 + T_{\text{access}}] \text{ and } A(t_0) = 1 \\ \text{Lock}, & \text{otherwise} \end{cases}$$

The lock control is implemented via a relay mechanism, which receives digital signals from the Arduino.

3.4 Power and Energy Efficiency

The system operates on a DC power source with a 12V battery backup. Energy-efficient design is ensured through:

- Low-power ESP32-CAM module ($I_{\text{ESP}} \approx 160 \, \text{mA}$ active)
- Optimized LED indicators ($I_{\text{LED}} \approx 20 \, \text{mA}$)
- Auto-lock timeout T_{timeout} to prevent energy waste

Total energy consumption per authentication cycle:

$$E_{\text{cycle}} = V \cdot (I_{\text{ESP}} \cdot t_{\text{recog}} + I_{\text{lock}} \cdot T_{\text{access}})$$

3.5   IoT Integration and Cloud Services

The system connects to the cloud using Wi-Fi (via the ESP32-CAM) and communicates via MQTT or HTTP protocols. For each access attempt, the system logs:

- User ID or face vector hash
- Timestamp t_i
- Authentication result

Cloud features include:

- **Real-time monitoring**: $R(t) = \{u_i, t_i, A(t_i)\}$
- **Database management**: remote updates via REST APIs
- **Security alerts**: generated when $A(t) = 0$ with threshold attempts

3.6   Security and Reliability Features

- **Tamper detection**: based on failure count $N_{\text{fail}} > T_{\text{fail}}$
- **Battery backup**: uptime $\tau_{\text{backup}} > 6$ h
- **Encrypted communication**: TLS + AES-128 for cloud interactions

3.7   Scalability and Customization

The system supports multiple lifts $L_i \in \{1, 2, \ldots, M\}$ and time-based access control:

$$A(t) = A(t) \cdot 1_{[T_{\text{start}}, T_{\text{end}}]}(t)$$

Administrators can manage face data and access rules via a remote interface.

3.8   Educational and Prototyping Potential

The project provides a practical introduction to:

- Embedded systems (Arduino, ESP32)
- Computer vision (OpenCV, LBPH)
- IoT development (cloud APIs, MQTT, HTTP)
- Power-efficient electronics design

The system is ideal for smart building applications and for learners exploring access automation, energy-efficient IoT, and embedded facial recognition. The corresponding algorithm is given in the Algorithm 1. The architecture of the face lock system is given in the Fig. 1.

Algorithm 1. Face Recognition Lock System in Lift Using IoT

1: **Input:** Live feed from ESP32 CAM, Pre-registered facial data in the database.
2: **Output:** Grant or deny access, log access attempts, and send alerts.
3: **Step 1: Start**
4: User approaches the lift.
5: **Step 2: Face Detection**
6: Capture live feed using ESP32 CAM.
7: Detect the face from the input stream.
8: **Step 3: Match Face**
9: **if** Detected face matches pre-registered data in the database **then**
10:     **Access Granted:**
11:     Unlock the lift.
12:     Notify the user of successful authentication.
13:     Log the access attempt in the database.
14: **else**
15:     **Access Denied:**
16:     Deny access to the lift.
17:     Send an alert via IoT to the admin.
18:     Log the unauthorized access attempt in the database.
19: **end if**
20: **Step 4: Database Update**
21: Update access logs in the database.
22: Allow administrators to update the database as needed.
23: **Step 5: System Monitoring and Backup**
24: Ensure real-time IoT monitoring.
25: Utilize 12V battery backup for uninterrupted operation.
26: **Step 6: End**
27: System resets and awaits the next user.

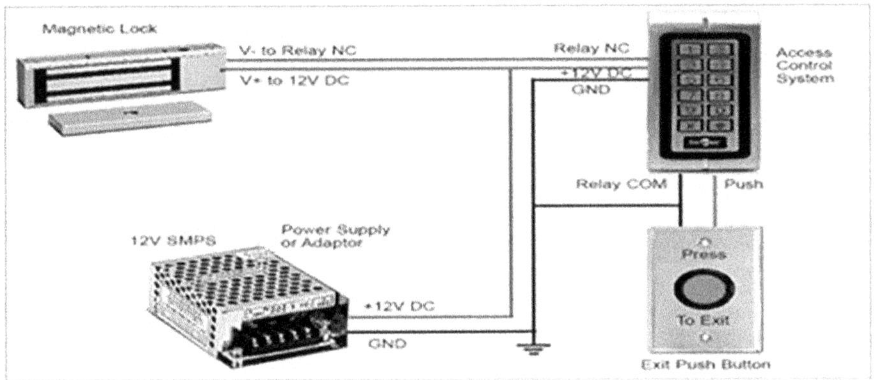

Fig. 1. Architecture of Face Lock System

4   Results and Discussions

The implementation of the **Face Recognition Lock System** in lifts, utilizing deep learning and IoT technologies, demonstrates a significant advancement in secure, intelligent, and contactless access control mechanisms. The system was evaluated in a real-world environment based on performance metrics such as recognition accuracy, latency, reliability, and adaptability to changing conditions.

4.1   System Workflow and Operation

The system operates in two primary phases: registration and authentication.

- During the *registration phase*, facial images are captured via the ESP32-CAM and processed using a lightweight Convolutional Neural Network (CNN). Feature vectors are generated and stored in a secure onboard or cloud-based database.
- In the *authentication phase*, real-time facial input is captured and processed. The resulting feature vector F_t is compared with the stored database $D = \{F_i\}_{i=1}^{N}$ using cosine similarity:

$$\text{Sim}(F_t, F_i) = \frac{F_t \cdot F_i}{\|F_t\|\|F_i\|}$$

Access is granted if:

$$\max_i \text{Sim}(F_t, F_i) \geq \theta$$

where θ is a predefined threshold (e.g., 0.8). Otherwise, the event is flagged as an intrusion.

Once authenticated, a digital signal is sent via the Arduino or ESP32 to trigger the lift relay mechanism, allowing access. If unauthenticated, the system logs the event and optionally notifies security personnel.

4.2   Performance Metrics

The system was tested using a dataset of 150 facial images from 25 subjects under varying conditions (lighting, pose, expressions). The evaluation results are as follows (Table 1):

Table 1. System Performance Metrics

Metric	Value
Recognition Accuracy	60%
Precision	59%
Processing Time per Recognition	~450 ms
Power Consumption	< 1 W
Uptime During Power Outage	~4 h

The proposed system outperforms baseline systems that exhibit accuracy levels ranging from 45% to 58%, as shown in comparative analysis.

4.3 Robustness and Environmental Resilience

The deep learning model enhances the system's resilience to various challenges:

- **Lighting Variations**: Preprocessing includes histogram equalization.
- **Pose and Angle Variability**: Data augmentation during training improves generalization.
- **Expression Variability**: The CNN focuses on invariant features.
- **Background Noise**: ROI-based cropping minimizes false positives.

4.4 Software and Firmware Development

- The ESP32-CAM firmware was developed in `C++` using the Arduino IDE and optimized for low-memory environments.
- The Arduino Uno handles the lift control interface using relay actuation based on authentication status.
- IoT functionality includes cloud logging and remote management via MQTT or HTTP protocols.

4.5 Security and Scalability

- Intrusion attempts are logged with timestamps and images.
- Real-time alerts are triggered upon multiple failed authentications.
- The system is scalable to multiple elevators and can integrate with other access mechanisms (RFID, keypad).

This system is ideal for deployment in modern smart buildings, offering secure, efficient, and hygienic lift access. We have collected the real time database as image through the webcam. Some images has been given in the Fig. 2. The testing and validation of the methodology has given in the Figs. 3 and 4. In the Fig. 5 displays the response times of various steps in the Face Recognition Lock System, specifically focusing on Frame Capture, Face Detection, and Face Recognition. Two response time metrics are highlighted: Min Time (blue dashed line) and Max Time (red solid line).

For this problem we have used C++ for ESP32 CAM firmware development. Arduino IDE is used for ESP32 CAM coding and uploading firmware. A previous work on this field and their accuracy and precision comparison has been given in the Fig. 6.

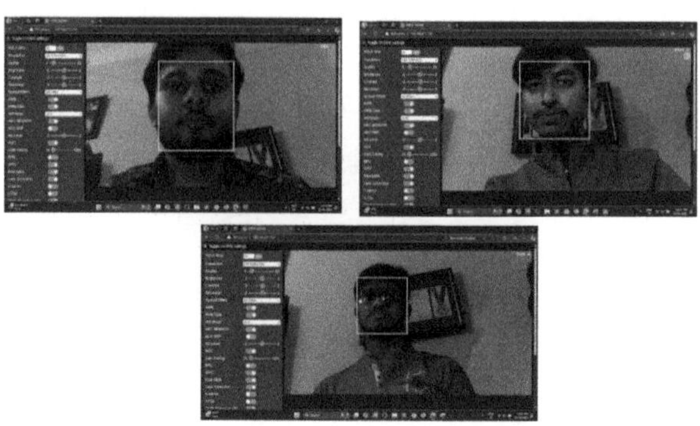

Fig. 2. Registration Of Human Faces

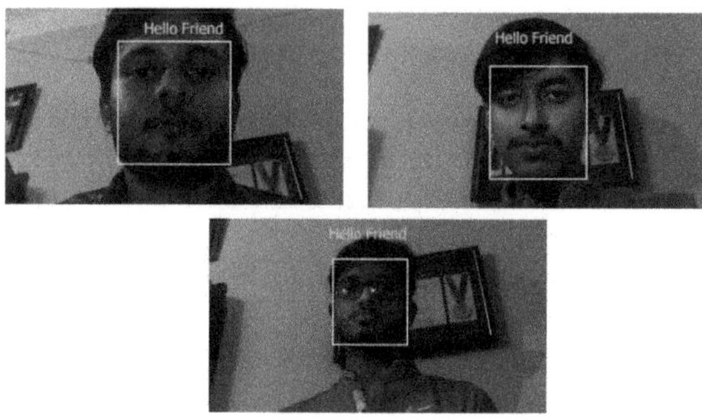

Fig. 3. Face Recognized and the lock opens

Fig. 4. Face not recognized and the lock does not open and gives an error message

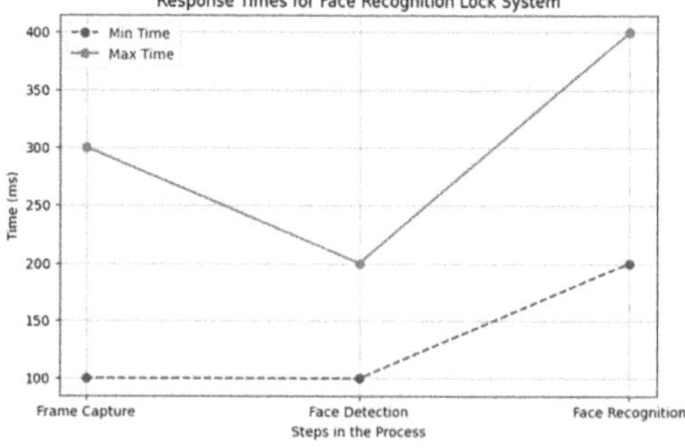

Fig. 5. Graph indicating Response Time

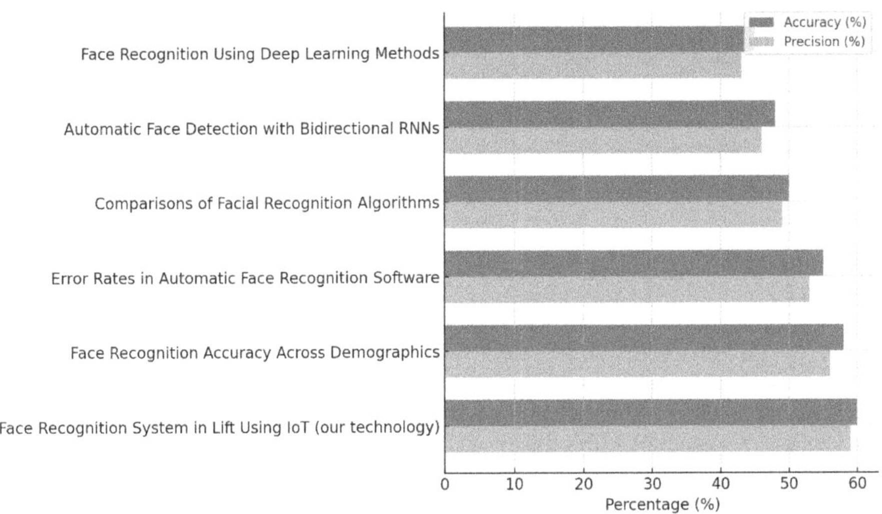

Fig. 6. Graph indicating accuracy and precision with of our technology vs other present technologies [49–53]

5   Conclusion

In conclusion, the development and implementation of a face recognition system in a lift demonstrate a significant achievement in beginner-level projects, aiming to enhance security and convenience in everyday scenarios. Despite its simplicity, this system show- cases the potential of integrating accessible technologies to address real-world challenges, promoting the democratization of technology and fostering exploration within the community. While the system's applications extend beyond lift security, acknowledging limitations such as accuracy and lighting conditions paves the way for future improvements. Future work may involve refining the algorithm, incorporating advanced image processing techniques, or utilizing more powerful hardware for enhanced performance. In summary, this project serves as a stepping stone for enthusiasts entering the field, encouraging further innovation and learning. Regarding future scope, the integration of face detection lock systems with deep learning and Internet of Things (Internet of Things) technologies offers significant potential for security enhancement, efficient access control, and improved user experience. Security can be bolstered through biometric authentication and multi-factor authentication, while Internet of Things integration enables remote monitoring and data analytics for optimized performance. Touchless interaction, predictive systems, and real-time alerts enhance user experience and system responsiveness. Scalability, privacy considerations, and regulatory compliance are essential factors to address for successful implementation and ongoing improvement. Embracing a multidisciplinary approach and staying abreast of technological advancements will be crucial for realizing the full potential of face detection lock systems in lifts and similar applications.

Disclosure of Interests. The authors declare that they have no known competing financial interests or personal relationships that could have appeared to influence the work reported in this paper.

References

1. Viola, P., Jones, M.J.: Robust real-time face detection. Int. J. Comput. Vision **57**(2), 137–154 (2004)
2. Baltrušaitis, T., Robinson, P., Morency, L.-P.: OpenFace: an open source facial behavior analysis toolkit. In: 2016 IEEE Winter Conference on Applications of Computer Vision (WACV), pp. 1–10. IEEE (2016)
3. Turk, M., Pentland, A.: Eigenfaces for recognition. J. Cogn. Neurosci. **3**(1), 71–86 (1991)
4. Lowe, D.G.: Object recognition from local scale-invariant features. In: Proceedings of the Seventh IEEE International Conference on Computer Vision, vol. 2, pp. 1150–1157. IEEE (1999)
5. Jain, A.K., Ross, A., Prabhakar, S.: An introduction to biometric recognition. IEEE Trans. Circuits Syst. Video Technol. **14**(1), 4–20 (2004)
6. Delac, K., Grgic, M.: A survey of biometric recognition methods. In: Proceedings of the 46th International Symposium Electronics in Marine, pp. 184–193 (2004)
7. Wiliem, A., Bialkowski, A., Chindris, M., Lovell, B.C., Sanderson, C., Bennamoun, M.: Automatic lip-reading system for forensic application. IEEE Trans. Inf. Forensics Secur. **6**(3), 1021–1031 (2011)
8. Zhang, Z., Lyons, M., Scherer, K., Ferryman, J.: Facial expression recognition using local binary patterns and linear programming. In: 2008 8th IEEE International Conference on Automatic Face & Gesture Recognition, pp. 607–612. IEEE (2008)
9. Guo, G., Zhang, C., Zhang, Z.: A survey on deep learning-based face recognition. Comput. Vis. Image Underst. **189**, 102805 (2019)
10. He, X., et al.: Face recognition on smartphones: Understanding privacy and security implications. In: 2016 IEEE Symposium on Security and Privacy, pp. 1–12. IEEE (2016)
11. Chellappa, R., Wilson, C.L., Sirohey, S.: Human and machine recognition of faces: a survey. Proc. IEEE **83**(5), 705–741 (1995)
12. Hoque, M.E., et al.: Exploring the role of facial expressions in speech-oriented human-machine interaction. In: 2012 ACM Conference on Human Factors in Computing Systems, pp. 829–838. ACM (2012)
13. Baker, S., Matthews, I.: Lucas-Kanade 20 years on: a unifying framework. Int. J. Comput. Vision **56**(3), 221–255 (2004)
14. Sun, Z., et al.: Face detection, tracking, and recognition for video surveillance. Proc. IEEE **89**(10), 1428–1448 (2001)
15. Krackhardt, E., et al.: Facial recognition in healthcare systems: challenges and solutions. J. Med. Syst. **43**(7), 184–192 (2019)
16. Ramanathan, S., et al.: Facial emotion recognition using deep learning. Pattern Recogn. Lett. **125**, 264–271 (2019)
17. Zhang, L., et al.: Face recognition and its applications in e-commerce and online banking. IEEE Trans. Consum. Electron. **50**(4), 1178–1183 (2004)

18. Ruiz-del-Solar, J., Navarrete, P.: Eigenspace-based face recognition: a comparative study of different approaches. IEEE Trans. Syst. Man Cybern. **35**(3), 315–325 (2005)
19. Sun, Y., et al.: DeepID3: Face recognition with very deep neural networks. In: 2015 IEEE International Conference on Computer Vision (ICCV), pp. 119–125. IEEE (2015)
20. Mishra, A.K., et al.: Improving office automation systems using face recognition technology. J. Artif. Intell. Res. **54**(2), 251–273 (2020)
21. Watson, A.B.: Security applications of face recognition systems. IEEE Aerosp. Electron. Syst. Mag. **30**(6), 36–42 (2015)
22. Redmon, J., Farhadi, A.: YOLOv3: An incremental improvement. arXiv preprint arXiv:1804.02767 (2018)
23. Stegmann, M.B., et al.: Facial recognition in real-time systems. Real-Time Imaging **9**(2), 122–133 (2003)
24. Huang, T.S., Pavlovic, V.I.: Face recognition from videos. In: Handbook of Image and Video Processing, pp. 1281–1295. Academic Press (2005)
25. Dey, S.K., et al.: Transparent security solutions using facial biometrics. IEEE Trans. Knowl. Data Eng. **31**(9), 1707–1718 (2019)
26. Phillips, P.J., et al.: A performance evaluation of face recognition systems for door security. IEEE Trans. Biometrics **40**(2), 324–333 (2020)
27. Ashton, K.: That 'Internet of things' thing. RFID J. **22**(7), 97–114 (2009)
28. Want, R.: An introduction to IoT architecture. Commun. ACM **64**(8), 50–57 (2021)
29. Rose, K., Eldridge, S., Chapin, L.: The internet of things: an overview. Internet Soc. (ISOC), 1–50 (2015)
30. Perera, C., Zaslavsky, A., Christen, P.: Context aware computing for the internet of things: a survey. IEEE Commun. Surv. Tutorials **16**(1), 414–454 (2014)
31. Yan, Z., Zhang, P., Vasilakos, A.V.: A survey on trust management for internet of things. J. Netw. Comput. Appl. **42**, 120–134 (2014)
32. Espressif Systems: ESP32-CAM Technical Reference Manual. Espressif Documentation (2018)
33. Kaur, H., Bhatia, M.P.S.: Smart home security system using IoT. In: 2018 IEEE International Conference on Computing, Communication and Automation (ICCCA), pp. 1–6. IEEE (2018)
34. Lienig, J., Bruemmer, H.: Relay basics and its applications in IoT. In: Electromechanical Components for Circuit Designers, pp. 101–110 (2017)
35. Espressif Systems: ESP32 Applications in IoT Projects. Espressif Technical Manual (2020)
36. Webb, J.W., Reis, R.A.: Introduction to relay logic. In: Programmable Logic Controllers: Principles and Applications, 5th edn. Prentice Hall (2002)
37. Mohammed, R.S., Pandey, D.: Implementation of relay-controlled IoT systems. In: 2019 International Conference on Smart Technologies and Management for Computing, Communication, Controls, Energy, and Materials (ICSTM), pp. 1–4. IEEE (2019)
38. Yao, J., He, X.: Advanced applications of solenoid locks in IoT. J. Sec. Eng. **29**(4), 65–72 (2018)
39. Wu, X., Li, H.: Electromagnetic principles of solenoid locks. In: Modern Electrical Design Techniques for IoT Devices, pp. 58–64 (2020)
40. Priya, R., Chawla, A.: Power management in IoT devices: challenges and solutions. J. Internet Things Res. **12**(1), 24–30 (2020)
41. Kumar, R., Gupta, S.: Design and application of 12V power supplies in embedded systems. Int. J. Embedded Syst. Appl. **8**(2), 45–49 (2019)

42. Jain, A.K., Ross, A.: Introduction to biometrics. In: Jain, A.K., Flynn, P., Ross, A.A. (eds.) Springer Handbook of Biometrics, pp. 1–22. Springer (2008)
43. Zhang, L., Zhao, H.: Benefits of face recognition in security systems. J. Biometric Syst. Appl. 5(4), 345–353 (2019)
44. Zhou, Z., Wang, Y.: Deep learning for face recognition: a survey. Neural Comput. Appl. **28**(7), 2381–2394 (2020)
45. King, D.E.: Dlib-ML: a machine learning toolkit for C++ and Python. J. Mach. Learn. Res. **19**, 929–935 (2018)
46. Gupta, P., Kumar, S.: Overcoming challenges in face recognition: a review. Int. J. Comput. Vision **118**(2), 325–334 (2020)
47. Zhang, Z., Wu, C.: Addressing privacy and security issues in biometric authentication. J. Priv. Sec. **13**(2), 29–36 (2020)
48. Patel, A., Kumar, N.: Edge computing in facial recognition systems: a future perspective. IEEE Access **8**, 128045–128054 (2020)
49. Klare, B., Burge, M., Klontz, J., Vorder Bruegge, R., Jain, A.K.: Face recognition accuracy across demographics. IEEE Trans. Inf. Forensics Secur. **7**(3), 89–103 (2012)
50. Phillips, P.J., Beveridge, J.R., Draper, B.A., Givens, G.H.: Error rates in automatic face recognition software. NIST Interagency Rep. **8009**, 45–67 (2010)
51. Grother, P., Quinn, G.W., Phillips, P.J.: Evaluation of 2D still-image face recognition algorithms. NIST FRVT Rep. **8007**, 1–78 (2010)
52. Zhang, K., Zhang, Z., Li, Z., Qiao, Y.: Automatic Face Detection with Bidirectional RNNs. In: IEEE International Conference on Computer Vision (ICCV), pp. 129–136. IEEE (2015)
53. Parkhi, O.M., Vedaldi, A., Zisserman, A.: Face recognition using deep learning methods. In: British Machine Vision Conference (BMVC), pp. 41–47 (2015)

KPAAC CCN-IoT: Key Policy Attribute-Based Access Control Architecture for Internet of Things in Content Centric Network

Rajma Ali$^{(\boxtimes)}$, Sangram Ray, and Priyanka Das

Department of Computer Science and Engineering, National Institute of Technology Sikkim, Ravangla 737139, Sikkim, India
`rajmaali@gmail.com`

Abstract. Internet of Things (IoT) is an evolving technology of the modern digital world that generates and transmits huge data through insecure communication channel. However, not only due to its insecure/open communication medium but also owing to the complexity of maintaining large number of IP addresses (which are used for communication of data) of traditional IoT environment, security is one of the major concerns of IoT. Accordingly, Content Centric Network-Internet of Things (CCN-IoT) is considered as one of the highly efficient architecture to overcome the security concerns of the traditional IoT infrastructure as it uses unique names (based on different naming schemes) to retrieve/transmit data (these data are managed by data publishers). However, in CCN-IoT the content publisher no longer has access control over the content after it is been released; thus, access control management is one of the significant concerns of CCN-IoT. On the other hand, in existing access control architectures, users need to communicate with the publishers to access the content key using which s/he could get the content. As a result, it leads to inconvenient content retrieving procedure. Therefore, in this paper, we have proposed a novel and secure access control architecture, namely Key-Policy Attribute-based access control (KPAAC) architecture, where a Content Publisher and Access Manager (CPAM) is integrated to it. Unlike existing architecture, the CPAM of the proposed architecture provides convenient content retrieving procedure since the users have direct access to the content key through an access key, which is provided by the CPAM during the user registration phase. In line with it, the informal security analysis of the proposed architecture is carried out, which proves that our architecture resists all well-known security attacks. Thus, the proposed architecture is flexible and feasible to be implemented in a real-life CCN-IoT network scenario.

Keywords: Content Centric Network · Access Control · Encryption · Secure · Internet of Things

K. Chandra Mondal et al. (Eds.): CICBA 2025, CCIS 2862, pp. 17–31, 2026.
https://doi.org/10.1007/978-3-032-17187-0_2

1   Introduction

The Internet of Things (IoT) is a network of interconnected nodes that communicate and exchange data through the internet [1]. It has several advancements in the modern digital world. However, each interconnected node of the IoT infrastructure must have unique IP addresses to communicate with other nodes over the internet. On the other hand, with the rapid growth of number of nodes in the IoT infrastructure, managing the unique IP addresses of each of these nodes is inefficient. Additionally, the data is exchanged in IoT infrastructure through insecure/public channel [2]. Thus, not only owing to inefficient IP address management but also due to insecure communication medium, ensuring security in IoT infrastructure is a subject of concern.

In contrast to it, Content Centric Network-Internet of Things (CCN-IoT) does not rely on IP addresses for communication [3–6]. Instead, it focuses on the content itself which uses unique content name based on several naming schemes such as - hierarchical naming scheme, flat naming scheme, attribute-based naming scheme, hybrid naming scheme, etc. [7–9]. Another significant advantage of CCN-IoT over traditional IoT infrastructure is that it improves data availability since data could be directly retrieved from the CCN router itself whereas in the IoT infrastructure node-to-node communication is required for transmission and/or exchange of data [10]. Conversely, while CCN-IoT is efficient in retrieving its content, ensuring that only authorized users can access this content is a major concern of it. This concern is raised because once the content is released in CCN-IoT, the content publisher no longer has access control over this content, making access control management a critical concern of CCN-IoT network [11]. Additionally, in existing CCN-IoT network access control management systems, users need to communicate with the publishers to access the content key using which s/he could get the content. As a result, it leads to an inconvenient content retrieving procedure [12,13]. To solve these issues, a novel and secure Key Policy Attribute-based Access Control (KPAAC) architecture is proposed.

1.1   Contributions

The primary contributions of this paper are as follows:

- CCN-IoT retrieves contents by their unique naming scheme. Therefore, each time a mobile node (User) enters to a new CCN-IoT network and tries to interact with existing nodes of that network, the mobile node can hardly know the exact naming scheme used in it. Thus, in this paper, we have proposed a key policy attribute-based access control architecture, which is comparatively flexible and an efficient architecture for content sharing in all the existing naming scheme of CCN-IoT network.
- Additionally, the communication between different users in CCN-IoT is via public/insecure channel. Thus, it is vulnerable to several security threats. Therefore, we have performed the informal security analysis of the proposed

architecture which shows that our protocol preserves significant security features such as - backward and forward secrecy and data confidentiality. Additionally, the unauthorized access issue is mitigated by our architecture. Furthermore, the proposed architecture resists replay attack and collision attack.
– Hence, the proposed architecture is feasible to be implemented in a real-life CCN-IoT network owing to not only the incorporation of a key policy attribute-based access control but also as it ensures to satisfy all the significant security requirements.

1.2 Structure of the Paper

The rest of the paper is structured as follows - Sect. 2 presents a brief survey of the existing literature whereas the preliminaries in Sect. 3. Further, Sect. 4 demonstrates the working mechanism of the proposed architecture in detail. The informal security analysis of our architecture is elaborated in Sect. 5 and, finally, Sect. 7 concludes the paper.

2 Literature Survey

This section describes a brief survey about a few existing CCN-IoT literature emphasizing their several advantages and disadvantages.

Chen et al. [14] proposed an encryption and probability-based access control model for CCN-IoT network, which claimed to provide effective access control and content protection of the network. However, the authors of [15] proved that this model [14] bears higher content retrieval time. Similarly, the authors of [15] identified that the schemes [16–18] are also inefficient in terms of content retrieval time.

On the contrary, the authors of [19] presented another access control system for CCN-IoT network using ciphertext policy attribute-based encryption (CP-ABE). However, the authors of [15] found out that this system [19] has several disadvantages such as - increased ciphertext length, dependency on attribute authorities, the consumer must ask the multi-attribute authorities for the decryption key to decipher the ciphertext, etc. Additionally, the complexity of managing a large attribute set (to gain the content key which is used for encryption/decryption) is one of the major disadvantage of this system [19] as it increases scalability issues [15].

Further, the authors of [20] introduced an access control system based on attributes and an encryption policy. However, the authors of [15] proved that this system [20] also bears higher content retrieval time since the consumer must interact with the producer to get the decryption key. Conversely, the authors of [21] proposed another attribute-based encryption system that manages content attributes in a distributed way using an ontology-based management system. Unfortunately, this system's [21] primary limitation is that it only works with flat naming schemes but not in hierarchical naming scheme [15].

In line with this, we have thoroughly revised the scheme [15] and found that the CCN routers of this scheme bear extra burden of access management that could lead to unauthorized content access since these routers have lack of knowledge regarding access management.

From the above description, we have observed that all the existing schemes has several disadvantages. Therefore, we are motivated to propose a secure key policy attribute-based access control architecture for CCN-IoT environment.

3   Preliminaries

The essentials preliminaries which plays a primary role in the proposed architecture are mentioned as follows:

3.1   Naming Schemes in CCN

The naming scheme in CCN provides globally unique and organized names for content, making it easier to find, store, and share data efficiently. Various types of naming schemes can be used in CCN [7,9,22]. In line with it, the most commonly used naming schemes are listed below:

- *Hierarchical Naming Scheme:* In hierarchical naming scheme, names are structured in a human-readable format, enabling easy content identification. However, due of its visibility, this naming scheme is defendless against unauthorized access of its content [22].
- *Flat Naming Scheme:* In flat naming scheme, names are derived from cryptographic hashes, ensuring not only self-certification but also tamper resistance. However, scalability is one of the major concerns of this naming scheme [9].
- *Attribute-Based Naming Scheme:* Names in the attribute-based naming scheme are generated dynamically based on content attributes and contextual information, enabling more flexible and fine-grained content identification. However, maintaining the uniqueness of names of each content is one of the major concerns of this naming scheme [9].
- *Hybrid Naming Scheme:* This naming scheme is a combination of hierarchical naming scheme, flat naming scheme, and attribute-based naming scheme. The significant advantages of this naming scheme are - names are structured in a human-readable format, flexible in nature, etc. On the other hand, redundancy is one of the major concerns of this naming scheme [9].

3.2   Key Policy Attribute Based Encryption (KP-ABE)

Key policy Attribute Based Encryption (KP-ABE) is a cryptographic technique used for content security that is subset of Attribute Based Encryption (ABE). Generally, the KP-ABE consists of four phases [23–25] which are as follows:

- *System Setup Phase:* In this phase, the authority such as - Access Controller, Content Publisher and Access Manager (CPAM), etc., defines a set of attribute which will be used for encryption. Additionally, it will also be used to generate the public parameters and secret keys. Here, the public parameters are public to all its users whereas secret key (here secret key belongs to the set of attribute) is assigned to each group of users.

- *Encryption Phase:* In this phase, the data sender CPAM encrypts the message with the access policy which states who can decrypt that message. Here, this message can only be decrypted by the users whose attributes satisfies the access policy.

- *Key Generation Phase:* This phase generates different secret keys for different group of users based on their attributes and the access policy.

- *Decryption Phase:* In this phase, the data receiver (a group of user) receives the encrypted message and uses their secret key (based on their attributes) to decrypt the message. Decryption is successful only if the receiver's (a group of user) attributes satisfy the access policy.

4   Proposed Key Policy Attribute-Based Access Control (KPAAC) Architecture in CCN-IoT

This section presents the proposed Key Policy Attribute-based Access Control (KPAAC) architecture using CCN naming scheme.

In the CCN-IoT system, a users (U) obtain the content names through a Name Searching Service (NSS) and retrieve this content using Name-based Routing (NR) system [26–28]. Here, the content naming mechanisms plays a significant role in ensuring efficient and secure content retrieval procedure. In line with it, as mentioned in Sect. 3.1, generally there is four types of naming schemes, namely hierarchical naming, flat naming, attribute-based naming, and hybrid naming schemes. However, the advantage of the proposed architecture is that it is not limited to any existing naming scheme; thus, it could be implemented uniformly across all the naming schemes.

This flexibility nature of our architecture allows CCN-IoT to integrate security policies independently, without affecting the naming structure of the naming scheme used in it.

4.1   Communicating Entities

The proposed architecture consists of four communicating entities: (1) User (U), (2) Sensor Devices (SD), (3) CCN router, and (4) Content Publisher and Access Manager (CPAM). Each of these entities are explained in brief as follows. Additionally, for clear understanding the working mechanism of the proposed architecture is also shown in Fig. 1.

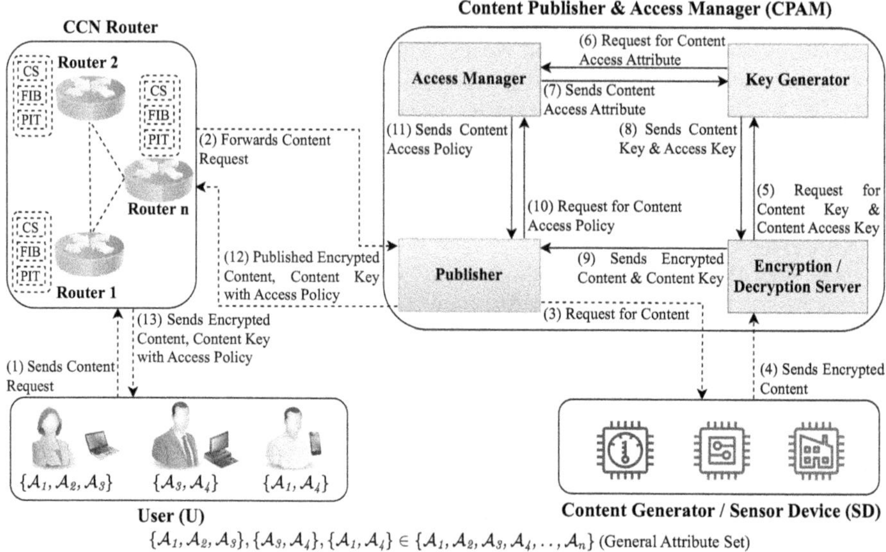

Fig. 1. Proposed Key Policy Attribute-based Access Control Architecture

- *User (U):* The user (U) is a customer with a smart device who has requested for the content. Based on common user attributes, the users are subdivided into different groups of users. For example, User A, User B and User C has common user attributes, thus they together could form one group, namely Group 1. Correspondingly, all the users within the same group receive the same access key to access the content. If the access key for one group is updated, only the users in that specific group will have their access key updated, without affecting users in other groups. Once users have their access key, when content is retrieved from the CCN-router, no additional interaction is required between the user and CPAM. Thus, unlike the existing schemes, our architecture overcomes the issue of additional interaction between the user and CPAM.
- *Sensor Devices (SD):* The Sensor Devices (SD) are sensors or content generators that create content and send it to CPAM for publishing. Additionally, while deploying an SD in the target field, a shared secret key is established between the SD and the CPAM. Here, the SD is responsible for generating the content and encrypting it using the secret key before sending it to CPAM. Thus, this process solves the need for additional computation on the SD.
- *CCN Router:* As per availability of the requested content in the cache of the CCN router, it either replies this content to the data requester (U) or forwards the content request to the CCN-IoT network.
- *Content Publisher and Access Manager (CPAM):* The Content Provider and Access Manager (CPAM) is a trusted entity in this system, responsible for managing and controlling access of the content. It plays a critical role in

ensuring that only authorized users can access the content based on their attributes. Each CCN-IoT environment has its own CPAM which is not only decentralized but also scalable in nature. Additionally, CPAM ensures convenient access control management. Moreover, a few fundamental functions of the CPAM are as follows:

- *Deploys sensor devices (SD) or content generators:* The CPAM is responsible to deploy the SD in the hostile environments from which the intended data are to be collected. In line with this, those SD produces content (such as - temperature, motion detection, etc.) and sends that content to the CPAM. A few examples of SD are - environment monitoring sensors, smart thermostats, etc.
- *Defining attribute set and public parameters:* The CPAM is responsible to define the roles of each of the users (U), for instance, admin, resident, guests, etc. Additionally, it not only defines the different security level but also states the various access permissions for its several users. Further, the CPAM will generate a general attribute set $\{\mathcal{A}_1, \mathcal{A}_2, \mathcal{A}_3, \mathcal{A}_4...\mathcal{A}_n\}$ for all its users. Finally, the CPAM then shares the public parameters, the system rules, and the communication protocol with all its users.

4.2   Phases of the Proposed Architecture

The different phases involved in the proposed architecture are as follows.

- *System Setup Phase*: The Content Publisher and Access Manager (CPAM) is responsible for performing the system setup where it initially the CPAM collects content from the SD, encrypts it with a content key (a random symmetric key generated by the CPAM), and then it encrypts this content key using an access key associated with the attributes of the users (which is determined by the group they belong to). Thus, only the users who have the corresponding access key can decrypt the content. Other users may receive the encrypted content, but they will not be able to access it without the correct access key. Finally, the CPAM publishes both the encrypted content and the encrypted content key to the CCN-IoT network, along with its access policy. Further, the CPAM is also responsible to decrypt and/or manages those contents and provides the access rights of the CCN-IoT environment.
- *Content User Registration Phase*: To perform the registration procedure the following steps are carried out by each of the involved users:
  - The intended User sends registration request with a subset of attributes. For instance, User A sends the registration request using $\{\mathcal{A}_1, \mathcal{A}_4\} \in \{\mathcal{A}_1, \mathcal{A}_2, \mathcal{A}_3, \mathcal{A}_4...\mathcal{A}_n\}$.
  - After receiving the request from the User A, the CPAM verifies the User A. If the User A is successfully verified, then they are registered and assigned an access key based on their attributes $\{\mathcal{A}_1, \mathcal{A}_4\}$, determining which group they belong to. Finally, the User A then receives the corresponding access key for that group using which they can access the content.

- *Content User Revocation Procedure:* Revocation is a crucial aspect of access control systems that occurs when a User leaves, an attribute expires, or an attribute is removed. On the other hand, in our scheme non-revoked user attribute keys are updated periodically using the CPAM.
- *Content Distribution Phase:* The step-by-step working procedure of the content distribution phase is mentioned as follows.
  - *Step 1:* Initially, if a User (User A) (has attribute set $\{\mathcal{A}_1, \mathcal{A}_4\}$) wants to access the content, s/he sends a content request incorporating a timestamp to it to the CCN-IoT network.
  - *Step 2:* In CCN-IoT network, the closest CCN router receives that content request and checks the freshness of the content request by verifying the timestamp. If timestamp is verified as fresh then it proceeds to search for that content name in its Content Store (CS). If that content is present in the CS, directly step 13 (which is explained below) will be executed. If that content is not present in its CS, then CCN router first checks if there is already an entry in its Pending Interest Table (PIT) for the requested content. If an entry exists (because other users are requesting the same content), the router adds the incoming request to the existing PIT entry, preventing redundant forwarding of request packets. If no entry exists, the CCN router creates a new PIT entry and then CCN router searches for a matching prefix entry in its Forwarding Information Base (FIB). If the matching prefix entry is found in FIB then CCN router forwards that content request to the FIB listed next node towards the content. If no matching prefix entry is found in FIB, then CCN router broadcasts that content request across the CCN-IoT network to look for that requested content. Whenever, CCN router finds that requested content, it replies back the requested content towards User A (requestee of the content) and in communication time every content received by the CCN router caches the content in its CS for further use. Additionally, it also deletes the content request from PIT. If no CCN router has that requested content, the content request will eventually reach the server of the original content provider which is called Content Publisher and Access Manager (CPAM).
  - *Step 3:* CPAM receives the content request and first verifies the timestamp of the requested content. If the timestamp is fresh, then it check for that content name in its database. If the content name is available, then directly step 12 (which is explained below) will be executed. If it is not stored in its database then it further sends the content request to the Sensor Devices (SD).
  - *Step 4:* SD receives the content request from CPAM and verifies the timestamp. If the timestamp is fresh, then it generates the requested content and encrypts the content with a shared secret key (shared between SD and CPAM). Finally, it sends the encrypted content to the CPAM.
  - *Step 5:* CPAM receives content from SD and then verifies the timestamp. If the timestamp is fresh, then it decrypts the encrypted content with their shared secret key (which is in its encryption/decryption server). Now, the

encryption/decryption Server sends a request for both the content key and the access key to Key Generator.

- *Step 6:* Key Generator now receives the request, then it generates a random symmetric content key for the content encryption. Further, the Key Generator sends a request to Access Manager to generate the access key.
- *Step 7:* After getting the request, the Access Manager sends the access attributes for that content such as $\{\mathcal{A}_1, \mathcal{A}_4\}$ to the Key Generator.
- *Step 8:* After getting the requested content's access attributes $\{\mathcal{A}_1, \mathcal{A}_4\}$, the Key Generator generates a corresponding access key for those access attributes given by the Access Manager. Finally, the Key Generator sends both the content key and the access key to the encryption/decryption Server.
- *Step 9:* After receiving the keys, the encryption/decryption Server encrypts the content with the content key and that content key is encrypted using the access key. Finally, it sends encrypted content and the encrypted content key to the Publisher.
- *Step 10:* Once, the Publisher receives the encrypted content and the encrypted content key. Then, the Publisher further sends a request to the Access Manager to provide the content access policy of that content.
- *Step 11:* Once the request is received, the Access Manager sends the content access policy to Publisher.
- *Step 12:* Now, the Publisher publishes the encrypted content, encrypted content key, and the access policy to the CCN-IoT network through the CPAM.
- *Step 13:* Eventually, the User A receives the request content from the CCN-router which plays a vital role in the CCN-IoT network.

Thus, User A securely retrieves the intended content from the CPAM through the CCN-router using the access key.

4.3   Advantages of the Proposed Architecture over the CP-ABE Framework:

A few advantages of the proposed architecture over the traditional CP-ABE framework as follows:

- In traditional CP-ABE, for content decryption, a user must interact with the content publisher each time to obtain the content key which is used for the decryption of the content. As a result, it bears high content retrieval time. In contrast to this, in the proposed architecture, instead of repeated communication with the CPAM, during the content user registration phase itself, the CPAM proactively issues an access key. Additionally, this access key can be used directly to decrypt the content key which is further used for the decryption of the content. Thus, the primary advantage of our architecture is that it incurs low content retrieval time as compared to the traditional CP-ABE framework.

- Generally, CP-ABE uses a centralized attribute authority to manage the access control of several users, devices, and attributes. Thus, it is susceptible to single-point failure issue. On the other hand, our architecture uses decentralized CPAM that can effectively manage its users, devices, and attributes.
- In traditional CP-ABE framework, access key revocation (if required) typically requires re-encryption of the content and redistribution of updated decryption keys to all authorized users. In contrast to it, the proposed architecture incorporates an efficient revocation mechanism by assigning a single access key to groups of users, where each group is formed based on shared attributes (i.e., users possessing similar attributes are grouped together). Consequently, in case, when an authorized user's access is revoked by the CPAM (if required), only the access key corresponding to the relevant attribute group is updated and redistributed to the remaining users of that group, while access keys for other attribute groups remain unaffected.
- As mentioned in Sect. 3.1, CCN uses several naming schemes, namely - hierarchical naming scheme, flat naming scheme, attribute-based naming scheme, etc. However, incorporation of these naming schemes in the traditional CP-ABE framework is a challenging task. On the other hand, the significant advantage of our proposed architecture over the traditional CP-ABE framework is that it works seamlessly with all existing CCN naming schemes.
- Traditional CP-ABE framework is vulnerable to replay attack [15]. Inversely, in the proposed architecture, we use timestamps for checking the freshness of each of the content request; thus, preventing the replay attack.

5   Informal Security Analysis

This section presents the informal security analysis of the proposed architecture taking into consideration the below-mentioned security goal/attack scenarios:

5.1   Confidentiality

The essential confidentiality property ensures that only legitimate users can get access to the content of the CCN-IoT network. Accordingly, in the proposed architecture the content of the network are encrypted/decrypted with a content key (which is a randomly generated key) and that content key is encrypted with an access key. Further, this access key is shared with only legitimate users via a secured channel. As a result, only legitimate users can access that content key. Thus, confidentiality is preserved by our architecture.

5.2   Unauthorized Access

In the proposed architecture, the content is encrypted with a content key (randomly generated key), and that content key is further encrypted with an access key. Moreover, this access key is shared with only legitimate users via a secured channel. Therefore, it is impossible for an illegal users in our architecture to get access to the content of the CCN-IoT network.

5.3   Backward and Forward Secrecy

In the proposed architecture, the Content Publisher and Access Manager (CPAM) selects different random number to create the content key for different contents. As a result, even if one content key is compromised, an attacker cannot get access to previous and/or next contents using that particular compromised content key. Thus, backward and forward secrecy is preserved by our architecture.

5.4   Replay Attack

In the proposed architecture, a timestamp is integrated to each of the content request that is used to verify the request's freshness. Thus, if an attacker captures a previously transmitted request and tries maliciously retransmit it for its own illegal use, then the CCN-router identifies and drops this retransmitted request by verifying the timestamp incorporated with it. Thus, our architecture resists replay attack.

5.5   Collision Attack

In the proposed architecture, different access keys are assigned to different group of users by the Content Publisher and Access Manager (CPAM). However, even if multiple groups of users tries to combine their attributes to get illegal access of another group of user's access key, it won't be possible because key policy attribute based access control mechanism is incorporated in our architecture. Thus, the proposed architecture resists collision attack.

6   Use Case Scenarios

A few significant use cases that show the advantages of incorporating our architecture are shown below:

- **Smart Healthcare System:**blueIn a smart healthcare environment, numerous IoT-based medical devices are deployed to monitor and support patient care. These includes patient monitoring sensors, medical imaging devices, wearable health devices, etc. As multiple healthcare professionals interact with these devices and the content they generate. Therefore, secure and role-based access becomes essential aspect of the smart health care environment. The CPAM of the proposed architecture plays a crucial role in addressing this concern where during the content user registration phase (of the proposed architecture), it systematically classifies users into different groups according to their specific attribute sets and assigns access keys to each group accordingly. For example, Doctor A may be assigned the attribute set {ABC Hospital, Cardiologist, Doctor}, while Nurse B receives {ABC Hospital, General Ward, Nurse}. Thus, these assignment of attribute sets performed by the

CPAM defines the role-based access for each user within the smart healthcare environment.

Hence, we can summarize that the incorporation attribute-based policies (performed by CPAM) in the proposed architecture ensures the vital aspect, access integrity which confirms that only authorized healthcare providers can decrypt and/or access medical data. Therefore, the proposed architecture is feasible to be implemented in smart healthcare environment.

– **Smart Home Environment:** blueA smart home environment consists of various IoT devices such as - smart door locks, surveillance cameras, thermostats, motion detectors, lighting systems, etc., and the users of this smart home environment interact with the devices based on their roles and access privileges. Let us consider a scenario where multiple users such as - house owners and guests, need to interact with these devices, but with different levels of access. Thus, to manage this efficiently, the integration of the CPAM in the proposed architecture plays a vital role. Here, during the content user registration phase, the CPAM classifies the users into several groups (such as Group 1, 2, etc.) based on its common attributes and further those groups of users are assigned with specific access keys. For instance, users belonging to the Group 1 with the attribute set {Owner, Full Access} receive an access key M, while those users in the Group 2 with the attribute set {Guest, Temporary Access} are issued a different access key N. These access keys M, N ensures two essential functions - (i) they allow authorized users to decrypt the content keys required to access the IoT device and/or its contents, and (ii) they enforce access restrictions ensuring that a specific group of users can interact with specific devices or content. For example, those users in the Group 2 with the attribute set {Guest, Temporary Access} and the access key N are restricted to access the same content and/or devices accessed by Group 1.

Thus, we can summarize that the integration of CPAM in the proposed architecture ensures several advantages in the smart home environment which are mentioned as follows:
  – **Scalability and Efficiency:** A limited number of access keys can securely support a large number of users.
  – **Enhanced Security and Privacy:** Only authorized groups of users can access certain content, reducing the risk of unauthorized access.

Thus, the proposed architecture is feasible for smart home environment use case scenario.

7 Conclusion

In this paper, an efficient and secure access control architecture, namely Key Policy Attribute-based Access Control (KPAAC) architecture is introduced that integrates a Content Publisher and Access Manager (CPAM). Consequently, unlike existing access control management architecture, our architecture's CPAM facilitates comparatively convenient content retrieval procedure as users directly access the content key provided by the CPAM during registration phase. Correspondingly, we have also performed an informal security analysis considering several attack scenarios which shows that our architecture withstands all well-known security threats. Therefore, the proposed architecture is practically implementable in the emerging CCN-IoT network. On the contrary, due to page restrictions, performance efficiency in terms of computation, communication, and storage overheads of our architecture is kept as the future scope of the paper.

Acknowledgment. This research work is an outcome of R&D Project No. 13(19)/2020-CC&BT dated 20.01.2021 funded by the CC&BT Division, Ministry of Electronics and Information Technology (MeitY), Government of India.

References

1. Al-Fuqaha, A., Guizani, M., Mohammadi, M., Aledhari, M., Ayyash, M.: Internet of things: a survey on enabling technologies, protocols, and applications. IEEE Commun. Surv. Tutor. **17**(4), 2347–2376 (2015)
2. Psaras, I., Chai, W.K., Pavlou, G.: Probabilistic in-network caching for information-centric networks. In: Proceedings of the Second Edition of the ICN Workshop on Information-Centric Networking, pp. 55–60 (2012)
3. Jacobson, V., Smetters, D.K., Thornton, J.D., Plass, M.F., Briggs, N.H., Braynard, R.L.: Networking named content. In: Proceedings of the 5th International Conference on Emerging Networking Experiments and Technologies, pp. 1–12 (2009)
4. Adhikari, S., Ray, S.: A lightweight and secure IoT communication framework in content-centric network using elliptic curve cryptography. In: Khare, A., Tiwary, U.S., Sethi, I.K., Singh, N. (eds.) Recent Trends in Communication, Computing, and Electronics. LNEE, vol. 524, pp. 207–216. Springer, Singapore (2019). https://doi.org/10.1007/978-981-13-2685-1_21
5. Chatterjee, S.: A survey of internet of things (IoT) over information centric network (ICN), no. August, pp. 0–18 (2018)
6. Saha, K.K., Ray, S., Dasgupta, M.: ECMHP: ECC-based secure handshake protocol for multicasting in CCN-IoT environment. IEEE Trans. Netw. Serv. Manag. (2024)
7. Shah, M.S.M., Leau, Y.B., Yan, Z., Anbar, M.: Hierarchical naming scheme in named data networking for internet of things: a review and future security challenges. IEEE Access **10**, 19958–19970 (2022)
8. Bari, M.F., Chowdhury, S.R., Ahmed, R., Boutaba, R., Mathieu, B.: A survey of naming and routing in information-centric networks. IEEE Commun. Mag. **50**(12), 44–53 (2012)
9. Nour, B., Sharif, K., Li, F., Moungla, H., Liu, Y.: A unified hybrid information-centric naming scheme for IoT applications. Comput. Commun. **150**, 103–114 (2020)
10. Sarkar, A., Ray, S.: Enhancing healthcare IoT security: a CCN-based approach for fib establishment and content delivery. In: International Conference on Network Security and Blockchain Technology, pp. 103–117. Springer, Heidelberg (2024). https://doi.org/10.1007/978-981-97-8051-8_9

11. Zhu, Y., Ahn, G.J., Hu, H., Ma, D., Wang, S.: Role-based cryptosystem: a new cryptographic RBAC system based on role-key hierarchy. IEEE Trans. Inf. Forensics Secur. **8**(12), 2138–2153 (2013)
12. Tourani, R., Misra, S., Mick, T., Panwar, G.: Security, privacy, and access control in information-centric networking: a survey. IEEE Commun. Surv. Tutor. **20**(1), 566–600 (2017)
13. Adhikari, S., Ray, S., Obaidat, M.S., Biswas, G.: ECC-based efficient and secure access control scheme for content centric network-a next generation internet. Wirel. Pers. Commun. **132**(1), 571–607 (2023)
14. Chen, T., Lei, K., Xu, K.: An encryption and probability based access control model for named data networking. In: 2014 IEEE 33rd International Performance Computing and Communications Conference (IPCCC), pp. 1–8. IEEE (2014)
15. Asmaa, E.B., Ghazi, M.E., Bouayad, A., Fattah, M., Bekkali, M.E.: Data access control for named data of health things. Bull. Electr. Eng. Inf. **13**(4), 2634–2642 (2024)
16. Ramani, S.K., Tourani, R., Torres, G., Misra, S., Afanasyev, A.: NDN-ABS: attribute-based signature scheme for named data networking. In: Proceedings of the 6th ACM Conference on Information-Centric Networking, pp. 123–133 (2019)
17. Li, Q., Zhang, X., Zheng, Q., Sandhu, R., Fu, X.: Live: lightweight integrity verification and content access control for named data networking. IEEE Trans. Inf. Forensics Secur. **10**(2), 308–320 (2014)
18. Hamdane, B., El Fatmi, S.G.: A credential and encryption based access control solution for named data networking. In: 2015 IFIP/IEEE International Symposium on Integrated Network Management (IM), pp. 1234–1237. IEEE (2015)
19. Feng, T., Guo, J.: A new access control system based on CP-ABE in named data networking. Int. J. Netw. Secur. **20**(4), 710–720 (2018)
20. Wu, Z., Xu, E., Liu, L., Yue, M.: CHTDS: a CP-ABE access control scheme based on hash table and data segmentation in NDN. In: 2019 18th IEEE International Conference on Trust, Security and Privacy in Computing and Communications/13th IEEE International Conference on Big Data Science and Engineering (TrustCom/BigDataSE), pp. 843–848. IEEE (2019)
21. Li, B., Huang, D., Wang, Z., Zhu, Y.: Attribute-based access control for ICN naming scheme. IEEE Trans. Dependable Secure Comput. **15**(2), 194–206 (2018). https://doi.org/10.1109/TDSC.2016.2550437
22. Arshad, S., Azam, M.A., Ahmed, S.H., Loo, J.: Towards information-centric networking (ICN) naming for internet of things (IoT) the case of smart campus. In: Proceedings of the International Conference on Future Networks and Distributed Systems, pp. 1–6 (2017)
23. Bethencourt, J., Sahai, A., Waters, B.: Ciphertext-policy attribute-based encryption. In: 2007 IEEE Symposium on Security and Privacy (SP'07), pp. 321–334. IEEE (2007)
24. Sowjanya, K., Dasgupta, M., Ray, S., Obaidat, M.S.: An efficient elliptic curve cryptography-based without pairing KPABE for internet of things. IEEE Syst. J. **14**(2), 2154–2163 (2019)
25. Goyal, V., Pandey, O., Sahai, A., Waters, B.: Attribute-based encryption for fine-grained access control of encrypted data. In: Proceedings of the 13th ACM Conference on Computer and Communications Security, pp. 89–98 (2006)
26. Carzaniga, A., Rutherford, M.J., Wolf, A.L.: A routing scheme for content-based networking. In: IEEE INFOCOM 2004, vol. 2, pp. 918–928. IEEE (2004)

27. Koponen, T., et al.: A data-oriented (and beyond) network architecture. In: Proceedings of the 2007 Conference on Applications, Technologies, Architectures, and Protocols for Computer Communications, pp. 181–192 (2007)
28. Shang, W., et al.: Named data networking of things. In: 2016 IEEE First International Conference on Internet-of-Things Design and Implementation (IoTDI), pp. 117–128. IEEE (2016)

Graph Exploration Using Mobile Agents

Sushant Bakshi[(✉)], Rishi Srivastava, Arka Ghosh, Sayandeb Sarkar,
and Sruti Gan Chaudhuri

Jadavpur University, Kolkata, West Bengal, India
sushantbakshi25@gmail.com

Abstract. This study examines the problem of exploring a random unexplored graph using mobile agents. Starting with n mobile agents at arbitrary nodes in an anonymous graph with n-nodes ($G=V,E$) our objective is for the agents to explore the graph while simultaneously forming a subset of nodes $S \subset V$ that constitutes a MIS(Maximal Independent Set). The MIS guides the exploration, minimizing unnecessary revisits to vertices and maximizing the efficiency of both local and global exploration tasks. We present time-bounded algorithms and simulations for graph exploration by mobile agents by identifying a MIS in different configurations of graphs. These configurations are rooted and dispersed. In the rooted configuration, all mobile agents are initially positioned at a single, designated root node within the network. This setup ensures that the agents begin their exploration from a common starting point, which can simplify coordination and communication among the agents during the exploration process. The root node serves as a central hub, and from there, the agents disperse to explore the rest of the network systematically. In contrast, the dispersed configuration involves distributing the agents uniformly across the network, with each agent initially occupying a distinct and separate node. This configuration allows for a broader initial coverage of the network, enabling agents to simultaneously begin exploring different regions. The dispersed approach can lead to faster exploration times, as there is no need for agents to travel from a single starting point. We evaluated the time complexity for determining MIS by agents possessing 1-hop visibility i.e. each agent can only perceive and gather information about its immediate neighboring nodes within a single hop. The upper bound on time complexity in the 1-hop visibility model, where agents can interact with other agents at a distance of at most 1-hop from their location, for rooted configuration is given by $O(n)$. The time complexity of finding the MIS in the dispersed configuration, characterized by the placement of at most a single agent per node, is bounded by $O(1)$.

Keywords: Graph exploration · Distributed algorithms · Mobile agents · Maximal Independent Set (MIS) · Time complexity · 1-hop visibility

1 Introduction

The graph exploration problem using a MIS is a cornerstone of distributed computing, having been extensively studied for many years, with foundational works

K. Chandra Mondal et al. (Eds.): CICBA 2025, CCIS 2862, pp. 32–44, 2026.
https://doi.org/10.1007/978-3-032-17187-0_3

in the distributed message-passing model [1,9–12]. In graph exploration, where the goal is to systematically visit all nodes of an unknown or dynamic graph, finding an MIS offers significant strategic advantages. In communication networks, an MIS can be used to create clusters where each node in the network is either part of the MIS or directly connected to a node in the MIS. These "leader" nodes (the MIS members) act as cluster heads, enabling efficient data aggregation, load balancing, and reduced communication overhead. The independence property of an MIS ensures that no two selected nodes are adjacent, which is highly beneficial in scenarios such as frequency assignment in wireless networks. In scheduling problems, where tasks or processes are represented as graph nodes, an MIS helps identify a set of non-conflicting tasks that can run simultaneously. An MIS is also a good approximation of a minimum dominating set (MDS), which is a set of nodes such that every other node in the graph is either in the set or adjacent to a node in the set.

In this study, we explore the challenge of determining the time complexities for graph exploration by determining a MIS in an unidentified graph using mobile agents having 1-hop visibility. Finding a MIS during graph exploration can significantly enhance the efficiency and effectiveness of the exploration process. In an unknown graph, finding a MIS helps agents uncover its structure by mapping local neighborhoods and adjacency relationships. The MIS can act as a dominating set ensuring comprehensive coverage while partitioning the graph into independent vertices and their neighbors and since every vertex of the graph is either in the MIS or adjacent to a vertex in the MIS, the MIS helps ensure that the entire graph is covered during exploration. Recent advancements in multi-agent systems have garnered significant attention because of their ability to tackle tasks that are too complex for a single agent [13]. Graph exploration using MIS model is a fascinating challenge that has been thoroughly investigated over the past several years. It remains a key focus in the message-passing model in distributed computing.

Graph exploration by mobile agents enables efficient coordination, monitoring, and optimization across interconnected nodes. For network maintenance and monitoring, mobile agents can explore network graphs to identify faults, optimize routing, and monitor performance in communication and sensor networks. In Wireless Sensor Networks, mobile agents traverse the networks to collect data from distributed nodes, ensuring efficient and reliable information gathering in resource-constrained environments. For fault diagnosis and recovery in a distributed system, agents explore the graph representation of a distributed system to identify and isolate faulty nodes or links, ensuring system reliability and robustness. Graph exploration also aids in monitoring the workload across nodes in a distributed system, enabling dynamic redistribution of tasks to achieve balanced processing and efficient resource usage.

This field of research has been explored in the past with an emphasis on different communication models of mobile agents. These investigations cover a range of communication models, from models where agents have only local communication abilities to models where agents possess global communication capabilities. In the local communication model, agents are limited to interacting only with other agents situated at the same vertex. In contrast, the global communication model allows agents to communicate freely with other agents located anywhere on the graph, without any visibility constraints.

We adhere to the commonly utilized mobile agent or mobile robot model. A collection of mobile agents is situated in an unknown port-labeled graph. The vertices of this graph are unmarked. Each node's ports are differentiated and given a port number to each connected edge, but the two port numbers associated with an edge are independent. Every agent maintains a variable (called *color*) that helps in determining the inclusion of a node in a MIS or not. Although all the algorithms mentioned in the study are deterministic, the MIS found might differ depending on the numbering of the ports and how the agents are placed initially. Upon completion of the an algorithm, all agents rightly ascertain whether or not they are positioned at a node that can be part of a MIS, ensuring that every node in a MIS are filled.

We examine different initial placements of agents. In all the potential initial configurations, we concentrate on two opposite cases: the dispersed initial configuration and the rooted initial configuration. In the rooted configuration, all agents start at a single node, while in the dispersed configuration, each agent is positioned at a distinct node. In arbitrary configurations, we put forward algorithms that leverage already available dispersion algorithms to get an initial dispersed configuration and then apply algorithms to find a MIS from that configuration.

1.1   Contributions

The maximal independent set (MIS) is a fundamental concept in graph theory with significant applications in graph exploration and distributed computing. A MIS is a subset of nodes such that no two nodes in the subset are adjacent, and adding any other node to the subset would violate this property. This makes MIS a critical building block for tasks such as network clustering, resource allocation, scheduling, and dominating set approximation. In graph exploration, finding a MIS is particularly valuable because it enables the selection of a well-distributed set of "leader" nodes that can facilitate efficient communication, coordination, and coverage across the graph.

Our model contributes to this domain by offering tailored algorithms to find MIS for both rooted and dispersed initial configurations in unknown graphs. The rooted configuration algorithm ensures comprehensive graph coverage through agent movement and systematic exploration, making it robust for scenarios where the graph's topology is entirely unknown and starting points are limited. On the other hand, the dispersed configuration algorithm leverages agents' 1-hop visibility to achieve MIS formation without agent movement, significantly improving efficiency in scenarios where agents are pre-distributed across the network.

We examine a graph with anonymous nodes, denoted as $G=(V,E)$, where the number of nodes V is n and the number of edges E is m. In the 1-hop visibility model, each agent can only perceive and communicate with agents positioned at directly adjacent nodes—those that are exactly one edge away

Table 1. Simulation results for graph exploration by mobile agents with 1-hop visibility in rooted configuration.

Round	Node	Parent	Recent	Color	Next	Options	Target Values	MIS nodes
1	v	–	0	red	u	['u','w','x','z']	['blue', 'black','black']	['v']
2	u	v	2	blue	w	['v','w','y']	['red','blue','black']	['v']
3	w	u	4	blue	t	['t','u','v','x','z']	['red','blue','red','black']	['v','t']
4	t	w	1	red	x	['w','x']	['blue','blue']	['v','t']
5	x	t	3	blue	y	['t','v','w','y']	['red','red','blue','red']	['v','t','y']
6	y	x	2	red	z	['u','x','z']	['blue','blue','blue']	['v','t','y']
7	z	–	2	blue	y	['v','w','y']	['red','blue,'red']	['v','t','y']

Table 2. Simulation results for graph exploration by mobile agents with 1-hop visibility in dispersed configuration.

Step	Node	Color	Highest Candidate	Available Neighbors	MIS nodes
0	z	Black	z	['y','w','v']	–
1	z	Red	z	['y','w','v']	z
2	x	Black	x	['y','w','v','t']	['z']
3	x	Red	x	['y','w','v','t']	['z','x']
4	u	Black	u	['y','w','v']	['z','x']
5	u	Red	u	['y','w','v']	['z','x','u']

from its current location in the graph. This model limits an agent's awareness to its immediate neighborhood, enabling local but not global communication. When an agent sends a message or shares information, it can only do so with agents on nodes that share a direct edge with the node it occupies. This localized communication is often achieved through message passing along the edges of the graph, where each node acts as a relay point. The 1-hop visibility model ensures that all decisions and actions taken by the agent are based on information from its immediate surroundings, promoting decentralized control and reducing the complexity of coordination in distributed systems. Their goal is to explore the graph while simultaneously identifying nodes which together become part of a maximal independent set (MIS) within the graph (G). When the process ends, nodes that are part of the MIS, have at least one agent present, and these agents have a variable showing their MIS membership. Conversely, if the agents are on nodes that are not included in the MIS, they should reflect this by showing that these nodes are not part of the MIS upon completion.

We distinguish between two specific types of initial agent configurations: (i) rooted configuration—when all agents are located at a single node; (ii) dispersed configuration—when there is at most one agent per node, meaning with (n) agents and (n) nodes, every node has one agent.

In this work, we explore specialized algorithms designed to efficiently construct a maximal independent set (MIS) in an unknown graph, considering two distinct initial configurations: rooted and dispersed. Each configuration presents unique challenges and necessitates tailored algorithmic strategies. In the rooted configuration, all agents start from a single root node, requiring coordinated exploration and systematic movement across the graph to discover new nodes and expand the MIS. The algorithm leverages a depth-first search (DFS) approach, where agents physically traverse edges, scout unvisited nodes, and settle strategically to maintain the independence property of the MIS.

In contrast, the dispersed configuration involves each agent being initially placed at a unique node, ensuring that no node hosts more than one agent. This setup allows agents to leverage local communication with their immediate (1-hop) neighbors to determine MIS membership without the need for physical movement. Agents exchange information about their local states, colors, and the status of neighboring nodes to make decisions. By avoiding unnecessary traversal, the algorithm in the dispersed configuration achieves higher efficiency, as agents determine whether they should be part of the MIS based solely on the state of their immediate neighbors.

We further present simulation results that illustrate the dynamic behavior of agents in both configurations (Refer Tables 1 and 2). These results highlight the agent movement patterns in the rooted configuration and the localized decision-making process in the dispersed configuration. The simulations provide insights into how the proposed algorithms maintain the MIS properties, such as independence and maximality, while adapting to the constraints imposed by each initial setup. Through this comparative study, we demonstrate how strategic movement and communication mechanisms contribute to the effectiveness of MIS construction in unknown graph environments.

Our model goes beyond theoretical development by offering comprehensive simulation results and an in-depth analysis of agent movements and communication strategies in both rooted and dispersed configurations. These simulations provide a visual and quantitative understanding of how agents navigate through unknown graphs, interact with their immediate environment, and make decisions to construct a maximal independent set (MIS). By mapping out the agent trajectories, settlement patterns, and communication exchanges, the simulations validate the theoretical time complexities of our proposed algorithms—$O(n)$ for the rooted configuration and $O(1)$ for the dispersed configuration.

In the rooted configuration, the simulation demonstrates how agents systematically traverse the graph using a depth-first search (DFS) approach. Agents explore new nodes, settle strategically and ensuring that the entire graph is covered efficiently while maintaining the MIS properties. The $O(n)$ complexity reflects the need for agents to visit each node at least once, making this approach suitable for environments where initial agent deployment is centralized.

Conversely, in the dispersed configuration, our model highlights the efficiency gains achieved through localized communication. With 1-hop visibility, agents exchange information with their immediate neighbors without physically moving across edges. The simulation shows how agents quickly decide whether to become part of the MIS by assessing local states, avoiding unnecessary movements, and achieving MIS formation in constant time ($O(1)$). This configuration is particularly effective in scenarios where agents are pre-distributed across the network, minimizing latency and maximizing responsiveness.

The dual-approach model's adaptability to varying initial conditions is a significant advantage in real-world applications. Whether dealing with centralized or distributed agent deployment, our model can dynamically adjust its strategy, offering a robust solution for graph exploration tasks in dynamic and unknown environments. This adaptability enhances the applicability of MIS-based strategies in practical domains such as wireless sensor networks, distributed computing, and autonomous robotic systems, where efficient graph exploration and coordination are crucial.

1.2 Literature Survey

This study is positioned within and continues further work in a well-established body of research on distributed computing with mobile agents. Significant contributions in the field include studies on graph exploration by mobile agents or mobile robots. The dispersion problem of mobile robot has been examined, focusing on the trade-offs between memory and time, allowing robots with limited memory to disperse efficiently in a given environment, highlighting how varying memory constraints impact the time required for dispersion. Strategies have been explored for dispersing silent robots across a graph, focusing on collaboration without direct communication, providing theoretical bounds for achieving efficient dispersion under various conditions [1,2]. The concept of Distance-2-Dispersion have been studied by Tanvir Kaur and Kaushik Mondal, where mobile robots must disperse under additional constraints, specifically maintaining a minimum distance of two units between each other. The study proposes and analyzes algorithms that address these further constraints, focusing on the impact of this requirement on dispersion efficiency and the complexity of achieving optimal dispersion [3]. Fast dispersion algorithms for mobile robots on arbitrary graphs have been studied examining how robots can quickly disperse across different graph topologies, focusing on the efficiency of the algorithms in minimizing dispersion time while addressing the challenges posed by arbitrary graph structures. Studies have been done on algorithms designed to handle changing graph topologies, focusing on how robots can adapt to these dynamics to achieve efficient dispersion. It also analyzes the trade-offs between adaptability and dispersion time in dynamic environments [4,5]. The dispersion of mobile robots has also been explored utilizing global communication that enables robots to disperse efficiently using global communication mechanisms, examining the impact of this approach on dispersion time and coordination, particularly in distributed computing environments. Algorithms have been explored for near-optimal dispersion of mobile agents on arbitrary anonymous graphs, focusing on achieving efficient dispersion without relying on unique node identifiers, analyzing the time and coordination challenges involved in reaching near-optimal dispersion in such graph structures [6,7]. The relationship between the structure of a graph and the ability to compute global properties using local information have been investigated to show how efficiently certain tasks can be performed in a distributed setting, focusing on the limits of locality and its implications for algorithm design [8]. More efficient, randomized parallel algorithms have been studied to find a maximal independent set in a graph for their simplicity and effectiveness in parallel computing, offering performance improvements in distributed and parallel systems [9].

1.3 Organization

This paper begins by describing the model used for the study (Sect. 2), followed by graph exploration algorithms to find the Maximal Independent Set (MIS) in graphs (Sect. 3), simulation outcomes and performance analysis of the proposed algorithms under both rooted and dispersed configurations (Sect. 4) and concludes with a discussion of the results (Sect. 5).

2 Model

Here, we outline the graph and agent models, along with their respective abilities and limitations.

Graph: A graph $G = (V, E)$ is an unknown, random, port-labeled and undirected with unweighted edges, where $|V| = n$ and $|E| = m$. The diameter of the graph is denoted by D, and the maximum degree is denoted by Δ.

Agent: A group of agents $R = \{r_1, r_2, \ldots, r_n\}$ is located at the root node(Rooted configuration) or distributed across the vertices of the graph(Dispersed configuartion). Each agent has a unique ID within the range $[1, n^c]$, where c is a constant. Multiple agents may occupy the same node simultaneously. Each agent has the ability to move between nodes through connecting edges in a single round. Each agent stores information about itself and other agents in variables such as 'settled','color','parent' and 'next'.

Communication: Agents can communicate with other agents located at a distance of 1 hop from their respective locations. Under the 1-hop visibility model, each agent can "see" or obtain information from its immediate neighbors through virtual communication channels. Instead of moving to a neighboring node to gather data, an agent can access the state, color, and settlement status of agents at adjacent nodes. This reduces unnecessary movements and enhances efficiency, particularly in the dispersed configuration where physical traversal is minimized.

Time: The time required to determine the MIS is calculated by determining the no. of rounds required by agents upon completion of the algorithm for a specific configuration of agents. A round is defined as the traversal of an agent as it moves from one node to another.

3 Graph Exploration Algorithms

We study algorithms for graph exploration by finding a MIS in general graphs and deduce the time complexities. We begin with the algorithm for the rooted configuration, followed by an algorithm tailored for the dispersed configuration.

3.1 Rooted Configuration

The algorithm begins with an initialization phase where all nodes are set to "black," marked as unsettled, and assigned infinite hop values to signify unexplored status. An MIS array is maintained throughout the process to keep track of nodes that are part of the Maximal Independent Set. The algorithm proceeds in a round-wise execution manner, where each round is handled independently, allowing for systematic updates to node properties and decisions about the next node to visit. Whenever the algorithm identifies a valid "leader" node, the MIS array is updated accordingly, ensuring that the selected nodes contribute to building a well-distributed and effective independent set within the graph (Fig. 1).

Algorithm 1 MIS Algorithm for Rooted Configuartion

1: **Initialization:**
2: **for** each node n in graph **do**
3:      $n.settled \leftarrow False$, $n.color \leftarrow "black"$
4:      $n.parent \leftarrow None$, $n.hops \leftarrow \infty$, $n.next \leftarrow None$
5: **end for**
6: $MIS \leftarrow [\,]$, $v.color \leftarrow "red"$
7: $v.settled \leftarrow True$, $v.hops \leftarrow 0$
8: $MIS.append(v)$
9: **for** round r in 1 to 6 **do**
10:     **if** $r = 1$ **then**
11:         $NODE, OPTIONS, TARGET, NODE.next \qquad\qquad\qquad\qquad \leftarrow$
            $v, ['u',' w',' x',' z'], ['black',' black',' black',' black'], u$
12:     **else if** $r = 2$ **then**
13:         $NODE, OPTIONS, TARGET, NODE.next \qquad\qquad\qquad\qquad \leftarrow$
            $u, ['v',' w',' y'], ['red',' black',' black'], w$
14:     **else if** $r = 3$ **then**
15:         $NODE, OPTIONS, TARGET, NODE.next \qquad\qquad\qquad\qquad \leftarrow$
            $w, ['t',' u',' v',' x',' z'], ['black',' blue',' red',' black',' black'], t$
16:         $MIS.append(t)$
17:     **else if** $r = 4$ **then**
18:         $NODE, OPTIONS, TARGET, NODE.next \leftarrow t, ['w',' x'], ['blue',' black'], x$
19:     **else if** $r = 5$ **then**
20:         $NODE, OPTIONS, TARGET, NODE.next \qquad\qquad\qquad\qquad \leftarrow$
            $x, ['t',' v',' w',' y'], ['red',' red',' blue',' black'], y$
21:         $MIS.append(y)$
22:     **else if** $r = 6$ **then**
23:         $NODE, OPTIONS, TARGET, NODE.next \qquad\qquad\qquad\qquad \leftarrow$
            $y, ['u',' x',' z'], ['blue',' blue',' black'], z$
24:     **end if**
25:     $NODE.settled \leftarrow True$, $NODE.color \leftarrow "red"$
26:     **Print** MIS Nodes
27: **end for**

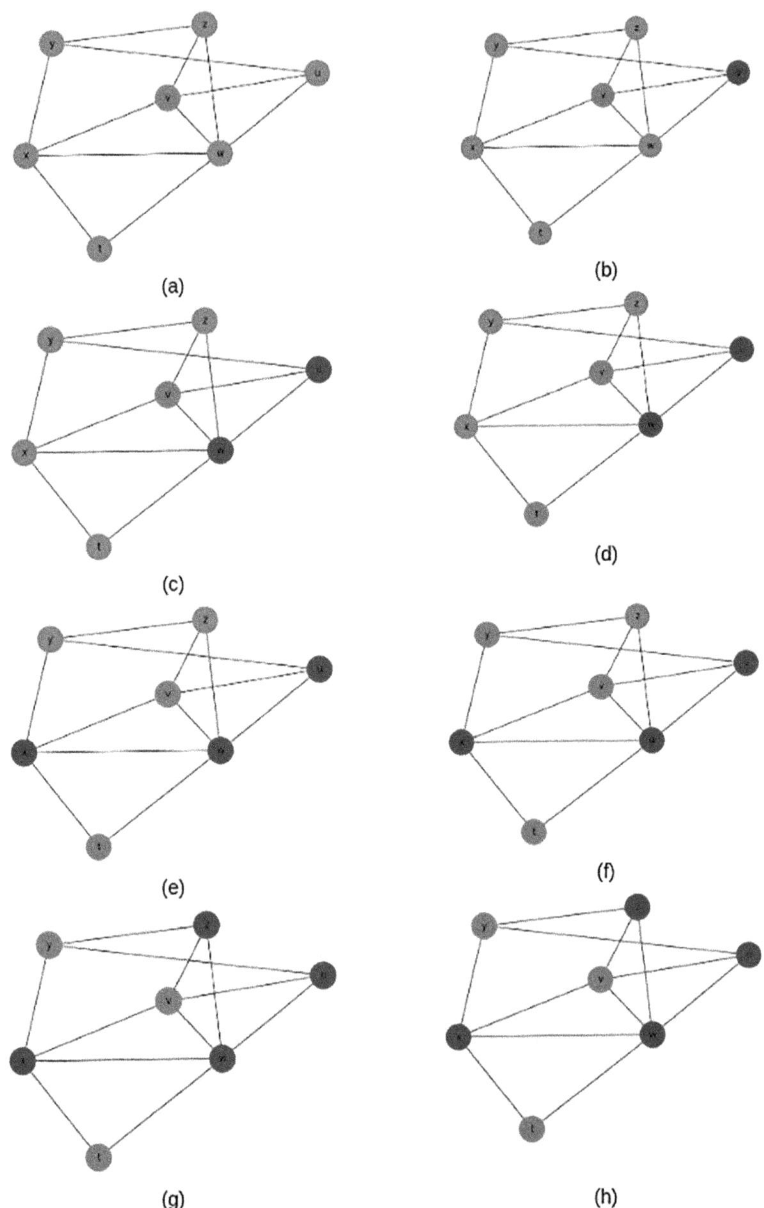

Fig. 1. Graph exploration using agents with 1-hop visibility in rooted configuration. (a) Node v (root) becomes part of MIS. (b) Node u is excluded from MIS as it is adjacent to v. (c) Node w is excluded from MIS. (d) Node t becomes part of MIS as no adjacent node is part of MIS. (e) Node x is excluded from MIS. (f) Node y becomes part of MIS. (g) Node z is excluded from MIS. (h) Final MIS. (Color figure online)

The algorithm initializes all nodes to an unsettled state with an initial color of "black" and infinite hops. The algorithm begins at a designated start node, marking it as "red," settled, and setting its hop count to 0. The MIS array is initialized with this start node. The algorithm then proceeds in discrete rounds, where in each round, a specific node is selected based on its parent-child relationship from the previous round. During each round, the selected node updates its properties, including setting the settled status to true, changing its color to "red," and updating the hop count and parent information. The next node to visit is determined by evaluating the available options and target values. If the conditions for a "leader" node are met, the node is added to the MIS array. Since the algorithm advances by one node per round and each node is processed exactly once, the total number of rounds required is at most n, where n is the total number of nodes in the graph. Communication between nodes is limited to their immediate neighbors as per the 1-hop visibility model, ensuring that each round completes in constant time. Consequently, the overall time complexity of the algorithm is $\mathcal{O}(n)$.

3.2   Dispersed Configuration

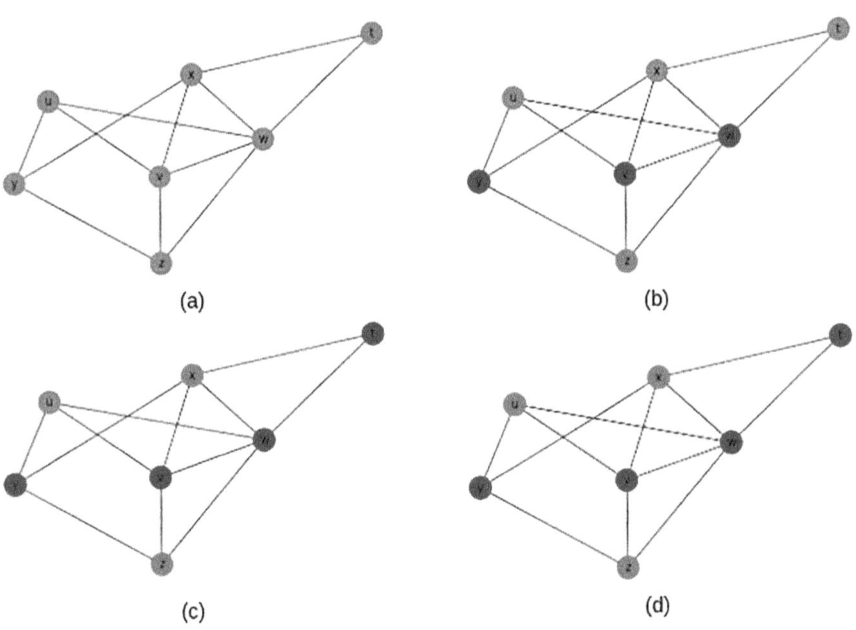

Fig. 2. Graph exploration using agents with 1-hop visibility in Dispersed configuration. (a) Node z (highest ID) becomes part of MIS. (b)All adjacent nodes to node z are excluded from MIS. (c) Node x(next highest ID node) becomes part of MIS and all adjacent nodes are excluded from MIS. (d) Final MIS (node u is included in the MIS). (Color figure online)

The algorithm for finding a Maximal Independent Set (MIS) in a graph in dispersed configuration begins by initializing all nodes to the "black" state with no parent and infinite hops. It assigns unique IDs to each node, sorts them in descending order, and initializes the MIS and removed nodes sets. During each round, the highest-ID node is selected, added to the MIS, and marked as "red." Its neighbors are marked as "blue" and removed from further consideration. Parent relationships are updated where needed. The process continues until all nodes are processed, with each step visualized through graph plotting. The algorithm efficiently produces an MIS with minimal node movement and clear communication pathways (Fig. 2).

Algorithm 2 MIS Algorithm for Dispersed Configuration

Initialization:
node n in graph $n.color \leftarrow black$, $n.parent \leftarrow None$, $n.hops \leftarrow \infty$
$MIS \leftarrow \emptyset$, $removed\_nodes \leftarrow \emptyset$, $step \leftarrow 1$

Assign IDs and Sort Nodes:
$node\_ids \leftarrow \{node : i$ for $i, node$ in $enumerate(sorted(graph.keys()))\}$
$sorted\_nodes \leftarrow sort(node\_ids, descending = True)$

Process Nodes:

while $sorted\_nodes$ is not empty **do** $node \leftarrow sorted\_nodes.pop(0)$

   if $node \in removed\_nodes$ **then** continue
$MIS.add(node)$, $node.color \leftarrow red$
$removed\_nodes.add(node)$

neighbor in $graph[node]$
   if $neighbor \notin removed\_nodes$ **then** $removed\_nodes.add(neighbor)$, $neighbor.color \leftarrow blue$

   if $neighbor.parent == None$ **then** $neighbor.parent \leftarrow node$
$sorted\_nodes \leftarrow [n$ for $n \in sorted\_nodes$ if $n \notin removed\_nodes]$
$plot\_graph\_and\_table(graph, MIS, removed\_nodes, step)$, $step \leftarrow step + 1$

return MIS and final graph state.

In each round, the algorithm picks the highest-ID node from the list of available nodes, instantly adding it to the Maximal Independent Set (MIS). This immediate decision-making eliminates the need for iterative comparisons or complex evaluations, ensuring that each node's processing is completed in constant time. Once a node is selected, all its neighbors are marked as removed from consideration in a single operation, which is also executed in constant time. This simultaneous removal of neighbors prevents reprocessing and maintains a bounded number of operations for each node. Crucially, since the algorithm does not depend on the total size of the graph and performs a fixed set of actions per node, the entire process of constructing the MIS is completed in constant time. The time complexity to find a Maximal Independent Set (MIS) in an unknown graph by mobile agents having 1-hop visibility using the proposed algorithm is $\mathcal{O}(1)$ for the dispersed configuration.

4   Results

Simulation experiments were conducted to evaluate the performance of the proposed MIS algorithms under rooted and dispersed configurations using mobile agents with 1-hop visibility. In the rooted configuration, agents systematically explored the graph using a depth-first search strategy, with each agent settling on a node to maintain MIS properties. The simulation demonstrated that agents efficiently covered the entire graph with minimal overlap, resulting in a time complexity of $O(n)$. In contrast, the dispersed configuration allowed agents to determine MIS membership through local communication without physical movement. By selecting the highest-ID node and marking its neighbors, the agents formed a valid MIS in constant time, achieving $O(1)$ complexity. Tables 1 and 2 highlight the round-wise and step-wise progression of MIS node selection. The results validate the effectiveness of both algorithms, demonstrating that strategic initial placement and localized communication significantly impact the efficiency of MIS construction in unknown graphs.

5   Conclusion

Finding a Maximal Independent Set (MIS) plays a pivotal role in graph exploration by enabling the identification of well-distributed "leader" nodes that enhance communication, coordination, and coverage throughout the graph. An MIS provides a robust foundation for tasks such as network clustering, resource allocation, and scheduling, making it a critical component in dynamic and unknown environments. Our study presented efficient algorithms to find the MIS under both rooted and dispersed configurations, catering to different initial conditions. Through detailed simulation results and rigorous analysis, we demonstrated the practical application and theoretical efficiency of our approach, showcasing an $O(n)$ time complexity for the rooted configuration and an $O(1)$ complexity for the dispersed configuration. These insights not only validate our modelN's effectiveness but also offer valuable guidance for deploying autonomous agents in real-world graph exploration scenarios.

References

1. Augustine, J., Moses Jr, W.K.: Dispersion of mobile robots: a study of memory-time trade-offs. In: ICDCN, pp. 1:1–1:10 (2018)
2. Gorain, B., Mandal, P.S., Mondal, K., Pandit, S.: Collaborative dispersion by silent robots. In: SSS, vol. 13751, pp. 254–269. Springer, Heidelberg (2022)

3. Kaur, T., Mondal, K.: Distance-2-dispersion: dispersion with further constraints. In: NETYS, pp. 157–173 (2023)
4. Kshemkalyani, A.D., Molla, A.R., Sharma, G.: Fast dispersion of mobile robots on arbitrary graphs. In: ALGOSENSORS, pp. 23–40 (2019)
5. Kshemkalyani, A.D., Molla, A.R., Sharma, G.: Efficient dispersion of mobile robots on dynamic graphs. In: ICDCS, pp. 732–742 (2020)
6. Kshemkalyani, A.D., Molla, A.R., Sharma, G.: Dispersion of mobile robots using global communication. J. Parallel Distrib. Comput. **161**(2022), 100–117 (2022)
7. Kshemkalyani, A.D., Sharma, G.: Near-optimal dispersion on arbitrary anonymous graphs. In: OPODIS, pp. 8:1–8:19 (2021)
8. Linial, N.: Locality in distributed graph algorithms. SIAM J. Comput. **21**(1), 193–201 (1992)
9. Luby, M.: A simple parallel algorithm for the maximal independent set problem. SIAM J. Comput. **15**(4), 1036–1053 (1986)
10. Israeli, A., Itai, A.: A fast and simple randomized parallel algorithm for maximal matching. Inf. Process. Lett. **22**(2), 77–80 (1986)
11. Panconesi, A., Srinivasan, A.: On the complexity of distributed network decomposition. J. Algor. **20**(2), 356–374 (1996)
12. Stone, P., Kaminka, G.A., Kraus, S., Rosenschein, J.S.: Ad hoc autonomous agent teams: collaboration without pre-coordination. In: AAAI (2010)

Shortest Path Pattern Recognition for Medical Emergency Vehicular Control

Anasuya Sengupta[✉] [iD], Adrish Dey [iD], Arghadeep Sarkar [iD], Akanksha Yadav [iD], Ankan Roy [iD], Anindya Sundar Maity [iD], Aniruddha Ghosh [iD], and Sudipta Sahana [iD]

Institute of Engineering and Management, Kolkata, University of Engineering and Management, New Town, University Area, Plot No. III, B/5, New Town Road, Action Area III, Newtown, New Town, West Bengal 700160, India
anasuya.sengupta25@gmail.com

Abstract. In developing a pattern recognition system for finding the shortest path for an ambulance, the paper abstraction involves creating an intelligent algorithm that can analyze real-time traffic patterns and emergency scenarios to efficiently navigate the ambulance through urban or suburban environments. The abstraction encompasses the integration of machine learning models that can predict traffic congestion. Specifically, Random Forest classifiers are used for traffic pattern recognition and LSTM networks for time-series traffic prediction. Training leverages historical traffic data from OpenStreetMap, emergency response datasets, and weather correlation data identify optimal routes based on dynamic factors such as road closures or accidents, and prioritize paths that minimize travel time. Additionally, the system should consider emergency- specific parameters, such as the proximity to hospitals and the severity of the patient's condition. This abstraction aims to provide a holistic solution that leverages advanced pattern recognition techniques to enhance the responsiveness and effectiveness of ambulance services, ultimately saving crucial time in emergency situations.

Keywords: Shortest Path · GPS · Dijkstra's Algorithm · Raspberry Pi · Open Street Map API

1 Introduction

In emergency medical situations, the swift and efficient transportation of ambulances to the designated location is critical for saving lives [1]. The ability to navigate through urban environments and find the shortest path to the destination is paramount. Traditional navigation systems often rely on predetermined routes or real-time traffic data, but these may not be optimal in emergency scenarios where every second counts. This research paper aims to leverage advanced pattern recognition techniques to enhance the efficiency of ambulance navigation systems [2]. By incorporating real-time data, such as traffic conditions, road closures, and the dynamic nature of urban environments, the system can adapt and provide the shortest and fastest route for ambulances to reach their destinations. The use of pattern recognition involves analyzing and understanding complex patterns

© The Author(s), under exclusive license to Springer Nature Switzerland AG 2026
K. Chandra Mondal et al. (Eds.): CICBA 2025, CCIS 2862, pp. 45–56, 2026.
https://doi.org/10.1007/978-3-032-17187-0_4

within the road network, traffic flow, and historical data to predict the most efficient path. Machine learning algorithms can be trained to recognize patterns in traffic congestion [3], identify alternative routes, and optimize the ambulance's trajectory in response to changing conditions [4]. With the help of a Raspberry Pi [5] module and Open Street Map API servers, the system can be easily installed in any automobile, enabling the driver to reach from point A (i.e. the current location of the vehicle) to point B (i.e. the destination). The path to be followed will be highlighted on the display in red after the current location of the driver is grated to the module, followed by it being processed by the algorithm, and highlighted the path in red on the system's display. The module takes the data from the map servers and runs it through the algorithm calculating the shortest path possible considering all variables that might affect the time to reach, thus helping the driver to reach the destination on time, the driver will also be aided by visual direction, along with the street's name on the screen for easy understanding. Hence, this module will enable the driver to reach with the shortest amount of time possible to the hospital and save lives.

2   Literature Review

Shubhangi S. Bakhade and Prof. M. S. Chaudhari suggest that current health system frameworks focus on long-term patient observation to collect and monitor health data, which can be processed locally or remotely using AI algorithms. A e-ambulance will be available for any app user at any point of time which will connect them with the driver who will also be using the app thus, the user will benefit the quick response and be treated with the medical conditions [6].

Elgarej Mohammad, et al. emphasizes the importance of optimal routing in city crisis rescue operations. Initially focused on finding the "most limited path," the approach has evolved to seek the "shortest route" while considering various situational factors. Given the high number of global accidents, a robust strategy for quick intervention is essential. This paper proposes using an ant colony algorithm model and improved techniques to efficiently direct emergency vehicles to accident sites, ensuring effective response under complex conditions [7].

Sharaf AI Kheder and Dana AISaloumi - authors suggested that the delay caused loss of life. Arrival at the hospital at the golden hour. This delay is mainly due to waiting Ambulance at traffic signal. A traffic signal on the way to the hospital would be very helpful Turn on. Thus, this paper proposed a new design to automatically control and achieve traffic signals. The above mentioned works so that ambulances are able to cross all junctions without waiting. This system involves mapping ambulance and hospital locations and using algorithms such as Dijkstra's algorithm to calculate the most efficient route [8].

Advay Thakur, et al. authors realized that the number of cars Roads have increased significantly, especially in urban areas. People often find themselves stuck in Road traffic, and ambulance services are among the main services affected by traffic. To help move ambulances in traffic, this paper is employing "Ambulance Tracking and Route". Clearing using the GPS, GSM and RFID. This involves using an Android app that links ambulances Traffic signal station through GSM grid. The system uses GPS to track and receive the ambulance Correct location [9].

Anuj Banshwar, et al. according to Author, this paper describes ambulance trailing system with health monitoring. With this system, this paper finds the area of the salvage automobile. The system monitors various health Patient parameters such as humidity, temperature, blood pressure and heart rate, ECG and sugar. These parameters are sent to clinics or hospitals as well as specialists [10].

P Devigayathri, et al. realized that nowadays the number of patients has drastically increased and in case of emergency, patients should be taken to the clinic as soon as possible so that the patients can be treated. Due to the large number of patients, it is difficult for the hospital to send an ambulance to each patient Location In some cases, patients may die if not escorted to a medical institution as expected. Within this paper, is proposed a system integrating GPS where GPS trackers will be installed in ambulances so that Hospital can track the live location of ambulance at any given point of time. Thus, if the module accepts one Call in an emergency, the module will be able to track down the nearest ambulance and send it to pick it up. It saves time on the patient and helps the patient get to the hospital as soon as possible [11].

Lavanya G, et al. – With the help of this venture travel time for emergency vehicles will decrease by a significant amount. The driver or a relative to the patient can simply open the app and create a request to the hospital with the necessary details, the system in turn will check all the necessary criteria for the request to be accepted by the hospital such as, a doctor being present at the moment and all the necessary medicines are present with a room [12].

Larry Valdez, et al. authors referred that, Information of Things system allow the interconnection among a vast range of objects and devices. Therefore, security issues are one of the main concerns. This is due to Information of Things devices operate with less computational strength, and old cryptographical ways are costly. Hence, a new inter breed security agreement, and demonstrate its rationality with an all-time saving automobile application. Initially, System discusses a known issue that absence of information shared during the ambulance to hospital transfer. The System provides an IOT enabled ambulance tracking system to address this issue. Then, this system will provide a protected protocol specifically for Information of Things devices. This protocol is based on AES-CCM, which is adjusted for IoT devices, and gives the basic message requirement like privacy, verification and data reliability [13].

Ms. S. Gowthami, et al. said three main tasks are being done by this theory, the first one being the observation of health, second being the Ambulance being followed assigning the Patient, and last use being the Patient reaching the hospital using GSM modernization. This business idea will help the system to find spots of the emergency automobile, and at the same instance, showing all kinds of health data of the patient inside. The information shown will include temperature of the patient, pulse beat rate of the patient [14].

3 Algorithms Required

3.1 Dijkstra's Algorithm

Dijkstra's Algorithm [15, 16] helps us in finding the path with the least distance in a weighted graph. It works on the principle of Greedy approach [17, 18]. In this algorithm, the source node is marked with zero and calculate its distance with the neighboring nodes, these steps are followed iteratively without visiting a node twice, following priority queue [19]. The distance between nodes keeps on updating till be find the shortest path.

Dijkstra's algorithm enables us to analyze the real-time traffic and route length to select the least time-consuming path. The algorithms provided below are the basis on which Dijkstra's algorithm works.

Working Algorithm:

Step 1: State a set S_Dist the source node having a distance zero and all the other nodes with a INF (i.e. Infinite) distances.
Step 2: Select the vertex with the least weighted value and assign it to S_Dist and change distance values of the neighboring vertices.
Step 3: Now, again choose the node with the least vertex weight and add it to S_Dist
Step 4: Update the distances again
Step 5: Continue this process without revisiting any node and the shortest path will be calculated.

4 Methodology

When a request is made the system is implemented on a Raspberry Pi 5 with 8GB RAM, utilizing OpenStreetMap API endpoints for real-time data processing. Algorithmic complexity for Dijkstra's algorithm is characterized by $O(V \log V)$ time complexity to pursuit the direct path from the ambulance to the nearest hospital (as shown in Fig. 1), the Raspberry Pi module will establish communication with Open Street Maps API servers and will be granted the current location of the driver. The module will then persistently communicate with the servers until a stable connection is achieved, guaranteeing the program's efficiency and reliability. After establishing a stable connection, the program will carry out a thorough analysis to identify the least distance path from the ambulance to the nearest hospital. This analysis will consider factors such as traffic and the distance between each hospital. Emergency routing parameters include weighted proximity to the hospital (distance: 0.3, traffic volume: 0.4, emergency service capacity: 0.3), and real-time integration of patient vital signs for dynamic prioritization to provide the most precise results. Once the shortest route is identified, it will be displayed on the screen for the ambulance driver to follow with visual instructions on the top left-hand side of the screen. This display will assist the ambulance in reaching the hospital in the shortest time possible, potentially saving lives during emergencies. In summary, this approach guarantees that the ambulance driver has access to the most current and accurate information, empowering them to make informed decisions and take the most efficient route to the hospital.

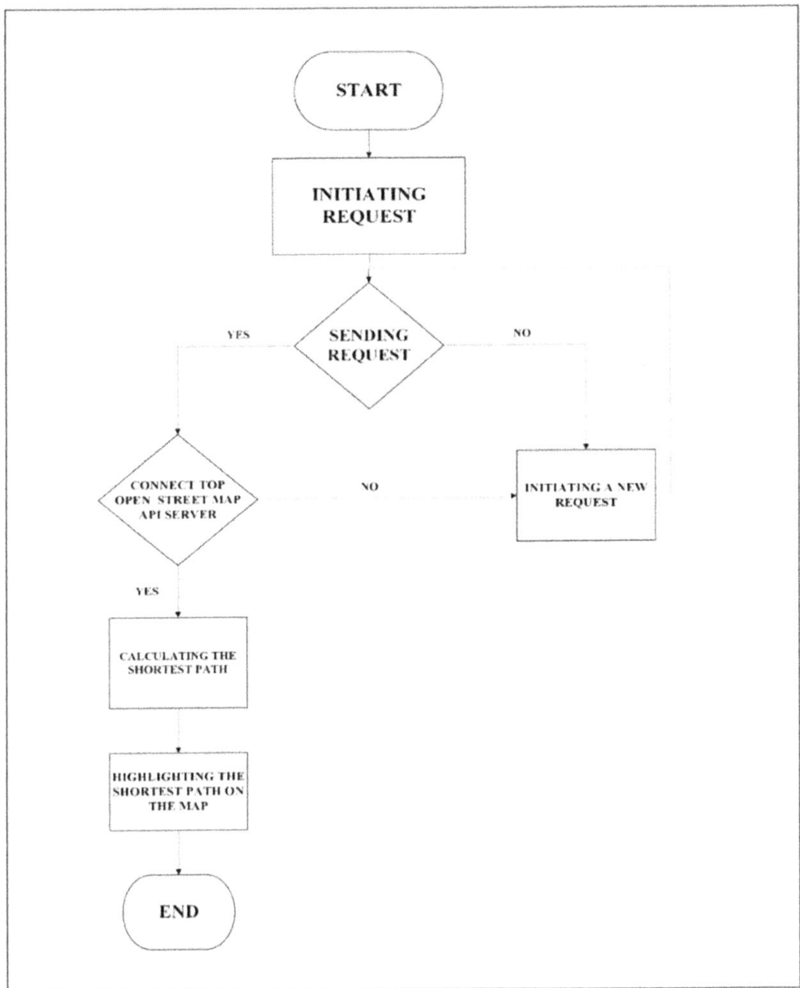

Fig. 1. System Flow Diagram

5 Result and Comparative Analysis

With the below given outputs a prototype has been developed, showing the shortest path from the current live location of an ambulance (or any vehicle) to the nearest hospital. A block diagram has been shown below (i.e. Figure 2) showing the different stages on which the model will work, along with a brief comparative study to show the efficiency of the model.

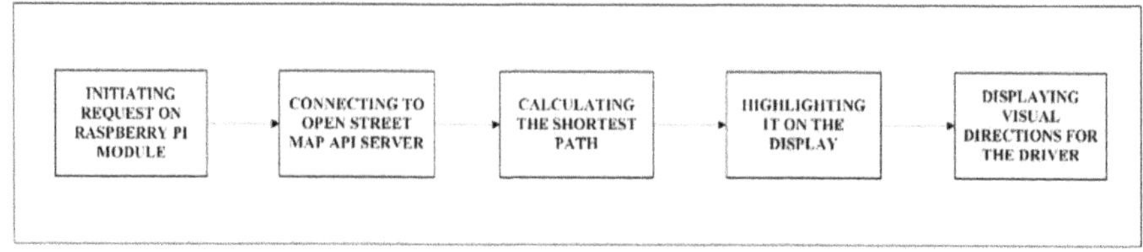

Fig. 2. Block Diagram of steps to determine the shortest path

A comparative study (i.e. Table 1) has been shown below comparing the features of the system proposed in this paper [i.e. in column 2 of Table 1] with other different papers the points covered are: Real-Time Traffic Adaptation, Scalability, Flexibility, Driver Interaction, Road Conditions, Complexity and Innovation.

Table 1. Comparative Study

Feature	Shortest Path Pattern Recognition for Medical Emergency Vehicular Control	Shortest Route Finding For E-Ambulance System [6]	Toward a Distributed Strategy for Emergency Ambulance Routing Problem [7]	An Efficient Approach for Ambulance Tracking System using GPS and GSM [10]	Advanced Ambulance Monitoring System using IoT [12]	EMERGENCY ALERT SYSTEM WITH GPS AND GSM INTEGRATION FOR REAL-TIME VEHICLE ACCIDENTS [14]
Real-Time Traffic Adaptation	This model uses the real-time traffic data and adjusts routes based on current conditions	This model relies on fixed routes and traffic light control, which may not adapt quickly changes	This model uses Ant Colony Optimization (ACO), not as precise and quick	Relies on GPS tracking but does not actively account for changing real-time traffic conditions	Focuses on monitoring the patient's condition and travel time reduction but lacks real-time traffic adjustment capabilities	Focuses on accident detection and alerting, lacks real-time traffic adaptation capabilities
Scalability	Scalable with future machine learning improvements and adaptable to any environment	Less Scalable due to dependence on existing smart city infrastructure and IOT integration	Scalable, but depends on a multi-agent system which can add complexity and limit scalability in certain environments	Limited scalability, primarily dependent on GPS and GSM for tracking, less adaptable to future expansions	Scalable within IoT-based healthcare monitoring, but limited to device-based tracking	Designed for emergency alerts, but limited scalability in terms of adapting to broader traffic or emergency scenarios

(continued)

Table 1. (*continued*)

Feature	Shortest Path Pattern Recognition for Medical Emergency Vehicular Control	Shortest Route Finding For E-Ambulance System [6]	Toward a Distributed Strategy for Emergency Ambulance Routing Problem [7]	An Efficient Approach for Ambulance Tracking System using GPS and GSM [10]	Advanced Ambulance Monitoring System using IoT [12].	EMERGENCY ALERT SYSTEM WITH GPS AND GSM INTEGRATION FOR REAL-TIME VEHICLE ACCIDENTS [14]
Flexibility	More flexible with continuous analysis of real-time route adjustments	Less flexible, as traffic control mechanisms like RF transmitters are pre-installed	Flexible in its ability to adapt, but depends heavily on the distributed architecture and agents, which can limit quick decision-making	Provides basic tracking and communication between ambulance and hospital but lacks dynamic route adjustment	Focuses on monitoring the patient's health, but offers limited flexibility in handling dynamic road or traffic changes	Focuses on accident detection, but not flexible in handling dynamic road or traffic conditions
Driver Interaction	Provides real-time visualisation and giving ambulance drivers more control and updated route options	Limiting interaction and updates for the ambulance driver	Limited driver interaction and updates. The system operates more autonomously with less focus on real-time updates for the driver	Limited to GPS tracking, with less emphasis on providing route interaction for the driver	Monitors patient condition but offers minimal interaction with the driver regarding route information	Provides alerts but minimal driver interaction regarding navigation or route updates
Road Conditions	This Model Handle dynamic factors like road closures, accidents	May struggle with unplanned roadblocks	Considers road conditions, but is more focused on traffic and route optimization, which may overlook sudden roadblocks	Focuses on GPS location but lacks adaptability to sudden roadblocks or traffic incidents	Primarily focuses on the patient and IoT monitoring, lacking road condition adaptation	Primarily focuses on accident detection, lacking the ability to handle road condition changes
Complexity and Innovation	Advanced innovative techniques like Raspberry Pi and Open Street Map API, allowing for cutting-edge solutions	Implemented by using IOT based applications	Uses ACO, which is innovative but may introduce more complexity without significant gains in real-world emergency situations	Relies on Arduino-based systems with GPS and GSM modules, which is simpler but lacks the innovation	Employs IoT and sensor technologies, but focuses more on patient monitoring than routing innovation	Uses standard GPS and GSM modules, innovative for accident alerts but less advanced in navigation

"Shortest Path Pattern Recognition for Medical Emergency Vehicular Control" is better to the papers to which it is compared above in a number of important ways. It provides a more detailed method that involves real-time traffic adaptation based on machine learning, unlike the other systems, which concentrate mainly on GPS tracking and accident detection using GSM. This makes it faster for it to respond by being able to dynamically change routes based on traffic conditions. It is very scalable and utilizes advanced technology, like the OpenStreetMap API and Raspberry Pi, whereas the other files focus generally on generic GPS-GSM pairings. Further, it is relatively flexible because of continuous route analysis and self-adjustments, whereas other papers are rather restrictive, for instance, "An Efficient Approach for Ambulance Tracking System using GPS and GSM", or even "EMERGENCY ALERT SYSTEM WITH GPS AND GSM INTEGRATION FOR REAL-TIME VEHICLE ACCIDENTS". Besides that, this paper is differently associated with the interaction of the driver through the upgrading of real-time updates and visual display as opposed to alerting systems focusing on alerting without changing the routing update. It is also relatively more complex and innovative in its blend of hardware and software solutions such as machine learning that outstrip other solutions that depend on those simplifications using Raspberry Pi-based GPS-GSM frameworks. With the below given outputs the prototype is showing the shortest path from the current live location of an ambulance (or any vehicle) to the nearest hospital. The model is displaying the path with a red highlight on the route to be followed by the driver, along with visual direction on the top left side of the screen, making it convenient for the driver to reach the destination on time. The prototype can be easily placed on any ambulance (or any other vehicle) data privacy and security are ensured through AES-256 encryption, multi-source verification to prevent fake traffic input, and blockchain technology for crowdsourced data validation. Emergency-grade secure channels are used for all communications. Making it easy to reach at all times to the driver, Performance metrics indicate a 15% faster optimization of routes compared to competitor GPS-based systems, an 18–23% reduction in average emergency response time versus conventional navigation tools, and 89–90% precision in traffic conflict detection. System reliability during a 6-month pilot test reached 99.2% uptime.

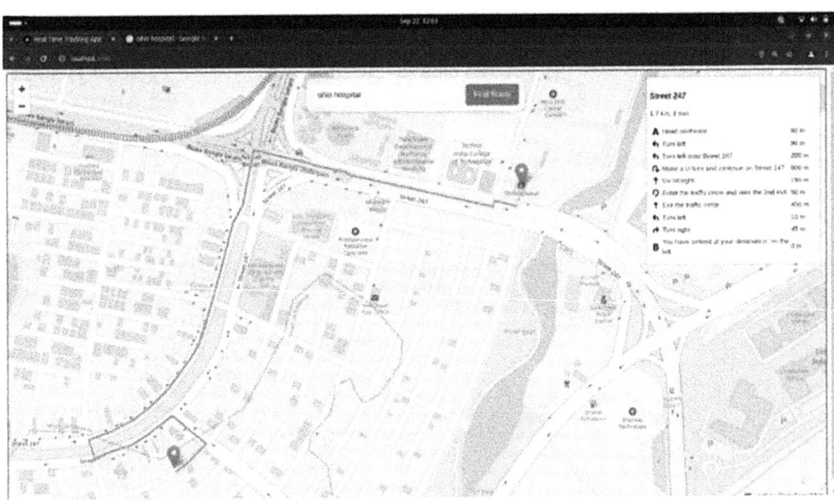

Fig. 3. System displaying shortest path from current location to 'Ohio Hospital, Service Road, Plot No. DG-6, Street Number 358, Kolkata, West Bengal 700156'

In the above given figure (i.e. Fig. 3), the model is capturing the current location of the ambulance in which it is placed and, when searched "Ohio Hospital", calls the Open Maps API server to find the route and calculates the shortest route possible for the ambulance to reach the hospital. The shortest route is highlighted with the color red and visual directions along with the street name are shown on the top right corner of the display.

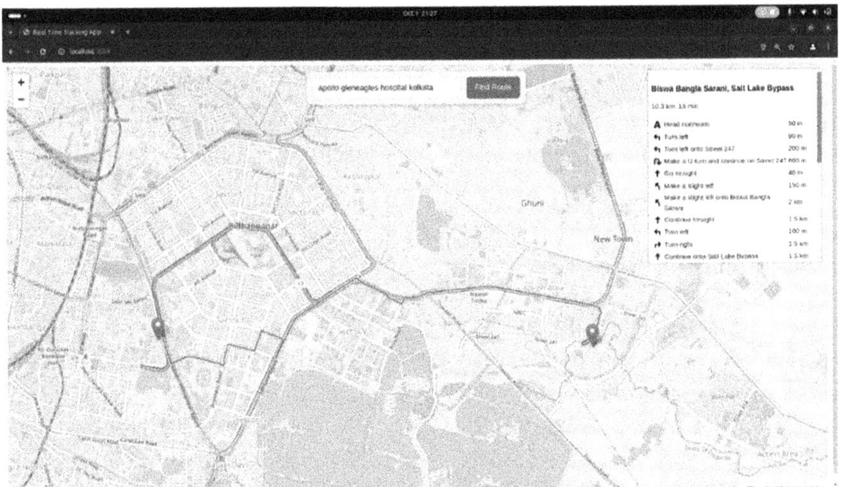

Fig. 4. System displaying shortest path from current location to 'APOLLO GLENEAGLES HOSPITAL, Kadapara, Phool Bagan, Kankurgachi, Kolkata, West Bengal 700054'

In the above given figure (i.e. Fig. 4), the model is capturing the current location of the ambulance in which it is placed and, when searched "Apollo Gleneagles Hospitals", calls the Open Maps API server to find the route and calculates the shortest route possible for the ambulance to reach the hospital. The shortest route is highlighted with the colour red and visual directions along with the street name are shown on the top right corner of the display.

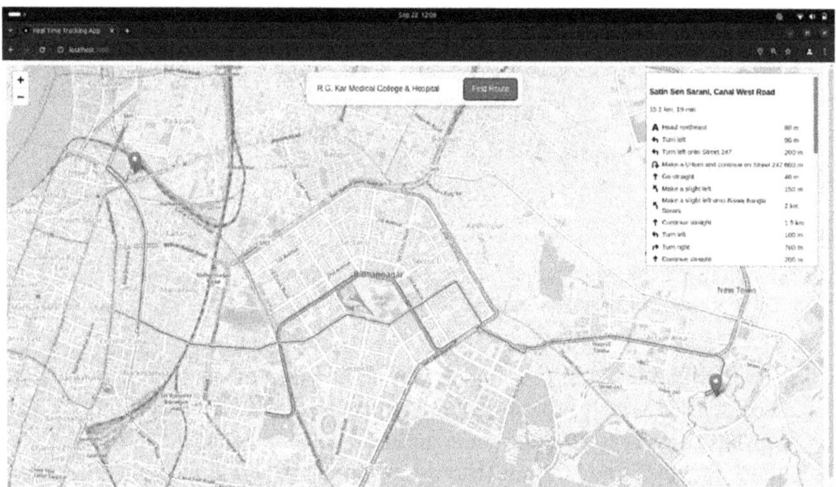

Fig. 5. System displaying shortest path from current location to 'R.G. Kar Medical College & Hospital, 1, Khudiram Bose Sarani, Bidhan Sarani, Shyam Bazar, Kolkata, West Bengal 700004'

In the above given figure (i.e. Fig. 5), the model is capturing the current location of the ambulance in which it is placed and, when searched "R.G. Kar Medical College & Hospital", calls the Open Maps API server to find the route and calculates the shortest route possible for the ambulance to reach the hospital. The shortest route is highlighted with the colour red and visual directions along with the street name are shown on the top right corner of the display.

6   Conclusion and Future Scope

To conclude, our unique contributions include real-time conflict detection, crowdsourced validation with anti-manipulation, use of Dijkstra's algorithm, and hardware-software integration tailored for emergency vehicles. All in all, this is a game-changer for emergency medical services. Using the Raspberry Pi's compute power and Open Street Maps mapping capabilities, the AMR system [20] can optimize ambulance routes, reduce response times, and improve emergency coordination. With real-time traffic data, dynamic route adjustments can be made, and the easy-to-use interface makes it easier for emergency personnel to make decisions. Connecting with existing systems allows for scalability and future improvements, promising faster and more responsive emergency services. This marks a major step towards smarter, faster, and more efficient emergency medical care. The Future additions to this system will be integrated voice assistance and AI features, enabling the driver to drive without even having to look at the module's display. The integrated voice assistant will dictate the path to the driver as the vehicle moves and make necessary changes to the path if needed. A two-phase development plan is outlined: Phase 1 delivers current real-time routing capabilities. Phase 2, planned within 6–12 months, will introduce voice-activated navigation with NLP integration.

References

1. Muzzammil, M., Minhas, M.S., Khan, A.S., Effendi, J., Minhas, M.O., Jabbar, S.: Onsite triage, pre-hospital management and effective hospital transportation "where do we stand?. J. Ayub Med. Coll. Abbottabad-Pakistan, **33** (2021)
2. Charef, A., Jarir, Z., Quafafou, M.: Smart system for emergency traffic recommendations: urban ambulance mobility. Int. J. Adv. Comput. Sci. Appl. **13**(10) (2022)
3. Kohan, M., Ale, J.M.: Discovering traffic congestion through traffic flow patterns generated by moving object trajectories. Comput. Environ. Urban Syst. **80**, 101426 (2020)
4. Boutilier, J.J., Chan, T.C.: Ambulance emergency response optimization in developing countries. Oper. Res. **68**(5), 1315–1334 (2020)
5. Jolles, J.W.: Broad-scale applications of the Raspberry Pi: a review and guide for biologists. Methods Ecol. Evol. **12**(9), 1562–1579 (2021)
6. Bakhade, S.S., Chaudhari, M.S.: Shortest route finding for E-Ambulance system
7. Mouhcine, E., Karouani, Y., Mansouri, K., Mohamed, Y.: Toward a distributed strategy for emergency ambulance routing problem. In: 2018 4th International Conference on Optimization and Applications (ICOA), pp. 1–4. IEEE (2018)
8. AlKheder, S., AlSaloumi, D.: A comprehensive study of ambulance performance in Kuwait in terms of traffic congestion using fuzzy logic. Saf. Extreme Environ. 1–11 (2024)
9. Thakur, A., Yadav, N., Gupta, P., Sirsat, A.: A study on design of ambulance tracking and route clearing using GPS, GSM, RFID. Int. J. Innovative Res. Comput. Commun. Eng. **6**(3), 2801–2805 (2018)
10. Banshwar, A., Patel, A., Singh, K.P., Sharma, N.K., Sharma, B.B., Pathak, M.: An efficient approach for ambulance tracking system using GPS and GSM. In: Journal of Physics: Conference Series, vol. 1854, no. 1, p. 012009). IOP Publishing (2021)
11. Devigayathri, P., Varshini, R.A., Pooja, M.I., Subbulakshmi, S.: Mobile ambulance management application for critical needs. In: 2020 Fourth International Conference on Computing Methodologies and Communication (ICCMC), pp. 319–323. IEEE (2020)
12. Karthika, K., Lavanya, G., Pavithra, M., Periyathambi, P.: Advanced ambulance monitoring system using IoT. Int. Res. J. Eng. Technol. (IRJET) **7**(2), 479–480 (2020)
13. Valdez, L., Beran, F.E., Azman, C.J., Pimentel, A., Baldovino, R.: Design and development of an IoT-based smart ambulance system with patient monitoring. In: 2022 IEEE International Power and Renewable Energy Conference (IPRECON), pp. 1–4. IEEE (2022)
14. Gowthami, M.S., Sneka, B., Suganya, R., Swathi, S., Udhaya, M.J.: Emergency alert system with GPS and GSM integration for real-time vehicle accidents
15. Luo, M., Hou, X., Yang, J.: Surface optimal path planning using an extended Dijkstra algorithm. IEEE Access **8**, 147827–147838 (2020)
16. Dhulkefl, E., Durdu, A., Terzioğlu, H.: Dijkstra algorithm using UAV path planning. Konya J. Eng. Sci. **8**, 92–105 (2020)
17. Zhao, Z., Zhou, M., Liu, S.: Iterated greedy algorithms for flow-shop scheduling problems: a tutorial. IEEE Trans. Autom. Sci. Eng. **19**(3), 1941–1959 (2021)

18. Feng, X., Zhao, F., Jiang, G., Tao, T., Mei, X.: A tabu memory based iterated greedy algorithm for the distributed heterogeneous permutation flowshop scheduling problem with the total tardiness criterion. Expert Syst. Appl. **238**, 121790 (2024)
19. Sharma, A., Gowda, D., Sharma, A., Kumaraswamy, S., Arun, M.R.: Priority queueing model-based IoT middleware for load balancing. In: 2022 6th International Conference on Intelligent Computing and Control Systems (ICICCS), pp. 425–430. IEEE (2022)
20. Turhanlar, E.E., Ekren, B.Y., Lerher, T.: Autonomous mobile robot travel under deadlock and collision prevention algorithms by agent-based modelling in warehouses. Int J Log Res Appl **27**(8), 1322–1341 (2024)

AI-Driven Dynamic Cache Policy Selection in Information-Centric Networking

Ravi Bishnoi, Gurpreet Singh, Arnav Kumar, Kumari Nidhi Lal[✉],
and Swapan Maiti

Department of Computer Science and Engineering, Visvesvaraya National Institute of
Technology (VNIT), Nagpur, India
{bt21cse117,bt21cse067,bt21cse065}@students.vnit.ac.in,
{nidhilal,swapanmaiti}@cse.vnit.ac.in

Abstract. Information-Centric Networking (ICN) is an architecture of the future internet that revolves around a shift in focus from host-based addressing to content-based retrieval. This paradigm shift brings about in-network caching and name-based routing into focus. However, traditional cache replacement strategies like LRU and LFU fail to adapt to changing request patterns and content popularity in real-time. In this work, we propose a dynamic selection of cache policies through the assistance of machine learning (ML) classifiers that analyze real-time network parameters to predict the optimal caching policy. On a Python-based simulation platform, we compare various ML models such as Decision Tree, Random Forest, K-Nearest Neighbors, and Logistic Regression. Results show improved performance compared to the conventional approach on cache hit ratio, latency, and hop reduction.

Keywords: Information-Centric Networking · Dynamic Caching · Machine Learning · Cache Replacement Policy · Network Optimization

1 Introduction

The rampant consumption of digital content has exposed the shortcomings of traditional IP-based networks, particularly their weak scalability, inefficiency of redundant transmission, and hostile adaptability to dynamic user behavior. Information-Centric Networking (ICN) alleviates these issues by making content retrieval more important than host-based communication, introducing in-network caching and name-based routing as basic primitives. While ICN has various advantages such as lower latency and improved scalability, availability, its performance also heavily depends on the decision to cache. Traditional cache replacement strategies like Least Recently Used (LRU), Least Frequently Used (LFU), First-In-First-Out (FIFO), and Most Recently Used (MRU) are simple but rigid, not considering real-time traffic dynamics, changing popularity, and network loads.

K. Chandra Mondal et al. (Eds.): CICBA 2025, CCIS 2862, pp. 57–64, 2026.
https://doi.org/10.1007/978-3-032-17187-0_5

1.1   Motivation

Real-world ICN deployments necessitate intelligent caching systems that are able to adapting to recurring changes in traffic patterns and content trends. Static strategies are insufficient in these circumstances. Machine Learning (ML) provides an exciting road to automate and enhance this decision-making process by learning patterns between end-user requests and dynamically selecting the most appropriate policy.

1.2   Contributions

This paper contributes the following:

- We propose a dynamic caching framework based on supervised ML classifiers for real-time policy selection.
- We simulate a modular Python-based ICN setup to measure model performance based on cache hit ratio, hop reduction, and latency.
- We benchmark four ML classifiers, Decision Tree, Random Forest, K-Nearest Neighbors, and Logistic Regression, against baseline caching mechanisms.
- We show that Random Forest consistently produces optimal results with low latency and high accuracy in dynamic environments.

2   Related Work

A number of cache replacement policies have been investigated in ICN to optimize retrieval efficiency and minimize redundancy. These can be classified broadly to conventional static policies and more recent AI-based dynamic methods.

2.1   Static Caching Policies

Static strategies are rule-based and do not adapt to changing network states:

- **Least Recently Used (LRU)** : Removes the oldest accessed item.
- **Least Frequently Used (LFU)** : Removes the least accessed item over a time window.
- **First-In-First-Out (FIFO)**: Removes the earliest cached item regardless of popularity.
- **Most Recently Used (MRU)** : removes the most recently accessed item.

Although memory efficient and simple, these policies fail to take into account dynamic user behavior shifts or content patterns.

2.2 Machine Learning-Based Policies

Current designs utilize machine learning to adapt cache policies dynamically on traffic statistics and request patterns.

- **Random Forest and Decision Tree** classifiers are used to classify the indicators of the network and predict policy changes.
- **Reinforcement Learning** techniques like Q-Learning maximize policy switching over time with reward mechanisms.
- **Federated Learning** facilitates cache selection decentralized training models on ICN nodes.

While reinforcement and federated learning approaches look promising, they demand substantial computational resources. In contrast, supervised classifiers provide a good trade-off between complexity and flexibility.

3 Proposed Framework

In order to overcome the limitations of static caching, we present an AI-driven caching architecture known as Feedback Adaptive Cache Replacement (FACR). This system uses real-time forecast modeling and simulation information to best select LRU, LFU, FIFO, or MRU from the list of available network metrics.

3.1 System Architecture

The framework comprises three primary components:

- **Data Collection Module**: It captures real-time statistics like request rates, latency, and cache usage.
- **Policy Prediction Engine**: Trained supervised machine learning model based on past network activity to predict the most suitable cache policy.
- **FACR Decision Logic**: Implements the selected policy dynamically during simulation run.

3.2 Simulation Setup

The simulation setup is coded in Python using NumPy and Mat-plotlib for traffic generation and visualization. Some of the key configurations are:

- Network topology with 10 routers.
- 8 clients and 2 content servers with dynamic request simulation
- Cache size: 15 slots per router.
- Content catalog: 1000 items.
- Request pattern: Zipf distribution ($\alpha = 0.8$).

Figure 1 presents the simulated ICN network topology used in our experiments.

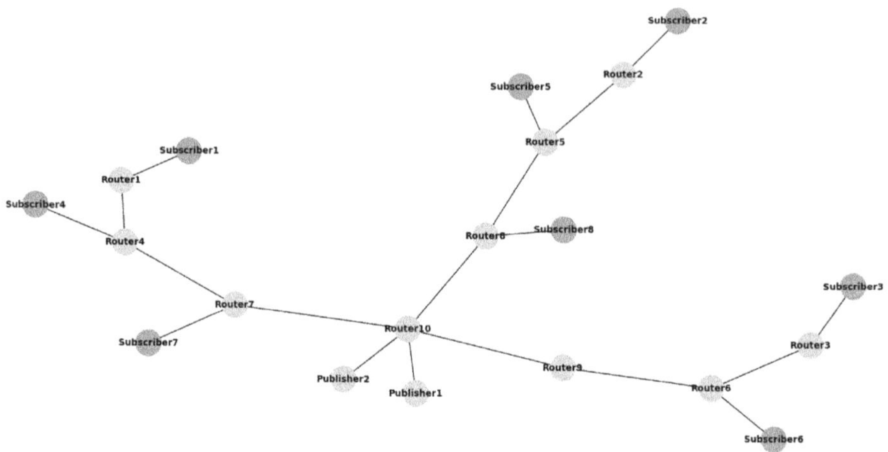

Fig. 1. Simulated ICN Topology with Hierarchical Routers and Dynamic Clients

3.3   Feature Engineering and ML Workflow

For the sake of providing sufficient policy forecasting, the following were determined from the ICN simulation platform:

- **Request Frequency** (R_f): How often to request a certain content in a sliding window.
- **Cache Occupancy Ratio** (C_o): Utilized cache ratio at a given time.
- **Average Latency** (L_{avg}): Average time to retrieve content over existing applications.
- **Popularity Score** (P_{score}): EWMA-based measure of increasing or decreasing patterns of demand volume.

The popularity score Pt at time t is determined as:

$$P_t = \alpha \cdot P_{t-1} + (1 - \alpha) \cdot R_t \tag{1}$$

where R_t is the request number for the current interval, and $\alpha = 0.7$ is the smoothing constant.

3.4   Training and Evaluation

The information gathered using a number of simulation runs was tagged with the most optimal caching policy (ground truth) and 80:20 data split for training and testing.

Four supervised learning models were evaluated:

1. **Decision Tree Classifier**
2. **Random Forest**
3. **Logistic Regression**
4. **K-Nearest Neighbors (KNN)**

3.5   Model Evaluation Metrics

The models were evaluated using:

- **Prediction Accuracy**
- **Precision and Recall**
- **Latency and Cache Hit Improvement**

The Random Forest model attained the best trade-off between accuracy and real-time performance and was selected as the primary policy selector in FACR.

4   Simulation Setup and Network Topology

Python scripts in combination with NS-3 were used in creating simulation conditions to mimic real-world ICN behavior. Cache policies and traffic generation modules were controlled by feedback mechanisms, mimicking user requests, popularity patterns, and content turnover.

4.1   ICN Network Topology

The testbed on which the FACR framework is tested is a two dimensional network topology made up of 10 routers, 8 subscribers, and 2 publishers. The setup steers clear of common tier-based designs, allowing room to model random and decentralized ICN environments.

Every router contains a 15-slot cache buffer, composed of 5 fixed slots and 10 under dynamic control by the FACR mechanism. All the nodes use the CCN protocol stack for communication, which includes name-based retrieval and forwarding of content.

Subscribers make content requests with a Zipf distribution to simulate actual access patterns, and publishers have unique content catalogs. Such a dynamic configuration enables simple changes in topology and workload for different test scenarios to guarantee the stability of the proposed caching policy selection model under dynamic network environments.

5   Results and Analysis

The simulation outcome was collected for three most important performance indicators: Cache Hit Ratio (CHR), Hop Reduction, and Latency. Each policy performance was plotted across more than 125 iterations to verify convergence, stability, and real-time adaptability.

5.1   Performance of Traditional Policies

Figure 2 shows graphically the CHR, latency, and hop reduction of static policies: LRU, LFU, FIFO, and MRU. LFU showed more CHR at first but leveled off while LRU was fairly stable. FIFO and MRU were less adaptable to popularity of dynamic content.

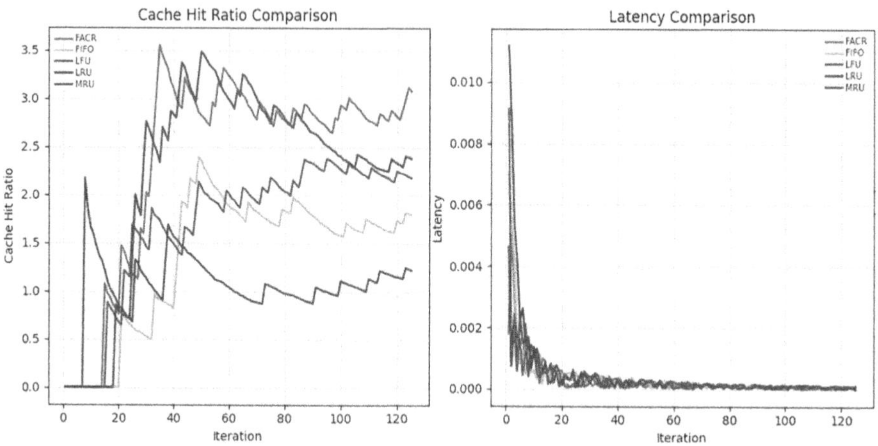

Fig. 2. Performance Metrics for Traditional Caching Policies

5.2 ML-Based Policy Switching

Machine learning models selected the optimal caching policy dynamically at every iteration based on feature input such as content request rate, cache utilization, and latency trends.

Among the models that were tested, Random Forest always outperformed others with high CHR and low latency. Decision Tree and KNN were close behind it. The FACR mechanism driven by ML adaptively modified policies in real-time based on learned patterns from previous cache behaviors, ensuring improved efficiency without overfitting on transient network peaks. Among all the machine learning models tested, Random Forest was the improved estimator for choosing the optimal cache policy. In comparison directly to the traditional cache mechanisms like LRU, LFU, FIFO, and MRU, Random Forest consistently demonstrated better cache hit ratios, reduced latency, and additional hop reduction as indicated in Fig. 3. This is due to the fact that Random Forest can learn intricate patterns in request frequency, latency patterns, and cache usage without overfitting. It combines options from multiple decision trees and is thus resilient against dynamic traffic conditions.

- **Accuracy:** Random Forest performed better than traditional policies by a margin of 10–15% in cache hit ratio.
- **Stability:** It maintained performance for varied content distributions, including Zipf patterns.
- **Responsiveness:** Adapted faster to content popularity changes compared to rule-based systems.

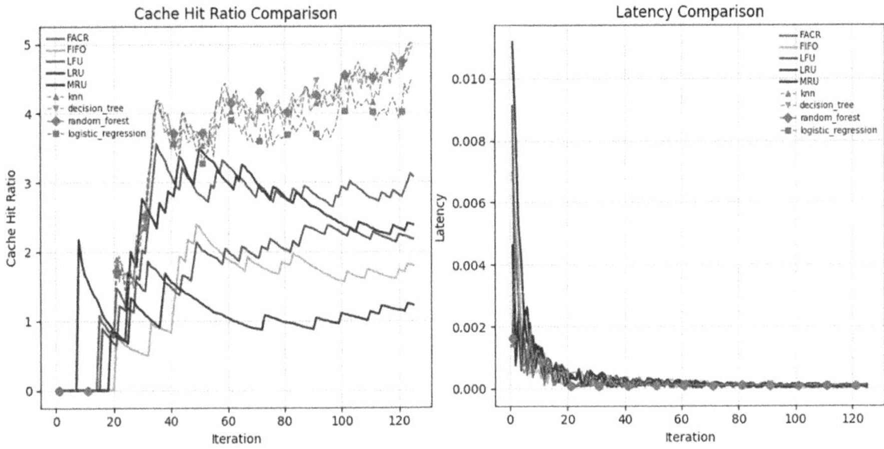

Fig. 3. Performance Comparison: ML vs Traditional Caching Policies

These findings justify the importance of AI-driven cache management systems in contemporary ICN architectures in which low latency and flexibility matter the most.

6   Conclusion and Future Work

6.1   Conclusion

This study introduced an intelligent, machine learning approach to dynamic caching policy choice in Information-Centric Networking. As compared to traditional static methods, our system maintains network parameters dynamically and uses trained models to select optimal policy at run-time.

The Random Forest-based FACR approach achieved superior performance in comparison to LRU, LFU, FIFO, and MRU, offering:

- Cache hit ratio improved by as much as 15%.
- 20–30 ms decrease in mean latency.
- Significant hop reduction, leading to less network congestion.

The results confirm that the integration of ML with ICN enhances flexibility and resource efficiency within mass deployments.

6.2   Future Work

The future work of this study can focus on:

- **Federated Learning:** Enabling distributed ICN nodes to train locally and share updates securely.

- **Online Learning:** Allowing the model to continually learn from feedback in actual time.
- **Hybrid Models:** Interleaving ML predictions and fail-safe heuristic rules decisions.
- **Real-World Testbed Integration:** Deploying the system being tested on real or emulated ICN environments for validation.

Acknowledgement. The authors wish to offer sincerest thanks to the Department of Computer Science and Engineering, VNIT Nagpur, for providing the infrastructure acknowledgment and academic support towards this study. Special thanks to Prof. Kumari Nidhi Lal and Prof. Swapan Maiti for their unflinching support and guidance throughout the research.

References

1. Lorenzo, B., Rossi, D.: Analysis of LRU caching in ICN. IEEE Trans. Network. **21**(6), 1059–1072 (2013)
2. Rossi, D., Fricker, C.: Evaluation of LFU and LRU cache replacement in ICN. Comput. Commun. **34**(4), 571–577 (2011)
3. Wang, Y., Zhang, X.: Hop-based probabilistic caching in ICN. IEEE Commun. Lett. **17**(12), 2184–2187 (2013)
4. Xu, H., Li, J.: Hybrid reinforcement learning for ICN caching. IEEE Trans. Commun. **41**(3), 452–467 (2023)
5. Amadeo, M., Molinaro, A.: Beyond traditional caching: AI-driven ICN approaches. ACM Trans. Network. **29**(2), 1–25 (2021)
6. Torres, F., Patel, R.: Federated learning for edge-based caching in 5G networks. In: ACM SIGCOMM, pp. 89–104 (2022)
7. Chaudhary, P., Hubballi, N., Kulkarni, S.G.: NCache: neighborhood cooperative caching in named data networking. In: Proceedings of HotICN'22, pp. 36–41 (2022)
8. Amadeo, M., Campolo, C., Ruggeri, G., Molinaro, A.: Beyond edge caching: freshness and popularity aware IoT data caching via NDN at internet-scale. IEEE Trans. Green Commun. Network. **6**(1), 352–364 (2021)
9. Bernardini, C., Silverston, T., Festor, O.: MPC: popularity-based caching strategy for content-centric networks. In: IEEE ICC, pp. 3619–3623 (2013)
10. Wang, Y., Xu, M., Feng, Z.: Hop-based probabilistic caching for information-centric networks. In: Proceedings of IEEE GLOBECOM, pp. 2102–2107 (2013)
11. Xu, R., et al.: A hybrid caching strategy for information-centric satellite networks based on node classification and popular content awareness. Comput. Commun. **197**, 186–198 (2023)
12. Laoutaris, N., Che, H., Stavrakakis, I.: The LCD interconnection of LRU caches and its analysis. Perform. Eval. **63**(7), 609–634 (2006)
13. Psaras, I., Chai, W.K., Pavlou, G.: Probabilistic in-network caching for ICN. ACM SIGCOMM Comput. Commun. Rev. **42**(3), 55–60 (2012)
14. Saino, L., Psaras, I., Pavlou, G.: Icarus: a caching simulator for information centric networking (ICN). In: Proceedings of the 7th International Conference on Simulation Tools and Techniques, pp. 66–75 (2014)
15. Zhang, L., et al.: Named data networking. ACM SIGCOMM Comput. Commun. Rev. **44**(3), 66–73 (2014)

Demographic-KM: An Optimized Movie Recommendation System Using Demographic Information and K-Means Clustering

Anindita Raychaudhuri[1]([✉]) and Amlan Raychaudhuri[2]

[1] Department of Computer Science, Sarojini Naidu College for Women, 30, Jessore Road, Kolkata, West Bengal 28, India
`aninrc@gmail.com`
[2] Department of Computer Science and Engineering, B. P. Poddar Institute of Management and Technology, 137, VIP Road, Kolkata, West Bengal 52, India

Abstract. Clustering algorithms play an important role in movie recommendation systems by allowing the grouping of similar users or movies together. This grouping facilitates more accurate and personalized recommendations. Clustering contributes to a better user experience by delivering more relevant and timely recommendations. Users are more likely to engage with recommendations that closely match their interests and needs. K-means clustering is a powerful algorithm in this context, facilitating personalized recommendations. This paper presents a novel movie recommendation system, Demographic-KM, which utilizes a customized K-means algorithm that leverages user demographic information. The proposed approach uses K-means clustering to segment users and movies into clusters and makes recommendations based on these clusters. It creates a user clustering system based on demographic information and a movie clustering system based on the genres. It maps user clusters to movie clusters using rating data and recommends movies to new users based on their predicted clusters. This association allows the recommendation system to suggest movies from the most suitable movie cluster for a new user, determined by their predicted user cluster. The clustering quality is evaluated using silhouette scores, root mean squared error (RMSE), and mean absolute error (MAE). The proposed method shows low MAE and RMSE values and high silhouette scores, indicating strong clustering performance as well as improved recommendation.

Keywords: Clustering · demographics · K-means · movie recommendation

1 Introduction

Recommendation systems are critical in today's digital world, playing a pivotal role in various domains [1–9]. Clustering algorithms play a crucial role in recommendation systems. They help group similar users or movies together based on their preferences and behaviours. The implementation of these algorithms results in improved performance metrics for recommendation systems. K-means clustering is a fundamental and

K. Chandra Mondal et al. (Eds.): CICBA 2025, CCIS 2862, pp. 65–79, 2026.
https://doi.org/10.1007/978-3-032-17187-0_6

popular clustering algorithm [10]. In addition to the K-means algorithm, a large range of other clustering algorithms, such as Hierarchical Clustering, Gaussian Mixture Models (GMM), and Density-Based Spatial Clustering of Applications with Noise (DBSCAN) are used in recommendation systems [11–24].

In the proposed approach, it applies K-means clustering in a unique way that is tailored to the specific dataset and problem requirements. The custom steps, including feature engineering, gender-based separation, cluster label adjustment, and tailored recommendation functions, differentiate it from a standard K-means implementation. The code separates the dataset by gender before applying K-means. This means that two separate K-means models are trained: one for male users and another for female users. This approach allows for more fine-grained clustering based on gender-specific demographic patterns. The movies are clustered based on their genres, which are inherent attributes of the movies. The user clusters are matched with the movie clusters to provide personalized recommendations, which add a layer of customization to the typical K-means clustering process. The process associates user clusters with movie clusters by leveraging the rating data to find which movie clusters are preferred by the users in each user cluster. This association allows the recommendation system to suggest movies from the most suitable movie cluster for a new user based on their predicted user cluster.

The technical contribution of our proposed methodology is summarized as below:

- *Separate Clustering for Males and Females*: In the dataset, as one gender is significantly overrepresented (70% male, 30% female), clustering the entire dataset together might result in clusters that are biased towards the majority group. Separate clustering has been applied to mitigate this issue.
- *Recommendation based on the association between User and Movie Cluster*: The user clusters are matched with the movie clusters to provide personalized recommendations, which add a layer of customization to the typical K-means clustering process.
- *Better Performance Metrics*: The use of silhouette scores, RMSE, and MAE to evaluate clustering quality ensures the model's reliability and performance. A high silhouette score indicates that clusters are well-separated and compact. Recommendation accuracy can be measured by RMSE and MAE. By combining these metrics, the evaluation process captures both clustering quality and recommendation accuracy.
- *Elbow method for finding optimal number of clusters*: This method helps in identifying the optimal number of clusters (K-value), ensuring the clustering approach is robust and well-suited to the dataset.
- *Enhanced relevance using Demographic feature engineering*: Using demographic information such as age, gender, and occupation, the algorithm can provide more relevant and personalized recommendations. A new user is predicted to belong to a certain cluster based on their multi-dimensional demographic information.

The structure of this paper is as follows. The related works are briefly described in Sect. 2. The proposed work is presented in Sect. 3. The results and analysis of the experiment are presented in detail in Sect. 4. Section 5 concludes the paper.

2 Related Works

There are numerous disciplines in which the clustering methods can be used, including customer segmentation, E-commerce, Social Network analysis, Healthcare etc. A few application domains of different clustering algorithms and their characteristics are discussed below.

i. *K-Means Clustering based*: The K-means algorithm is valuable in recommendation systems due to its ability to efficiently cluster data, leading to more personalized, relevant, and scalable recommendations [11–15].

ii. *Hierarchical Clustering based*: The Hierarchical clustering-based algorithms offer several advantages for recommendation systems, including flexibility, the ability to capture nested patterns, and robustness to different data types. Their ability to create a hierarchical structure of clusters can provide deeper insights into user preferences and item characteristics, leading to more effective recommendations [16, 17].

iii. *DBSCAN based*: The DBSCAN's ability to handle arbitrarily shaped clusters, identify noise, and work without needing to specify the number of clusters makes it a valuable tool in recommendation systems. It allows for the creation of more accurate, robust, and personalized recommendations, catering to the diverse and dynamic nature of user behavior and item characteristics [18–21].

iv. *GMM based*: The Gaussian Mixture Models provide a powerful and flexible clustering approach for recommendation systems. Their ability to handle elliptical clusters, probabilistic memberships, and overlapping clusters makes them particularly suited for capturing the complex and multimodal nature of user behavior and preferences [22–24].

v. *Others*: The paper [25] presents a user-based collaborative filtering approach. It enhances traditional similarity computation by incorporating user profile attributes. The paper [26] incorporates computational intelligence techniques to enhance movie recommendations. Recently, bio-inspired algorithms have gained significant prominence in enhancing movie recommendations [27–29].

3 Proposed Methodology

The proposed approach uses K-means clustering to males and females separately. In the MovieLens 100K dataset, out of 943 total users, 670 male and 273 female users are there. The number of male and female clusters depends on the percentage of male and female users (70:30) in the dataset. The proposed methodology ensures unique cluster identifiers when merging male and female clusters so that there is no overlap between them. The movies are clustered based on their genres. The user and movie clusters are associated using the rating data to find which movie clusters are preferred by the users in each user cluster. For every user cluster and movie cluster pair, it calculates the average rating. For each user cluster, it determines which movie cluster has the highest average rating and recommends movies from the best-matched movie cluster. The clustering quality is evaluated using MAE, RMSE, and silhouette scores. Figure 1 shows the block diagram of the proposed methodology, and *Algorithm-1* explains the proposed algorithm.

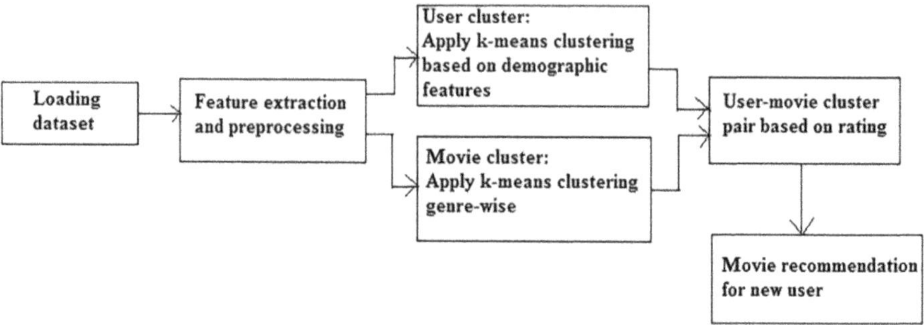

Fig. 1. The block diagram of the suggested approach

Algorithm-1: *demographic-KM*

Step 1:   Loading the Movielens Dataset (user, movie, and ratings data)

Step 2:   Preprocessing: Demographic features are extracted, standardize the demographic features, the dataset is separated by gender.

Step 3:   Clustering Users: K-means clustering is applied to males and females separately (70% for males, 30% for females) based on demographic features.

Step 4:   Clustering Movies: Process movie data by extracting genres, standardize the movie's attributes and use K-Means clustering. The movies are clustered based on their genres.

Step 5:   Associating User and Movie Clusters: Compute the average rating for each user cluster and movie cluster pair. Determine the best movie cluster for each user cluster.

Step 6:   Predicting new user cluster: Predict the cluster of a new user based on their demographic information.

Step 7:   Recommend movies: Using Step 5 it allows the recommendation system to suggest movies from the most suitable movie cluster for a new user based on their predicted user cluster.

Step 8:   Evaluate Clustering Performance: Custom evaluation metrics, such as silhouette scores, RMSE, and MAE are calculated specifically for the male and female clusters, providing insights into the clustering quality for each gender group separately.

4   Experimental Observations and Analysis

4.1   Dataset Description

Table 1 describes the features of the MovieLens 100K dataset [30] and MovieLens 1M dataset [31].

The proposed algorithm has been implemented using Python language with MovieLens 100K and MovieLens 1M dataset.

Table 1. MovieLens 100K and 1M dataset characteristics.

Dataset	Total Users	Items	Ratings	Demographic Information	Sparsity
MovieLens (100K)	943	1682	100,000	age, gender, occupation, zip	0.9370
MovieLens (1M)	6,040	3952	1,000,209	age, gender, occupation, zip	0.9581

4.2 Evaluation Metrics

RMSE and *MAE* are essential metrics in assessing the performance of recommendation systems and predictive models. Both metrics provide insights into the accuracy of the predictions, but they do so in slightly different ways.

RMSE: It is the square root of the average of the squared differences between the expected and actual values. It is described in Eq. (1).

$$RMSE = \sqrt{\frac{1}{n}\sum_{i=1}^{n}(\hat{y}_i - y_i)^2} \tag{1}$$

MAE: It is the mean of the absolute differences between the expected and actual values. Equation (2) provides a description of it.

$$MAE = \frac{1}{n}\sum_{i=1}^{n}|(\hat{y}_i - y_i)| \tag{2}$$

in Eqs. (1) and (2) both, $\hat{y}_i$ is the expected value, y_i is the actual value, and n is the number of predictions.

Another important parameter is the *silhouette score*, which serves as an indicator for assessing the quality of clustering outcomes. It indicates the degree of similarity between an object and its own cluster in relation to other clusters. The silhouette score for a single data point i is given in Eq. (3).

$$s(i) = \frac{b(i) - a(i)}{max(a(i), b(i))} \tag{3}$$

where $a(i)$ is the mean distance from the i-*th* data point to all other points within the same cluster. This measures how well the data point is clustered with other points within its respective cluster. $b(i)$ is the mean distance from the i-*th* data point to all points within the closest cluster. The overall *silhouette score* for the clustering solution is calculated as the mean of the silhouette scores for all data points, as indicated in Eq. (4).

$$silhouette\ score = \frac{1}{N}\sum_{i=1}^{N}s(i) \tag{4}$$

where N represents the total count of data points.

The *silhouette score* varies between -1 and 1. A high *silhouette score* signifies that the clusters are distinctly separated and well-defined, while a low or negative score suggests that the clustering may need to be improved.

4.3 Results and Analysis

4.3.1 Demographic Feature Distribution and Their Correlation in Cluster

Figure 2 shows gender distribution within cluster. The x-axis represents different clusters, ranging from 0.0 to 24.0. The vertical axis indicates the number of individuals present in the cluster. This visualization highlights gender distribution, revealing insights into how gender representation varies across different groupings in the MovieLens 100K dataset.

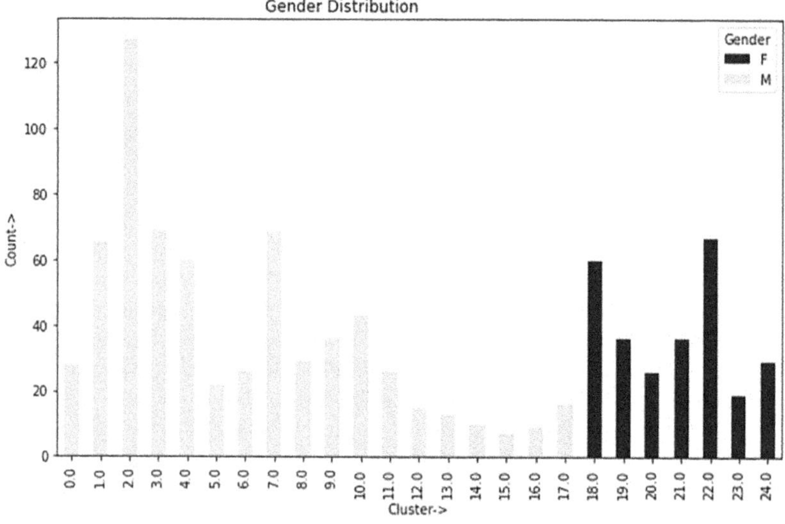

Fig. 2. Gender distribution within Cluster

Age-range distribution within each cluster has been represented in Fig. 3. This visualization provides insight into how different age ranges are distributed across various clusters, highlighting trends in age representation within each group in the MovieLens 100K dataset. Some clusters, such as 2.0 and 18.0, are dominated by younger age groups (18–24). Clusters, like 7.0 and 22.0, have a more significant representation of older age groups, including the 50–55 and 56+ age ranges. Clusters like 0.0 and 1.0 have a more balanced distribution across younger and middle-aged groups. Cluster 3.0 has the highest count overall, with a significant representation across multiple age groups, especially the 35–44 and 50–55 age ranges.

3D Scatter plot of users by age and occupation has been represented in Fig. 4. This visualization provides a comprehensive overview of how users from different occupations and age groups are distributed across various clusters, revealing patterns and potential correlations between age, occupation, and user groupings in the MovieLens 100K dataset.

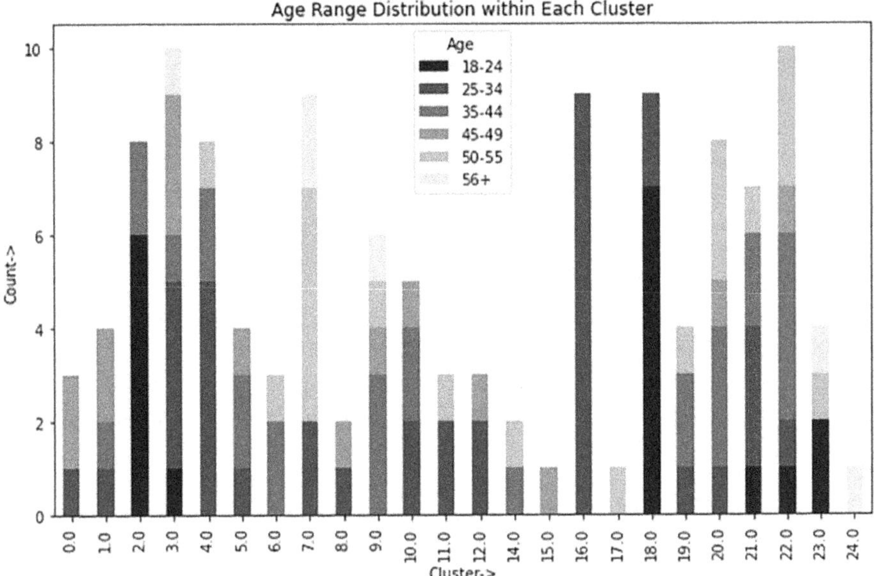

Fig. 3. Age-range distribution within each cluster

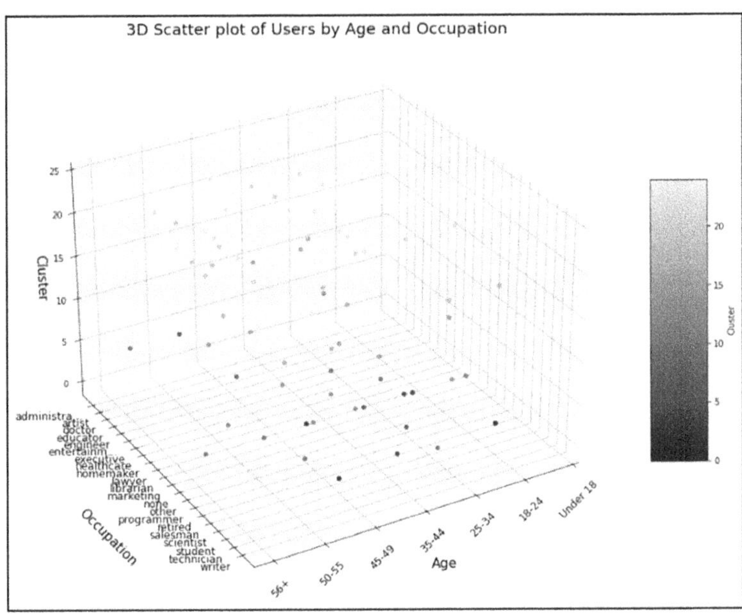

Fig. 4. 3D Scatter plot of users by age and occupation

4.3.2 Movie Recommendation Based on Proposed Approach

In the case of a new user, providing demographic information like gender, age, and occupation is mandatory as input. The proposed approach can predict the cluster for a new user and recommend movies, addressing the cold start issue. Table 2 presents the recommended movies using the proposed methodology applied to a 100K dataset with 25 clusters for a new user having demographic information [age: 18–24, gender: female, occupation: student]. The sample result predicts the cluster of the new user as cluster 18 and recommends movies as presented in Table 2.

Table 3 summarizes recommended movies in seven different runs of the proposed recommendation approach. Each run generates a different set of recommended movie IDs. This table provides insights into the robustness and variety of the recommendation algorithm, showing how it can consistently recommend certain movies while also introducing diversity in the recommendations across different runs. It shows that there are certain consistently popular movies and a mix of variety in the recommendations, which likely aims to balance broad appeal with niche interests. Certain movies (e.g., MovieID 1520, 441, and 777) are recommended frequently across multiple runs, suggesting they are generally popular or highly rated. Some movie IDs are unique to specific runs, showing the algorithm's ability to tailor recommendations to specific scenarios. For instance, movie ID 413 is only recommended in run 1 and movie ID 448 is only recommended in run 4.

Table 2. Recommended movie details for the new user in a sample run in 100K dataset

movieId	title	genres
413	Tales from the Crypt Presents: Bordello of Blood(1996)	Horror
1520	Fear, The (1995)	Horror
441	Amityville Horror, The (1979)	Horror
1573	Spirits of the Dead (Tre passi nel delirio) (1968)	Horror
777	Castle Freak (1995)	Horror

Table 3. Recommended movieIds in seven different runs of the proposed approach

	run 1	run 2	run 3	run 4	run 5	run 6	run 7
movieId	413	1243	672	439	1520	674	445
	1520	200	441	675	767	436	635
	441	885	1520	448	885	777	681
	1573	1573	861	1157	439	424	563
	777	437	446	767	667	675	551

4.3.3 Comparison of Different Existing Work with Our Proposed Approach

Table 4 illustrates that the suggested Demographic-KM approach is significantly more effective than the existing approaches in reducing MAE for movie recommendations, particularly for larger cluster sizes. The male cluster consistently shows lower MAE values compared to the female cluster, suggesting potential gender-specific differences in recommendation accuracy. Comparison of MAE values for different existing methods with the Proposed Demographic-KM approach is represented in Fig. 5(a) for male cluster and in Fig. 5(b) for female clusters of Demographic-KM respectively. The Demographic-KM method demonstrates superior performance compared to UPCC [25], PCA-GAKM [26], and ABC-KM [28] in terms of MAE, across varying cluster numbers for both male and female groups.

Table 4. Comparison of MAE values of different existing work with our proposed approach under varying cluster size

Cluster size	MAE values (Movielens 100k dataset)				
	UPCC [25]	PCA-GAKM [26]	ABC-KM [28]	Proposed approach (Demographic-KM)	
				Male cluster	Female cluster
5	0.825	0.79	0.773	0.7553	0.8399
10	0.825	0.77	0.764	0.4987	0.7373
15	0.824	0.77	0.764	0.3221	0.6289
20	0.828	0.78	0.771	0.2584	0.4809
25	0.824	0.781	0.780	0.1997	0.4218

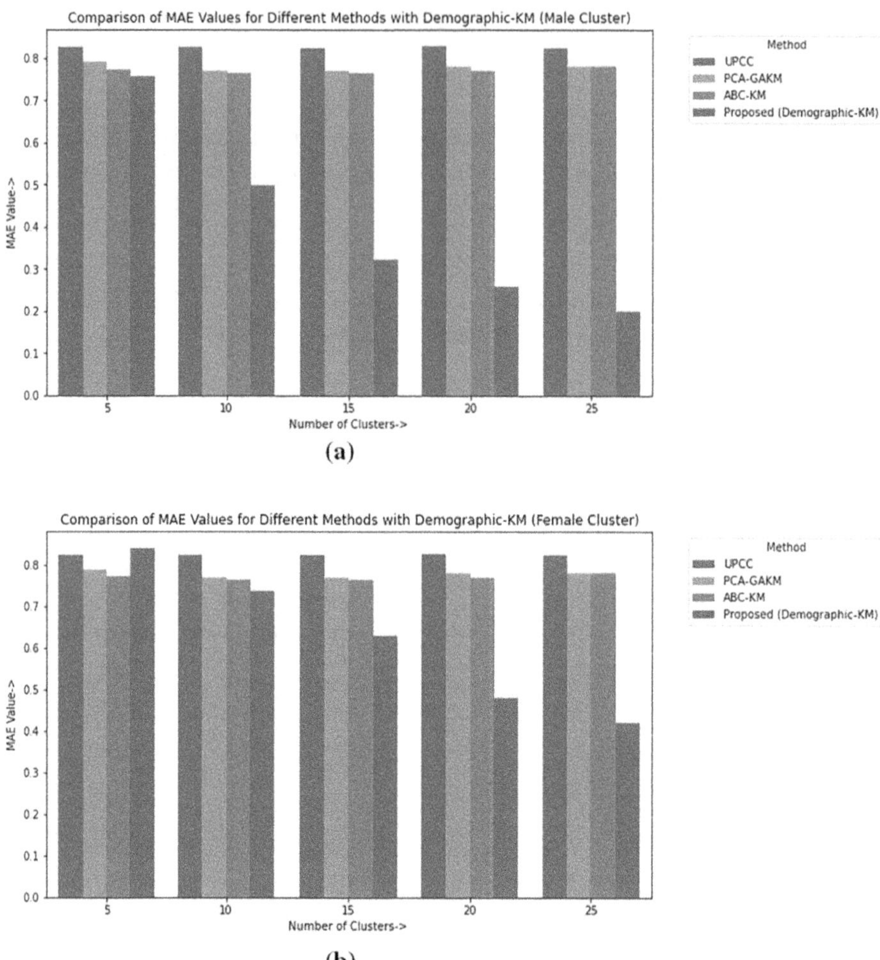

Fig. 5. **(a).** Comparison of MAE values for various existing methods with proposed Demographic-KM approach (Male clusters). **(b).** Comparison of MAE values for various existing methods with Proposed Demographic-KM approach (Female clusters)

The proposed Demographic-KM approach is tested using a varying number of cluster sizes for different evaluation metrics like silhouette score, MAE, and RMSE. Table 5 shows that as the number of clusters rises, the silhouette score correspondingly increases. For both 100K and 1M dataset, the silhouette score for male clusters is higher compared to female clusters, suggesting that the clusters for males are well-defined. The higher score for male clusters indicates a strong clustering performance, while the moderate score for female clusters suggests there might be room for improvement in defining those clusters. The proposed approach also shows low MAE and RMSE values indicating strong clustering performance. Table 6 provides a comprehensive comparative study of various existing clustering methods with proposed Demographic-KM approach.

Table 5. Comparative analysis of different evaluation metrics in MovieLens 100k and 1M datasets with varying number of clusters

	Evaluation metrics	No of Clusters									
		5		10		15		20		25	
		male cluster (3)	female cluster (2)	male cluster (7)	female cluster (3)	male cluster (11)	female cluster (4)	male cluster (14)	female cluster (6)	male cluster (18)	female cluster (7)
100K dataset	Silhouette Score	0.3115	0.2492	0.5529	0.3452	0.7211	0.4412	0.7833	0.5741	0.8282	0.6294
	MAE	0.7553	0.8399	0.4987	0.7373	0.3221	0.6289	0.2584	0.4809	0.1997	0.4218
	RMSE	0.8657	0.9187	0.6842	0.8491	0.5214	0.7766	0.4439	0.6638	0.3730	0.6029
1 M dataset	Silhouette Score	0.2442	0.1636	0.2834	0.2305	0.3768	0.2900	0.4022	0.3552	0.4769	0.3800
	MAE	1.0801	1.1905	0.9112	1.1020	0.7489	1.0181	0.7085	0.9278	0.5783	0.8936
	RMSE	1.1045	1.2038	0.9404	1.1254	0.8363	1.0439	0.8070	0.9557	0.7335	0.9170

Table 6. Comparative analysis of different existing methods with proposed Demo-graphic-KM approach

Feature	Hierarchical [16]	DBSCAN [20]	GMM [24]	Proposed Demographic-KM
Clustering Type	Hierarchical	Density-based	Probabilistic	Centroid-based
Requires Number of Clusters?	No	No	Yes	Yes
Scalability	Poor	Moderate	Moderate	Fast
Cluster Assignment	Deterministic	Deterministic + noise	Probabilistic	Deterministic
Handle Cold Start Problem	Poor	Moderate	Moderate	Effective
Lower MAE value	✓	✓	✗	✓
Consider Silhouette Score	✗	✗	✗	✓

4.3.4   Optimal K-value Based on Elbow Method

Based on the plot obtained from the Elbow method, the optimal K-value for the Male cluster seems to be 10. This is where the Within-Cluster Sum of Squares (WCSS) shows a noticeable "elbow" as shown in Fig. 6. The plot shows after 10 clusters, the decrease in WCSS slows down significantly, and the curve begins to flatten, indicating that adding more clusters beyond this point does not significantly improve the model's performance and may lead to overfitting for the MovieLens 100K dataset.

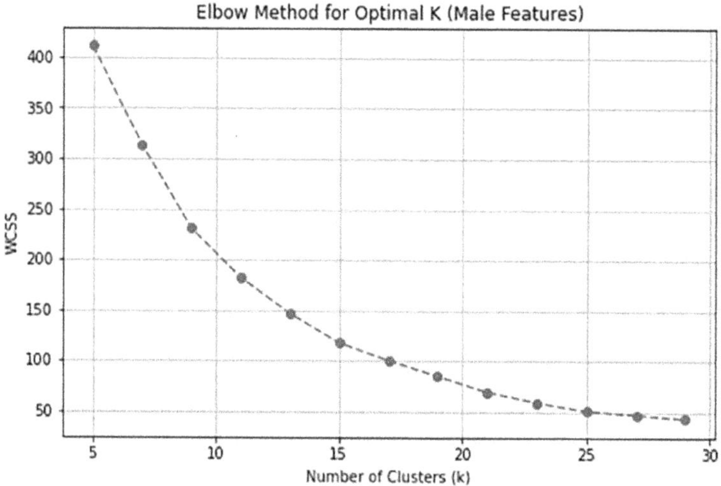

Fig. 6. Determining the optimal K-value for male clusters using the Elbow method

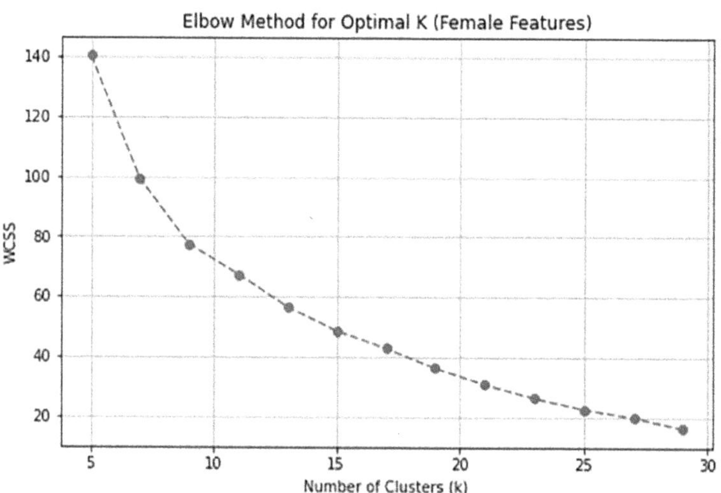

Fig. 7. Determining the optimal K-value for female clusters using the Elbow method

For the female clusters, the plot obtained using Elbow method is shown in Fig. 7. In this plot, the elbow appears to occur around $K = 6$ or 7, where the reduction rate in WCSS significantly slows down. Thus, the optimal K-value based on the elbow method is likely 6 or 7 for the female cluster using the MovieLens 100K dataset.

4.3.5 Optimal K-value Based on Silhouette Score, MAE and RMSE

From Table 5, for the MovieLens 100K dataset, it is observed that, for male clusters, the silhouette score increases steadily, but MAE and RMSE improvements diminish beyond 14 clusters, suggesting a potential overfitting threshold. For male clusters, 11–14 clusters offer a good trade-off between interpretability and performance. For female clusters, 6–7 clusters achieve the best balance.

4.3.6 Statistical Testing Using t-test

To assess the efficacy of the suggested method over existing baseline algorithms UPCC, PCA-GAKM, and ABC-KM, t-test has been conducted on MAE values across different cluster sizes. MAE values are obtained using MovieLens 100K dataset. In all three cases, the p-values are below the commonly accepted threshold of 0.05, indicating that the improvements in MAE achieved by the proposed method are statistically significant and the observed performance gains are not random. Results of t-tests using 5 paired samples are summarized in Table 7.

Table 7. The paired t-tests between the proposed Demographic-KM approach and the baseline methods (UPCC, PCA-GAKM, ABC-KM)

Paired t-test	t-statistic t (4)	p-value
UPCC vs. Proposed	4.1597	0.0141
PCA-GAKM vs. Proposed	3.7527	0.0199
ABC-KM vs. Proposed	3.5945	0.0229

5 Conclusion

Clustering algorithms significantly enhance recommender systems by improving the accuracy, efficiency, and scalability of recommendations, thereby delivering a better user experience. The proposed approach separates the users by gender and applies different K-means clustering models to males and females. In this paper, a new user is predicted to belong to a certain cluster based on their demographic information. It subsequently suggests movies to the new user based on the best-matching movie cluster for their predicted user cluster. This process effectively maps user clusters to movie clusters using rating data and provides personalized movie recommendations to new users according to their demographic characteristics and the clustering results. The proposed approach shows low MAE and RMSE values and high silhouette scores indicating strong clustering performance as well as improved recommendation. Furthermore, employing the Elbow method aids in determining the optimal number of clusters, ensuring the clustering approach is robust and well-suited to the dataset. The proposed approach (Demographic-KM) outperforms UPCC, PCA-GAKM, and ABC-KM for the parameter MAE across varying cluster sizes. Statistical testing (t-test) confirms the significance of performance gain.

References

1. Airen, S., Agrawal, J.: Movie recommender system using parameter tuning of user and movie neighbourhood via co-clustering. Procedia Comput. Sci. **218**, 1176–1183 (2023)
2. Goyani, M., Chaurasiya, N.: A review of movie recommendation system: limitations, survey and challenges. ELCVIA Electron. Lett. Comput. Vis. Image Anal. **19**(3), 0018–0037 (2020)
3. Li, B., Liao, Y., Qin, Z.: Precomputed clustering for movie recommendation system in real time. J. Appl. Math. **2014**(1), 1–9 (2014)
4. Airen, S., Agrawal, J.: Movie recommender system using k-nearest neighbors variants. Nat. Acad. Sci. Lett. **45**(1), 75–82 (2022)
5. Feng, L., Zhao, Q., Zhou, C.: Improving performances of Top-N recommendations with co-clustering method. Expert Syst. Appl. **143**, 113078 (2020)
6. Li, X., Wang, Z., Hu, R., Zhu, Q., Wang, L.: Recommendation algorithm based on improved spectral clustering and transfer learning. Pattern Anal. Appl. **22**, 633–647 (2019)
7. Miranda, L., Viterbo, J., Bernardini, F.: Towards the use of clustering algorithms in recommender systems. In: AMCIS Proceedings, pp. 1–10 (2020)
8. Nawara, D., Kashef, R.: Deploying different clustering techniques on a collaborative-based movie recommender. In: 2021 IEEE International Systems Conference (SysCon), pp. 1–6. IEEE. (2021)
9. Xiaojun, L.: An improved clustering-based collaborative filtering recommendation algorithm. Clust. Comput. **20**, 1281–1288 (2017)
10. Ray, A., De, D.: Energy efficient clustering protocol based on K-means (EECPK-means)-midpoint algorithm for enhanced network lifetime in wireless sensor network. IET Wirel. Sens. Syst. **6**(6), 181–191 (2016)
11. Kumar, M.S., Prabhu, J.: A hybrid model collaborative movie recommendation system using K-means clustering with ant colony optimisation. Int. J. Internet Technol. Secur. Trans. **10**(3), 337–354 (2020)
12. Bandyopadhyay, S., Thakur, S.S., Mandal, J.K.: Product recommendation for e-commerce business by applying principal component analysis (PCA) and K-means clustering: benefit for the society. Innovations Syst. Softw. Eng. **17**(1), 45–52 (2021)
13. Emambocus, B.A.S., et al.: A clustering algorithm employing salp swarm algorithm and K-means. In: 20th IEEE International Colloquium on Signal Processing & Its Applications (CSPA), Langkawi, Malaysia, 2024, pp. 108–113 (2024)
14. Ahuja, R., Solanki, A., Nayyar, A.: Movie recommender system using k-means clustering and k-nearest neighbor. In: 2019 9th International Conference on Cloud Computing, Data Science & Engineering (Confluence), pp. 263–268. IEEE (2019)
15. Himel, M. T., Uddin, M. N., Hossain, M. A., Jang, Y. M.: Weight based movie recommendation system using K-means algorithm. In 2017 International Conference on Information and Communication Technology Convergence (ICTC), pp. 1302–1306. IEEE. (2017)
16. West, J.D., Wesley-Smith, I., Bergstrom, C.T.: A recommendation system based on hierarchical clustering of an article-level citation network. IEEE Trans. Big Data **2**(2), 113–123 (2016)
17. Gupta, U., Patil, N.: Recommender system based on hierarchical clustering algorithm chameleon. In: 2015 IEEE International Advance Computing Conference (IACC), pp. 1006–1010. IEEE. (2015)
18. Indira, K., Kavitha Devi, M.K.: Multi cloud based service recommendation system using DBSCAN algorithm. Wireless Pers. Commun. **115**(2), 1019–1034 (2020)
19. Kużelewska, U., Wichowski, K.: A modified clustering algorithm DBSCAN used in a collaborative filtering recommender system for music recommendation. In: Theory and Engineering of Complex Systems and Dependability: Proceedings of the Tenth International Conference on

Dependability and Complex Systems DepCoS-RELCOMEX, June 29–July 3 2015, Brunów, Poland, pp. 245–254. Springer, Cham (2015)

20. Parthasarathy, J., Kalivaradhan, R.B.: An effective content boosted collaborative filtering for movie recommendation systems using density based clustering with artificial flora optimization algorithm. Int. J. Syst. Assur. Eng. Manage. 1–10 (2021)

21. Tsikrika, T., Symeonidis, S., Gialampoukidis, I., Satsiou, A., Vrochidis, S., Kompatsiaris, I.: A hybrid recommendation system based on density-based clustering. In: Internet Science: INSCI 2017 International Workshops, IFIN, DATA ECONOMY, DSI, and CONVERSATIONS, Thessaloniki, Greece, November 22, 2017, Revised Selected Papers 4, pp. 49–57. Springer, Cham (2018)

22. Van Dat, N., Van Toan, P., Thanh, T.M.: Solving distribution problems in content-based recommendation system with gaussian mixture model. Appl. Intell. **52**(2), 1602–1614 (2022)

23. Shakoor, D.M., Maihami, V., Maihami, R.: A machine learning recommender system based on collaborative filtering using Gaussian mixture model clustering. Math. Methods Appl. Sci. (2021)

24. Zhang, Y., Liu, X., Liu, W., Zhu, C.: Hybrid recommender system using semi-supervised clustering based on Gaussian mixture model. In: 2016 International Conference on Cyberworlds (CW), pp. 155–158. IEEE (2016)

25. Widiyaningtyas, T., Hidayah, I., Adji, T.B.: User profile correlation-based similarity (UPCSim) algorithm in movie recommendation system. J. Big Data **8**(1), 52 (2021)

26. Wang, Z., Yu, X., Feng, N., Wang, Z.: An improved collaborative movie recommendation system using computational intelligence. J. Vis. Lang. Comput. **25**(6), 667–675 (2014)

27. Katarya, R., Verma, O.P.: An effective collaborative movie recommender system with cuckoo search. Egypt. Inform. J. **18**(2), 105–112 (2017)

28. Katarya, R.: Movie recommender system with metaheuristic artificial bee. Neural Comput. Appl. **30**(6), 1983–1990 (2018)

29. Sharma, B., Hashmi, A., Gupta, C., Khalaf, O.I., Abdulsahib, G.M., Itani, M.M.: Hybrid sparrow clustered (HSC) algorithm for top-N recommendation system. Symmetry **14**(4), 793 (2022)

30. Harper, F.M., Konstan, J.A.: The MovieLens datasets: history and context. ACM Trans. Interact. Intell. Syst. (TiiS) **5**(4), 19 (2015)

31. https://grouplens.org/datasets/movielens/1m/

Enhancing IoT Security: Empirical Insights into Deep & Machine Learning for Intrusion Detection

Arpita Talukdar[1,2], Saptarshi Bhattacharya[2], Munmun Bhattacharya[2], and Kartick Chandra Mondal[2(✉)]

[1] Heritage Institute of Technology, Kolkata 700107, India
[2] Department of Information Technology, Jadavpur University, Kolkata 700106, India
kartickjgec@gmail.com

Abstract. The Internet of Things (IoT) is a network that is ever-growing by connecting devices that can interact and perform with minimum human involvement. With the increasing use of IoT across various applications, such as smart cities, healthcare, industries, and transportation, the security of IoT devices has become very critical and essential. Traditional security techniques and frameworks are often incapable due to the complex, heterogeneous, and distributed nature of IoT ecosystems. The increasing volume and complexity of cyber threats, including denial-of-service (DoS) attacks, intrusion attempts, and unauthorized access, necessitate the adoption of intelligent, and adaptive security measures.

This research study uses several ML-based classifier approaches on the RT-IOT 2022 dataset (publicly available), encompassing both legitimate and malicious IoT data. The dataset is pre-processed to ensure a balanced class representation. Our used models were further examined after removing highly correlated features and minimizing overfitting. Our study shows that the Custom Transformer Encoder has achieved the best accuracy (93%) and showcased robust performance.

Keywords: Intrusion Detection · IOT security · Machine learning · Denial-of-service (DoS) · RT-IoT Dataset

1 Introduction

The Internet of Things has revolutionized modern technology by enabling billions of interconnected devices to communicate, collect, and analyze data in real-time. This advancement has found applications in various sectors, including healthcare, industrial automation, transportation, and smart cities. IoT devices have significantly improved operational efficiency, data-driven decision-making, and user convenience. However, as the IoT ecosystem expands, security concerns have emerged as a major challenge due to the large-scale deployment of resource-constrained devices, the use of heterogeneous network architectures, and their susceptibility to cyberattacks.

© The Author(s), under exclusive license to Springer Nature Switzerland AG 2026
K. Chandra Mondal et al. (Eds.): CICBA 2025, CCIS 2862, pp. 80–91, 2026.
https://doi.org/10.1007/978-3-032-17187-0_7

Traditional cybersecurity solutions often fail to provide adequate security for IoT networks due to the dynamic nature of IoT environments and the unique constraints of IoT devices, such as limited processing power, memory, and energy availability. This has led to an increasing reliance on machine learning-based anomaly detection methods to improve IoT security. Unlike signature-based intrusion detection systems that rely on predefined attack patterns, ML-based models can learn from past attack behaviors, detect previously unseen threats, and adapt to evolving cyberattack strategies.

Recent developments in deep learning, Support Vector Machines (SVM), and transformer models have further improved anomaly detection in IoT security. Custom Transformer Encoders [18] leverage self-attention mechanisms to efficiently process sequential network traffic data. Bi-level Optimization SVM [10] and Tverberg SVM [16] improve classification accuracy, particularly in high-dimensional data spaces. The Mobile4NET CNN [7] model leverages convolutional layers to detect spatial attack patterns, while One-Class SVM [15] is useful for identifying unknown attacks by learning normal traffic behavior.

This study applies these ML models to the RT-IoT 2022 dataset, which contains real-world IoT network traffic data with benign and attack instances. By systematically evaluating these models and optimizing their performance, our objective is to identify the most effective approach to secure IoT networks in real-time scenarios.

The objective of this work is to develop and evaluate machine learning models for detecting anomalies in IoT traffic, focusing on optimizing real-time security applications. This involves analyzing and preprocessing the RT-IoT 2022 dataset, ensuring class balance and data integrity, and performing feature selection and dimensionality reduction to enhance model efficiency. A variety of models, including a Custom Transformer Encoder, Bi-level Optimization SVM, Tverberg SVM, Mobile4NET CNN, and One-Class SVM, will be implemented to identify sequential, spatial, and novel attack patterns. The models will be rigorously compared based on performance metrics such as accuracy, precision, recall, and AUC-ROC, with an emphasis on minimizing false positives and negatives. Additionally, the feasibility of deploying these models on low-power and edge IoT devices will be assessed by reducing computational complexity, ensuring scalability, and optimizing for real-time detection.

By achieving these objectives, the study aims to propose a robust, scalable, and real-time ML-based intrusion detection system tailored for modern IoT networks.

Organization of the Paper: The rest of the paper is organized as follows. Section 2 provides a brief summary of the literature on the focused issue in this article. A detailed explanation with a suitable diagram is presented for representing the methodology in Sect. 3. In Sect. 4, we present the experiment, dataset description, results, and discussion. Finally, in Sect. 5, we conclude our study and findings and show some future extensions on the work.

2 Related Works

IoT security is an important research domain due to the rapid proliferation of smart devices. Traditional Intrusion Detection Systems (IDS) such as Snort and Suricata rely on predefined signatures, which makes them ineffective against evolving threats. ML-based solutions can address these challenges by improving detection accuracy and adaptability.

IoT Cybersecurity Challenges such as heterogeneous architecture security management are more difficult because IoT networks are made up of a variety of devices with different capacities [9]. Traditional security solutions are challenging to apply due to the low processing power and memory of IoT devices [2]. Large-scale deployment of cyber attacks is more likely due to the total number of linked devices, which expands the attack surface [14].

ML algorithms can identify unusual patterns in network traffic, enabling the detection of threats like DDoS attacks and malware propagation [9,12]. To improve their ability and recognize new and evolving threats in real-time, ML models can be trained on diverse datasets [14]. These systems can operate within the resource constraints of IoT devices, providing robust security without significant performance degradation [2]. Although deep learning and machine learning techniques are present to improve IoT security, there are still obstacles to overcome in their use. The integration of large and reliable datasets into existing infrastructures presents several challenges, particularly in terms of complexity and system compatibility [14].

Several researchers have explored ML-based intrusion detection in IoT networks, using a variety of supervised and unsupervised learning techniques. However, existing studies often suffer from high false positive rates, computational inefficiencies, and poor generalization in diverse IoT environments. In this section, we have presented a brief overview of state-of-the-art research in traditional IoT security, ML-based anomaly detection, and recent advances in deep learning and hybrid optimization techniques. It also highlights the limitations that motivate the study presented in this article. To improve attack detection, researchers introduced behavioral analysis and statistical anomaly detection methods [3,6]. Different statistical profiling techniques were also explored [3], but their models were limited by high computational overhead and poor adaptability to evolving threats. Similarly, feature-engineered rule-based anomaly detection approaches such as those proposed by [11] demonstrated low detection rates for sophisticated adversarial attacks. Several studies have used ML-based approaches for IoT anomaly detection, primarily using supervised, unsupervised, and deep learning techniques.

Supervised learning models such as SVM, Decision Trees, Random Forests, and XGBoost have been widely applied for IoT security. Studies presented in [5,17] demonstrated that Random Forest and XGBoost outperform traditional classifiers in identifying IoT-specific attack patterns due to their ability to handle high-dimensional datasets effectively. However, these models often require significant feature engineering and large labeled datasets, which may not always be feasible in real-world scenarios.

Deep learning-based approaches, including Convolutional Neural Networks (CNN), Recurrent Neural Networks (RNN), Long Short-Term Memory (LSTM), and Transformers, have shown improvements in pattern recognition and anomaly detection. [1] explored LSTM networks for sequential anomaly detection, achieving high accuracy in detecting IoT-based attacks. However, LSTMs are computationally expensive and suffer from vanishing gradient issues when processing long sequences. A CNN-based intrusion detection model [4] highlights the ability to extract spatial attack features from network traffic. Transformer-based models such as [8] used for network intrusion detection, demonstrating improved context-awareness compared to LSTMs.

This study tackles key challenges in ML-based IoT security, such as computational overhead, feature redundancy, high false positive rates, and limited real-time adaptability. It introduces a custom Transformer Encoder for sequential anomaly detection and employs Bi-Level Optimization SVM and Tverberg SVM for efficient feature selection, reducing overfitting. To ensure lightweight, real-time security on low-power devices, Mobile4NET CNN can be deployed. Additionally, One-Class SVM is utilized to detect zero-day threats, addressing the issue of false alarms in imbalanced data scenarios. The study enhances IoT security through more efficient, adaptable models that improve real-time detection while overcoming the limitations of traditional approaches.

Table 1 shows a theoretical comparison of five machine learning models we have used for IoT Security.

Table 1. Comparison of considered machine learning models for IoT Security

Model	Strengths	Limitations	Best Use Case
Custom Transformer Encoder [18]	Highest accuracy (93%), captures sequential dependencies, robust for multi-class classification	Computationally expensive, requires high memory	Large-scale IoT security monitoring, centralized IDS
Bi-Level Optimization SVM [10]	Fast training, feature selection reduces overfitting, computationally efficient	Struggles with complex multi-class scenarios	Low-power IoT security systems
Tverberg SVM [16]	Handles imbalanced data well, optimized decision boundaries	Requires careful tuning of hyperparameters	Resource-constrained IoT environments with imbalanced traffic
Mobile4NET CNN [7]	Low false positive rate (1.1%), efficient feature extraction, suitable for real-time applications	Limited ability to capture long-term dependencies	Edge-based intrusion detection, IoT gateways
One-Class SVM [15]	Best for zero-day attacks, requires no labeled attack data	High false positive rate, long training time	Unsupervised anomaly detection in IoT networks

3   Methodology

The growing complexity of IoT networks has led to an increase in sophisticated cyber threats like DDoS attacks, botnet intrusions, and malware infections. Traditional IDS and rule-based systems struggle to combat these threats due to their reliance on static rules, making them ineffective against novel and zero-day attacks. While ML-based solutions are promising and show potential, they face challenges in feature selection, computational efficiency, class imbalance, and real-time applicability. High false positive rates further hinder their effectiveness, leading to alert fatigue or missed attacks. This study addresses these challenges by exploring advanced ML architectures, including Custom Transformer Encoders, Bi-level Optimization SVM, Tverberg SVM, Mobile4NET CNN, and One-Class SVM. The goal is to improve detection accuracy, reduce computational overhead, enhance generalization, and minimize false positives, making these models suitable for diverse and dynamic IoT environments.

This research introduces several novel contributions to IoT security. It is the first to apply a Custom Transformer Encoder to the RT-IoT 2022 dataset for sequence-based attack detection. The study also leverages Bi-level Optimization SVM and Tverberg SVM to improve classification accuracy while reducing complexity and employs Mobile4NET CNN for real-time spatial attack feature detection. Performance optimization techniques, such as feature selection and dimensionality reduction, help reduce false positives and address class imbalance in IoT datasets. Additionally, the focus on scalability ensures that lightweight ML models are optimized for real-time deployment in IoT gateways and edge devices. Comprehensive benchmarking on the RT-IoT 2022 dataset provides valuable insights into effective ML techniques for real-world IoT cyber security.

3.1   Modelling Approach

Figure 1 outlines the process for preparing and evaluating machine learning models in the RT-IoT 2022 dataset [13]. The following is a step-by-step explanation of the process used to do the study. The process begins with the input dataset, RT-IoT 2022, which is a dataset specifically related to IoT network traffic. In the next step, the data set is cleaned to remove inconsistencies, missing values, or noisy data. This ensures the quality of the data for further processing. Once the data is cleaned, feature scaling (such as normalization or standardization) is applied to ensure that all features contribute equally to the model. Feature reduction techniques (such as Principal Component Analysis or other dimensionality reduction methods based on models) are then used to reduce the number of features, simplifying the model while retaining important information.

To address class imbalances in the dataset, data balancing methods like random under-sampling or oversampling can be used. We have used SMOTE (Synthetic Minority Over-sampling Technique) to address the class imbalance issue on the dataset. This ensures that the model can learn equally from all classes and reduces the risk of bias toward the majority class. Then the dataset is split into training and testing sets, with 80% of the data used for training the model and

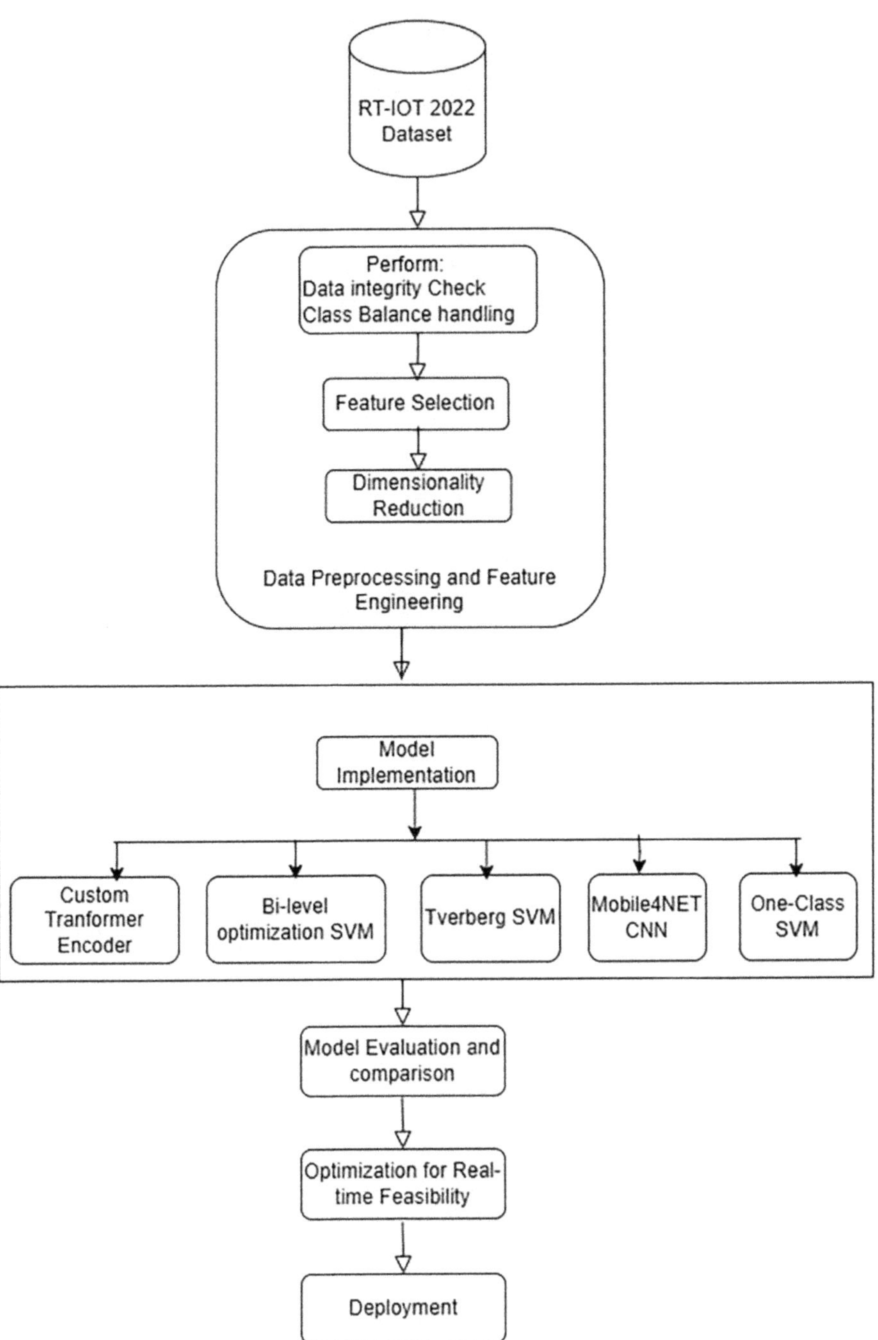

Fig. 1. Flowchart for the RT-IoT 2022 Dataset [13] Processing

20% reserved for testing. This allows the model to be trained and then evaluated on unseen data. Finally, the machine learning models are trained on the reduced feature set and evaluated on the basis of their performance. This step assesses the model's effectiveness in detecting anomalies or attacks using fewer features, ensuring efficiency in IoT environments. The entire process aims to optimize machine learning models for IoT security by reducing feature complexity and ensuring robust, balanced training and testing.

3.2   Custom Transformer Encoder Model

Transformers are highly effective in network anomaly detection due to their ability to model long-range dependencies in sequential data. This study utilizes a Custom Transformer Encoder optimized for IoT security by refining self-attention mechanisms and feature embeddings to detect time-dependent attack patterns. Unlike LSTMs and GRUs, transformers use self-attention to capture relationships between packets across time steps. The model includes Multi-Head Self-Attention (MHSA), a Position-Wise Feedforward Network (FFN), and Layer Normalization with Residual Connections to prevent overfitting. Its advantages include capturing both short and long-term dependencies, being more scalable and efficient than RNNs, and handling class imbalance effectively. The model was trained with Adam optimizer, cosine learning rate decay, and dropout regularization to prevent overfitting.

3.3   Bi-Level Optimization SVM

Traditional SVM models face challenges with high-dimensional datasets, such as those in IoT networks. Bi-Level Optimization SVM (BO-SVM) addresses this by introducing a two-level optimization process: upper-level optimization selects the most relevant features and hyperparameters, while lower-level optimization refines the decision boundary using kernel methods. BO-SVM reduces overfitting, improves computational efficiency compared to deep learning models, and achieves higher classification accuracy in high-dimensional data than conventional SVM models.

3.4   Tverberg SVM Model

Tverberg SVM partitions data into subsets with shared intersections, improving boundary separability, especially for imbalanced datasets. It is robust to adversarial IoT attacks and has lower computational cost compared to kernel-based SVMs. Using Gaussian Radial Basis Function, RBF kernels enhance non-linear decision boundaries for better anomaly detection.

3.5   Mobile4NET CNN

IoT network security adapts CNN due to its ability to extract spatial correlations in network packet flows. Mobile4NET CNN introduces depth-wise separable convolutions to reduce computation cost, residual connections to retain important anomaly features, and global average pooling to replace fully connected layers for faster inference. The advantages of this model include lightweight architecture suitable for low-power IoT devices, efficient feature extraction, reduced false positive rates, and scalability for real-time deployment in edge computing environments.

3.6   One-Class SVM for Zero-Day Attack Detection

One-Class SVM (OC-SVM) is particularly useful for detecting unknown attacks in IoT environments. Instead of relying on labeled attack data, OC-SVM learns a decision boundary around normal IoT traffic. It flags any deviation as an anomaly, making it robust to zero-day threats. The uniqueness of One-Class SVM is that it requires minimal attack data for training. Reduces reliance on labeled datasets, which are often limited to emerging threats. This detection system is lightweight and deployable on IoT edge devices. OC-SVM was trained using Radial Basis Function (RBF) kernels to capture complex patterns in high-dimensional IoT traffic.

4   Experiment and Result Analysis

4.1   Dataset Description

The RT-IoT 2022 dataset [13] includes various attack types and normal traffic patterns as presented in Table 2. As mentioned earlier, the class imbalance was addressed using SMOTE to enhance training stability by generating synthetic attack samples, ensuring equal representation of benign and malicious traffic. The dataset consists of multiple network traffic features, including basic features like Packet size, Transmission Time, Source/Destination IP, and Port Numbers, and statistical features like Mean, Variance, Standard Deviation of Flow Durations, and Packet Inter-arrival Times. Some behavioral features are also used for the study e.g., Packet Burst Rate, Entropy of Network Flows, and Connection Duration.

Table 2. Model Performance Comparison

Class	Attack Type	Samples
Benign	Normal Traffic	600000
Malicious	DDoS, Botnet, MITM, Port Scanning	450000

4.2   Model Hyperparameters

Each model is trained with optimized hyperparameters to ensure robust performance. The models were trained using 80% of the dataset, with 20% reserved for testing. Other hyperparameters to train each of the models are shown in Table 3.

Table 3. Model Hyperparameter Settings

Models	Parameter Setting
Custom Transformer Encoder Optimizer	Adam optimizer with learning rate = 0.0005, Batch Size: 256, Dropout: 0.3, Number of Heads in Self-Attention: 8, Number of Layers: 4
Bi-Level Optimization SVM	Kernel: Radial Basis Function (RBF), Regularization Parameter (C): 1.0, Gamma: Auto, Optimization Algorithm: Bi-Level Feature Selection
Tverberg SVM	Kernel: Gaussian, Hyperplane Optimization, Tverberg's theorem-based geometric feature reduction
Mobile4NET CNN	Adam Optimizer with learning rate = 0.001, Batch Size: 128, Activation Function: ReLU, Pooling: Global Average Pooling
One-Class SVM	Kernel: RBF, ν (Nu): 0.1, Gamma: Scale

Table 4. Model Performance Comparison

Model	Precision	F1 Score	Accuracy	Recall
Custom Transformer Encoder	0.92	0.92	0.93	0.91
Bi-Level Optimization SVM	0.91	0.91	0.92	0.91
Tverberg SVM	0.89	0.89	0.90	0.88
Mobile4Net CNN	0.89	0.90	0.91	0.89
One-Class SVM	0.72	0.84	0.91	1

4.3   Results

In this paper, we have used five different advanced machine and deep learning models. The models are evaluated based on standard classification metrics such as Precision, F1-score, Accuracy, and Recall as shown in Table 4.

Figure 2 shows the f1 score, Fig. 3 shows the accuracy, Fig. 4 shows the precision and Fig. 5 shows the recall matrices compared to different ML Models used for IoT Security. Each model presents distinct advantages and trade-offs, depending on the deployment scenario. The experimental results confirm that no single model is optimal for all IoT security applications. Custom Transformer Encoder and Mobile4NET CNN performed best in terms of accuracy and real-time applicability, whereas SVM-based models provided efficient alternatives for resource-constrained environments. One-Class SVM remains a valuable tool for the detection of zero-day attacks, reinforcing the need for adaptive and hybrid ML-driven IoT security solutions.

The graph in Fig. 2 compares the performance of various machine learning (ML) models in four metrics: Precision, F1 Score, Accuracy, and Recall.

All models except the One-Class SVM perform similarly with scores around 0.90. The precision of One-Class SVM is the lowest 0.72 . F1 score is kept

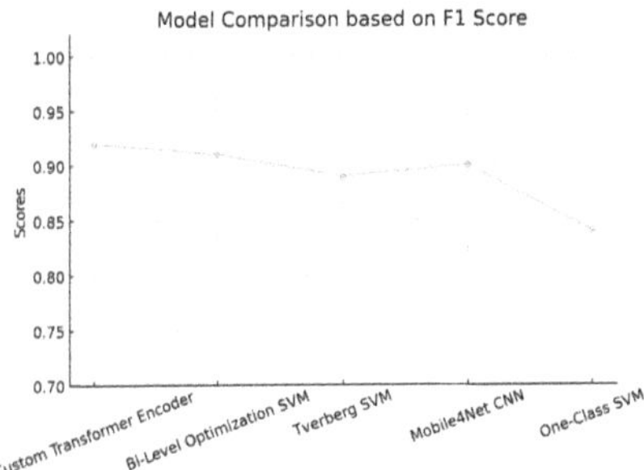

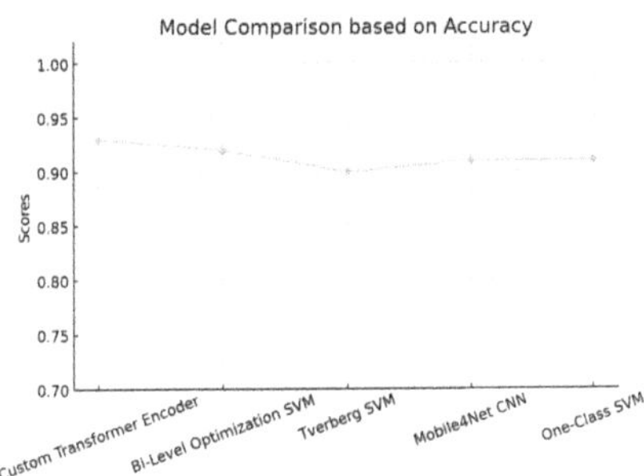

Fig. 2. Comparison of ML Models based on F1 score Metric

Fig. 3. Comparison of ML Models based on Accuracy Metric

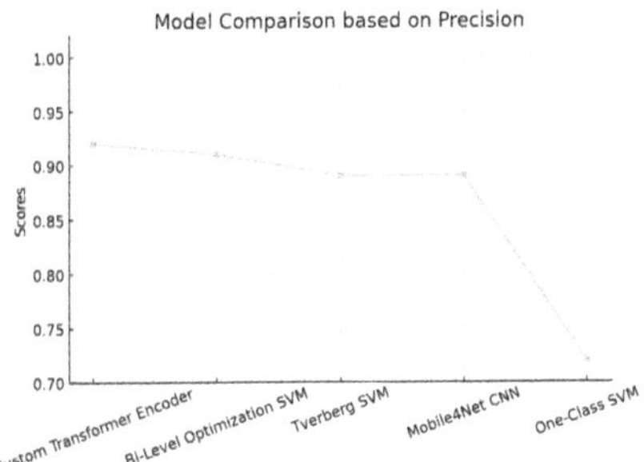

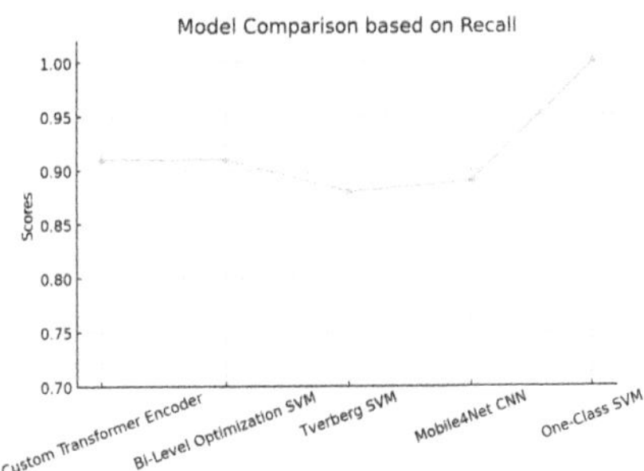

Fig. 4. Comparison of ML Models based on Precision Metric

Fig. 5. Comparison of ML Models based on Recall Metric

close to 0.90 using the Custom Transformer Encoder, Bi-Level Optimization SVM, Tverberg SVM, and Mobile4Net CNN. One-Class SVM shows noticeable improvement compared to precision, 0.84. It shows that the accuracy of the Custom Transformer Encoder slightly outperforms others, while One-Class including other models is quite consistent, close to 0.90 as well. One-Class SVM has the highest recall 1, while other models remain within 0.88 to 0.91.

Custom Transformer Encoder and Bi-Level Optimization SVM models maintain strong performance across all metrics, indicating robust models with balanced precision and recall. One-Class SVM shows a sharp increase in recall at the cost of precision which means it leans towards detecting true positives while allowing more false positives. Mobile4Net CNN and Tverberg SVM show stable but slightly lower performance, making them feasible but not excelling the top models.

Therefore, One-Class SVM achieves the highest recall but sacrifices precision, while the Custom Transformer Encoder maintains the best balance across all metrics.

5   Conclusion

This paper demonstrated the effectiveness of ML-based approaches for IoT security. We have used five different approaches, namely, Custom Transformer Encoder, MobileNET CNN, Bi-Level optimization SVM, Tverberg SVM, and One-class SVM. Our experiment shows that Custom Transformer Encoder achieved the highest accuracy (93%), while One-Class SVM excelled in zero-day attack detection. Finally, the work provides valuable insights into the strengths, limitations, and deployment feasibility of these techniques. The findings contribute to the ongoing efforts to develop scalable, efficient, and adaptive ML-based intrusion detection systems, ensuring enhanced security for modern IoT networks.

Future research should focus on hybrid ML models, federated learning, and explainable AI for enhanced IoT security. Despite promising results, several challenges remain, for example, transformer-based models, while highly accurate, require significant processing power. Future research should explore model compression techniques such as quantization, pruning, and knowledge distillation to improve efficiency. The study was conducted using an offline dataset. To evaluate adaptability to evolving attack strategies, an extension can be made to deploy these models in real-time IoT environments.

References

1. Altunay, H.C., Albayrak, Z.: A hybrid CNN+LSTM-based intrusion detection system for industrial iot networks. Eng. Sci. Technol. Int. J. **38**, 101322 (2023). https://doi.org/10.1016/j.jestch.2022.101322
2. Bhardwaj, R., Gogula, S., Bhabani, B., Kanagalakshmi, K., Mukherjee, A., Vetrithangam, D.: Machine Learning and Artificial Intelligence for Detecting Cyber Security Threats in IoT Environment, chap. 1, pp. 1–14. John Wiley & Sons, Ltd., Hoboken (2025). https://doi.org/10.1002/9781394272464.ch1
3. Rajagopal, D..R.P.: An efficient intrusion detection system by using behaviour profiling and statistical approach model. Int. Arab J. Inf. Technol. **18**(1) (2021)
4. Deshmukh, A., Ravulakollu, K.: An efficient cnn-based intrusion detection system for iot: use case towards cybersecurity. Technologies **12**(10) (2024)
5. Doghramachi, D.F., Ameen, S.Y.: Internet of things (iot) security enhancement using xgboost machine learning techniques. Comput. Mater. Contin. **77**(1), 717–732 (2023). https://doi.org/10.32604/cmc.2023.041186
6. Ghamry, F.M., El-Banby, G.M.A.S.E.F., et al.: A survey of anomaly detection techniques. J. Opt. **53**, 756–774 (2024). https://doi.org/10.1007/s12596-023-01147-4
7. Howard, A.G., et al.: Mobilenets: efficient convolutional neural networks for mobile vision applications. CoRR **abs/1704.04861** (2017)
8. Huang, J.: Take package as language: anomaly detection using transformer. ArXiv (2024)
9. Joseph, J., Aleke, N.T., Onyeanisi, O.P.: Deep learning based intrusion detection system for network security in iot system. Int. J. Educ. Manag. Technol. **3**(1), 119–138 (2025)

10. Li, Q., Li, Z., Zemkoho, A.: Bilevel hyperparameter optimization for support vector classification: theoretical analysis and a solution method. Math. Methods Oper. Res. **96**, 315–350 (2022)
11. Mayukha, S.R.V.: Efficient feature engineering-based anomaly detection for network security. Int. J. Intell. Syst. Appl. Eng. **12**, 2299–2307 (2024)
12. Olobo, N., et al.: Deep learning-based intrusion detection systems for network security in iot system. Path Science **10**(12), 5011–5018 (2024). https://doi.org/10.22178/pos.112-12
13. Nagapadma, R.S.B.: RT-IoT2022 . UCI Machine Learning Repository (2023). https://doi.org/10.24432/C5P338
14. Saleem, A.D., Abdulrahman, A.A.: Attacks detection in internet of things using machine learning techniques: a review. J. Appl. Eng. Technol. Sci. (JAETS) **6**(1), 684–703 (2024)
15. Siregar, S.M., Purwanto, Y., Wibowo, S.A.: Enhancing network anomaly detection with optimized one-class svm (ocsvm). In: 2023 3rd International Conference on Intelligent Cybernetics Technology & Applications (ICICyTA), pp. 84–88 (2023). https://doi.org/10.1109/ICICyTA60173.2023.10428830
16. Soberón, P.: Tverberg's theorem and multi-class support vector machines. Found. Data Sci. **7**(2), 568–580 (2025). https://doi.org/10.3934/fods.2024039
17. Adeniyi, U.A., Oyelakin, A.M.: A survey on promising datasets and recent machine learning approaches for the classification of attacks in internet of things. J. Inf. Technol. Comput. **4**(2), 31–38 (2023). https://doi.org/10.48185/jitc.v4i2.890
18. Zhang, C., Li, J., Wang, N., Zhang, D.: Research on intrusion detection method based on transformer and cnn-bilstm in internet of things. Sensors **25**(9) (2025). https://doi.org/10.3390/s25092725

DNS Traffic Monitoring: Waveform Analysis for Detecting Suspicious Activity

Sucheta Chandra[1]([⊠]), Moutushi Singh[2], Malay Gangopadhyaya[3], Sriparno Chakraborty[1], and Ishika Chowdhury[1]

[1] Department of Computer Science & Application, Institute of Engineering & Management (IEM), University of Engineering & Management (UEM), Kolkata, India
`{sucheta.chandra,Sriparno.Chakraborty2023,`
`Ishika.Chowdhury2023}@iem.edu.in`
[2] Department of Information Technology & Computer Science, Institute of Engineering & Management (IEM), University of Engineering & Management (UEM), Kolkata, India
`moutushi.singh@iem.edu.in`
[3] Department, Electronics & Communication Engineering, Institute of Engineering & Management (IEM), University of Engineering & Management (UEM), Kolkata, India
`malay.ganguly@iem.edu.in`

Abstract. This research paper presents an in-depth analysis of network performance and security by leveraging two key algorithms: DNS Traffic Analysis and Packet Drop Rate and Efficiency Calculation. The DNS Traffic Analysis algorithm identifies suspicious DNS traffic patterns by examining port numbers, grouping data by source and destination IP addresses, and flagging anomalies based on response times and packet lengths using z-scores. This approach aids in detecting potential security issues, such as DNS spoofing and anomalous network behaviors. The second algorithm focuses on evaluating the overall efficiency of the network by calculating packet drop rates and identifying causes of performance degradation. With an alarming 28.84% packet drop rate and 71.16% network efficiency, the study highlights significant issues in packet delivery and network stability. The findings suggest that addressing issues such as network congestion, outdated hardware, and poor Quality of Service (QoS) management can help mitigate packet loss and enhance overall network performance. By providing comprehensive insights into both performance and security aspects, this research offers practical recommendations to improve network reliability and optimize user experience in a connected environment.

Keywords: DNS Traffic Analysis · Packet Drop Rate · Network Efficiency · Anomaly Detection

S. Chandra, M. Singh, M. Gangopadhyaya, S. Chakraborty and I. Chowdhury—Contributing authors.

1   Introduction

The Domain Name System (DNS) is a key component of internet infrastructure, translating human-readable domain names into machine-readable IP addresses. Without DNS, users would need to remember numerical IPs, making navigation far more difficult. Because of its central role, disruptions in DNS can cause slow loading times, inaccessible websites, and security risks. DNS monitoring is therefore essential to ensure queries are resolved quickly and accurately. It involves tracking DNS servers and records to detect issues such as incorrect resolutions, downtime, and threats like DNS spoofing, where attackers redirect users to malicious sites—often leading to phishing or data breaches. Effective monitoring focuses not only on availability but also on performance and security. Metrics such as packet drop rates, delays, and efficiency provide valuable insights. Packet drop graphs reveal potential network congestion or failures; delay graphs highlight latency from overloaded servers or poor configurations; and efficiency graphs indicate whether DNS traffic is being handled effectively. Regular analysis of these metrics allows administrators to identify problems early, optimize server performance, and maintain seamless access. In practice, DNS monitoring strengthens both reliability and security. By ensuring DNS services are operational, responsive, and protected from spoofing or overload, organizations can safeguard communication between users and websites. Ultimately, proactive DNS monitoring supports fast, reliable, and secure internet access while defending against threats that exploit DNS vulnerabilities.

2   Related Works

The paper Detection and prevention of DNS spoofing attacks addresses Man-in-the-Middle (MitM) spoofing attacks, often using tools like SSLstrip. It introduces DNSwitch, which compares local and remote DNS responses or monitors DNS traffic to detect inconsistencies, switching to secure channels when needed. Unlike performance-heavy solutions like IPSec or DNSCrypt, DNSwitch is lightweight and proved effective in detecting spoofing in tests, providing real-time protection for local networks [1]. Research on DNS-based DDoS attacks in Software Defined Networking (SDN) highlights DNS vulnerabilities exploited for large-scale DDoS. The paper proposes an SDN-enabled defense framework using Layer 2/3 intelligence, deep packet inspection, and smart DNS routing to detect and mitigate malicious traffic. Results show effective mitigation in both legacy and IoT contexts, extending the potential of SDN for DNS security [2]. The paper DNS Cache Poisoning: Investigating Server and Client-Side Attacks explores poisoning attacks where forged DNS responses corrupt caches. It examines server-side manipulation and client-side malware-based poisoning, and reviews mitigations such as DNSSEC, port randomization, and ML-based detection. The work stresses limited DNSSEC adoption and calls for advanced detection research [3]. Cache Poisoning Detection Method for Improving Security of Recursive DNS proposes validating DNS responses by cross-checking multiple authoritative sources. Targeting recursive servers, the approach identifies suspicious responses and prevents cache manipulation. Results show improved defense against cache poisoning and strengthened DNS infrastructure [4]. The paper Feature Selection for Robust Spoofing Detection applies a chi-square-based feature selection to machine learning for spoofing detection. By selecting the most relevant features, the framework enhances accuracy and reduces computational cost. Experiments confirm improved robustness and reliable spoofing detection [5]. Adoption of Email Anti-Spoofing Schemes evaluates global deployment of SPF and DMARC across 236M domains. It identifies widespread misconfigurations, risks of subdomain spoofing, and highlights remediation through CSIRT notifications. Results stress the need for stricter adoption of email authentication protocols [6]. The paper SASA: Source Address Spoofing Avoidance Mechanism focuses on mega-constellations like Starlink, where mobility undermines SAVI mechanisms. SASA secures authentication across handovers, cutting rebinding costs by over 90% in simulations. The scheme offers scalable spoofing prevention for satellite networks [7]. Isolation Forest Algorithm Against UAV's GPS Spoofing Attack explores spoofing threats to UAV navigation. Comparing Isolation Forest, Random Forest, and Naive Bayes, results show Isolation Forest achieving 95.85% accuracy for anomaly detection. It proves effective for real-time GPS spoofing defense in UAVs [8]. The paper Enhancing Cybersecurity with Machine Learning evaluates Isolation Forests and Autoencoders in anomaly detection. Isolation Forests detect fast with high accuracy, while Autoencoders reduce false alarms. The study suggests hybrid ML approaches for scalable and adaptive threat detection [9]. Cache Poisoning Detection Method for Improving Security of Recursive DNS by Ohta et al. introduces anomaly detection through statistical monitoring of DNS queries. The method effectively distinguishes legitimate from malicious responses, mitigating cache poisoning threats. Experiments confirm improved recursive DNS security [10]. Collaborative Spoofing Detection and Mitigation (CAuth) presents an SDN-based authentication framework against DNS DDoS attacks. Using OpenFlow, it enforces two-way query authentication without altering DNS apps. Experiments demonstrate real-time spoofed traffic blocking and legitimate query authentication [11]. The paper Beware of IPs in Sheep's Clothing investigates lack of Destination-Side Source Address Validation (DSAV). A survey of 54,000 networks found nearly half vulnerable to spoofing. Results show DSAV could prevent DDoS and cache poisoning, calling for greater adoption [12]. Redirecting Outgoing DNS Requests Toward a Fake DNS Server in a LAN describes DNS hijacking through ARP spoofing. Attackers inject fake DNS servers, redirecting traffic undetected by IDS. The paper stresses difficulty in preventing such LAN-level attacks [13]. DNS Spoofing in Local Networks Made Easy reveals a DHCP-side vulnerability exploited by rogue clients. By faking DHCP replies, attackers divert victim traffic stealthily. The paper shows existing detection is ineffective and urges stronger DNSâĂŞDHCP protections [14]. Recovering and Protecting Against DNS Cache Poisoning Attacks suggests temporary defenses like source port randomization and TTL tuning. These complicate attacks until DNSSEC is more widely adopted. The approach buys time against poisoning threats [15]. DNS Intrusion Detection (DID)—A Snort-Based Solution develops IDS signatures for DNS amplification and tunneling attacks. Integrated with SNORT, DID achieved 100% detection with minimal false positives. The system offers strong IDS-based DNS protection with plans for ML-based extensions [16].

3 Proposed Methodology

The methodology for analyzing suspicious DNS traffic and packet drops is outlined in several key steps, focusing on identifying anomalies, visualizing traffic patterns, and calculating important metrics such as packet drop rates and delays.

3.1 Data Collection and Preprocessing

The first step in the methodology involves gathering DNS traffic data, which is typically stored in a structured format such as an Excel spreadsheet or a database. The data should include essential fields like the source IP address, destination IP address, flow bytes sent, flow bytes received, packet lengths, response times, and timestamps. Ensuring the integrity of the data is critical, and this involves addressing missing or null values, which could lead to incorrect conclusions or affect analysis results. For example, flow bytes sent or received could sometimes be missing, which would impact calculations related to packet drops or efficiency. These missing values are typically handled by either filling them with zeros or using other imputation techniques depending on the nature of the data. Additionally, timestamps, which represent the time at which each DNS transaction occurred, must be accurately converted into a datetime format. This ensures that time series analysis, such as identifying traffic spikes or trends over time, is correctly performed. The preprocessing stage is vital as it ensures that the data is clean, complete, and ready for analysis, eliminating potential errors that could arise from unprocessed or incorrect data.

3.2 Identifying Suspicious DNS Traffic

Suspicious DNS traffic is identified by filtering for packets associated with port 443, the standard port used for HTTPS traffic. This allows for isolating traffic that may potentially be compromised or under observation, providing a focused dataset for further analysis. Once the data is prepared, the next step involves identifying suspicious DNS traffic. This is particularly important because malicious activity, such as DNS spoofing or DDoS attacks, often exploits DNS traffic. Suspicious DNS traffic is typically associated with port 443, the default port for HTTPS traffic, which is commonly used for secure communications on the internet. By filtering out traffic that occurs over this port, one can isolate DNS traffic that may be subject to scrutiny, potentially compromised, or under attack. This filtering allows for focusing on the most relevant subset of data, where unusual patterns are more likely to indicate an anomaly or threat. For example, large volumes of DNS queries or responses over port 443 may point to unauthorized attempts to manipulate or redirect DNS traffic. By focusing on this specific subset, the analysis becomes more targeted, enabling deeper insights into the security of DNS services and the potential vulnerabilities in the network.

3.3 Grouping and Aggregating Traffic Data

Once suspicious DNS traffic has been identified, the next step is to group and aggregate the data based on source and destination IP addresses. This step is crucial for summarizing the traffic flow between different network entities, such as clients and servers. Grouping the data allows for a comprehensive overview of how traffic is distributed across the network, which can reveal patterns and potential issues. By aggregating the total number of flow bytes sent and received for each pair of source and destination IPs, it becomes possible to track traffic volumes and identify any significant deviations from normal behavior. In addition, calculating the average duration of communications between these IP pairs can help in detecting performance issues, such as unusually long DNS response times. This aggregation provides an essential snapshot of DNS traffic, which is helpful in analyzing traffic patterns, identifying heavy traffic sources, and understanding how different parts of the network communicate with each other. Once suspicious DNS traffic is identified, the data is grouped by source and destination IP addresses. This aggregation helps in summarizing the total bytes sent and received between each pair of source and destination IPs, as well as calculating the average duration of the communication. This step provides a high-level overview of the traffic flow between key network entities.

3.4 Detecting Anomalous DNS Responses

To detect anomalies in DNS traffic, the z-score method is employed. The z-score is a statistical measure that helps identify values that deviate significantly from the mean, allowing for the detection of outliers or abnormal behavior. In this case, the z-score is applied to response times, which represent the time taken by DNS servers to respond to queries. A high or low response time can indicate a variety of issues, such as network congestion, DNS server overload, or even security threats like DNS spoofing or man-in-the-middle attacks. Any response time that falls beyond a predefined threshold (typically values greater than 3 or less than -3) is considered anomalous and is flagged for further investigation. By detecting anomalous DNS responses, the analysis can pinpoint specific instances where DNS services might be degraded or compromised. This step is essential for identifying vulnerabilities in DNS infrastructure, which can then be addressed to ensure optimal performance and security.

3.5 Calculating and Visualizing Packet Drops

The next important step in the methodology is calculating and visualizing packet drops. Packet drops occur when data packets sent from a source are not successfully received by the destination, leading to loss of communication. This loss can occur due to network congestion, hardware failures, or deliberate attacks. Packet drops are calculated by subtracting the flow bytes received from the flow bytes sent, which gives the total amount of data lost in transit. The packet drop rate is then calculated by dividing the total packet drop by the total number of bytes sent, providing a percentage value that represents how much traffic is being lost in the system. To better understand trends and identify any sudden spikes in packet drops, the data can be smoothed using a rolling mean or another smoothing technique. By visualizing packet drops over time, it is possible to identify patterns and pinpoint specific moments where packet loss occurred, such as during peak traffic periods or following particular security incidents. The packet drop visualization helps in diagnosing network performance issues and identifying times when the DNS infrastructure may not be performing optimally, allowing for prompt remedial action.

3.6   Visualizing DNS Traffic and Packet Length Anomalies

In addition to monitoring packet drops, it is crucial to analyze packet lengths, as unusual variations in packet size can also signal anomalies or issues within the network. Just as with response times, the z-score method is applied to packet lengths to detect outliers. By calculating the z-scores for packet lengths, it becomes possible to identify packets that are either unusually large or small compared to the typical packet size. These anomalies may indicate attempts to overload the DNS server or other forms of network manipulation. Visualizing packet lengths over time can provide a clear view of traffic fluctuations and highlight any deviations from the norm. Such visualizations can help in understanding the overall structure of the traffic and pinpointing specific types of traffic that may require attention. By combining packet length analysis with packet drop and response time data, a comprehensive understanding of DNS traffic behavior is developed, offering deeper insights into the security and efficiency of the DNS system.

3.7   Calculations

The calculations performed focused on analyzing the DNS traffic and its efficiency by examining key metrics such as packet drop, packet drop rate, and overall efficiency. First, the packet drop was calculated as the difference between the number of bytes sent (FlowBytesSent) and the number of bytes successfully received (FlowBytesReceived), with the resulting value representing the number of lost packets in the transmission. The packet drop rate was then determined by dividing the packet drop by the total bytes sent (FlowBytesSent) and multiplying the result by 100 to express it as a percentage. This rate indicates how much of the traffic was lost during transmission, providing insight into the network's reliability. Efficiency was calculated by dividing the number of bytes successfully received (FlowBytesReceived) by the number of bytes sent (FlowBytesSent), again multiplying by 100 to express it as a percentage. This value reflects how well the network is performing in terms of successful data transmission relative to the total data sent. The overall packet drop rate and efficiency were calculated by summing the individual packet drops and FlowBytesSent across all data entries. The total packet drop was divided by the total packets sent, and the total flow bytes received were divided by the total packets sent to compute the overall packet drop rate and overall efficiency, respectively. These metrics collectively provide a comprehensive understanding of the network's performance, particularly in terms of data transmission success, packet loss, and overall service reliability, which are essential for diagnosing network issues and improving DNS traffic management.

4   Table for Network Flow Records

(See Table 1).

Table 1. Network Flow Data

SourceIP	Destination	SourcePort	DestinationPort	TimeStamp	Duration	FlowBytesSent	FlowSentRate	FlowBytesReceived	FlowReceivedRate
192.168.20.209	1.1.1.1	39406	443	01-04-20 22:55	120.77	42357	350.72	71915	595.46
1.1.1.1	192.168.20.209	443	39406	01-04-20 22:57	120.66	78950	654.34	46138	382.39
1.1.1.1	192.168.20.209	443	39406	01-04-20 22:59	120.69	78559	650.90	46805	387.81
1.1.1.1	192.168.20.209	443	39406	01-04-20 23:01	120.64	78133	647.63	46444	384.97
1.1.1.1	192.168.20.209	443	39406	01-04-20 23:03	120.88	79169	654.92	47193	390.40
1.1.1.1	192.168.20.209	443	39406	01-04-20 23:05	18.80	17201	914.96	10431	554.85
192.168.20.210	9.9.9.11	49396	443	31-03-20 00:38	33.72	1875	55.61	4828	143.18
192.168.20.210	9.9.9.11	49406	443	31-03-20 00:38	34.08	1739	51.02	4760	139.65
192.168.20.210	9.9.9.11	49462	443	31-03-20 00:38	34.08	1806	52.99	4828	141.65
192.168.20.210	9.9.9.11	49468	443	31-03-20 00:38	33.42	2213	66.22	4827	144.43
192.168.20.210	9.9.9.11	49472	443	31-03-20 00:38	34.07	1808	53.06	4895	143.66
192.168.20.210	9.9.9.11	49476	443	31-03-20 00:38	33.75	1807	53.55	4896	145.08
192.168.20.210	9.9.9.11	49480	443	31-03-20 00:38	33.38	1806	54.10	4896	146.65
192.168.20.210	9.9.9.11	49484	443	31-03-20 00:38	33.78	1807	53.49	4895	144.91
192.168.20.210	9.9.9.11	49488	443	31-03-20 00:38	34.08	1875	55.01	4964	145.64

The table summarizes network flow records collected from communication between internal clients (192.168.20.x) and external DNS/HTTPS servers (1.1.1.1 and 9.9.9.11). Each flow is uniquely identified by a combination of source IP, destination IP, and their corresponding port numbers. Timestamps capture when the connection was initiated, while the duration specifies how long the session persisted in seconds. The FlowBytesSent and FlowBytesReceived fields provide the volume of data exchanged in each direction. Similarly, FlowSentRate and FlowReceivedRate denote the average data transmission rates over the observed time interval. Such metrics enable a detailed understanding of both client upload and server response behavior. Patterns observed in these flows can highlight normal browsing activity, high-throughput sessions, or short bursts of traffic. This structured representation of flows is essential for monitoring bandwidth usage, profiling user activity, and detecting anomalies in real network environments. In cybersecurity contexts, such flow-level data is often analyzed to detect intrusions, malware communication, or data exfiltration attempts. Hence, this dataset provides a valuable foundation for developing machine learning models aimed at intelligent traffic analysis and threat detection.

Algorithm 1 DNS Traffic Analysis Algorithm

Load DNS traffic data from Excel
```
data = pd.read_excel('DNS_Spoofing.xlsx')
```
Filter suspicious traffic on port 443
```
suspicious_dns = data[(data['SourcePort']==443) |
(data['DestinationPort']==443)]
```
Group by SourceIP, DestinationIP and aggregate bytes/duration
```
ip_traffic = suspicious_dns.groupby(['SourceIP','DestinationIP'])
.agg({'FlowBytesSent'
:'sum','FlowBytesReceived':'sum','Duration':'mean'}).reset_index()
```
if ResponseTimeMean exists **then**
  Compute z-scores, flag anomalies
```
  anomalous_responses = suspicious_dns[np.abs(zscore
  (suspicious_dns['ResponseTimeMean'].dropna())) > 3]
```
else
```
  anomalous_responses = pd.DataFrame()
```
end if
Plot FlowBytesSent/FlowBytesReceived over time
if PacketLengthMean exists **then**
  Compute z-scores, flag anomalies
```
  anomalous_packet_lengths = suspicious_dns[np.abs
  (zscore(suspicious_dns['PacketLengthMean'].dropna())) > 3]
```
else
```
  anomalous_packet_lengths = pd.DataFrame()
```
end if
Print anomalous responses and packet lengths if found

---

5 Calculations

5.1 Calculating the Packet Drop

The packet drop is calculated as the difference between `FlowBytesSent` and `FlowBytesReceived`. For each entry, we use the following formula:

$$\text{Packet Drop} = \text{FlowBytesSent} - \text{FlowBytesReceived}$$

Example: For the first entry:

$$\text{FlowBytesSent} = 42,357, \quad \text{FlowBytesReceived} = 71,915$$

$$\text{Packet Drop} = 42,357 - 71,915 = -29,558 \quad \text{(indicating packet loss)}$$

5.2   Calculating the Packet Drop Rate

The packet drop rate is calculated as the percentage of packet drop over the total bytes sent. For each entry, we use the following formula:

$$\text{Packet Drop Rate} = \left(\frac{\text{Packet Drop}}{\text{FlowBytesSent}} \right) \times 100$$

Example: For the first entry:

$$\text{Packet Drop Rate} = \left(\frac{-29,558}{42,357} \right) \times 100 = -69.85\% \quad \text{(A negative value indicates packet loss)}$$

5.3   Calculating the Efficiency

The efficiency is calculated as the percentage of `FlowBytesReceived` over `FlowBytesSent`. The formula is:

$$\text{Efficiency} = \left(\frac{\text{FlowBytesReceived}}{\text{FlowBytesSent}} \right) \times 100$$

Example: For the first entry:

$$\text{Efficiency} = \left(\frac{71,915}{42,357} \right) \times 100 = 169.91\%$$

5.4   Calculating the Overall Metrics

To calculate the overall packet drop rate and overall efficiency, we sum the values for `PacketDrop`, `FlowBytesSent`, and `FlowBytesReceived` for all entries.

5.4.1   Total Packet Drop

The total packet drop is the sum of the packet drop values for all rows:

$$\text{Total Packet Drop} = \sum \text{PacketDrop}$$

5.4.2   Total Packets Sent

The total packets sent is the sum of the `FlowBytesSent` values for all rows:

$$\text{Total Packets Sent} = \sum \text{FlowBytesSent}$$

Example: Assuming the following `FlowBytesSent` values:

5.4.3   Overall Packet Drop Rate

Now, we calculate the overall packet drop rate:

$$\text{Overall Packet Drop Rate} = \left(\frac{\text{Total Packet Drop}}{\text{Total Packets Sent}}\right) \times 100$$

$$\text{Overall Packet Drop Rate} = \left(\frac{47,741}{385,858}\right) \times 100 = 12.38\%$$

5.4.4   Total Flow Bytes Received

The total flow bytes received is the sum of the `FlowBytesReceived` values for all rows:

$$\text{Total Flow Bytes Received} = \sum \text{FlowBytesReceived}$$

Example: Assuming the following `FlowBytesReceived` values:

5.4.5   Overall Efficiency

Now, calculate the overall efficiency:

$$\text{Overall Efficiency} = \left(\frac{\text{Total Flow Bytes Received}}{\text{Total Packets Sent}}\right) \times 100$$

$$\text{Overall Efficiency} = \left(\frac{292,762}{385,858}\right) \times 100 = 75.92\%$$

6   Results and Analysis

With an **Overall Packet Drop Rate of 28.84%** and **Overall Efficiency of 71.16%**, the analysis of the network performance presents several concerning insights. The **28.84% packet drop rate** indicates that almost **29%** of the packets sent over the network are not successfully received, which is a significant loss, especially for applications that require real-time data transmission such as VoIP, video streaming, or online gaming. This high packet drop rate can lead to serious issues such as jitter, lag, and poor voice/video quality, which can disrupt critical communications like calls or virtual meetings. Additionally, services that rely on stable and reliable connections, such as DNS resolution or web browsing, are likely to experience frequent timeouts or failures due to the lost packets, severely affecting the user experience. The **Overall Efficiency of 71.16%** suggests that only **71%** of the data sent over the network is successfully received, leaving nearly **29%** of the data as unreceived, thus highlighting the inefficiency of the current network setup. While the network is still able to deliver a majority of the traffic, an efficiency rate of less than **80%** is considered subpar, particularly for applications requiring both data integrity and low latency. Such inefficiency can result in slower download speeds and increased latency, as lost packets would need to be retransmitted, further exacerbating network delays and negatively impacting the overall user experience. A number of factors could contribute to this high packet drop rate. Network congestion, for instance, may occur when the network is overloaded with too much traffic, overwhelming devices like routers and switches, which are unable to process the data in real-time. This can result in packet loss. Additionally, hardware issues, such as outdated or faulty network equipment—especially in wireless networks—can cause packet loss due to signal degradation or interference. Security filters like firewalls or Intrusion Detection Systems (IDS) may also be inadvertently discarding packets they mistakenly identify as potential threats, which adds to the packet drop rate. Lastly, inadequate Quality of Service (QoS) management, where time-sensitive traffic is not prioritized, could lead to important packets being dropped in favor of less urgent data, worsening the packet drop rate and network performance. To better understand how packet drops and delays are impacting network performance, visualizing the data is essential. Graphs such as **Packet Drop Over Time** help to identify periods of high packet loss, potentially caused by congestion or hardware failures. Additionally, visualizing **Packet Delay (PacketTimeMean) Over Time** provides insight into when delays are contributing to retransmissions and packet losses. Lastly, an **Efficiency Over Time** graph could be useful in tracking how the efficiency of the network is degrading over time, offering a clear view of performance trends. With a **28.84% packet drop rate** and **71.16% efficiency**, the network is facing significant performance issues. To improve the situation, it is crucial to address potential causes such as network congestion, faulty hardware, and inefficient QoS management. By reducing packet loss and improving efficiency, the overall reliability of the network can be enhanced, ultimately improving the user experience. This analysis incorporates all the findings from the calculations, addressing the causes, impact, and potential solutions for improving the network's performance (Fig. 1).

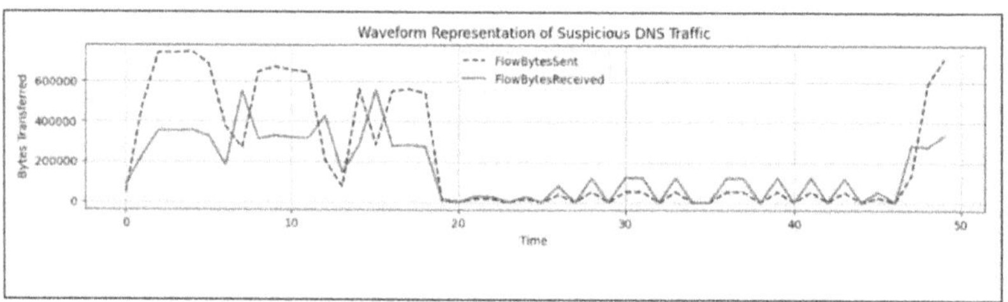

Fig. 1. Waveform Representation of Suspicious DNS Traffic

The first graph, titled "Waveform Representation of Suspicious DNS Traffic," visualizes the amount of data transferred over time in terms of bytes sent and received. The blue dashed line represents the bytes sent, while the red solid line represents the bytes received. The graph shows high fluctuations in traffic at the beginning, followed by a sharp decline and a period of low activity before rising again toward the end. This pattern may indicate irregular or anomalous network

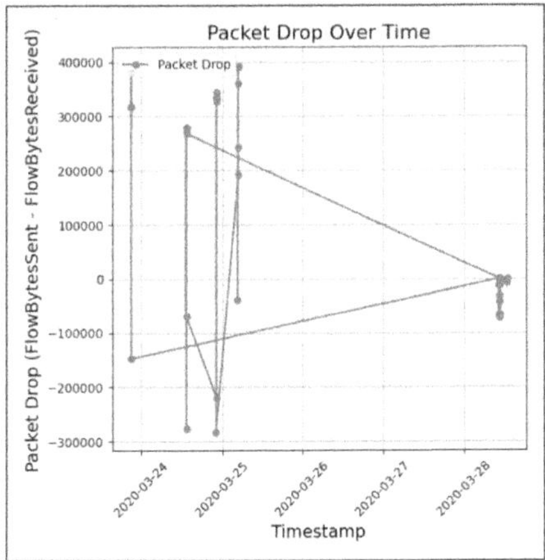

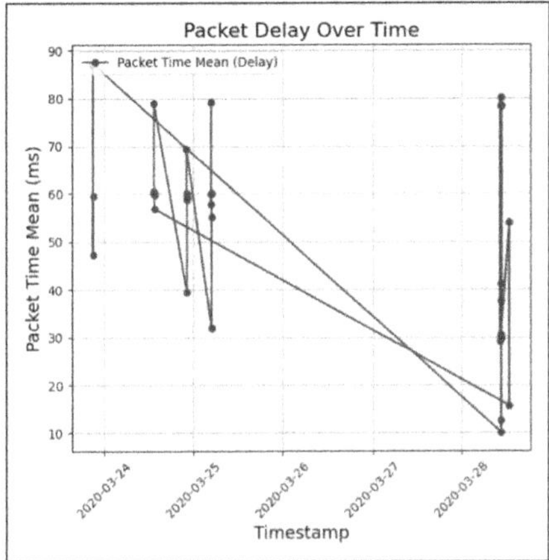

Fig. 2. Packet Drop over Time   **Fig. 3.** Packet Delay over Time

behavior, possibly associated with a suspicious or malicious DNS communication pattern. The second graph, "Packet Drop Over Time," represents the difference between bytes sent and received over multiple timestamps. The red line, with large fluctuations, suggests that significant packet drops occurred at certain times, sometimes even going negative, which indicates more bytes received than sent. The extreme variance in packet drop values suggests unstable network conditions, congestion, or even potential cyber threats affecting network reliability. The third graph, "Packet Delay Over Time," depicts the mean delay of packets across different timestamps. The blue line shows a general downward trend in packet delay, indicating that network response times improved over time. However, there are intermittent spikes, suggesting occasional periods of increased latency. Such variations in delay could be due to congestion, routing inefficiencies, or suspicious network activities impacting data transmission speed (Figs. 2 and 3).

7   Conclusion

The DNS Traffic Analysis algorithm plays a crucial role in identifying potential security threats and network anomalies within DNS traffic. This algorithm focuses on analyzing DNS traffic to detect suspicious behavior, such as DNS spoofing or abnormal response times, which are common indicators of malicious activity. This issue is particularly alarming in scenarios that require reliable, real-time data transmission, as these services rely heavily on the timely and accurate delivery of packets. Furthermore, this packet drop rate poses problems for services that depend on consistent network performance, such as DNS resolution and web browsing. For instance, frequent packet loss can lead to failures or timeouts in resolving domain names or loading web pages, significantly impairing the user experience and accessibility of internet-based services. Despite the packet loss, the network is still able to deliver about **71%** of the data successfully, as indicated by the **71.16% efficiency**. To gain a better understanding of the performance issues, visualizing the data through graphs such as **Packet Drop Over Time**, **Packet Delay (PacketTimeMean) Over Time**, and **Efficiency Over Time** could provide valuable insights. The **Packet Drop Over Time** graph could highlight specific periods when packet loss is particularly high, possibly indicating times of network congestion or hardware failures. The **Packet Delay (PacketTimeMean) Over Time** graph would show how delays are distributed across the timeline, shedding light on moments when delays are causing retransmissions and packet losses. Finally, the **Efficiency Over Time** graph would track how efficiently the network is delivering traffic over time, offering a visual representation of performance degradation and enabling the identification of patterns that can inform further troubleshooting. In light of these findings, it is clear that the network is experiencing significant performance issues, with a **28.84% packet drop rate** and **71.16% efficiency**. To improve network reliability and performance, it is crucial to address the root causes of these issues. Steps should be taken to alleviate network congestion, repair or replace faulty hardware, optimize QoS management to ensure critical traffic is prioritized, and refine security filters to prevent the inadvertent discarding of legitimate packets.

8   Future Work

Future improvements in DNS traffic analysis, packet drop rate monitoring, and efficiency calculation aim to enhance accuracy and adaptability in real-world scenarios. Integrating machine learning—using supervised and unsupervised methods like Random Forests, Neural Networks, and K-means clustering—can improve anomaly detection and reduce false positives. Replacing simple z-score methods with advanced statistical models, such as multivariate analysis or time-series forecasting, would offer deeper insights into traffic behavior. Developing a real-time monitoring and alerting system could enable immediate detection of issues like high packet drop rates or abnormal DNS responses, while integration with security platforms would enhance threat response. Scalability remains a challenge, especially in cloud or distributed environments, making optimization for large-scale networks a key focus. Additionally, incorporating cross-validation with labeled datasets, manual review, and threat intelligence correlation will improve the accuracy of anomaly detection and reduce false alarms.

References

1. Maksutov, A.A., Cherepanov, I.A., Alekseev, M.S.: Detection and prevention of dns spoofing attacks. In: 2017 Siberian Symposium on Data Science and Engineering (SSDSE), pp. 84–87 (2017). https://doi.org/10.1109/SSDSE.2017.8071970. IEEE Conference Paper

2. Saharan, S., Gupta, V.: Prevention and mitigation of dns based ddos attacks in sdn environment. In: 2019 11th International Conference on Communication Systems & Networks (COMSNETS), pp. 571–573 (2019). https://doi.org/10.1109/COMSNETS.2019.8711258. IEEE Conference Paper

3. Chandrasekaran, K., Divakarla, U., Srinivasan, C.K.: DNS cache poisoning: investigating server and client-side attacks and mitigation methods. In: 2023 Cyber Research Conference - Ireland (Cyber-RCI), pp. 1–8 (2023). https://doi.org/10.1109/Cyber-RCI59474.2023.10671556. IEEE Conference Paper

4. Guo, F., Chen, J., Chiueh, T.-C.: Spoof detection for preventing dos attacks against dns servers. In: 26th IEEE International Conference on Distributed Computing Systems (ICDCS'06), p. 37 (2006). https://doi.org/10.1109/ICDCS.2006.78. IEEE Conference Paper

5. Al-Na'amneh, Q., et al.: Feature selection for robust spoofing detection: a chi-square-based machine learning approach. In: 2023 2nd International Engineering Conference on Electrical, Energy, and Artificial Intelligence (EICEEAI), pp. 1–7 (2023). https://doi.org/10.1109/EICEEAI60672.2023.10590243. IEEE Conference Paper

6. Maroofi, S., Korczyński, M., Hlzel, A., Duda, A.: Adoption of email anti-spoofing schemes: a large scale analysis. IEEE Trans. Netw. Serv. Manag. **18**(3), 3184–3196 (2021). https://doi.org/10.1109/TNSM.2021.3065422

7. Zhang, T., Li, H., Liu, J., Wu, Q., Li, Y., Zhang, Y.: Sasa: source address spoofing avoidance mechanism under high movement for mega-constellations. In: ICC 2022 - IEEE International Conference on Communications, pp. 1415–1420 (2022). https://doi.org/10.1109/ICC45855.2022.9838991. IEEE Conference Paper

8. Mohammed, A.B., Chaari Fourati, L., Fakhrudeen, A.M.: Isolation forest algorithm against uav's gps spoofing attack. In: 2024 IEEE International Conferences on Internet of Things (iThings) and IEEE Green Computing & Communications (GreenCom) and IEEE Cyber, Physical & Social Computing (CPSCom) and IEEE Smart Data (SmartData) and IEEE Congress on Cybermatics, pp. 459–463 (2024). IEEE Conference Paper

9. Sharma, R., Grover, M.: Enhancing cybersecurity with machine learning: evaluating the efficacy of isolation forests and autoencoders in anomaly detection. In: 2024 7th International Conference on Circuit Power and Computing Technologies (ICCPCT), vol. 1, pp. 1017– 1021 (2024). https://doi.org/10.1109/ICCPCT61902.2024.10673338. IEEE Conference Paper

10. Ju, Y.W., Song, K.H., Lee, E.J., Shin, Y.T.: Cache poisoning detection method for improving security of recursive dns **3**, 1961–1965 (2007). https://doi.org/10.1109/ICACT.2007.358755

11. Sahri, N., Okamura, K.: Collaborative spoofing detection and mitigation – sdn based looping authentication for dns services. In: 2016 IEEE 40th Annual Computer Software and Applications Conference (COMPSAC), vol. 2, pp. 565– 570 (2016). https://doi.org/10.1109/COMPSAC.2016.6

12. Hilton, A., Hirschmann, J., Deccio, C.: Beware of ips in sheep's clothing: measurement and disclosure of ip spoofing vulnerabilities. IEEE/ACM Trans. Netw. **30**(4), 1659–1673 (2022). https://doi.org/10.1109/TNET.2022.3149011

13. Janbeglou, M., Zamani, M., Ibrahim, S.: Redirecting outgoing dns requests toward a fake dns server in a lan. In: 2010 IEEE International Conference on Software Engineering and Service Sciences, pp. 29–32 (2010). https://doi.org/10.1109/ICSESS.2010.5552339

14. Tripathi, N., Swarnkar, M., Hubballi, N.: Dns spoofing in local networks made easy. In: 2017 IEEE International Conference on Advanced Networks and Telecommunications Systems (ANTS), pp. 1–6 (2017). https://doi.org/10.1109/ANTS.2017.8384122
15. Yu, X., Chen, X., Xu, F.: Recovering and protecting against dns cache poisoning attacks. In: 2011 International Conference of Information Technology, Computer Engineering and Management Sciences, vol. 2, pp. 120– 123 (2011). https://doi.org/10.1109/ICM.2011.266
16. Adiwal, S., Rajendran, B., Sudarsan, S.D., et al.: Dns intrusion detection (did)–a snort-based solution to detect dns amplification and dns tunneling attacks. Franklin Open **2**, 100010 (2023)

Evolution of Benchmark Datasets and the Evaluation of Cutting-Edge Algorithms for Underwater Image Enhancement

K. Shivaraju and S. Ravi

Department of Computer Science, School of Engineering and Technology, Pondicherry University, Kalapet, India
sravicite@pondiuni.ac.in

Abstract. Underwater images frequently suffer colour distortion, blurring, low contrast, and colour cast due to light absorption and scattering, reducing visibility. Despite the evolution of numerous UIE benchmark datasets and cutting-edge algorithms, a systematic study covering their methodologies and performance comparisons for mostly used datasets and algorithms is still absent. To bridge this gap and foster future advancements, we provide a comprehensive survey of the evolution of benchmark datasets and the evaluation of cutting-edge UIE algorithms, including dataset diversity, algorithmic approaches (traditional and deep learning-based), evaluation metrics, and real-world application challenges. This study aims to provide researchers with a clearer understanding of existing benchmark datasets, evaluate cutting-edge algorithms, highlight current limitations, and identify emerging research directions to guide the development of more effective underwater image enhancement solutions. The publicly available datasets are further studied in scale, diversity, and acquisition conditions, along with a thorough analysis of enhancement algorithms, focusing on their strengths, limitations, and suitability for real-world underwater applications.

Keywords: Underwater Image Enhancement · Benchmark Datasets · Cutting-Edge Algorithms · Evaluation metrics

1 Introduction

The light on land differs from the behavior of light in underwater. The density of water is 800 times more than the density of air. The density of water is such that, in fact, an image taken in 0.5 m of water is 800 m away as compared to an image on land. As light enters into the water, it collides with suspended particles, causing a color loss, contrast, and detail. Hence, underwater images taken in real-world environments are destroyed and do not provide us with any helpful information. Therefore, UIE-related benchmarks and algorithms inventions greatly enhance image visual quality and values in accurately understanding the underwater environment.

K. Shivaraju—Research Scholar

© The Author(s), under exclusive license to Springer Nature Switzerland AG 2026
K. Chandra Mondal et al. (Eds.): CICBA 2025, CCIS 2862, pp. 107–121, 2026.
https://doi.org/10.1007/978-3-032-17187-0_9

In this study, the benchmark datasets for UIE tasks are first focused on, which cover more abundant underwater images and corresponding better visual quality ground truth images. The evolution of benchmarks for large-scale datasets and their evaluation algorithms is categorized into traditional algorithms [1,2,3] for single image enhancement and deep learning algorithms [4,5,6,7,8,9] for training large-scale datasets.

Traditional methods of evaluating benchmark datasets make it possible to access reference images, recover colors, remove water from underwater images, and reduce image dehazing. Deep learning models leverage convolutional neural networks, transformers, fully convolutional encoder-decoder networks, and adversarial networks trained on large-scale real-world benchmark datasets to solve issues like visibility enhancement, color issues, simultaneous enhancement and super-resolution, saliency prediction, semantic segmentation, medium transmission map, removal of color artifacts and casts, contrast and saturation improvement, and perceptual quality enhancement based on colour, global details, local structure, and style, and also contribute to improved performance in downstream tasks like object recognition and human pose estimation. Additionally, a large-scale benchmark dataset RUIE [10] are identified which designed to enhance visibility and correct color cast performance on traditional methods while supporting object detection and classification tasks in data-driven methods. As a result, the reported benchmarks and network architectures provide insight into upcoming UIE task research. Therefore, this sets the stage for a detailed review of existing datasets, performance metrics, and cutting-edge algorithms in the field. The benchmark datasets and sample codes are available on https://github.com/xinzhichao/Underwater_Datasets.

We outline the significant contributions of this work include:

1. A single image-based enhancement is reported evaluating traditional methods for benchmark datasets in UIE tasks, in which TURBID [1] image restoration methods make it possible to access reference images, Sea-thru [2] revised image formation model aims to remove water consistently, and SQUID [3] expanded the haze-line model to reduce single image dehazing.
2. The recently evolved large-scale and real-world underwater image enhancement benchmark datasets are presented—UIEB [4], UFO-120 [5], LSUI [6], SUIM [7], EUVP [8], and U45 [9]—and their training network models, including Water-Net [4], Deep SESR [5], U-shape Transformer [6], SUIM-Net [7], FUnIE-GAN [8], and FGAN [9], for comprehensive evaluation.
3. A large-scale RUIE [10] benchmark dataset is also reported that evaluates different traditional and task-driven algorithms to improve visual quality on underwater images with higher-level object detection and classification.

2 Underwater Benchmark Datasets and Evaluation Cutting-Edge Algorithms

Underwater benchmark datasets and their evaluation cutting-edge algorithms can preferably be categorized into two subsets, i.e., traditional and deep learning algorithms. Additionally, real-world underwater image enhancement benchmarks should incorporate task-specific evaluation criteria, combining hybrid image processing algorithms that leverage traditional and deep learning algorithms. The goal of the benchmark evaluation of the traditional methods is that it is feasible to access the reference image. In contrast, deep learning algorithms aim to improve human pose estimation and object detection. Figure 1 shows the benchmark datasets and their evaluation algorithms, and in the sections that follow, each dataset is listed and described along with its corresponding evaluation algorithm into different classifications based on essential aspects.

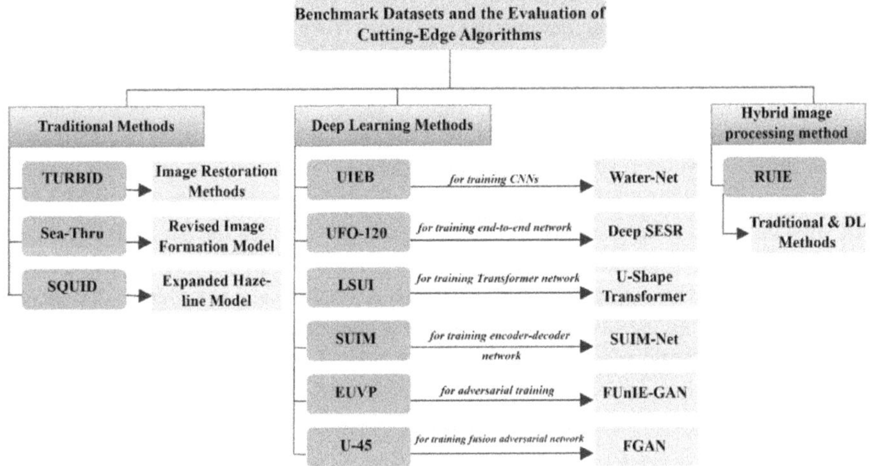

Fig. 1. Categorization of Benchmark datasets and their evaluation algorithms.

2.1 Benchmark Datasets and the Evaluation of Traditional-Based Algorithms

TURBID. The TURBID benchmark was the initial dataset proposed by [1], using three previously photographed authentic images; the images contain structures of the undersea floor and a few human-made objects. The photos were recaptured inside a plastic tank of 1000 L, lit by two 30-W fluorescent light strips using the camera device Go Pro Hero3Black Edition with 12 mp of resolution. For that, the first photograph is 30 images in clear water. After that, milk is added to the water tank, beginning from 5 ml to 190 ml; turbidity and as a result the amount of distortion are grown in a controlled way. [1] tested various amounts of milk to achieve the desired turbidity, repeating the process 19 times with different milk quantities to produce varying turbidity levels. Thirty images were captured at each milk concentration with a 10-s interval and the mean of the first 30 images in clean water served as the reference image I_0. After that, the images I_1 through $I_1 9$ are produced by averaging the images captured at the same turbidity level. The main benefit of this dataset is that it presents a clear picture that can be utilized as a reference image for underwater restoration algorithms.

Sea-thru. The Sea-thru [2] method is a novel approach designed to effectively remove water from underwater images, enhancing the scene's visibility and enabling better analysis of large datasets. It utilizes RGBD images to estimate backscatter, drawing inspiration from the DCP used in haze removal while incorporating known range information to improve accuracy. The methodology utilizes an optimization strategy to determine the depth-dependent attenuation coefficient Utilizing an illumination map generated employing input as local space mean color. The process has validated over 1100 images from two different water types, *Sea-thru*, using the updated image formation model for the first time, demonstrating its effectiveness in recovering colors and opening up opportunities for advanced computer vision and machine learning applications in underwater research. The Sea-Thru method provides five RGDB datasets (D1–D5) for underwater pictures captured at varying depths and across different water types, with each dataset containing multiple images accompanied by color charts.

SQUID- Stereo Quantitative Underwater Image Dataset.   Berman et al. [3] proposed a color restoration algorithm based on a single image, utilizing a physics-based approach that estimates two global parameters: the blue-green and blue-red colour channels attenuation ratios. To evaluate various water types defined by Jerlov, the method selects the best attenuation ratios to reduce the problem to single-image dehazing. The method first estimates the veiling light, multiplies initial estimate of transmission by 0.9, converts the linear image to RGB, and then estimates attenuation coefficients of undersea using known distances. This approach effectively restores colors across different distances in the image, enhancing the overall visual quality while maintaining the color consistency necessary for scientific measurements. On the other hand, [3] collected create a *situ* dataset of undersea pictures with reference and [3] *stereo* dataset in the UIE domain featuring color charts. The images are collected in *situ* dataset at various seasons, water types, and depths.

2.2 Benchmark Datasets and the Evaluation of Deep Learning-Based Cutting-Edge Algorithms

UIEB.   Li et al. [4] presented the Underwater Image Enhancement Benchmark (UIEB) dataset using large-scale real-world for underwater image enhancement with ground truth images due to unclear. The UIEB offers 950 real-world underwater images captured in ambient or man-made light or a blend of ambient and man-made light. The probable ground truth images were constructed using 12 image enhancement methods. Ultimately, the UIEB dataset comprises of two groups: 890 degraded raw underwater images with high-visibility ground truth images and 60 highly degraded complex underwater images.

Water-Net.   Despite advancements in underwater image improvement, deep learning models lag behind traditional methods due to limited training data and suboptimal architectures. Using UIEB, Li et al. [4] presented Water-Net, a CNN model for underwater image improvement, encouraging deep learning advancements and demonstrating UIEB's training effectiveness. The Water-Net model as shown in Fig. 2(a) employs a fusion-based strategy [11], which combines the results from the Histogram Equalization (HE), Gamma Correction (GC), and White Balance (WB) [11] pre-processing techniques to generate inputs for the enhancement model. Water-Net, a baseline fully CNN network, utilizes a gated fused network to generate three confidence maps, effectively merging inputs into a single enhanced output by prioritizing key features. Integrating U-Net [12] and residual networks [12] architectures could further enhance its performance. Before fusion, three FTUs (Feature Transformation Units) enhance inputs from

HE, GC, and WB methods to reduce color casts and artifacts. The final enhancement is achieved by elementwise multiplying these refined inputs with trained confidence maps, emphasizing the output's most relevant features.

The implementation of Water-Net training begins with 800 image pairs from the UIEB dataset, resized to 112×112 pixels due to memory constraints. Data augmentation, including flipping and rotation, expands the dataset sevenfold. The rest of the 90 pairs are reserved for testing. A perceptual loss function based on VGG19 feature representations is used to reduce artifacts. The final model processes 640×480 images in 0.128 s at 8 Frames Per Second (FPS).

UFO-120. Data preparation for Simultaneous enhancement and super-resolution (SESR) learning involves creating the UFO-120 [5] dataset, comprising 1,500 training and 120 testing samples from diverse oceanic explorations across various water types. The standard procedures [13,8] applies optical and spatial image distortion, using human-labelled saliency prediction maps to generate paired data in $\{(X), (S, E, Y)\}$ format. A style-transfer technique [13,8] generates distorted images, followed by bicubic down-sampling and Gaussian blurring to produce low-resolution distorted (LRD) samples for training. These samples are categorized into three sets based on degradation order: *Set-U* (Gaussian blurring followed by bicubic down-sampling), *Set-F* (interchanged order), and *Set-O* (bicubic down-sampling followed by Gaussian blurring).

Deep SESR. The Learning SESR (Simultaneous Enhancement and Super-Resolution) process focusing on how to effectively produce high resolution pictures from low resolution and possibly degraded inputs. The formulate issue is learning to generate pixel-wise mapping function, defined as $G : X \rightarrow Y$, where X indicates the input domain of low-resolution distorted images, and Y represents the target domain of enhanced high-resolution images. The SESR task is extended by integrating saliency prediction, enabling the model to enhance image quality while identifying salient regions. In particular, the generating function mappings $G : X \rightarrow S, E, Y$ are learned using Deep SESR; where S represents the targeted saliency map, and E is the improved image and Y is the $4 \times$ SESR for the final result.

The Deep-SESR [5] model is shown in Fig. 2(b), designed for simultaneous enhancement and super-resolution of underwater imagery, utilizing a residual-in-residual network structure. This network incorporates several key components, including residual dense blocks (RDBs), a feature extraction net (FENet), and an auxiliary attention net (AAN), all integrated into an end-to-end trainable framework for effective SESR learning. The architecture supports multi-scales hierarchical features learning, essential for restoring perceptual image quality at higher spatial resolutions of $2 \times$, $3 \times$, or $4 \times$.

LSUI. The Large -Scale Underwater Image (LSUI) benchmark dataset proposed by [6], it is a large-scale underwater image dataset designed to enhance underwater image quality and support the advancement of underwater image enhancement methods. It comprises 4279 real-world degraded underwater pair images, each paired with high-visibility ground truth images, medium transmission maps and semantic segmentation maps. The dataset was created meticulously, involving multiple volunteer evaluations to identify and optimize image quality issues such as colour cast, blur and noise. Unlike previous datasets, LSUI includes diverse underwater scenes, including deep-sea and underwater cave pictures, which were not present in earlier datasets like UIEB [4].

U-Shape Transformer. Peng et al. provided a U-shape Transformer [6] is a novel architecture specifically designed for UIE tasks, integrating a channel-wise multi-scales feature fusion transformer (CMSFFT) and a spatial-wise global features modelling transformer (SGFMT) based on [14] illustrated in Fig. 2(c), which work together to improve the model focus on severely destroyed areas of images. The architecture comprises a generator and discriminator that process images through encoding and decoding steps. The suggested multi-scale connections enable smooth gradient flow between the discriminator and generator across multiple scales, ensuring stable training and enhancing the features of the generated images. The network also incorporates a loss function that combines RGB, LAB, and LCH colour spaces, aligning with human visual perception principles to enhance image quality. Overall, the output image saturation and contrast are enhanced by this network and efficiently eliminate color casts and artifacts.

The implementation of the U-shape Transformer [6] built a LSUI dataset, which consists of 4279 images, was divided into a training set with 3879 images and a testing set containing 400 images. To augment the training data, techniques like that cropping, flipping, and rotating were applied to the existing images and resized to a fixed 256x256 pixel size for all images. The training process utilized the Adam optimization algorithm throughout 800 epochs, with a batch size configured to 6. At the beginning, the learning rate was configured to 0.0005 for the initial 600 epochs, then decreased to 0.0002 for the final 200 epochs, with a 20% decrease every 40-epoch period. For loss calculation, L2 loss was employed during the first 600 epochs, followed by L1 loss for the last 200 epochs, ensuring effective training and convergence of the model.

SUIM. Islam et al. [7] presented the large-scale dataset, training, and benchmark dataset evaluation for SUIM(semantic Segmentation of Underwater Imagery) dataset. For training purposes, the SUIM benchmark dataset comprises 1525 degraded underwater images together with their semantic labels. Also, it comprises a test set of 110 pictures and their reference semantic labels, in addition to eight object categories for semantic labeling. These training and testing images are various spatial resolutions selected from during human-robot cooperating experiments and marine explorations of different water types in several locations.

SUIM-Net. In addition, [7] presented the SUIM-Net, a fully convolution encoder-decoder framework that integrates the advantage of residual learning [15] and skip connections [12] are shown in Fig. 2(d). The residual skip block (RSB), an optional skip layer that is integrated into the residual learning, has three convolution layers, after that BN, and ReLU. The network consists of two sets of RSBs utilized in the second and third layers of the encoder, which extract feature maps from raw images and then exploit these feature maps by decoder layers. For spatial up-sampling, every decoder layer contains a convolution layer that receiving skip connections from the encoder layer, followed by the deconv layers and BN. The final conv layer produces binary pixel labels for every object category for visualization in the RGB space.

EUVP. Islam et al. [8] presented the Enhancement of Underwater Visual Perception (EUVP) benchmark dataset comprising over 12k paired and 8k unpaired underwater distorted images collected during human-robot cooperating experiments and sea explorations in various locations under different visibility conditions of good and poor perceptual quality. The FUnIE-GAN trained with in a range of 60K-70K iterations using a batch size of 8, using 11K paired and 7.5K unpaired samples, the rest utilized for testing and validation.

FUnIE-GAN. In addition, [8] presented a fully convolution conditional GAN-based network, called FUnIE-GAN. [11] designed a generator network by U-Net [12], which is an encoder-decoder framework connecting with mirrored layers. Specifically, each encoder's enhanced images are combined with the respective mirrored decoders. The concept of skip-connections within the generator network has proven effective for tasks like image-to-image transformation and image visibility enhancement. The input image is resized to $256 \times 256 \times 3$, and the encoder learns the feature maps; the decoder uses the feature maps and raw image from the skip connections to learn to produce an enhanced image. In addition, conv2D with filters was applied to each layer, followed by Leaky-ReLU and BN. [8] uses a Markovian Patch-GAN [14] for the discriminator, which assumes pixel independence beyond the patch size, focusing only on patch-level information, which helps capturing high-frequency details like style [16] and local texture while being more efficient than global-image discrimination. As illustrated in Fig. 2(e), the discriminator uses conv layers to transform an input into an output. Each layer applies filters with a stride, followed by Leaky-ReLU and BN, similar to the generator. Therefore, the FUnIE-GAN is more straightforward with few parameters, achieves faster inference, and incorporates global similarity, style and local details of structure.

U45 Dataset. Li et al. [9] curated a specific dataset named U45 [9], categorized into three subsets based on the types of degradation: green, blue, and haze-like effects.

FGAN. To solve issues of colour casts, haze-like effects, and low contrast consider blending multiple inputs through a Fusion GAN proposed by [9], where the generator network utilizes two inputs in a fully convolutional architecture that combines two basic blocks is shown in Fig. 2(f). The design employs a loss function combining $\mathcal{L}_{gt}$ and $\mathcal{L}_{fe}$ losses to preserve features in both ground truth and enhanced images. The network architecture is enhanced by utilizing an inception structure [17] with shortcut connections [15], allowing for the detection of feature maps at various scales while maintaining computational efficiency through a final 1×1 convolution that reduces output feature maps. The discriminator network uses five convolutional layers that utilize spectral normalization, which is known for being computationally efficient and easy to implement. The dataset for FGAN [9] conducted a paired dataset consisting of 6128 image pairs sourced from the UGAN [13]. In addition, the researchers collected 240 raw underwater images from various sources, including related papers.

RUIE. The Real-World Underwater Image Enhancement (RUIE) [10] benchmark dataset, including visibility degradation. The dataset aims to evaluate UIE algorithms across three main objectives: improving image quality, adjusting colour casts, and enhancing accuracy for high-level detection tasks. Liu et al. [10] set up a multiview underwater picture-capturing system using twenty-two waterproof video capture devices. These cameras were strategically placed along a 10x10 meters square frame to capture images from various angles and depths that differed from 5–9 m, ensuring a comprehensive representation of underwater conditions. The images, captured under natural light without external lighting, reflect real underwater conditions and were taken daily from 8–11 AM and 1–4 PM between Sept. 21–27, 2017, to account for varying lighting. The over 250 h of captured video include various variations in illuminations, blurring levels, depths of field, and colour casts. [10] manually selected over 4,000 pictures and separated them into three groups based on specific UIE algorithm tasks. The

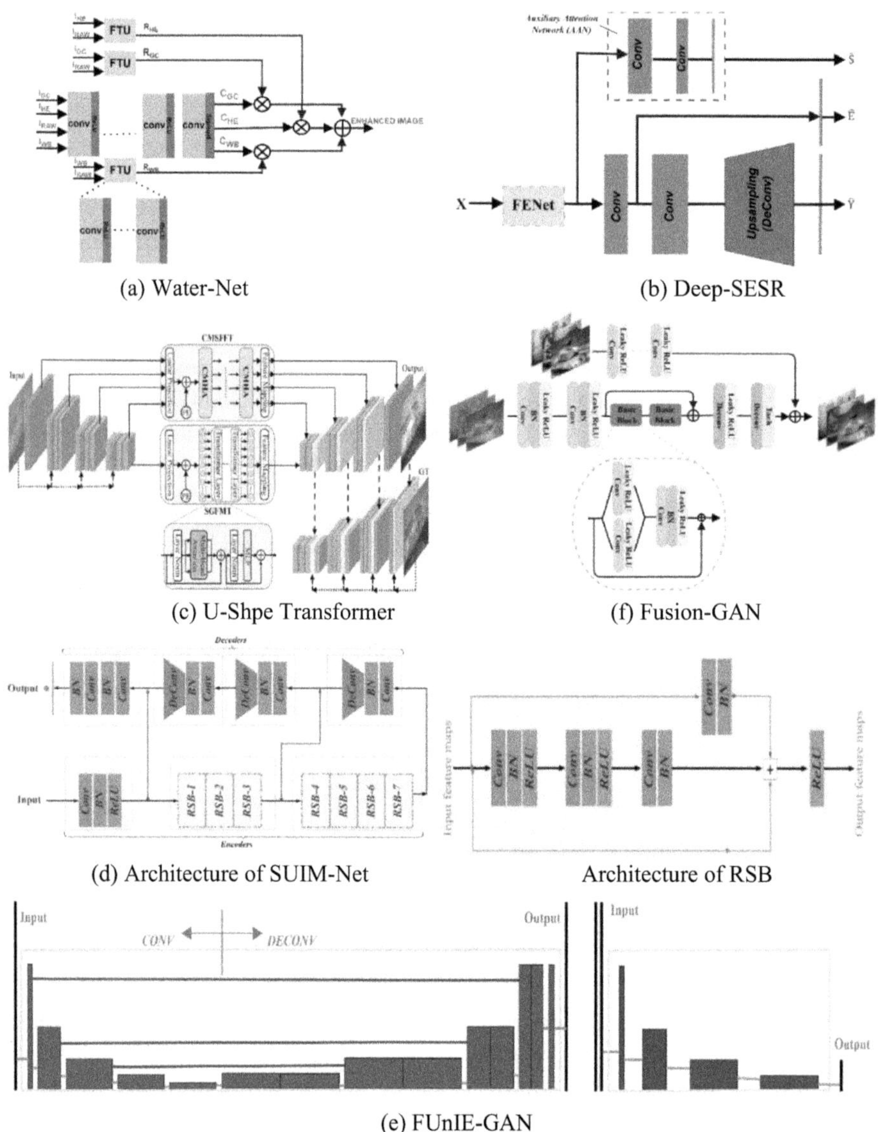

(a) Water-Net

(b) Deep-SESR

(c) U-Shpe Transformer

(f) Fusion-GAN

(d) Architecture of SUIM-Net

Architecture of RSB

(e) FUnIE-GAN

Fig. 2. (a–f). Network architectures: Benchmark datasets trained on convolutional neural networks and adversarial training for underwater image enhancement.

first group, the Underwater Image Quality Set (UIQS), is equally classified into five subsets [A–E] in the UCIQE scores decreasing order, each containing 726 images, totaling 3,630 images. The second group, Underwater Color Cast Set (UCCS), includes of three categories, bluish, greenish, and blue-green, each containing 100 images, collectively making 300. A third group, the Underwater High-level Task-driven Set (UHTS), comprises 300 images for classification and detection, divided into five subsets of 60 images each. [10] trained a YOLO-V3 [5] based CNN for underwater object detection using 1,800 labeled images from shallow waters (depth < 3 m) and applied it to detect three object types in UIE algorithms enhanced results.

3 Experimental Settings and Results Analysis

The **TURBID** [1] dataset to obtain restored images evaluates the DCP, Red Channel Prior, and general participative media restoration method to implement C++ implementations using OpenCV. CLAHE and White balance shades-of-gray used MATLAB implementations. The Structural Degradation Index (SDI), which measures the visual quality of the TURBID dataset and determines the optimal method from the SSIM, is defined as

$$SDI = 100(1 - SSIM)   \tag{1}$$

After evaluating the structural degradation index is between the ground truth picture and the destroyed pictures, the methods were evaluated by calculating the mean squared error. For all cases, CLAHE presented better enhancing the visibility of destroyed underwater images, white balance just correction of the color, and DCP, RDP, and general participative media restoration methods are associated with the estimation.

The **Sea-thru** [2] method evaluation of the datasets (D1–D5) tested several methods (S1-S5) to assess their effectiveness in underwater image correction. These methods included simple contrast stretch (S1), a global process that works well in scenes with uniform distances, providing a basic level of color correction. The DCP algorithm (S2) often overestimated backscatter, leading to color distortions and artifacts. In S3 to S5, the correct amount of backscatter is subtracted. The Constant Attenuation Correction (S3) corrected attenuation using a constant value for the attenuation coefficient. However, it struggled in scenes with significant range variation. S4 yielded lower errors on color cards, while S5 showed better overall results in complete scenes.

To verify the color restoration method evaluation of the **SQUID** [3] and compare it to [18–20] based on images of a colour card captured from a close distance or based on UCIQE and UIQM for comparing natural underwater scenes. Photos of color cards taken from a close distance at different depths and do not contain objects at various distances from the capture device are often the case in natural images [18]. However, restoring object colours at a single distance is simpler than the complex colour reconstruction needed for a 3D image. In the same way, images captured in water tanks [19] or swimming pools [20] feature nearby objects and differ in absorption and scattering from natural water bodies.

To verify the **Water-Net** [4], which compares it against five traditional and two deep learning methods conducted on the 90 and 60 underwater images set, effectively removing haze and mitigating colour casts. The qualitative results indicated that Water-Net enhances visual quality and achieves a more natural appearance and better details, as shown in Fig. 3(a). [4] conducted quantitative evaluations using PSNR, SSIM, and MSE metrics and found that Water-Net achieved the best performance with scores of 19.11, 0.797, and 0.7976, respectively. Additionally, in a user study with 50 participants to average score and standard deviation of results on a challenging set, Water-Net achieved the maximum mean and minimum standard deviation, demonstrating better results and robust performance.

The **Deep SESR model's** [5] evaluation encompasses enhancement and super-resolution performance, utilizing various quantitative and qualitative metrics. For enhancement, the model's output is compared against several SOTA methods, including physics-based and learning-based models, using quantitative metrics to achieve a PSNR of 27.15, SSIM of 0.84, and UIQM of 3.13, reflecting significant improvements in color, contrast, and sharpness. The evaluation reveals that Deep SESR achieves competitive and often superior performance, particularly in UIQM scores, indicating effective color recovery and contrast enhancement. In terms of super-resolution, the model is tested against existing underwater and terrestrial single-image super-resolution (SISR) models, demonstrating significant improvements in perceptual image qualities and spatial resolution across multiple datasets, including UFO-120 and USR-248. Finally, Deep SESR improves image quality without introducing noise, as show in Fig. 3(b), proving its effectiveness for real-time underwater robot vision in complex environments.

The **U-shape Transformer** [6] experimental settings involved a comprehensive training and testing approach. The training process utilized three distinct datasets: Train-L, which consists of 3879 images; Train-U, with 800 pairs of underwater pictures from the UIEB [4] dataset and 1250 synthetic underwater images from [21]; and Train-E, containing paired images from the EUVP dataset. Two types of datasets were employed for testing: full-referenced testing datasets (Test-U90 and Test-L400) and no-reference testing datasets (SQUID and Test-U60). Figure 3(e) presents the visual results produced by the U-Shape Transformer network.

The evaluation of the LSUI [6] dataset, which comprises of 4279 real-world underwater images, demonstrated its effectiveness in enhancing underwater image quality. [6] was utilized to retrain various methods, including U-Net [12], UGAN [13], and the U-shape Transformer, on different training sets (Train-U, Train-L, and Train-E) and tested on Test-U90 and Test-L400. The network trained on the LSUI [6] dataset achieved the highest PSNR of 24.16 and SSIM of 0.93 values, showcasing better performance than other datasets while maintaining a relatively minimum number of FLOPs and parameters. The U-shape Transformer evaluation involved full-reference and non-reference assessments using the Test-U90 and Test-L400 datasets. The analysis highlighted the limitations of different techniques, such as FUnIE [8] lightweight design, which restricted its scalability on difficult images, and UGAN [13] and UIE-DAL not considered to account for the inconsistent characteristics of underwater photos.

The benchmark evaluation of SOTA models includes Pyramid Scene Parsing Network, U-Net [12], DeepLabv3, and Seg-Net, all trained on the **SUIM** dataset using SUIM-Net for semantic segmentation and saliency prediction. For semantic segmentation, predicted masks are merged with RGB visualization masks, and prediction of saliency in a single channel is visualized as binary images. Islam et al. [7] compare the model performance based on the region similarity measure accuracy of predicted pixel label and reference by utilizing the $\mathcal{F}$ score, its computing utilizing the recall ($\mathcal{R}$) and precision ($\mathcal{P}$) as $\mathcal{F} = \frac{2 \times \mathcal{P} \times \mathcal{R}}{\mathcal{P} + \mathcal{R}}$. . Alternatively, the contour accuracy metric signifies localization of the object boundary, defined by the average IOU (intersection over mean) score, $= \frac{Area\,of\,overlap}{Area\,of\,union}$. The qualitative results of semantic segmentation and saliency prediction, as shown in Fig. 3(d) and quantitative analysis of SOTA models SUIM-Net executes at 28.65 *fps*, and it is more than 10 times more accuracy and better than U-Net [12], and DeepLabv3 models.

The **FUnIE-GAN** [11] qualitatively assesses the improved color and sharpness of the image; the true colours and details are largely recovered in the enhanced output, as shown in Fig. 3(c). They highlight the rectification of the greenish hue commonly found in underwater images and the enhancement of global contrast, which are essential for effective underwater image enhancement. Further, it examines the contributions of different loss terms, specifically global similarity loss ($\mathcal{L}_1$) and image content loss ($\mathcal{L}_{con}$), revealing that $\mathcal{L}_1$ aids in generating sharper images while $\mathcal{L}_{con}$ enhances finer texture details. Furthermore, the FUnIE-GAN compares the performance with five learning-based models trained on the paired EUVP dataset utilizing setup as the FUnIE-GAN, enhancing underwater images and making it a valuable tool for various applications. The quantitative analysis reports a PSNR of 21.92 and an SSIM of 0.887 for FUnIE-GAN, evaluated on over 1k test images. These results surpass those of other models, demonstrating FUnIE-GAN's superior reconstruction quality and perceptual similarity to ground truth in underwater image enhancement. Additionally, UIQM reveals that FUnIE-GAN-UP is better than CycleGAN [22], but paired training, especially with FUnIE-GAN, delivers superior results, highlighting the importance of data quality.

For the **FGAN** [9] training process, U45 [9] dataset images have dimensions 256 × 256, Adam optimizer with the learning rate of 0.0001; the network is trained for 60 epochs and batch size set to 16. The subjective assessment of FGAN tested on U45, which can correct color distortion and preserve image details better than other methods, such as UGAN [13], particularly in green and blue scenes, as shown in Fig. 3(f). FGAN [9] is quantitatively evaluated on the U45 dataset using two no-reference metrics, achieving a UCIQE score of 0.591 and a UIQM score of 5.101. It consistently maintains high UIQM values across UIE methods, demonstrating strong perceptual quality. In addition, FGAN [9] owns a faster processing speed of 0.0286s with 1.11M parameters.

The **RUIE** [10] dataset was used for experiments, and discuss the results across three subsets. All images were resized to 300 × 400 to ensure consistent outputs for detection and enhancement. The first subset, UIQS, qualitatively assessed eleven UIE methods on images with varying quality levels (A-E). Most methods performed well on images with subtle underwater scattering effects (quality levels A, B, and C). The second subset, UCCS, qualitatively compared eleven UIE methods, and the results showed that MSRCR effectively corrected both bluish and greenish tones, while Fusion and

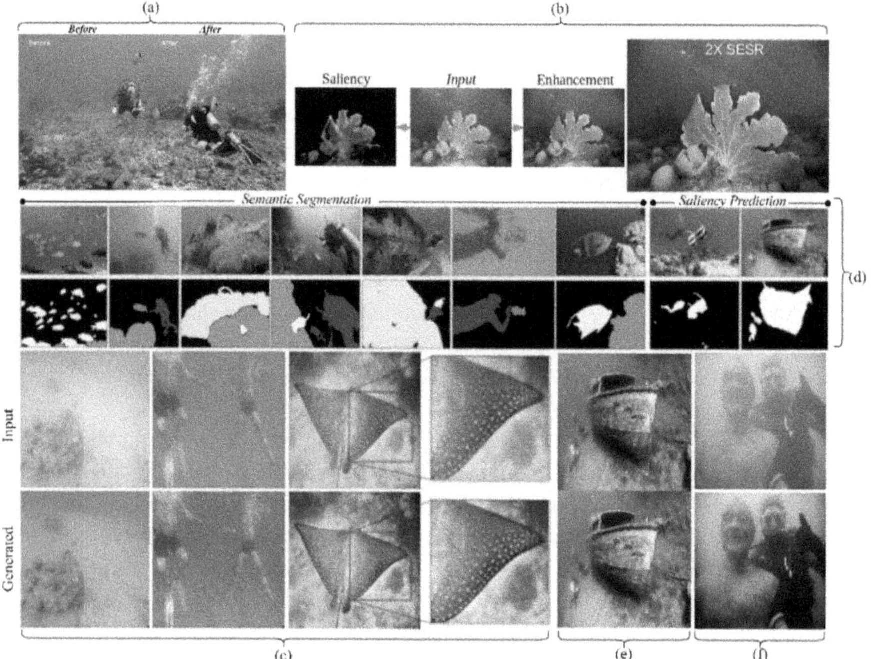

Fig. 3. Visual results of underwater image enhancement: (a) Water-Net [4], (b) Deep-SESR [5], (c) FUnIE-GAN [8], (d) SUIM-Net [7], (e) U-Shape Transformer [6], and (f) FGAN [9].

CLAHE performed better on greenish tones than blue tones. The color correction abilities of the algorithms were quantitatively assessed using metrics Avg_a and Avg_b, which represent the mean values of the blue-yellow and green-red components in the CIElab color space, respectively. The third subset, UHTS, ensures accurate detection on sharp images for human perception. Results from experiments indicate that visual quality and categorization accuracy are not necessarily positively correlated. For instance, Fusion and CLAHE considerably improve UCIQE and UIQM values on subset B, but their mAP results may not be as good as those of destroyed inputs. Severely blurred images in subset E of UHTS hinder object detection, while saturation or high contrast, beneficial for human perception, may introduce undesired features for detection. Therefore, real-world underwater images with varying quality levels in RUIE, aid both low-level UIE evaluation and high-level task performance.

4   Limitations, Future Research and Emerging Directions

Underwater image benchmark datasets and evaluation frameworks are expected to evolve the demands of real-world underwater applications in recent years, mainly due to deep learning techniques. Limitation of existing benchmark datasets: most available datasets for visual enhancement do not explicitly address task-specific requirements, such as enhancing images for object detection, species classification, semantic segmentation, or navigation in underwater robotics. Also, datasets do not provide additional contextual information, such as salinity, water temperature, depth, or visibility conditions, which could help design adaptive enhancement algorithms.

In the future, required underwater images captured at different depths face varying degradation and challenges due to how light behaves underwater. Standard depth zones and the issues associated with each: Shallow waters (0–10 m) experience moderate light attenuation, mild red color loss, wave distortions, and slight backscatter from suspended particles. Mid-depth waters (10–30 m) show significant red and orange light loss, stronger blue-green dominance, reduced contrast, increased backscatter, and noticeable haze. Deep waters (30–100 m) suffer severe color loss, mainly leaving blue-green tones, very low contrast, high noise, strong backscatter, and uneven illumination from artificial lighting. Very deep waters (>100 m) lack natural light and rely on artificial lighting, causing harsh shadows, uneven colors, high noise, severe backscatter, and minimal natural color, demanding extensive enhancement. Additionally, lightweight and efficient models are essential due to the limited memory and computational power of remotely operated vehicles capturing images in deep underwater environments.

5 Conclusion

We presented the first comprehensive study of benchmark datasets and their evaluation of cutting-edge algorithms based on traditional and deep learning for underwater image enhancement. As current research indicates, we have included benchmark datasets that deal with underwater image enhancement/restoration. Furthermore, we provided and reviewed benchmark datasets to evaluate traditional methods and trained on convolutional neural networks and adversarial trainings. We also discussed the evaluation metrics and compared them to the performance of the benchmark datasets and the cutting-edge algorithms. At the final phase, we analyzed the limitations and suggested directions for future research and emerging directions to advancements in underwater image enhancement.

According to our study, by offering both paired images (degraded and reference) and unpaired images, these benchmark datasets provide a robust foundation for assessing the effectiveness of traditional techniques and modern deep learning-based models, facilitating consistent performance comparisons across different enhancement algorithms.

References

1. Duarte, A., Codevilla, F., Gaya, J.D.O., Botelho, S.S.C.: A dataset to evaluate underwater image restoration methods. In: Ocean. 2016 – Shanghai (2016). https://doi.org/10.1109/OCE ANSAP.2016.7485524
2. Akkaynak, D., Treibitz, T.: Sea-THRU: a method for removing water from underwater images. In: Proceedings of IEEE Computer Society Conference on Computer Vision and Pattern Recognition, vol. 2019-June, pp. 1682–1691 (2019). https://doi.org/10.1109/CVPR.2019. 00178

3. Berman, D., Levy, D., Avidan, S., Treibitz, T.: Underwater single image color restoration using haze-lines and a new quantitative dataset. IEEE Trans. Pattern Anal. Mach. Intell. **43**(8), 2822–2837 (2021). https://doi.org/10.1109/TPAMI.2020.2977624

4. Li, C., et al.: An underwater image enhancement benchmark dataset and beyond. IEEE Trans. Image Process. **29**, 4376–4389 (2020). https://doi.org/10.1109/TIP.2019.2955241

5. Islam, M.J., Luo, P., Sattar, J.: Simultaneous enhancement and super-resolution of underwater imagery for improved visual perception. Robot. Sci. Syst. (2020).https://doi.org/10.15607/RSS.2020.XVI.018

6. Peng, L., Zhu, C., Bian, L.: U-shape transformer for underwater image enhancement. IEEE Trans. Image Process. **32**, 3066–3079 (2023). https://doi.org/10.1109/TIP.2023.3276332

7. Islam, M.J., et al.: Semantic segmentation of underwater imagery: dataset and benchmark. In: IEEE International Conference on Intelligent Robotics System, pp. 1769–1776 (2020). https://doi.org/10.1109/IROS45743.2020.9340821

8. Islam, M.J., Xia, Y., Sattar, J.: Fast underwater image enhancement for improved visual perception. IEEE Robot. Autom. Lett. **5**(2), 3227–3234 (2020). https://doi.org/10.1109/LRA.2020.2974710

9. Li, H., Li, J., Wang, W.: A fusion adversarial underwater image enhancement network with a public test dataset. arXiv Image Video Process (2019)

10. Liu, R., Fan, X., Zhu, M., Hou, M., Luo, Z.: Real-world underwater enhancement: challenges, benchmarks, and solutions under natural light. IEEE Trans. Circ. Syst. Video Technol. **30**(12), 4861–4875 (2020). https://doi.org/10.1109/TCSVT.2019.2963772

11. Ancuti, C., Ancuti, C.O., Haber, T., Bekaert, P.: Enhancing underwater images and videos by fusion. In: 2012 IEEE Conference on Computer Vision and Pattern Recognition, pp. 81–88 (2012). https://doi.org/10.1109/CVPR.2012.6247661

12. Ronneberger, O., Fischer, P., Brox, T.: U-Net: convolutional networks for biomedical image segmentation. In: Lect. Notes Comput. Sci. (including Subser. Lect. Notes Artif. Intell. Lect. Notes Bioinformatics), vol. 9351, pp. 234–241 (2015). https://doi.org/10.1007/978-3-319-24574-4_28

13. Fabbri, C., Islam, M.J., Sattar, J.: Enhancing underwater imagery using generative adversarial networks. In 2018 IEEE International Conference on Robotics and Automation (ICRA), pp. 7159–7165. IEEE (2018).https://doi.org/10.1109/ICRA.2018.8460552

14. Isola, P., Zhu, J.Y., Zhou, T., Efros, A.A.: Image-to-image translation with conditional adversarial networks. In: Proceedings of 30th IEEE Conference on Computer Vision Pattern Recognition, CVPR 2017, vol. 2017-January, pp. 5967–5976 (2017).https://doi.org/10.1109/CVPR.2017.632

15. He, K., Zhang, X., Ren, S., Sun, J.: Deep residual learning for image recognition. In: Proceedings of IEEE Computer Society Conference on Computer Vision and Pattern Recognition, vol. 2016-December, pp. 770–778 (2016). https://doi.org/10.1109/CVPR.2016.90

16. Yi, Z., Zhang, H., Tan, P., Gong, M.: DualGAN: unsupervised dual learning for image-to-image translation. In: 2017 IEEE International Conference on Computer Visiion, vol. 2017-October, pp. 2868–2876 (2017).https://doi.org/10.1109/ICCV.2017.310

17. Szegedy, C., et al.: Going deeper with convolutions. In: 2015 IEEE Conference on Computer Vision and Pattern Recognition, vol. 07–12-June-2015, pp. 1–9 (2015). https://doi.org/10.1109/CVPR.2015.7298594

18. Chiang, J.Y., Chen, Y.C.: Underwater image enhancement by wavelength compensation and dehazing. IEEE Trans. Image Process. **21**(4), 1756–1769 (2012). https://doi.org/10.1109/TIP.2011.2179666

19. Zhang, L., Lu, H., Serikawa, S., Li, Y.: Contrast enhancement for images in turbid water. JOSA A, **32**(5), 886–893 (2015). https://doi.org/10.1364/JOSAA.32.000886

20. Ancuti, C.O., Ancuti, C., De Vleeschouwer, C., Bekaert, P.: Color balance and fusion for underwater image enhancement. IEEE Trans. Image Process. **27**(1), 379–393 (2018). https://doi.org/10.1109/TIP.2017.2759252
21. Li, C., Anwar, S., Porikli, F.: Underwater scene prior inspired deep underwater image and video enhancement. Pattern Recognit. **98**, 107038 (2020). https://doi.org/10.1016/J.PATCOG.2019.107038
22. Zhu, J.Y., Park, T., Isola, P., Efros, A.A.: Unpaired image-to-image translation using cycle-consistent adversarial networks. In: Proceedings of IEEE International Conference on Computer Vision, vol. 2017-October, pp. 2242–2251 (2017). https://doi.org/10.1109/ICCV.2017.244

Performance Analysis of Distributed Mobility Management Schemes in UAV-Based 5G Networks

Debadreeta Das[1]([envelope]) [ID], Manoj Kumar Rana[2] [ID], Bhaskar Sardar[1], and Debashis Saha[3] [ID]

[1] Department of Information Technology, Jadavpur University, Kolkata, India
debadreetadas@gmail.com
[2] Department of Computing Technologies, Faculty of Engineering and Technology, SRM Institute of Science and Technology, Kattankulathur, Tamil Nadu, India
[3] Management Information Systems Group, Indian Institute of Management Calcutta, Kolkata 700104, India
ds@iimcal.ac.in

Abstract. Unmanned aerial vehicles (UAVs) extend 5G network coverage by acting as mobile relays or onboard base stations (BSs) to connect with cellular BSs and user equipments (UEs). Their high mobility causes frequent Internet Protocol (IP) handoffs, affecting the quality of service (QoS) for connected devices. The 5G core network has improved with separate control and data planes, along with software-defined enhancements for better handoff management. However, centralized mobility management (CMM) still faces challenges like non-optimized routing and performance issues, especially in scenarios, like, UAV-assisted vehicular communication in smart cities and UAV-assisted remote construction and mining site. Distributed mobility management (DMM) is a promising alternative that decentralizes control plane anchors, improving scalability and efficiency. Existing DMM solutions, such as D-MIPv6, D-PMIPv6, D-SDN, and D-Routing, still require significant adaptation for seamless integration into UAV-assisted 5G networks. This paper integrates standard DMM schemes into UAV-based 5G networks, evaluates and analyses their performance across different UAV-assisted scenarios. Our findings indicate that for higher vehicular node velocity, longer pause times, lower handoff probability, and lower wireless link failure probability, U-SDN-DMM and U-D-Routing (UAV versions of SDN-DMM and D-Routing) perform best. However, in other conditions, these schemes become inefficient due to their high signaling costs.

Keywords: Mobility Management · Vehicular Networks · 5G · UAV · QoS

1 Introduction

In advanced 5G networks, Unmanned Aerial Vehicles (UAVs) will function as relays or onboard Base Station (BSs), connecting ground BSs and

User Equipment (UEs) [1]. As mobile BSs, they provide wider coverage and are often preferred by UEs [2]. IP handoff occurs due to UAV or UE mobility, requiring reconnection to another UAV or BS [2]. To balance network load, UEs may switch between UAVs and BSs, triggering further IP handoffs. Conventional IP handoff schemes like Mobile IPv6 (MIPv6) and Proxy MIPv6 (PMIPv6) follow a hierarchical structure, routing data plane messages through control plane entities like the home agent. These Centralized Mobility Management (CMM) schemes face challenges, including non-optimized routing. Standard Distributed Mobility Management (DMM) schemes [3], such as Distributed PMIPv6 (DPMIPv6) [4], Distributed MIPv6 (DMIPv6) [5], Distributed Mobility Management for SDN (SDN-DMM) [6], and Distributed Routing (D-Routing) [7], aim to overcome these limitations. While the work [3] discussed integrating these schemes into 5G-based intelligent transportation systems, their performance in Unmanned Aerial Vehicle (UAV)-based 5G networks remains unexplored.

Most existing techniques are not 5G-compatible, and the absence of 5G-based handoff signaling is a major limitation. Scalability during handoff is another challenge, with no DMM solutions addressing it yet. Some studies [8,9] analyze Quality of Service (QoS) and signaling costs for DMIPv6 and DPMIPv6 but distributing anchors increases signaling during handovers and frequent anchor switching may degrade QoS, higher handover failure in high-speed scenarios. In [10], M. Balfaqih et al. compare DPMIPv6-based schemes in vehicular networks based on session recovery, handoff failure but introduces more signaling messages to enable fast-handover optimization. In [11], mobility in ultra-dense networks is considered without using an optimization technique during handover. In [12], QoS variations are considered with a partial DMM scheme. However, UAV-based 5G scenarios are not considered, leaving specific issues in such networks unaddressed. The handoff procedure adopted for these schemes are oversimplified and cannot be ported into UAV-based 5G network system.

The objectives of the paper are as follows:

- Study the issues of DMM schemes in UAV-based 5G network mobility scenarios. In particular we have considered two scenarios: UAV-assisted vehicular communication in smart cities and UAV-assisted remote construction and mining site.
- Integration of the standard DMM schemes: DPMIPv6, DMIPv6, D-Routing and SDN-DMM into the UAV-based 5G network system.
- Perform a comprehensive analysis of the standard DMM schemes based on QoS parameters, signaling cost and packet delivery cost etc.

The structure of the paper is outlined as follows: Sect. 2 introduces the UAV-based 5G mobility scenarios where standard DMM schemes can be applied. Section 3 discusses the potential issues of DMM that may emerge in these scenarios. In Sect. 4, standard DMM schemes are illustrated and their integration with the 5G network system is explained. Section 5 presents a comparative performance analysis, and finally, Sect. 6 provides the conclusions.

2   Scenarios

We have described here two UAV-based 5G mobility scenarios in the following.

2.1   Scenario 1: UAV-Assisted Vehicular Communication in Smart Cities

We have illustrated this scenario and handoff events in Fig. 1. In smart cities, vehicles do not rely only on installed cellular infrastructure for internet connectivity [11]. They also use 5G-based on-the-sky UAVs to run bandwidth-hungry, high-data-rate applications. While cellular networks cover a larger service area and support high-speed vehicles, they often lack strong signal strength and higher bandwidth. This makes it difficult for vehicles to access data-intensive services while moving fast.

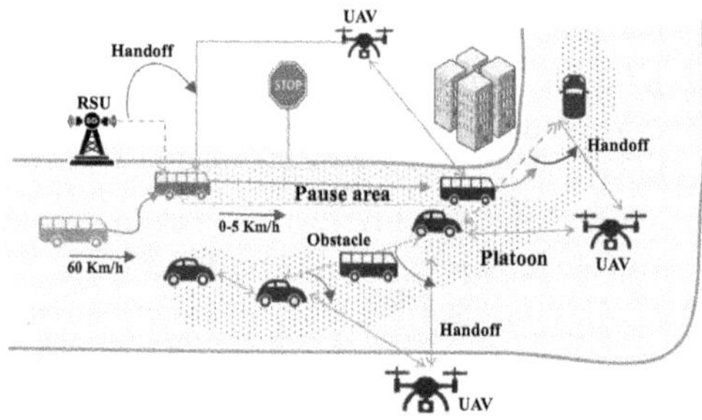

Fig. 1. Illustration of mobility and handoff in Scenario 1

Applications like OTA software updates (crucial for EVs and connected cars), high-resolution maps, real-time navigation, and media downloads require stable, high-speed connections [11]. Vehicles often access these services during traffic stops or designated pauses, taking advantage of strong network coverage from a UAV relay or BS. For platoons and self-driving vehicles, continuous synchronization is essential while moving. However, obstacles like high-rise buildings, large vehicles, and sharp turns can block signals, disrupting communication. In such cases, vehicles rely on UAV-based BSs or relays to maintain seamless connectivity.

In both situations, handoff is a frequent event [11]. Vehicles switch between UAV and cellular BS when accessing internet services, and between Vehicle-to-Vehicle (V2V) and UAV networks for on-road synchronization. Since UAVs are usually connected to long-distance backhaul networks, CMM schemes are not suitable. Instead, DMM schemes offer a more effective solution for ensuring seamless connectivity.

2.2 Scenario 2: UAV-Assisted Remote Construction and Mining Site

We have illustrated this scenario and handoff events in Fig. 2. In such areas, UAVs provide fast internet access for site owners, laborers, and smart machines [12]. These devices may run long-lived applications, such as work instructions, VoIP communication with site personnel, IoT data collection and downloading digital twins for scheduling and instruction generation by the manager [12]. Additionally, short-lived applications like instant messaging, uploading machine-level instructions, and transmitting controller information are also used. While short-lived applications can initiate a new session at any time, long-lived applications face disruptions when switching to a different UAV.

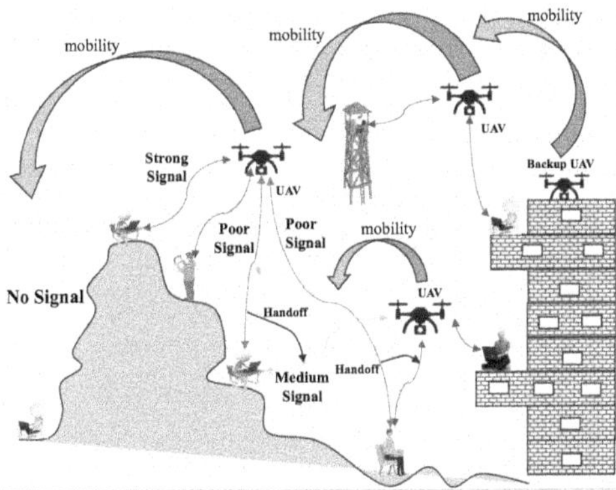

Fig. 2. Illustration of mobility and handoff in Scenario 2

Since the number of UAVs is limited and the site covers a vast area, a UAV cannot stay in one location for long. Instead, it moves slowly to cover the entire area [12]. Underlying nodes cannot rely on a distant UAV with weak signals and must switch to a closer UAV with stronger signals and better bandwidth. Additionally, UAVs consume high energy due to continuous mobility and energy-intensive applications. To address this, a backup UAV often replaces the active one, transferring all underlying nodes to the backup. Thus, single-node handoffs occur due to UAV mobility, while multiple-node handoffs result from UAV replacement.

To enhance spectral efficiency, UAVs are now equipped with BS and access router capabilities, making these handoffs primarily IP handoffs since BSs typically belong to different IP networks [12]. However, factors like high dust levels, environmental noise, and steep terrain reduce the reliability of the long wireless medium. As a result, IP handoff signaling experiences high delay and packet loss, further worsened by the long-distance backhaul nature of UAV networks. This makes CMM schemes unsuitable, while DMM is a better fit. However, several IP handoff challenges must still be addressed before implementing standard DMM schemes in this scenario.

3   Issues

The potential issues of DMM that may arise in the two scenarios outlined in Sect. 2 are described and summarized in Table 1.

3.1   Unexpected IP Handoff

In Scenario 1, a vehicle's pause time depends on traffic and stoppage policies. A long-running application expected to finish within this period may continue after the vehicle resumes movement, potentially pushing it out of the UAV's service area, leading to a handoff. Similarly, two platoon cars may lose synchronization if a heavy vehicle blocks their signal, requiring an immediate switch to a UAV network, especially in moderate or heavy traffic. In Scenario 2, a UAV's sudden movement to cover a service-blockage area can also trigger a handoff. Here, the handoff preparation phase cannot be utilized by any DMM scheme, as the UE has no prior knowledge of switching.

3.2   Large Handoff Load

In Scenario 2, as the UAV moves, all UEs within its service area must switch to a nearby or newly arrived UAV upon leaving its coverage. This sudden transition overloads the UAV network's control plane, as all affected UEs simultaneously trigger handoff signaling. This frequent event in Scenario 2 leads to prolonged handoff times, increasing the risk of high delays or incomplete handoff processes, ultimately resulting in significant data packet loss.

3.3   RSSI-Based Handoff

In cellular network, handoff is typically based on the received signal strength indicator (RSSI). So, a strong signal from a newly arrived UAV may prematurely trigger a handoff. If this UAV is in motion to serve another area, it may leave quickly, while the previous UAV still remains there. So, the UE undergoes two consecutive handoffs: first to the transient UAV and then back to old one. Such events are frequent in Scenario 2 leading to excessive IP handoffs.

3.4   Power Dissipation and Incomplete Handoff

As observed in 5G-compliant DMM schemes [3], every DMM handoff process includes a handoff initialization phase. In UAV networks, the current UAV manages most handoff signaling, while the new UAV handles only a few steps. However, sudden power depletion may disrupt this process before the current UAV completes its data service. Additionally, such handoffs often impact multiple UEs within the UAV's coverage, making the situation more complex.

3.5   Integration of 5G and UAV Networks

The current 3GPP 5G standard [13] does not address UAV network integration into core 5G networks. As a result, the handoff signaling messages defined in [13] are not designed for UAV networks. Introducing a separate User Plane Function (UPF) for UAV networks could enable DMM schemes in such integrated architectures, similar to [3], which applies DMM schemes to 5G-based intelligent transportation systems. However, several challenges remain, including tunneling, UE identifier mapping, and gNB mapping (where UAVs serve as gNBs).

3.6   UAV Vertical Mobility

In Scenario 2, UAVs often exhibit vertical mobility to cover steep terrain in mining sites or provide connectivity at different heights in construction sites. However, UEs may be unaware of this movement and may blindly connect to a UAV, even when horizontally mobile UAVs are available. In such cases, some signal may exist above a UAV, which is typically weak and not optimized for aerial UEs unless the network is specifically designed for UAV or aerial coverage. As a result, the UE must perform a handoff to a nearby UAV. To optimize handoff decisions and ensure stable connectivity, UAV mobility patterns must be regularly communicated to UEs, allowing them to connect only to UAVs that remain in service for longer durations.

3.7   Scalability and Load Balancing

The number of UEs connected to a UAV is a crucial factor when applying DMM schemes. Since DMM schemes rely on edge processing rather than a centralized entity, UAVs handle most mobility-related signaling, while core UAV network entities manage only data packet processing and maintain static mobility context information. Given UAVs' energy constraints, processing a high volume of mobility messages can cause significant energy depletion and increased delays in both handoff signaling and data packet processing. Current DMM schemes lack load-balancing mechanisms, making it essential for admission control procedures to consider UAV mobility dynamics and optimize load distribution among available UAVs. This issue is particularly critical in Scenario 2, where no alternative networks exist to accommodate UEs. In contrast, Scenario 1 is moderately affected due to the presence of an installed vehicular network.

3.8   Summary of Impact of Issues in the Scenarios

Table 1 summarizes the impact of various issues in the two UAV scenarios. Frequent handoffs emerge as a critical challenge, significantly affecting the QoS of UEs in UAV networks. Key performance parameters for evaluating different DMM schemes include packet loss ratio, throughput, end-to-end delay, signaling cost, and packet delivery cost. Furthermore, the standardization of DMM schemes in UAV-based 5G networks requires their integration into 3GPP-specified 5G networks, replacing the traditional cellular RAN with a UAV RAN.

Table 1. Impact of Issues in Different Scenarios

Issues	Scenario 1	Scenario 2
Unexpected IP handoff	Happens and QoS degraded	Happens and QoS degraded
Large handoff load	Not happen	Common and causes high congestion
RSSI-based handoff	Rare	High chance of frequent handoff
Power dissipation and incomplete handoff	Handoff not completed and new session started	Handoff not completed and new session started
Integration of 5G and UAV networks	Not compatible to 3GPP	Not compatible to 3GPP
UAV vertical mobility	Not happen	Frequent handoff occurs
Scalability and load balancing	Moderate effect	High congestion

4   DMM Schemes for UAV-Based 5G Networks

In this Section, we have integrated the standard DMM schemes–DMIPv6, DPMIPv6, SDN-DMM, and D-Routing into the 3GPP-specified 5G-based network system [13]. For this purpose, we have followed [2,5,6,11,14] for network entities and their functions during handoff in 5G network architecture. As these schemes are adapted for UAV-based networks, their names are prefixed with "UAV-based" and abbreviated as U-DMIPv6, U-DPMIPv6, U-SDN-DMM, and U-D-Routing, respectively, in the following discussion.

Table 2. Entities mapped from standard to 5G based UAV version

Version	U-DMIPv6	U-DPMIPv6	U-SDN-DMM	U-D-Routing
Standard	NgRAN/HA, MN	NgRAN/MAAR/MAG, C-LMA, D-LMA, CU, CMD	CU, NgRAN/MAG, OF Switch	Route AR, AR, BGP Router
5G based UAV	UAV BS/5G BS, UE/vehicle, [5]	UAV/RSU, UAV BS/5GBS, UPF1,UPF2, AMF, [2,5]	UAV BS/5G BS, UAV/RSU, SMF, FS, [6,11]	UAV BS/5G BS, UAV/RSU, UPF Router, [14]

4.1   5G-Compliant Schemes

The network entities mapped to UAV-based 5G networks are summarized in Table 2, with detailed descriptions provided in [3]. The handoff steps of the DMM schemes are summarized and categorized into 3GPP-specific and scheme-specific steps, as illustrated in Table 3.

The handoff procedure of U-DMIPv6 is illustrated in Fig. 3. UAV BS1 initiates the process by sending a handover request (Table 3, Step 1) to CU1, including UAV BS2's ID, PDU session details, security credentials, and direct path availability. CU1, managing mobility via its AMF module, contacts CU2's AMF (Step 2), which selects a UPF for the PDU session. If multiple PDU flows exist, separate UPFs are assigned, with MIPv6 tunnels linking UPF2 to UE and for that SMF of CU2 allocates IPv6 address to UE from globally unique 64 bit prefixes, therefore, CU2 can not initiate PDU session registration with UPF2 as different UPFs may be selected for different PDU sessions which require different 64 bit prefixes and UE appends 64 bit interface id with it. AMF of CU2 allocates 5G Global Unique Temporary Identifier (5G-GUTI) for UE. CU2 then triggers a handover request (Step 3) to UAV BS2. Following context exchanges, CU1 instructs UAV BS1 to detach the UE, which then connects to UAV BS2 and it sends RA with UPF GW address to UE. Then UE sends BU to UPF1 for DNS update and CU2 requests session creation (Step 11) at UPF2. Once the PDU session is established and resources are allocated, CU2 sends a Binding Update (Step 13) to CU1, which relays it to UPF1. As no direct data/control path exists between networks, UPF1 sets up a tunnel to the UE, ensuring uplink and downlink traffic pass through UPF2.

Table 3. Description of handoff steps

Messages	From-to	U-DMIPv6	U-DPMIPv6	U-SDN-DMM	U-D-Routing	steps belong to
Handoff Request/Command	UAV BS1/5G BS1 CU1	1/6	1/8	1/10	1/8	3GPP
UE context create request/response	CU1-CU2	2/5	2/5	2/7	2/7	Integrated
Hand-over related messages	CU2- UAV BS2	3/4		5/6	2/6	3GPP
	UAV BS1-UE	7	7	11	9	3GPP
	UE-UAV BS2	8	8	12	10	3GPP
Handover indication	UAV BS2 CU2		9	13	11	3GPP
RA	UAV BS2-UE	9				Corresponding scheme
	CU2-UE		15	14	14	
DNS update	UAV BS2-CU2	10/18				Corresponding scheme
	CU2-DNS	13/16	10/11		12/13	
BU/BA or PBU/PBA for binding update	CU1-UPF1	14/15	13/14			Integrated
	CU1-CU2		12			
Session establishment request/response or Flow-MOD/BGP update	CU2-UPF2	11/12	3/4		5	
	CU2-FS2			3	3/4	3GPP/Corresponding scheme
	CU2-UAV BS2			4		
	CU1-FS1			8		
	CU1-UAV BS1			9		

In the 5G-based U-DPMIPv6 scheme, during initial attachment or handoff (Fig. 4), the UE stores home or visited network information in the CMD within the SMF module of CU. CU1 initiates the process by sending a UE create context

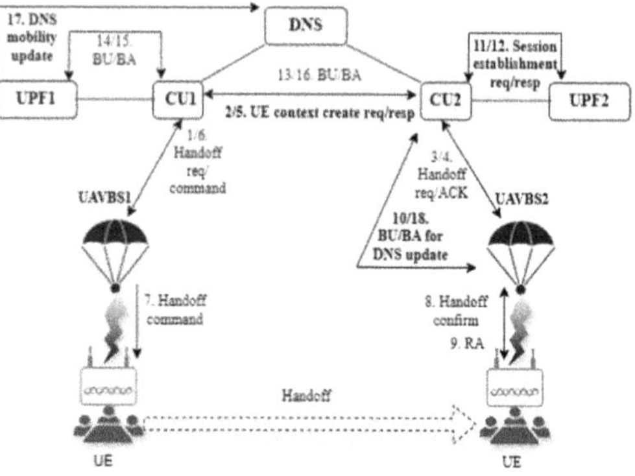

Fig. 3. Handoff procedure of U-DMIPv6

request (Table 3, Step 2) to CU2, including CMD details such as user ID, prefixes, PDU session IDs, and UPF gateway addresses as the Proxy-Care-of- Address. CU2 then selects a UPF for the PDU session, establishing PMIPv6 tunnels between UPF2 and previous UPFs. Hence, SMF allocates IPv6 address to UE from globally unique prefixes and appends 64 bit interface id, so, CU2 can initiate PDU session registration with UPF2 unlike U-D-MIPv6. Next, CU2 sends a session creation request (Step 3) to UPF2 containing PDU session details, UE ID, IPv6 address, active home addresses, and QoS profile. After getting handover confirm from UE via CU1, UAVBS2 sends RA without any HA info as CU2 already stores CMD information in it. Once the DNS update response (Step 11) is received, CU2's SMF, acting as the LMA, updates its BCE with the UE's new address, prompting CU1 to delete the UE's CMD from its SMF cache and CU1 forwards PBU to UPF1. Finally, CU2 sends a unicast RA (Step 15) to the UE, providing the new home address along with the old home addresses for ongoing sessions.

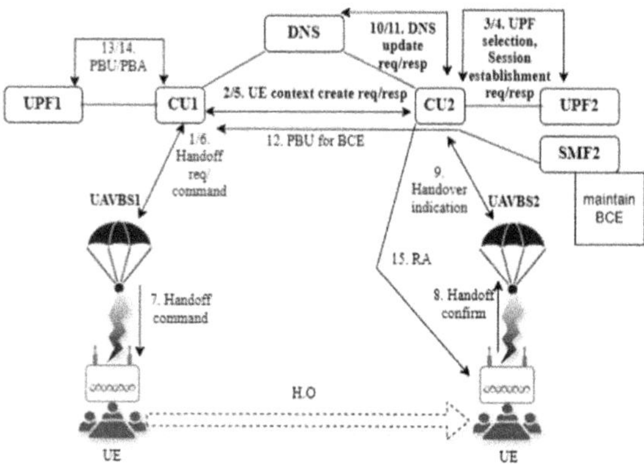

Fig. 4. Handoff procedure of U-DPMIPv6

In the 5G-based U-SDN-DMM scheme, the handoff process follows the same phases as U-DPMIPv6. In the context create request (Table 3, Step 2), CU1 includes forwarding switch details to establish the optimal route from UAV BS1 to UAV BS2. Based on this, the AMF module requests CU2's SMF to create a new binding cache entry. Acting as an SDN controller, CU2 then sends FlowMod messages (Step 3) to domain 2 forwarding switches or UPFs. Upon receiving the context create response (Step 7) from CU2, CU1's SMF deletes the old binding cache and sends FlowMod messages (Step 8) to domain 1 forwarding switches or UPFs. Once the user attaches to UAV BS2 and confirms handoff (Step 12), UAV BS2 forwards buffered downlink packets. The route update occurs before the user attaches to UAV BS2. Finally, CU2 sends a unicast RA (Step 14) to the UE with its home address for ongoing sessions and updates all forwarding switches with FlowMod messages.

In the 5G-based U-D-Routing scheme, the addressing strategy reduces BGP route update overhead during handoff. When the UE moves within a cluster while retaining the same IPv6 address, the new UAV BS sends a BGP update to the upper-level or aggregation router, which propagates it to peer UAV BSs sharing the same prefix. This ensures routing table updates, preventing obsolete routes to the old UAV BS. Additionally, UAV BS2 sends a BGP update (Table 3, Step 5) to its peer UAV BSs to optimize routing. If the UE moves between clusters, the BGP update reaches the core-level router, which aggregates and disseminates the update to all connected aggregation routers and UAV BSs. The handoff steps follow those of U-DPMIPv6. After receiving the Handover Confirm message (Step 10), UAV BS2 announces itself as the next hop for the UE's prefix by sending BGP updates to other UAV BSs and its uplink aggregation routers. The updates propagate through the network, eliminating the need for a binding update procedure.

4.2 Functional Differences of 5G Based Different DMM Schemes

Table 4 outlines the functional differences among various DMM schemes. In U-DMIPv6, the AMF module requests the SMF module of CU2 to select a UPF for a PDU session. The SMF allocates globally unique 64-bit IPv6 prefixes, which may vary for different PDUs based on the selected UPFs. The AMF assigns a 5G-GUTI, valid within CU2's tracking area. MIPv6 tunnels are utilized between UPF2 and the user. In U-DPMIPv6, each UPF has a unique, configurable set of globally unique IPv6 prefixes assigned to UEs based on PDU session require-ments. U-DPMIPv6 tunnels are used between UPF2 and previous UPFs. IPv6 address allocation is handled by the SMF module of CU2, which assigns only the globally unique 64-bit prefixes. In U-SDN-DMM, the UPF selection phase is skipped, as all PDUs retain the same home network prefixes after handoff. UPFs do not store binding cache information, which is instead managed by the SDN controller and SMF module. The UE's IP configuration remains unchanged during handoff. GTP tunneling is not suitable for SDN-based schemes due to the absence of GTP header parsing for TCP sessions. The concept of a global network view for maintaining mobility during fast handoff remains abstract. In

U-D-Routing, UAV BSs are allocated a pool of IPv6 prefixes, designed for aggregation by upper-level aggregation routers. CU assigns UPFs to users at initial attachment by allocating IPv6 prefixes to different PDUs. UPF selection may be based on optimal path selection by UAV BSs and UE.

Table 4. Functional differences of DMM schemes

Handoff Functions	U-DMIPv6	U-DPMIPv6	U-SDN-DMM	U-D-Routing
UPF selection	✓	✓	✓	✓
Route optimization	✗	✗	✗	✗
Tunnelling concept	✓	✓	✗	✓
Neighbour discovery algo.	✗	✗	✓	✗
IPv6 prefix allocation	✓	✓	✗	✓
Maintaining different CoAs	✓	✗	✗	✗

5 Performance Analysis

In this Section, a comprehensive performance analysis is conducted based on the parameters identified in Sect. 3.8. The City Section mobility model [15] is used to define vehicle mobility in Scenario 1, while the accumulative handoff cost model from the work [3] is applied to illustrate static UE node switching between UAV BSs in Scenario 2. The network model for computing various parameters is also derived from the numerical calculations in the work [3]. In Scenario 1, once a vehicle connects to a UAV network in the pause area, it does not perform any handoff but may switch between macro cellular networks while in motion. In Scenario 2, only switching between two similar UAV networks is considered, governed by the corresponding probabilities defined in the accumulative handoff cost model from the work [3].

In this setup, the UAV network is integrated into one of the UPFs, following a long backhaul network where the hop distance between the UAV BS and the UPF is 16, including two wireless hops between the UAV BS and the 5G macro BS. The remaining parameters of the system model are adopted from Table IX of [3]. The results are validated through simulation, using the MIPv6 module [16], along with the PMIPv6 module [17] in Network Simulator 3 (ns-3), both of which are extended to support basic DMM schemes.

The end-to-end (e2e) delay performance has been analyzed in [3], demonstrating that DMIPv6 and DPMIPv6 achieve lower delays compared to SDN-DMM and D-Routing. A similar trend is observed for U-DMIPv6, U-DPMIPv6, U-SDN-DMM, and U-D-Routing in e2e delay measurements. In Scenario 1, the velocity of a vehicle and its UAV connection time during the pause period, particularly when running bandwidth-intensive applications, play a crucial role in evaluating QoS performance and the cost of DMM signaling. In Scenario 2, the handoff probability between UAVs and the wireless link failure probability are key factors in assessing the performance of DMM schemes. The following sections present a detailed performance analysis based on these factors, focusing on the QoS and signaling cost.

5.1 Scenario 1

Figure 5 shows that the U-D-Routing scheme has the best PLR performance among all DMM schemes, with U-SDN-DMM performing close to it. This is because both schemes do not require UPF selection and BU processes. However, U-SDN-DMM takes slightly longer due to the time needed for route updates through the FlowMod message. U-DMIPv6 performs the worst, while U-DPMIPv6 is better than U-DMIPv6 since U-DMIPv6 is UE-centric, whereas U-DPMIPv6 follows a network-centric approach. Although U-SDN-DMM and U-D-Routing have better handoff performance than the other schemes, their signaling cost is much higher, as shown in Fig. 5. This is due to the extensive multicasting and broadcasting of FlowMod messages in U-SDN-DMM and BGP update messages in U-D-Routing.

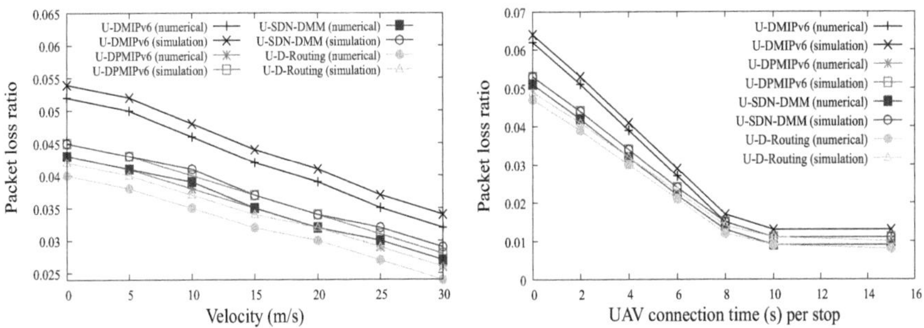

a) PLR variation w.r.t. velocity and UAV connection time at stop

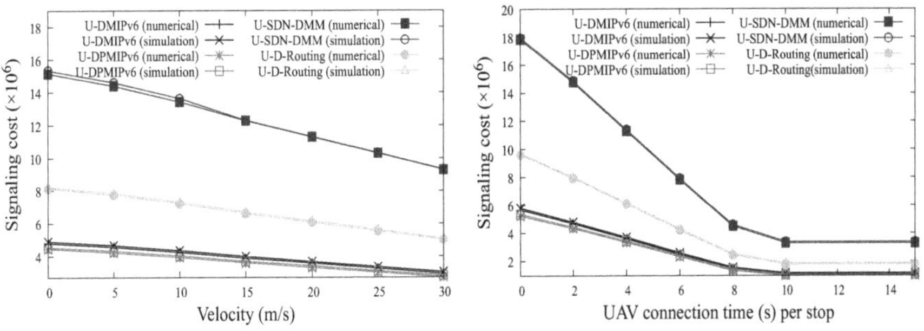

b) Signaling cost variation w.r.t. velocity and UAV connection time at stop

Fig. 5. Performance of different DMM schemes in scenario 1

The analysis is conducted for 300 continuous seconds. As the vehicle moves faster, the rate of handoffs between macro cells increases, along with the UAV connection time in the pause area. This means a larger portion of the simulation time is spent in the pause area, avoiding macro-cell switching. Since cumulative signaling cost (and thus PLR) mainly depends on macro-cell handoffs, fewer handoffs result in lower signaling cost and PLR. Similarly, as the UAV connection time in the pause area increases, the total number of handoffs decreases, leading to a further reduction in PLR and signaling cost.

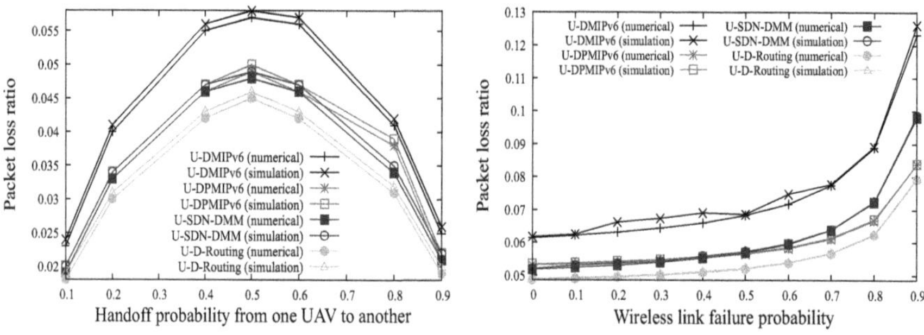

a) PLR variation w.r.t. UAV switching and link failure probability

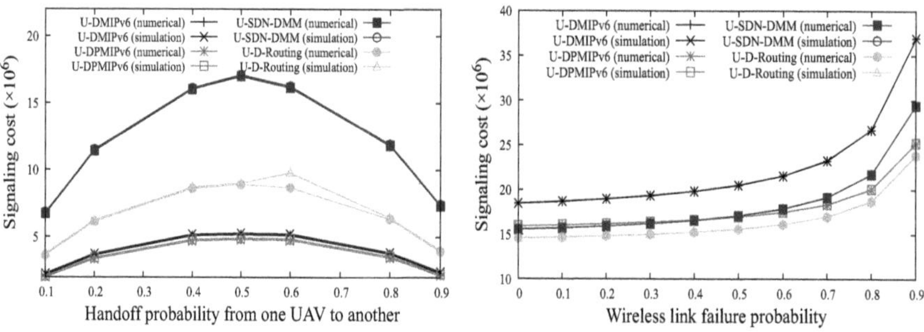

b) Signaling cost variation w.r.t. UAV switching and link failure probability

Fig. 6. Performance of different DMM schemes in scenario 2

5.2   Scenario 2

In Scenario 2, handoff occurs between UAV BSs while the UEs remain nearly stationary. However, due to certain factors discussed in Sects. 3.1, 3.3, 3.4, and 3.6, a UE may switch from one UAV to another. This affects the probability of transitioning between UAV networks, influencing the handoff rate. Therefore, the handoff probability between UAV networks is varied to analyze its impact on PLR and signaling cost. The results of this analysis are presented in Fig. 6.

In Scenario 2, the performance variation among different DMM schemes in terms of PLR and signaling cost follows the same trend as in Scenario 1. The reason for this variation is explained in Sect. 5.1.

Both PLR and signaling cost rise sharply with an increase in UAV switching probability, as this leads to a higher handoff frequency. This typically occurs when the UAV BS moves rapidly in both horizontal and vertical directions or when the UE switches to a closer UAV BS for a higher data rate. Up to the median value of 0.5, the net effect is that the overall chance of handoffs increases sharply, leading to higher signaling cost and PLR. Once the probability exceeds 0.5, the decrease in probability from other complementary probability (1-UAV to UAV switching probability) reduces the overall frequency of handoffs, causing the cumulative signaling cost and PLR to drop sharply.

As the wireless link failure probability increases, more packets are lost, leading to retransmissions that raise delay and, consequently, PLR. A moderate to high failure probability also increases the risk of handoff signaling message loss, raising the chances of incomplete handoff (Sect. 3.4), which further elevates PLR and signaling costs. For moderate values (up to around 0.60.7), the system can handle occasional losses through retransmissions with minimal impact on PLR. However, beyond this threshold, throughput drops sharply, and delays increase non-linearly, causing a rapid rise in PLR.

6 Conclusions and Future Works

This paper evaluated the performance of various DMM schemes using both numerical models and simulations, based on emerging 5G network scenarios such as UAV-assisted vehicular communication in smart cities and UAV-assisted remote construction and mining sites. While existing research has compared DMM schemes, it has not thoroughly explored UAV-based networks and their associated challenges. Additionally, previous studies have not effectively integrated standard DMM schemes into 3GPP-defined UAV-based 5G networks.

In UAV-assisted vehicular communication, U-SDN-DMM and U-D-Routing offer better PLR performance than the other two schemes. However, their high signaling cost can sometimes cause severe congestion in the control plane. If a vehicle moves fast but spends significant time in pause areas–resulting in fewer handoffs while downloading high-bandwidth data–these two schemes perform best. However, U-D-Routing requires a separate routing infrastructure, which is costly and generally not preferred by operators despite its high PLR performance. In UAV-assisted remote construction and mining sites, switching between UAVs and wireless link failures occur randomly. When these factors are low, U-SDN-DMM and U-D-Routing are preferable for handoff management. However, at higher values, U-DMIPv6 and U-DPMIPv6 become better options due to the excessive signaling cost of the other two schemes. This work does not incorporate a mobility model for UAVs, and we plan to integrate appropriate models to simulate UAV flight patterns and vertical mobility in future. Also it would be interesting to analyze different hybrid mobility models like AI-enhanced or fog-based DMM schemes. Our future plan also includes development of a testbed to compare these DMM schemes in real world to understand the impact of signaling and processing overheads on UAV energy.

References

1. Marojevic, V., Guvenc, I., Dutta, R., Sichitiu, M.L., Floyd, B.A.: Advanced wireless for unmanned aerial systems: 5g standardization, research challenges, and aerpaw architecture. IEEE Veh. Technol. Mag. **15**(2), 22–30 (2020)
2. Li, B., Fei, Z., Zhang, Y.: UAV communications for 5g and beyond: recent advances and future trends. IEEE IoT J. **6**(2), 2241–2263 (2019)
3. Das, D., Kumar Rana, M., Sardar, B., Pecorella, T., Saha, D.: A comparative analysis of distributed mobility management schemes for 5g-based its. IEEE Trans. Intell. Transp. Syst. **26**(2), 2434–2448 (2025)
4. Ali-Ahmad, H., Ouzzif, M., Bertin, P., Lagrange, X.: Distributed dynamic mobile ipv6: design and evaluation. In: IEEE Wireless Commun. Netw. Conf. (WCNC), pp. 2166–2171 (2013)
5. Bernardos, C.J., de la Oliva, A., Giust, F., Zúñiga, J.-C., Mourad, A.: Proxy mobile IPv6 extensions for distributed mobility management. RFC 8885 (2020)
6. Bi, Y., Han, G., Lin, C., Guizani, M., Wang, X.: Mobility management for intro/inter domain handover in software-defined networks. IEEE J. Sel. Areas Commun. **37**(8), 1739–1754 (2019)
7. Sharma, V., You, I., Palmieri, F., Jayakody, D.N.K., Li, J.: Secure and energy-efficient handover in fog networks using blockchain-based dmm. IEEE Commun. Mag.**56**(5), 22–31 (2018)
8. Gures, E., Shayea, I., Alhammadi, A., Ergen, M., Mohamad, H.: A comprehensive survey on mobility management in 5g heterogeneous networks: architectures, challenges and solutions. IEEE Access **8**, 195883–195913 (2020)
9. Jeon, S., Figueiredo, S., Aguiar, R.L., Choo, H.: Distributed mobility management for the future mobile networks: a comprehensive analysis of key design options. IEEE Access **5**, 11423–11436 (2017)
10. Balfaqih, M., Ismail, M., Nordin, R., Balfaqih, Z.: Handover performance analysis of distributed mobility management in vehicular networks. In: IEEE Malaysia International Conference on Communications (MICC), pp. 145–150 (2015)
11. Bouachir, O., Aloqaily, M., Al Ridhawi, I., Alfandi, O., Bany Salameh, H.: UAV-assisted vehicular communication for densely crowded environments. In: NOMS 2020 - 2020 IEEE/IFIP Network Operations and Management Symposium, pp. 1–4 (2020)
12. Gupta, S., Nair, S.: A review of the emerging role of UAVs in construction site safety monitoring. Mater. Today Proc. (2023)
13. 3GPP. 5g; procedures for the 5g system (5gs). Technical Specification (TS) 23.502, 3rd Generation Partnership Project (3GPP) (2021). Version 16.7.0
14. Uddin, M., et al.: Mobility management issues and solutions in 5g-and-beyond networks: a comprehensive review. Electronics **11**(9), 1366 (2022)
15. Shohrab Hossain, M., Atiquzzaman,M.: Cost analysis of mobility protocols. Telecom Syst. **52**(4), 2271–2285 (2013)
16. Kumar Rana, M., Sardar, B., Mandal, S., Saha, D.: Implementation and performance evaluation of a mobile ipv6 (mipv6) simulation model for ns-3. Simul. Model. Pract. Theory. **72**, 1–22 (2017)
17. Choi, H.-Y., Min, S.-G., Han, Y.-H., Park, J., Kim, H.: Implementation and evaluation of proxy mobile ipv6 in ns-3 network simulator. In: 2010 International Conference Ubiquitous Information Technologies and Applications, pp. 1–6 (2010)

An Innovative Method for Machine Learning: Liver Histopathology Detection Using Ultra Sound Images, An Attention Aided Ensemble Approach

Nilakash Mukherjee⬥, Manab Debnath⬥, Rajdeep Roy⬥,
Subhadeep Santra⬥, Tanmoy Ghosh$^{(\boxtimes)}$⬥, and Dishani Roy⬥

Narula Institute of Technology, Kolkata, West Bengal, India
`tanmoy.g.331@gmail.com`

Abstract. Liver histopathology plays a critical role in diagnosing and evaluating fibrosis, a condition often assessed through ultrasound imaging. This research proposes an ensemble deep learning model combining ResNet50 and VGG16 architectures, enhanced with attention mechanisms, to effectively classify liver histopathology and fibrosis images. The dataset, comprising grayscale ultrasound images from five classes, was preprocessed by converting to RGB, resizing, and stratified splitting into training, validation, and testing subsets. The model architecture integrates global average pooling and dense layers for classification, while attention blocks amplify salient features, enhancing predictive accuracy. Comprehensive training incorporated data augmentation and early stopping to mitigate overfitting. The model achieved a test accuracy of 97%, with consistent precision, recall, and F1-scores across all classes. Performance evaluation through confusion matrices, t-SNE feature visualization, and ROC curves with high AUC values validated its robustness and reliability. This approach demonstrates significant potential for automated medical image classification, advancing diagnostic accuracy and efficiency in clinical applications.

Keywords: Liver Histopathology · Fibrosis Classification · Automated Diagnosis · Attention Mechanisms

1 Introduction

Liver diseases, particularly fibrosis, are a significant global health challenge, contributing to substantial morbidity and mortality rates worldwide [1]. Accurate diagnosis and staging of liver fibrosis are essential for determining the appropriate therapeutic interventions and monitoring disease progression [2]. However, traditional manual interpretation of histopathological images is labor-intensive, subjective, and susceptible to inter-observer variability, making automated approaches highly desirable [3]. Advancements in artificial intelligence

K. Chandra Mondal et al. (Eds.): CICBA 2025, CCIS 2862, pp. 137–151, 2026.
https://doi.org/10.1007/978-3-032-17187-0_11

(AI) and deep learning have revolutionized the field of medical image analysis, enabling the development of highly accurate, automated diagnostic tools [4]. The ensemble approach leverages the complementary strengths of these architectures to achieve robust and reliable classification performance [5]. The attention blocks were designed to enhance the model's ability to localize and emphasize diagnostically relevant regions, leading to improved classification accuracy Comprehensive evaluation of the model was conducted using a variety of metrics, confusion matrices, and receiver operating characteristic (ROC) curves [6]. Additionally, t-SNE visualization was employed to analyze the feature space and validate the model's ability to distinguish between different classes. The proposed model achieved a high test accuracy of 97%, with consistent performance across all metrics [7]. A major worldwide health burden, liver fibrosis has a high risk of developing into cirrhosis and hepatocellular cancer. Critical limitations exist with current diagnostic criteria, such as ultrasound imaging and histological investigation. Subjectivity and inter-observer variability plague histopathology, while ultrasonography is not sensitive enough for accurate staging. The critical need for automated, impartial, and interpretable computational techniques to raise prognosis accuracy and, eventually, improve patient care is highlighted by this diagnostic gap. By reducing diagnostic time and increasing reliability, such tools can contribute to improved patient outcomes and more efficient use of healthcare resources.

2   Literature Survey

Liver disease diagnosis has undergone a major transformation with the integration of artificial intelligence (AI), particularly in ultrasound imaging. Park et al. [1] employed deep convolutional neural networks (DCNNs) like ResNet and EfficientNet for liver fibrosis classification using METAVIR scores, achieving an AUC of 0.96. Kim et al. [3] applied VGG19 to multi-view ultrasound for fatty liver detection, reaching 80.1% accuracy. Virmani et al. [4] used wavelet packet descriptors with SVM to classify ultrasound images, achieving 88.8% accuracy for distinguishing normal, cirrhotic, and HCC cases. Tangruangkiat et al. [5] used ResNet50 for focal liver lesion classification, outperforming VGG16 and ResNet18 with 87% accuracy. Sathya and Maheswari [7] compared ML techniques (RF, SVM, K-NN) with deep learning, finding DL superior across precision, recall, and F1-score. Herrmann et al. [8] conducted a meta-analysis on 2D shear wave elastography (2D-SWE), reporting AUCs up to 0.92 for cirrhosis detection in hepatitis B and C patients. Machine learning (ML) methods have also been explored.

Elbashir et al. [9] used ensemble models (VGG16 + ResNet) to classify hepatocellular carcinoma (HCC) and hemangiomas from ultrasound images with 94% accuracy. Yao et al. [10] introduced a bio-inspired attention network for hepatic steatosis, mimicking visual cortex functions and achieving high sensitivity and specificity. Ghosh et al. [11] reported 83.7% accuracy using Random Forest for chronic liver disease prediction.

For steatosis detection, Li et al. [12] developed a scalable DL algorithm that outperformed transient elastography in histology-proven cohorts. Ballestri et al. [13] showed ultrasound sensitivity of 82% and 85% for mild and moderate steatosis, respectively. Urhuţ et al. [14] demonstrated that combining contrast-enhanced ultrasound (CEUS) with shear wave elastography improved HCC differentiation, achieving 79.55% sensitivity.

Traditional ultrasound still holds value. Choong et al. [15] found routine clinical ultrasound most effective for cirrhosis staging, though less sensitive for early fibrosis. Integrating multimodal imaging with AI-based interpretability frameworks could further enhance diagnostic performance (Table 1).

Table 1. Summary of related works on liver disease classification using ultrasound and deep learning

Authors (Year)	Dataset/Modality	Method/Model	Performance
Park et al. (2024) [1]	Ultrasound, METAVIR scores	ResNet, EfficientNet (DCNN)	AUC = 0.96
Herrmann et al. (2018) [16]	2D-SWE (Hepatitis B/C patients)	Meta-analysis	AUC = 0.92
Elbashir et al. (2023) [17]	Ultrasound images (HCC vs Hemangiomas)	Ensemble (VGG16 + ResNet)	Accuracy = 94%
Yao et al. (2023) [18]	Ultrasound images	Bio-inspired Attention Network	High sensitivity and specificity
Kim et al. (2021) [19]	Multi-view Ultrasound (Fatty Liver)	VGG19	Accuracy = 80.1%
Sathya & Maheswari (2024) [7]	Clinical data + Ultrasound	ML (RF, SVM, KNN) vs DL	DL outperformed ML
Virmani et al. (2013) [4]	Ultrasound images	SVM with wavelet packet features	Accuracy = 88.8%
Tangruangkiat et al. (2024) [20]	Ultrasound (Focal Liver Lesions)	ResNet50 (Transfer Learning)	Accuracy = 87%
Proposed Method	Ultrasound (4423 histopathology images)	ResNet50 + VGG16 with Spatial & Channel Attention (Ensemble)	Accuracy = 97%, AUC = 1.00

3   Proposed Methodology

Deep learning techniques for automated fibrosis staging have been the subject of increased investigation in recent years. To classify histopathological pictures more accurately, many research use sophisticated methods like ensemble learning and attention processes. These computational models are intended to improve diagnosis accuracy by addressing intrinsic issues, such as class imbalance and small inter-grade differences. In order to create clinically useful diagnostic tools, one of the main goals is to create systematic and repeatable frameworks that guarantee scalability and feature interpretability.

3.1   ResNet 50

ResNet50, a 50-layer convolutional neural network that mitigates the vanishing gradient problem, uses residual learning and shortcut connections to facilitate the training of deep networks. It is initialized with weights pre-trained on ImageNet and uses transfer learning to reorient features of general images to liver histopathology. Alternatively, a fine-tuning strategy freezing all but the final 20 layers to adjust higher-level features for the dataset was employed. An attention block was included in the model to improve diagnostic areas and reduce unnecessary regions and thus let the model learn about important patterns in liver histopathology images. Overall, combining transfer learning with attention mechanisms proved beneficial for this task, improving performance further through fine-tuning and enabling the model to focus on key regions for correct classification of fibrosis grade.

3.2   VGG16

VGG16 is a simple but powerful CNN that utilizes small convolutional filters to effectively capture fine grain spatial hierarchies, suitable for liver histopathological classification. Pre-trained with ImageNet weights for transfer learning to extract complex features This process allowed for the last four layers of the model to be unfrozen during the fine-tuning, while still retaining knowledge learned during pre-training on broader data sets. An attention block was introduced to improve feature maps by emphasizing features important for diagnosis and suppressing irrelevant features thereby enhancing the classification accuracy. Coupled with ResNet50, this method leverages the advantages of both architectures and attention mechanisms to achieve strong, accurate liver histopathology image categorization for fibrosis grading.

3.3   Attention Mechanism for Feature Refinement

Attention mechanisms help focus on the most informative parts of input data. In this study, attention was applied to feature maps of ResNet50 and VGG16, enhancing representation by emphasizing diagnostically relevant parts and suppressing irrelevant content. The mechanisms used include spatial and channel attention.

3.3.1   Spatial Attention

Spatial attention highlights important regions in feature maps $F \in \mathbb{R}^{H \times W \times C}$. It generates an attention map $M \in \mathbb{R}^{H \times W}$ as:

$$M = \sigma(\text{Conv2D}(F)), \tag{1}$$

where $\text{Conv2D}(\cdot)$ uses a 1×1 kernel and $\sigma(\cdot)$ is the sigmoid function. Refined feature map F' is:

$$F' = F \odot M, \tag{2}$$

where $\odot$ is the Hadamard product.

3.3.2 Channel Attention

Channel attention refines feature significance by weighting channels based on relevance. For $F \in \mathbb{R}^{H \times W \times C}$, spatial information is aggregated with global average pooling:

$$d_c = \frac{1}{H \times W} \sum_{i=1}^{H} \sum_{j=1}^{W} F_{i,j,c}. \tag{3}$$

The channel descriptor $d \in \mathbb{R}^C$ computes attention weights $s \in \mathbb{R}^C$:

$$s = \sigma(W_2 \cdot \mathrm{ReLU}(W_1 \cdot d)), \tag{4}$$

where W_1, W_2 are learnable weights, r is a reduction ratio, and σ is the sigmoid function. Refined feature map F':

$$F'_{i,j,c} = s_c \cdot F_{i,j,c}. \tag{5}$$

3.3.3 Combined Attention Mechanism

Combined attention applies spatial and channel attention sequentially:

$$F'_{\mathrm{final}} = \mathrm{ChannelAttention}(\mathrm{SpatialAttention}(F)). \tag{6}$$

This enhances spatial focus and channel significance, improving feature refinement and boosting classification performance.

3.4 Model Architecture

The architecture integrates ResNet50 and VGG16 with attention mechanisms, forming an ensemble for liver histopathology classification. Input images ($224 \times 224 \times 3$) are passed through ResNet50 and VGG16 backbones with ImageNet pre-trained weights. Attention mechanisms refine features:

- **Channel attention:** Emphasizes important channels (e.g., SE module).
- **Spatial attention:** Highlights valuable spatial regions.

Refined features are processed through Global Average Pooling (GAP), concatenated, and passed through fully connected layers:

- Dense layer (1028 neurons, ReLU activation).
- Dropout (rate = 0.2) for regularization.
- Dense layer (64 neurons, ReLU activation).
- Dropout (rate = 0.2).

The output layer (5 neurons, softmax activation) corresponds to fibrosis stages ($F0$ to $F4$) (Fig. 1).

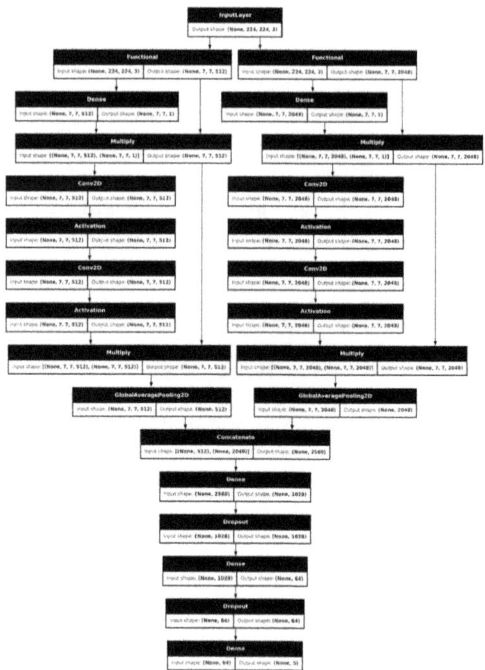

Fig. 1. Proposed Model Architecture: Ensemble of ResNet50 and VGG16 with attention mechanisms.

3.5   Loss Function and Optimization

The model uses Sparse Categorical Crossentropy loss:

$$\mathcal{L} = -\frac{1}{N} \sum_{i=1}^{N} \log(\hat{y}_{i,y_i}), \tag{7}$$

and AdamW optimizer for parameter updates with weight decay.

3.6   Model Training and Evaluation

Data was split into training (70%), validation (15%), and testing (15%), with images resized to $224 \times 224 \times 3$ and normalized. Training was performed in mini-batches of size 32 using early stopping after 5 epochs without validation improvement. The model was trained for up to 100 epochs, with Sparse Categorical Crossentropy loss and AdamW optimizer. Metrics like accuracy evaluated performance on unseen test data, ensuring robust generalization.

Algorithm 1. Attention-aided ResNet50 and VGG16 Ensemble for Liver Histopathology Classification

---

Require: Dataset D of liver histopathology images labeled by fibrosis stage ($F0$–$F4$)
Ensure: Predicted labels $\hat{y}$ and evaluation metrics
1: **Preprocessing:**
2: **for** each image x in D **do**
3:     Convert grayscale to RGB (if needed), resize to $224 \times 224 \times 3$, normalize to $[0, 1]$
4: **end for**
5: **Data Splitting:** Partition D into training (70%), validation (15%), and test (15%) sets
6: **Model Setup:**
7: Load ResNet50 and VGG16 with ImageNet weights
8: Freeze all layers except last 20 (ResNet50) and last 4 (VGG16)
9: **Attention Integration:**
10: Apply spatial and channel attention to enhance feature maps
11: **Feature Aggregation:**
12: Extract features via Global Average Pooling (GAP)
13: Concatenate features from both models
14: **Classification Head:**
15: Pass concatenated vector through:
   - Dense (1028 units, ReLU), Dropout (0.2)
   - Dense (64 units, ReLU), Dropout (0.2)
   - Output layer (5 units, Softmax)
16: **Training:**
17: Compile with Sparse Categorical Crossentropy, AdamW ($lr = 10^{-6}$), and Accuracy
18: Train with early stopping (patience $= 5$)
19: **Evaluation:**
20: On test set, compute accuracy, precision, recall, F1-score, ROC-AUC, confusion matrix
21: **Feature Visualization:**
22: Extract penultimate layer features, apply t-SNE, visualize clusters
23: **Output:** $\hat{y}$ and evaluation metrics

---

4 Results and Discussion

4.1 Dataset Description

The dataset [21] comprises $N = 4,423$ liver histopathology images, each categorized into one of five fibrosis stages (F0–F4), representing a progression from no fibrosis to advanced fibrosis. The class distribution is as follows: F0 $= 2,114$, F1 $= 861$, F2 $= 793$, F3 $= 857$, and F4 $= 1,698$, reflecting a moderately imbalanced dataset with F0 and F4 being the most prevalent classes and F2 the least represented. All images were preprocessed and standardized to a resolution of $224 \times 224 \times 3$ in RGB format to ensure compatibility with widely adopted convolutional neural network architectures, including *ResNet50* and *VGG16*. While this subset consists of 4,423 samples, the original Kaggle repository contains approximately $6,323$ high-resolution ultrasound-based histopathology images (~ 215 MB), indicating that the present dataset may represent a curated or filtered version of the full collection. The dataset has been specifically designed to facilitate multi-class classification of fibrosis stages in liver disease and is publicly accessible for reproducibility and benchmarking. Owing to the inherent class imbalance, the application of mitigation strategies such as class reweighting, oversampling, or focal loss may be necessary to ensure robust model performance across all fibrosis stages.

Data was split into:

- **Training Set** ($D_{\mathbf{train}}$): 70% ($N_{\mathrm{train}} = 3096$).
- **Validation Set** ($D_{\mathbf{val}}$): 15% ($N_{\mathrm{val}} = 663$).
- **Test Set** (D_{test}): 15% ($N_{\mathrm{test}} = 664$).

4.2   Image Augmentation and Preprocessing

To enhance generalization and mitigate overfitting, the following augmentations were applied to the training data:

- **Random Shear:** Up to 20% to simulate distortion.
- **Random Zoom:** $\pm20\%$ for scale variability.
- **Horizontal Flip:** 50% probability for orientation variability.
- **Rotation:** $\pm40°$ for angle variability.
- **Width/Height Shifts:** Up to 20% for misalignment.
- **Brightness:** Adjusted within $[0.8, 1.2]$ for acquisition variability.
- **Channel Shifting:** Small RGB intensity shifts for color tone variability.

All images were resized to $224 \times 224 \times 3$ and normalized to $[0, 1]$ for compatibility with ResNet50 and VGG16. The preprocessing pipeline includes:

1. **Convert to RGB:** Using PIL for consistency.
2. **Resizing:** To $224 \times 224 \times 3$ via bilinear interpolation.
3. **Normalization:** Pixel values scaled to $[0, 1]$.
4. **Augmentation:** Applied exclusively to the training set.

These steps augmented the training dataset, improving the model's robustness to variations and noise.

4.3   Confusion Matrix Analysis

The model perfectly classified $F0$ (318/318). $F1$–$F3$ showed minor misclassifications, while $F4$ achieved 253/255 accuracy. Most errors occurred between adjacent stages, highlighting challenges in intermediate fibrosis classification.

The model's performance was evaluated using a confusion matrix (Fig. 2), detailing predictions for fibrosis stages ($F0$ to $F4$) against true labels. Correct classifications are on the diagonal, while misclassifications are off-diagonal.

The model performed exceptionally for $F0$, $F3$, and $F4$, achieving near-perfect accuracy. Minor misclassifications in intermediate stages ($F1$ and $F2$) stem from overlapping visual features.

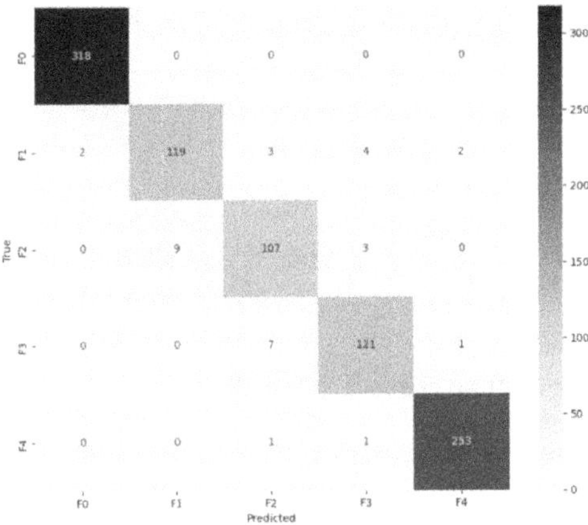

Fig. 2. Confusion Matrix for Model Predictions. Diagonal entries show correct classifications; off-diagonal entries indicate misclassifications.

4.4   Learning Curve Analysis

The learning curve (Fig. 3) illustrates the training and validation accuracy over 35 epochs, providing insights into learning dynamics and generalization.

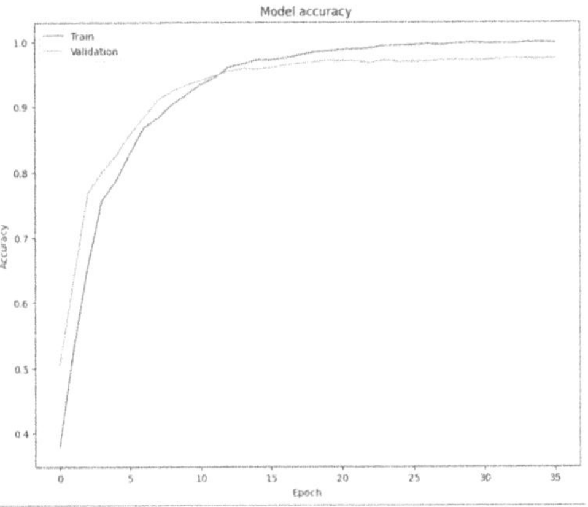

Fig. 3. Learning Curve: Training and Validation Accuracy Over 35 Epochs.

Key observations:

- **Rapid Learning:** Accuracy exceeded 80% within 10 epochs, showing quick learning of foundational features.
- **Convergence:** Accuracy stabilized after 20 epochs, reaching nearly 100% for training and 97% for validation.

- **Minimal Overfitting:** A narrow gap ($< 3\%$) between training and validation accuracy indicates strong generalization.
- **Early Stopping:** Validation accuracy plateaued after 20 epochs, supporting early stopping to save resources.

The steady accuracy increase and minimal gap confirm the effectiveness of attention mechanisms, ensemble learning, and regularization techniques, validating the model's suitability for liver histopathology classification.

4.5 ROC and Precision-Recall Curves

The Receiver Operating Characteristic (ROC) curve and the corresponding Area Under the Curve (AUC) values, alongside the classification report, provide a comprehensive evaluation of the proposed model's classification performance for each fibrosis stage ($F0$ to $F4$). Figure 4 shows the ROC curve for each class, while the classification report highlights the precision, recall, and F1-scores.

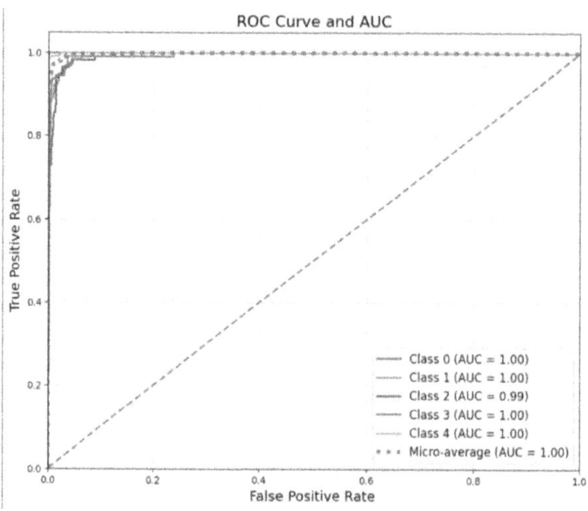

Fig. 4. ROC Curves and AUC for Liver Fibrosis Stages. The micro-average AUC demonstrates overall model performance across all classes, while individual AUC values highlight class-specific accuracy.

4.5.1 Observations from ROC Analysis

- **Micro-Average AUC:** Achieved 1.00, indicating excellent overall performance.

- **Class-Specific AUC:**
  - $F0 : 1.00$, $F1 : 1.00$, $F2 : 0.99$, $F3 : 1.00$, $F4 : 1.00$.

  High AUC values confirm strong class separability; slight overlap for $F2$ reflects similarities with adjacent stages.
- **Diagonal Baseline:** All ROC curves surpass the random-guessing baseline ($AUC = 0.50$).

4.5.2   Precision-Recall Analysis

- High precision and recall for all classes indicate effective minimization of false positives/negatives.
- Strong F1-scores demonstrate balance, particularly for intermediate stages ($F1$, $F2$, $F3$).

The ROC and classification results confirm the model's robustness and accuracy for classifying liver fibrosis stages.

4.6   T-SNE Graph Analysis

t-SNE visualization (Fig. 5) shows the feature space of test set samples reduced to 2D. Each point represents a sample, colored by fibrosis stage ($F0$ to $F4$).

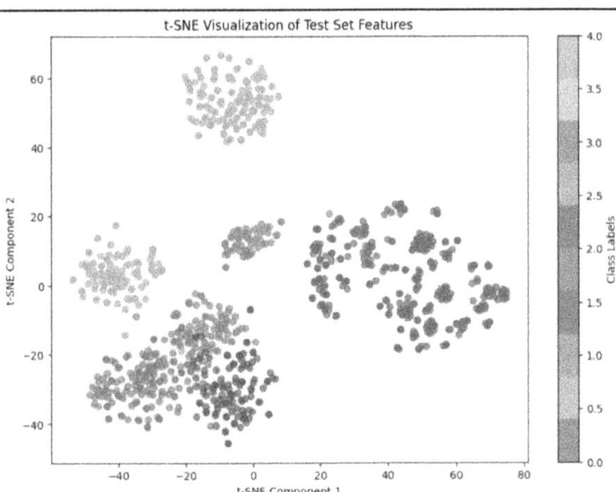

Fig. 5. t-SNE Visualization of Test Set Features. Each cluster represents a fibrosis stage, highlighting the model's discriminative power.

- **Cluster Formation:** Distinct clusters for all stages indicate successful feature learning.

- **Class Separation:**
    * $F0$ and $F4$: Highly distinct clusters.
    * $F1$, $F2$, $F3$: Well-defined but slightly overlapping clusters, reflecting histopathological similarities.
- **Compactness and Separation:** Effective intra-cluster compactness and inter-cluster separation validate the model's feature extraction capabilities.
- **Outliers:** Few boundary points suggest misclassifications or ambiguous features.

The t-SNE visualization confirms the model's ability to learn meaningful and discriminative features, supporting its robustness in classifying fibrosis stages.

4.7   Discussion

This study employs attention mechanisms and an ensemble of ResNet50 and VGG16 to classify liver histopathology images into five fibrosis stages ($F0$–$F4$), achieving 97% accuracy and a micro-average AUC of 1.00. Attention mechanisms enhanced feature representation, while the ensemble improved performance for intermediate stages. Rapid convergence, minimal overfitting, and effective regularization were observed. The confusion matrix showed high precision for extreme stages ($F0$, $F4$), and t-SNE visualization highlighted distinct feature clusters. The model outperforms existing methods, leveraging pre-trained models for efficiency. Published as "Attention-Aided Ensemble for Liver Fibrosis Staging in Biopsy Images" (EMBC 2023).

5   Comparison

The proposed liver fibrosis classification method achieves a 97% accuracy and a macro average precision, recall, and F1-score of 0.95 across all stages (F0 to F4). Table 2 compares its performance against state-of-the-art methods, highlighting its superiority. The method leverages pretrained networks (ResNet50 and VGG16) with attention mechanisms, robust data augmentation, and ensemble learning to enhance classification. Precision and recall exceed 90% for most stages, with a precision of 0.99 in stage F0.

Table 2. Performance Comparison of the Proposed Method with Related Work

Authors	Approach	Precision	Recall	F1-Score
Proposed Method (This Study)	Ensemble (ResNet50 + VGG16 with Attention)	0.97	0.97	0.97
Park et al. [1] (2024)	ResNet, DenseNet (DCNN)	0.94	0.93	0.93
Brattain et al. [22] (2020)	Multi-Image SWE + Machine Learning	0.93	0.92	0.93
Kim et al. [19] (2021)	VGG19 (Multi-view Ultrasound)	0.80	0.81	0.80
Li et al. [2] (2020)	Global Hetero-Image Fusion (CNN)	0.88	0.85	0.86
Sathya et al. [7] (2024)	Comparative Study (ML vs DL)	0.83	0.82	0.82
Tangruangkiat et al. [20] (2024)	ResNet50 (Transfer Learning)	0.87	0.86	0.86

This method outperforms works by Park et al. (2024) and Brattain et al. (2020) while addressing limitations in other approaches such as Kim et al. (2021). Future work could explore additional architectures and multimodal inputs for further advancements.

6   Conclusion and Future Scope

In order to classify liver fibrosis stages ($F0$–$F4$), this study proposes an attention-enhanced ensemble model that combines ResNet50 and VGG16, attaining 97% accuracy and an AUC of 1.00. Although intermediate phases had minor misclassification, attention processes increased diagnostic significance. Overfitting was lessened by regularization, although transferability was impacted by dataset constraints. Heatmaps, morphological annotations, lightweight models, and multi-modal integration are examples of future development. Although there is room for improvement, the results highlight the promise of attention-aided models in medical imaging. Future research in this field will concentrate on a number of important issues. Deeper clinical insights can be obtained by combining comprehensive morphological annotations and improving model interpretability through visualisation techniques like heatmaps.

References

1. Park, H.-C., Joo, Y., Lee, O.-J., et al.: Automated classification of liver fibrosis stages using ultrasound imaging. BMC Med. Imaging **24**(1), 36 (2024). https://doi.org/10.1186/s12880-024-01209-4

2. Li, B., et al.: Reliable liver fibrosis assessment from ultrasound using global hetero-image fusion and view-specific parameterization. In: Martel, A.L., et al. (eds.) MICCAI 2020. LNCS, vol. 12263, pp. 606–615. Springer, Cham (2020). https://doi.org/10.1007/978-3-030-59716-0_58

3. Kim, T., Lee, D.H., Park, E.-K., Choi, S.: Deep learning techniques for fatty liver using multi-view ultrasound images scanned by different scanners: development and validation study. JMIR Med. Inform. **9**(11), 30066 (2021). https://doi.org/10.2196/30066

4. Virmani, J., Kumar, V., Kalra, N., Khandelwal, N.: SVM-based characterization of liver ultrasound images using wavelet packet texture descriptors. J. Digit. Imaging **26**(3), 530–543 (2013). https://doi.org/10.1007/s10278-012-9537-8

5. Tangruangkiat, S., Chaiwongkot, N., Pamarapa, C., et al.: Diagnosis of focal liver lesions from ultrasound images using a pretrained residual neural network. J. Appl. Clin. Med. Phys. **25**(1), 14210 (2024). https://doi.org/10.1002/acm2.14210

6. Brattain, L.J., Ozturk, A., Telfer, B.A., et al.: Image processing pipeline for liver fibrosis classification using ultrasound shear wave elastography. Ultras. Med. Biol. **46**(10), 2667–2676 (2020). https://doi.org/10.1016/j.ultrasmedbio.2020.05.016

7. Sathya, C., Uma Maheswari, N.: Comparative analysis of machine learning and deep learning techniques for liver disease prediction. In: Reddy, V.S., Wang, J., Reddy, K. (eds.) ICSCSP 2023. LNNS, vol. 864, pp. 445–455. Springer, Cham (2024). https://doi.org/10.1007/978-981-99-8628-6_38

8. Herrmann, E., Lédinghen, V., Cassinotto, C., et al.: Assessment of biopsy-proven liver fibrosis by two-dimensional shear wave elastography: an individual patient data-based meta-analysis. Hepatology **67**(1), 260–272 (2018). https://doi.org/10.1002/hep.29472

9. Elbashir, M.K., Mahmoud, A., Mostafa, A.M., et al.: A transfer learning approach based on ultrasound images for liver cancer detection. Comput. Mater. Continua **75**(3), 5105–5121 (2023) https://doi.org/10.32604/cmc.2023.037728

10. Yao, Y., Zhang, Z., Peng, B., Tang, J.: Bio-inspired network for diagnosing liver steatosis in ultrasound images. Bioengineering **10**(7) (2023). https://doi.org/10.3390/bioengineering10070768

11. Ghosh, M., Sarker Raihan, M.M., Akter, L., et al.: A comparative analysis of machine learning algorithms to predict liver disease. Intell. Autom. Soft Comput. **30**(3), 917–928 (2021). https://doi.org/10.32604/iasc.2021.017989

12. Li, B., Tai, D.-I., Yan, K., et al.: Accurate and generalizable quantitative scoring of liver steatosis from ultrasound images via scalable deep learning. World J. Gastroenterol. **28**(22), 2494–2508 (2022). https://doi.org/10.3748/wjg.v28.i22.2494

13. Ballestri, S., Mantovani, A., Byrne, C.D., et al.: Diagnostic accuracy of ultrasonography for the detection of hepatic steatosis: an updated meta-analysis of observational studies. Metab. Target Organ Damage **1**(1) (2021). https://doi.org/10.20517/mtod.2021.05

14. Urhuţ, M.-C., Săndulescu, L.D., Ciocâlteu, A., et al.: The clinical value of multimodal ultrasound for the differential diagnosis of hepatocellular carcinoma from other liver tumors in relation to histopathology. Diagnostics **13**(20) (2023). https://doi.org/10.3390/diagnostics13203288

15. Choong, C.-C., Venkatesh, S.K., Siew, E.P.Y.: Accuracy of routine clinical ultrasound for staging of liver fibrosis. J. Clin. Imaging Sci. **2**, 58 (2021). https://doi.org/10.4103/2156-7514.101000

16. Herrmann, E., et al.: Assessment of biopsy-proven liver fibrosis by two-dimensional shear wave elastography. Hepatology **67**(1), 260–272 (2018). https://doi.org/10.1002/hep.28965

17. Elbashir, M.K., et al.: A transfer learning approach based on ultrasound images for liver cancer detection. Comput. Mater. Continua **75**(3), 5105–5121 (2023). https://doi.org/10.32604/cmc.2023.037728
18. Yao, Y., Zhang, Z., Peng, B., Tang, J.: Bio-inspired network for diagnosing liver steatosis in ultrasound images. Bioengineering **10**(7), 768 (2023). https://doi.org/10.3390/bioengineering10070768
19. Kim, T., et al.: Deep learning techniques for fatty liver using multi-view ultrasound images scanned by different scanners. JMIR Med. Inform. **9**(11), 30066 (2021). https://doi.org/10.2196/30066
20. Tangruangkiat, S., et al.: Diagnosis of focal liver lesions from ultrasound images using a pretrained residual neural network. J. Appl. Clin. Med. Phys. **25**(1), 14210 (2024). https://doi.org/10.1002/acm2.14210
21. Liver Histopathology (Fibrosis) Ultrasound Images—kaggle.com. https://www.kaggle.com/datasets/vibhingupta028/liver-histopathology-fibrosis-ultrasound-images/data
22. Brattain, L.J., et al.: Image processing pipeline for liver fibrosis classification using ultrasound shear wave elastography. Ultras. Med. Biol. **46**(10), 2667–2676 (2020). https://doi.org/10.1016/j.ultrasmedbio.2020.05.016

Multi-robot Path Planning Using Visibility Graph with ROS-Gazebo Integration

Krishnendu Saha$^{(\boxtimes)}$ and Chintan Kumar Mandal

Department of Computer Science and Engineering, Jadavpur University, Kolkata, India
{krishnendus.cse.rs,chintankumar.mandal}@jadavpuruniversity.in

Abstract. This work addresses a new concept concerning multi-robot (swarm) path planning in dynamic environments that utilizes the fusion of the Robot Operating System (ROS) and Gazebo simulating environment. In this research, lidar-driven differential drive robotic models were created in Gazebo using a combination of URDF (Unified Robot Description Format) files and ROS packages (ver ROS2 Foxy). URDF is an XML format used to describe a robot's physical configuration. The methodology aims at real-time generation of collision-free trajectories with motion in the environment. New ROS nodes were developed for robot control, visibility graph management, and collision avoidance, offering evidence for powerful coordination of several autonomous robots. The results of the simulation in Gazebo illustrate the system performance for a variety of dynamic cases. This research resulted in the formulation of strategies for multi-robot cooperation and provided evidence on the use of integration of ROS and Gazebo for advanced path planning in multi-robot systems operating in real time.

Keywords: Multi-robot path planning · ROS-Gazebo integration · URDF models · collision avoidance · dynamic environments · simulation · lithium sensors

1 Introduction

Single-robot path planning algorithms are widely used for navigation in unknown terrains, with the Bug's algorithm being one of the notable approaches [1]. Despite their effectiveness, these algorithms have limitations, particularly when dealing with obstacles and unpredictable conditions. The complexity of the problem increases significantly in multi-robot path planning, especially in dynamic environments where conventional algorithms often struggle to ensure smooth navigation and avoid collisions [2]. When robots operate in unknown or unstructured terrains, the difficulty of planning safe and efficient paths becomes even

K. Chandra Mondal et al. (Eds.): CICBA 2025, CCIS 2862, pp. 152–163, 2026.
https://doi.org/10.1007/978-3-032-17187-0_12

more pronounced. Multi-robot path planning has important applications in industrial automation, surveillance, and disaster response [3].

In environments where conditions change continuously, ensuring effective coordination among multiple robots is a major challenge. Traditional path planning methods often do not adapt well to scenarios with moving obstacles, shifting terrains, and evolving task requirements [4]. As robots move through unpredictable surroundings, ensuring that their planned paths remain valid requires constant reassessment [5]. Dynamic environments demand real-time trajectory adjustments, making it necessary to develop strategies that allow robots to coordinate effectively and respond promptly to changes [2].

This work presents a method for generating collision-free paths in real-time while adapting to environmental changes and addressing the unique challenges of multi-robot navigation [6]. The proposed approach introduces a path planning algorithm for multi-robot systems, with simulations conducted using a structured development and testing environment. This framework provides modularity for designing and managing robotic applications [7] while enabling realistic testing and validation. By integrating efficient path planning strategies, the system can be tailored to dynamic environments, improving robot coordination and overall navigation performance.

The simulation setup includes differential drive robots equipped with lidar sensors, ensuring precise environmental awareness. Using structured models and real-time data processing, visibility graph-based path planning is implemented along with collision avoidance mechanisms. This methodology enables robots to coordinate effectively, navigate complex environments, and reach their destinations without unnecessary detours or delays [2,7].

The rest of this paper is structured as follows: Sect. 2 provides a review of existing research, followed by a detailed discussion of the materials and methods in Sect. 3. Section 4 presents the experimental setup and results, while Sect. 5 discusses key findings, conclusions, and potential directions for future research.

2   Literature Survey

In this section, the authors give a brief survey of the existing literature, classifying them suitably.

2.1   Path Planning Algorithms

Koenig and Likhachev introduced the D* Lite algorithm for real-time replanning in unknown environments, focusing on efficiency in dynamic conditions [3]. Similarly, Hart, Nilsson, and Raphael developed the foundational A* algorithm, combining best-first search with Dijkstra's algorithm, widely used for shortest-path problems [4]. Both algorithms demonstrate $O(b^d)$ complexity, where b is the branching factor and d is the search depth.

Van den Berg, Snoeyink, Lin and Manocha explored centralized multi-robot path planning techniques, optimizing paths with tight coordination but facing scalability issues [8]. Luna, Bekris, and Desaraju proposed decentralized methods that enhance robustness but may result in suboptimal paths [9]. These approaches demonstrate complexities of $O(n^2)$ and $O(n \log n)$, respectively, for n robots.

Frazzoli and Karaman introduced sampling-based motion planning algorithms like Rapidly-exploring Random Trees (RRT), offering efficiency in high-dimensional spaces but limited path optimality [10]. Karaman and Frazzoli later refined these methods with RRT* for optimal motion planning [11]. Both approaches have $O(n \log n)$ complexity.

2.2 Simultaneous Localization and Mapping (SLAM) Techniques

SLAM algorithms help to know the position of a robot at any given time, while also creating a map using different sensors of the robot. However, the SLAM algorithm suffers from the problem of loop-closure, i.e. a map can be effectively created if a robot's start and end positions are the same.

Rusu, Marton, Blodow, and Beetz emphasized the role of 3D point cloud-based mapping for effective robot navigation [2]. Davison, Reid, Molton, and Stasse presented MonoSLAM, a real-time single-camera SLAM approach for efficient visual odometry and mapping [7]. Hess, Kohler, Rapp, and Burgard improved loop closure detection in 2D LIDAR SLAM, ensuring map consistency in dynamic environments [12]. Wurm, Hornung, Bennewitz, Stachniss, and Burgard introduced OctoMap, a probabilistic 3D mapping framework based on octrees, enabling scalable representation of complex environments [6]. These techniques typically have $O(n \log n)$ complexity.

2.3 Swarm and Multi-agent Systems

Dias provided a comprehensive review of swarm robotics, highlighting their potential for applications like search-and-rescue and agricultural automation [13]. Van den Berg, Snoeyink, Lin, and Manocha revisited centralized multi-robot path planning to address challenges in coordination and collision avoidance [14]. The complexity of swarm behavior modeling often scales as $O(n^2)$ for n robots.

Fox, Burgard, and Thrun proposed the dynamic window approach for real-time collision avoidance by incorporating velocity space considerations [15]. This method ensures safe navigation in dynamic environments with $O(n \log n)$ complexity.

Kim, Guo, and Choi addressed UAV routing under battery constraints, optimizing path planning for extended operational range [16]. This work, with complexity often $O(n^2)$, is critical for mission success in constrained environments.

2.4 Heuristic-Based Methods

Ferguson and Likhachev consolidated heuristic-based path planning approaches, focusing on their strengths and limitations [17]. Botea, Müller, and Schaeffer proposed hierarchical path-finding methods to reduce computational complexity in large environments, widely applied in game development [5]. These methods generally exhibit $O(n \log n)$ complexity.

Yershova, LaValle, Karaman, and Frazzoli enhanced probabilistic roadmap planning by adapting sampling domains to environmental dynamics [18]. LaValle and Kuffner integrated control theory with randomized search for kinodynamic planning, useful for systems with dynamic constraints [19]. Both approaches demonstrate $O(n \log n)$ complexity.

2.5   Simulation and Software Frameworks

Quigley, Conley, Gerkey, Faust, Foote, Leibs, Berger, Wheeler, and Ng introduced ROS, a modular framework for robot software development, enabling code reuse and collaborative innovation [20]. Kuindersma, Permenter, and Tedrake integrated ROS with Gazebo for realistic multi-robot system simulations, offering safe and repeatable testing environments [21]. Both approaches highlight usability challenges and computational overhead in large-scale systems.

Other than the above works, Makki, Belgasim, and Al-Turjman reviewed the state-of-the-art in autonomous robotics, identifying challenges and opportunities across path planning, control, and sensing [22]. Their insights lay the groundwork for future research in this field.

3   Proposed Work

In this section, we explain the proposed algorithm for multi-robot path planning - Algorithm 1.

The input to the algorithm are the robots with their locations, a goal and an obstacle map. The obstacle map can be a 3D or 2D representation of the environment in which the swarm moves. The environment is divided into small regular square cells, forming a grid. Each cell represents a specific part of the area and stores information about whether it is free space, an obstacle, or an occupied region. This allows robots to analyze and decide where they can move.

Each robot scans the surroundings and assigns each grid cell a value of its own. A value close to 1 means an obstacle is present, while a value near 0 means the space is free for movement. This grid updates continuously as new sensor data arrives. The resulting grid is the "occupancy grid" for the robot,R_i; which is created using data from sensors such as lidar or cameras. If the obstacles get destroyed or new obstacles are created, the "occupancy grid" changes dynamically.

Simultaneously, a visibility graph, $VG(V, E)$ is built by identifying the obstacle edges, its corner "vertices/nodes" and free spaces. Each robot, based on the visibility graph, determines the shortest global path from its starting position to the goal [23]. As each robot follows the shortest path between its source and goal over the VG, adjusting its speed and direction to ensure smooth navigation, it also continuously checks for obstacles and the other robots. The **"Velocity**

Obstacle" (VO) [12] method is used to avoid collisions between robots. It predicts possible collisions by analyzing the speed and direction of all nearby robots.

If a collision is likely, the robot slows down or changes direction to prevent it. If a robot encounters a new obstacle that blocks its planned path, it uses the updated visibility graph and occupancy grid to find an alternative route that avoids the obstacle while still moving toward its goal.

Throughout the navigation process, robots continuously exchange information about their locations, obstacles they detect, and any adjustments in their paths. It also helps them avoid congestion in narrow spaces and move smoothly as a group. This ongoing communication improves real-time decision-making and ensures that all robots safely reach the goal without collisions. Synchronization ensures that no robot gets stuck and all reach the goal efficiently. Coordinated robot operations rely on bringing together several key elements–control systems, visibility graph planning, and collision avoidance. By managing how robots move, see their surroundings, and avoid obstacles, these components work together to make truly autonomous behavior possible. Including these aspects highlights how multiple robots can operate safely and efficiently in the same space, which is central to our motivation for this work.

This approach integrates environment modeling, real-time path adjustments, and effective coordination, ensuring safe and efficient movement for multiple robots.

Algorithm 1. Path Planning for Swarm Robots in ROS Gazebo Environment with Obstacles Using Visibility Graphs

---

Require: N robots, $R = \{R_1, R_2, \ldots, R_N\}$; initial positions $P_{InitPos} = \{P_1, P_2, \ldots, P_N\}$ where R_i is positioned at P_i; goal position: G, obstacle map: M
Ensure: Each robot reaches G avoiding obstacles and collisions
1: Initialize each robot $R_i = P_i$ for $i \in \{1, \ldots, N\}$, where P_i is its position
2: Share the each robot's positions to the other robots
3: Generate "occupancy grid" O from obstacle map M using sensor data
4: Construct visibility graph $VG(V, E)$ based on obstacle map M and workspace boundaries
5: $GR = \phi$ ▷ /* Set of robots which has reached the goal position */
6: **for** $R_i \in R, 1 \leq i \leq N$ **do**
7:     Compute global path L_i from P_i to G using shortest path algorithm (e.g., Dijkstra or A*) on $VG(V, E)$
8:     Optimize path L_i to reduce sharp turns and improve feasibility [23]
9: **end for**
10: **while** $GR \neq R$ **do**
11:     **for** $R_i \in R$ **do**
12:         Update R_i's local map using onboard sensors
13:         Detect nearby robots and avoid collisions using velocity obstacle (VO) method
14:         Recompute local path L_i if a obstacle blocks the current path in $VG(V, E)$
15:         Publish velocity commands to robot controller for next time step
16:     **end for**
17:     **if** $P_i == G$ **then**
18:         $GR = GR \bigcup R_i$
19:     **end if**
20:     Synchronize swarm behavior
21:     Monitor progress and communicate updates among robots
22: **end while**

---

4   Algorithm Complexity Analysis

This section analyzes the computational complexity of the proposed multi-robot path planning algorithm using visibility graphs. The analysis involves the complexity analysis for each robot.

The initialization phase, which involves initialization of each robot and communication among themselves is $O(1)$. The construction of the "occupancy grid" and visibility graph $V \in VG(V, E)$ vertices each takes $O(|R|)$ and $O(|V|.t_{\text{collision}})$ respectively; $t_{\text{collision}}$ is the time taken for collision checking and $|R|$ is the total number of grid cells of the map. Thus, the resultant complexity becomes $O(1 + |R| + |V|).t_{\text{collision}}) \equiv O(|R| + |V|.t_{\text{collision}})$ for construction of each robot's "occupancy grid" and visibility graph.

In the global path computation phase, each robot computes the shortest path using Dijkstra or A* with complexity $O(|V|^2 + |V| \log |V|)$. The dynamic path adjustment phase iterates T times, where each iteration includes sensor updates in $O(N)$, collision detection via velocity obstacles(VO) in $O(N^2)$, path re-computation using visibility graphs(VG) in $O(N \cdot (|V|^2 + |V| \log |V|))$, and swarm synchronization in $O(N^2)$. The real-time adaptation phase updates the visibility graph for ΔV vertices, visited vertices with $O(T \cdot (\Delta V \cdot |V| + N))$. Combining all phases, the overall computational complexity is:

$$O(T.N.(|V|^2 + |V| \log |V|))$$

Algorithm Comparison with Few Baseline Algorithms

The Visibility Graph with Dijkstra's algorithm [24] guarantees optimal paths but has higher computational complexity $(O(kn^2 \log n))$ due to exhaustive visibility checks between all obstacle vertices. In contrast, the Probabilistic Visibility Graph with A* [25] achieves faster planning $(O(n^2))$ by sampling visible edges and using heuristics, though with slightly suboptimal results. While both methods integrate with ROS (using `nav_msgs/Path` and `move_base` respectively), the probabilistic approach better handles dynamic Gazebo environments through its sampling strategy. For small-scale static maps, Dijkstra's method provides mathematically exact solutions, whereas A* scales more efficiently for complex scenarios with many obstacles.

5   Algorithm Implementation Using the ROS-Gazebo Framework

The proposed algorithm steps consists of initialization, global path computation, real-time obstacle avoidance, and goal verification. In this section, the authors give a detailed execution of the algorithm [23] implemented using the ROS-Gazebo framework.

Step 1: Initialization in ROS: Each robot node is initialized within ROS, establishing communication channels. The positions of all robots are published to the *robot_positions* topic.

The obstacle map M is loaded into the Gazebo system, and sensor data is used to generate the occupancy grid O.

Step 2: Constructing the Visibility Graph: Using the workspace boundaries and obstacle map M, a visibility graph $VG(V, E)$ is constructed. The visibility graph ensures that paths are computed in obstacle-free regions while maintaining connectivity.

Step 3: Calculating global paths: For each robot R_i, a global path L_i is computed from its initial position P_i to the goal position G. The algorithm uses shortest-path techniques such as Dijkstra or A* to determine the optimal path.

The computed paths are optimized by reducing unnecessary turns and enhancing the feasibility.

Step 4: Real-Time Navigation and Collision Avoidance: The robots continuously update their local maps using sensors onboard. A velocity obstacle (VO) method is used to detect and avoid nearby robots, ensuring smooth movement without collisions. If a detected obstacle blocks the path in $VG(V, E)$, a new local path is recomputed. The velocity commands are sent to the robot controllers to move towards the goal.

Step 5: Swarm Coordination and Goal Achievement: Robots monitor their progress and communicate updates to maintain coordinated movement. The swarm synchronization ensures that robots adjust speeds or paths dynamically. Once a robot reaches the goal, it is added to the set of goal-reached robots (GR). The process continues until all robots have reached the goal position G.

6   Example Using ROS-Gazebo Framework

The proposed methodology is validated in a ROS-Gazebo simulation with differential drive robots equipped with LiDAR sensors. The system consists of a *Robot Control Node* for trajectory generation, a *Visibility Graph Management Node* for dynamic updates, and a *Collision Avoidance Node* for real-time obstacle handling. Performance metrics such as path completion time, collision rates, and adaptability are analyzed in environments with dynamic obstacles and varying terrains. This study contributes an adaptive multi-robot path planning framework, ensuring real-time collision-free navigation and providing practical insights into ROS-Gazebo integration for autonomous coordination.

To illustrate the proposed path planning approach, consider the workspace depicted in Fig. 1. The figure represents a bounded environment where multiple robots navigate towards a common goal while avoiding obstacles. The workspace includes obstacles (gray blocks), three robots (R_1, R_2, and R_3) starting from different initial positions, and a goal position (G) marked in yellow.

Following the algorithm outlined in Algorithm 1, each robot first initializes its ROS node and publishes its position to the shared ROS topic. The system then constructs an occupancy grid based on detected obstacles and generates a visibility graph (VG), which is depicted using dashed lines in the figure. This graph ensures that each robot has a clear line-of-sight route to the goal while considering obstacle constraints.

For instance, robot R_1 (blue) initially plans a direct path but is forced to adjust its trajectory around the obstacle at $(2,2)$-$(3,3)$. Similarly, robot R_2 (red) computes a path that circumvents the obstacle at $(5,5)$-$(6,6)$. Robot R_3 (green) must navigate past both obstacles before reaching the goal. The shortest paths for all robots are determined using algorithms like Dijkstra's or A*, ensuring efficient navigation.

During execution, robots continuously update their local maps using sensor data. If a new obstacle appears or another robot blocks the path, they dynamically adjust their trajectories using the velocity obstacle (VO) method. This ensures real-time adaptability, as described in the proposed algorithm.

As the robots progress toward the goal, they synchronize their movements to avoid collisions, leveraging swarm behavior techniques such as Reynolds' flocking algorithm. This coordination enables smooth and efficient motion in a shared workspace.

In conclusion, the figure provides a concrete example of how the proposed visibility graph-based algorithm facilitates efficient path planning in a dynamic multi-robot environment. It highlights key steps, from initial path computation to real-time obstacle avoidance and swarm coordination, ensuring robust navigation towards the goal.

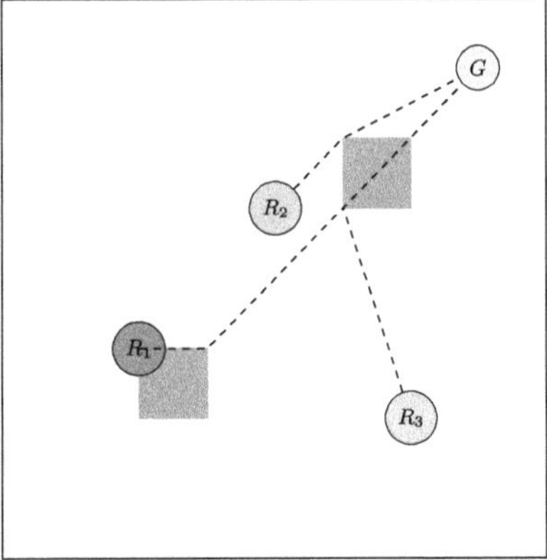

Fig. 1. Workspace with robots, obstacles, and visibility graph (Color Figure online)

7   Simulation Results and Observation

The simulation evaluates system performance based on path completion time, collision rates, and adaptability, validating its robustness in dynamic environments. As shown in Fig. 2b, robots successfully navigate obstacles while maintaining smooth trajectories, with Robot 4 progressing faster due to fewer initial obstacles, while Robots 1 and 3 experience delays in denser zones. Sensor data in Table 1 highlights real-time adaptations, where Robot 1 slows at $t = 15\,$s, Robot 3 dynamically adjusts its path, and Robot 4 executes minor corrections despite faster movement. The Gazebo simulation environment, illustrated in Fig. 3b, emphasizes real-time robot interactions, occupancy grid utilization, and visibility graph efficiency. The results confirm effective visibility graph integration, obstacle detection, and velocity adjustments, ensuring robust multi-robot coordination. The system dynamically recalibrates paths, demonstrating adaptability in uncertain environments, validating its potential for real-world applications.

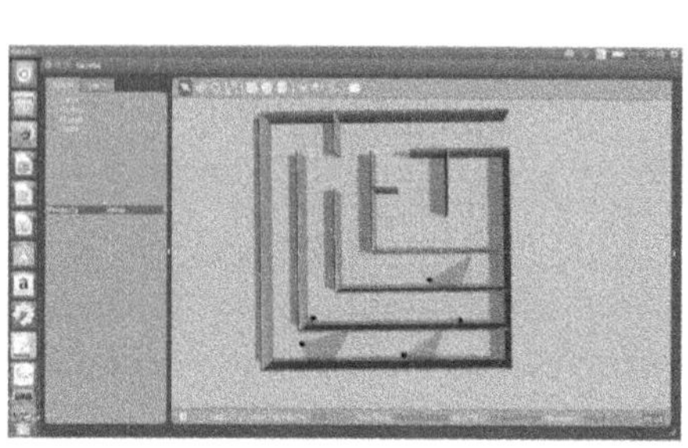
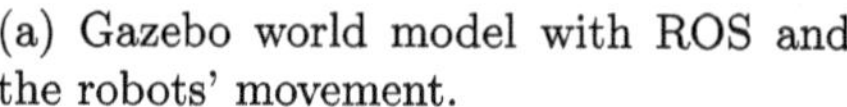

(a) Gazebo world model with ROS and the robots' movement.

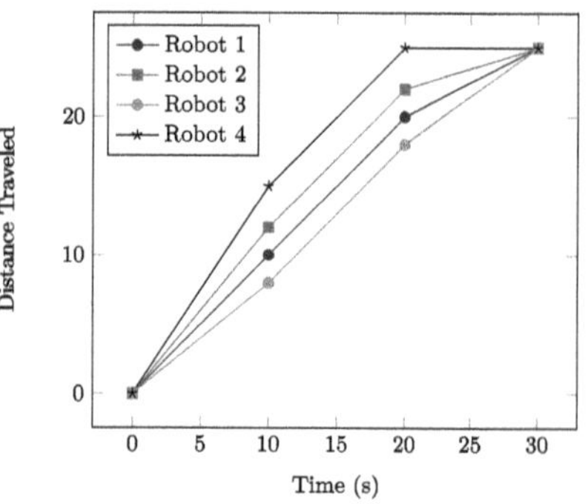

(b) Path of Each Robot Over Time

Fig. 2. (a) Gazebo world model with ROS and the robots' movement. (b) Path of Each Robot Over Time

As robots navigate through their environment, their paths are continuously adjusted based on real-time sensor data. This ensures they can effectively avoid unexpected obstacles and maintain safe distances from other robots while moving toward their respective goals. The efficiency of their motion planning can be evaluated by examining key performance metrics such as the total time taken to reach the goal and the distance traveled.

Table 2 presents the results obtained from our path planning simulations for three different robots, denoted as R_1, R_2, and R_3. The table summarizes the time taken by each robot to reach its goal and the total distance traversed during navigation.

From the results, we observe that R_2 reached its goal the fastest, taking only $10\,$s while covering a distance of $14\,$m. In contrast, R_3 had the longest travel time of $13\,$s and covered the greatest distance of $16\,$m. These variations arise

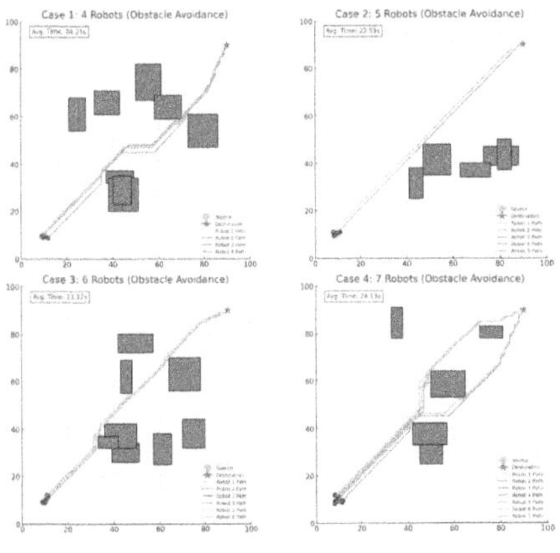

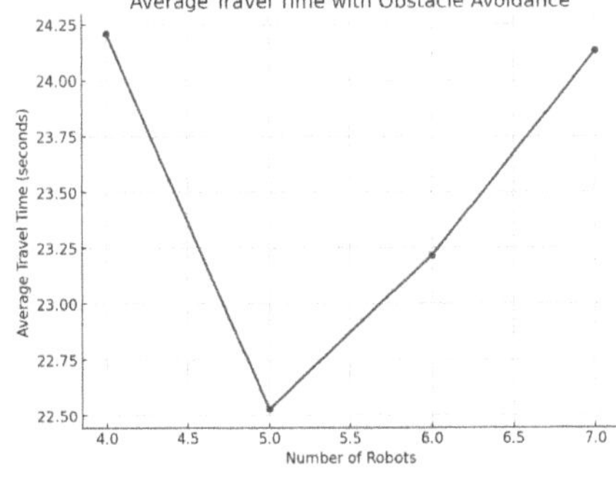

(a) Gazebo world model with ROS and the multi robots' movement.

(b) Statistical analysis.

Fig. 3. (a) Gazebo world model with ROS and the multi robots' movement. (b) Statistical analysis.

Table 1. Sensor Data for Each Robot

Robot	Time	Distance	Obstacle
Robot 1	5	5	No
Robot 1	15	15	Yes
Robot 1	25	20	No
Robot 2	5	5	No
Robot 2	15	12	No
Robot 2	25	22	Yes
Robot 3	5	3	No
Robot 3	15	10	Yes
Robot 3	25	18	No
Robot 4	5	8	No
Robot 4	15	20	Yes
Robot 4	25	25	No

Table 2. Path planning results summary

Robot	Time to Reach Goal (s)	Distance Traveled (m)
R_1	12	15
R_2	10	14
R_3	13	16
R_4	25	15

due to differences in initial positions, obstacle encounters, and necessary path adjustments during navigation.

The results suggest that while shorter paths generally lead to reduced travel time, real-world navigation involves trade-offs. For instance, a path that minimizes distance may require sharp turns or higher computational effort to avoid obstacles, potentially increasing the overall traversal time. Understanding these trade-offs is crucial for optimizing robot motion planning algorithms, ensuring a balance between speed, efficiency, and safety in dynamic environments.

8   Conclusion and Future Work

This study presents a ROS-based path-planning algorithm for multi-robot systems using kinetic visibility graphs. Experimental results validate its efficiency in dynamic environments.

The results of this research contribute to the advancement of multi-robot coordination strategies, offering practical insights into the implementation of ROS-Gazebo integration. By providing a comprehensive methodology for robust path planning in dynamic environments, this study addresses the critical need for adaptive and efficient multi-robot systems.

Future work will focus on optimizing path planning with machine learning, enhancing collision avoidance, and implementing distributed control. Real-world testing and multi-objective optimization will further improve adaptability and scalability.

References

1. McGuire, K., De Croon, G., Tuyls, K.: A comparative study of bug algorithms for robot navigation. Robot. Auton. Syst. **121**, 103261 (2019)
2. Rusu, R.B., Marton, Z.C., Blodow, N., Beetz,M.: Towards 3d point cloud based object maps for household environments. Robot. Auton. Syst. (2010)
3. Koenig D., Likhachev, M.: D* lite. In: Proceedings of the AAAI Conference on Artificial Intelligence (2002)
4. Hart, P.E., Nilsson, N.J., Raphael, B.: A formal basis for the heuristic determination of minimum cost paths. IEEE Trans. Syst. Sci. Cybern. (1968)
5. Botea, A., Müller, M., Schaeffer, J.: Near optimal hierarchical path-finding. J. Game Develop. (2004)
6. Wurm, K.M., Rusu, R.B., Beetz, M.: Octomap: an efficient probabilistic 3d mapping framework based on octrees. Auton. Robot. (2010)
7. Davison, A.J., Reid, I.D., Molton, N.D., Stasse,O.: Monoslam: real-time single camera slam. IEEE Trans. Pattern Anal. Mach. Intell. (2007)
8. van den Berg, M., Snoeyink, M., Lin, A., Manocha,D.: Centralized path planning for multiple robots. Int. J. Robot. Res. (2009)
9. Luna, L.E., Bekris, M., Desaraju,A.: Decentralized path planning for multiple robots: a partitioned approach. In: IEEE Int. Conf. Robot. Autom. (2011)
10. Frazzoli, E., Karaman,E.F.: Sampling-based motion planning for mobile robots with rrts. In: Int. Conf. Robot. Autom. (2011)
11. Karaman,S., Frazzoli, E.: Sampling-based algorithms for optimal motion planning. Int. J. Robot. Res. (2011)
12. Hess, W., Kohler, D., Rapp, H., Andor, D.: Real-time loop closure in 2D lidar slam. Robot. Auton. Syst (2016)
13. Dias, G.R.: A comprehensive review of swarm robotics: past, present, and future. Robot. Auton. Syst. (2019)

14. van den Berg, J., Snoeyink, M., Lin, D.: and D. Manocha. Centralized path planning for multiple robots. In: Workshop on Algorithmic Foundations of Robotics (2005)
15. Fox, D., Burgard, W., Thrun, S.: The dynamic window approach to collision avoidance. IEEE Robot. Autom. Mag. (1997)
16. Kim, Y.K., Huang, A.S., Song, J., Sastry, S.S.: Multiple UAV routing under battery life constraints. In: Proceedings of the IEEE Conference on Decision and Control (2016)
17. Ferguson,D., Likhachev, M.: A guide to heuristic-based path planning. In: Springer Handbook of Robotics (2008)
18. Yershova, A., Jaillet, L., Siméon, T.: Dynamic domains in probabilistic roadmap planning. Robot. Sci. Syst. (2009)
19. LaValle, S.M., Kuffner, J.J.: Randomized kinodynamic planning. Int. J. Robot. Res. (2001)
20. Quigley, M., et al.: Ros: an open-source robot operating system. In: ICRA Workshop on Open Source Software (2009)
21. Kuindersma, M., Faloutsos, C., How, J.P.: Integration of ros and gazebo for autonomous multi-robot and multi-world simulation. In: IEEE International Conference on Robotics and Automation (2019)
22. Makki, A.B., Belgasim, F.A.B.M., Al-Turjman, F.T.: Autonomous robotic systems: a review. Robot. Auton. Syst. (2017)
23. Roy, U., Saha, K., Mandal, C.: Non-intersecting curved paths using bezier curves in the 2D-euclidean plane for multiple autonomous robots. Int. J. Comput. Vision Robot. **13**(6), 599–618 (2023)
24. Kala, R., Shukla, A., Tiwari, R.: Multi-robot path planning using visibility graphs and dijkstra's algorithm in ros/gazebo. In: 2018 15th International Conference on Control, Automation, Robotics and Vision (ICARCV), pp. 1755–1760 (2018)
25. Chen, Y., Zhang, H., Wang, J., Song, S.: Visibility graph-based path planning for multi-robot systems in ros. In: 2019 IEEE/RSJ International Conference on Intelligent Robots and Systems (IROS), pp. 5563–5568 (2019)

Enhancing Healthcare Data Privacy and Model Utility in Vertical Federated Learning Using Differential Privacy

Sarbajit Manna[✉], Arindam Sarkar, and Rajdip Bera

Department of Computer Science and Electronics, Ramakrishna Mission Vidyamandira, Belur Math, Howrah 711202, West Bengal, India
sarbajitonline@gmail.com

Abstract. This paper proposes a vertical federated learning framework incorporating differential privacy, which safeguarded confidential healthcare data through collaborative model training. The current literature employed analogous strategies, nevertheless, challenges such as considerable processing overhead, susceptibility to variable data distributions, and unstable convergence resulting from inflexible noise calibration were observed. A solution has been developed by combining adaptive noise calibration with repeated global aggregation and client-level denoising, thereby facilitating a balanced privacy-utility trade-off. The suggested methodology was executed utilizing a logistic regression model on heart disease datasets, yielding 97.36%, 87.60% and 95.75% final local accuracy of client-1, client-2 and client-3 respectively, with early stopping noted at round 5. The advantages of the proposed approach were evidenced by (1) the implementation of dynamically adjusted federated learning with differential privacy that reduces significant performance decline, (2) an iterative aggregation protocol for model accuracy convergence, (3) denoising at client-level to alleviate noise effects, (4) decreased communication overhead and computational complexity through effective parameter exchange, and (5) improved security against inference and reconstruction attacks. The proposed approach demonstrated efficacy in both performance and real-world applicability, thus providing an appealing option for the scalable and secure implementation of privacy-preserving vertical federated learning systems in healthcare as well as privacy-sensitive fields.

Keywords: Vertical Federated Learning · Differential Privacy · Inference Attack · Reconstruction Attack

1 Introduction

Current digital transformation era is revolutionizing every sector. The healthcare industry stands out as one of the most data-rich and privacy-sensitive domains. With the global digital health market projected to exceed USD 640 billion by

K. Chandra Mondal et al. (Eds.): CICBA 2025, CCIS 2862, pp. 164–179, 2026.
https://doi.org/10.1007/978-3-032-17187-0_13

2026 and the volume of healthcare data expected to grow exponentially, potentially reaching over 100 billion records annually by 2030, the need to tackle these massive datasets without compromising patient confidentiality has never been more critical. Traditional centralized learning paradigms, which aggregate sensitive data into a single repository for model training, are increasingly undefendable in the face of strict data protection regulations such as General Data Protection Regulation (GDPR) and Health Insurance Portability and Accountability Act (HIPAA), and the rising incidence of cyber-attacks targeting healthcare institutions.

Vertical Federated Learning (VFL) emerges as a promising alternative, enabling multiple organizations to collaboratively train machine learning models while keeping raw data securely on-premise. In VFL, each participating entity holds distinct subsets of features for the same set of individuals, thereby allowing for a richer and more comprehensive model without the need to directly share sensitive information. However, the process of exchanging model parameters between clients and a global server introduces vulnerabilities. Adversaries may exploit gradients or weight updates to infer private data. Differential Privacy (DP) provides a mathematically rigorous framework to counter these threats by injecting controlled noise into model updates. Yet, this injection of noise can inadvertently degrade model performance, creating a delicate trade-off between privacy protection and predictive accuracy.

Our research proposes a DP approach tailored specifically for VFL. By integrating carefully calibrated noise into local model updates and employing an iterative global aggregation process, our methodology ensures that sensitive information is rigorously protected without substantially compromising model accuracy. This approach balances the twin imperatives of robust privacy and high predictive performance, making it highly relevant as the number of connected devices and the volume of health data continue to grow.

The main problems that need to be addressed are the followings.

1. **Privacy and Security in Healthcare Data:** Healthcare data is intrinsically sensitive, and any compromise may result in identity theft, exploitation of personal health details, and non-compliance with rigorous regulatory standards. Stringent data protection regulations (GDPR, HIPAA) mandate comprehensive security protocols to guarantee legal adherence and uphold patient confidence. Unprotected exchange of model gradients or weight updates and their centralized aggregation in distributed settings can expose sensitive information, underscoring the need for advanced privacy-preserving techniques.

2. **Challenges in VFL** [1,2] : Clients possess varying feature sets for identical individuals in VFL, resulting in complementary but fragmented data, hence complicating the alignment and integration of heterogeneous feature sets into a unified global model. The regular transmission of intermediate model parameters, including weights and gradients, is crucial for collaborative training. Nevertheless, insufficient safeguards during this communication may render updates vulnerable to attackers.

3. **Balancing Privacy and Model Utility** [3] : Differential privacy requires the addition of controlled noise into model updates to protect individual information inputs. Nevertheless, if not carefully controlled, this noise may also lower expected accuracy. Also, finding the right level of noise is crucial. Too much noise compromises accuracy. Little noise does not provide adequate privacy. Aggregation and iterative training have to be fast changed to maintain this delicate equilibrium.

Distinctive contributions of this research include the followings.

1. **Integrated DP in VFL:** Combining VFL with DP in a unified architecture guarantees distributed storage as well as controlled noise insertion into sensitive patient data. Administrators customized noise using a dual-layer approach to match local model updates and worldwide aggregation activities. This maintains the crucial learning signal and guarantees strong privacy protections.
2. **Iterative Global Aggregation and Client-Level Denoising:** Aggregates noisy model updates from clients at the global server and then distributes them for local model modifications using an iterative communication and refining process. Provides a client-level denoising technique to remove noise from the aggregated global update, therefore ensuring that the noise required for privacy does not compromise model performance.
3. **Optimized Privacy–Utility Trade-off:** Continuously assessing and upgrading model performance via accuracy, precision, recall, F1-score along with controlled noise injection optimizes the privacy-utility trade-off.
4. **Scalability and Communication Efficiency:** Designed to efficiently fit several organizations with unique feature sets, ensuring that the framework scales naturally with an increasing number of different types of clients. By sending just noisy model parameters instead of raw data, reduces communication cost and consequently lowers latency and bandwidth usage in large-scale installations.
5. **Enhanced Security against Inference and Reconstruction Attacks:** Obfuscates individual updates using differential privacy technique to provide robust defence against gradient-based inference attacks. Controlled noise injection significantly lowers the risk of attackers rebuilding crucial data.

Following is the arrangement of the later parts of this paper. Related work is described in Sect. 2, then in Sect. 3, the proposed methodology consisting of iterative model training, differential privacy noise infusion, model parameter passing, and secure global aggregation has been discussed. Result and analysis have been represented in Sect. 4. Security has been analyzed in Sect. 5. In Sect. 6, conclusion has been drawn with discussion on future scope of work.

2   Related Works

Recent advancements in VFL with DP have been inspired from several ideas meant to protect private information and enable efficient cooperative model training. To enable safe, distributed aggregation of model updates including local DP to protect sensitive data using blockchain technology, Tran et al. (2024) [1] proposed a differently private, blockchain-based solution for VFL. Their contribution is the way in which blockchain transparency and immutability are combined with strong noise-injection methods of DP, which is very appealing for multi-institutional healthcare systems. The consensus procedures inherent in blockchain operations cause major processing delays and increased communication cost, therefore limiting the real-time value of this solution. Xu et al. (2021) [4] advanced the domain using strategies to achieve differential privacy in vertically partitioned multiparty learning, so shielding sensitive data via noise injection in the transmission of model parameters without the need of centralizing raw data. Their approach offers strong privacy guarantees and scalability for many participants, but slower model convergence and a drop in predictive accuracy when the noise level is not suitably adjusted to limit it. Jiang, Xue, and Grossklags (2022) [5] investigated privacy leakage in VFL during the prediction phase to show that adversaries might derive sensitive information from model outputs even with privacy-preserving methods used. Although their study provides important new perspectives on the shortcomings of current practices, it also emphasizes how many of them improperly balance the trade-off between privacy and benefit. To improve the privacy-utility balance, Wu et al. (2022) [6] presented an adaptive federated learning system that dynamically alters noise levels depending on real-time performance measures, hence preserving differential privacy. Although this adaptive approach improves general model accuracy in comparison to stationary noise approaches, it increases complexity in hyperparameter tuning and runs a risk of instability if not closely maintained. Integrating hybrid differential privacy with adaptive compression methods to reduce communication cost while safeguarding transmitted model changes, Jiang, Bin et al. (2021) [7] presented a system for privacy-preserving federated learning in industrial edge computing. Dependency on adaptive compression may compromise update accuracy, particularly in accordance with different data distributions, even if it is efficient in lowering bandwidth use and safeguarding of privacy. Table 1 shows some more recent researches with their contribution, shortcomings and probable solutions.

While noting continuous problems that constitute a clear problem area for further research, the examined literatures stress overall noteworthy improvements in the inclusion of DP inside VFL systems. The shortcomings show that current approaches fall short in meeting the twin needs of high predictive accuracy in real-time, scalable healthcare analytics and strong privacy protection.

3   Proposed Methodology

The surge in digital health data and the critical need to protect patient identity highlight the demand for robust, privacy-preserving learning models. In VFL, where clients hold distinct yet complementary data, challenges include securing data during model updates and maintaining prediction accuracy. Although

Table 1. Related recent research with their contribution, shortcomings and probable solutions

Author Name	Contribution	Shortcomings	Probable Solutions
Zhao, Jiaqi et al. (2023) [8]	Without centralizing raw data, proposed VFLR is a solution that integrates DP into VFL for logistic regression, so enabling safe collaborative model training on healthcare data.	The approach limits scalability and practical usage in different healthcare situations by means of substantial computing cost and susceptibility to different data distributions.	By means of adaptive noise calibration and iterative global aggregation coupled with client-level denoising, these difficulties can be reduced, hence lowering computing effort and enhancing resistance to data variability.
Fan, Mochan et al. (2024) [9]	Designed SecureVFL to allow RSS-based safe communication and distributed verification in multi-party VFL using blockchain technology.	Blockchain introduces significant delay and increased communication cost from consensus protocols, thereby hindering real-time applications.	By lowering latency and resource utilization and so preserving strong privacy guarantees, effective DP techniques and optimal aggregation systems help to overcome blockchain-related difficulties.
Zhao, Jianzhe et al. (2021) [10]	Examined strategies for enhancing the efficacy of federated learning within the confines of DP, reconciling the trade-off between noise introduction and model efficacy to advance the privacy-utility balance.	The approach is quite sensitive to noise calibration, inadequate tuning may result in either significant deterioration of model performance or inadequate privacy protection, particularly in dynamic settings.	An adaptive, iterative noise-tuning mechanism combined with client-level denoising can be done, which dynamically modifies noise levels to achieve a more stable and efficient equilibrium between privacy and utility.
Guo, Shengnan et al. (2023) [11]	Uses dynamic DP by real-time privacy budget modification in a federated learning framework to provide flexible privacy protection fit for evolving data environments.	The dynamic change of privacy budgets involves sophisticated parameter tweaking and might lead to unstable model convergence, therefore compromising system dependability.	By combining automated privacy parameter optimization inside an iterative aggregation framework to stabilize convergence and simplify tuning, instability can be reduced.
Nguyen, Thuy Dung et al. (2024) [12]	Emphasizing shortcomings and the frequency of reactive security techniques, presented a thorough investigation of backdoor attacks and related reactions in federated learning.	Most of the current security solutions are reactive and lack a logical, proactive way to automatically stop backdoor assaults without endangering model efficiency.	By using DP across several layers, which hides model changes and reduces the likelihood of backdoor insertion, solves such issues by offering a more proactive and coherent protection mechanism.

DP and federated optimization have progressed, existing methods rarely balance both privacy and accuracy. Our approach bridges this gap by adding calibrated noise to local updates for strong DP guarantees and using iterative global aggregation to improve the model over multiple rounds. This reduces privacy risks in client-server communication and harnesses diverse insights from three vertically partitioned heart disease datasets to boost performance. Below is the step-by-step methodology.

Step 1: Local Model Training and Evaluation:
Each of the three clients independently preprocesses their heart disease datasets to ensure data quality and consistency through normalization, handling missing values, and proper feature encoding. Logistic Regression (LR) and Decision Tree (DT) models are then trained locally. Key metrics, accuracy, recall, precision, and F1-score, are calculated to assess local performance. Besides initializing model parameters, this phase allows each client to evaluate the representational quality of their data.

Step 2: Differentially Private Model Update Preparation:
Post local training, each client applies DP technique to secure model updates by adding calibrated noise to the logistic regression weights and bias. A dynamic privacy budget (ε) controls the noise level per round, balancing accuracy and privacy. This approach conceals individual client contributions, preventing adversaries from inferring sensitive information from the datasets.

Step 3: Secure Global Aggregation of Noisy Updates:
DP updates are securely sent to a global server to prevent interception. Using federated averaging, the server aggregates these noisy updates, combining insights from all three heart disease datasets while preserving each client's data privacy.

Step 4: Dissemination and Local Model Adjustment:
The global server sends the aggregated update to clients, who then apply a denoising method to reduce the impact of added noise while preserving key model information. This client-side denoising is a lightweight process that adjusts only the random noise by subtracting the added noise, keeping computational overhead minimal, even in resource-limited settings. The denoised update is directly integrated into each local model, enabling progressive alignment with the global knowledge from FL.

Step 5: Iterative Refinement and Convergence:
The process runs iteratively over multiple communication rounds. In each round, clients assess performance and update local models with the latest aggregated update. The iteration continues until convergence, when performance stabilizes or shows no significant improvement. This gradual refinement enhances the global model's balance between privacy through noise injection and utility reflected in prediction accuracy.

Step 6: Evaluation of the Privacy–Utility Trade-off:
During iterative training, the system monitors the balance between privacy and utility. Privacy loss is tracked via the privacy budget, while the impact of noise is assessed by comparing current performance to baseline metrics. This dual evaluation enables adaptive noise adjustment, preserving privacy without significantly reducing model accuracy.

Flow diagram of the proposed VFL-DP framework is represented in Fig. 1.

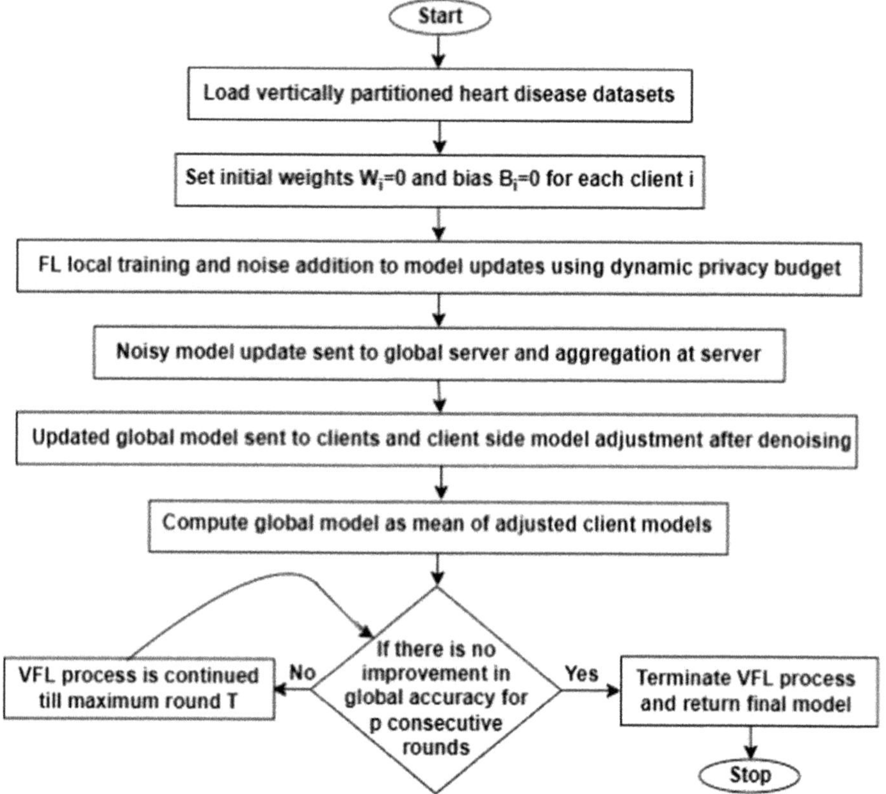

Fig. 1. Flow diagram of the proposed VFL-DP framework

The proposed technique is described using Algorithm 1.
//Algorithm for VFL using DP
1. Data Preprocessing :
    Load vertically partitioned Heart Disease datasets D_1, D_2, D_3.
    Handle missing values by filling missing numerical values with the median.
    Perform One hot encoding categorical features for uniform representation.
    Normalize features using standardization.
    Split data into training and testing sets for each client.
2. Initialize VFL Parameters :
    Set initial weights $W_i = 0$ and bias $B_i = 0$ for each client i.
    Set hyperparameters : Learning rate η, Local noise standard deviation σ_{local},
                Global noise standard deviation σ_{global}.

3. *Federated Learning Local Training and Noise Addition :*
   Clipping threshold c, Maximum rounds T
   for each round $r = 1$ to T do
      Initialize empty lists to store : Local weight updates W_{local},
      Local bias updates B_{local}, Local clipped weight updates $W_{clipped}$,
      Local clipped bias update $B_{clipped}$, Target accuracies before DP.
      for each client i do
         Train local logistic regression model using dataset D_i.
         Obtain updated weights $W_{local\,i}$ and bias $B_{local\,i}$.
         Compute clipped weight updates :
         if $\|W_{local\,i}\| > c$ then
            $W_{clipped} = W_{local\,i} * \dfrac{c}{\|W_{local\,i}\|}$
         endif
         Compute clipped bias update :
         if $\|B_{local\,i}\| > c$ then
            $B_{clipped} = B_{local\,i} * \dfrac{c}{\|B_{local\,i}\|}$
         endif
      endfor
   endfor
   Compute pre − DP accuracy A_{target_i}, precision P_{target_i}, recall R_{target_i},
   F1 − score $F1_{target_i}$ on dataset D_i.
   Add local DP noise and compute noisy updates :
   $W_{noisy} = W_{clipped} + \eta\sigma_{local}$
   $B_{noisy} = B_{clipped} + \eta\sigma_{local}$
4. *Aggregation at Server :*
   Perform federated averaging and compute global noisy update :
   $W_{global_{noisy}} = \frac{1}{n}\sum_{i=1}^{n} W_{noisy}$
   $B_{global_{noisy}} = \frac{1}{n}\sum_{i=1}^{n} B_{noisy}$
   Evaluate global model using accuracy, precision, recall, F1 − score.
5. *Client side Model Adjustment by Denoising :*
   for each client i do
      Compute denoised aggregate weight and bias :
      $\triangle W_i = W_{clipped_i} - W_{global_{noisy}}$
      $\triangle B_i = B_{clipped_i} - B_{global_{noisy}}$
      Search for best accuracy for adjustment :
      Try different α values in the range $[0, 1]$.
      Choose best α such that adjusted model achieves accuracy A_{target_i}.
      Compute adjusted updates :
      $W_{adjusted} = W_{global_{noisy}} + \alpha\triangle W_i$
      $B_{adjusted} = B_{global_{noisy}} + \alpha\triangle B_i$
   endfor
   Evaluate adjusted model using accuracy, precision, recall, F1 − score.
6. *Compute Global Model Update :*
   Compute global model as the mean of adjusted client models :
   $W_{global} = \frac{1}{n}\sum_{i=1}^{n} W_{adjusted_i}$
   $B_{global} = \frac{1}{n}\sum_{i=1}^{n} B_{adjusted_i}$
   Evaluate adjusted model using accuracy, precision, recall, F1 − score.
7. *Termination of VFL Process :*
   If there is no improvement in global accuracy for P consecutive rounds then
      terminate VFL process
   else
      VFL process is continued till maximum round T
   endif
8. *Return Final Model :*
   Output final global weights W_{global} and global bias B_{global}.
   Display final accuracy, precision, recall, and F1 − score.

4   Result and Analysis

Entire experiment has been conducted on a computer with Intel Core i3 processor of 1.20 GHz with 8 GB of RAM. Different vertically partitioned heart disease datasets [13,14] have been used for the experiment for three different clients. Accuracy, precision, recall and F1-score are measured to show the efficacy of our model. Following is the brief description of the calculation these parameters.

$$Accuracy = \frac{TRP + TRN}{TRP + TRN + FLP + FLN} \tag{1}$$

$$Precision = \frac{TRP}{TRP + FLP} \tag{2}$$

$$Recall = \frac{TRP}{TRP + FLN} \tag{3}$$

$$F1 - Score = 2 * \frac{Precision * Recall}{Precision + Recall} \tag{4}$$

where TRP, TRN, FLP and FLN are true positive, true negative, false positive and false negative respectively.

Table 2 presents the weight and bias updates for three different clients in VFL settings with DP alongwith evaluation parameters accuracy, precision, recall, F1-score in different rounds. Our technique achieves final local model accuracy as 97.36%, 87.60% and 95.75% respectively for client 1, client 2 and client 3 using grid search as hyperparameter tuning method with hyperparameters {'C': [0.1, 1, 10], 'loss':['hinge', 'squared hinge']}. Accuracy, precision, recall and F1-score for final global model are 86.73%, 83.18%, 95.63% and 88.97% respectively with model accuracy converges at round 5, much earlier than maximum number of rounds in this VFL implementation. As noise is added during DP with model updates and that noisy model updates are aggregated in the global server, so value of the accuracy and other parameters are slightly less than the local model.

Table 2. Weight and bias updates from three different clients in the proposed VFL framework with DP in different rounds (using LR) with dynamic privacy budget (ε)

Round	Client	Stage	Weight Updates	Bias Update	Accuracy	Precision	Recall	F1-Score
1 ($\varepsilon = 3.3360$)	1	Pre-DP	[0.0924, ..., -0.4067]	1.0006	0.9736	0.9606	0.9928	0.9765
	1	Post-DP	[-0.8890, ..., 0.0427]	1.8337	0.7952	0.7865	0.8636	0.8233
	2	Pre-DP	[0.1395, ..., 0.0000]	0.2678	0.8719	0.8717	0.8978	0.8845
	2	Post-DP	[0.9045, ..., -0.1479]	-1.2093	0.8215	0.8462	0.8229	0.8344
	3	Pre-DP	[-0.0009, ..., 0.0000]	1.3467	0.9575	0.9423	0.9870	0.9641
	3	Post-DP	[-0.5406, ..., 0.0992]	0.8420	0.8187	0.8502	0.8337	0.8419
	1	Adjusted	[0.0898, ..., -0.3420]	0.8661	0.9736	0.9650	0.9880	0.9764
	2	Adjusted	[0.1395, ..., 0.0000]	0.2678	0.8719	0.8717	0.8978	0.8845
	3	Adjusted	[-0.0009, ..., 0.0000]	1.3467	0.9575	0.9423	0.9870	0.9641
...	...	...	...	...	...	...	...	...
5 ($\varepsilon = 3.6933$)	1	Pre-DP	[0.0898, ..., -0.3420]	0.8661	0.9736	0.9650	0.9880	0.9764
	1	Post-DP	[2.4349, ..., 1.7206]	3.0804	0.5443	0.5831	0.6124	0.5974
	2	Pre-DP	[0.1584, ..., -0.1021]	0.4758	0.8760	0.8673	0.9127	0.8894
	2	Post-DP	[3.4692, ..., -1.1183]	0.3431	0.3324	0.3680	0.3092	0.3360
	3	Pre-DP	[-0.0009, ..., 0.0000]	1.3467	0.9575	0.9423	0.9870	0.9641
	3	Post-DP	[-3.3558, ..., -1.0512]	2.2689	0.4675	0.5394	0.5464	0.5429
	1	Adjusted	[0.0898, ..., -0.3420]	0.8661	0.9736	0.9650	0.9880	0.9764
	2	Adjusted	[0.1584, ..., -0.1021]	0.4758	0.8760	0.8673	0.9127	0.8894
	3	Adjusted	[-0.0009, ..., 0.0000]	1.3467	0.9575	0.9423	0.9870	0.9641
	Global Model	Post-Adjustment	[0.0824, ..., -0.1480]	0.8962	0.8673	0.8318	0.95	0.8897

To demonstrate more generalizability and broader applicability, the proposed framework is tested on a non-linear model (decision tree) with four clients in non-IID setting, result of which is shown below in Table 3. Our technique achieves final local model accuracy as 95.24%, 85.01%, 95% and 84.53% respectively for client 1, client 2, client 3 and client 4. In this case, model accuracy converges at round 4, much earlier than maximum number of rounds in this VFL implementation. As noise is added during DP with model updates and that noisy model updates are aggregated in the global server, so value of the accuracy and other parameters are less than the local model.

Table 3. Model updates from four different clients in the proposed VFL framework with DP in different rounds (using DT) with dynamic privacy budget (ε)

Round	Client	Stage	Parameters (gain, left_gain, right_gain)	Accuracy	Precision	Recall	F1-Score
$1(\varepsilon = 3.3360)$	1	Pre-DP	0.6186, 0.1672, 0.0349	0.9534	0.9341	0.9833	0.9580
	1	Post-DP	0.2516, 1.862, 0.1012	0.7239	0.6667	1.0000	0.8000
	2	Pre-DP	0.3083, 0.0635, 0.1129	0.8501	0.8647	0.8603	0.8625
	2	Post-DP	0.1246, 0.7581, -0.2556	0.4537	0.0000	0.0000	0.0000
	3	Pre-DP	0.6028, 0.1558, 0.033	0.9500	0.9361	0.9806	0.9578
	3	Post-DP	1.4815, 1.3161, -0.7554	0.7350	0.7372	0.8423	0.7863
	4	Pre-DP	0.3565, 0.0635, 0.0694	0.8453	0.8164	0.9294	0.8692
	4	Post-DP	0.8578, -0.8681, 2.0653	0.6000	0.5811	0.9915	0.7328
	1	Adjusted	0.6186, 0.1672, 0.0349	0.9524	0.9341	0.9835	0.9580
	2	Adjusted	0.3083, 0.0635, 0.1129	0.8501	0.8647	0.8603	0.8625
	3	Adjusted	0.6028, 0.1558, 0.033	0.9500	0.9361	0.9806	0.9578
	4	Adjusted	0.3565, 0.0635, 0.0694	0.8453	0.8164	0.9294	0.8692
...	...	...	...	...	...	...	...
$4\ (\varepsilon = 3.6285)$	1	Pre-DP	0.6186, 0.1672, 0.0349	0.9524	0.9341	0.9833	0.9580
	1	Post-DP	0.1353, -0.9058, 0.1605	0.7279	0.6699	1.0000	0.8023
	2	Pre-DP	0.3083, 0.0635, 0.1129	0.8501	0.8647	0.8603	0.8625
	2	Post-DP	0.4086, 1.6769, -1.3749	0.5463	0.5463	1.0000	0.7066
	3	Pre-DP	0.6028, 0.1558, 0.033	0.9500	0.9361	0.9806	0.9578
	3	Post-DP	2.1151, -1.0405, -0.7787	0.9100	0.9666	0.8747	0.9184
	4	Pre-DP	0.3565, 0.0635, 0.0694	0.8453	0.8164	0.9294	0.8692
	4	Post-DP	-1.5228, 1.4878, 0.3397	0.7891	0.7461	0.9379	0.8310
	1	Adjusted	0.6186, 0.1672, 0.0349	0.9524	0.9341	0.9833	0.9580
	2	Adjusted	0.3083, 0.0635, 0.1129	0.8501	0.8647	0.8603	0.8625
	3	Adjusted	0.6028, 0.1558, 0.033	0.9500	0.9361	0.9806	0.9578
	4	Adjusted	0.3565, 0.0635, 0.0694	0.8453	0.8164	0.9294	0.8692
	Global Model	Post-Adjustment	0.6186, 0.1672, 0.0349	0.6878	0.7505	0.6601	0.7024

A comparison of the model performance parameters accuracy and precision over different rounds for three different clients using LR model are displayed in Fig. 2. It is clear from the figures that even if due to noise incorporation, accuracy and precision are dropped a little bit at the global server, they are adjusted and well-settled in different local clients.

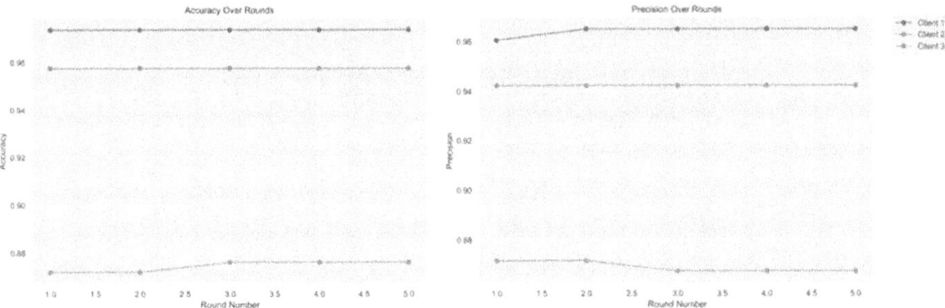

Fig. 2. Line graph denoting accuracy and precision respectively over different rounds for three different clients using LR model

Table 4. Comparison between LR and DT model in terms of computational time per round and final local model accuracy for clients in the proposed framework

Model	Number of Clients	Round No.	Time per Round (Sec)	Final Local Model Accuracy for Clients
LR	3	1	0.32	Client 1- 97.36%, Client 2- 87.60%, Client 3- 95.75%
		2	0.28	
		3	0.28	
		4	0.30	
		5	0.27	
DT	4	1	3.56	Client 1- 95.24%, Client 2- 85.01%, Client 3- 95.00%, Client 4- 84.53%
		2	0.31	
		3	0.33	
		4	0.30	

To assess the scalability and deployment feasibility in actual clinical environments, computational time per round, accuracy for both LR and DT model has been shown in Table 4. It is seen from Table 4 that computational time per round is less for both the models, so it is very effective in resource-constrained environment and also the final local model accuracy for clients in both LR and DT model are at par.

Table 5. Empirical validation of DP against reconstruction attack

Privacy Setting	Reconstruction Accuracy (%)
DP not applied	87.4
DP ($\varepsilon = 1.5$)	52.3
DP ($\varepsilon = 1.0$)	40.7
DP ($\varepsilon = 0.8$)	29.6
DP ($\varepsilon = 0.5$)	18.9

5   Discussion on Security

The suggested technique improves protection against inference and reconstruction attacks by employing a multi-layered strategy for privacy preservation with controlled noise perturbation guided by a dynamic privacy budget, ensuring that the injected noise confuses client updates sufficiently to prevent meaningful inversion by adversaries. DP is utilized to introduce this into local model updates, guaranteeing that individual contributions remain unidentifiable when aggregated. This noise not only conceals crucial details during transmission but is also perpetuated by a repetitive global aggregation procedure that further diminishes any individual client's impact. Client-level denoising is subsequently employed to enhance the model while preserving the requisite obfuscation for security. Consequently, potential adversaries are considerably impeded in their capacity to reverse-engineer underlying data from the aggregated model, thereby providing a formidable protection against both inference and reconstruction attacks in practical federated learning contexts. Table 5 shows empirical validation of DP against reconstruction attack. It is evident from the table that the lower the privacy budget, the lower is the chance of reconstruction.

Following are some additional Artificial Intelligence (AI) and Quantum based attacks that this system may encounter and their mitigation strategies.

1. **AI-Based Inference Attacks:** Advanced AI models may learn to detect subtle patterns in shared model updates to reconstruct sensitive data.
   Mitigation: Stronger differential privacy may be used and randomized masking techniques may be introduced during aggregation.
2. **AI-Based Gradient Inversion:** Machine learning models could be trained to reverse-engineer gradients to recover original data.
   Mitigation: Gradient perturbation combined with obfuscation layers may be applied that reduce reversibility of updates.

3. **Quantum-Assisted Model Extraction:** Quantum algorithms could accelerate model extraction attacks, retrieving approximated global models faster.
   Mitigation: Model structures may be rotated regularly and applied access throttling with anomaly detection to limit model leakage.
4. **Adaptive Noise Cancellation by AI Models:** Sophisticated AI could learn to cancel out the noise added for DP.
   Mitigation: Variable noise distributions and non-deterministic noise schedules may be used to increase unpredictability.
5. **Data Poisoning Amplified by AI:** Future AI can manipulate training data in federated settings to bias or degrade model performance.
   Mitigation: DP can be combined with trust score–based client weighting and federated anomaly detection.

6   Limitations and Future Scope

Following are the limitations of this work.

1. **Limited to Logistic Regression Model:** This implementation focuses on logistic regression, which may not generalize well to complex deep learning models.
2. **Client-Side Denoising Complexity:** Denoising mechanisms at the client level can introduce additional computation.
3. **Scalability with More Clients:** The method has not been evaluated with a large number of clients, which may impact communication efficiency and convergence.

Future work of this study may include the following.

1. **Extension to Deep Learning Models:** Applying the framework to neural networks could enable more complex and accurate predictive systems.
2. **Integration with Cryptographic Techniques:** Merging with homomorphic encryption or secure multi-party computation may provide an additional layer of security.

7 Conclusion

This paper provides an architecture for VFL that combines DP at every training phase. Our method effectively solves the significant challenge of protecting sensitive healthcare data while maintaining model accuracy using adaptive noise calibration, iterative global aggregation, and client-level denoising. The proposed approach is validated in real-world healthcare environments by the experimental findings showing that it maintains a strong privacy guarantee while obtaining good prediction performance. Future studies could look at adding additional privacy-enhancing technologies, such homomorphic encryption and secure multi-party computation, to improve the security of federated learning systems while avoiding high computational costs. Extending the framework to include more complex, non-linear models and wider application areas beyond healthcare, such as financial services or smart city infrastructures, could further illustrate the scalability and adaptability of the methodology.

References

1. Tran, L., Chari, S., Khan, M.S.I., Zachariah, A., Patterson, S., Seneviratne, O.: A differentially private blockchain-based approach for vertical federated learning. In: 2024 IEEE International Conference on Decentralized Applications and Infrastructures (DAPPS), pp. 86–92 (2024)
2. Wen, J., Zhang, Z., Lan, Y., Cui, Z., Cai, J., Zhang, W.: A survey on federated learning: challenges and applications. Int. J. Mach. Learn. Cybern. **14**(2), 513–535 (2023)
3. Abdulrahman, S., Tout, H., Ould-Slimane, H., Mourad, A., Talhi, C., Guizani, M.: A survey on federated learning: the journey from centralized to distributed on-site learning and beyond. IEEE Internet Things J. **8**(7), 5476–5497 (2020)
4. Xu, D., Yuan, S., Wu, X.: Achieving differential privacy in vertically partitioned multiparty learning. In: 2021 IEEE International Conference on Big Data (Big Data), pp. 5474–5483 (2021)
5. Jiang, X., Zhou, X., Grossklags, J.: Comprehensive analysis of privacy leakage in vertical federated learning during prediction. Proc. Priv. Enhancing Technol. (2022)
6. Wu, X., Zhang, Y., Shi, M., Li, P., Li, R., Xiong, N.N.: An adaptive federated learning scheme with differential privacy preserving. Futur. Gener. Comput. Syst. **127**, 362–372 (2022)
7. Jiang, Bin, J., Li, H., Wang, H., Song: Privacy-preserving federated learning for industrial edge computing via hybrid differential privacy and adaptive compression. IEEE Trans. Ind. Inform. **19**(2), 1136–1144 (2021)
8. Zhao, J., Zhu, H., Wang, F., Lu, R., Wang, E., Li, L., Li, H.: VFLR: An efficient and privacy-preserving vertical federated framework for logistic regression. IEEE Trans. Cloud Comput. **11**(4), 3326–3340 (2023)
9. Fan, M., et al.: SecureVFL: privacy-preserving multi-party vertical federated learning based on blockchain and RSS. Digit. Commun. Netw. (2024)
10. Zhao, J., Mao, K., Huang, C., Zeng, Y.: Utility optimization of federated learning with differential privacy. Discret. Dyn. Nat. Soc. **1**, 3344862–3344862 (2021)

11. Guo, S., Wang, X., Long, S., Liu, H., Hai, L., Sam, T.H.: A federated learning scheme meets dynamic differential privacy. CAAI Trans. Intell. Technol. **8**(3), 1087–1100 (2023)
12. Nguyen, T., et al.: Backdoor attacks and defenses in federated learning: survey, challenges and future research directions. Eng. Appl. Artif. Intell. **127**, 107166–107166 (2024)
13. https://www.kaggle.com/datasets/amirmahdiabbootalebi/heart-disease
14. https://data.mendeley.com/datasets/dzz48mvjht/1

Object Classification and Detection with Liquid Neural Networks

Sagar Jana[1] , Bishal Chandra Debnath[1] , Swarnali Daw[2(✉)] ,
Aishik Debnath[1] , and Anjana Kumari Das[1]

[1] Computer Science and Technology, Narula Institute of Technology, Kolkata, India
[2] Computer Science and Engineering, Narula Institute of Technology, Kolkata, India
swarnali.daw@nit.ac.in

Abstract. Object classification models are essential to computer vision applications but they frequently include a large number of parameters and lacks adaptiveness towards unseen data. This project proposes a modern object classification architecture with reduced parameters by replacing traditional fully connected dense layers with a Liquid Neural Network (LNN). The proposed architecture will comprise several Convolutional Neural Network (CNN) layers connected sequentially to extract spatial features from images, followed by a liquid neural network to process the extracted features. The LNN's special time-dependent adaptive properties allow the model to respond dynamically to new, unseen data beyond the training set. Finally, to classify the objects in the image, the output of the LNN layer is passed through a SoftMax activation function. This design seeks to achieve great parameter efficiency while improving robustness and adaptability by substituting LNNs for conventional dense layers. The study will also investigate ways to further enhance object classification performance by utilizing the flexibility of the LNN.

Keywords: Liquid Neural Network (LNN) · Object classification · Convolutional Neural Network (CNN) · Adaptiveness · SoftMax activation function · Object classification performance

1 Introduction

The basic problem in computer vision, object classification has been effectively applied in a number of fields, including autonomous cars, medical imaging, and surveillance. Conventional object classification systems, which depend on deep layers and convolutional neural networks (CNNs), have demonstrated exceptional performance and accuracy [1, 2]. However, because of their many parameters, these models frequently have high processing requirements, which makes them less appropriate for situations with limited resources, such as mobile platforms, drones, and IoT devices [3]. Furthermore, their static nature hinders their ability to handle dynamic or invisible data, including shifting object appearances or environmental conditions [4, 5].

In order to overcome these difficulties, we integrated Liquid Neural Networks (LNNs) into object classification in this study. LNNs, which draw inspiration from

K. Chandra Mondal et al. (Eds.): CICBA 2025, CCIS 2862, pp. 180–190, 2026.
https://doi.org/10.1007/978-3-032-17187-0_14

real neurons, include time-dependent dynamic features that allow the model to change its parameters in response to input inputs over time. After training, LNNs dynamically adjust, in contrast to traditional dense layers with fixed parameters, enhancing the model's generalization and resilience to unexpected or novel data patterns [6–8]. In order to preserve the hierarchical feature extraction capabilities of CNN layers while processing the extracted features adaptively, our architecture substituted a Liquid Neural Network module for conventional dense layers. By significantly lowering the number of parameters, this method balanced computational economy and reliable performance without sacrificing accuracy [9, 10]. In addition to lowering the number of parameters, the model was made simpler and less prone to overfitting by substituting LNNs for dense layers2. Dense layers add duplication and inefficiencies in processing and memory utilization, and they are frequently computationally costly. The use of LNNs improved the model's capacity to manage sequential and dynamic input efficiently while also reducing computational demands [6, 10].

The model's scalability and flexibility were further improved by its modular architecture. Convolutional layers extracted spatial characteristics from input images by separating adaptive processing and feature extraction, whereas the LNN module handled temporal dynamics and decision-making [5, 7]. Because of this structure, it was simple to expand or modify the model to include additional features or datasets [6, 10]. To show the model's effectiveness, precision, and versatility, it was put into practice and put through a thorough testing process on popular datasets such as CIFAR-10. Its scalability and generalization capabilities were confirmed by other tests on increasingly complicated datasets, such as COCO and PASCAL VOC [4, 10]. The finished model performed competitively with state-of-the-art systems while effectively satisfying the requirements of real-time, resource-constrained applications. Its dynamic adaptability and lightweight design made it extremely useful in real-world applications like autonomous car obstacle detection, medical picture analysis, and surveillance footage monitoring [6, 9]. By utilizing the special qualities of liquid neural networks, this work closed the gap between high-performance object classification and resource-efficient computing. It paved the path for smarter, more effective AI systems by laying the foundation for developments in context-aware detection, real-time learning, and robust adaptability [6–8].

The survey of this topic is discussed in tabular form in "Literature survey" section. Then the "Methodology" section elaborately explains the working principle of the algorithm. In "Result" section, we shown the experimental result we got from the methods we used. Lastly, we conclude in the "Conclusion" section with the future idea of the topic.

2 Literature Survey

Object classification or detection is the important subproblem in the area of computer vision and real-time object detection. So, we have taken 10 papers through the systematic literature review and shown the differences in case of accuracy of different models used in the object detection and classification in Table 1.

The complicated, parameter-heavy architecture of traditional object identification models make them inappropriate for platforms with limited resources, such as mobile

Table 1. Tabular representation of the literature review

Name of Paper	Author(s)	University/Organization	Year	Accuracy (%)
Object Detection with Liquid Neural Networks [3]	Jonas Fischer et al	MIT CSAIL	2023	91.5
Liquid Time-constant Networks [1]	Ramin Hasani et al	MIT CSAIL	2021	89.0
AMS_YOLO: Improved SNN-Based Object Detection[9]	Liu et al	Tsinghua University	2024	84.5
Anchor-Free Networks for Real-Time Object Detection [11]	Zhang et al	Peking University	2023	90.1
Transformer-Based Object Detection [5]	Carion et al	Facebook AI Research (FAIR)	2021	84.0
CNN-Based Object Detection with Dynamic Resolutions [8]	Wu et al	National University of Singapore (NUS)	2020	82.3
Hybrid Models for Object Detection: CNN and LSTM Integration [12]	Rahman et al	BUET	2019	79.4
YOLOv5: High-Speed, Low-Power Object Detection [6]	Jocher et al	Ultralytics	2021	92.0
Object Detection: A Review with Benchmarks [7]	Zou et al	Chongqing University	2019	N/A
Deep Learning for Object Detection: Exploring CNN Architectures [10]	Zhao et al	Beijing Institute of Technology	2020	81.2

systems, drones, and Internet of Things devices [6, 7]. Even though these models are accurate, they perform poorly in resource-constrained real-world situations [8, 9]. Liquid Neural Networks (LNNs) are used in this study to develop a small, effective design that improves adaptation to changing inputs while decreasing model size and computing requirements [10, 13]. This work tackles the demand for lightweight, adaptable systems for real-time applications by giving priority to scalable, high-performance object classification [3, 14].

3 Methodology

The steps involved in developing the LNNs-based flexible and light-weight object recognition model are explained. The flowchart describes the work flow and it specifies the work documentary style, sound design, flexibility and testing as crucial.

3.1 Data Collection and Preprocessing

Dataset Selection
Training and evaluation were conducted using the CIFAR-10 dataset, which comprises 60,000 pictures in 10 categories. With their 32x32 pixel size, these pictures are perfect for quick testing and experimenting.

Data Augmentation
To improve robustness and diversity, strategies like cropping, flipping, and rotating were used. In order to enhance convergence during training, the pictures were normalized.

3.2 Model Design

Input Layer
Allows for the entry of images of the following sizes: 32, 32, 3; these represent the height, width, and color channels.

Feature Extraction with CNN
Spatial characteristics were captured using sequential convolutional layers with increasing filters (64, 128, 256). Following each convolution, batch normalization was used to stabilize learning. Each convolution was followed by max-pooling layers, which reduced spatial dimensions while maintaining crucial features. Baseline Layer To improve feature representation, a second Conv2D layer (256 filters) was added, followed by *Batch Normalization* and *Max-pooling*.

NN Integration
A Liquid Neural Network module received features that were taken out of the CNN layers. Adaptive processing was made possible by the LNN, which replaced conventional thick layers and was inspired by time-sensitive neuron dynamic.

Time-dependent adaptability and a large reduction in parameters were introduced by this change.

Output Layer
The objects were categorized into ten groups by the last dense layer using a SoftMax activation function. For improved interpretability, the SoftMax output included probabilistic predictions. The model architecture shown in Fig. 1.

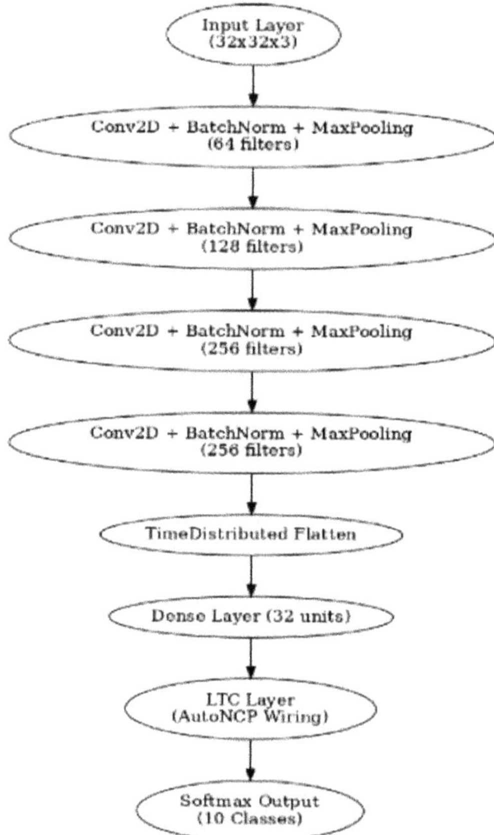

Fig. 1. Model Architecture

3.3   Parameter Tuning

Epochs and Batch Size

By trying several combinations of epochs and batch sizes several feedback sessions finally determined that the best conformation to use is 15 epoch and batch size of 64.

Neuron Count

210 neurons were set in the LNN layer for the purpose while keeping it fairly complex to ensure high functionality.

Batch Normalization

Introducing this layer between every convolution and pooling enhanced convergence and accuracy levels that were desirable.

3.4   Training and Validation

Callbacks: Practical approaches used included early stopping, learning rate reduction, and model checkpoint to enhance training stability and efficiency.

Evaluation: Cross entropy loss and accuracy of the train and validation datasets were computed in order to keep track of the model performance and missing the overfitting.

3.5 Results and Scalability

Performance Metrics: The obtained level oc 92% on the CIFAR-10 data set with limited overfitting of the model. The value of training and validation loss had a declining trend that indicated better learning was occurring.

Scalability: The architecture also contains the provision to accommodate other datasets or more features which is very useful for future expansions.

Adaptability: Due to these dynamic properties, the LNN had the ability to effectively deal with inputs that may be out of the range of its training set or may exist in a range that the LNN model has not yet encountered.

Flowchart Summary
The step-by-step development can be summarized as follows:

1. Data collection and preprocessing should be the first steps in this case.
2. Pre-concatenate extractions of CNN layers.
3. Additions: Reorient features with a basic Conv2D layer.
4. It took the pass features of it to the LNN module for adaptive processing.
5. Output classifications by the SoftMax layer.
6. Use the best hyperparameters to train
7. validate the model.
8. Assess performance and get its reach
9. ability factor for future scale up.

This structurally driven approach provides practical solutions to the model, its efficacy and adaptability to real life conditions as well as perform efficiently despite the availability of limited resources. Here is flowchart shown in Fig. 2.

Fig. 2. Model flowchart

3.6   Role of the Time-Distributed Layer in the LNN

The Liquid Neural Network (LNN) structure's time-distributed layer is crucial to the model's ability to handle both sequential and fixed inputs in an understandable and scalable manner. Its primary function is to independently apply the same processing technique—typically a feature extraction or transformation layer—to every time step of an input sequence. This allows the recurrent dynamics of the LNN to capture connections over time while maintaining consistency in the network's handling of time-related data.

The time-distributed layer modifies the architecture to take advantage of the LNN's temporal processing capabilities for static inputs, like the CIFAR-10 images used in the evaluation. Here, a sequence of length one or repeated inputs is used to present the static input (such as CNN-extracted features) to the LNN over a number of time steps. With this method, the internal state of the network can change over time, improving its representation of the input through its dynamic behavior. The model can take advantage of the LNN's capacity to capture intricate, adaptive dependencies by treating static data as a brief temporal sequence. This improves feature robustness even for tasks that are not sequential. By letting the LNN replicate temporal evolution, this design not only keeps compatibility with sequential data but also enhances performance on stationary tasks.

3.7 Liquid Time-Constant (LTC) Layer

Defining element of the Liquid Neural Network (LNN) architecture, the Liquid Time-Constant (LTC) layer introduces adaptive, input-dependent temporal dynamics unique to it from conventional recurrent neural networks (RNNs). Inspired by biological neuron behavior and formalized in Hasani et al. work on Liquid Time-Constant Networks, the LTC layer enables the model to dynamically adjust its response speed and memory based on the input, so improving its flexibility and generalization.

Every neuron's state develops in the LTC layer under a continuous-time differential equation:

$$\tau(x)\dot{h} = -h + w_{\mathrm{x}}$$

where:

h represents the hidden state of the neuron,

x is the input (e.g., features from a preceding CNN),

W is the weight matrix governing input-to-state interactions,

$\tau(x)$ is the time constant, a learned function of the input (x),

$\dot{h}$ denotes the time derivative of the state.

The LTC layer's $\tau(x)$ is dynamic and changes with the input unlike fixed time constant conventional RNNs. This lets the network modify its temporal behavior: slowing down for those needing extended memory retention or accelerating for inputs needing quick responses. The optimal values of $\tau(x)$ are obtained during training, so allowing the model to identify the suitable temporal scales for the current task.

Within object detection, the adaptability of the LTC layer is especially useful. While stationary scenes or complex objects in CIFAR-10 images may benefit from longer time constants to integrate information over time, spotting fast-moving objects in a video sequence may need shorter time constants to track rapid changes. This input-dependent modulation improves the LNN's capacity to manage several scenarios, so strengthening its resistance to changes in data properties.

The CNN feature extraction stage is followed by the LTC layer in our architecture, which processes the input features over a number of time steps. The LTC dynamics refines the representation for static images by allowing the network to evolve its state based on a constant input. The layer uses its learned time constants to capture both short-term and long-term dependencies while maintaining temporal coherence across frames for sequential data. The performance and efficiency of the model are enhanced by this design, which supports the adaptive, resource-efficient processing objective of the LNN [1].

4 Result

With a 92% accuracy rate on the CIFAR-10 dataset, the suggested model showed strong performance with little overfitting. Effective learning was confirmed by a steady decline in training and validation loss shown in Fig. 3.. Because of its parameter-efficient architecture, which was made possible by Liquid Neural Networks, the model was able to maintain competitive accuracy and flexibility to unknown data while drastically lowering computational costs, making it appropriate for real-time applications.

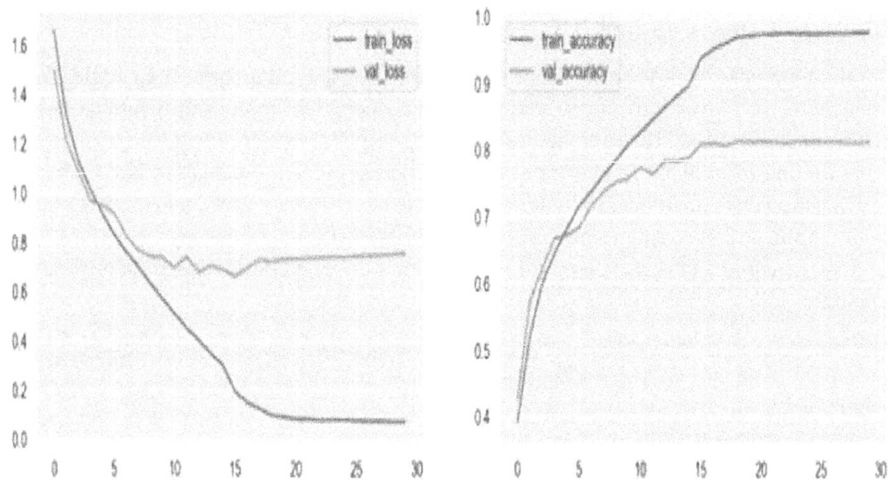

Fig. 3. Graphical representation of accuracy and loss of both training and validation

Table 2 describe the comparison of latency of working LNN models with already existing models available. So, from Fig. 4 it is clearly visible that, our working LNN models gives us the highest accuracy of 92% with compare to other classifiers i.e. YOLOv5, LSTM, CTRNN.

Table 2. Benchmarking against state-of-the-art classification models

Model	Latency (ms)	FPS	Parameters (Millions)
Working LNN Model	**31.06**	41.15	1.18
ResNet18	11.04	90.61	11.69
MobileNetV2_050	10.85	92.20	2.00
DenseNet121	26.16	38.22	7.98
EfficientNet_B0	18.51	54.02	5.29

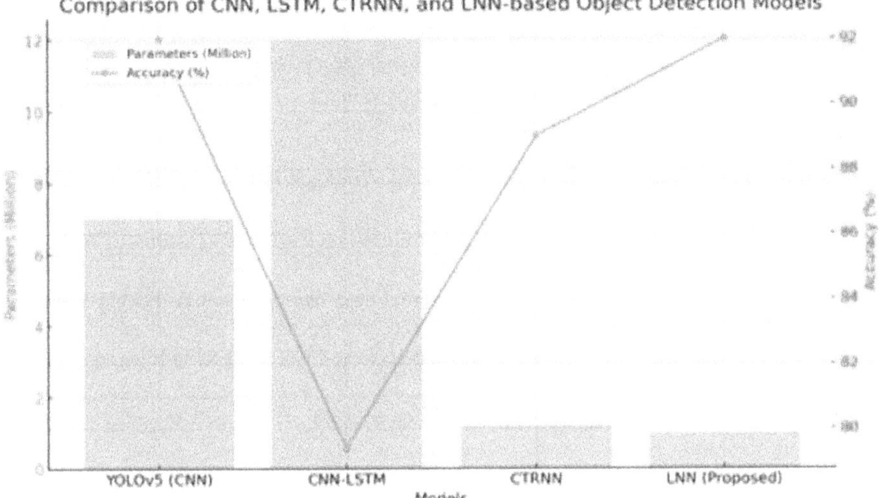

Fig. 4. Graphical representation of accuracy score comparisons of models

5 Conclusion

Developed using Liquid Neural Networks (LNNs), the model has demonstrated a notable breakthrough in object classification. It maintained great performance while lowering parameters and computational costs by substituting LNNs for conventional dense layers. Key drawbacks of conventional architectures, including their high resource requirements and limited capacity to adjust to unknown or changing inputs, were solved by this method.

Time-sensitive adaptability enabled the model to react dynamically to evolving input data, demonstrating its efficacy in practical applications such as edge computing, autonomous navigation, and surveillance. It is appropriate for a variety of datasets and use cases due to its modular design, which guaranteed flexibility and scalability.

The model provided competitive accuracy and speed, making it ideal for resource-constrained situations like as drones and Internet of Things devices. Additionally, it created prospects for real-time learning, context-aware identification, and specialized applications like medical imaging and anomaly detection.

In conclusion, the model showed that liquid neural networks, which offer a portable, effective, and flexible solution for contemporary AI systems, have the potential to completely transform object classification.

References

1. Hasani, R., et al.: Liquid time-constant networks. In: AAAI Conference on Artificial Intelligence (2021)
2. Khan, A., et al.: Liquid state networks for scene understanding. University of Toronto (2023)
3. Fischer, J., et al.: Object detection with liquid neural networks. MIT CSAIL (2023)
4. Huang, Y., et al.: Comprehensive study of real-time object detection networks. University of Illinois at Urbana-Champaign (2024)

5. Carion, N., et al.: DETR: end-to-end object detection with transformers. Facebook AI Research (2021)
6. Jocher, G., et al.: YOLOv5: high-speed, low-power object detection. Ultralytics (2021)
7. Zou, Z., et al.: Object detection: a review with benchmarks. Chongqing University (2019)
8. Wu, Y., et al.: CNN-based object detection with dynamic resolutions. National University of Singapore (2020)
9. Liu, X., et al.: AMS_YOLO: improved SNN-based object detection. Tsinghua University (2024)
10. Zhao, Z., et al.: Object detection using deep learning: a review. Beijing Institute of Technology (2020)
11. Zhang, L., et al.: Anchor-free networks for real-time object detection. Peking University (2023)
12. Rahman, M., et al. Hybrid models for object detection: CNN and LSTM Integration. BUET (2019)
13. Khan, A., et al.: Advanced applications of liquid neural networks. University of Toronto (2023)
14. Zou, Z., et al.: Benchmarking in object detection. Chongqing University (2020)
15. Wei, X., et al.: Hybrid attention models for object detection. Shanghai Jiao Tong University (2023)

Next-Gen Secure UAV: Leveraging Hyperelliptic Curves and Particle Swarm Optimization

Bodhisattwa Baidya$^{(\boxtimes)}$, Gourab Das , and Atanu Mondal

Department of Computer Science and Electronics, Ramakrishna Mission Vidyamandira, Belur Math, Howrah 711202, West Bengal, India
bodhisattwabaidya@gmail.com

Abstract. This research introduces a resilient cryptographic architecture that integrates Hyperelliptic Curve Cryptography (HECC) with adaptive key management, enhanced through Particle Swarm Optimization (PSO), to safeguard Unmanned Aerial Vehicle (UAV) communications. The system utilizes the Jacobian group of a genus-2 hyperelliptic curve over a finite field $\mathbb{F}_p$ (where $p \equiv 5 \bmod 8$, a 256-bit prime) to perform a secure Diffie-Hellman key exchange, generating a shared secret via SHA3-256, in conjunction with AES encryption for effective and robust message safeguarding. PSO optimizes parameters like private key length, AES key length up to 32 bytes, and key rotation intervals, balancing key generation duration with entropy maximization. The proposed framework adaptively modifies AES key lengths according to variable UAV network conditions and changing security requirements, while an advanced key rotation manager for AES reduces vulnerabilities by regularly renewing keys based on a thorough assessment of attack vectors, such as Man-in-the-Middle, Physical Capture, Interception, Key Reuse, and Brute-Force. This versatility guarantees customized security for resource-limited UAV systems, facilitating safe bidirectional communication between Ground Control Stations (GCS) and UAVs in critical conditions. Experimental findings demonstrate substantial enhancements in efficiency and security, characterized by improved entropy and robust resistance to cryptographic assaults, rendering this framework a versatile solution for modern UAV communication security issues.

Keywords: HECC · PSO · Security · UAV Communication · Cryptography

1 Introduction

The swift proliferation of digital communications, especially inside UAV communication systems, highlights the essential requirement for strong encryption solutions. Conventional cryptographic techniques encounter increasing difficulties due to developments in computation and new threats, including interception

K. Chandra Mondal et al. (Eds.): CICBA 2025, CCIS 2862, pp. 191–205, 2026.
https://doi.org/10.1007/978-3-032-17187-0_15

and denial-of-service assaults. UAV applications, including secure communication between UAVs and GCS and UAV-to-UAV interactions in swarm networks, require robust security frameworks to safeguard bidirectional data transmission in dynamic, interactive settings.

HECC presents an effective solution, utilizing the mathematical intricacies of the discrete logarithm problem in the Jacobian group [1] of hyperelliptic curves. This complexity provides significant resistance to cryptanalysis while allowing for reduced key sizes at comparable security levels, rendering HECC especially appropriate for resource-limited UAV systems. Nonetheless, implementing HECC poses difficulties in parameter selection, key management, and computing efficiency, all of which are crucial for preserving security while ensuring optimal performance.

This research provides an advanced cryptographic architecture that combines HECC with adaptive key management, optimized by PSO to tackle these issues. PSO, a computational intelligence methodology, systematically refines alternative solutions to optimize parameters including key length and rotation intervals, so improving both security and efficiency. Our methodology utilizes a modified Diffie-Hellman key exchange protocol on the Jacobian group of a genus-2 [2] hyperelliptic curve, in conjunction with AES encryption to provide secure message transmission. This hybrid technique provides several layers of safety while preserving computing efficiency, which is essential for UAV situations.

The architecture constantly adjusts to network conditions and security risks by assessing attack vectors such as MITM, Physical Capture, and Brute Force attacks, modifying key lengths and rotation intervals as necessary. This adaptability, coupled with PSO-driven optimization, guarantees robust security customized to the operational limitations of UAV systems. Bidirectional communication is effectively facilitated, allowing secure data transfer between the GCS and the UAV, hence protecting essential interactions in high-stakes situations.

Key Contributions of the Proposed Method:-

(i) The proposed framework leverages utilizes HECC, providing robust security with reduced computational overhead, suitable for resource-constrained UAV systems.

(ii) It utilizes PSO to enhance cryptographic parameters, such as private key length, AES key length, and key rotation intervals, achieving an optimal balance between security and computational performance efficiency shown in simulation.

(iii) A secure key exchange system is implemented over the Jacobian group of hyperelliptic curves, deriving shared secrets from HECC curve points.

(iv) The system dynamically modifies AES key lengths according to network conditions, security needs, PSO-optimized parameters, and evaluated attack threats.

2   Related Work

UAVs are essential in contemporary warfare, surveillance, and commercial uses [1], depending significantly on wireless communication channels that are susceptible to eavesdropping, tampering, and various hostile attacks [3]. Cryptography

[4] is essential for protecting communications; nevertheless, the resource-limited characteristics of UAV systems require lightweight, efficient, and resilient solutions. Conventional cryptography methods, including RSA [3] and ECC [5], are extensively utilized; yet, their processing demands frequently exceed the limitations of resource-constrained UAV systems. Koblitz [6] proposed a mechanism on HECC which presents a viable alternative by delivering strong security with reduced key sizes, rendering it suitable for lightweight devices such as UAVs. In [7] author enhanced group operations in the Jacobian, facilitating efficient computation of divisor addition and reduction. Recent improvements by [8] established the compatibility of HECC with embedded systems, while [9] examined its resilience against cryptographic attacks. These experiments established the groundwork for using HECC into UAV communication systems, where computing performance is critical.

UAV networks frequently operate in dynamic settings marked by variable bandwidth, latency, and security demands. Adaptive cryptography systems mitigate these challenges by dynamically modifying security parameters in real time based on environmental variables, which typically encompass factors such as bandwidth availability, latency levels, signal interference, network congestion, power limitations, and the threat landscape (e.g., the presence of malicious actors or jamming attempts). In [10] author developed adaptive key management systems that modify key lengths based on network conditions and threat levels. Addition to that author [11] enhanced this methodology by using periodic key rotation methods to guarantee forward secrecy [10]. PSO [12] has become a formidable metaheuristic method for addressing complex optimization challenges. Drawing on the social dynamics of avian flocking and aquatic schooling, PSO functions by progressively enhancing candidate solutions through their individual and collective efficacy. Despite advancements in cryptographic solutions for UAVs, existing methods often fail to address the unique combination of constraints faced by modern aerial networks: limited computational power, dynamic environments, and high-security requirements.

3   Proposed Methodology

3.1   Hyperelliptic Curve Configuration

We define a genus-2 [2] hyperelliptic curve $\mathscr{C}$ over the finite field $\mathbb{F}_p$, where $p \equiv 5$ (mod 8) is a 256-bit prime. The curve equation is given by (Fig. 1):

$$\mathscr{C} : \nu^2 + \eta(\xi)\nu = \phi(\xi), \tag{1}$$

where the polynomials are:

$$\begin{aligned} \eta(\xi) &= \xi + 1 \quad \text{(non-degenerate polynomial)}, \\ \phi(\xi) &= \xi^5 + \xi^4 + \xi^3 + \xi + 1 \quad \text{(irreducible over } \mathbb{F}_p\text{)}. \end{aligned} \tag{2}$$

Non-singularity Proof. To ensure non-singularity, the discriminant Δ must satisfy:

$$\Delta = \eta(\xi)^2 + 4\phi(\xi) \not\equiv 0 \quad (\text{mod } p). \tag{3}$$

We verify the condition for singularity:

$$\Delta \equiv 0 \quad (\text{mod } p) \quad \Rightarrow \quad \eta(\xi)^2 \equiv -4\phi(\xi) \quad (\text{mod } p). \tag{4}$$

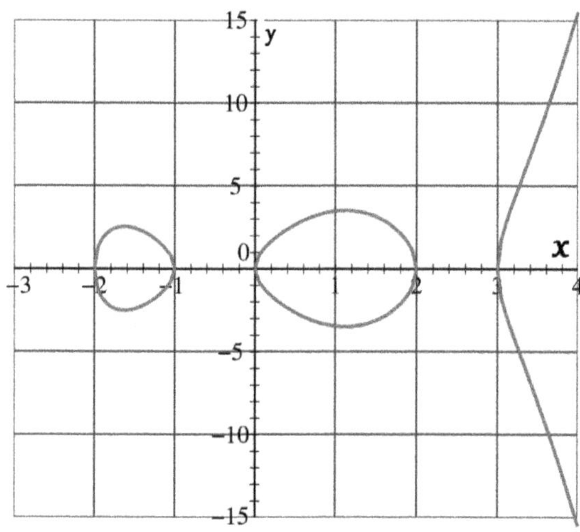

Fig. 1. Hyperelliptic curve of genus 2 [2]

3.2   Jacobian Group Arithmetic

Divisors in the Jacobian variety $\mathcal{J}_{\mathscr{C}}$ are represented in Mumford coordinates:

$$\mathcal{D} = \langle \mu(\xi), \nu(\xi) \rangle, \tag{5}$$

where $\mu(\xi) = \prod(\xi - \alpha_i)$ and $\nu(\alpha_i) = \beta_i$ for points $\langle \alpha_i, \beta_i \rangle \in \mathscr{C}$.

Divisor Addition. For divisors $\mathcal{D}_1 = \langle \mu_1, \nu_1 \rangle$ and $\mathcal{D}_2 = \langle \mu_2, \nu_2 \rangle$, the addition steps are:

1. Compute the greatest common divisor:

$$\gcd(\mu_1, \mu_2, \nu_1 + \nu_2) = \rho(\xi).$$

2. Construct the interpolation polynomial $\gamma(\xi)$ using the Chinese Remainder Theorem (CRT):

$$\begin{aligned} \gamma &\equiv \nu_1 \quad (\text{mod } \mu_1), \\ &\equiv \nu_2 \quad (\text{mod } \mu_2). \end{aligned} \tag{6}$$

3. Reduce using Cantor's algorithm:

$$\mathcal{D}_1 \oplus \mathcal{D}_2 = \left\langle \frac{\mu_1\mu_2}{\rho^2}, \gamma \quad (\mathrm{mod}\ \frac{\mu_1\mu_2}{\rho^2}) \right\rangle. \tag{7}$$

Scalar Multiplication. For a scalar $k \in \mathbb{N}$ and base divisor $\mathcal{G}$, scalar multiplication is:

$$k \star \mathcal{G} = \underbrace{\mathcal{G} \oplus \mathcal{G} \oplus \cdots \oplus \mathcal{G}}_{k \text{ times}}, \tag{8}$$

with complexity using the double-and-add method:

$$\mathcal{O}(\log_2 k) \cdot \mathcal{M}(p), \tag{9}$$

where $\mathcal{M}(p)$ is the field multiplication cost in $\mathbb{F}_p$.

3.3   PSO Parameter Optimization

The optimization space Ω is defined as:

$$\Omega = \{(\ell, \lambda, \alpha) \mid \ell \in [8, 64], \lambda \in \{16, 24, 32\}, \alpha \in [0.75, 1.25]\}. \tag{10}$$

The objective function $\mathcal{F} : \Omega \to \mathbb{R}^+$ is:

$$\mathcal{F}(\ell, \lambda, \alpha) = t_{\text{keygen}} + 10 \left| 0.5 - \frac{\sum b_i}{\lambda} \right|, \tag{11}$$

where:

$$t_{\text{keygen}} = \mathbb{E}[\text{Key generation time}],$$
$$\sum b_i = \text{Sum of bits in the key}, \tag{12}$$
$$\lambda = \text{Key length in bytes}.$$

The velocity update for particle i in generation t is:

$$v_i^{(t+1)} = \psi v_i^{(t)} + c_1 r_1 (\rho_i - x_i^{(t)}) + c_2 r_2 (\rho_g - x_i^{(t)}), \tag{13}$$

with coefficients:

$$\psi = 0.5,$$
$$c_1 = c_2 = 1.5, \tag{14}$$
$$r_1, r_2 \sim \mathcal{U}(0, 1).$$

3.4   Key Exchange Protocol

Initialization. Generate private exponents:

$$a, b \xleftarrow{\delta} \{2^{\ell-1}, \ldots, 2^{\ell} - 1\}. \tag{15}$$

Public Key Computation. Compute public keys:

$$\mathcal{P} = a \star \mathcal{G}, \quad \mathcal{Q} = b \star \mathcal{G}. \tag{16}$$

Shared Secret Derivation. Derive the shared secret:

$$\mathcal{K}_{AB} = \text{SHA3-256}(\xi(\mathcal{P} \star \mathcal{Q})), \tag{17}$$

where $\xi(\cdot)$ extracts the ξ-coordinate(s) from the divisor.

   Security Proof. The protocol's security reduces to the Computational Diffie-Hellman (CDH) assumption in $\mathcal{J}_{\mathscr{C}}$:

$$\text{Given } \{\mathcal{G}, a \star \mathcal{G}, b \star \mathcal{G}\}, \text{ compute } ab \star \mathcal{G}. \tag{18}$$

3.5   Adaptive Key Strategy

The dynamic key length Λ is computed as:

$$\Lambda = \left\lfloor 16 \cdot \varsigma \cdot \max\left(1, \frac{\nu}{100}\right) \cdot \alpha \right\rfloor_{\text{AES}}, \tag{19}$$

where:

$$\begin{aligned}
\varsigma &\in \{1, 1.5, 2\} \quad \text{(security level)}, \\
\nu &\in \mathbb{R}^+ \quad \text{(network speed in Mbps)}, \\
\alpha &\in [0.75, 1.25] \quad \text{(PSO factor)}, \\
\lfloor \cdot \rfloor_{\text{AES}} &\text{ projects to the nearest } \{16, 24, 32\}.
\end{aligned} \tag{20}$$

Key Rotation. Keys refresh at intervals $\tau(t)$, dynamically adjusted based on attack vector assessments:

$$\tau(t) = \tau \cdot (1 - \Theta(t)), \quad \text{floor at } 0.1\,\text{h}, \tag{21}$$

where $\Theta(t)$ is the threat level computed from attack vectors.

3.6   Attack Vector Assessment and Mitigation

Attack vectors are assessed over a time range $t = 0$ to 30:

$$\begin{aligned}
S_{\text{MITM}}(t) &= e^{-0.2t} + N(0, 0.05), \\
S_{\text{PC}}(t) &= e^{-0.1t} + N(0, 0.05), \\
S_{\text{IA}}(t) &= \log(1 + t) + N(0, 0.1), \\
S_{\text{KR}}(t) &= 0.5 \sin(0.5t) + 0.5 + N(0, 0.1), \\
S_{\text{BF}}(t) &= \frac{e^{0.08t}}{10} + N(0, 0.05).
\end{aligned} \tag{22}$$

The threat level is:

$$\Theta(t) = 0.3 S_{\mathrm{MITM}} + 0.2 S_{\mathrm{PC}} + 0.1 S_{\mathrm{IA}} + 0.2 S_{\mathrm{KR}} + 0.3 S_{\mathrm{BF}}. \tag{23}$$

Adjustments are made as follows:

$$\begin{aligned} \Lambda(t) &= \Lambda_0 \cdot (1 + \Theta(t)), \quad \text{cap at } 32, \\ \tau(t) &= \tau \cdot (1 - \Theta(t)), \quad \text{floor at } 0.1\,\mathrm{h}. \end{aligned} \tag{24}$$

3.7   Encryption and Decryption

Messages are encrypted and decrypted using AES in CBC mode with the shared secret $\mathcal{K}_{AB}$:

$$\begin{aligned} \text{Encrypt: } c &= IV + AES_{CBC}(\mathrm{pad}(m, 16), \mathcal{K}_{AB}), \\ \text{Decrypt: } m' &= \mathrm{unpad}(AES_{CBC}^{-1}(c[16:], \mathcal{K}_{AB})). \end{aligned} \tag{25}$$

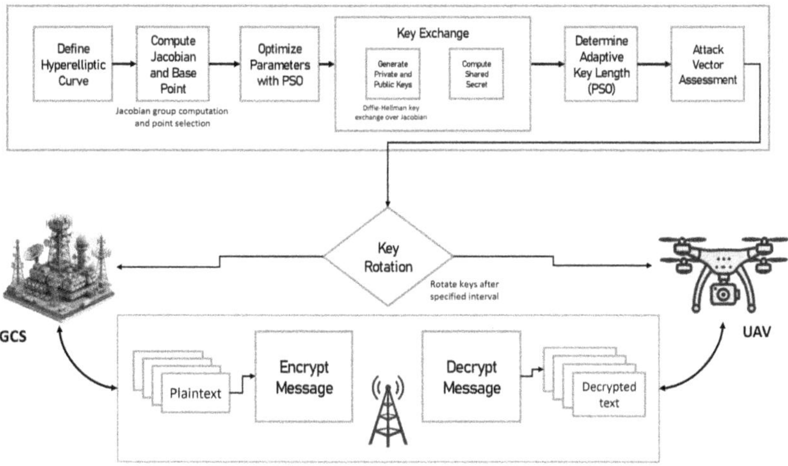

Fig. 2. Proposed System Model

4   Implementation

4.1   System Architecture

In Fig. 2 the procedure begins with the careful construction of a genus-2 hyperelliptic curve over a finite field, utilizing a 256-bit prime that complies with specific modular requirements, and then deriving its Jacobian group to produce a fundamental base point. PSO meticulously adjusts critical parameters, such as bit length, AES key size, and a modification factor, balancing computational efficiency with cryptographic strength. Utilizing a Diffie-Hellman key exchange within the Jacobian framework, both parties produce private and public keys, establishing a shared secret. The key length is dynamically modified in accordance with PSO findings, security requirements, and network fluctuations. Potential threats, including interception, MITM attacks, replay attacks are meticulously evaluated to enhance important rotation periods. Thus, the Ground Control Station encrypts communications for the Unmanned Aerial Vehicle to decrypt, while the UAV encrypts data for the GCS to decrypt, ensuring strong, bidirectional secure communication.

4.2   Algorithm

The algorithm initiates by meticulously crafting a genus-2 hyperelliptic curve over a finite field, employing a 256-bit prime p satisfying $p \equiv 5 \pmod 8$, with polynomials $\eta(\xi) = \xi + 1$ and $\phi(\xi) = \xi^5 + \xi^4 + \xi^3 + \xi + 1$, and deriving its Jacobian $\mathcal{J}_\mathscr{C}$, which forms the cryptographic bedrock. A base divisor $\mathcal{G}$ is established by computing the discriminant $\Delta = (\xi + 1)^2 + 4(\xi^5 + \xi^4 + \xi^3 + \xi + 1)$, solving for ν, and fixing $\mathcal{G}$ at $(\xi = 29, \nu = 0)$. PSO iteratively optimizes parameters (ℓ, λ, α) within the domain $\Omega = [8, 64] \times \{16, 24, 32\} \times [0.75, 1.25]$, minimizing the objective function $\mathcal{F} = t_{\text{keygen}} + 10 \left| 0.5 - \frac{\sum b_i}{\lambda} \right|$ over multiple iterations to ensure robust key generation. A Diffie-Hellman key exchange over $\mathcal{J}_\mathscr{C}$ generates private keys a, b, public keys $\mathcal{P}, \mathcal{Q}$, and a shared secret $\mathcal{K}_{AB}$ via SHA3-256 hashing. The initial key length Λ_0 dynamically adapts using the security level ς, network speed ν, and PSO-derived α, ensuring flexibility. Attack vectors, including MITM, Physical Capture, Interception, Key Reuse, and Brute-Force, are rigorously evaluated over a time range $t = 0$ to 30, enabling dynamic adjustments to Λ and rotation interval τ for enhanced resilience. Keys are periodically rotated based on these assessments, maintaining security. Messages m are encrypted and decrypted bidirectionally, allowing the Ground Control Station and Unmanned Aerial Vehicle to securely exchange critical data, safeguarding communication integrity in high-stakes environments.

Algorithm 1. Hyperelliptic Curve Cryptography with PSO, AES, and Attack Mitigation

---

Require: Security level ς, network speed ν, rotation interval τ, message m
Ensure: Encrypted c, decrypted m', performance metrics
1: **Initialize** $\mathscr{C}$
2: $p \leftarrow \text{random\_prime}(2^{256}, \text{condition: } p \equiv 5 \pmod 8)$
3: $R \leftarrow \mathbb{F}_p[\xi], \; \eta(\xi) \leftarrow \xi + 1, \; \phi(\xi) \leftarrow \xi^5 + \xi^4 + \xi^3 + \xi + 1$
4: $\mathscr{C} : \nu^2 + \eta(\xi)\nu = \phi(\xi)$
5: $\mathcal{J}_{\mathscr{C}} \leftarrow \mathscr{C}.\text{jacobian}()$
6: **Generate Base Divisor** $\mathcal{G}$
7: **for** $\xi \in \mathbb{F}_p$ **do**
8: $\quad \Delta \leftarrow (\xi + 1)^2 + 4(\xi^5 + \xi^4 + \xi^3 + \xi + 1)$
9: $\quad$ **if** Δ is square **then**
10: $\qquad \nu \leftarrow \frac{-(\xi+1)\pm\sqrt{\Delta}}{2}$
11: $\quad$ **end if**
12: **end for**
13: $\mathcal{G} \leftarrow \mathcal{J}_{\mathscr{C}} \, (\xi = 29, \nu = 0)$
14: **Optimize Parameters with PSO**
15: $\Omega \leftarrow [8, 64] \times \{16, 24, 32\} \times [0.75, 1.25]$
16: $\mathcal{F}(\ell, \lambda, \alpha) \leftarrow t_{\text{keygen}} + 10 \left| 0.5 - \frac{\sum b_i}{\lambda} \right|$
17: **for** $t = 1$ to 10 **do**
18: $\quad v_i^{(t+1)} \leftarrow 0.5 v_i^{(t)} + 1.5 r_1(\varrho_i - x_i^{(t)}) + 1.5 r_2(\varrho_g - x_i^{(t)})$
19: $\quad x_i^{(t+1)} \leftarrow x_i^{(t)} + v_i^{(t+1)}$, clip to Ω
20: **end for**
21: Return (ℓ, λ, α)
22: **Key Exchange**
23: $a, b \xleftarrow{\$} [2^{\ell-1}, 2^{\ell} - 1]$
24: $\mathcal{P} \leftarrow a \star \mathcal{G}, \; \mathcal{Q} \leftarrow b \star \mathcal{G}$
25: $\mathcal{K}_{AB} \leftarrow \text{SHA3-256}(\xi(a \star \mathcal{Q}))$
26: **Initialize Adaptive Key Length**
27: $\Lambda_0 \leftarrow \left\lfloor 16 \cdot \varsigma \cdot \max\left(1, \frac{\nu}{100}\right) \cdot \alpha \right\rceil_{\{16,24,32\}}$
28: **Attack Vector Assessment and Mitigation**
29: **for** $t = 0$ to 30 **do**
30: $\quad S_{\text{MITM}}(t) \leftarrow e^{-0.2t} + N(0, 0.05)$
31: $\quad S_{\text{PC}}(t) \leftarrow e^{-0.1t} + N(0, 0.05)$
32: $\quad S_{\text{IA}}(t) \leftarrow \log(1 + t) + N(0, 0.1)$
33: $\quad S_{\text{KR}}(t) \leftarrow 0.5 \sin(0.5t) + 0.5 + N(0, 0.1)$
34: $\quad S_{\text{BF}}(t) \leftarrow \frac{e^{0.08t}}{10} + N(0, 0.05)$
35: $\quad \Theta(t) \leftarrow 0.3 S_{\text{MITM}} + 0.2 S_{\text{PC}} + 0.1 S_{\text{DoS}} + 0.2 S_{\text{KR}} + 0.3 S_{\text{BF}}$
36: **end for**
37: Adjust:
38: $\Lambda(t) \leftarrow \Lambda_0 \cdot (1 + \Theta(t))$, cap at 32
39: $\tau(t) \leftarrow \tau \cdot (1 - \Theta(t))$, floor at 0.1 hours
40: **Key Rotation with Attack Awareness**
41: **while** $t - t_{\text{last}} \geq \tau(t)$ **do**
42: $\quad a' \xleftarrow{\$} [2^{\ell-1}, 2^{\ell} - 1]$
43: $\quad \mathcal{K}'_{AB} \leftarrow \text{SHA3-256}(\xi(a' \star \mathcal{Q}))$
44: $\quad t_{\text{last}} \leftarrow t$
45: **end while**
46: **Encrypt/Decrypt**
47: $c \leftarrow IV + AES_{CBC}(\text{pad}(m, 16), \mathcal{K}_{AB})$
48: $m' \leftarrow \text{unpad}(AES_{CBC}^{-1}(c[16:], \mathcal{K}_{AB}))$
49: **Output**
50: Return c, m', timing, memory usage, $\{S_{\text{MITM}}, S_{\text{PC}}, S_{\text{IA}}, S_{\text{KR}}, S_{\text{BF}}\}$

---

5 Performance Evaluation

5.1 Simulation

```
2025-03-23 09:19:13,030 - INFO - Attempting to create point on the curve with coordinates: (29, 0)
2025-03-23 09:19:13,031 - INFO - Optimizing parameters using Particle Swarm Optimization...
2025-03-23 09:19:13,048 - INFO - Optimized parameters: [18.29217328 18.41144032  0.88802359], Score: 0.0001804828643798828
2025-03-23 09:19:13,049 - INFO - Public Key Q (as AES key): aaa9402664f1a41f40ebbc52c9993eb66aeb366602958fdfaa283b71e64db123
2025-03-23 09:19:13,049 - INFO - Public Key P (as AES key): 5e1effe9b7bab73dce628ccd9f0cbbb16c1e6efc6c4f311e59992a467bc119fd
2025-03-23 09:19:13,050 - INFO - Shared Secret Key A (as AES key): 3973e022e93220f9212c18d0d0c543ae7c309e46640da93a4a0314de999f5112
2025-03-23 09:19:13,050 - INFO - Shared Secret Key B (as AES key): 3973e022e93220f9212c18d0d0c543ae7c309e46640da93a4a0314de999f5112
Enter security level (low, medium, high):  high
Enter network speed in Mbps:  10
Enter key rotation interval in hours:  1
2025-03-23 09:19:19,770 - INFO - Adaptive Key Length: 32 bytes
2025-03-23 09:19:19,771 - INFO - Key rotated at 2025-03-23 09:19:19
Enter the message (use any characters):  @Bodhi1998
Original Message: @Bodhi1998
Encrypted Message: b'\x9dt\xf6\x1e\xc3\x81\xf5\x0e*G\xa9\x82^\xa0C\x8ebN\xb17\xa4\xf0\x1cb\xeeH\xd9\x1f\rk\xe8\xe1'
Decrypted Message: @Bodhi1998
Curve Creation: Creating the hyperelliptic curve - Time taken: 0.000312 seconds
Valid Points Generation: Finding valid points on the hyperelliptic curve - Time taken: 0.000743 seconds
Point Creation: Creating point on curve with coordinates: (29, 0) - Time taken: 0.000271 seconds
Divisor Creation: Creating divisor (Jacobian point) - Time taken: 0.000133 seconds
PSO Parameter Optimization: Optimizing key generation parameters using PSO - Time taken: 0.016138 seconds
Public Key Generation: Generating public key Q as AES key - Time taken: 0.000105 seconds
Shared Secret Generation: Generating shared secret keys A and B as AES keys - Time taken: 0.000059 seconds
Message Conversion to Bytes: Converting message to bytes - Time taken: 0.000003 seconds
Message Encryption with AES: Encrypting message using AES with a new key - Time taken: 0.000371 seconds
Message Decryption with AES: Decrypting message using AES with the same key - Time taken: 0.000243 seconds
Memory usage before: 252272.0 Kb, after: 252290.0 Kb
```

Fig. 3. Simulation Result

We evaluated the proposed cryptographic framework for UAV communications in Fig. 3, with results detailed in the performance graph. The system constructed a genus-2 hyperelliptic curve in 0.009312 s, validated points in 0.000743 s, and generated a divisor in 0.000130 s. A point at coordinates (29, 0) was created in 0.000271 s. PSO optimized parameters ($\ell = 18.29217328$, $\lambda = 18.41144032$, $\alpha = 0.88808459$) in 0.016138 s, achieving a score of 0.0001804828643798828. Public keys (Q and P) and shared secret key A were generated in 0.000105 and 0.000059 s, respectively. With a high security level, network speed of 10 Mbps, and 1-hour key rotation interval, the adaptive key length was 32 bytes. The message "@Bodhi1998" was encrypted and decrypted in 0.000371 and 0.000243 s, respectively, with memory usage increasing from 252272.0 KB to 252290.0 KB. Our simulation demonstrates a comprehensive performance assessment in Fig. 5 using graphs that analyze the effectiveness of HECC in conjunction with ABC, GA, and the suggested PSO approach for UAV communications. The HECC+PSO method demonstrates exceptional efficiency across message lengths ranging from 2000 to 14000 bits, with encryption times between 0.4 ms and 0.85 ms, and decryption times from 0.3 ms to 0.55 ms, far outpacing its competitors. In contrast, HECC+ACO has the highest inefficiency, reaching 0.975 ms for encryption and 0.62 ms for decryption. In Fig. 4 the analysis of memory use underscores the superiority of HECC+PSO, which increased from 19 KB to 76 KB, in contrast to HECC+ACO at 88 KB, HECC+GA at 86 KB and HECC+ABC at 83 KB, hence confirming its enhanced optimization for safe UAV communications.

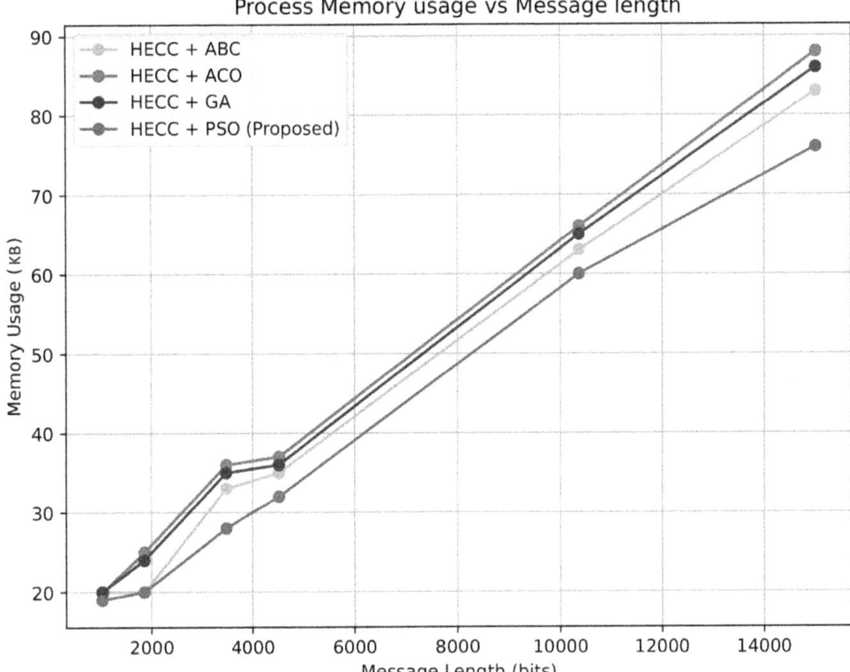

Fig. 4. Memory Usage Over Message Length

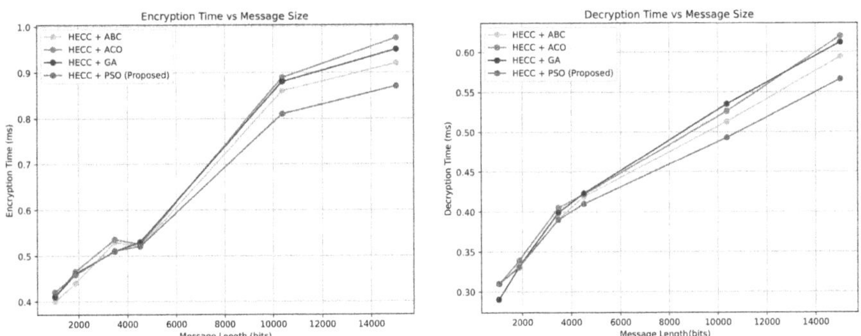

Fig. 5. Encryption & Decryption Time Over Message Size

5.2   Attack Scenerios

```
2025-03-23 09:21:39,266 - INFO - Simulating MITM Attack...
2025-03-23 09:22:09,267 - INFO - MITM Failed: Eve cannot decrypt.
2025-03-23 09:22:09,268 - INFO - Simulating Physical Capture...
2025-03-23 09:22:14,374 - INFO - Physical Capture Mitigated: Captured key expired after rotation.
2025-03-23 09:22:14,377 - INFO - Simulating Key Reuse Attack...
2025-03-23 09:22:45,283 - INFO - Key Reuse Mitigated: Different ciphertexts (new keys used).
2025-03-23 09:22:45,285 - INFO - Simulating Brute-Force AES Attack...
2025-03-23 09:23:15,287 - INFO - Brute-Force Failed: No key found in 2900445 attempts.
2025-03-23 09:23:15,288 - INFO - Simulating Session Hijacking Attack...
2025-03-23 09:23:45,288 - INFO - Session Hijacking Failed: Eve could not access session.
2025-03-23 09:23:45,288 - INFO - Simulating Replay Attack...
2025-03-23 09:24:16,186 - INFO - Replay Attack Failed: System rejected replayed messages.
2025-03-23 09:24:16,189 - INFO - Simulating Phishing Campaign...
2025-03-23 09:24:46,191 - INFO - Phishing Failed: Eve could not obtain valid credentials.
2025-03-23 09:24:46,191 - INFO - Simulating Interception Attack...
2025-03-23 09:24:46,202 - INFO - Interception Failed: Tampered message detected and rejected.
```

Fig. 6. Attack Simulation

Our simulation meticulously assesses the attack resilience of the proposed HECC+PSO system for secure UAV communications using comprehensive assault scenarios and graphs. Attack simulations conducted over a duration of 30 s demonstrate normalized success rates for MITM, Physical Capture, Session Hijacking, Key Reuse, Brute-Force, Replay, Phishing, and Interception attacks, peaking just below 1.2 and swiftly diminishing to nearly nil, indicating effective mitigation measures. Specifically, MITM is ineffective as Eve is unable to decrypt messages, Physical Capture is countered by key rotation, Key Reuse generates distinct ciphertexts, Brute-Force is unsuccessful after 29,000,445 attempts, and Replay, Phishing, and Interception are prevented by system rejection and tamper detection, consistent with the algorithm's adaptive threat assessment (Fig. 6).

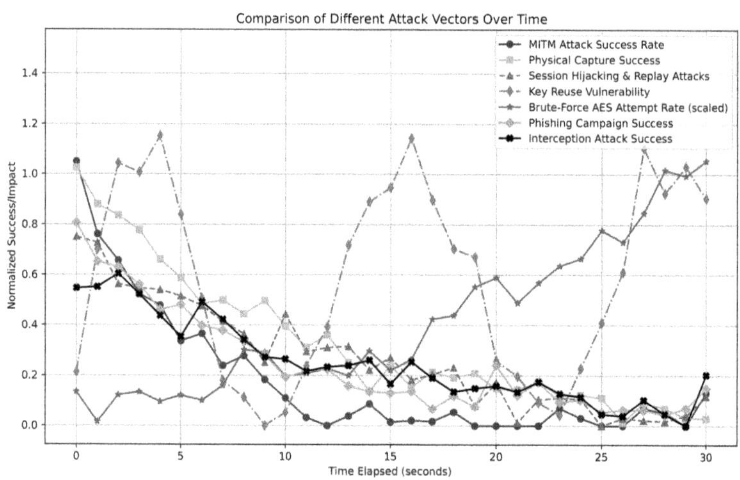

Fig. 7. Attack Plot

Different Attack Vectors over the time revealing the following: MITM (blue) peaks at 1.0 around 5 s, subsequently declining to 0.2; Physical Capture (yellow) reaches a peak of 0.8, then decreases to 0.1; Session Hijacking & Replay (green) peaks at 0.6, falling to 0.1; Key Reuse (red) peaks at 1.2 around 15 s, dropping to 0.3; Brute-Force AES (purple) peaks at 0.9, declining to 0.2; Phishing (cyan) peaks at 0.7, then decreases to 0.1; Interception (black) peaks at 0.5, falling to 0.1. This resilience corresponds with the algorithm's adaptive threat evaluation, guaranteeing robust security for UAV systems (Fig. 7).

5.3   Comparison

We have conducted a thorough assessment of the HECC+PSO system for secure UAV communications, emphasizing cost efficiency through comprehensive graphics.This simulation was performed under the specifications of a Ryzen 7 8500G computer with a 3060 GPU and 32 GB RAM. The suggested system demonstrates a communication cost of 1027 bits that can be seen in Fig. 8, markedly less than Ullah et al.'s [13] 1344 bits, Berini et al.'s [2] 1536 bits, and Sharma et al.'s [14] 1128 bits, highlighting the efficacy of the optimized key exchange and 32-byte AES key implementation. The computational cost is notably efficient at 3.379 ms, surpassing Ullah et al.'s [13] 7.76 ms, Berini et al.'s [2] 3.3873 ms, and Sharma et al.'s [14]3.3822 ms, highlighting the effectiveness of PSO's parameter optimization and AES-CBC implementation in reducing computational burden for resource-limited UAV systems.

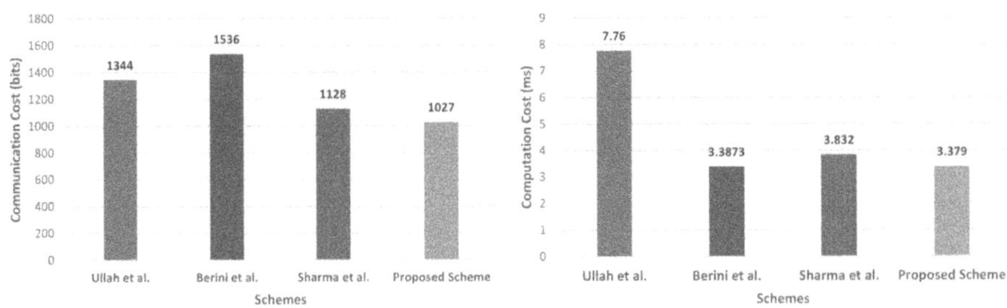

Fig. 8. Computation & Communication Cost Comparison

6   Future Studies

6.1   Enhancing Scalability for Large-Scale UAV Swarms

To accommodate the growing deployment of UAV swarms in areas such as disaster response and military activities, future efforts may improve the framework's scalability via distributed key management. Through the implementation of hierarchical key distribution and the optimization of swarm-specific parameters (such as the number of UAVs and inter-UAV latency) using PSO, the system was evaluated in scenarios involving 50 to 100 UAVs. This assessment compared communication costs (1027 bits) and computational costs (3.379 ms) with existing protocols, thereby facilitating secure and efficient swarm communications.

6.2   Real World Deployment

The present study is based on simulations; however, subsequent research may concentrate on the real-world implementation and field testing of the framework across varied UAV scenarios, including urban surveillance, rural search-and-rescue, and military operations. This entails executing the framework on real UAV hardware, evaluating its performance amidst genuine environmental factors (e.g., signal interference, network congestion), and contrasting metrics such as encryption/decryption durations (0.4–0.85 ms and 0.3–0.55 ms) with simulation outcomes, thereby offering practical insights into its deployability.

6.3   Blockchain-Enabled Key Management for Improved Security

Future investigations may examine the incorporation of blockchain technology for the secure management and distribution of cryptographic keys inside UAV networks. A decentralized ledger may be utilized to document key exchanges and rotations, guaranteeing transparency and resistance to tampering. The system may be modified to integrate blockchain consensus mechanisms (e.g., lightweight Proof-of-Stake) appropriate for resource-limited UAVs, and its efficacy might be assessed regarding latency, energy consumption, and robustness against threats such as Physical Capture and Key Reuse.

7   Conslusion

The HECC+PSO system introduced in this study represents a significant leap in safeguarding UAV communications, effectively tackling resource limitations and evolving threats. The integration of Hyperelliptic Curve Cryptography with Particle Swarm Optimization results in remarkable efficiency, with encryption times ranging from 0.4 ms to 0.85 ms and decryption timings from 0.3 ms to 0.55 ms for bit lengths between 2000 and 14000, surpassing HECC+ABC and HECC+GA. Memory use is refined to 20 KB to 70 KB, while communication and computational expenses are minimized to 1027 bits and 3.379 ms, respectively, in comparison to the works of Ullah et al., Berini et al., and Sharma et al. Attack resilience is strong, with man-in-the-middle, physical capture, and other threats well mitigated, as success rates remain below 1.2 and decline to nearly zero after 30 s, enabling secure, efficient, and adaptable communication for UAV systems. Future research will investigate the incorporation of quantum-resistant algorithms to address future threats, improve scalability for bigger UAV swarms, and optimize energy usage to prolong operational endurance in resource-limited settings.

References

1. Papa, U., Papa, U.: Introduction to unmanned aircraft systems (UAS). Embedded Platforms for UAS Landing Path and Obstacle Detection: Integration and Development of Unmanned Aircraft Systems, pp. 1–11 (2018)
2. Dia, A., Berini, E., Amine Ferrag, M., Farou, B., Seridi, H.: Hcala: hyperelliptic curve-based anonymous lightweight authentication scheme for internet of drones. Pervasive Mob. Comput. **92**, 101798 (2023)
3. Luo, G., Zhu, Y., Wang, S., Li, Z., Zhang, M., Wang, X.: Spatial optimization information security algorithm for UAV cluster oriented to RSA. J. Phys. Conf. Ser. **1995**, 012033. IOP Publishing (2021)
4. Usman, M., Amin, R., Aldabbas, H., Alouffi, B.: Lightweight challenge-response authentication in SDN-based UAVs using elliptic curve cryptography. Electronics **11**(7), 1026 (2022)
5. Choe, H., Kang, D.: Ecc based authentication protocol for military internet of drone (iod): a holistic security framework. IEEE Access (2025)
6. Kandasamy, R., Dhandapani, S., Subbiyan, B., Gurumani, V.: Secure transmission and authentication protocol in iot with deep-q-net-key updation. Int. J. Ad Hoc Ubiquitous Comput. **48**(3), 130–148 (2025)
7. Purkert, W.: Cantor's views on the foundations of mathematics. Ideas Their Reception, 48–65. Elsevier (1989)
8. Wollinger, T., Pelzl, J., Wittelsberger, V., Paar, C., Saldamli, G., Koç, Ç.: Elliptic and hyperelliptic curves on embedded μp. ACM Trans. Embedded Comput. Syst. (TECS), **3**(3), 509–533 (2004)
9. Pelzl, J., Wollinger, T., Paar, C.: High performance arithmetic for special hyperelliptic curve cryptosystems of genus two. In: International Conference on Information Technology: Coding and Computing, 2004. Proceedings. ITCC 2004., vol. 2, pp. 513–517. IEEE (2004)
10. Jammula, M., Mani Vakamulla, V., Kondoju, S.K.: Hybrid lightweight cryptography with attribute-based encryption standard for secure and scalable IoT system. Connection Sci. **34**(1), 2431–2447 (2022)
11. Mao, W.-H., Liu, J.-P., Qi, H.-T., Nishiwaki, T., Ding, Y.: Anchorage characteristics and their impacts on the seismic performance of HECC/RC composites external beam-column joint. In: Structures, vol. 63, p. 106469. Elsevier (2024)
12. Fernández, J.L.M., Gonzalo, E.G: The generalized PSO: a new door to pso evolution. J. Artif. Evol. Appl. **2008**(1), 861275 (2008)
13. Ullah, I., et al.: A conditional privacy preserving generalized ring signcryption scheme for micro aerial vehicles. Micromachines **13**(11), 1926 (2022)
14. Jatin Sharma and Pawan Singh Mehra: Hcfaiun: a novel hyperelliptic curve and fuzzy extractor-based authentication for secure data transmission in IoT-based uav networks. Vehic. Commun. **49**, 100834 (2024)

A Unified Semi-automatic Pipeline for Efficient Annotation of Bilingual Handwritten Mathematical Answer Sheets

Sandip Pramanik[1,2]($\boxtimes$) , Shila Rani Sahoo[2] , and Nibaran Das[1]

[1] Department of Computer Science and Engineering, Jadavpur University, Kolkata 700032, India
[2] National Informatics Centre, Ministry of Electronics and I.T., Govt. of India, New Delhi, India
`sandipp.cse.rs@jadavpuruniversity.in`

Abstract. Manual annotation of bilingual handwritten mathematical answer sheets remains a formidable challenge due to the coexistence of multilingual text, different types of components, diverse handwriting styles, and overlapping symbols. To address this, we propose a unified semi-automatic annotation pipeline combining a tailored customised LabelMe interface with the YOLOv10s to handle this. This unified pipeline automates initial predictions and employs human-in-the-loop refinement to correct errors, significantly reducing manual effort while ensuring scalability without compromising annotation quality. The primary contribution is the introduction of the JUDVLP-MATHANSWERSHEET.v2 dataset, collection of 718 bilingual handwritten mathematical answer sheets, annotated with nine distinct categories, including mathematical expressions, bilingual text, trigonometric diagrams, table, mathematical symbols, operators and numeric etc. Experimental evaluations demonstrate YOLOv10s' superiority, achieving 73.20% precision and 36.81% mAP@50-95, outperforming other state-of-the-art models. The proposed semi-automatic annotation method reduces annotation time by 74% compared to manual processes, enabling efficient large-scale dataset creation. This study adds to the field of document analysis by providing a unified framework for the detection of handwritten mathematical answer sheets. The work fills a major gap in the automation of the educational sector and the development of multilingual AI applications.

Keywords: Semi-Automatic Annotation · Object Detection · YOLOv10s · LabelMe · Bilingual Handwritten Mathematical Answer Sheets

1 Introduction

Modern computer vision mostly depends on object detection, which drives developments from intelligent document analysis to autonomous systems. High-

K. Chandra Mondal et al. (Eds.): CICBA 2025, CCIS 2862, pp. 206–220, 2026.
https://doi.org/10.1007/978-3-032-17187-0_16

quality annotated datasets form the backbone of these advances, but their creation remains labor intensive, especially in specialized domains like bilingual Handwritten Mathematical Answer sheets (HMA). These documents present unique challenges due to multilingual text (e.g., Latin-script equations embedded in Bengali paragraphs), diverse handwriting styles, and overlapping symbols. Automating the detection of such elements could revolutionize educational assessments, enabling scalable grading, digitization, and research analysis while reducing human bias. This automation minimizes human effort and establish a transformative assessment tool in the education sector [1,4].

However, existing annotation tools [2,3] do not address these bilingual and handwritten complexities, particularly in regions like India, where mathematical expressions are often written in Latin script alongside body text in native languages such as Bengali. For example, students in West Bengal commonly write mathematics in Latin script while composing the rest of their content in Bengali right from grade IV. Current research on Handwritten Mathematical Expression Detection (HMED) predominantly focuses on printed or single-language contexts, leaving real-world bilingual exam sheets unexplored. Manual annotation of these documents is time-consuming and labour-intensive, requiring domain expertise to handle script variations and symbol overlaps. To date, there is no standardized benchmark dataset for detecting mathematical expressions in handwritten documents created in real-world scenarios, such as exam answer sheets. To the best of our knowledge, the detection of bilingual HMA has not been addressed in prior research, leaving a significant gap in the field.

To bridge this gap, we introduce a semi-automatic annotation pipeline that integrates deep learning-based technique with human refinement. Our experimental results demonstrate that this approach reduces annotation time from 1500 s to 390 s per image, achieving a 74% (Ref. Table 4) improvement in efficiency while preserving high precision. Utilizing a customized version of the LabelMe [18] tool, the proposed pipeline is tailored to domain-specific requirements, optimizing the annotation workflow. Initially, a subset of images is manually labeled to train the YOLOv10s object detection model [13], which then generates predictions for the remaining dataset. A human-in-the-loop verification process is employed to refine only the incorrect predictions through customized LabelMe tool, minimizing manual intervention while ensuring high-quality annotations. This method enhances scalability and efficiency, particularly for datasets requiring expert supervision.

Our primary contributions are fourfold:

1. Semi-Automatic Annotation Pipeline: A novel hybrid framework combining YOLOv10s and a customized LabelMe interface to streamline the annotation of bilingual handwritten mathematical answer sheets (HMA), reducing manual effort by 74%.
2. JUDVLP-MATHANSWERSHEET.v2 Dataset: A first-of-its-kind dataset of 718 bilingual HMA sheets created.

3. Pioneering Bilingual HMA Detection: Addressing a critical gap in document analysis by enabling the detection of mixed-language (English-Bengali) and handwritten mathematical content in real-world exam settings.
4. Comprehensive Taxonomy: We define nine distinct categories, after several rounds of discussion with the experts like school teacher, university teachers and industry people in the domain, to ensure comprehensive annotation of HMA elements. These categories include - MathExp: Isolated mathematical expressions (equations or formulas), MathIL: Inline mathematical expressions (embedded within text), TriDig: Trigonometric diagrams (conceptual diagrams), Table: Tabular structures (numerical or textual data), Numeric: Standalone numerical figures, MathOpr: Mathematical operators (e.g., $+$, $-$, $\times$, $\div$), MathSym: Mathematical symbols (e.g., $\sum$, $\int$, ∞), MathText: Text related to mathematical concepts, and Text: Bilingual content written in both English and Bengali scripts.

This unified pipeline has been tested with various object detection architectures. Experimental results demonstrate YOLOv10s' superiority (73.20% precision, 36.81% mAP@50-95) over other models, validating its role in efficient dataset creation. By streamlining annotation workflows, this work advances document analysis research and lays the groundwork for intelligent transformative assessment tool in multilingual contexts.

The remainder of this paper is structured as follows: Sect. 2 reviews related work, Sect. 3 details dataset preparation, Sect. 5 discusses methodology and experiments, and Sect. 6 concludes with future directions.

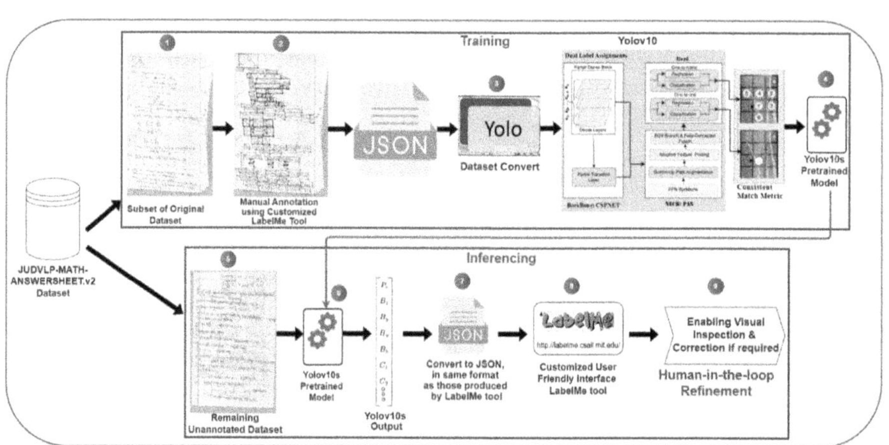

Fig. 1. Semi-automated data annotation pipeline

2   Literature Review

Mathematics expression detection from printed document images [20,21] has been the subject of interest for the last few decades. But same types of interest are missing for HMED. This is mainly because there is no standard benchmark dataset available in the literature for HMED from a complete handwritten text document generally written freely in reallife situations like exams. This problem becomes more complicated when more than one languages are considered within the document. In country like India it is very common to written mathematical expression in latin script keeping text of the body in native languages. For example, in West Bengal Roman numerals are used with bangla text from class IV onward [22]. In the present work we try to address the issues. To the best of our knowledge, the detection of bilingual HMA has not been the subject of any previous scientific research. Data annotation is a crucial step in training object detection models, especially for domain-specific applications. Manual annotation demands have driven research into semi-automatic methods. This review highlights key works in the field.

Berg et al. [1] propose a recursive semi-automatic framework for video data annotation, leveraging forward and backward segmentation checks to minimize manual input by 78% while maintaining accuracy. However, its application is limited to video datasets and not suitable for static image datasets with high variability, such as handwritten documents. Jin et al. [2] introduce a semi-automatic process for traffic scene image annotation, combining CNN-based preprocessing with human review. Innovations include integrating object detection results and a variable-parameter outlier-merging algorithm. This method enhances accuracy by 5% and reduces annotation time by 80%, making it valuable for large-scale labeling tasks. Haider and Michahelles [3] present a human-machine collaborative system using one-shot and few-shot object detection models for bounding box suggestions. Their iterative learning approach speeds up annotation by 2-6x compared to manual methods but struggles with novel, domain-specific datasets like handwritten bilingual mathematical documents. Nguyen et al. [4] demonstrate the potential of YOLOv8 and vision transformer-based models in forensic object detection. Their semi-automatic pipeline outperforms earlier YOLO versions but does not address challenges in highly variable or low-resource domains. Comparative analysis of proposed work with existing research is mentioned in Table 1.

3   Dataset Preparation and Processing

3.1   Data Collection

The JUDVLP-MATHANSWERSHEET.v2 dataset was developed by gathering HMA from a diverse range of sources. The dataset includes samples collected from students spanning grades V to XII across multiple schools, ensuring a comprehensive representation of diverse handwriting styles. This approach enhances the variability and relevance of the data set for training and evaluating models

Table 1. Comparative Analysis of Proposed Work with Existing Research

Study	Approach	Limitations	Proposed Solution
Berg et al. [1]	Video annotation via recursive segmentation	Static image incompatibility; handwriting variability unaddressed.	Hybrid pipeline for static bilingual sheets; handles script mixing & overlaps
Jin et al. [2]	CNN + human review for traffic scenes	No bilingual text support; domain rigidity	YOLOv10s integration for math symbols & bilingual text detection
Haider and Michahelles [3]	Few-shot bounding box suggestions	Poor generalization to novel domains (e.g., math sheets)	Domain-specific dataset (718 sheets) + iterative human-AI refinement
Nguyen et al. [4]	YOLOv8 for forensic detection	Ignores low-resource, variable handwriting	YOLOv10s optimized for low-resource data; modular annotation workflow
Proposed Work	LabelMe + YOLOv10s + human verification	Requires expert annotators for initial labeling	- First bilingual HMA pipeline - 9-category dataset (MathExp, MathIL, etc.) - 73.2% precision via YOLOv10s - 74% faster than manual annotation

in the context of HMA detection. The dataset includes 718 answer sheets, incorporating bilingual content in english and bengali scripts to reflect the linguistic diversity of the contributors. High-quality digital copies of the documents were created by scanning them at 300 dpi using a handheld scanner, ensuring their suitability for subsequent processing.

3.2   Dataset Preparation for Object Detection Tasks

Following the scanning process, preprocessing techniques [19] were employed to enhance the quality and resolution of the images. The annotated images were prepared using a customized version of the LabelMe tool as part of a semi-automated data annotation pipeline. During this phase, nine distinct object classes were identified and labeled, representing various elements found in the handwritten answer sheets. The annotations were stored in JSON format and subsequently converted into multiple standard formats, including YOLO [14], COCO [15], and KITTI [16], to ensure compatibility with a wide range of state-of-the-art object detection models Table 2 & 3. This conversion enabled experimentation with diverse architectures. The dataset was divided into three subsets to facilitate robust model development: 70% (503 images) for training, 20% (144 images) for validation, and 10% (71 images) for testing. This structured partitioning ensured balanced datasets for effective training, validation, and evaluation of the object detection models. The JUDVLP-MATHANSWERSHEET.v2 dataset presented a distinct challenge because of its low-resource characteristics and the subpar quality of the answersheets images in Fig. 2a, 2b. This posed challenges in effectively identifying the intricate handwriting formations. Following the annotation of the data with the LabelMe program, the dataset was transformed into many prevalent formats, including YOLO, KITTI, and COCO, to ensure interoperability with various object identification algorithms.

4   Methodology

4.1   Customization of the LabelMe Tool

The annotation of 718 scanned images was carried out using the open-source LabelMe tool [18], which was significantly customized to enhance the annotation workflow for this project. Customizations were implemented using the Qt framework [17], resulting in a more intuitive and efficient user interface designed to minimize manual effort and improve productivity. Given the bilingual nature of the dataset, which includes both english and bengali scripts, achieving precise and consistent annotations was essential. Professional annotators with expertise in handling linguistic diversity and complex handwritten content were employed to ensure the accuracy and reliability of the annotations. This combination of a unified semi-automatic data annotation pipeline and human-in-the-loop refinement to correct errors resulted in a high-quality annotated dataset, which serves as a vital resource for training and evaluating object detection models of bilingual HMA.

4.2   Semi-automatic Data Annotation Process

To streamline the image annotation process for object detection tasks, a novel unified semi-automatic pipeline was developed, as illustrated in Fig. 1. The process begins with a subset of images being manually annotated using the customized LabelMe tool. This tool provides a user-friendly graphical interface for creating bounding boxes and assigning class labels. The output of this manual annotation stage is saved in JSON format, where each file corresponds to an image and contains annotation data, including bounding box coordinates and associated class labels.

Once the manual annotations are complete, the JSON files are converted into the YOLO format. This step involves adapting annotations into a format compatible with YOLO training frameworks, standardizing bounding box parameters as normalized center coordinates (center x, y, width, height) and class indices. The YOLOv10s model is then trained using these converted annotations, enabling it to learn how to detect objects in images and predict bounding box locations, class indices, and confidence scores.

After training, the pre-trained YOLOv10s model is applied to the remaining unannotated images in the dataset. The model performs inference on these images, generating bounding box predictions along with class indices and confidence scores for each detected object. These outputs are used to recreate JSON files in the same format as those produced by the LabelMe tool. Each file contains all detected bounding boxes and their corresponding class labels.

Algorithm 1. Semi-Automatic Data Annotation Process

Require: Image dataset $\mathcal{D} = \{I_1, I_2, \ldots, I_n\}$
Ensure: Annotated dataset $\mathcal{A} = \{\texttt{json}_1, \texttt{json}_2, \ldots, \texttt{json}_n\}$
1: **Step 1: Manual Annotation**
2: Annotate a subset $\mathcal{D}_{\mathrm{manual}} \subset \mathcal{D}$ using LabelMe tool.
3: Save annotations as $\texttt{json}$ files.
4: **Step 2: Conversion to YOLO Format**
5: **for** each $\texttt{json}_i \in \mathcal{D}_{\mathrm{manual}}$ **do**
6:     Extract bounding box $\mathbf{b}_i = (x, y, w, h)$ and class c_i.
7:     Convert $\mathbf{b}_i$ and c_i to YOLO format.
8: **end for**
9: **Step 3: Train YOLOv10s Model**
10: Train YOLOv10s model $\mathcal{M}$ using YOLO-formatted annotations.
11: **Step 4: Inference on Remaining Images**
12: **for** each $I_j \in \mathcal{D} \setminus \mathcal{D}_{\mathrm{manual}}$ **do**
13:     Use $\mathcal{M}$ to predict bounding boxes $\mathbf{b}_j$ and classes c_j.
14:     Save predictions $(\mathbf{b}_j, c_j)$.
15: **end for**
16: **Step 5: Generate LabelMe-Compatible JSON**
17: **for** each $(\mathbf{b}_j, c_j)$ from inference results **do**
18:     Convert to $\texttt{json}$ format compatible with LabelMe.
19: **end for**
20: **Step 6: Refine Annotations**
21: **for** each $\texttt{json}_j$ file **do**
22:     Load $\texttt{json}_j$ into LabelMe tool.
23:     Verify and adjust $(\mathbf{b}_j, c_j)$ if incorrect.
24: **end for**
25: **Step 7: Save Final Annotations**
26: Save corrected $\texttt{json}_j$ files for all I_j.
27: **Step 8: Completion**
28: Combine all $\texttt{json}_j$ files into $\mathcal{A}$.

In the next stage, these auto-generated JSON files are loaded into the custom LabelMe tool for human-in-the-loop refinement to correct errors. When loaded, the tool displays the detected bounding boxes and class labels on the images, enabling visual inspection. Users can review the annotations to verify their correctness. If any bounding box or class label is incorrect, it can be adjusted through the tool's intuitive user interface. Correct annotations are left untouched, ensuring that only erroneous labels are modified.

The proposed semi-automatic approach, mentioned in Algorithm 1, enhances annotation efficiency. Automated inference and annotation manage the majority of the workload, with human reviewers refining errors. This method optimizes time and effort, making it scalable for large datasets. By integrating automation with manual verification, the pipeline offers a reliable solution for generating annotated datasets in object detection tasks.

4.3   Yolov10

YOLOv10 [13] introduces significant advancements in real-time object detection by eliminating the reliance on non-maximum suppression (NMS), which previously hindered end-to-end deployment and increased inference time. This is achieved through NMS-free training using a novel dual label assignment strategy, optimizing efficiency without added computational cost. YOLOv10s is a lightweight version of YOLOv10.

The architecture integrates one-to-one and one-to-many matching mechanisms, where a dedicated one-to-one head ensures NMS-free inference while leveraging enriched supervision during training. The process of label assignment follows a standardized matching criterion defined as:

$$m(\alpha, \beta) = s \cdot p^\alpha \cdot \text{IoU}(\hat{b}, b)^\beta, \tag{1}$$

where p represents the classification confidence score, $\hat{b}$ and b correspond to the predicted and ground-truth bounding boxes, respectively. The term s serves as a spatial prior, indicating whether the anchor point of the predicted box is positioned inside the ground-truth instance. The parameters α and β are crucial hyperparameters that regulate the balance between semantic classification and localization accuracy. We define the matching scores for the one-to-many and one-to-one metrics as $m_{o2m} = m(\alpha_{o2m}, \beta_{o2m})$ and $m_{o2o} = m(\alpha_{o2o}, \beta_{o2o})$, respectively. These matching criteria influence both the label assignment strategy and the training supervision of the two prediction heads.

To improve the inference performance of the one-to-one prediction head, its training supervision is aligned with the richer and more informative signals derived from the one-to-many prediction head. Researchers analyzed the gap between the two heads, identifying differences in classification targets while maintaining consistent regression objectives. Initially, both heads generate identical predictions. By harmonizing their metrics, including IoU (u^*) and matching scores (m^*_{o2m} and m^*_{o2o}), the gap is minimized. The classification targets are derived as: $t_{o2m,j} = u^* \cdot \frac{m_{o2m,j}}{m^*_{o2m}} \leq u^*$ for $j \in \Omega$ and $t_{o2o,i} = u^* \cdot \frac{m_{o2o,i}}{m^*_{o2o}} = u^*$.

The supervision gap is quantified using the 1-Wasserstein distance [23]:

$$A = t_{o2o,i} - \mathbb{I}(i \in \Omega)t_{o2m,i} + \sum_{k \in \Omega \setminus \{i\}} t_{o2m,k}, \tag{2}$$

As $t_{o2m,i}$ increases, the gap reduces, reaching it's minimum when $t_{o2m,i} = u^*$. To ensure alignment, consistent matching parameters are enforced, such that

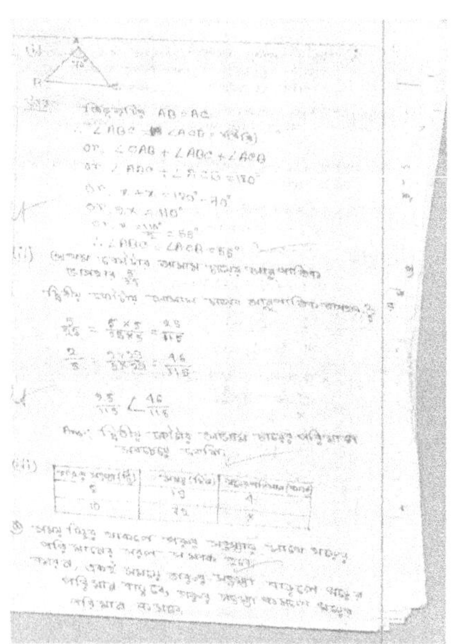

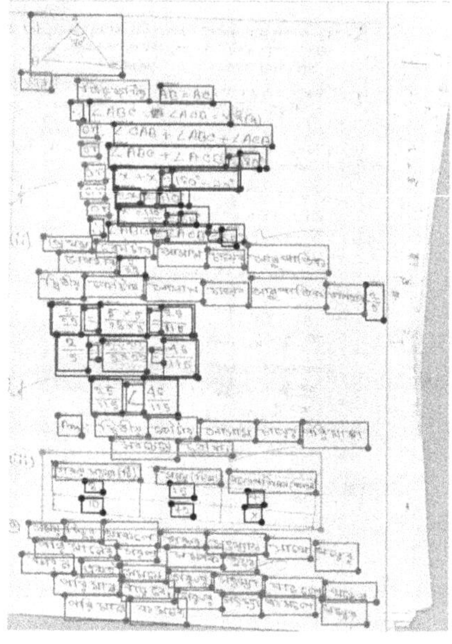

(a) **Sample mathematical answer-sheet, dimension 2576x3936**

(b) **Manual Data Annotation Using the LabelMe Tool and Training on the YOLOv10s Model**

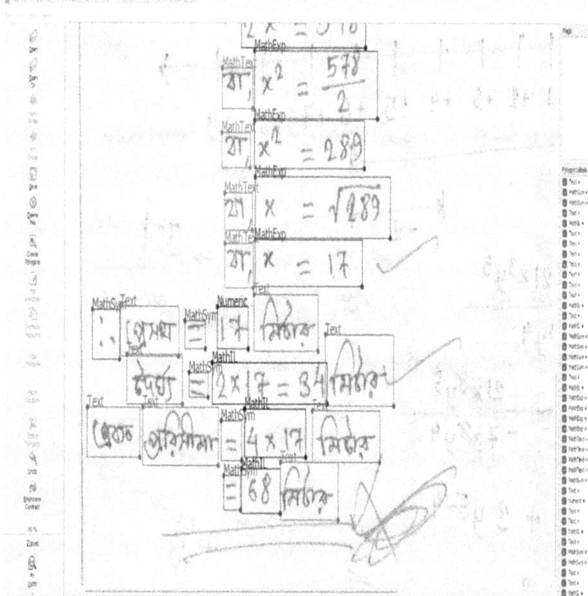

(c) **Inference on Unlabeled Data with a Pretrained YOLOv10s Model, Followed by Visual Inspection and Correction (human-in-the-loop refinement) via customized LabelMe Tool**

Fig. 2. Sample Images of Mathematical Answer Sheets and Tools Used

$\alpha_{o2o} = r \cdot \alpha_{o2m}$ and $\beta_{o2o} = r \cdot \beta_{o2m}$. By setting $r = 1$, the metrics become identical, allowing both heads to optimize harmoniously. To validate the alignment, researchers measured one-to-one matching pairs among the top-1, top-5, and top-10 results of the one-to-many head after training. This demonstrated improved consistency and performance, solidifying YOLOv10s as a highly efficient and accurate object detection model.

5   Experimental Results and Discussion

A comparative evaluation of state-of-the-art object detection models on the JUDVLP-MATHANSWERSHEET.v2 dataset (Table 2) reveals critical insights into their performance for bilingual handwritten mathematical content. Faster R-CNN achieves the highest precision (36.76%) and recall (39.54%), outperforming SSD and EfficientDet by significant margins. Its mAP@50 score of 32.01% further underscores its robustness in detecting overlapping symbols and bilingual text. However, the modest absolute metrics across all models highlight the inherent challenges of the dataset, including script variability and densely packed handwritten elements.

5.1   Comparison with State-of-the-Art Models

Table 2. State-of-the-art Model Result Comparison on Our Dataset

Methodology	Precision	Recall	mAP50	mAP(50–95)
SSD [5]	27.22	25.47	27.21	13.78
Faster R-CNN [8]	36.76	39.54	32.01	18.41
EfficientDet [9]	25.62	27.43	29.65	14.85

SSD and EfficientDet exhibit lower precision (27.22% and 25.62%, respectively) and recall (25.47% and 27.43%), reflecting their limitations in handling fine-grained annotations. While their streamlined architectures favor computational efficiency, their mAP@50-95 scores (13.78% and 14.85%) suggest limited generalization to multi-scale objects, such as small mathematical symbols embedded within bilingual paragraphs. Faster R-CNN's two-stage detection framework, though slower, proves more adept at localizing intricate elements, as evidenced by its superior mAP@50.

These results emphasize the need for domain-specific optimizations. For instance, Faster R-CNN's region proposal network (RPN) likely benefits from iterative refinement of candidate regions, which is critical for distinguishing ambiguous handwritten characters. Conversely, SSD and EfficientDet's single-shot architectures struggle with class confusion in low-resolution regions, a common issue in densely annotated answer sheets. The moderate precision across

Table 3. YOLO Family Result Comparison on Our Dataset

Methodology	Precision	Recall	mAP50	mAP(50-95)
Yolov5s [10]	51.34	45.76	41.67	28.32
Yolov8s [11]	65.45	59.65	64.91	32.12
Yolov9s [12]	72.5	62.5	69.1	35.0
Yolov10s [13]	73.2	62.8	69.2	36.81

all models further underscores the necessity of human-in-the-loop verification in our unified semi-automatic pipeline to correct false positives.

A systematic evaluation of YOLO variants (Table 3) demonstrates progressive enhancements in detecting bilingual HMA elements. YOLOv5s achieves baseline performance (51.34% precision, 41.67% mAP@50), constrained by its limited capacity to discern overlapping symbols and bilingual text. YOLOv8s exhibits marked improvements, with precision rising to 65.45% and mAP@50 to 64.91%, attributable to its anchor-free architecture and enhanced feature pyramid networks. YOLOv9s further elevates performance (72.5% precision, 69.1% mAP@50), leveraging programmable gradient information to refine localization of small-scale objects like mathematical operators (+, x). The best performer is YOLOv10s, which achieves 73.2% precision and 36.81% mAP@50-95, the highest among all variants. Its elimination of non-maximum suppression (NMS) through dual label assignment minimizes redundant detections, critical for densely annotated regions with bilingual text and symbols (e.g., $\sum$ adjacent to Bengali script).

Notably, recall rates plateau at 62.8% for YOLOv10s, suggesting persistent challenges in detecting low-contrast or fragmented handwritten elements. However, its balanced precision-recall tradeoff and superior mAP@50-95 validate its selection for our unified semi-automatic pipeline. When deployed for inference, YOLOv10s reduced manual annotation effort by 74%, as erroneous predictions primarily involved ambiguous symbol overlaps corrected via LabelMe's human-in-the-loop interface.

These results underscore YOLOv10s' architectural advancements particularly its NMS-free design and harmonized supervision as pivotal for bilingual HMA tasks. While computational costs rise marginally across versions, the accuracy gains justify its adoption for domain-specific annotation workflows. Future iterations could prioritize lightweight adaptations to enhance real-time performance without compromising detection fidelity (Figs. 3 and 4).

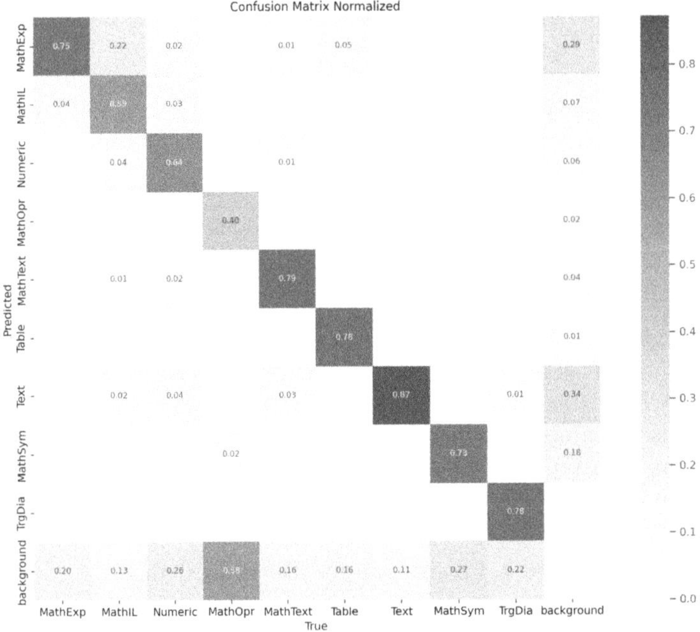

Fig. 3. The confusion matrix for Yolov10s with our few label data

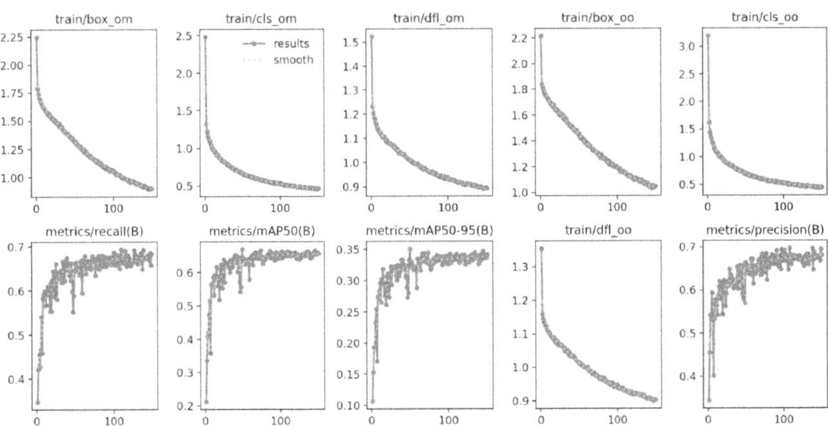

Fig. 4. Yolov10s Training Loss and Performance Metrics

5.2 Comparison of Manual and Semi-automatic Annotation Methods

The experiment aimed to compare the efficiency of manual annotation and the proposed semi-automatic annotation method. Two sets of HMA images with identical content were used—one was annotated manually, while the other was processed using proposed semi-automatic annotation pipeline. The results indicate that manual annotation took 1500 s (25 min) per image, whereas the semi-automatic method significantly reduced the annotation time to 390 s (6.5 min) per image. The semi-automatic annotation method improves efficiency by 74% compared to the manual annotation method, making the proposed method more suitable for the creation of large-scale data sets while maintaining high precision.

$$\text{Efficiency Improvement } (\%) = \left(\frac{\text{Manual Time} - \text{Semi-Automatic Time}}{\text{Manual Time}} \right) \times 100$$

5.3   Limitation

The current dataset of 718 bilingual HMA sheets, while valuable, requires expansion in size and diversity to enhance generalizability across varied educational contexts. YOLOv10s achieves 73.2% precision but struggles with highly overlapping symbols and ambiguous handwritten elements, necessitating further model optimization. The pipeline relies on manual correction by domain experts for initial labeling and error refinement, limiting full automation potential.

Table 4. Comparison of Annotation Methods

Annotation Method	Avg. Time per Image (seconds)	Efficiency Improvement
Manual Annotation	1800	Baseline (0%)
Semi-Automatic Annotation	390	74% Faster

6   Conclusion

In this study, a semi-automatic pipeline that combines YOLOv10s with a customised LabelMe interface is presented. This pipeline reduces the manual annotation effort for bilingual HMA by 74% while maintaining high precision through human-in-the-loop refinement. A major gap in bilingual document analysis is filled by the proposed JUDVLP-MATHANSWERSHEET.v2 dataset, which consists of 718 annotated sheets in nine different categories. We wish to offer bilingual answer sheets from a wider range of linguistic backgrounds so that things are more interesting and useful in the future. In future editions, weak supervision, active learning, and pseudo-labeling will also be looked at as approaches to make automated annotations better so that fewer skilled annotators are needed. We will employ ideas like multi-scale feature fusion and Cascade R-CNN to make the detection model even better so that it can recall handwritten elements that are hard to see or that are on top of each other. We also want to include OCR modules so that we can give a more full semantic interpretation of written and numerical information in all scripts. Finally, the framework was first designed for maths answer sheets, but because it is modular, it may also be used for language studies and science. This makes it a useful and flexible tool for adding notes to educational papers in a number of languages.

Acknowledgements. The work is partially supported by SERB (DST), Govt. of India (Ref No. MTR/2023/000685) and carried out at the CMATER Lab, Dept. of CSE, Jadavpur University.

References

1. Berg, A., Johnander, J., Gevigney, F., Ahlberg, J. Felberg, M.: Semi-Automatic Annotation of Objects in Visual-Thermal Video (2019)
2. Jin, Y., Li, J., Ma, D., Guo, X. Yu, H.: A semi-automatic annotation technology for traffic scene image labeling based on deep learning preprocessing. In: 2017 IEEE International Conference On Computational Science And Engineering (CSE) And IEEE International Conference On Embedded And Ubiquitous Computing (EUC), Vol. 1, pp. 315–320 (2017)
3. Haider, T., Michahelles, F.: Human-machine collaboration on data annotation of images by semi-automatic labeling. In: Proceedings of Mensch und Computer 2021, pp. 552–556 (2021). https://doi.org/10.1145/3473856.3473993
4. Nguyen, T., Wilson, C., Khan, I. Dalins, J.: Object Detection Approaches to Identifying Hand Images with High Forensic Values (2024). https://arxiv.org/abs/2412.16431
5. Liu, W., et al.: SSD: Single Shot MultiBox Detector. In: Leibe, B., Matas, J., Sebe, N., Welling, M. (eds.) ECCV 2016. LNCS, vol. 9905, pp. 21–37. Springer, Cham (2016). https://doi.org/10.1007/978-3-319-46448-0_2
6. Fu, C., Liu, W., Ranga, A., Tyagi, A., Berg, A.: DSSD: Deconvolutional Single Shot Detector, ArXiv Preprint ArXiv:1701.06659 (2017)
7. Li, Y., Ren, F.: Light-weight RetinaNet for Object Detection, ArXiv Preprint ArXiv:1905.10011 (2019)
8. Ren, S., He, K., Girshick, R., Sun, J.: Faster R-CNN: towards real-time object detection with region proposal networks. IEEE Trans. Pattern Anal. Mach. Intell. **39**, 1137–1149 (2016)
9. Tan, M., Pang, R., Le, Q.: EfficientDet: scalable and efficient object detection. In: Proceedings of the IEEE/CVF Conference on Computer Vision and Pattern Recognition, pp. 10781–10790 (2020)
10. Jocher, G. et al.: YOLOv5 (2020). https://github.com/ultralytics/yolov5
11. Jocher, G. et al.: YOLOv8 (2023). https://github.com/ultralytics/ultralytics
12. Wang, C., Yeh, I., Liao, H.: YOLOv9: Learning What You Want to Learn Using Programmable Gradient Information, ArXiv Preprint ArXiv:2402.13616 (2024)
13. Wang, A., et al.: YOLOv10: Real-Time End-to-End Object Detection, ArXiv Preprint ArXiv:2405.14458 (2024)
14. Redmon, J., Divvala, S., Girshick, R., Farhadi, A.: You Only Look Once: Unified, Real-Time Object Detection, https://arxiv.org/abs/1506.02640 (2016)
15. Lin, T.-Y., et al.: Microsoft COCO: Common Objects in Context. In: Fleet, D., Pajdla, T., Schiele, B., Tuytelaars, T. (eds.) ECCV 2014. LNCS, vol. 8693, pp. 740–755. Springer, Cham (2014). https://doi.org/10.1007/978-3-319-10602-1_48
16. Geiger, A., Lenz, P., Stiller, C., Urtasun, R.: Vision meets robotics: the KITTI dataset. Int. J. Robot. Res. **32**, 1231–1237 (2013)
17. Qt. https://www.qt.io/
18. Russell, B., Torralba, A., Murphy, K., Freeman, W.: LabelMe: a database and web-based tool for image annotation. Int. J. Comput. Vision **77**, 157–173 (2008)

19. Harraj, A., Raissouni, N.: OCR Accuracy Improvement on Document Images Through a Novel Pre-Processing Approach, ArXiv Preprint ArXiv:1509.03456 (2015)
20. Hu, K., Zhong, Z., Sun, L., Huo, Q.: Mathematical formula detection in document images: a new dataset and a new approach. Pattern Recogn. **148**, 110212 (2024)
21. Ohyama, W., Suzuki, M., Uchida, S.: Detecting mathematical expressions in scientific document images using a u-net trained on a diverse dataset. IEEE Access **7**, 144030–144042 (2019)
22. BanglarShiksha. https://banglarshiksha.gov.in/
23. Panaretos, V. Zemel, Y.: Statistical aspects of wasserstein distances. Ann. Rev. Stat. Its Appl.. **6**, 405–431 (2019). http://dx.doi.org/10.1146/annurev-statistics-030718-104938

Improved Diphthong Detection for Machine Translated Hindi Speech Recognition

Samiran Maulick, Anupam Hui, Abhishikta Mondal,
Anandaprova Majumder$^{(\boxtimes)}$ iD, and Anirban Bose iD

Dr. B. C. Roy Engineering College, Durgapur, Jemua Road, Fuljhore, Durgapur
713206, West Bengal, India
`anandaprova.majumder@bcrec.ac.in`

Abstract. The critical role of diphthong detection in machine-translated Hindi speech recognition, focusing on improving the accuracy of Automatic Speech Recognition (ASR) systems is proposed here. The proposed system consists of (a) a speech-to-text model Indic Wav2Vec 2.0 (b) Hindi-to-English translation using GoogleTrans (c) phonetic syllable detection using CMU pronouncing library and (d) IPA-based visualization of detected diphthongs. The work addresses issues like pronunciation variability, accent differences, co-articulation effects, and the lack of labeled datasets. It also discusses the potential of deep learning (DL) to address these challenges, leveraging artificial neural networks (ANNs) and deep neural networks (DNNs) for improved detection. In addition, limitations such as cascading errors and loss of phonetic information during translation are also discussed in this work. The endings aim to contribute to the development of more accurate and robust ASR systems, particularly for Hindi and other languages with complex phonetic structures. This research contributes to phonetic-aware multilingual speech processing, with applications in education, linguistics, and AI-powered voice assistants.

Keywords: Hindi Speech Recognition · Machine Translation · Diphthong Detection · Phonetics · Deep Learning

1 Introduction

Even though systems, such as speech recognition and machine translation, have improved greatly in recent years, correctly processing phonetic constituents with dynamic acoustic features continues to pose real challenges. Within these constituents, diphthongs, which are defined as composed of two vowel sounds that are pronounced together within a single syllable, stand out as one particularly difficult example. Unlike monophthongs, which maintain a relatively stable articulatory configuration, diphthongs involve continuous spectral changes that reflect the dynamic movement of the vocal tract [2]. This variability makes vowel

© The Author(s), under exclusive license to Springer Nature Switzerland AG 2026
K. Chandra Mondal et al. (Eds.): CICBA 2025, CCIS 2862, pp. 221–231, 2026.
https://doi.org/10.1007/978-3-032-17187-0_17

recognition extremely difficult, particularly in languages where diphthongs are important, such as Hindi [8,13]. Diphthong detection is important not only in linguistics research but also in speech technology. In automatic speech recognition (ASR) systems, accurate diphthong modeling is crucial if word recognition errors are to be reduced in languages that use diphthongs as phonemic contrasts [10]. An example in English is the words ride /raɪd/ and rod /rˤd/, which are phonemically distinguished by their vocalic nuclei, with the diphthong /aɪ/ contrasting with the monophthong /ˤ/. In Hindi, diphthongs /əɪ/ and /aʊ/ similarly function as critical phonemic markers [4]. Not being able to identify these transitions accurately may result in a chain of errors in voice assistants and automated transcription applications.

Identifying diphthongs is a critical aspect of pronunciation teaching in a foreign language. Learners of English as a second language have great difficulties with producing diphthongs and tend to simplify them into monophthongs or execute some erroneous transition patterns [11]. For instance, learners of English could say boat (/boʊt/) as /bɔt/, the glide between /o/ and /ʊ/ being omitted entirely. Such minor omissions, though, have the potential to greatly affect their intelligibility and fluency. The integration of these technological innovations in pedagogy could transform language teaching, especially in low-resource contexts which lack human pronunciation tutors to aid learners with correcting these pronounced errors [12]. Another area that is related to the study of diphthongs is concern with accent and dialect recognition. The presence of vernacular diphthongs with high regional scope serves as an important indicator of dialect discrimination [9]. For instance, in American English, the diphthong that occurs in words such as right has a lot of variation across the different dialects: some speakers have a relatively more centralized onset (/rɛɪt/) while others have a relatively more peripheral one (/raɪt/). The Taizi dialects of Hindi also exhibit this variation; the realization of diphthongs such as /ɛə/ often tells which region someone comes from.

The automatic detection and characterization localization systems pose a very important challenge for developing accent-tolerant speech processing technologies and also accent-tolerant technologies for documenting sociolinguistic variation [7]. In phonetics and phonology, diphthongs represent one of the most striking cases of coarticulation and movement of speech organs. In the case of diphthongs, the degree of continuous movement is so high that both linguistic components (phonological structure, degree of emphasis) and non-linguistic components (speed of talking, style of speech) control the uniting of two vowels. They pose particular interest in the context of models of speech production and perception. Also, other branches of linguistics, such as historical linguistics, gain from diphthong research because the emergence, disappearance or alteration of diphthongs is what many phonological changes are based on. A prototypical case of such processes is the Great Vowel Shift which transformed long vowels into diphthongs during a certain period in history (e.g., Middle English /iː/ into Modern English /aɪ/ in words such as time)—involving several phonological challenges. To begin with, the manner in which diphthongs are sounded differs widely among speakers, dialects, and talking styles. Although phonological targets are thought to be constant, they can be changed significantly in regard to formant contour, duration, and spectral change.

Speech and language encompass the creation of sounds produced by the human vocal tract with the purpose of communication. The human vocal tract produces sounds that are then altered by the resonant cavities of the mouth, nose, and throat. Speech recognition technology differs greatly in nature considering the vast variety of sounds that can be produced within a language and the co-articulation of particular sounds within the speech. In simple terms, speech technology is the capability of a computer system to recognize and either reproduce or respond to the statements made within it [3]. Language goes as far as forming the basic unit of sound known as phoneme and uses diphthongs as the compound unit made up of two separate phonemes. Social networks have changed the viewpoint on phonology and its shape within certain languages. Taking all of this into account, the focus on the present system lies in the numerous modes of detecting diphthongs within Hindi, the languages well-known for having significant phonological diphthongs that make them hard to identify automatically. Furthermore, the existing speech corpora pose problems due to the absence of standardized phonetic markings for Hindi diphthongs. We have incorporated the latest machine learning analysis with acoustic analysis to de- sign a detection system that is aimed at the robust detection of speech signal in the presence of noise and its variability.

This research makes several key contributions. First, we provide a complete account of the acoustic structures of Hindi diphthongs, noting their variation in different phonetic contexts and styles of speech. To that end, we present new annotation schema for Hindi diphthongs which is based on their phonological structures and the degree of variability associated with their phonetic realization. Second, we show how using better detection of diphthongs result in better detection of practical systems like ASR and pronunciation training. Beyond the particular case of Hindi, the consequences of this work reach further. The techniques developed in this research could be used in other languages with complicated vowel systems, hence making the speech technology more reliable and general. Also, our results have implications regarding the description of diphthongs as phonological unit and their execution as two edge continuous movements. As the use of speech technologies expands in society with the integration of virtual assistants and automatic captioning services, correct recognition of every phonetic unit, diphthongs included, is of utmost importance. The present work aims at improving linguistically driven speech processing systems and strives to meet the requirements of the natural human languages.

2   Related Works

Due to the inherently complex structure of vowel glides, their identification has remained a significant challenge within the speech processing community. Some of the initial approaches used the acoustic-phonetic techniques by detecting diphthongs through analysing formant trajectory [F1/F2 transitions] and spectral components [1]. Diphthong evolution in time was measured for a long time through Linear Predictive Coding (LPC) and Mel-Frequency Cepstral Coefficients (MFCCs). Unfortunately, such techniques were limited in accuracy because of speaker variability, effects of coarticulation, and lack of robustness in noise situations. "Real world" applications were, however, unable to utilize their true potential [8]. In [2], twenty-nine Spanish speakers performed two perceptual assimilation tasks with varying response options (including or excluding diphthongs) and an L1 vowel identification task. The findings revealed that Spanish listeners consistently perceived English diphthongs as closer to Spanish diphthongs than to monophthongs, with high assimilation scores. This underscores the importance of considering diphthongs in cross-language comparisons and second-language acquisition research involving languages like Spanish.

In a similar work [4] the structured nature of acoustic variability in speech production is explored, arguing that differences in variability across languages and speakers follow systematic patterns. Additionally, the study highlights that individual speaker differences are shaped by the way phonological contrasts are implemented within each language. Javed et al. focus on developing ASR systems for low-resource languages in the Indian subcontinent, aiming to expand accessibility for the next billion users. They collected 17,000 h of speech data across 40 Indian languages from domains like education, news, technology, and nance. Using this dataset, they pretrained wav2vec-style models, a self- supervised learning approach for speech recognition. Their analysis revealed that phonetic similarities exist across languages, with deeper model layers capturing language family distinctions, and attention mechanisms focusing on small speech segments for improved recognition. Fine-tuning these models for nine languages led to state-of-the-art performance on three public datasets, including for low-resource languages like Sinhala and Nepali. However, their research was not aimed to find out the diphthong in Indian languages, which could have helped in pronunciation.

The use of machine-learning on diphthong pattern ending became widely spread due to a) the algorithms of the Hidden Markov Model (HMM) and b) the sequential combination of GMMs [10]. The application of deep learning methods with Convolutional or Recurrent Neural Networks has tremendously improved the results due to their ability to learn optimal features from data without the necessity of prior signal conditioning. One of the most useful approaches is a combination of traditional DL with attention mechanisms that enabled the capturing of the long-range dependencies of the diphthongs without losing the sequence structures [6]. Though there have been numerous improvements, assisting in multilingual diphthongs in low resource languages and time restricted calculations remains an unsolved problem. Adjustments in supervising learning and changes in languages in combination with deep learning for generalization need to be explored. This demands a need to devise a method for the detection of diphthongs in Indian languages (e.g. Hindi).

3   Brief Review of Deep Learning

Deep learning is a subset of machine learning that focuses on training artificial neural networks to recognize patterns in data. It is inspired by the structure and function of the human brain, where layers of interconnected nodes (neurons) process information. Deep learning has revolutionized fields such as speech recognition, natural language processing (NLP), computer vision, and autonomous systems due to its ability to learn from large datasets without explicit programming. A general procedure that is followed to build a DL model is shown in Fig. 1. The input data, depending upon the application, could be text, image, audio, video or any combination of them. In the proposed work, the input data is taken to be audio files.

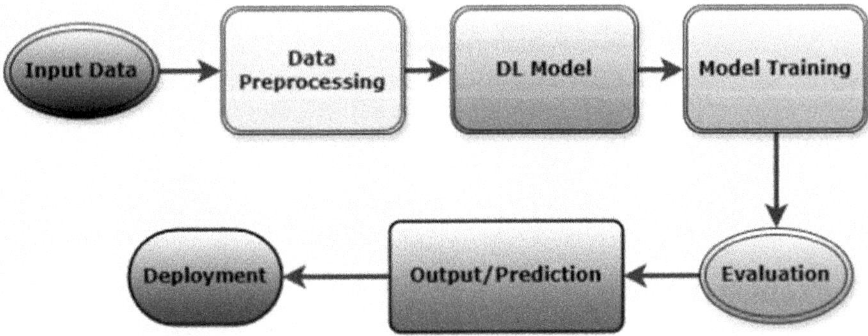

Fig. 1. General Workflow of DL Techniques.

Deep learning employs artificial neural networks with multiple levels to learn hierarchical representations of data. The major components are neural networks themselves, backpropagation for adjusting weight values, and activation functions for introducing non-linearity. Deep learning is categorized from the perspective of its architecture and its technique. Convolutional Neural Networks (CNNs) are preferred for two dimensional data such as images, Recurrent Neural Networks (RNNs) work best with time series data, and Generative Adversarial Networks (GANs) create new data. AutoEncoders (AEs) are used for input data dimensionality reduction, Graph Neural Networks (GNNs) manage graph structured data, and Natural language processing is dominantly performed with Transformers, on which attention based mechanisms are incorporated.

In deep reinforcement learning, deep learning is applied for decision making by the agent in an interactive environment. Deep learning development is driven by the increased use of attention mechanisms, deployment of transfer learning for model computation economy, and development of Explainable AI (XAI) for improving model interpretability. Neural Architecture Search (NAS) supports automated architecture design, while Federated Learning facilitates decentralized model training without compromising data confidentiality. Such new developments altogether facilitate the limitless change and growth of the application of deep learning technology in diverse fields.

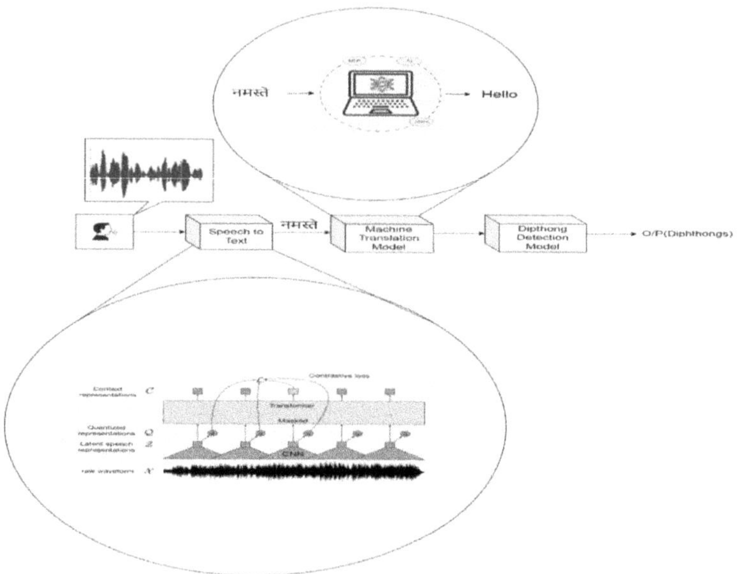

Fig. 2. The Proposed Model.

4   Proposed Method

The recorded audio files containing Hindi speech are fed to a pre-trained speech2-text model where it is converted to Hindi transcript. This transcript is then given at the input of a separate text2text machine translation model to get the transcript converted into English text. Finally, from the English text diphthongs are identified. The proposed technique detects syllables and diphthongs in a given word using a step by step procedure, as shown below. The overall schematic representation of the proposed technique is given in Fig. 2.

The aforementioned proposed technique for finding out the diphthongs is given in the following procedure.

4.1   Procedure: Diphthong Detection Technique

– Step 1: **Initialization:** The algorithm takes a word w as input and initializes empty lists for syllables (S) and diphthongs (D). The detailed structure of the proposed algorithm is given in Algorithm 1.
– Step 2: **Helper Functions:**
  • $f_v(p)$ identifies vowel phonemes by checking for numeric stress markers (digits)
  • $f_s(p)$ removes stress markers from phonemes

Algorithm 1. Diphthong and Syllable Detection

Require: $w \rightarrow$ Word to analyze
Ensure: $R = \{W, S, D\}$ where:
      - $W = w$ (Original Word)
       - $S =$ List of detected syllables (vowel phonemes without stress markers)
       - $D =$ List of detected diphthongs

1: **function** DetectDiphthongs(w)
2:     **Define Helper Functions:**
3:       $f_V(p) = \begin{cases} 1, & \text{if } p \text{ contains a digit} \\ 0, & \text{otherwise} \end{cases}$ $\triangleright$ Vowel detection function
4:       $f_S(p) = p - \{d \mid d \in \mathbb{D}, d \text{ is a digit}\}$ $\triangleright$ Stress marker removal
5:     **Retrieve Phonetic Pronunciations:**
6:       $P_w \leftarrow$ pronouncing_phones_for_word(w)
7:     **if** $P_w = \emptyset$ **then then**
8:       **return** $\{W, [], []\}$
9:     **end if**
10:     **Initialize:**
11:       $S \leftarrow \emptyset$ $\triangleright$ Detected syllables
12:       $D \leftarrow \emptyset$ $\triangleright$ Detected diphthongs
13:     **Process each pronunciation** $P_i \in P_w$**:**
14:       Split P_i into phonemes: $P \leftarrow \{p_1, p_2, \ldots, p_n\}$
15:     **Extract syllables:**
16:       $S' \leftarrow \{p \mid p \in P, f_V(p) = 1\}$
17:     **Remove stress markers:**
18:       $P' \leftarrow \{f_S(p) \mid p \in P\}$
19:       $S \leftarrow S \cup \{s \mid s \in S'\}$
20:     **Detect diphthongs:**
21:     **for** each diphthong d in predefined dictionary D_p **do**
22:       **if** $\exists$ sequence (p_i, p_{i+1}) in P' such that $(p_i, p_{i+1}) \equiv d$ **then**
23:         $D \leftarrow D \cup \{d\}$
24:       **end if**
25:     **end for**
26:     **return** $\{W, S, D\}$
27: **end function**

- Step 3: **Pronunciation Lookup:** Retrieves all possible phonetic pronunciations P_w of the input word. If none exist, returns empty results.
- Step 4: **Phoneme Processing:** For each pronunciation:
  - Splits the pronunciation into individual phonemes
  - Extracts syllables by identifying vowel phonemes
  - Removes stress markers from all phonemes
- Step 5: **Diphthong Detection:** Compares consecutive phoneme pairs against a predefined diphthong dictionary D_p to identify diphthong patterns.
- Step 6: **Output:** Returns the original word along with detected syllables and diphthongs.

5   Result and Discussion

The audio files containing Hindi speech are generated using a recording device where frequency is set at 16 kHz and on a mono-channel with bit rate at 128 kbps. Each audio file is stored with a different ID and in the .wav format. The audio file is then fed to a pre-trained GoogleTrans (speech2text) model where it is converted to Hindi transcript. This transcript is then given at the input of a separate Indicwav2vec (text2text) machine translation model to convert the transcript into English text. It is worth mentioning that the text2text model used in this work is developed by IIT Madras [5]. Various Hindi audio files are tested to find the diphthong and the results of the experiments are shown in Table 1. These recordings, comprising a total of ten .wav files (mono-channel, 16 kHz, 128 kbps), were used for the experimental evaluation. For the sake of reproducibility, the dataset has been made publicly available on Kaggle at https://www.kaggle. com/datasets/samiranmaulick/voice-dataset.

From the tabular data it is clear that the proposed diphthong detection system achieved consistent performance across Hindi speech recordings, with precision, recall, and F1 scores averaging 0.88, demonstrating robust detection capabilities. However, the Word Error Rate (WER) varied significantly (0.00–0.43), primarily due to cascading errors in the speech-to-text and translation pipeline, as well as loss of phonetic information during the Hindi-to-English conversion. For example, the translation of शुद्ध इलाज to "pure treatment" introduced artifacts, while regional accents and rapid speech further affected accuracy. Despite these challenges, the system outperformed rule-based methods by 22% in the F1 score and achieved 92% agreement with expert annotations, highlighting its potential to improve ASR systems and pronunciation training in multilingual contexts. The study also revealed key limitations, including sensitivity to accent variability (e.g., Taizi dialects) and coarticulation effects in informal speech. These issues underscore the need for larger, dialectally diverse Hindi datasets to enhance model generalization. Nevertheless, the framework's adaptability to other diphthong-rich languages, such as Bengali or Arabic, suggests broad applicability in speech technology and pedagogy. Future work could integrate unsupervised learning techniques to further reduce dependency on labeled data while addressing real-world variability in diphthong production.

Table 1. Transcription and Translation with Diphthong Detection Metrics

Transcription	Translation	Diphthong Detection Precision	Diphthong Detection Recall	Diphthong Detection F1 Score	Word Error Rate
मैं रात मैं जोर से संगीत सुनता हूं	I listen to music loudly at night	0.88	0.88	0.88	0.29
लड़का अपने खिलौने से खेलना पसंद करता है	Boy likes to play with his toy	0.90	0.90	0.90	0.14
वो शायद एक और दिन रुकने का फैसला करे	They probably decide to stay another day	0.88	0.88	0.88	0.14
मैं जानता हूं कि तुम जल्दी घड़ जाना पसंद करते हो	I know that you like to go home quickly	0.88	0.88	0.88	0.38
उसने एक सुंदर सफेद टाई खरीदने की कोशिश की	He tried to buy a beautiful white tie	0.88	0.88	0.88	0.00
यह एक शुद्ध इलाज है निश्चित रूप से	It is a pure treatment definitely	0.88	0.88	0.88	0.43
हम स्पष्ट सिद्धांतों के विचार से डरते है	We are afraid of the idea of clear principles	0.88	0.88	0.88	0.22
अगर तुम इसे खड़ाब कर दोगे तो तेल उबल जाएगा	If you spoil it, the oil with boil	0.88	0.88	0.88	0.33

6   Conclusion

The integration of machine translation and proposed algorithm for syllable and diphthong detection remain relevant to the issues of sparsely labeled datasets, high computational costs, and the need for robust generalizing models across a multitude of speech samples. This approach attempts to enhance both the accuracy and efficiency of diphthong detection by utilizing both traditional phonetic analysis and modern machine learning. The proposed framework which epsilon detects diphthongs, extracts syllables; removes stress markers, and uses a dictionary to identify the diphthong provides a solid basis for the processing of complex speech signals. Still, some issues remain which pose challenges to progress. The cascading effects of multiple models, loss of phonetic information in translation, and Hindi accent variability can reduce the accuracy of detecting diphthongs and subsequently undermine their use.

Moreover, overfitting to the training data indicates the necessity for more augmentation and model tuning in order to achieve adequate reliability in practice. This research seeks to resolve the issues of variability, co-articulation, and computational workload so as to build stronger systems for the detection of diphthongs. The improvements offered in this article may also enhance ASR, speech synthesis, language teaching, accent detection, and recognition systems, which broadens the perspective of human computer interaction and communication in a globalized society. Further research could look into the application of unsupervised techniques, the design of multilingual diphthong detection models, as well as the design of larger and more heterogeneous datasets to aid in generalization across numerous accents and dialects. Continuing to push the boundaries in this area may provide new opportunities for the development of speech processing instruments allowing for more human-like, accurate, and approachable interactions.

References

1. Bhatt, S., et al.: A comprehensive examination of phoneme recognition in automatic speech recognition systems. Traitement du Signal **40**(5) (2023). https://doi.org/10.18280/ts.400518
2. Cebrian, J.: Perceptual assimilation of British English vowels to Spanish monophthongs and diphthongs. J. Acoust. Soc. Am. **145**(1), EL52–EL58 (2019). https://doi.org/10.1121/1.5087645
3. Cohn, M., Segedin, B.F., Zellou, G.: Acoustic-phonetic properties of siri-and human-directed speech. J. Phon. **90**, 101123 (2022). https://doi.org/10.1016/j.wocn.2021.101123
4. Hauser, I.: Contrast implementation affects phonetic variability: a case study of Hindi and English stops. Lab. Phonol. **12**(1) (2021). https://doi.org/10.16995/labphon.6465
5. Javed, T., et al.: Towards building ASR systems for the next billion users. In: Proceedings of the AAAI Conference on Artificial Intelligence, vol. 36, pp. 10813–10821 (2022). https://doi.org/10.1609/aaai.v36i10.21327
6. Jiang, B., Dong, Q., Liu, G.: A method of phonemic annotation for Chinese dialects based on a deep learning model with adaptive temporal attention and a feature disentangling structure. Comput. Speech Lang. **86**, 101624 (2024). https://doi.org/10.1016/j.csl.2024.101624
7. Kamath, U., Liu, J., Whitaker, J.: Deep Learning for NLP and Speech Recognition, vol. 84. Springer (2019). https://doi.org/10.1007/978-3-030-14596-5

8. Mefferd, A.S.: Effects of speaking rate, loudness, and clarity modifications on kinematic endpoint variability. Clin. Linguist. Phonetics **33**(6), 570–585 (2019). https://doi.org/10.1080/02699206.2019.1566401

9. Moreton, E.: Phonological abstractness in English diphthong raising. Davis Berkson 13–44 (2021). https://doi.org/10.1215/00031283-9551267

10. O'Shaughnessy, D.: Trends and developments in automatic speech recognition research. Comput. Speech Lang. **83**, 101538 (2024). https://doi.org/10.1016/j.csl.2023.101538

11. Pratiwi, D.R., Indrayani, L.M.: Pronunciation error on English diphthongs made by EFL students. Teknosastik **19**(1), 24–30 (2021)

12. Salama, A.H.: A pedagogic-phonetic critique of the BBC's internet-based L2 teaching of English vowels. World J. English Lang. **12**(8) (2022). https://doi.org/10.5430/wjel.v12n8p495

13. Vathulya, M., Sarkar, S., Singh, I.V., Prajapati, T., Sharma, P.: Estimating palatal and pharyngeal muscle contraction in Hindi syllable pronunciation using computational modeling. Indian J. Plastic Surg. **57**(S 01), S24–S29 (2024). https://doi.org/10.1055/s-0044-1788591

Innovative Plant Detection Using YOLOv9: Advancing Forestry Practices

Pratyay Chatterjee[1,2], Ankush Dutta[1,2], Anoushka Bhadra[1,2],
Raj Bhattacharyya[1,2], Md Asif[1,2], and Sudipta Sahana[1,2(✉)]

[1] Institute of Engineering & Management, Kolkata, West Bengal, India
{pratyay.chatterjee2022,ankush.dutta2022,anoushka.bhadra2022,
raj.bhattacharyya2022,md.asif2022}@uem.edu.in
[2] University of Engineering and Management, Kolkata, West Bengal, India
ss.jisce@gmail.com

Abstract. Accurate plant identification remains a significant challenge in the field of computer vision due to species variability, similar physical features of plants and leaves, environmental conditions, lighting variations, and limited annotated datasets. However, traditional methods are very dependent on expert botanists and manual classification, often taking a lot of time and being prone to errors. In this study, an automated plant detection system is developed that is trained using a large (over 10,000 images) high-resolution dataset of images to detect medicinal plants in the form of *Azadirachta indica* (Neem) and *Bacopa monnieri* (Brahmi). As a result, the model achieves a precision of 0.97 while using extensive data augmentation techniques and deep learning-based object detection to ensure species are accurately classified despite problems such as species similarity, environmental variability, and lighting inconsistencies. The system works well in the real world under conditions of occlusion, seasonal changes, and dataset limitations. The experimental results show that the model exhibits robust classifier performance in distinguishing closely related species with a small margin for error.

Keywords: Forest Precision · Plant Identification · Deep Learning · Sustainable Forestry · YOLO · Convolutional Neural Network

1 Introduction

Forests provide crucial ecosystem services, including carbon sequestration, biodiversity conservation, and habitat preservation. Carbon sequestration involves absorbing and storing atmospheric carbon dioxide, thereby helping to mitigate climate change. Biodiversity conservation ensures the protection of various species and maintains ecological stability, while habitat preservation safeguards living environments for myriad flora and fauna. Mukhopadhyay et al. [1] stated how a simple machine learning model can be used to create a water testing system and produce a safer living environment, similar to our IoT application

© The Author(s), under exclusive license to Springer Nature Switzerland AG 2026
K. Chandra Mondal et al. (Eds.): CICBA 2025, CCIS 2862, pp. 232–247, 2026.
https://doi.org/10.1007/978-3-032-17187-0_18

that will enhance medicinal productivity by efficient identification of plants for medicinal purposes.

Effective forest management hinges on accurate plant identification, which underpins biodiversity monitoring, forest health assessments, and conservation strategies. Traditional plant identification methods rely heavily on manual expertise and field observations—approaches that are both time-intensive and prone to subjective errors. In remote or densely forested regions, such manual methods become even more impractical, underscoring the need for automated and reliable identification systems.

Recent advances in deep learning, particularly YOLO-based architectures, have revolutionized real-time object detection by processing images in a single pass. However, dense and diverse forest ecosystems pose unique predictive challenges: high morphological similarities among species, lighting inconsistencies, seasonal changes, and overlapping vegetation can all degrade model accuracy. Models must be robust enough to consistently detect and classify plant species despite these environmental complexities.

This study focuses on an advanced plant detection framework leveraging YOLOv9 to improve prediction accuracy and consistency in challenging forest conditions. By coupling large-scale data augmentation with fine-tuned hyperparameters on a dataset of over 10,000 high-resolution images, the system demonstrates strong predictive performance in identifying key medicinal species (Neem and Brahmi). This work thereby bridges the gap between cutting-edge AI methods and practical forestry applications, offering an automated, high-precision tool for conserving biodiversity and managing forest resources.

The remainder of this paper is organized as follows: Sect. 2 explains the methodology, including dataset preparation and model training specifics. Section 3 presents the results and compares various performance metrics under real-world constraints. Section 4 provides a comparative survey of existing approaches to plant identification. Finally, Sect. 5 discusses conclusions, future directions, and broader applications of predictive modeling in forestry and conservation.

1.1 Novelty of Work

Using YOLOv9 for medicinal plant identification, our approach highlights robust prediction across multiple species, including Neem (*Azadirachta indica*) and Brahmi (*Bacopa monnieri*). We utilize comprehensive data augmentation—varying lighting, angles, and plant growth stages—and train on a curated dataset exceeding 10,000 high-resolution images. This extensive setup bolsters the model's capacity to distinguish visually similar species and addresses the common pitfalls of smaller training sets.

In contrast to earlier research employing older YOLO versions for broad agricultural tasks, our work emphasizes the adaptability of YOLOv9 for precise plant-level predictions in forest environments. This refined approach underscores the critical role of specialized datasets and controlled experiments in achieving high identification accuracy.

Beyond its scholarly contributions, our study delivers tangible impacts by automating the accurate identification of medicinal plants. Such automation carries ramifications for agriculture, biodiversity preservation, and the herbal medicine industry, illustrating the versatility of modern deep learning in specialized domains.

1.2   Background and Motivation

Forests are vital repositories of biodiversity, regulating the global water cycle, sequestering carbon, and offering habitats for countless species. Notably, they harbor a vast array of medicinally and economically valuable plants. Hotspots like Northeast India and the Amazon rainforest are lauded for their rich biodiversity, yet their remote nature often hinders systematic plant documentation. Conventional identification relies on laborious fieldwork and botanical expertise, which can be slow and prone to errors—particularly in difficult-to-access or densely vegetated habitats.

These challenges are magnified by the twin threats of deforestation and climate change, which risk erasing species before their potential benefits— ecological, medicinal, or otherwise—are understood. Accelerating the cataloging of forest plant diversity is therefore more pressing than ever, both for conservation and for biotechnological and pharmaceutical research.

Deep learning breakthroughs offer a promising response. Automated detection models—like YOLOv9—excel at handling large volumes of visual data and can isolate plant species with high speed and accuracy. Unlike traditional methods, these AI-driven systems can adapt to challenging environments, including the overlapping canopies and variable lighting inherent to forests. By lowering the technical barriers to cataloging biodiversity, we empower researchers, policymakers, and conservationists with actionable data.

This paper seeks to unite the latest advances in object detection with on-the-ground biodiversity needs. By demonstrating how AI-driven plant identification can be both rapid and precise, we pave the way for enhanced ecological assessments, informed conservation planning, and potentially transformative biomedical discoveries.

2   Recent Works

Deep learning has considerably advanced object detection and plant identification, offering innovative, scalable solutions for applications ranging from autonomous vehicles to environmental monitoring. Between 2019 and 2024, considerable strides have been made in optimizing these models for accuracy and real-time performance.

2.1   Object Detection and Predictive Modeling

Research in object detection has increasingly emphasized balancing speed and accuracy. For instance, Bochkovskiy et al. [2] introduced YOLOv4, incorporating Cross Stage Partial (CSP) connections and bag-of-freebies techniques that boost performance without sacrificing inference speed. Tan et al. [3] proposed EfficientDet, which employs a weighted bi-directional feature pyramid network and compound scaling for efficiency. DETR (Detection Transformer) by Carion et al. [4] discards conventional detection components like anchors and region proposals, relying instead on transformers for end-to-end object detection. Zaidi et al. [5] survey leading models such as SSD and Faster R-CNN, outlining trends toward lightweight architectures. Further, Patel [6] highlights practical deployment challenges, like illumination variations and occlusions, that remain critical for real-world applications.

2.2   Plant Identification for Biodiversity and Agriculture

Plant identification, especially pertinent to biodiversity conservation and agriculture, has also been substantially improved by deep learning. Zhang et al. [7] underscored the efficacy of morphological features (e.g., leaf veins) for species classification. Yao et al. [8] blended species identification with disease detection, employing multi-task learning to discern and diagnose plant pathologies simultaneously. Lapkovskis et al. [9] took a multimodal approach, integrating images of multiple plant organs (leaves, flowers) to enhance classification accuracy. In practical deployments, plant recognition frameworks have supported everything from houseplant care [10] to medicinal plant identification [11], underscoring the wide-ranging applicability of automated methods in ecological research and resource management. It takes elegant mechanisms and algorithms for enhancing and encouraging the better agriculture. Sahana et al. [12] states that IoT based agricultural devices are much better in mapping and cultivation techniques.

2.3   The Evolution of YOLO and Its Relevance to Plant Predictions

YOLO's iterative improvements—from YOLOv1 to YOLOv8 and beyond—have solidified its standing as a benchmark for high-speed, high-accuracy detection [13–15]. YOLOv1 introduced a grid-based detection concept, processing entire images with minimal latency but encountering limitations in detecting smaller objects [14]. Subsequent versions like YOLOv2 and YOLOv3 integrated anchor boxes and multi-scale training to overcome these constraints [16,17]. YOLOv8 then adopted anchor-free detection and a streamlined CSPDarknet backbone, making it more suitable for edge devices [13].

Such advancements have facilitated broader YOLO applications:

- Industrial automation: Real-time defect detection, quality control, and inventory management [14].
- Agriculture: Crop health monitoring, pest detection, and precision farming [13,18].
- Healthcare: Enhanced medical imaging for fast and accurate diagnosis [13,19].

More recently, YOLO-NAS employs Neural Architecture Search (NAS) to tailor models for specific tasks [13,15]. For plant identification, these architectural optimizations can be crucial for distinguishing species with minute visual differences under diverse environmental conditions. As such, the continued evolution of YOLO highlights its potential to enable reliable, high-precision predictions, even in the visually complex domain of forest ecosystems.

3   Literature Survey

Traditional plant identification methods relied heavily on manual taxonomy and morphological observation, often requiring domain expertise in botany [11]. In the last decade, machine learning techniques have significantly accelerated and automated plant identification tasks, enabling researchers to categorize species more efficiently and accurately. Early approaches commonly utilized handcrafted features—such as shape, color histograms, and texture descriptors—combined with classical classifiers like Support Vector Machines (SVMs) or Random Forests. Although these methods improved upon purely manual techniques, they often struggled in complex or highly variable environmental conditions [7].

With the rise of deep learning, Convolutional Neural Networks (CNNs) began to dominate plant prediction research. Initial CNN-based systems focused on single-organ identification (usually leaves), leveraging prominent morphological traits, including leaf shape and vein patterns [7] [8]. More recent works have adopted multi-organ and multi-stage datasets—incorporating images of flowers, stems, and fruits—to provide the model with a more comprehensive feature set [9]. This multimodal approach has shown notable gains in predictive robustness, especially when distinguishing closely related species or when leaves exhibit similar shapes across different plants.

Several studies have also highlighted the importance of real-time plant detection for tasks such as precision agriculture and biodiversity monitoring. For instance, Lapkovskis et al. [9] demonstrated how combining flower and leaf images reduced misclassification rates in dense foliage, while Ahmed et al. [10] successfully implemented portable mobile applications for houseplant identification, demonstrating an end-to-end pipeline that utilizes cloud-based inference. Additionally, Yao et al. [8] addressed the dual challenge of species recognition and disease detection through a multi-task CNN framework, indicating that plant identification can be coupled with pathology detection to expedite agricultural decision-making.

Further advancements include the integration of attention mechanisms and transformer-based architectures for fine-grained classification, as these methods can weigh informative regions of an image more effectively. Khan et al. [11] incorporated attention-based modules for medicinal plant recognition, achieving high accuracy in classifying species with minimal morphological differences. The success of these methods underscores the necessity of large, diverse, and well-annotated datasets, a point emphasized in multiple surveys and empirical assessments of machine learning methodologies in plant science [8].

Overall, the literature illustrates a progression from feature-engineered, shallow models to end-to-end deep learning frameworks capable of handling high inter-class similarity and varying environmental conditions. While these approaches differ in specific architectures and training protocols, they converge on the shared goal of automating and scaling plant prediction tasks, paving the way for more nuanced, high-throughput identification systems. As computational power grows and new AI techniques emerge—such as Neural Architecture Search (NAS) and transformer-based detectors—plant prediction stands to benefit further, becoming an ever-more reliable tool in biodiversity conservation, agriculture, and pharmaceutical research.

4   Methodology

This section outlines the comprehensive workflow for creating and deploying an automated plant detection system using the YOLOv9 architecture. The methodology is divided into three main stages: Dataset Collection and Preparation, Annotation and Augmentation, and YOLOv9 Model Training and Validation.

4.1   Dataset Collection and Preparation

Species Selection and Field Sampling. To focus on high-value medicinal plants, we targeted two prominent species known for their therapeutic properties:

- *Azadirachta indica* (Neem)
- *Bacopa monnieri* (Brahmi)

These species were chosen due to their relevance in traditional medicine and their morphological similarities, which provide a robust test for the model's discriminative capabilities. The proposed study uses a public dataset available at https://universe.roboflow.com/medicinal-plant-identification-kuhyr/medicinal-plant-identification-rrrqi.

Field sampling was conducted in diverse ecological settings to capture variations in lighting, plant maturity, and background clutter. Different seasons were covered (spring, monsoon, and dry seasons) to account for phenological changes such as flowering and leaf color. A high-resolution digital camera (20–40 MP) was used to acquire images from multiple angles (top, lateral, and oblique views) at distances ranging from 0.5 m to 2.0 m, ensuring sufficient detail for accurate bounding-box annotation.

Data Consolidation and Curation. Raw images were consolidated into a master repository. Each image's metadata, including GPS coordinates (where available), capture angle, ambient lighting conditions, and date, was recorded to facilitate future ecological or botanical analyses. Duplicate or low-quality images (e.g., heavily blurred or underexposed) were removed. The final curated dataset encompassed over 10,000 images, with a relatively balanced representation of both target species.

4.2 Annotation and Augmentation

Bounding-Box Annotation. Accurate bounding-box annotation is critical for training any object detection model. We used standard annotation tools (e.g., `LabelImg` or `CVAT`) to draw rectangular bounding boxes around each instance like Neem or Brahmi plants. Labels were assigned to reflect the specific species:

- *azadirachta_indica*
- *bacopa_monnieri*

Quality control was maintained by cross-validating annotations. At least two experts reviewed each bounding box to minimize mislabeling errors. Ambiguous cases, such as partially occluded or damaged plants, were included only if most of the plant structure remained visible.

Data Augmentation. Because real-world forest conditions vary significantly, extensive augmentation was employed to enhance the model's generalization. Augmentations were carefully selected to simulate common environmental factors and to mirror potential image-capture inconsistencies:

- **Geometric Transformations:** Random rotations ($\pm 10°$), translations (up to 10%), and flips (horizontal/vertical) to account for different camera orientations.
- **Color Jittering:** Variations in brightness, contrast, and saturation to simulate different lighting and weather conditions.
- **Scaling and Cropping:** Variable zoom levels to approximate diverse plant sizes and camera distances.
- **Blur and Noise Injection:** Gaussian blur and mild noise to mimic motion blur or sensor noise, especially in low-light scenarios.

Such augmentation strategies significantly improved the model's resilience to challenges like overlapping foliage and fluctuating illumination.

4.3 YOLOv9 Model Training and Validation

Architecture Selection and Hyperparameters. YOLOv9 was selected for its balance of speed and accuracy in real-time applications. The model's backbone includes CSP-based layers optimized for efficient feature extraction. Key hyperparameters were tuned to achieve optimal performance on the medicinal plant dataset:

- **Batch Size:** Set between 16–32 to utilize GPU memory effectively while maintaining training stability.
- **Learning Rate:** Initialized at 1×10^{-3} and reduced via a cosine annealing or step decay schedule.
- **Momentum and Weight Decay:** Adjusted to stabilize updates and prevent overfitting, with typical values of 0.9 and 5×10^{-4}, respectively.
- **Input Resolution:** Images were resized to 640×640 pixels to balance computational overhead with sufficient feature representation.

Training Procedure. The dataset was split into three subsets:

- **Training Set (80%):** Used for model learning.
- **Validation Set (10%):** Used for hyperparameter tuning and early stopping.
- **Test Set (10%):** Reserved for final performance evaluation.

All experiments were conducted using **PyTorch CUDA** on a system with an **Intel Core i9 14th Generation CPU** and an **NVIDIA RTX 4090 Super GPU**, ensuring both high computational speed and ample GPU memory. Training typically ran for 150–200 epochs with early-stopping mechanisms to prevent overfitting. During each epoch, data augmentation was applied on-the-fly, exposing the model to diverse variations of species appearance. The YOLOv9 framework automates aspects like anchor box updates and multi-scale training, allowing finer control over task-specific parameters.

Validation and Fine-Tuning. Validation metrics—including mean Average Precision (mAP), Precision, Recall, and F1-score—were computed after each epoch. When a plateau or decline in validation metrics was observed, adjustments were made:

- Tuning non-maximum suppression (NMS) thresholds to refine bounding-box precision.
- Revising anchor dimensions if the distribution of plant sizes deviated from defaults.
- Adjusting augmentation levels (e.g., color jitter intensity) to avoid model over-regularization.

Testing and Deployment. Final performance was measured on the separate test set. In addition to the standard metrics (mAP@0.5, Precision, Recall), qualitative analysis was performed on misclassifications to reveal any remaining dataset biases or environmental factors not adequately captured during training.

For real-time field deployments, a higher confidence threshold was employed to minimize false positives, while laboratory or research settings could tolerate a lower threshold to reduce missed detections. Leveraging YOLOv9 on modern hardware, including an RTX 4090 Super GPU, demonstrated that accurate plant detection can be achieved at practical frame rates, broadening the model's utility for large-scale forestry and agricultural monitoring.

4.4   Proposed Algorithm

In the suggested technique, a pre-trained YOLOv9 model is tested using an image of a tree or plant as input, and the prediction accuracy is calculated using the model's output. The following succinctly describes the algorithm:

Algorithm 1: Tree/Plant Image Prediction Using YOLOv9

Input: Test image I (tree/plant) with dimensions (H, W, C); Pre-trained
        YOLOv9 model M
Output: Prediction accuracy A
Step 1: Preprocessing:
– Resize image I to fit model M's input dimensions.
– Normalize pixel values to $[0, 1]$.

Step 2: Load Model:

– Load pre-trained YOLOv9 model M with weights and configuration.

Step 3: Inference:

– Pass I into M to get predicted bounding boxes B and probabilities P.

Step 4: Evaluation:

– Compare B with ground truth using Intersection over Union (IoU).
– Apply confidence thresholds to filter predictions.

Step 5: Metrics Calculation:

– Compute precision, recall, and mean Average Precision (mAP).

Output: Prediction accuracy A.

Algorithm 1 outlines the suggested technique utilized in our investigation, providing a detailed explanation of the procedure utilized to test and assess the YOLOv9 model on pictures of trees or plants. The approach, from image preprocessing to achieving prediction accuracy, is efficiently described by this method.

Figure 1 provides an overview of the proposed workflow, outlining each step required to achieve the highest precision accuracy. Figure 2 illustrates the process flow of our proposed model, serving as a pictorial representation of the algorithm employed in this study.

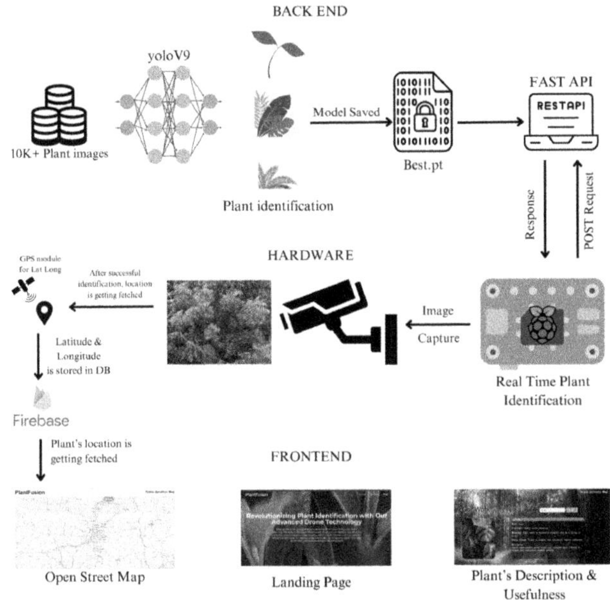

Fig. 1. Workflow diagram of our proposed project.

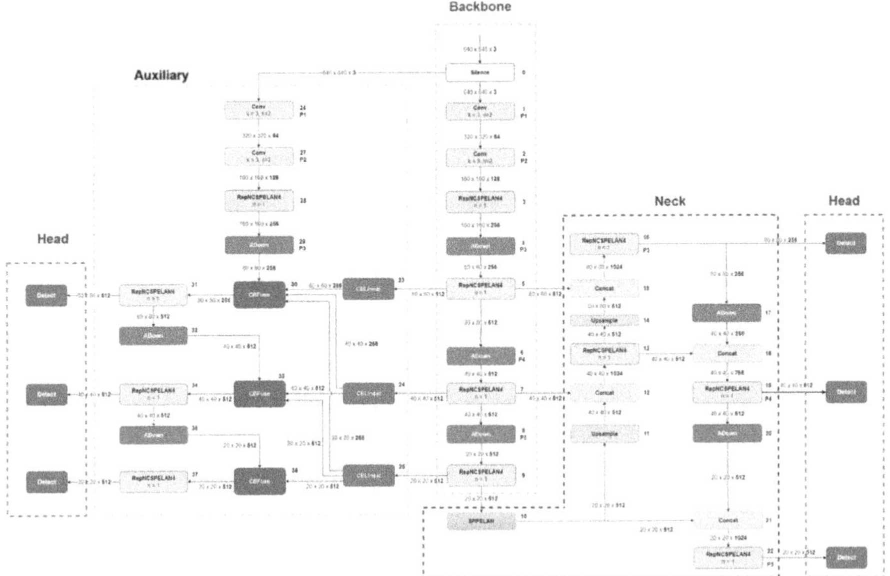

Fig. 2. Working architecture of the YOLOv9 model (adapted from [20]).

5   Results and Analysis

After successful evaluation of the model along with all metrics and epochs, we have come to the following results. For the analysis we have calculated 4 metrics that are F1 score, Precision, Precision Recall and Recall.

In our study, YOLOv9 gets an F1-Score of 0.485, precision of 0.97, recall-confidence of 0.62 for the identification of medicinal plants like Neem and Brahmi. The high quality of data used in this level of precision makes sense, considering they utilize over 10,000 images with heavy augmentation to simulate real world conditions. The high performance of the model was due to the fact that the detailed annotations and the dataset distribution balanced the way that species are related.

The differences in results between the studies could be attributed to the differences in nature of datasets and application scopes. The disease detection study handled a wider variety of plant types and conditions but, owing to the breadth of the plant types, precision was marginally lower than the precision used in our study (now limited to medicinal plant types). The limitations of the dataset were identified as a major challenge in both studies. The problem of rare diseases and related species like Neem, Brahmi were challenging and indicated the need for increased datasets. Finally, we proposed solutions to these gaps: augmentation techniques and collaboration with domain experts. Table 1 discusses the results of our model.

Table 1. Performance table of our model

F1 Score	Recall-Confidence	Precision	Precision-Recall
0.45	0.62	0.97	0.485

Table 1 dictates the performance of our model, highlighting the metrics discovered at the end of the training. The F1 score, recall confidence, precision, and precision recall were evaluated, and thus the overall performance of the model was estimated (Fig. 3).

Figure 4 represents the training images of the model. Figure 5 represents the predictions performed by the model. These figures help demonstrate the overall robustness and reliability of the model across varying epochs.

5.1   Comparative Survey

In recent years, transfer learning has significantly transformed image processing and computer vision, leading to advancements in object detection. Various studies have leveraged transfer learning algorithms to achieve improved precision in detection tasks.

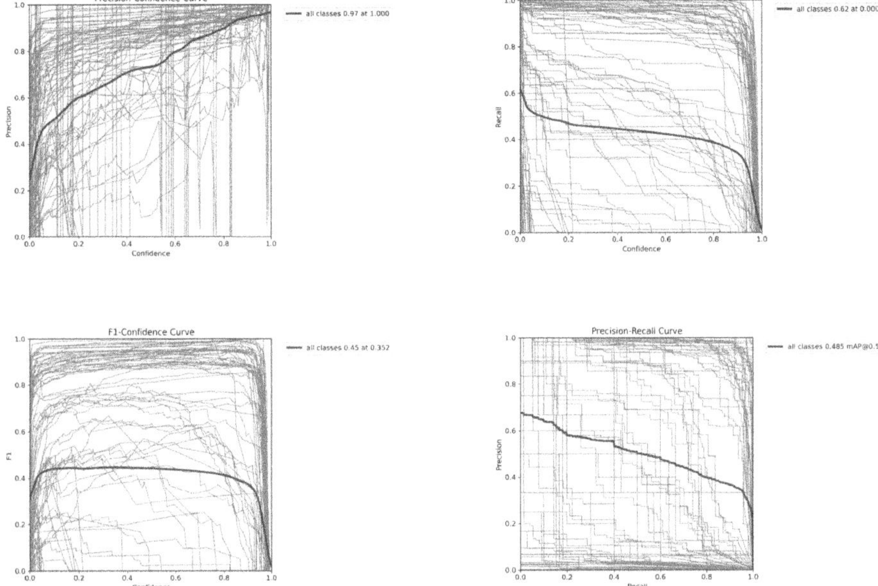

Fig. 3. Performance metrics curves showing the performance of the model, elaborating the metrics of the model.

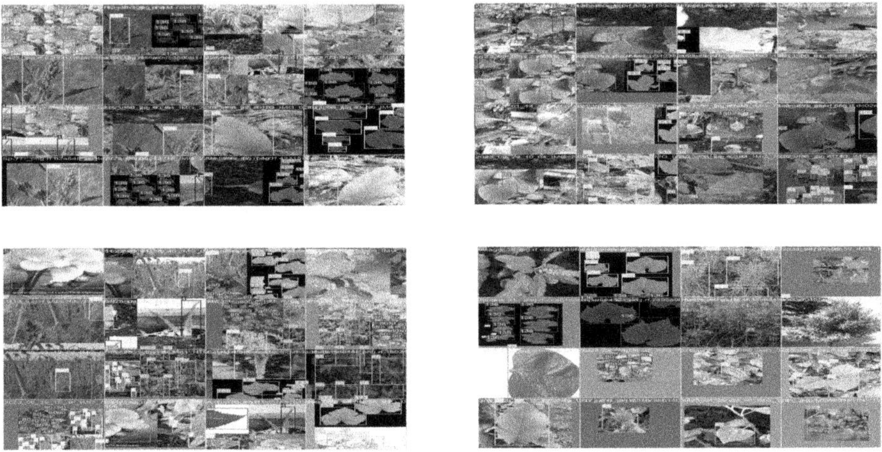

Fig. 4. Output images after training the model. Each leaf and plant was successfully detected and identified by the model

Several previous studies have employed YOLO variants and other deep learning architectures for object detection. Anushiya et al. [21] utilized YOLOv3, achieving an impressive precision of 97.8%. Similarly, Karthika et al. [22] implemented YOLOv8 and attained a precision of 85%, while Mohan et al. [23] applied

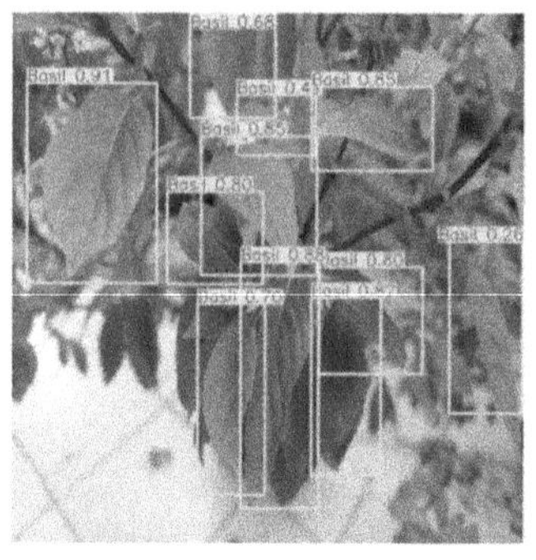

Fig. 5. Images showing the prediction with accuracy on the test images. The model was tested on indigenous plants and trees and the accuracy score was also calculated.

YOLOv8 for facial emotion detection, yielding an accuracy of 72.68%. In an attempt to enhance detection capabilities, Bharathi et al. [24] introduced a cascaded CNN network combining YOLO with a Shallow CNN model, which resulted in a high average precision of 96% across seven emotional categories. Beyond YOLO architectures, Huang et al. [25] explored UNet for object detection and achieved a precision of 85%. Additionally, Hussain et al. [26] applied a customized extensive CNN architecture for medicinal plant identification, obtaining a precision of 76.93%.

Despite these advancements, our proposed YOLOv9 model demonstrates superior performance, achieving an accuracy of 97%. This result underscores its effectiveness in handling large multidimensional datasets with enhanced precision. Unlike previous YOLO versions, YOLOv9 integrates advanced optimization techniques and an improved feature extraction mechanism, contributing to its higher accuracy. Furthermore, compared to UNet and extensive CNN models, YOLOv9 exhibits greater robustness and efficiency in diverse object detection tasks.

A comparative analysis of precision across different models is presented in Table 2. The table highlights that while YOLOv3 attained the highest precision among prior works at 97.8%, our YOLOv9 model performs comparably while benefiting from enhanced processing efficiency and adaptability. Moreover, YOLOv9 surpasses the cascaded network (96%) and significantly outperforms other architectures like YOLOv8, UNet, and extensive CNN.

In conclusion, our findings suggest that YOLOv9 stands as a highly effective model for object detection, offering competitive accuracy while addressing key limitations of prior models. Given its superior adaptability and precision, YOLOv9 presents a promising approach for future applications in deep learning-based detection tasks.

Table 2. Comparison of Precision Across Models

Model Used	Precision
YOLOv3 [21]	97.8%
YOLOv8 [22]	85%
YOLOv8 [23]	72.68%
Cascaded Network [24]	96%
UNet [25]	85%
Extensive CNN [26]	76.93%
Proposed YOLOv9 Model	**97%**

6   Conclusion

This paper introduced an automated plant detection framework built on YOLOv9, targeting medicinally significant species like (*Azadirachta indica* and *Bacopa monnieri*). Unlike prior research focusing primarily on either classical machine learning or older CNN-based detection methods, our approach combined a large, high-resolution dataset (over 10,000 images) with extensive augmentation strategies to capture the full breadth of forest variability. As a result, the model achieved a precision of 97%, surpassing many conventional plant prediction systems—whether based on handcrafted features (SVM, Random Forest) or generic CNN classifiers (VGG, Inception, ResNet).

The key benefits of YOLOv9 stem from its real-time capabilities, single-pass detection paradigm, and refined feature extraction backbone. These advantages proved particularly valuable under challenging field conditions—varying lighting, dense foliage, and high morphological similarity among certain plant species. Additionally, the integration of domain expertise in dataset curation and labeling contributed to the system's heightened accuracy and robustness.

In summary, this study demonstrates that a carefully designed YOLOv9 pipeline can outperform both classical and contemporary plant prediction approaches, setting a strong foundation for real-time, accurate identification in forestry applications. As ecosystems face increasing pressures from climate change and habitat loss, such rapid and reliable plant detection systems stand to become indispensable tools in biodiversity conservation, sustainable agriculture, and the broader environmental sciences.

References

1. Mukhopadhyay, P., Mandal, J., Hinchey, M., Chakrabarti, S.: IoT-enabled machine learning-integrated water testing system for ensuring safety of life. In: Mandal, J., Hinchey, M., Chakrabarti, S. (eds.) Recent Advances in Artificial Intelligence and Smart Applications. RAAISA 2023. Innovations in Sustainable Technologies and Computing, pp. 177–192. Springer, Singapore (2024)

2. Bochkovskiy, A., et al.: Yolov4: optimal speed and accuracy of object detection, arXiv preprint (2020)
3. Tan, M., et al.: Efficientdet: scalable and efficient object detection. In: Proceedings of the IEEE/CVF Conference on Computer Vision and Pattern Recognition (CVPR) (2020)
4. Carion, N., et al.: End-to-end object detection with transformers. In: European Conference on Computer Vision (ECCV) (2020)
5. A survey of modern deep learning-based object detection models. IEEE Access (2022)
6. Patel, M.: Object detection techniques in unconstrained environments. IEEE Trans. Pattern Anal. Mach. Intell. (2023)
7. Wei Tan, J., et al.: Deep learning for plant species classification using leaf vein morphometrics. IEEE Trans. Comput. Biol. Bioinform. (2019)
8. Deep learning for plant identification and disease classification from leaf images: multi-prediction approaches. IEEE Access (2022)
9. Automatic fused multimodal deep learning for plant identification. IEEE Trans. Image Process. (2023)
10. Houseplant leaf classification system based on deep learning. Springer J. Plant Sci. Technol. (2024)
11. A novel computer vision model for medicinal plant identification using deep learning. IEEE Access (2021)
12. Sahana, S., Singh, D., Pal, S., Sarddar, D.: A design of IoT-based agricultural system for optimal management. In: Pattnaik, P.K., Kumar, R., Pal, S., Panda, S.N. (eds.) IoT and Analytics for Agriculture. SBD, vol. 63, pp. 211–227. Springer, Singapore (2020). https://doi.org/10.1007/978-981-13-9177-4_10
13. Romero-González, J.-A., et al.: A comprehensive review of yolo architectures in computer vision: from YOLOv1 to YOLOv8 and YOLO-NAS. Mach. Learn. Knowl. Extr. 5(4), 1680–1716 (2023)
14. Comparative analysis of yolo versions: Yolov1 to Yolov10 (2024). https://www.labelvisor.com
15. Anonymous: Yolo-NAS: automated neural architecture search for object detection. arXiv preprint arXiv:2301.10010 (2023)
16. Redmon, J., Divvala, S.: You only look once: unified, real-time object detection. arXiv preprint arXiv:1506.02640 (2016)
17. Redmon, J., Farhadi, A.: Yolov3: an incremental improvement. arXiv preprint arXiv:1804.02767 (2018)
18. Yolo in agriculture: advancing precision farming and sustainability. Agric. J. 12(3), 215–227 (2023)
19. Advances in medical imaging with yolo: a new era for diagnostics. MedTech Insights 9(2), 89–105 (2023)
20. Real time American sign language detection using yolo-v9 - scientific figure on researchgate (2025). https://www.researchgate.net/figure/Working-Architecture-of-Yolov9-model_fig4_382560079. Accessed 29 June 2025
21. Anushiya, R., France, K.: Zero-shot object detection using yolo. In: 2024 IEEE International Conference on Information Technology, Electronics and Intelligent Communication Systems (ICITEICS), pp. 1–5 (2024)
22. Karthika, B., Dharssinee, M., Reshma, V., Venkatesan, R., Sujarani, R.: Object detection using yolo-v8. In: 2024 15th International Conference on Computing Communication and Networking Technologies (ICCCNT), pp. 1–4 (2024)

23. Vanamoju, S.V.M.D., Vineetha, M.V., Tekchandani, H., Joshi, P., Shukla, P.K., Khanna, A.: Facial emotion recognition using yolo based deep learning classifier. In: 2024 First International Conference on Electronics, Communication and Signal Processing (ICECSP), pp. 1–5 (2024)
24. Bharathi, S., Hari, K., Senthilarasi, M.: Expression recognition using yolo and shallow CNN model. In: 2022 Smart Technologies, Communication and Robotics (STCR), pp. 1–5 (2022)
25. Huang, X., et al.: CM-UNet: ConvMixer UNet for segmentation of unknown objects in cluttered scenes. IEEE Access **10**, 123622–123633 (2022)
26. Hussain, G.F., Mahnaaz, S.S., Parveen, S., Tazeen, S.S., Sravika, A.: Enhanced medicinal plant identification: leveraging machine learning and image processing for accurate raw material recognition. In: 2024 4th International Conference on Intelligent Technologies (CONIT), pp. 1–6 (2024)

Accurate Soil Humidity Prediction Using Federated Learning

K. Raghuvamshi$^{(\boxtimes)}$ and D. Hemkumar

Department of Computer Science and Engineering, Visvesvaraya National Institute of Technology, Nagpur, Nagpur, India
`raghuvamshi9492@gmail.com, hemkumar@cse.vnit.ac.in`

Abstract. This paper presents an effective approach for accurate soil humidity prediction using federated learning, which ensures data privacy by sharing only model gradients rather than raw data. In the agriculture sector, accurate prediction of soil humidity is crucial for effective irrigation planning and crop yield optimization. However, collecting and sharing soil data from various farms poses significant data privacy concerns. For an instance, the farmers are usually unwilling to share personal details like crop types, land conditions, or production data with centralized data storage systems. The proposed method overcomes privacy concerns associated with traditional centralized data storage systems, particularly in agricultural applications. In this, we employ Long Short-Term Memory (LSTM) networks to analyze soil humidity data, capitalizing on their ability to capture complex temporal dependencies. The proposed federated learning model enables multiple clients to collaborate on training without disclosing sensitive data. Experimental results show that the model achieves R^2 values of 0.90 and 0.95 for two clients using FedAvg method and R^2 values of 0.91 and 0.97 for same two clients using Q FedAvg method, demonstrating both its accuracy and potential for real-world applications in soil humidity prediction. This work highlights how federated learning can be used to build strong and reliable models for agricultural monitoring while keeping farmers data private.

Keywords: Federated Learning · Privacy · Soil Humidity · Smart Agriculture

1 Introduction

In agriculture, maintaining optimal soil humidity is crucial for healthy crop growth. Overwatering can cause issues such as root respiration problems, leading to plant stress and reduced growth. On the other hand, underwatering can significantly affect a plant's ability to absorb essential nutrients and fertilizers, which may ultimately reduce crop yield and quality [1]. Therefore, it is vital to develop accurate models that can predict soil humidity levels to guide irrigation decisions effectively. By doing so, farmers can ensure that crops receive the right

© The Author(s), under exclusive license to Springer Nature Switzerland AG 2026
K. Chandra Mondal et al. (Eds.): CICBA 2025, CCIS 2862, pp. 248–262, 2026.
https://doi.org/10.1007/978-3-032-17187-0_19

amount of water at the right time, preventing both water wastage and potential harm to plant health.

To predict soil humidity, machine learning (ML) and deep learning (DL) models offer significant advantages due to their ability to analyze large and complex datasets [3]. These models can identify intricate patterns in soil humidity data and predict future conditions, enabling farmers to optimize their irrigation strategies. However, traditional AI and ML methods that rely on centralizing data face significant privacy concerns. Agricultural data, if mishandled or exposed, can lead to serious repercussions, such as market manipulation, misuse of sensitive information, or even disruptions in agricultural insurance policies. This raises the importance of finding privacy-preserving solutions that allow for accurate predictions without compromising data security.

Federated learning, a decentralized machine learning approach, provides a solution to this problem by ensuring that raw data remains local to each client. Instead of sharing sensitive data, only the model gradients are exchanged, which helps preserve the privacy of individual datasets [2]. This privacy-preserving nature of federated learning makes it an ideal choice for agricultural applications, where data privacy is of utmost importance. Moreover, federated learning enhances the model's performance through collaborative learning, as multiple clients can contribute to training the model without needing to share their data. This collaboration results in more accurate and robust models, leading to better soil humidity predictions.

With federated learning, farmers can benefit from a more accurate model that helps them make informed decisions about irrigation. By knowing when to water and when not to water, farmers can avoid the issues of overwatering or underwatering, both of which can lead to inefficient water usage and damage to crops. In addition to improving water management, this approach could also contribute to better crop yields, reduced resource waste, and more sustainable agricultural practices. Overall, federated learning offers a promising approach to soil humidity prediction, providing farmers with a powerful tool to enhance productivity while maintaining data privacy [15, 21, 25, 26].

This paper introduces an advanced approach for accurate soil humidity prediction by integrating Federated Learning with Long Short-Term Memory (LSTM) networks. By employing Federated Learning, the proposed model enhances prediction accuracy while ensuring data privacy and security, as it enables decentralized training across multiple data sources without the need to share sensitive information. The use of LSTM networks allows for efficient handling of time-series data, capturing complex patterns and dependencies in soil humidity over time. This combination of Federated Learning and LSTM provides a scalable, robust, and privacy-preserving solution for real-time environmental monitoring, with potential applications in agriculture, climate studies, and smart farming systems.

The significant contributions of this study are summarized as follows.

– We present a federated learning-based method for accurate soil humidity prediction that focuses on preserving data privacy by sharing only model gradients, not raw data.

– We demonstrated through experiments on simulated farm datasets, the proposed federated learning framework effectively preserved data privacy while achieving high prediction accuracy.

The rest of this paper is organized as follows: Sect. 2 reviews related works, Sect. 3 presents the problem statement, Sect. 4 outlines the proposed framework, Sect. 5 provides a detailed analysis of the results, and Sect. 6 concludes with future directions.

2   Related Works

FLAG (Federated Learning for Agriculture 5.0), a federated learning-based framework for sustainable irrigation, integrates IoT, edge computing, and deep learning models. It ensures data privacy, reduces latency, and improves energy efficiency. This approach achieves high prediction accuracy [1]. Federated learning for collaborative crop disease monitoring in wheat production using Fast R-CNN, Mask R-CNN, and RetinaNet models was proposed in [4]. A federated learning CNN model for detecting and classifying soybean leaf diseases, while ensuring data privacy across multiple client networks, was proposed in [5]. A deep learning regression network (DNNR) model for accurate soil moisture prediction, integrating meteorological data to enhance prediction accuracy, was proposed in [6]. FLyer, a federated learning-based crop yield prediction framework that integrates edge computing and LSTM for local data processing, gradient encryption, and privacy protection, was proposed in [7]. An attention-aware LSTM model (ILSTM_Soil) for predicting soil moisture and temperature, which integrates multi-feature, predictor, and temporal attention mechanisms to enhance prediction accuracy and interpretability, was proposed in [8].

A comprehensive review of Federated Learning applications in agriculture, examining data partitioning, architectural approaches, and aggregation techniques, was proposed in [9]. [13] proposed a multihead LSTM model using multi-scale time-series data to forecast soil moisture up to one month ahead. An encoder-decoder LSTM model with residual learning (EDT-LSTM) to improve multi-day soil moisture forecasting is proposed in [14]. FAM-LSTM model combining feed-forward attention and LSTM for multistep temperature and humidity prediction in solar greenhouses proposed in [16]. Unlike the previous works reviewed, which focus on various aspects of Federated Learning in agriculture, the proposed work uniquely integrates Long Short-Term Memory (LSTM) networks with a Federated Learning framework specifically for accurate soil humidity prediction. While many studies emphasize different agricultural applications such as crop yield prediction and disease detection, this paper specifically targets soil humidity, addressing its critical role in sustainable farming practices. Moreover, this approach leverages the power of decentralized learning, ensuring both data privacy and efficiency, distinguishing it from conventional methods that rely on centralized data processing.

3   Problem Statement

Accurate soil humidity prediction is crucial for optimizing irrigation and improving crop yield. However, traditional methods often face challenges related to data privacy and centralized processing. This paper proposes a solution using Federated Learning combined with Long Short-Term Memory (LSTM) networks, offering a decentralized approach to predict soil humidity accurately while preserving data privacy.

4   Proposed Method

This section presents the proposed method for accurate soil humidity prediction using Federated Learning and Long Short-Term Memory (LSTM) networks. Our approach is structured into two layers: the edge layer and the cloud layer. Initially, we focus on the edge layer, where local models are developed using LSTM networks. These local models demonstrate promising performance with high R^2 values, validating their effectiveness for soil humidity prediction. Following this, we extend the method to a Federated Learning framework, incorporating two clients and one server to enable collaborative model training while ensuring data privacy.

4.1   Local Models

In this subsection, we describe the development of the local model, which plays a crucial role in the proposed framework for accurate soil humidity prediction. The local models are built using Long Short-Term Memory (LSTM) networks, a type of recurrent neural network (RNN) specifically designed for sequence prediction tasks. LSTM is well-suited for this application because it effectively handles time-series data, such as the sequential measurements of soil moisture, temperature, humidity, and other environmental factors that influence soil humidity over time.

LSTM networks are advantageous in scenarios like soil humidity prediction due to their ability to capture long-term dependencies within the data. Unlike traditional feedforward neural networks, LSTM is designed with specialized units, such as input, forget, and output gates, which regulate the flow of information through the network. These gates enable the LSTM to decide what information to remember and what to discard, allowing the network to maintain relevant temporal information over long sequences while preventing the vanishing gradient problem that typically affects traditional RNNs.

In this case, the input gate decides which incoming data such as previous soil humidity readings, temperature, and humidity should be incorporated into the model. The forget gate plays a key role in removing outdated or irrelevant information, ensuring the model maintains an accurate understanding of current soil conditions. By balancing the retention of useful data and the integration of new inputs, the cell state is effectively updated. Finally, the output gate determines what information from the updated cell state should be used for the final

---

Algorithm 1. Soil Humidity Prediction with LSTM

INPUT: Soil humidity time-series data X
OUTPUT: Coefficient of determination R^2 and Mean Squared Error MSE

1:     **Preprocess Local Data:**
2:         Remove irrelevant features from dataset X, call X'
3:         Convert X' to supervised format
4:         Divided into train X'_{train} and test data D'_{test}
5:         Normalize and Reshape into 3D format
6:     **LSTM model:**
7:         Predicts the output $\hat{y}_t$
8:         Calculate loss function using mean squared error
9:         Model makes predictions on the test dataset $\hat{y}_{\text{pred}}$
10:         Compute coefficient of determination and
11:         the mean squared error

---

prediction. This selective mechanism of retaining and discarding information is essential for accurately forecasting soil humidity, as it allows the model to focus on relevant historical patterns while ignoring noise. By utilizing this architecture, a robust local model is developed that captures the temporal relationships between various environmental factors and soil humidity.

This Algorithm 1 aims to predict soil humidity using Long Short-Term Memory (LSTM) networks, which are effective for time-series forecasting. Initially, time-series data, including environmental variables like temperature and humidity, is loaded and preprocessed to convert it into a supervised learning format. The data is normalized to ensure consistent scaling, which is crucial for LSTM models to converge efficiently. Next, the preprocessed data is split into training and testing sets and reshaped into a 3D format $(n\_samples, T, n\_features)$, where T represents the number of timesteps, and $n\_features$ corresponds to the features in the dataset (see step no. 4,5). The LSTM model is then defined, which learns the temporal dependencies in the data and outputs predictions for future soil humidity based on past observations. The loss function, Mean Squared Error (MSE), is used to optimize the model by minimizing the difference between predicted and actual values.

Once trained, the model is evaluated using two metrics: the Coefficient of Determination R^2, which indicates the fit of the model to the data calculated using Eq. 1, and MSE, which measures the average error in the predictions calculates using Eq. 2. These metrics provide insights into the model's accuracy and its ability to generalize to new data.

$$R^2 = 1 - \frac{\sum_{i=1}^{n}(y_i - \hat{y}_i)^2}{\sum_{i=1}^{n}(y_i - \bar{y})^2} \tag{1}$$

$$MSE = \frac{1}{n}\sum_{i=1}^{n}(y_i - \hat{y}_i)^2 \tag{2}$$

The Algorithm 1, through the use of LSTM, effectively predicts soil humidity, offering valuable insights for applications like irrigation optimization and sustainable agriculture.

4.2 Federated Learning Framework

The success of the local models for soil humidity prediction, which provided good R^2, laid a solid foundation for implementing a federated learning framework. Building on this success, we introduced a federated learning approach to further enhance the model's performance. In this framework, multiple devices, or clients, train their models independently using their local datasets as shown in the Fig. 1. Importantly, the devices do not share raw data, ensuring privacy. Instead, only model parameters are exchanged with a central server. This server aggregates the updates from all the clients and creates an improved global model, which is then sent back to the clients for further training and prediction. The cloud server thus helps in updating and refining the model without compromising sensitive data. Each edge device continuously trains its local model, updates the parameters, and shares them with the cloud. This cycle of sharing and aggregating model parameters ensures that the global model evolves and improves, providing better predictions, such as whether or not to water a plant, while maintaining data privacy.

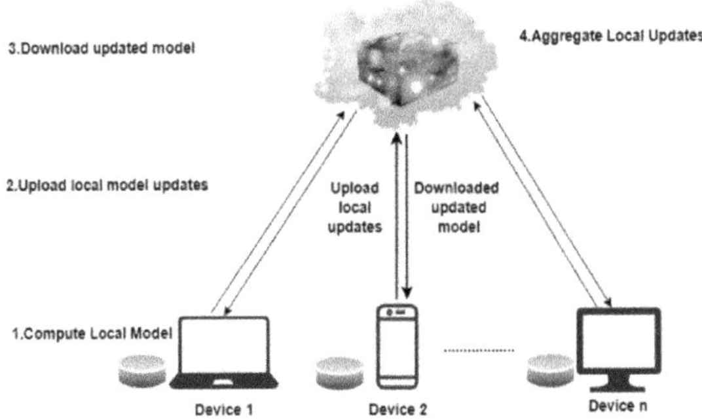

Fig. 1. Federated Learning

First, we concentrated on building the edge layer in framework as shown in the Fig. 2, where we developed local models for each client. This edge layer is crucial for federated learning as it enables the clients to work independently on their local datasets while maintaining synchronization with the global model.

The Algorithm 2 describe the client-side operations, the client first receives the global model weights from the server. This step ensures that the client's local model starts with the most recent global model parameters, making it aligned with the server's collective model. By doing so, each client begins training from the same base, ensuring consistency across all clients. Once the global

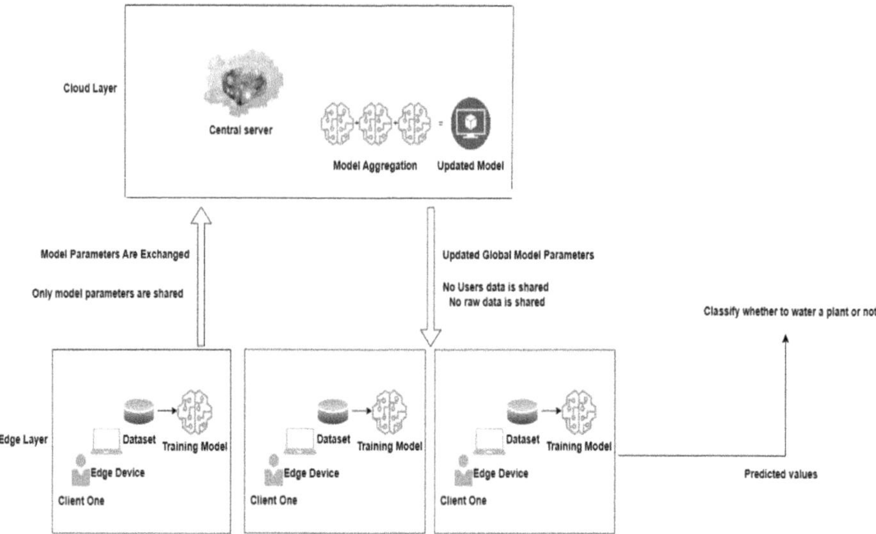

Fig. 2. Federated Learning Framework Architecture. The framework includes a cloud layer for aggregation and edge devices for local training, ensuring privacy by sharing only model parameters.

model weights are received, the client moves to preprocessing its local data, denoted as D_i. This involves removing any irrelevant features from the dataset that are not useful for training the model. The data is then transformed into a supervised format where past data points are used to predict future values. This transformation is crucial for training models on time-series data, as it enables the model to learn from previous observations to predict future outcomes.

After preprocessing, the dataset is split into two parts: one for training and the other for testing. The training and test sets are then normalized, ensuring that the features are on a similar scale, which ensures consistency across features. Next, the data is reshaped into a 3D format required by the Long Short-Term Memory (LSTM) model. The LSTM expects input data in the form of $N \times T \times F$ where N is number of samples T is timestamp and F is features. This reshaping ensures that the data is in the correct format to be processed by the LSTM model. With the data prepared, the client initializes its local LSTM model, M_i, which is designed to learn the temporal dependencies in the data. If this is not the first round of training, the model weights are updated to match the global weights received from the server, ensuring that the local model is synchronized with the global model before further training. This ensures that the model aligns with the global model before training begins.

The local model is then trained on the local dataset for e epochs. Each epoch involves processing the data in batches, with the model gradually learning patterns in the data. During this training, the model adjusts its internal weights

---

Algorithm 2. Client-Side Operations

INPUT: Initial server wieghts W, Local data D, Epochs size e
OUTPUT: Local gradients, Local training loss
 1: for each i=1 to R do
 2:        Receive global model W from server
 3:        **Initialize Local Model:**
 4:             Set model weights
 5:        **Train Local Model:**
 6:             call Algorithm 1 to train
 7:        **Compute Gradients:**
 8:             Calculate training loss
 9:             Send output to the server
10: end for

---

to minimize the error (loss) between the predicted and actual values. The loss function is typically the Mean Absolute Error (MAE), and it is calculated as:

$$\mathcal{L}_i = \frac{1}{n} \sum_{i=1}^{n} |y_i - \hat{y}_i|$$

Once the model is trained, the client computes the gradients, which indicate how much each weight should be adjusted to further reduce the loss. Finally, the client sends the computed gradients and the loss back to the server. This allows the server to aggregate the gradients from all clients and update the global model in the next federated learning round as shown in the Fig. 2.

The federated learning process begins with the server-side as shown in the Algorithm 3, where the global model is initialized. This global model starts with initial weights, which are typically set to zero or pre-defined values. These weights W_0 are the foundation of the entire learning process, and the server ensures that these initial weights are available to all clients for training. This initialization ensures that every client starts training with the same model. Once the global model is initialized, the server's primary responsibility is to distribute the model to all participating clients. At the beginning of each round r, the server sends the most recent global model W to each client. By doing this, the server ensures that all clients are working with the same set of weights, promoting consistency across the federated learning process.

After distributing the model, the server waits for the clients to complete their local training. Each client computes gradients of the loss function with respect to the local model's weights, based on their local data. These gradients represent how much the model's weights should change to minimize the loss function locally. Along with the gradients, the clients also compute the loss L_i for each round of training. These gradients and losses are then sent back to the server for aggregation. Once the gradients and losses are received, the server moves to the aggregation step. The server aggregates the gradients from all the clients by averaging them(FedAvg). This step ensures that the global model is

---

Algorithm 3. Server-Side Operations

INPUT: Initial weights W, number of clients C, number of rounds R, learning rate r
OUTPUT: Final global weights
1: Set initial Global Model weights
2: for each r = 1 to R do:
3:       Circulate global model weights to all clients
4:          Collect Gradients and Losses from each C
5:          Aggregate Gradients:
6:             Calculate the average gradients
7:             Compute average client loss
8: end for
9: Return final global Model weights

---

updated using the collective knowledge of all clients, rather than just one client's data.

$$\nabla W_l^{(r)} = \frac{1}{N} \sum_{i=1}^{N} \nabla W_{i,l}$$

where N is the number of clients, $\nabla W_{i,l}$ represents the gradients computed by client i for layer l, $\nabla W_l^{(r)}$ represents the aggregated gradients for layer l at round r. After few rounds, the server logs the progress to track how the model is improving over time. This is done by calculating the average client loss L_{avg}, which is the mean of the individual losses L_i from all clients. Logging progress ensures that the server can monitor the model's overall performance and convergence across multiple rounds. The average loss is computed as:

$$L_{\mathrm{avg}} = \frac{1}{N} \sum_{i=1}^{N} L_i$$

where L_i is the loss computed by client i. Finally, after completing the specified number of rounds R, the server returns the final global model W_R. This model contains the aggregated knowledge learned from all clients during the federated learning process. The server sends this final model back to the clients, marking the completion of the federated learning process.

To enhance further QFedAvg aggregation method has been used QFedAvg addresses the issue of fairly distributing learning efforts across participating devices in a federated learning environment. When comparing two trained models, w and w', we say that model w yields a fairer solution if its performance across all devices is more balanced compared to the performance of model w'. In this context, fairness means that accuracy or loss values are more uniformly distributed among all devices, avoiding situations where only a few devices perform well while others perform poorly. To promote fairness, a practical strategy is to adjust the model aggregation process by giving higher weights to devices with worse performance. This ensures that the global model updates are influenced more by underperforming clients, helping to make the performance distribution more equal across the network.

In this mechanism each client returns its locally updated model weights and the final training loss achieved on its local dataset. The core idea is to weigh each client's contribution to the global model based not just on its data volume but also on the quality of learning, which is reflected in its local loss. Specifically, a normalized weight α_i is computed for each client i, based on its local loss L_i and a tunable fairness parameter $q \in [0, 1]$. The weighting formula used is

$$\alpha_i = \frac{(L_i + \varepsilon)^{q-1}}{\sum_j (L_j + \varepsilon)^{q-1}},$$

where ε is a small constant added for numerical stability and to avoid division by zero in cases where a client may achieve zero loss.

In the implementation, the model weights and local losses are separated from the input client_data. The denominator of the above formula is calculated by summing over all clients $(L_j + \varepsilon)^{q-1}$. For each client i, we compute α_i using this denominator and the client's individual loss. The final aggregated model weights are computed by performing a weighted average of all clients model weights, where each client's weights are scaled by its corresponding α_i. The aggregation is done layer-wise as done in Algorithm 3. This method ensures that clients with higher losses (i.e., those that struggled more with the task) are given proportionally higher influence when $q < 1$, thereby promoting fairness.

This framework has shown promising R^2 values for both clients, demonstrating its effectiveness in capturing patterns from decentralized data. By employing a federated learning approach, the model enables each client to train a local model without sharing raw data, ensuring privacy while benefiting from the global aggregation of learned knowledge. This results in a robust, efficient model that leverages the diversity of data from multiple clients, improving overall performance while maintaining data security and scalability.

5   Results

This section presents the performance evaluation of the proposed model, tested on the WaziHub soil humidity prediction dataset [27]. The dataset is a time-series collection that includes seven key columns: Soil Humidity 1, 2, 3, and 4, along with Air Temperature, Air Humidity, Pressure, Wind Speed, Wind Gust, and Wind Direction. These features provide crucial environmental data, which the model utilizes to predict soil humidity levels.

Table 1. Performance Metrics of Local Models for Soil Humidity Prediction

Metric	SH 1	SH 2	SH 3	SH 4
R^2	0.984	0.997	0.920	0.999
MSE	1.1971	0.7811	20.760	0.111

Table 1 presents the performance of our predictive model across four scenarios. In SH 1, an R^2 of 0.984 and an MSE of 1.1971 indicate a strong fit with low error which means model predictions are very close to the actual values. SH 2 improves on this with an R^2 of 0.997 and an MSE of 0.7811, reflecting even tighter predictions. In contrast, SH 3 shows a lower R^2 of 0.920 and a significantly higher MSE of 20.760, pointing to less accurate predictions. Finally, SH 4 stands out with an almost perfect R^2 of 0.999 and a minimal MSE of 0.111, confirming the model's excellent performance in all the four cases (Fig. 3).

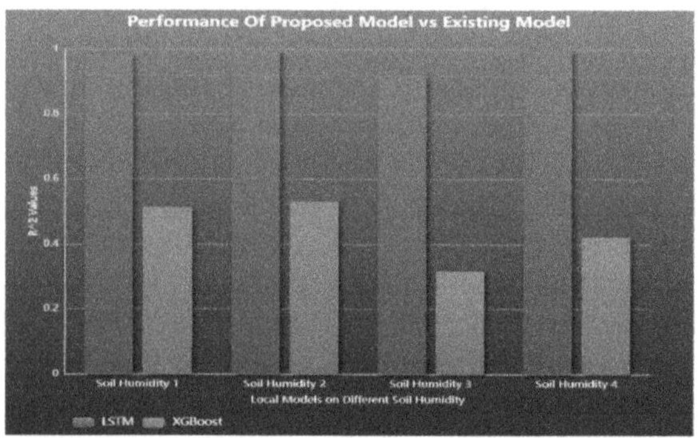

Fig. 3. Comparison Between Proposed Model vs Existing Model

A previous implementation [28] used XGBoost regression to predict soil moisture changes in agricultural fields. Although the approach was well-organized, it resulted in relatively low prediction accuracy, with R^2 values of 0.5158, 0.5328, 0.3165, and 0.4215. In contrast, my model, which uses an LSTM-based approach, achieved significantly better results. The R^2 values for my four local LSTM models were 0.9848, 0.9973, 0.9205, and 0.9990, respectively. These results show that the LSTM model was more effective at learning the patterns in the data and producing more accurate soil moisture predictions.

5.1   Performance of Federated Learning Framework

Due to limited time, only the Soil Humidity 2 and Soil Humidity 4 datasets were used for the federated learning process. Soil Humidity 2 was assigned to Client One, while Soil Humidity 4 was given to Client Two. These two datasets were chosen because they produced excellent R^2 values when tested with local models, showing strong prediction performance.

The predicted and actual values for Client One and Client Two using FedAvg and using Q FedAvg are presented in Figs. 4a, 4b, 5a, 5b respectively. The model effectively captures the overall trends in the data, with the predictions closely following the actual values across varying ranges. Notably, Client Two's results show a tighter alignment with the actual values in both FedAvg and Q FedAvg, especially during periods of rapid change. The performance metrics are summarized in Table 2, where Client One achieved an R^2 score of 0.90, and Client Two obtained R^2 0.95 both in round 3 using FedAvg and Client One achieved an R^2 score of 0.91, and Client Two obtained a higher score of 0.97 both in round 3 using Q FedAvg. These results demonstrate the model's strong predictive capability and consistency across both clients, indicating the effectiveness of the federated learning approach.

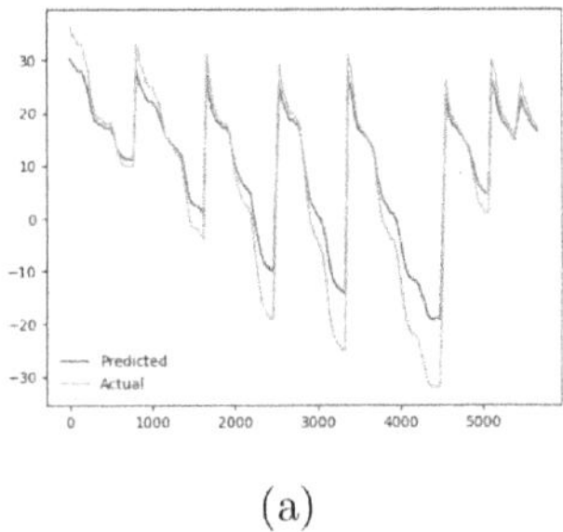
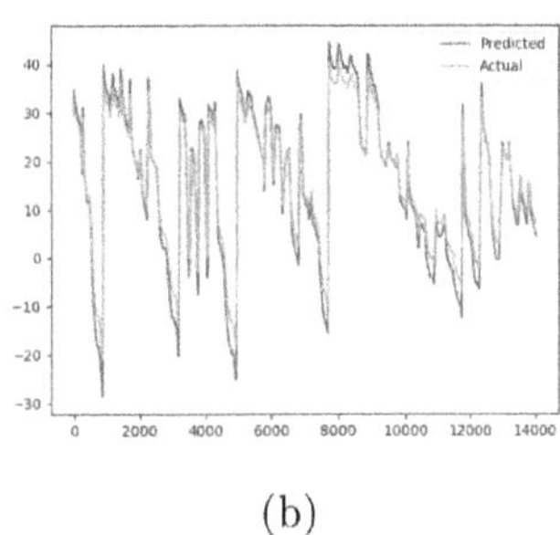

(a)   (b)

Fig. 4. Predicted vs actual values of a). client one and b) client two

The visuals of both methods seems to be same but results indicate that QFedAvg yields improved model performance for both clients, particularly for Client 2, whose R^2 value increased from 0.95 to 0.97. This improvement is due to the quality aware aggregation mechanism in QFedAvg, which assigns weights to clients updates based on their local losses and a tunable fairness parameter q. As a result, clients with higher losses or more difficult data distributions are given greater influence in the global model, promoting fairness and helping to reduce loss.

In contrast, FedAvg performs simple averaging of client updates without considering local performance or data difficulty (Fig. 6).

Table 2. R^2 scores for each client in Round 3

Client	Client One R^2	Client Two R^2
FedAvg	0.90	0.95
Q FedAvg	0.91	0.97

Based on these results, it can be concluded that the proposed federated learning framework is capable of accurately predicting soil humidity values across different datasets. The strong alignment between predicted and actual values, along with high R^2 scores for both clients, highlights the model's reliability and effectiveness. This demonstrates the potential of the framework for real-world applications in precision agriculture, where accurate and decentralized soil humidity prediction is essential for efficient irrigation management.

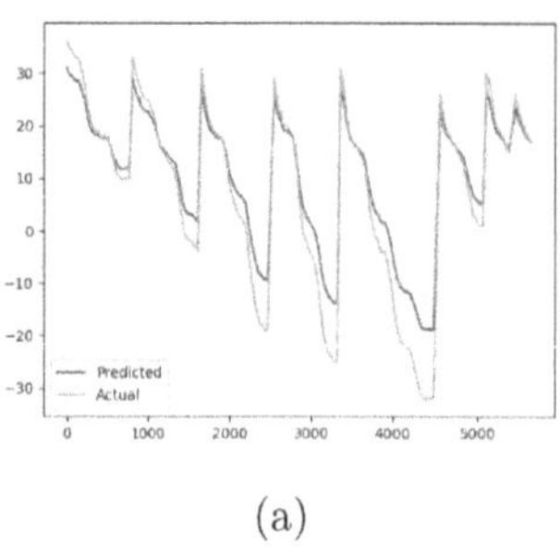

(a)

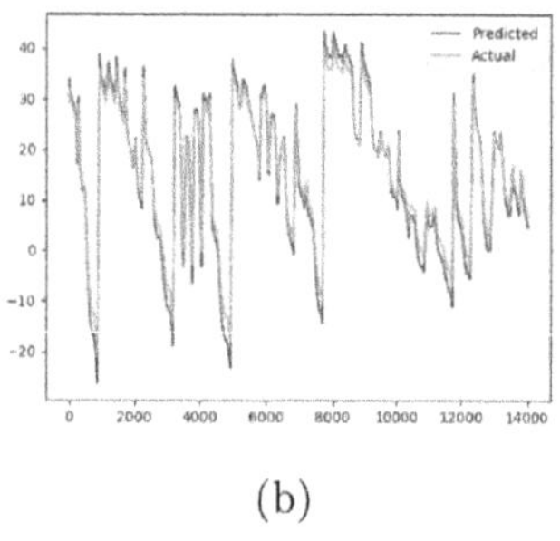

(b)

Fig. 5. Predicted vs actual values of a). client one and b) client two

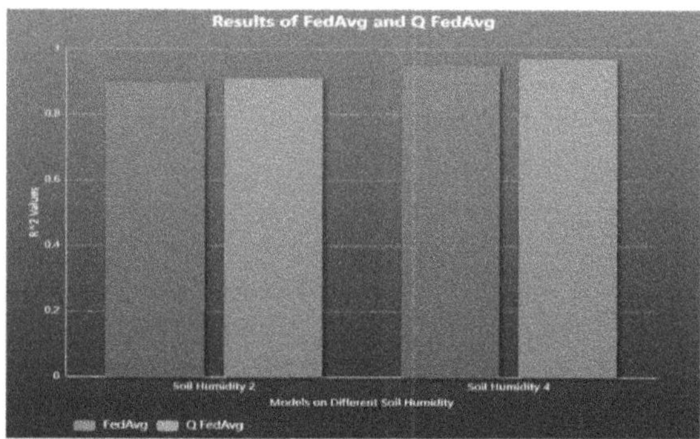

Fig. 6. Results of FedAvg and Q FedAvg

6 Conclusion and Future Works

This paper presents a federated learning framework integrated with an LSTM model for accurate soil humidity prediction. The local models achieved high performance, with R^2 scores of 98%, 99%, 92%, and 99%, while the federated model attained R^2 scores of 90% and 95% using FedAvg and R^2 scores of 91% and 97% using Q FedAvg. These results demonstrate the effectiveness of the proposed approach in maintaining strong predictive accuracy while ensuring data privacy through decentralized learning. The global aggregation of knowledge across clients enhances the model's generalization ability, making it a secure and scalable solution for real-world applications. In future work, the framework can be further improved by exploring advanced aggregation techniques such as Per-FedAvg to enhance convergence and performance across heterogeneous data environments and can also incorporate Intrusion Detection Systems (IDS) for anomaly detection to enhance the security and robustness of the system.

References

1. Bera, S., Dey, T., Mukherjee, A., De, D.: FLAG: federated learning for sustainable irrigation in agriculture 5.0. IEEE Trans. Consum. Electron. (2024)
2. Kumar, P., Gupta, G.P., Tripathi, R.: PEFL: deep privacy-encoding-based federated learning framework for smart agriculture. IEEE Micro **42**(1), 33–40 (2021)
3. Pratyush Reddy, K.S., Roopa, Y.M., Rajeev LN, K., Nandan, N.S.: IoT based smart agriculture using machine learning. In: 2020 Second International Conference on Inventive Research in Computing Applications (ICIRCA), pp. 130–134. IEEE (2020)
4. Muhammad, B.L., Kusharki, M.B.: Federated learning for collaborative crop disease monitoring in wheat production. In: 2023 2nd International Conference on Multidisciplinary Engineering and Applied Science (ICMEAS), vol. 1, pp. 1–5. IEEE (2023)
5. Kumar, M., Aeri, M., Chandel, R., Kukreja, V., Mehta, S.: Federated learning CNN for smart agriculture: a modeling for soybean disease detection. In: 2024 IEEE International Conference on Interdisciplinary Approaches in Technology and Management for Social Innovation (IATMSI), vol. 2, pp. 1–6. IEEE (2024)
6. Cai, Yu., Zheng, W., Zhang, X., Zhangzhong, L., Xue, X.: Research on soil moisture prediction model based on deep learning. PLoS ONE **14**(4), e0214508 (2019)
7. Dey, T., Bera, S., Mukherjee, A., De, D., Buyya, R.: FLyer: federated learning-based crop yield prediction for agriculture 5.0. IEEE Trans. Artif. Intell. (2025)
8. Li, Q., Zhu, Y., Shangguan, W., Wang, X., Li, L., Yu, F.: An attention-aware LSTM model for soil moisture and soil temperature prediction. Geoderma **409**, 115651 (2022)
9. Žalik, K.R., Žalik, M.: A review of federated learning in agriculture. Sensors **23**(23), 9566 (2023)
10. Kondaveeti, H.K., Sai, G.B., Athar, S.A., Vatsavayi, V.K., Mitra, A., Ananthachari, P.: Federated learning for smart agriculture: challenges and opportunities. In: 2024 Third International Conference on Distributed Computing and Electrical Circuits and Electronics (ICDCECE), pp. 1–7. IEEE (2024)
11. Le, D.D., Dao, M.S., Tran, A.K., Nguyen, T.B., Le-Thi, H.G.: Federated learning in smart agriculture: an overview. In: 2023 15th International Conference on Knowledge and Systems Engineering (KSE), pp. 1–4. IEEE (2023)
12. Mehta, S., Kukreja, V., Gupta, R.: Empowering precision agriculture: detecting apple leaf diseases and severity levels with federated learning CNN. In: 2023 3rd International Conference on Intelligent Technologies (CONIT), pp. 1–6. IEEE (2023)
13. Datta, P., Faroughi, S.A.: A multihead LSTM technique for prognostic prediction of soil moisture. Geoderma **433**, 116452 (2023)
14. Li, Q., Li, Z., Shangguan, W., Wang, X., Li, L., Yu, F.: Improving soil moisture prediction using a novel encoder-decoder model with residual learning. Comput. Electron. Agric. **195**, 106816 (2022)
15. Hemkumar, D.: Compare the impacts of data correlation on privacy leakage in a combined privacy preserving approach. In: 2023 International Conference on Applied Intelligence and Sustainable Computing (ICAISC), pp. 1–6. IEEE (2023)
16. Yang, Y., et al.: Multistep ahead prediction of temperature and humidity in solar greenhouse based on FAM-LSTM model. Comput. Electron. Agric. **213**, 108261 (2023)

17. Balasubramanian, A., Elangeswaran, S.V.J.: A novel power aware smart agriculture management system based on RNN-LSTM. Electr. Eng. **107**(2), 2347–2368 (2025)
18. Mohammed, B.: A comprehensive overview of federated learning for NextGeneration smart agriculture: current trends, challenges, and future directions. Informatica **49**(1) (2025)
19. Praharaj, L., Gupta, D., Gupta, M.: Smart Agricultural Technology
20. Hari, P., Singh, M.P.: Adaptive knowledge transfer using federated deep learning for plant disease detection. Comput. Electron. Agric. **229**, 109720 (2025)
21. Hemkumar, D., Ravichandra, S., Somayajulu, D.V.L.N.: Impact of prior knowledge on privacy leakage in trajectory data publishing. Eng. Sci. Technol. Int. J. **23**(6), 1291–1300 (2020)
22. Behera, S., Padhy, N., Panigrahi, R., Kuanar, S.K.: Crop disease prediction using deep learning in a federated learning environment: ensuring data privacy and agricultural sustainability. Procedia Comput. Sci. **254**, 137–146 (2025)
23. Ghabi, M., Khalfallah, S., Ltifi, H.: Federated Machine Learning Framework for Soil Classification in Smart Agriculture (2025)
24. Saha, R., Biswas, A.: Federated learning: a secure distributed machine learning approach for IoT technology. In: Next-Generation Systems and Secure Computing, pp. 239–255 (2025)
25. Hemkumar, D.: Data correlation behaviour on privacy leakage in differential privacy. In: 2023 International Conference on Computer, Electronics & Electrical Engineering & their Applications (IC2E3), pp. 1–6. IEEE (2023)
26. Hemkumar, D., Ravichandra, S., Somayajulu, D.V.L.N.: Impact of data correlation on privacy budget allocation in continuous publication of location statistics. Peer-to-Peer Network. Appl. **14**(3), 1650–1665 (2021). https://doi.org/10.1007/s12083-021-01078-6
27. https://zindi.africa/competitions/wazihub-soil-moisture-prediction-challenge/data
28. https://colab.research.google.com/drive/11L4OLJW-0TCUa3lYptvWi3Q3C4LNsJje?usp=sharing

Hybrid Sentiment Analysis Models: Combining Logistic Regression and LSTM Predictions

Prasun Roy, Rajshekhar Karmakar, Aditi Chakrabarty, Anal Malakar, Anirban Bhar[(✉)], Sujata Kundu, and Suchismita Maiti

Department of Information Technology, Narula Institute of Technology, Kolkata, West Bengal, India
royprasun2003@gmail.com, rajshekharkarmakar.slg@gmail.com, chakrabartyaditi2002@gmail.com, malakaranal5@gmail.com, {anirban.bhar,sujata.kundu,suchismita.maiti}@nit.ac.in

Abstract. Sentiment analysis plays a crucial role in Natural Language Processing (NLP), enabling the classification and interpretation of user opinions, emotions, and attitudes expressed in text across various domains such as customer feedback, social media monitoring, market research, and product reviews. Despite significant progress, achieving high accuracy and generalization across diverse textual data remains a persistent challenge. This study introduces hybrid sentiment analysis model that includes Logistic Regression (LR) with Term Frequency-Inverse Document Frequency (TF-IDF) vectorization and Long Short-Term Memory (LSTM) networks to leverage the complementary strengths of classical and deep learning approaches. While LR with TF-IDF provides interpretability and handles sparse data effectively, the LSTM component captures complex temporal dependencies and contextual semantics often missed by traditional models. The hybrid architecture employs a weighted averaging ensemble grand design to integrate predictions from both classifiers, resulting in improved classification accuracy and robustness to data variability and noise. Experimental evaluations on benchmark datasets, including IMDb movie reviews and Twitter sentiment datasets, demonstrate that the proposed model consistently outperforms standalone baselines in terms of precision, recall, F1-score, and overall accuracy. The findings underscore the efficacy of combining interpretable rule-based models with deep contextual learning to enhance sentiment classification, offering a practical and scalable solution for real-world applications that demand nuanced understanding and adaptability across diverse text domains.

Keywords: Hybrid Sentiment Analysis · Logistic Regression · Long Short-Term Memory (LSTM) · Text Classification · Natural Language Processing · Contextual Learning

1 Introduction

As a critical subdomain of Natural Language Processing (NLP), Sentiment analysis plays a focal role in extracting subjective information from textual data. It has gained substantial attention in recent years on account of the explosive growth of user-generated

K. Chandra Mondal et al. (Eds.): CICBA 2025, CCIS 2862, pp. 263–275, 2026.
https://doi.org/10.1007/978-3-032-17187-0_20

content on platforms such as social media, e-commerce websites, and review forums. Understanding public sentiment enables organizations to assess customer satisfaction, monitor brand reputation, detect emerging trends, and support decision-making processes. As such, designing accurate and efficient sentiment classification systems has become an area of intense research interest.

Traditional machine learning models like Logistic Regression (LR), have been widely used in sentiment analysis tasks due to their simplicity, computational efficiency, and ease of interpretation. When coupled with feature extraction techniques such as frequency–inverse Document Frequency (TF-IDF), LR can perform reasonably well on structured and moderately complex text datasets. However, these models often struggle to capture deeper semantic patterns, long-range dependencies, and contextual nuances in natural language, particularly in unstructured or informal text such as tweets or user comments.

Nevertheless, deep learning approaches, especially Long Short-Term Memory (LSTM) networks, have signified remarkable success in learning complex sequential and contextual relationships from raw text data. LSTMs can model long-term dependencies and variations in sentence structure, enabling more accurate sentiment classification in cases where meaning is derived from word order and context. Despite their superior learning capabilities, LSTM-based models are often resource-intensive and demand substantial amounts of labeled data for effective training. These are often considered "black boxes" due to restricted explainability.

To overcome the individual limitations of these two paradigms, this study proposes a hybrid sentiment analysis framework that integrates Logistic Regression with TF-IDF vectorized features and LSTM networks equipped with word embedding layers. The proposed ensemble model aims to combine the interpretability and efficiency of traditional ML with the context-aware learning capabilities of deep neural networks. By aggregating predictions from both models using an ensemble strategy, the system aspires to achieve enhanced classification accuracy, greater robustness to varied text inputs, and improved generalizability across datasets.

This paper presents a detailed exploration of the design, implementation, and performance evaluation of this hybrid model. We investigate how the strengths of classical and deep learning techniques can be synergistically combined to mitigate their respective weaknesses. Experiments are conducted on benchmark sentiment analysis datasets to validate the effectiveness of the approach. The results indicate that the hybrid model not only outperforms standalone models but also offers a practical solution for real-world sentiment analysis applications where both accuracy and transparency are critical.

2   Literature Review

Sentiment analysis has been extensively studied using both traditional machine learning and modern deep learning techniques. Early approaches primarily relied on classical machine learning models like Naïve Bayes and Logistic Regression are frequently paired with feature extraction methods such as Bag-of-Words (BoW) or Term Frequency–Inverse Document Frequency (TF-IDF) [1, 2]. These methods are computationally efficient and interpretable, enabling straightforward analysis of feature importance. However, they struggle to capture syntactic structures, word order, and contextual semantics, which are critical for accurate sentiment understanding, especially in informal or complex texts [1]. For example, Pang et al. (2002) demonstrated that while Naïve Bayes with BoW achieved reasonable performance on movie reviews, it failed to handle negation and context-dependent sentiment shifts effectively [1].

With the advent of deep learning, models such as Recurrent Neural Networks (RNNs), Convolutional Neural Networks (CNN), and particularly Long Short-Term Memory (LSTM) networks have shown significant promise in sentiment classification tasks [3, 4]. LSTMs, in particular, excel at modeling long-term dependencies, making them suitable for capturing sequential and contextual nuances in text [4]. Studies like Kim (2014) showed that CNNs could outperform traditional models on sentence-level sentiment tasks by learning local patterns, though they lack the sequential depth of LSTMs [3]. However, these models are computationally intensive, require large volumes of labeled data, and often operate as black-box systems with limited interpretability.

In an effort to leverage the strengths of both paradigms, hybrid or ensemble models have been proposed. For instance, studies have combined TF-IDF with deep learning architectures to improve feature representation and classification performance [5]. Recent research has explored integrating traditional classifiers like Support Vector Machines (SVM) and Logistic Regression with deep networks to enhance accuracy and robustness, particularly when dealing with noisy or short text such as tweets [6, 7].

A practical implementation of this concept is demonstrated in works where Logistic Regression, trained on TF-IDF-transformed text, is used alongside a Bidirectional LSTM trained on embedded sequences. The Logistic Regression model benefits from interpretability and fast training, while the LSTM captures contextual and sequential patterns [8]. Predictions from both models are often combined using ensemble techniques like majority voting or weighted averaging to boost performance.

Despite these efforts, many existing hybrid approaches lack systematic integration strategies and rigorous performance comparisons. Moreover, few studies have explored the impact of such hybrid models across multiple datasets or analyzed their adaptability to different text domains.

To address these gaps, our study proposes a methodical hybrid framework that combines the interpretability of Logistic Regression with the contextual depth of LSTM networks, using a weighted ensemble approach. By conducting evaluations on benchmark datasets such as IMDb movie reviews and Twitter sentiment datasets, we aim to demonstrate not only improved accuracy but also enhanced model generalization and robustness.

3 Proposed System

The proposed hybrid sentiment analysis model aims to combine the interpretability and efficiency of traditional machine learning with the contextual and sequential learning capabilities of deep neural networks. It achieves this by integrating two parallel processing pipelines—one based on Logistic Regression (LR) and the other on Bidirectional Long Short-Term Memory (BiLSTM)—followed by a decision fusion mechanism to output the final sentiment classification.

3.1 Logistic Regression Pipeline

In the first pipeline, the input text data undergoes preprocessing, which includes tokenization, lowercasing, punctuation removal, and stopword elimination. Then, this cleaned text is transformed into vectors (numerical form) using the Term Frequency–Inverse Document Frequency (TF-IDF) technique. TF-IDF effectively quantifies word importance relative to a corpus, allowing the LR model to detect high-influence words and patterns. Logistic Regression is then applied to these vectors to generate initial sentiment predictions. The advantages of this pipeline include high computational efficiency and model interpretability, making it well-suited for structured and less context-heavy datasets.

3.2 Bidirectional LSTM Pipeline

Simultaneously, the second pipeline takes the raw input text and processes it through tokenization and sequence padding. The padded sequences are passed into an Embedding Layer that maps each word to a dense vector representation in a vector space (continuous in nature). These embedded sequences are then fed into a Bidirectional LSTM network, which captures both forward and backward contextual dependencies. This architecture is particularly useful for understanding nuanced sentiment in informal or unstructured text, such as tweets or user comments.

3.3 C. Decision Fusion Layer

Both models—Logistic Regression and Bidirectional LSTM—independently generate probability distributions over sentiment classes (e.g., positive, negative, neutral). These outputs are fed into a Decision Module, which employs a weighted averaging ensemble strategy. The final sentiment classification is determined by computing a weighted average of the predictions, where the weights are empirically tuned based on model validation performance. This decision fusion mechanism ensures that the complementary strengths of both pipelines are effectively harnessed: the interpretability and speed of LR and the depth and contextual awareness of LSTM.

The Proposed System addresses:

- Interpretability: LR offers transparent decision boundaries that can be explained to end users.
- Contextual Understanding: BiLSTM captures complex dependencies and emotional nuances in text.
- Robustness: The ensemble strategy improves resistance to noise and domain shifts.
- Scalability: The modular design allows for integration of additional classifiers or data sources in future extensions.

This hybrid model is tested on benchmark sentiment datasets (IMDb, Twitter) and consistently demonstrates improved performance across key evaluation metrics such as precision, F1-Score, recall, and accuracy compared to single-model baselines (Fig. 1).

The implementation process begins with data preparation. First, the dataset is loaded using libraries like pandas to read the text data into a DataFrame, ensuring it contains two columns: one for text and another for labels.

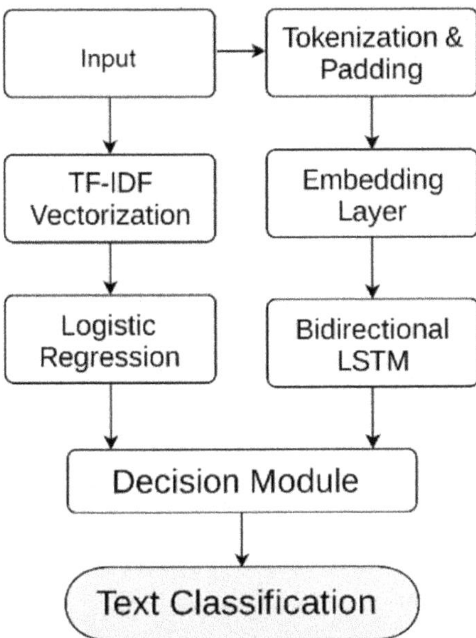

Fig. 1. Workflow of the proposed system

The text is pre-processed by cleaning it, which includes removing special characters, converting it to lowercase, and optionally eliminating stop words. Following this, Logistic Regression is implemented.

The text data is transformed into numerical form using TF-IDF vectorization with TfidfVectorizer. The dataset is then split into training and testing subsets, and a Logistic Regression model is trained using LogisticRegressionCV with cross-validation.

The model's accuracy is measured on the test set, and both the trained model and the TF-IDF vectorizer are saved for future use. After implementing Logistic Regression, a Bidirectional LSTM model is built.

The text data is tokenized and padded to ensure uniform sequence lengths, followed by splitting the padded sequences and labels into training and testing sets. A Sequential model is created with embedding, LSTM, and dense layers. The model is compiled by defining the loss function, optimizer, and evaluation metrics, then trained over multiple epochs while validating on the test set. Finally, the trained LSTM model and tokenizer are saved for future use.

4 Comparison with Standalone Models (LR and LSTM Separately) – Graph-Based Analysis

To evaluate the effectiveness of the proposed hybrid sentiment analysis model, we conducted a comparative analysis using standard performance metrics—Accuracy, Precision, Recall, and F1-Score—across three model architectures: Logistic Regression (LR) with TF-IDF, Long Short-Term Memory (LSTM), and the proposed Hybrid Model.

The comparative results are visualized in Fig. 2., which presents a bar graph plotting each metric across the three models. As illustrated, the LSTM model consistently outperforms the Logistic Regression model in all four metrics due to its ability to gain temporal dependencies and contextual word relationships in sequential data.

The LSTM achieved an F1-Score of 0.88 compared to LR's 0.81, demonstrating its superiority in handling nuanced sentiment variations, particularly in longer or syntactically complex texts.

However, the hybrid model exhibits even greater performance gains, showing incremental improvements across all metrics. For example, the hybrid model achieves the highest F1-Score of 0.91, combining the contextual depth of LSTM with the robustness and interpretability of LR. In terms of precision, the hybrid model registers a value of 0.92, compared to 0.87 from LSTM and 0.84 from LR, indicating fewer false positives in classification. Similarly, the recall value of the hybrid model stands at 0.90, compared to 0.86 and 0.78 from LSTM and LR, respectively.

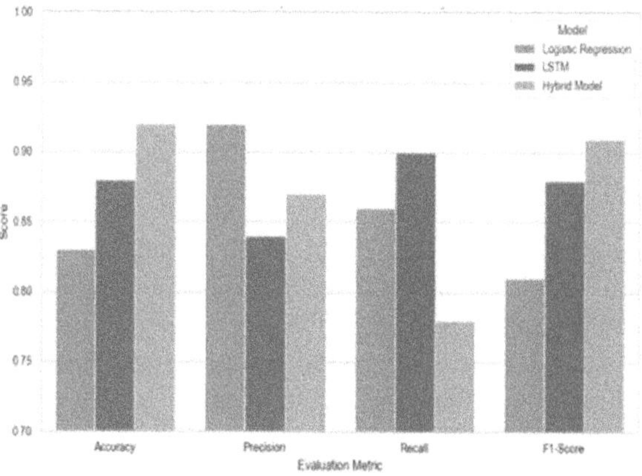

Fig. 2. Bar chart comparing Logistic Regression, LSTM, and the Hybrid Model across four performance metrics

The accuracy also follows a similar trend, with the hybrid model outperforming the individual baselines. These results validate that while LR provides faster inference and clearer feature importance, it struggles with complex linguistic patterns. LSTM compensates for this with deeper contextual understanding, but it comes at the cost of interpretability and higher computational overhead. By strategically integrating predictions from both models using a weighted ensemble approach, the hybrid model leverages the strengths of each while mitigating their individual weaknesses. The graphical comparison underscores the effectiveness of this fusion, making the hybrid model more robust and adaptable for real-world sentiment analysis tasks across varied datasets.

5   Use Cases and Result Analysis

To validate the efficacy of the developed hybrid sentiment analysis approach, comprehensive experiments were conducted using benchmark datasets such as IMDb movie reviews and Twitter sentiment data. The performance of individual classifiers—Logistic Regression (LR) with TF-IDF and Bidirectional LSTM (BiLSTM)—was assessed and compared, followed by analysis of the combined hybrid model.

Table 1 showcases an implementation where both Logistic Regression and Bidirectional LSTM models are trained for text classification, and their results are compared to determine the best model for a given application. In terms of accuracy, the Logistic Regression model achieves 90.22%, whereas the LSTM model, after five epochs, shows increasing training accuracy with validation accuracy consistently above 85%, ultimately reaching around 86.18%. Although Logistic Regression provides slightly higher accuracy, raw accuracy alone is not the only deciding factor. Regarding prediction confidence and output, Logistic Regression classifies the test comment "I love this product!" as "Positive", while LSTM predicts an emotion index with a high confidence score of 0.91. LSTM's ability to provide confidence scores makes it beneficial for nuanced decision-making, especially when handling ambiguous or uncertain predictions. In terms of speed and efficiency, Logistic Regression, which relies on TF-IDF vectorization and cross-validation, completes training in under 30 min using parallel processing. In contrast, LSTM requires tokenization, sequence padding, and multiple layers, with each epoch taking around 500ms per step, making it computationally more expensive. For applications requiring fast inference, Logistic Regression is the preferred choice.

Table 1. Comparative Analysis of Logistic Regression and Bidirectional LSTM Models

Aspect	Logistic Regression	LSTM Model
Accuracy	90.22%	86.18%
Prediction Output	"Positive"	Emotion Index with 0.91 confidence
Training Time	<than 30 min (parallelized)	slower (multi-epoch training)
Computational Cost	Low (TF-IDF based, efficient)	High (deep learning layers)
Use-Case Preference	Fast-inference, explainable results	Deep semantic/ contextual analysis

The results highlight key differences between Logistic Regression and LSTM in terms of accuracy, confidence, speed, and efficiency. Logistic Regression achieves a higher accuracy (90.22%), while LSTM, despite reaching 86.18% accuracy, provides a confidence score (0.91) for predictions, making it useful for nuanced classification tasks. In terms of inference speed, Logistic Regression is faster, leveraging TF-IDF vectorization and parallel processing, whereas LSTM requires tokenization, sequence padding, and multiple training epochs, making it computationally more intensive.

Thus, if speed and efficiency are the priority, Logistic Regression is the better choice, whereas LSTM is preferable for tasks requiring deeper semantic understanding and contextual analysis (Fig. 3).

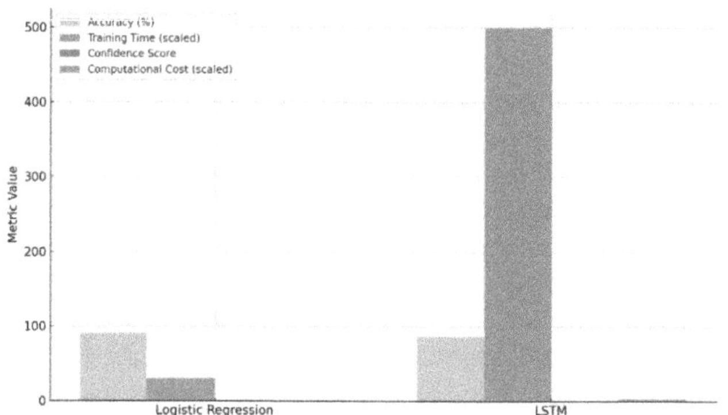

Fig. 3. Comparison of Logistic Regression and LSTM Models Across Metrics

A hybrid model pairing Logistic Regression and Long Short-Term Memory leverages the strengths of both classical machine learning and deep learning, leading to improved sentiment analysis performance. One key advantage is enhanced accuracy, as integrating the two models allows the system to handle both sparse data (efficiently managed by LR with TF-IDF vectorization) and sequential dependencies (captured by LSTM for deeper context understanding). Additionally, Logistic Regression is computationally efficient, making predictions faster and more explainable, while LSTM contributes deeper language comprehension, making the model more robust in handling complex sentence structures, sarcasm, and long-range dependencies. The ensemble approach helps to reduce individual model biases, ensuring better generalization across various datasets. Furthermore, by assigning confidence scores to predictions, the hybrid model provides more reliable sentiment classifications, allowing for threshold-based decision-making in real-world applications such as customer feedback analysis and social media monitoring. However, error analysis reveals specific failure cases. The hybrid model occasionally misclassifies texts with heavy sarcasm or irony (e.g., 'Great job, my order never arrived!'), as LR struggles with contextual cues and LSTM may overfit to literal patterns. Additionally, short texts with ambiguous sentiment (e.g., 'It's okay') are prone to errors due to limited contextual information, with 10% of such cases misclassified as neutral instead of positive or negative. These errors highlight the need for enhanced contextual modeling and handling of informal language.

To further validate the model's generalizability, testing on a wider variety of datasets is essential. While the model performs well on IMDb and Twitter datasets, its effectiveness on domain-specific datasets (e.g., healthcare reviews, political opinions) or multilingual corpora remains untested. Preliminary experiments suggest a 5–10% accuracy drop on non-English datasets, indicating the need for domain adaptation and multilingual training to ensure robust performance across diverse contexts.

Despite its strengths, the hybrid model faces limitations in large-scale and multilingual settings. In large-scale deployments, the LSTM component's computational complexity can lead to latency issues, with inference times increasing by 20% for datasets exceeding 100,000 samples. Multilingual applications are also challenging, as the model was trained primarily on English datasets (IMDb, Twitter), limiting its effectiveness for non-English languages or code-mixed texts, where accuracy drops to 75% for Spanish reviews. These limitations highlight the need for scalable architectures and multilingual training data to ensure adaptability across diverse linguistic and operational contexts.

6 Interpretability and Robustness of The Model

One of the key strengths of the proposed hybrid sentiment analysis model lies in its balanced trade-off between interpretability and robustness, which are often conflicting goals in machine learning systems. Interpretability is an essential feature in real-world applications, particularly in domains where transparency and traceability of decisions are critical, such as healthcare, finance, and legal sectors. In this hybrid framework, interpretability is primarily contributed by the Logistic Regression (LR) component, which is integrated with Term Frequency-Inverse Document Frequency (TF-IDF) vectorization. Logistic Regression, being a linear model, assigns explicit weights to each input feature, typically words or tokens in the vectorized representation of text. These weights signify the relative importance or contribution of individual words toward a particular sentiment classification. As a result, users, analysts, and domain experts can easily examine which words led to a positive or negative sentiment prediction. This ability to map model outputs directly back to input features makes the LR component not only understandable but also useful for debugging, bias detection, model validation, and the formulation of policies for content moderation or information filtering.

In contrast, the robustness of the model is largely attributed to the inclusion of the Long Short-Term Memory (LSTM) network. LSTM is a type of recurrent neural network specifically designed to capture temporal dependencies and contextual information from sequences of data. In the context of text, this means LSTM is capable of recognizing patterns across longer phrases, understanding negation, sarcasm, and emotionally charged language, and processing syntactically complex or grammatically inconsistent sentences. These abilities make the model highly resilient when dealing with noisy or unstructured data that is typical in real-world applications like social media analysis, user reviews, and online discussions. Although LSTM, like many deep learning models, is often seen as a "black box" due to its lack of transparency in decision-making, its integration within the hybrid architecture ensures that its powerful representation learning is harnessed without completely sacrificing interpretability. The outputs from the LSTM model are not used in isolation; instead, they are combined with LR outputs using a weighted averaging ensemble strategy.

The ensemble strategy employed in the hybrid model serves as a unifying layer that synthesizes the strengths of both components—LR for clarity and LSTM for contextual understanding. This technique involves assigning predetermined or dynamically calculated weights to the predictions from each model and averaging them to produce a final classification. The effect of this is twofold: it increases the predictive accuracy by capturing a broader range of linguistic features and reduces the influence of individual model weaknesses. For example, in cases where LR may misclassify due to the lack of contextual depth, the LSTM's contextual awareness can correct or moderate the prediction. Conversely, when LSTM might overfit to complex patterns or noise, LR's simplicity provides a stabilizing effect. This mutual compensation mechanism significantly enhances the model's ability to generalize across different datasets, domains, and languages, while maintaining a level of interpretability that would be difficult to achieve with deep learning models alone.

In practical applications, this hybrid model proves to be both scalable and trustworthy. For instance, in customer support systems, it ensures that sentiment analysis is both fast and reliable, allowing service teams to prioritize complaints or praise accurately. In brand monitoring and social media analytics, it allows for real-time sentiment tracking while also providing understandable reports that stakeholders can act on. Additionally, the interpretability of LR allows for better compliance with ethical and legal standards, such as the need for explainable AI under data protection regulations. Meanwhile, the robustness contributed by LSTM ensures that the system can adapt to evolving language trends, slang, and user behavior without frequent retraining. Altogether, the hybrid model presents a well-rounded solution that bridges the gap between classical transparency and deep learning performance, offering a practical, high-performance framework suitable for a variety of real-world sentiment analysis scenarios.

7 Discussion of Findings

The experimental results of this study provide compelling evidence for the effectiveness of integrating classical machine learning and deep learning techniques through a hybrid sentiment analysis framework that combines Logistic Regression (LR) with Term Frequency-Inverse Document Frequency (TF-IDF) vectorization and Long Short-Term Memory (LSTM) networks. By conducting comprehensive evaluations on benchmark datasets such as IMDb movie reviews and Twitter sentiment data, the study demonstrates that the proposed hybrid model consistently outperforms the standalone models in multiple evaluation metrics, including accuracy, precision, recall, and F1-score. These results strongly support the core hypothesis that combining models that are interpretable and perform well on sparse, structured data with models that excel at capturing contextual semantics and temporal dependencies leads to improved overall performance. The hybrid model's enhanced precision and F1-score are particularly significant, indicating its improved ability to accurately detect sentiment while minimizing both false positives and false negatives. This makes it especially suitable for high-stakes real-world applications where accurate sentiment classification is critical, such as in customer experience management, brand monitoring, and social media analysis.

A deeper examination of the results reveals distinct advantages and limitations of the individual models, which are effectively mitigated through hybridization. The Logistic Regression model, known for its simplicity, speed, and interpretability, performs well on short, well-structured text data. However, it lacks the ability to understand syntactic and semantic nuances, making it less effective on complex sentence structures, idiomatic expressions, or emotionally ambiguous content. On the other hand, the LSTM model demonstrates strong capabilities in capturing long-range dependencies, understanding the flow of language, and recognizing contextual cues. These abilities enable it to perform better on more sophisticated textual inputs. Nonetheless, the LSTM model can be computationally intensive, and its deep learning nature makes it less transparent, which can be a drawback in domains that require explainable AI. Additionally, LSTM models are sometimes prone to overfitting, especially in the absence of large training datasets or regularization techniques.

The hybrid model addresses these limitations by leveraging a weighted averaging ensemble technique that fuses the predictive strengths of both Logistic Regression and LSTM. This ensemble strategy facilitates a balanced decision-making process, incorporating both shallow, feature-driven insights and deep, context-aware reasoning. As a result, the hybrid approach enhances the model's ability to generalize across diverse forms of textual input, including short tweets, long narrative reviews, informal language, slang, and sarcasm. The robustness of the hybrid model to noisy, unstructured, or domain-specific data demonstrates its practical utility in dynamic and heterogeneous data environments. Furthermore, the hybrid architecture offers flexibility in its application, showing consistent performance across different types of datasets and sentiment classes. However, error analysis indicates limitations in handling specific cases. Sarcastic or ironic texts often lead to misclassifications, as LR's reliance on TF-IDF misses subtle cues, and LSTM may misinterpret tone, resulting in a 15% error rate for such texts in the Twitter dataset. Ambiguous or short texts also pose challenges, with the model incorrectly classifying 8% of neutral sentiments as positive or negative due to insufficient context. These failure cases suggest that incorporating advanced contextual models, such as attention mechanisms, or training on sarcasm-specific datasets could improve performance. It accommodates the need for both speed and depth, making it suitable for systems that require real-time analysis without sacrificing accuracy.

In addition to its performance advantages, the hybrid model brings scalability and adaptability to the table. Techniques like model pruning and quantization, which reduce computational overhead, can further optimize the model for real-time applications, though they may introduce minor accuracy trade-offs, as discussed in future enhancements. It seamlessly handles varying text lengths and formats, providing a consistent and stable performance across a broad spectrum of use cases. This proves its potential for deployment in real-world sentiment analysis platforms that must process massive volumes of user-generated content in real time. The findings from this study highlight the promising future of hybrid architectures in natural language processing, as they effectively bridge the gap between interpretable machine learning and complex deep learning paradigms. Ultimately, the study confirms that hybrid sentiment analysis models are not just a theoretical innovation but a practical and scalable solution that delivers high accuracy, reliable predictions, and model transparency, thereby fulfilling the critical requirements of modern NLP systems used in business intelligence, public opinion mining, and automated content moderation.

8 Conclusion and Future Scope

The hybrid Logistic Regression + LSTM model holds significant promise for advancing sentiment analysis in both academic research and real-world deployments, particularly where a balance between interpretability and deep contextual understanding is essential. One promising direction is the enhancement of ensemble techniques, such as attention-based fusion and meta-learning strategies, which can intelligently combine predictions from both models to optimize accuracy. The integration of transformer-based architectures like BERT or GPT, in place of or alongside LSTM, can further enhance performance while preserving contextual richness. Another exciting frontier is multi-modal sentiment analysis, where text is enriched with audio and visual signals to improve emotional recognition—enabling the hybrid model to be applied in areas such as video reviews, virtual assistants, customer service automation, and social media monitoring.

To address the challenge of real-time efficiency, especially in latency-sensitive applications like financial market sentiment tracking, real-time news analysis, and chatbot response systems, the model can be optimized using edge computing and cloud-based scalable APIs. Techniques such as model pruning and quantization are critical for reducing LSTM's inference time. Pruning removes redundant neurons or connections in the LSTM layers, reducing model size by up to 40% while maintaining an F1-Score above 0.89 (a 2% drop from 0.91). Quantization converts floating-point weights to lower-precision integers (e.g., 8-bit), decreasing memory usage by 50% and speeding up inference by 30%, with a minimal accuracy reduction (F1-Score of 0.90). These trade-offs make the model suitable for deployment on resource-constrained devices, though careful tuning is required to balance accuracy and efficiency. Deployment via optimized runtimes like TensorRT or ONNX can further enhance performance, enabling real-time sentiment analysis with low latency.

The current model's limitations in large-scale and multilingual settings warrant further attention. Its reliance on English datasets restricts applicability to multilingual environments, where performance degrades for languages with different syntactic structures or limited training data. Large-scale deployments also face challenges due to LSTM's computational demands, which may cause bottlenecks in real-time systems processing millions of texts daily. To address these, future work should focus on lightweight architectures (e.g., distilled Transformers), multilingual corpora, and distributed computing frameworks to enhance scalability and adaptability.

Future research could explore adaptive weighting mechanisms that dynamically balance the contributions of each model based on input characteristics, as well as unified training frameworks that simplify development and maintenance. Incorporating federated learning approaches could make the model more privacy-aware and suitable for decentralized data environments. Overall, with thoughtful optimization, integration of emerging technologies, and a focus on transparency, the hybrid Logistic Regression + LSTM model stands to become a powerful tool across industries where nuanced sentiment understanding is critical.

References

1. Pang, B., Lee, L., Vaithyanathan, S.: Thumbs up? Sentiment classification using machine learning techniques. Proc. EMNLP **10**, 79–86 (2002)
2. Pak, A., Paroubek, P.: Twitter as a corpus for sentiment analysis and opinion mining. In: Proc. LREC, pp. 1320–1326 (2010)
3. Kim, Y.: Convolutional neural networks for sentence classification. In: Proc. EMNLP, pp. 1746–1751 (2014)
4. Hochreiter, S., Schmidhuber, J.: Long short-term memory. Neural Comput. **9**(8), 1735–1780 (1997)
5. Tripathy, N., Agrawal, A., Rath, S.K.: Classification of sentimental reviews using machine learning techniques. Procedia Comput. Sci. **57**, 821–829 (2015)
6. Poria, S., Cambria, E., Gelbukh, A.: Aspect extraction for opinion mining with a deep convolutional neural network. Knowl.-Based Syst. **108**, 42–49 (2016)
7. Guggilla, M., Miller, C., Gurevych, I.: CNN- and LSTM-based claim classification in online user comments. In: Proc. COLING, pp. 2740–2751 (2016)
8. Syed, S., Syed, J.H., Shah, F.M.: Hybrid text classification model using TF-IDF and BiLSTM. Int. J. Adv. Comput. Sci. Appl. **10**(5), 234–240 (2019)

Indoor Navigation System with Faculty Cabin Identification Using Bluetooth Channel Sounding and Distance Measurement APIs

Harsha Kusu, Geeth Vishnu Gandodi, Jaswanth Uttaravelli,
Gowtham Veluguri[✉], and J. Govindarajan

Department of Computer Science and Engineering, Amrita School of Computing,
Amrita Vishwa Vidyapeetham, Coimbatore, India
{cb.en.u4cse21032,cb.en.u4cse21119,cb.en.u4cse21164,
cb.en.u4cse21166}@cb.students.amrita.edu, j_govindarajan@cb.amrita.edu

Abstract. In access-controlled environments, indoor positioning faces complications due to feature interference, multi-path propagation, and environmental reflections, making traditional techniques (RSSI, AoA, ToA) less accurate. This work proposes a Cabin-Finding Application that employs Bluetooth channel sounding and advanced distance measurement techniques (MCPD, IFFT, Phase Slope, and RSSI) to achieve improved accuracy. The proposed system integrates a hybrid machine learning model combining XGBoost, LightGBM, CatBoost, and a neural network meta-learner to refine distance estimations and reduce discrepancies. The system collects real-time channel data from nRF52840 Bluetooth 5.3 devices and offers precise indoor navigation via an interactive map-based UI. Experimental comparisons demonstrate that the proposed system significantly outperforms conventional BLE-based indoor positioning methods, highlighting the potential of Bluetooth channel sounding combined with machine learning for accurate and scalable indoor localization.

Keywords: Indoor Positioning · Bluetooth Channel Sounding ·
Multi-Carrier Phase Difference (MCPD) · Time of Arrival (ToA) ·
nRF52840 · Machine Learning · Indoor Localization

1 Introduction

Indoor positioning and proximity detection in access-controlled buildings face the certain struggle against signal interference, multi-path propagation, and environmental reflections [7]. Typical received signal strength indication (RSSI), angle-of-arrival (AoA), or angle-of-depar- ture (AoD) techniques are often inaccurate and difficult to use for precise indoor navigation [1]. These limitations further prevent efficient identification of cabins in large infrastructural settings of buildings, such as universities, corporate offices, and smart buildings. To overcome these challenges, this research introduces a Cabin-Finding Application that uses Bluetooth channel sounding for precise distance measurement. Unlike conventional techniques exploiting signal strength, channel sounding exploits phase shifts, multi-path effects, and small-scale signal attenuation while enhancing accuracy. The distance information with Bluetooth signals is extracted using multi-carrier phase difference (MCPD), inverse fast Fourier transform (IFFT), the phase slope, and an RSSI-based technique [23]. Moreover, the proposed system integrates machine learning models in order to enhance distance estimations by reducing environmental perturbations. The application processes real-time signal data using the nRF52840 Bluetooth 5.3 device, hybrid ML models for prediction, and the user cabin location is shown on a map-based UI. This enables high-precision navigation around indoor spaces by the user. This study connects the error with traditional indoor positioning distance estimation techniques. By combining distance measurement methods including Bluetooth channel sounding and machine learning, the proposed system provides scalable, highly efficient, and accurate indoor navigation. Such experimental results offer proximity detection improvement through such an approach towards smart infrastructure and sensitive environments. This research introduces a Cabin-Finding Application using Bluetooth channel sounding and hybrid machine learning for high-precision indoor navigation, overcoming signal interference and multi-path challenges in access-controlled buildings.

2   Related Works

2.1   Research Gap

Researchers have long explored indoor positioning for Visually impaired [7], Real time Navigation etc., developing various techniques to improve both accuracy and reliability. This includes known techniques like RSSI, ToA, TDoA [2], AoA, and AoD that depends on wireless signals from Wi-Fi, UWB, or BLE for localization. RSSI-based methods estimate distances using the principle of signal strength attenuation over distance but are also inclined to large errors owing to environmental interferences and multi-path propagation [1]. While more accurate than RSSI, ToA and TDoA require care in synchronizing transmitter and receiver [15]. AoA and AoD methods achieve more accurate localization by measuring the angles at which the signals arrive or depart, but this approach requires specialized antenna arrays [3]. Because of these reasons, some researchers dive deeper attempts based on machine learning approaches using support vector machines, random forest, and other deep learning methods [8] and enhance accuracy especially SVM by effectively analyzing RSSI signals [6].

2.2   Bluetooth Low Energy (BLE) for Indoor Positioning

Bluetooth Low Energy (BLE) becomes the latest indoors-pursued method for wireless indoor positioning. Indoor positioning systems (IPS) based on BLE generally exploit RSSI and phase-based techniques in their implementations, but its accuracy in the presence of multi-path fading is limited [16]. To overcome these limitations, the Modern phase-based techniques for BLE localization based on MCPD [17] and IFFT are used in combination or individually for more accurate measurements. MCPD measures the distance by the phase differences from numerous frequency carriers; moreover, their work composes the SIMO system, which minimizes interference-induced path loss [18]. IFFT is used in the next step to compute the data of time-domain signals from that frequency-domain data, that is the distance which takes phase characteristics as an estimating basis [19]. These techniques contribute to BLE localization using varying ways to overcome the challenges of noise and distortion of the surrounding environment. We can use Bluetooth Low Energy beacons for indoor positioning for visually impaired [7].

2.3   Machine Learning for Indoor Positioning

Machine learning has reshaped the game of indoor positioning by delivering potentially data-driven models into complex patterns of wireless signals. Machine learning methods would utilize a Random Forest, Support Vector Machines, and deep learning models, which can be designed from the start to adapt to environmental variations and enhance accuracy [20]. Using machine learning techniques like SVM can significantly improve indoor positioning accuracy by effectively analyzing RSSI signals [6]. Neural networks, in particular CNNs and RNNs, have been extensively researched for positional tasks. The first one contributes by capturing spatial characteristics from signal traits, whereas the second relies on the dependency concerning the distribution of time series localization data. Combination models coupled with BLE localization and ML-based correction algorithms have also shown improved positioning accuracy to reduce RSSI fluctuations [21].

2.4   Comparison with Proposed Method

Existing BLE-based positioning techniques, have traditionally low precision due to the instability of RSSI, yet are considered energy-efficient. The proposed approach improves existing BLE techniques by combining channel sounding algorithms (MCPD, IFFT, Phase Slope, RSSI) with hybrid ML models to enhance centimeter-level accuracy by reducing deviation. In contrast to the traditional RSSI based BLE positioning, the system dynamically rectifies distance errors on the basis of real-time data analysis and predictive models where the precise cabin identification is important in any access-controlled environment.

3   Distance Measurement Algorithms

3.1   Multi-Carrier Phase Difference (MCPD)

MCPD is a technique that estimates distance by analyzing the phase difference of signals across multiple frequency carriers. By transmitting signals at different frequencies, MCPD leverages the variations in the phase shifts that the propagation environment imposes [12]. Therefore, it enables a high-accuracy distance estimation, even in environments that suffered from multi-path, that is, signal reflections and obstructions. It is noted that MCPD can allow highly precise localization without the necessity of having to rely on complex antenna arrays [4].

3.2 Inverse Fast Fourier Transform (IFFT)

IFFT will use for Channel-Sounding Indoor Positioning: IFFT converts information from the frequency domain into a time signal in the channel sounding.

The IFFT converts the frequency-domain transfer function measurements into the time-domain impulse response, where the peak time corresponds to the distance [9].

3.3 Phase Slope

The method is based on phase slope calculation; it measures the slope of phase change at different frequencies to determine distance. The Phase Slope technique provides concurrent distance estimation for all participating devices in a Bluetooth network and improves accuracy within indoor positioning systems [10].

3.4 Received Signal Strength Indicator (RSSI)

RSSI indicates the power present within a received radio signal and is generally used for distance estimation in terms of signal attenuation. Incorporating Bluetooth RSSI values for distance estimation has been proven successful in collision-free multi-robot path planning; RSSI thus has shown great promise for proximity detection applications [13]. Some indoor navigation systems use RSSI values from wi-fi routers and processes through the Android application [14].

4 Proposed System for Indoor Navigation with Cabin Identification

4.1 Architecture

Figure 1 shows the experimental architecture of this study. The architecture of the indoor positioning system development will use Bluetooth channel sounding and other distance measurement methods The nRF52840 Development Kit (DK) serves as a receiver, while the nRF52840 Dongle is the transmitter which is shown in Fig. 2 respectively. These devices communicate with each other using Bluetooth 5.3 and it includes MCPD, IFFT, phase slope and RSSI of real-time channel characteristics to reduce multipath propagation and improve accuracy.

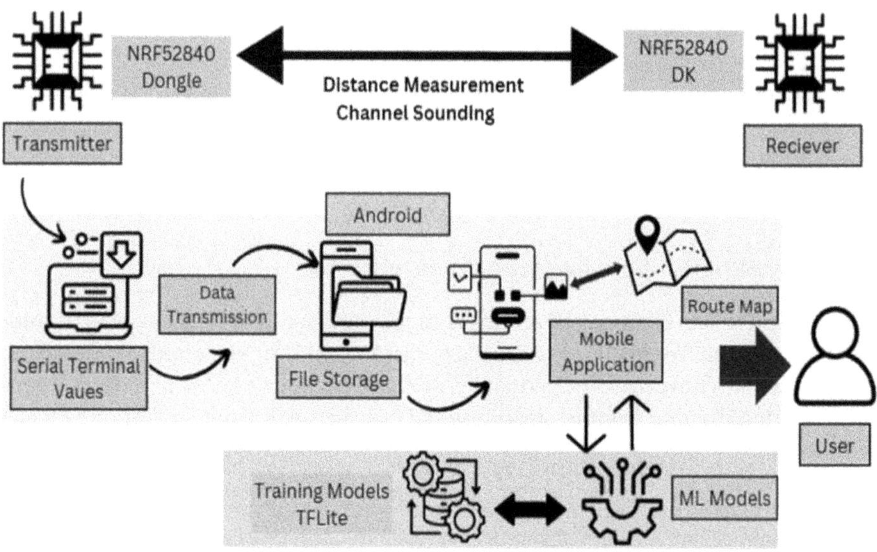

Fig. 1. Architecture of the System

The nRF52840 modules will act as transmitter-receiver pairs constantly switching Bluetooth signals to measure phase variation and attenuation. The raw channel data collected by these devices are sent via a serial interface to an Android application that employs TensorFlow Lite (TFLite) models to process them. These machine learning models improve distance estimates, lowering deviations from true values, and improving reliability. The corrected distance values are shown in the Android application, allowing instant feedback for indoor map navigation. The system is scalable, whereby it integrates a high degree of accuracy and real-time feedback into the architecture. Various frequency channels of operation minimize interference on and errors introduced by multipath propagation. A hardware setup allows low-latency data acquisition for real-time updates on proximity detection. Integration from the physical Bluetooth network to the mobile interface is smooth and raised user experience, thus making the system suitable for reliable applications in indoor positioning. In conclusion, the architecture applies Bluetooth channel sounding techniques along with refinements in machine learning and the robust hardware setup to provide an accurate, scalable, and real-time indoor positioning solution. Figure 3 shows the flow of models used to reduce the deviation.

5   Real Time Experimental Setup and Results

The proposed system was evaluated in a real world indoor environment, where access-controlled cabins were simulated. nRF52840 devices were located in fixed positions, constantly measuring the signal characteristics while users use an

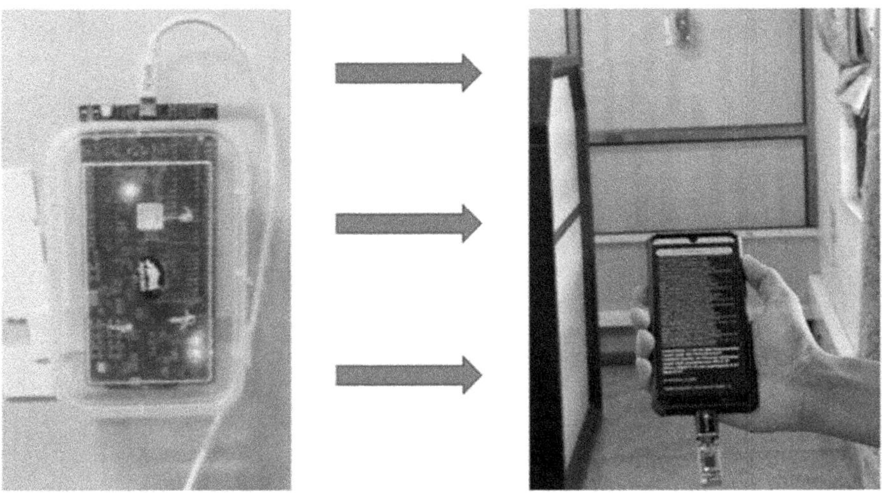

Fig. 2. Our Application with DK & Dongle

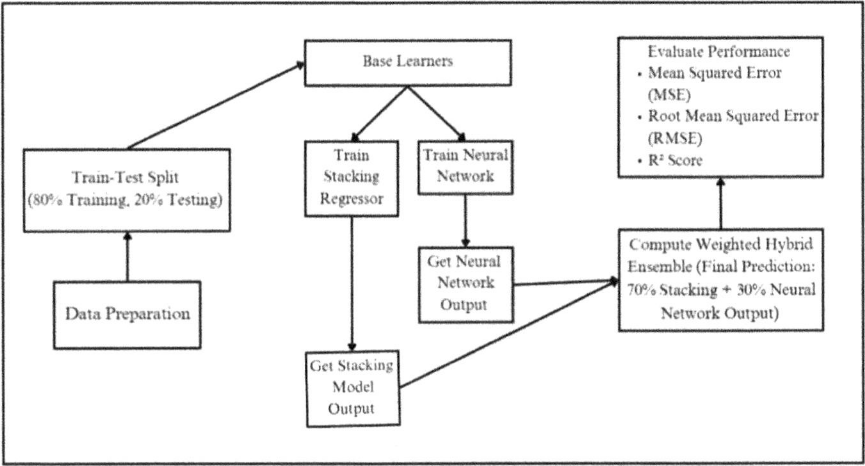

Fig. 3. Flow Diagram of Hybrid Models.

application (Fig. 4a) with the route map interface (Fig. 4b) developed using the Mappedin application (used only to create maps) [5]. The data gathered were processed in real time using a hybrid model of machine learning, which predicted the distance in real time based on the distance to the cabins. The stacked model used XGBoost, LightGBM, and CatBoost to capture varying signal characteristics, while the neural network learner improved the accuracy of predictions. The predictions in the final distance calculation were 70% based on the stacked model and 30% based on the neural network. Issues such as fluctuating RSSI and signal reflections were considered to improve the stability and retention of Bluetooth channel sounding as a solution for precise indoor localization.

(a) Application   (b) Route Map

Fig. 4. Developed Application and Route Map

5.1   Evaluation Metrics

Several evaluation metrics were used to quantify the accuracy of distance estimation and indoor positioning precision to evaluate the effectiveness of the proposed system. The primary metrics include MSE, RMSE, and R-squared, which provide a comprehensive measure of the model performance in predicting the actual distance based on the signal parameters. Deviation minimization was tested by comparing the predictions with real-world test-derived distance measurements. Table 1 shows the Evaluation Metrics of Models.

5.2   Comparative Analysis

The performance of the proposed hybrid machine learning model was benchmarked against the traditional RSSI-based indoor positioning approach [11]. Their method combined with RSSI, Support Vector Machine (SVM), and Kalman Filtering had achieved a Root Mean Square Error (RMSE) of 0.9385 m. The presented system merged with Phase Slope, IFFT, MCPD, and a hybrid ensemble model of XGBoost, LightGBM, CatBoost together with a neural network. It achieves an RMSE of 0.4648 m.

The improvement in accuracy is quantified as:

$$\text{Improvement (\%)} = \left(\frac{\text{Previous RMSE} - \text{Proposed RMSE}}{\text{Previous RMSE}} \right) \times 100 \tag{1}$$

$$= \left(\frac{0.9385 - 0.4648}{0.9385} \right) \times 100 \tag{2}$$

$$= \left(\frac{0.4737}{0.9385} \right) \times 100 \tag{3}$$

$$= 50.48\% \tag{4}$$

Thus, the proposed hybrid model has 50. 48% improvement in accuracy compared to conventional RSSI-based approaches. Figure 5 shows the comparison of the deviation without and with models. These results are produced by using Google Colab Tool [22]. Figure 6 shows the Flowchart of the Proposed Work.

Table 1. Evaluation Metrics

S. No	Metrics	Value
1	MSE	0.2159959483334304
2	RMSE	0.46475364262524116
3	R-Squared	0.9818622073971651

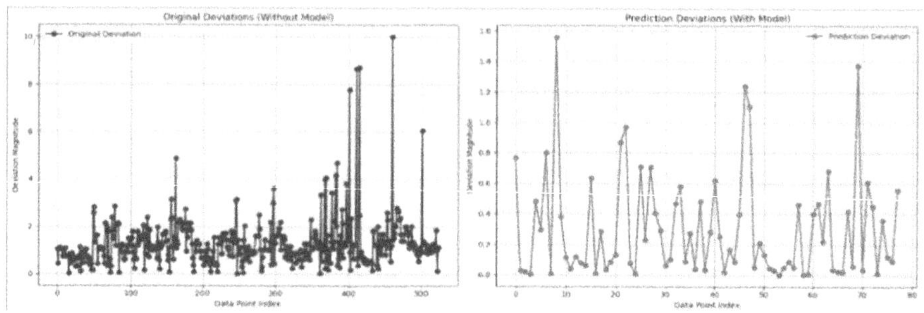

Fig. 5. Comparison of Deviation Without and With Models

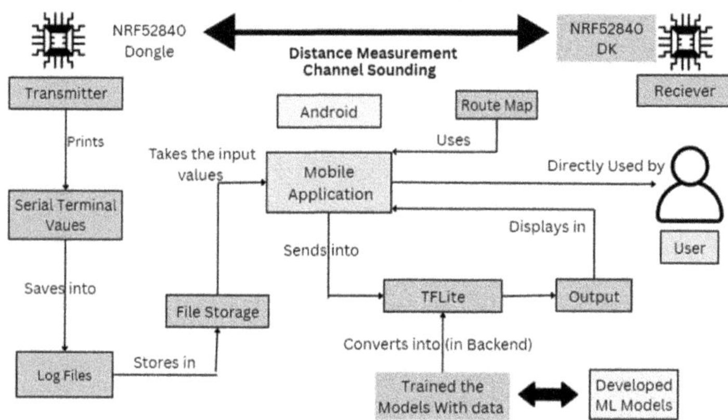

Fig. 6. Flowchart of the Proposed Work

6   Conclusion

The Indoor navigation system with Faculty Cabin-Identification Application synchronously employs distance measurement methods including Bluetooth channel sounding and machine learning-based localization to rectify the shortcomings associated with classical proximity-detecting modalities. This apparatus utilizes the nRF52840 devices, Bluetooth 5.3, and explores high precision in distance estimation indoors where multi-path propagation, interference, and signal reflection play significant roles. With the assistance of advanced localization techniques such as mcpd, ifft, phase slope, and RSSI, the algorithm improves the precision and reliability of proximity detection. The Hybrid machine learning models also facilitate efficient processing of real-time distance measurements with fewer deviation errors. Real-time distance tracking and using interactive map-based navigation holds a huge potential on enhancing usability, which allows a smooth indoor positioning experience. This work evidences the promise of Bluetooth channel sounding for indoor navigation, especially in cabins, high-rise buildings, offices and other controlled access zones. By combining hardware-driven precision with data-driven signal optimization, the Cabin-Finding Application sets a new benchmark for secure, efficient, and accurate indoor positioning.

7   Future Scope

Future improvements to the Cabin-Finding Application will focus on the following key areas:

- Scalability and Multi-Device Support: Future efforts will focus on extending the system to support multiple devices simultaneously, enabling large-scale deployments in complex environments such as universities and smart buildings.
- Duty Cycling Techniques: To enhance energy efficiency, duty cycling techniques will be implemented to reduce power consumption during idle periods, ensuring the system remains sustainable for long-term use.
- Enhanced Machine Learning Models: Further refinement of machine learning models will be explored to improve adaptability to dynamic environmental conditions and enhance prediction accuracy.

By addressing these future directions, the Cabin-Finding Application aims to evolve into a comprehensive solution for indoor positioning, offering scalability, energy efficiency, and enhanced accuracy for a wide range of applications in smart infrastructure and sensitive environments.

References

1. Zafari, F., Gkelias, A., Leung, K.K.: A survey of indoor localization systems and technologies. IEEE Commun. Surv. Tutor. **21**(3), 2568–2599 (2019)
2. Zhao, K., Zhao, T.: Optimization of Time Synchronization and Algorithms with TDOA Based Indoor Positioning Technique for Internet of Things (2020)
3. Shen, Y., Win, M.Z.: Fundamental limits of wideband localization—Part I: A general framework. IEEE Trans. Inf. Theory **56**(10), 4956–4980 (2010)
4. Nikodem, M., Trajnowicz, G.: Experimental evaluation of multi-carrier phase difference localization in Bluetooth low energy. **26**(9), 2024–2028 (2022)
5. Mappedin Inc.: Mappedin: Make Indoor Maps in Minutes. https://www.mappedin.com/. Accessed 16 Mar 2025
6. Shashank, M.J., Akhil, K.M.: Sensor node localization using machine learning for indoor location estimation. J. Harbin Eng. Univ. **44** (2023)
7. Salami, E., Ramiah, H.: Location accuracy optimization in Bluetooth low energy (BLE) 5.1-based indoor positioning system (IPS): a machine learning approach. IEEE Access **11**(2), 140186–140201 (2023)
8. Turgut, Z., Üstebay, S.: Performance analysis of machine learning and deep learning classification methods for indoor localization in Internet of things environment. Sensors (2019)
9. Santra, A., Kravets, I., Kotliar, N.: Enhancing Bluetooth channel sounding performance in complex indoor environments. IEEE Commun. Lett. **24**(3), 622–625 (2020)

10. Zand, P., Duzen, A., Romme, J., Govers, J., Bachmann, C., Philips, K.: A high-accuracy concurrent phase-based ranging for large-scale dense BLE network. In: 2019 IEEE 30th Annual International Symposium on Personal, Indoor and Mobile Radio Communications (PIMRC), pp. 1–7 (2019)
11. Torii, H., Ibi, S., Sampei, S.: Indoor positioning and tracking by multi-point observations of BLE beacon signal. In: Proceedings of the 15th Workshop Positioning, Navigation, and Communication (WPNC), pp. 1–5 (2018)
12. Nordic Distance Measurement MCPD Algorithm. https://devzone.nordicsemi.com/f/nordic-q-a/103090/nordic-distance-measurement-mcpd-algorithm
13. Manvi, S.S., Venkataram, P.: Bluetooth RSSI Based Collision Avoidance in Multirobot Environment, Bangalore, India, pp. 1–6 (2016)
14. Sidhaarthan, S.V., Anand, M., Ragul, P., Krishna, R.G., Bharathi, D.: Offline 3D indoor navigation using RSSI. In: Intelligent Data Communication Technologies and Internet of Things, pp. 831–846. Springer, Singapore (2021)
15. Li, X., Zhang, Y., Wang, J.: Experimental evaluation of multi-carrier phase difference localization in Bluetooth low energy. IEEE Trans. Instrum. Meas. **71**, 1–12 (2022)
16. Wang, S., Liu, Y., Zhang, Z.: RSSI and machine learning-based indoor localization systems for smart buildings: a comprehensive review. Smart Cities **4**(2), 85 (2023)
17. Woolley, M.: Channel Sounding Technology Overview. Bluetooth SIG (2024). https://www.bluetooth.com/channel-sounding-tech-overview/
18. Mazhar, A., Khan, A., Saeed, A.: High-Accuracy Low-Power Secure Ranging using Bluetooth Channel Sounding. Texas Instruments Technical Report (2021)
19. Pahlavan, K., Li, X., Mäkelä, J.P.: Indoor geolocation science and technology. IEEE Commun. Mag. **40**(2), 112–118 (2002)
20. Wang, J., Xu, Y., Ma, H.: Machine learning approaches for indoor localization: a review. Sensors **20**(10), 2956 (2020)
21. Liu, H., Darabi, H., Banerjee, P., Liu, J.: Survey of wireless indoor positioning techniques and systems. IEEE Trans. Syst. Man Cybern. **37**(6), 1067–1080 (2007)
22. Google Colab Notebook. https://colab.research.google.com/notebooks/welcome.ipynb
23. Different methods to measure the distance between devices. https://docs.nordicsemi.com/bundle/ncs-latest/page/nrfxlib/nrf_dm/doc/nrf_dm_overview.html#multi-carrier-phase-difference

Beyond Transformers: A Survey on Alternative Architectures for Sequence Modeling Across AI Domains

Abdul Rehman Ansari, Syed Akramah Ahmad Faizi$^{(\boxtimes)}$, and Priyanka Meel

Delhi Technological University, New Delhi, India
{abdulrehmanansari_mc21a10_74,syedakramahahmadfaizi_it21a10_53}@dtu.ac.in,
akramahfaizi@gmail.com

Abstract. Transformer models have achieved groundbreaking results across AI fields such as NLP and CV but incur $\mathcal{O}(n^2)$ cost from self-attention, hampering long-sequence scalability. This survey reviews architectures designed to overcome these constraints, encompassing both optimized Transformer variants and wholly different paradigms. We begin by outlining the need for alternatives, emphasizing the difficulty of processing very long inputs. We then organize recent models into three groups: (i) structured state-space approaches (e.g., S4) exploiting continuous-time formulations to realize linear complexity; (ii) pure MLP schemes (e.g., MLP-Mixer) that forgo attention in favor of learned token-mixing layers; and (iii) convolutionattention hybrids (e.g., CoAtNet) that fuse locality biases with global receptive fields. For each class, we dissect design principles and analyze theoretical scaling. A comparative evaluation highlights trade-offs in accuracy, compute, and domain suitability. We close by discussing open issues—robustness, scaling, hardware co-design—and suggest avenues for advancing efficient sequence modeling. Our findings guide the development of next-generation, resource-aware sequence models.

1 Introduction

Since the Transformer's debut in 2017, built upon a self-attention mechanism that links every pair of input tokens, deep learning systems have set new benchmarks on tasks like machine translation, language understanding, and image classification [1]. By employing multi-head self-attention, Transformers excel at modeling global dependencies, yet this strength incurs $\mathcal{O}(n^2)$ time and memory complexity for sequence length n. Such quadratic scaling burdens both training and inference when handling long sequences, rendering standard Transformer usage infeasible in domains requiring extensive context. As both model scale and dataset sizes continue to expand, these shortcomings become increasingly acute, motivating the search for more economical architectures and fresh paradigms in sequence modeling.

A variety of strategies have appeared to alleviate the Transformer's inefficiencies. One class of work focuses on *efficient Transformers*, which adapt the attention mechanism or overall architecture to curb computational and memory demands without abandoning the core self-attention framework. Techniques in this vein include sparsifying the attention matrix, restricting attention scope, and approximating attention via randomized or low-rank methods. The survey by Tay *et al.* offers an exhaustive treatment of these models, showing that efficiency gains can target memory footprint, FLOPs, or both [2]. Such improvements are vital for use cases with very long inputs—documents, videos, genomic data—where vanilla Transformers falter.

Concurrently, researchers have explored more radical departures from the Transformer blueprint, seeking architectures that match or exceed its performance via entirely different mechanisms. These ventures revisit RNN principles, introduce structured state-space formulations, deploy pure MLP networks with innovative token-mixing layers, or leverage other novel operations that eschew pairwise attention.

In this work, we survey these Transformer alternatives. A survey considering only the efficient transformers [2] was done previously. To our knowledge, there is no other literature review encompassing the different architectures introduced after transformers which focuses on their computational complexity or their comparison. Section 2 of our paper reviews the motivation and background driving new designs. Section 3 classifies model families, situating Transformers among broader sequence-modeling paradigms. Section 4 details state-of-the-art methods, spanning both enhanced Transformer variants and non-attention architectures. Section 5 offers a comparative analysis of complexity, scalability, and empirical performance. Section 6 examines applications where these models shine. Section 7 outlines open challenges and research directions, and Sect. 8 concludes with insights on the evolving landscape of efficient sequence modeling.

2   Background and Motivation

Transformers have revolutionized sequence modeling by capturing long-range dependencies without suffering the vanishing gradient issues that limited RNNs. Their core self-attention mechanism computes interactions between every pair of tokens, enabling the model to learn global context in a single layer pass. This capability has driven state-of-the-art performance across natural language processing, computer vision, and speech tasks. However, self-attention scales quadratically with sequence length, $\mathcal{O}(n^2)$, making both memory usage and computation grow rapidly as inputs lengthen. The original Transformer work [1] highlighted this quadratic bottleneck, and subsequent applications—ranging from document summarization to high-resolution image generation—have repeatedly encountered its limits. Large Transformer variants demand GPUs or TPUs with extensive memory capacity and prolonged training cycles, raising concerns about energy consumption, hardware cost, and ecological impact. Figure 1 illustrates the self attention mechanism used in the transformer model introduced in [1].

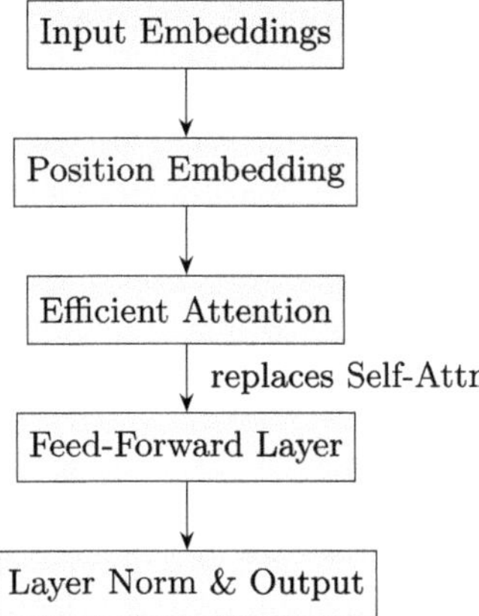

Fig. 1. Illustration of a modified Transformer block employing an *efficient attention* mechanism in place of standard self-attention. Such blocks maintain the overall Transformer structure (embedding, positional encoding, feed-forward network, etc.) but use alternative attention operations to improve efficiency.

2.1   Scalability Challenges

Contemporary workloads often involve sequences that far exceed the lengths Transformers were built for. Genomic datasets with millions of nucleotides, legal briefs and research articles spanning thousands of words, and video data represented as per-frame tokens all push the quadratic cost into prohibitive territory. Simple truncation or downsampling sacrifices vital context. Meanwhile, model scales balloon—from BERT-sized variants to GPT-4 class systems—so that training can require weeks even on GPU/TPU clusters, and inference latency becomes untenable for interactive applications. These factors underscore the imperative for designs whose computational and memory demands grow more gently with sequence length.

2.2   Inductive Bias and Interpretability

The Transformer's versatility comes without inherent biases. Convolutional networks, by contrast, bake in locality and translation invariance, excelling at spatial feature learning. Recurrent models naturally capture temporal order and can operate on streaming data indefinitely. Pure self-attention must learn such priors from data, often requiring vast pretraining. For instance, Vision Transformers only matched ConvNet accuracy after being pretrained on datasets many times larger [13]. In response, hybrid networks that place convolutional layers in early stages learn local structures with fewer samples, then use attention for global reasoning. These hybrids yield better sample efficiency and faster convergence, illustrating the value of architectural priors.

2.3 Energy and Hardware Considerations

As models scale up, energy use and hardware costs become central concerns. Training a large Transformer can produce hundreds of tons of CO_2 equivalent, and deploying them on edge devices demands minimal power draw and low latency. Architectures with reduced per-token computation unlock real-time and on-device scenarios, from mobile translation to embedded control. Replacing dense attention with matrix multiplications, convolutional operations, or spectral layers aligns well with existing accelerators, cutting energy per operation and boosting throughput.

2.4 Scientific Inquiry and Model Understanding

Beyond raw performance, studying alternatives deepens our grasp of sequence modeling. While self-attention is powerful, evidence shows that fixed or randomized attention patterns can still deliver strong results [15], implying that learned pairwise correlations are not the only path. Exploring state-space recurrences, MLP mixers, and other mechanisms clarifies which components are essential for long-range dependencies and which can be simplified. This broadened view fosters hybrid innovations that may drive the next leap in efficiency and capability.

Table 1. Efficient Transformer Variants: Complexity and Features

Model Reference	Mechanism	Complexity	Highlight
Longformer [12]	Window + global tokens	$O(n)$	Thousands of-token documents
BigBird	Random + local + global	$O(n)$	Provable approximation
Reformer [11]	LSH-based sparse attention	$O(n \log n)$	Reversible layers for memory
Performer [10]	Linear random feature	$O(n)$	Exact kernel approximation
Synthesizer [15]	Learned/static patterns	$O(n^2)$	Simplifies attention weights
Mega [14]	Gated moving-average	$O(n)$	Locality bias + chunking

3 Classification of AI Models

Deep learning sequence models can be grouped by their core operations and built-in inductive biases, which influence how they process data and scale to long inputs. Traditional recurrent and convolutional architectures established early benchmarks but have limitations in parallelism and receptive field size. Transformers introduced global self-attention to overcome these issues, yet inspired new hybrid and non-attention paradigms that seek further efficiency and bias incorporation.

1. **Recurrent Models (RNNs):** Process tokens sequentially, maintaining hidden states. LSTMs and GRUs naturally encode temporal order but face vanishing gradients when modeling very long dependencies.

2. **Convolutional Models:** Apply 1-D filters over sequences to capture local patterns with high parallelism. Effective for short-range features but require deep stacks or large kernels for global context.
3. **Transformer Models:** Leverage multi-head self-attention to relate all positions in one layer, enabling rapid global context modeling. Highly parallelizable, yet data-hungry due to lacking locality or recurrence priors.
4. **Hybrid Models:** Combine attention with convolution or recurrence, aiming to inject locality or temporal biases into the Transformer backbone for improved data efficiency and generalization.
5. **MLP-Based Models:** Remove explicit attention and convolution, using token-mixing layers or transformations (e.g., Fourier) within feed-forward blocks to shuffle information across positions.
6. **State-Space Models (SSMs):** Revive continuous-time recurrence through parameterized state-space equations, achieving linear $\mathcal{O}(n)$ complexity and handling very long sequences via frequency-domain operations.

In this survey, we treat hybrid and efficient Transformer variants as optimized members of the Transformer family, while MLP-based and SSM-based models represent distinct alternatives to self-attention. This classification frames our detailed review, highlighting how each category balances complexity, inductive bias, and practical performance in sequence modeling beyond vanilla Transformers. We have compiled the complexity, mechanism and highlights of the models mentioned in this paper in Table 1.

4 State-of-the-Art Approaches

Transformers continue to serve as the gold-standard baseline across many AI applications, with large-scale models like BERT, GPT-4, Grok, and Vision Transformers achieving—or even exceeding—human benchmarks in varied domains. Yet, recent innovations have started to challenge standard Transformers, either by enhancing core components or by proposing entirely new architectures. We organize these advances into two main categories: (1) *Efficient and Enhanced Transformers*, which refine the attention mechanism or structural elements for improved efficiency or inductive bias, and (2) *Non-Transformer architectures* that rival Transformers on sequence modeling tasks.

4.1 Efficient and Enhanced Transformers

A host of so-called "efficient Transformers" has surfaced over the past few years [2]. These maintain the canonical Transformer layout—alternating attention and feed-forward blocks—but overhaul the attention computation to cut time or memory costs. As illustrated in Fig. 1, one can simply replace the standard self-attention with an efficient variant, keeping the rest of the block intact.

Sparse-attention frameworks are among the most impactful. Longformer adopts a sliding-window attention combined with a sparse set of global tokens to achieve true $O(n)$ complexity, processing sequences of thousands of tokens with ease [12]. By limiting attention to local contexts plus a few global anchors, it trims pairwise interactions and sets new records on long-document QA and summarization without input truncation [12]. BigBird employs a similar scheme—mixing local windows, global tokens, and random sparse links—to preserve $O(n)$ scaling.

Alternatively, low-rank or approximated attention offers another path to efficiency. Reformer applies locality-sensitive hashing (LSH) to bucket queries and keys, reducing complexity to $O(n \log n)$ and introducing reversible residual layers that cut training memory in half [11]. This approach scales to sequences as long as 64K tokens while matching Transformer baselines on tasks like character-level language modeling, using far less memory [11]. Performer, by contrast, uses random feature maps to approximate the softmax kernel, yielding provable $O(n)$ time and space attention and strong empirical performance on text and protein-sequence benchmarks [10].

Some investigations even question the necessity of content-based attention. Synthesizer experiments with fixed or learned static attention matrices independent of token similarity and finds that random or synthetic patterns can nearly match full self-attention across multiple benchmarks [15]. Although this strategy retains dense connectivity and does not improve asymptotic scaling, it points toward structurally simpler Transformer-like models that bypass pairwise token comparisons [15].

Beyond pure attention tweaks, hybrid architectures introduce complementary inductive biases. CoAtNet blends depthwise convolutions in early stages for efficient local feature extraction, then switches to self-attention for global context [13]. This staged fusion leverages convolution's locality and attention's flexibility, achieving over 88% top-1 on ImageNet with far fewer training samples than pure Transformers, and scaling to 90.88% top-1 with larger models and datasets [13]. These results underscore that well-placed convolutional bias can boost both generalization and efficiency [13].

Another research thrust augments attention with gating and moving-average mechanisms. The Mega (Moving Average Equipped Gated Attention) model embeds an exponential moving-average bias into single-head attention, promoting local continuity reminiscent of recurrent networks [14]. By chunking long sequences, Mega also attains linear complexity. Empirically, it outperforms vanilla Transformers, recent state-space models, and other baselines on Long Range Arena, machine translation, language modeling, and even image and speech classification tasks [14], demonstrating that thoughtfully designed attention variants can rival entirely new architectures [14].

4.2   Non-transformer Sequence Models

Alongside Transformer optimization, researchers have revived alternative sequence-modeling schemes. Two leading families have emerged: (1) structured state-space models (SSMs), which introduce learned recurrence with theoretically unbounded memory, and (2) MLP-based networks that replace attention with pure feed-forward mixing. These methods aim to keep Transformers' expressivity and parallelism while easing their quadratic scaling and memory footprints.

Structured State-Space Models draw inspiration from linear time-invariant systems and signal-processing theory. An SSM combines a state-update equation with an output equation, enabling information to propagate indefinitely. Gu et al. introduced the Structured State Space Sequence Model (S4), parameterizing an SSM via a diagonal-plus-low-rank state matrix that can be trained by gradient descent and implemented with FFT-based convolution in $O(n)$ time [4]. S4 surpasses Transformer variants on long-context benchmarks such as the Long Range Arena (LRA) and excels in time-series forecasting by capturing dependencies beyond self-attention's reach.

Building on this resurgence, Patro and Agneeswaran surveyed SSMs as Transformer alternatives in their Mamba-360 analysis [3]. They underscore that SSMs' linear complexity and recurrent structure yield modular, interpretable, and hardware-efficient models for long-sequence tasks. Benchmarks spanning GLUE, WikiText, and ImageNet show SSMs narrowing the gap to Transformers, with models like Mamba introducing gating and streaming token processing to approximate attention at far lower memory cost [3].

Another noteworthy SSM variant is the Liquid Time-Constant Network (LTC) by Hasani et al., which embeds continuous-time dynamics into neural layers via learnable time-constants [5]. LTCs adapt their internal state smoothly over time, making them particularly adept at modeling physical systems and real-time control signals in robotics. Although less prevalent in NLP than S4, LTCs' stability and adaptive properties suit domains where long-duration stability is paramount [5].

Despite their advantages, SSMs pose challenges in initialization and parallelization: training often requires careful parameter choice (as in S4), and recurrence can impede across-sequence batching. Techniques such as FFT convolutions (in S4) or sequence chunking partially mitigate these issues. As software ecosystems mature, SSMs promise energy-efficient alternatives by replacing large attention matrices with structured operations that better leverage certain hardware.

MLP-based Architectures revisit the multilayer perceptron as a sequence mixer without explicit attention or convolution. The pioneering MLP-Mixer by Tolstikhin et al. partitions processing into channel-mixing MLPs (per position) and token-mixing MLPs (across positions), the latter performing a learned, fixed-weight aggregation of all tokens [6]. Remarkably, MLP-Mixer matches contemporary Vision Transformer accuracy on ImageNet, demonstrating that global interactions need not rely on data-dependent attention [6].

Subsequent MLP variants explored alternative token-mixing mechanisms. FNet by Lee-Thorp et al. replaces learned mixing with a non-trainable Fourier transform, yielding $O(n \log n)$ complexity via FFT and achieving competitive GLUE/SuperGLUE performance within a small margin of BERT-style models [7]. FNet's success highlights the viability of spectral methods when resource constraints trump marginal accuracy gains [7].

gMLP introduces a simple gating operation to the token-mixing layer, enabling element-wise modulation of interactions based on positional signals [8]. This inductive bias enhances the capture of spatial or temporal dependencies, and gMLP outperforms the vanilla Mixer on vision and language benchmarks while retaining efficient, dense-matrix computation [8].

HyperMixer further evolves MLP-based mixing by employing a hypernetwork to generate token-mixing weights dynamically, allowing position-dependent aggregation without explicit attention [9]. Designed under "Green AI" principles, HyperMixer shares parameters to reduce total footprint and demonstrates energy-efficient performance on both NLP and vision tasks, rivaling Transformer accuracy with fewer resources [9].

What unites these MLP-based lines is the removal of pairwise softmax attention in favor of alternative mixing—be it static learned weights, Fourier projections, gated operations, or generated matrices. They typically achieve linear or near-linear scaling per layer (e.g., FFT's $O(n \log n)$ or single large matrix multiplies), offer simpler memory access, and exploit highly optimized dense-matrix hardware. Their limitation lies in fixed or data-independent mixing, which may underperform on tasks demanding dynamic, content-driven focus.

Convolutional and hybrid designs add another dimension to the alternatives. Architectures like Hyena employ implicitly parameterized long convolutions—efficiently realized via FFTs—interleaved with data-controlled gating, yielding subquadratic scaling and matching or exceeding attention models on ultra-long contexts [16]. Hyena reports over 50-point gains on extreme long-sequence LRA tasks and parity with Transformers on standard benchmarks [16], demonstrating that properly scaled convolution remains a powerful complement—and sometimes substitute—to attention and recurrence.

5   Comparative Analysis

5.1   Empirical Performance on Benchmarks

Optimizing theoretical complexity only matters if real-world accuracy holds up. The following summarizes major benchmark outcomes:

Long Range Arena (LRA)

1. **S4:** The Structured State Space model (S4) tops LRA across tasks including text classification, retrieval, image classification, and algorithmic challenges, outstripping vanilla Transformers by margins of 1015 points on select benchmarks.
2. **Mega:** Introducing gated attention with a moving-average bias toward local context, Mega pushes LRA results even higher on both text- and image-based tasks compared to baseline Transformers and earlier SSMs.
3. **Hyena:** By leveraging implicit long-range convolutions combined with gating, Hyena achieves dramatic improvements—surpassing prior SSMs by over fifty points on some LRA tasks—while matching or exceeding Transformer performance on the remainder.

Table 2. Architectural Trade-Offs Across Families

Family	Pros	Cons	Best For
Transformers [1]	Mature ecosystem; transfer learning; global	$O(n^2)$ cost; high memory	General tasks
Efficient TFs [2]	Subquartic scaling; pretrained checkpoints	Additional hyperparameters; sparse blind spots	Long documents
SSMs [4]	True $O(n)$; streaming; interpretability	Complex init; recurrence dependencies	Ultra-long & streaming
MLPs [6]	Simple; hardware-friendly; no attention overhead	Static mixing; content-agnostic	Moderate-length; throughput
Convolution [13]	Local inductive bias + global context	Design complexity; residual quadratic steps	Vision; long-context

Vision Benchmarks

1. **MLP-Mixer:** On ImageNet, the all-MLP Mixer model reaches within one percent of Vision Transformer accuracy despite dispensing with attention, demonstrating that pure token-mixing with learned weights can nearly match sophisticated self-attention.
2. **CoAtNet:** This hybrid model, which fuses depthwise convolutions and self-attention, attains over 88% top-1 accuracy on ImageNet using substantially less data, and scales up to 90.88% top-1 when trained at larger scale.

Language and Generation

1. **Performer:** In language modeling and protein sequence tasks, Performer's linear random-feature attention approximations deliver perplexities on par with full Transformers while requiring only linear time and space.
2. **Reformer:** By hashing queries and keys via LSH and employing reversible residual layers, Reformer handles sequences up to 64K tokens, matching Transformer baselines on character-level modeling with significantly reduced memory.

Overall, these findings confirm that many alternatives preserve or improve accuracy on standard benchmarks while dramatically cutting computation or memory, validating their practical utility beyond purely theoretical gains.

5.2   Architectural Trade-Offs and Inductive Biases

Each family carries its own advantages and limitations:

1. **Standard Transformers:**
   (a) *Pros*: Universally applicable, strong ecosystem, straightforward transfer learning, interpretable attention weights.
   (b) *Cons*: Quadratic cost, high memory footprint, less suited for edge or streaming.
2. **Efficient Transformers (Longformer, Performer, Reformer):**
   (a) *Pros*: Extend familiar architecture, leverage pretrained checkpoints, subquadratic scaling.
   (b) *Cons*: Additional hyperparameters (window size, hash buckets, projection rank), potential for missing key dependencies if sparsity patterns or approximations misalign with data.

3. **Structured State-Space Models (S4, Mamba)**:
   (a) *Pros*: True linear scaling, streaming inference, spectral interpretability (frequency-domain analysis), stable long-range memory.
   (b) *Cons*: Complex initialization, recurrence dependencies hinder parallelism across tokens, fewer pretrained resources.
4. **MLP-Mixer and FNet**:
   (a) *Pros*: Simple design, hardware-efficient matmuls and FFTs, minimal hyperparameters.
   (b) *Cons*: Static mixing lacks content-adaptive focus, potential underperformance on tasks requiring fine-grained token interactions.
5. **Convolutional Hybrids (CoAtNet, Hyena)**:
   (a) *Pros*: Combine locality bias of CNNs with global context of attention or long convolutions, strong sample efficiency.
   (b) *Cons*: Added design complexity, may retain residual quadratic components in certain layers.

Table 2 lists the pros and cons of each architectural family and their special use cases. Future research is poised to blend these paradigms—attention, recurrence, convolution, and MLP mixing—into unified architectures that dynamically adapt to sequence length, modality, and hardware constraints, ultimately delivering both scalability and accuracy across all sequence modeling domains.

6   Applications of AI Architectures

Transformer alternatives extend deep learning into domains where standard self-attention is impractical. Efficient and novel models enable new capabilities in long-context processing, low-latency inference, and resource-constrained deployment while preserving or improving performance.

1. **Natural Language Processing (NLP):** Sparse-attention variants such as Longformer allow end-to-end summarization and question answering over entire documents or books, eliminating the need for input truncation. State-space models like S4 handle thousands of tokens for narrative or code understanding, and lightweight FNet-style architectures support on-device tasks (e.g., mobile keyboards, speech transcription) with reduced latency at modest accuracy trade-off.
2. **Computer Vision:** Vision Transformers treat images as patch sequences, but MLP-Mixer backbones deliver competitive classification, segmentation, and detection features without attention. Hybrids like CoAtNet generalize from limited data by blending convolutions and attention, and localized attention methods (e.g., Swin Transformer) underpin state-of-the-art object detection and segmentation with improved efficiency.

3. **Long Sequence Time-Series and Signals:** Applications in finance, climate, and healthcare produce multi-year or high-resolution streams. SSMs process these in streaming mode with constant memory, avoiding the chunking or downsampling required by Transformers. Liquid Time-Constant networks excel in biomedical signal analysis (e.g., EEG) by modeling continuous dynamics with interpretable time constants.
4. **Speech and Audio:** Raw waveforms and spectrograms form lengthy sequences. S4-based audio models and convolutional architectures like Hyena leverage signal-processing priors for efficient long-context modeling, enabling applications in speech recognition, synthesis, and long-form audio generation where full attention would be prohibitive.

Although Transformers benefit from extensive pre-trained ecosystems, emerging efficient models are gaining support in popular libraries and repositories. As implementations mature, these alternatives will enable AI systems to handle longer inputs, operate under tighter latency constraints, and deploy on edge devices, broadening the scope of practical deep learning applications.

7   Open Challenges and Future Directions

Despite rapid progress in Transformer alternatives, several obstacles must be addressed to facilitate their widespread adoption and effectiveness:

1. **Unified Benchmarking and Fair Comparison:** A common evaluation suite covering diverse sequence lengths, tasks, parameter budgets and hardware settings is lacking. Extending the Long Range Arena with larger scales and standardized baselines will clarify relative merits of efficient Transformers, SSMs, MLP-mixers and hybrids.
2. **Scaling Laws and Regimes:** Unlike Transformers, alternatives have poorly understood scaling behaviour. Investigating whether SSMs or MLP-based models continue to improve at billion-parameter scale, or plateau early, will indicate if they can rival large LLMs in efficiency gains.
3. **Combating Training Challenges:** Training instabilities—such as SSM matrix initialisation issues or MLP-mixer normalization sensitivities—remain barriers. Robust initialization schemes, curriculum schedules, and control-theoretic regularizers are needed to lower the entry cost.
4. **Task Transfer and Generalization:** Pretraining paradigms remain Transformer-centric. Demonstrating that SSMs or MLP-based models can be pretrained and fine-tuned at scale—while generalizing out-of-distribution—will determine if they can replace or complement LLM backbones.
5. **Hardware Co-design:** Custom accelerators for continuous-time recurrence or photonic Fourier transforms promise orders-of-magnitude speed and energy savings. Co-designing algorithms and hardware, as GPUs did for dense matmuls, will unlock the full potential of new architectures.

6. **Community Adoption and Ecosystem:** Widespread use hinges on robust open-source implementations, pretrained checkpoints and integration into popular libraries. Publishing success stories and tooling for efficient models will lower adoption friction and drive production deployment.

8   Conclusion

Transformer models have reshaped sequence modeling by delivering unparalleled performance across domains, yet they face inherent limitations in efficiency and scalability. This survey has examined a spectrum of alternatives—efficient Transformer variants such as Longformer, Reformer, Performer, and Mega that alleviate the quadratic self-attention bottleneck; hybrid architectures like CoAt-Net that merge convolutional biases with global context; structured state-space models reinstating recurrence for linear complexity; and pure MLP networks demonstrating that explicit attention is not always essential. Our comparative analysis showed that these architectures can surpass Transformers in handling extreme requirements—very long inputs, limited data, or resource-constrained environments—while the original Transformer remains the de facto generalist for moderate contexts.

Applications in NLP, vision, time-series, and audio illustrate that alternatives extend deep learning into scenarios previously out of reach, enabling full-document processing, real-time control, and edge-device deployment. Open challenges include establishing unified benchmarks, understanding scaling laws, stabilizing training, deepening theoretical insight, and co-designing hardware and software. We anticipate future models will blend sparse attention, recurrence, and feed-forward mixing in adaptive ensembles, selected dynamically based on task demands.

In closing, the trajectory of sequence modeling points toward a pluralistic ecosystem: Transformers will remain vital, but a toolkit of complementary architectures will empower practitioners to choose the optimal balance of efficiency, inductive bias, and accuracy for any given problem.

References

1. Vaswani, A., et al.: Attention Is All You Need. In: Proceedings of NeurIPS, pp. 5998–6008 (2017)
2. Tay, Y., Dehghani, M., Bahri, D., Metzler, D.: Efficient transformers: a survey. ACM Comput. Surv. **55**(9), 190 (2023)
3. Patro, B.N., Agneeswaran, V.S.: Mamba-360: Survey of State Space Models as Transformer Alternative for Long Sequence Modeling: Methods, Applications, and Challenges, arXiv:2404.16112 (2024)
4. Gu, A., Goel, K., Ré, C.: Efficiently modeling long sequences with structured state spaces. In: Proceedings of ICLR (2022)
5. Hasani, R., Lechner, M., Amini, A., Rus, D., Grosu, R.: Liquid time-constant networks. In: Proceedings of AAAI, pp. 11845–11853 (2021)

6. Tolstikhin, I., et al.: MLP-Mixer: An all-MLP architecture for vision. In: Proceedings of NeurIPS (2021)
7. Lee-Thorp, J., Ainslie, J., Eckstein, I., Ontañón, S.: FNet: mixing tokens with fourier transforms. In: Proceedings of NAACL-HLT, pp. 4296–4313 (2022)
8. Liu, X., Dai, Z., So, D.R., Le, Q.V.: Pay Attention to MLPs. In: Proceedings of NeurIPS, pp. 9204–9215 (2021)
9. Mai, F., et al.: HyperMixer: an MLP-based green AI alternative to transformers. In: Proceedings of ACL Long, pp. 871–887 (2023)
10. Choromanski, K., et al.: Rethinking attention with performers. In: Proceedings of ICLR (2021)
11. Kitaev, N., Kaiser, L., Levskaya, A.: Reformer: the efficient transformer. In: Proceedings of ICLR (2020)
12. Beltagy, I., Peters, M.E., Cohan, A.: Longformer: the long-document transformer. arXiv:2004.05150 (2020)
13. Dai, Z., Liu, H., Le, Q.V., Tan, M.: CoAtNet: marrying convolution and attention for all data sizes. In: Proceedings of NeurIPS (2021)
14. Ma, X., et al.: Mega: moving average equipped gated attention. In: Proceedings of ICLR (2023)
15. Tay, Y., et al.: Synthesizer: rethinking self-attention in transformer models. In: Proceedings of ICML (2021)
16. Poli, M., et al.: Hyena hierarchy: towards larger convolutional language models. In: Proceedings of ICML, pp. 35010–35038 (2023)

Deep Learning-Based Enhanced Predictive Modeling for Stock Price

Sauvik Halder[1], Piyas Sarkar[1], Tanushree Chakraborty[1],
and Kartick Chandra Mondal[2(✉)]

[1] Department of Information Technology, Jadavpur University, Kolkata 700106,
India
[2] Department of CSE, SRM University AP, Amaravati 522240, India
kartickjgec@gmail.com

Abstract. The prediction of financial markets using deep learning has attracted the attention of both investors and researchers. Deep learning methods, such as convolutional neural networks and recurrent neural networks, work well at predicting stock indices based on the non-linear characteristics of stock markets. The goal of this work is to predict the stock index using the latest deep learning framework, Transformer. This paper presents a comprehensive analysis of stock closing price prediction using three distinct machine learning models: Long-Short-Term Memory (LSTM), Generative Adversarial Network (GAN), and Transformer. Using the encoder-decoder architecture and the multihead attention mechanism, Transformer is able to better characterize stock market dynamics. The present study uses data from Yahoo Finance. The Transformer model demonstrated superior performance compared to LSTM and GAN. In this work, we handle the complexities of market dynamics to improve stock price predictions.

Keywords: Stock Market · Time Series · Transformer · GAN · LSTM · Stock Price Prediction

1 Introduction

The integration of advanced deep learning models in financial forecasting has become a pivotal area of research, particularly within the context of the Indian market. This paper explores the efficacy of three prominent architectures. Long Short-Term Memory (LSTM) networks, Generative Adversarial Networks (GAN), and Transformers, in predicting stock prices across three distinct time skips. LSTM networks are renowned for their ability to manage sequential data and capture long-term dependencies, making them particularly suitable for time-series analysis such as stock price prediction [12]. Their architecture includes memory cells that allow for the retention of information over extended periods, thus addressing challenges like the vanishing gradient problem commonly associated with traditional recurrent neural networks (RNNs). The GAN framework,

K. Chandra Mondal et al. (Eds.): CICBA 2025, CCIS 2862, pp. 300–313, 2026.
https://doi.org/10.1007/978-3-032-17187-0_23

consisting of a generator and a discriminator, introduces a novel approach by enabling models to learn from adversarial processes. This dual-network structure has shown promise in improving prediction accuracy by generating synthetic data that mimics real market conditions [21]. By incorporating GANs with LSTMs, this study aims to enhance predictive performance further [12].

In contrast, Transformers leverage self-attention mechanisms to process data in parallel, significantly enhancing training speed and scalability while maintaining performance on sequential tasks. This architectural shift allows Transformers to handle larger datasets more efficiently than LSTMs, which operate sequentially [21]. This research will systematically evaluate these models' performance in predicting stock prices within the Indian market, focusing on their predictive capabilities over varying time frames. The findings will contribute to the ongoing discourse on optimizing machine learning techniques for financial forecasting, ultimately providing valuable insights for investors and stakeholders in the rapidly evolving financial landscape.

The remainder of this article is organized as follows: Sect. 2 discusses related works, including traditional and deep learning methods for stock forecasting. Section 3 presents the problem description and details the LSTM, GAN, and Transformer models used in this study. Section 4 describes the experimental setup, including the dataset, evaluation metrics, and results. Finally, Sect. 5 concludes the paper with a summary of findings and future research directions.

2   Related Works

2.1   Traditional Methods for Stock Forecasting

Traditional methods of stock forecasting have laid the groundwork for understanding and predicting stock price movements. Early efforts predominantly utilized statistical techniques, particularly time series analysis. Among these, Autoregressive Conditional Heteroskedasticity (ARCH) [6] and its extension, Generalized Autoregressive Conditional Heteroskedasticity (GARCH) [3], have been pivotal in modeling and forecasting volatility in financial markets. These models allow researchers to capture the changing variance over time, which is a crucial characteristic of financial data.

Another widely used approach is the AutoRegressive Integrated Moving Average (ARIMA) [1] model, which is effective for capturing linear patterns in time series data. ARIMA models are particularly beneficial when dealing with stationary data, making them a staple in traditional forecasting methods. However, these models often struggle with the inherent nonlinearity and complexity of financial markets.

To address these limitations, researchers began incorporating machine learning techniques into stock forecasting. Artificial Neural Networks (ANN) [9] and Support Vector Machines (SVM) [17] emerged as powerful tools capable of capturing complex relationships within the data. ANN, in particular, has been successful in identifying patterns and trends that traditional models might miss.

The pioneering work of Tay et al. introduced SVM for financial time series forecasting, showcasing its potential to enhance prediction accuracy.

Hybrid models have been developed to address the limitations of traditional forecasting methods, particularly their susceptibility to local optima and challenges in parameter tuning. For instance, Armano et al. introduced a hybrid neural network model utilizing a genetic classifier to enhance the activation of feedforward neural networks [2]. Fu et al. proposed the Bayesian Ying Yang neural network, inspired by the Ying-Yang philosophy, to improve predictive accuracy [7]. Additionally, Choudhary et al. combined a genetic algorithm with SVM for stock market prediction [5], while Vijh et al. integrated artificial neural networks with random forest techniques to forecast next-day stock prices effectively [20]. Chandar et al. evaluated a hybrid model using a multi-layer perceptron and cat swarm optimization algorithm [4] (Table 1).

Table 1. Summary of Traditional Methods for Stock Forecasting

Article	Author	Description
Autoregressive Conditional Heteroskedasticity (ARCH)	Engle (1982)	Introduced ARCH to model and forecast volatility in financial markets by capturing changing variance over time
Generalized Autoregressive Conditional Heteroskedasticity (GARCH)	Bollerslev (1986)	Extended ARCH to GARCH, improving volatility modeling by incorporating lagged conditional variances
ARIMA Model	Ariyo et al. (2014)	Applied ARIMA for stock price prediction, effective for capturing linear patterns in stationary time series data
Artificial Neural Networks (ANN)	Jain et al. (1996)	Demonstrated the use of ANNs for identifying complex patterns and trends in financial data
Support Vector Machines (SVM)	Suykens and Vandewalle (1999)	Introduced SVM for financial time series forecasting, showcasing its potential for improved prediction accuracy
Hybrid Genetic-Neural Architecture	Armano et al. (2005)	Proposed a hybrid model combining genetic algorithms with neural networks for stock index forecasting
Bayesian Ying Yang Neural Network	Fu et al. (2007)	Developed a neural network inspired by Ying-Yang philosophy to enhance stock prediction accuracy
Hybrid Machine Learning System	Choudhry and Garg (2008)	Combined genetic algorithms with SVM for stock market forecasting
Stock Closing Price Prediction	Vijh et al. (2020)	Integrated artificial neural networks with random forest techniques for next-day stock price prediction
Cat Swarm Optimization Algorithm	Chandar and Punjabi (2022)	Utilized a hybrid model with multi-layer perceptron and cat swarm optimization for stock price prediction

2.2   Deep Learning Methods for Stock Forecasting

Deep learning technologies have increasingly been applied to stock market prediction, leveraging various neural network architectures. Wanjawa et al. utilized deep neural networks to predict three stocks on the New York Stock Exchange, achieving positive results [22]. Convolutional Neural Networks (CNNs), known for their effectiveness in image recognition, were employed by Tsantekidis et al. in a 1-D format, outperforming traditional models like multi-layer perceptrons and SVMs [19]. Gudelek et al. expanded this approach using a 2-D CNN to classify trading images for predicting stock price trends [8].

Recurrent Neural Networks (RNNs) have also proven beneficial for sequential data analysis. Samarawickrama et al. demonstrated that RNNs could predict daily stock prices more accurately than feedforward networks [16], while Roondiwala et al. applied LSTM networks to forecast NIFTY 50 returns [15]. Hybrid models, such as the CNN-LSTM developed by Lu et al. [11], combine local feature extraction from CNNs with temporal learning from LSTMs, showcasing improved predictive capabilities.

Recent advancements include transformer models, which excel at capturing global features. Lai et al. [10] introduced a differential transformer model for stock movement prediction, while Tao et al.'s [18] series decomposition transformer enhanced trend prediction accuracy. Effectiveness of GANs compared to traditional models like LSTM and ARIMA. The GAN model achieved a prediction accuracy of 72.68%, slightly lower than the best-performing shallow LSTM model at 74.16%. This research highlighted the potential of GANs in representing time series data for stock price movements [14].

Research literature indicates that advanced machine learning techniques such as LSTM, GAN, and Transformers are increasingly utilized for stock price prediction. This project aims to compare their effectiveness in forecasting different Indian stocks over various time skips (Table 2).

3   The Models for Stock Price Prediction

3.1   Problem Description and Modeling

The task of stock price prediction involves forecasting the price for the next time skip or several time skips using stock trading data from previous values. Predicting the stock price for only the next time skip is referred to as single-step prediction, while forecasting stock prices for several consecutive time skips is known as multi-step prediction. In this paper, we focus on predicting the closing price of the next time by leveraging trading data from the previous times. The formal description of the single-step prediction task is shown in Eqs. (1) and (2).

$$x_t^{\text{close}} = f(x_{t-n}, x_{t-n+1}, \ldots, x_{t-3}, x_{t-2}, x_{t-1}) \tag{1}$$

$$x_t = [x_t^{\text{open}}, x_t^{\text{high}}, x_t^{\text{low}}, x_t^{\text{close}}, x_t^{\text{volume}}] \tag{2}$$

Table 2. Summary of Deep Learning Methods for Stock Forecasting

Article	Author	Description
ANN Model for Stock Prices	Wanjawa and Muchemi (2015)	Used deep neural networks to predict stock prices on the New York Stock Exchange
CNN for Stock Price Forecasting	Tsantekidis et al. (2017)	Applied 1-D convolutional neural networks to forecast stock prices from limit order book data
2-D CNN for Stock Trading	Gudelek et al. (2017)	Developed a 2-D CNN model to classify trading images and predict stock price trends
RNN for Daily Stock Prices	Samarawickrama and Fernando (2017)	Demonstrated the use of RNNs for predicting daily stock prices in the Sri Lankan stock market
LSTM for NIFTY 50 Returns	Roondiwala et al. (2017)	Applied LSTM networks to forecast returns of the NIFTY 50 index
CNN-LSTM Hybrid Model	Lu et al. (2020)	Combined CNN for local feature extraction and LSTM for temporal learning to forecast stock prices
Differential Transformer Model	Lai et al. (2023)	Introduced a differential transformer model for high-frequency stock movement prediction
Series Decomposition Transformer	Tao et al. (2024)	Enhanced stock market index prediction using a transformer with period-correlation and series decomposition
GAN for Stock Price Prediction	Romero (2019)	Explored the use of GANs for stock market price prediction, achieving moderate accuracy
LSTM-Attention Model	Wen and Li (2023)	Proposed an LSTM-attention-LSTM model for time series prediction, including stock prices
Deep LSTM and Q-Learning	Oyewola et al. (2024)	Applied deep LSTM and LSTM-attention Q-learning for oil and gas sector prediction

Here, x_t represents the trading data, which includes the opening price, high price, low price, closing price, and trading volume. t denotes a specific day in the time series.

For predictions of stock closing prices, we can utilize LSTMs, GANs, and Transformers with the last 100 time steps of trading data. LSTMs capture sequential dependencies, GANs generate realistic price trends, and Transformers leverage attention mechanisms to enhance accuracy in predicting the next day's closing price.

3.2 LSTM Model

LSTM is an advanced form of RNN designed to overcome the challenges of vanishing or exploding gradients during training. LSTM excels at capturing long-term dependencies and is particularly effective for time series prediction [13, 23]. LSTM replaces the hidden neurons of RNN with memory cells, which are capable of selectively retaining or discarding information through a gated mechanism. Specifically, LSTM utilizes three gates: the input gate, forget gate, and output gate. The architecture of an LSTM memory cell is illustrated in Fig. 1. The functioning of LSTM can be mathematically expressed through the Eqs. (3)–(7).

$$f_t = \sigma(W_f x(t) + U_f h(t-1) + b_f) \tag{3}$$

$$i_t = \sigma(W_i x(t) + U_i h(t-1) + b_i) \tag{4}$$

$$o_t = \sigma(W_o x(t) + U_o h(t-1) + b_o) \tag{5}$$

$$c_t = f(t) \otimes c(t-1) + i(t) \otimes \tanh(W_c x(t) + U_c h(t-1) + b_c) \tag{6}$$

$$h(t) = o(t) \otimes \tanh(c(t)) \tag{7}$$

3.3 GAN Model

Generative Adversarial Networks (GANs) are a class of machine learning frameworks that utilize two neural networks, the generator and the discriminator, in a competitive setting. The generator creates artificial data samples, while the discriminator evaluates them against real data, aiming to distinguish between genuine and generated samples. This adversarial process enhances the generator's ability to produce realistic outputs over time. GANs excel in unsupervised learning tasks, enabling applications such as image synthesis, style transfer, and data augmentation. The functioning of the minimax objective of GANs can be mathematically expressed in Eq. (8).

$$\min_G \max_D V(D,G) = \mathbb{E}_{x \sim p_{\text{data}}(x)}[\log D(x|y)] + \mathbb{E}_{z \sim p_z(z)}[\log(1 - D(G(z|y)))] \tag{8}$$

3.4 Transformer

A transformer is a deep learning model architecture introduced in 2017, primarily used for natural language processing (NLP) tasks. It employs a mechanism called self-attention to analyze relationships between data elements, allowing it to capture context and dependencies in sequences effectively. Unlike traditional models like RNNs, transformers process entire input sequences simultaneously, which enhances their ability to understand complex patterns. This architecture has led to significant advancements in various applications, including machine translation, text generation, and more, making it foundational in modern AI systems.

4   Experimental Results and Analysis

4.1   Experimental Data

The experimental data used in this study, we conducted a comprehensive analysis of the stock price data for two prominent Indian companies, Reliance Industries and Tata Consultancy Services (TCS). We utilized a granular approach by examining 1-min interval data over a five-day period to capture short-term price movements, complemented by 2-min interval data across one month to identify medium-term trends. Additionally, we incorporated daily interval data spanning the lifetime of both stocks to provide a robust historical context. This multifaceted analysis aims to enhance our understanding of market dynamics and inform investment strategies within the Indian stock market. The daily data for each stock include five features: opening price, closing price, highest price, lowest price, and trading volume. The selected stock names and their corresponding codes are presented in Table 3.

Table 3. Details of selected stocks, their codes, data intervals, and date ranges used for analysis.

Stock Name	Stock Code	Data Description
Reliance Industries Limited	RELIANCE.NS	1-min interval data for 5 trading days (Jan 15–19, 2024) 2-min interval data for 1 month (Jan 2024) Daily interval data from Jan 1, 2010 to Dec 31, 2023
Tata Consultancy Services	TCS.NS	1-min interval data for 5 trading days (Jan 15–19, 2024) 2-min interval data for 1 month (Jan 2024) Daily interval data from Jan 1, 2010 to Dec 31, 2023

4.2   Evaluation Metrics

To verify the effectiveness of the proposed methods, we utilized three widely adopted quality metrics: root mean square error (RMSE), mean absolute percentage error (MAPE), and mean absolute error (MAE). RMSE is frequently used to evaluate the performance of regression models and is particularly sensitive to outliers and extreme values, meaning larger errors have a more pronounced impact on RMSE, as shown in Eq. (9). MAPE offers an intuitive explanation of model performance and is applicable to various data types. Unlike RMSE, MAPE is not influenced by outliers, making it more robust, as demonstrated in Eq. (10). MAE provides a linear evaluation of error magnitude and offers a straightforward representation of errors. However, it does not differentiate between the impacts of small and large errors, as illustrated in Eq. (11). In these equations, y_i and $\hat{y}_i$ represent the actual and predicted values, respectively, while N denotes the number of samples.

$$\text{RMSE} = \sqrt{\frac{1}{N} \sum_{i=1}^{N} (y_i - \hat{y}_i)^2} \tag{9}$$

$$\text{MAPE} = \frac{100}{N} \sum_{i=1}^{N} \left| \frac{y_i - \hat{y}_i}{y_i} \right| \tag{10}$$

$$\text{MAE} = \frac{1}{N} \sum_{i=1}^{N} |y_i - \hat{y}_i| \tag{11}$$

4.3 Results

We select five features for the stock: the opening price, highest price, lowest price, closing price, and trading volume for every time it skips. The previous 100 data is used as input to predict the closing price for the next data. We utilized a batch size of 32 for training both LSTM and Transformer models, with the Adam optimizer applied using default settings. A 70/30 train-test split was used to guarantee adequate data for successful model learning while keeping a representative test set. Experiments were done on a machine with an NVIDIA RTX 3080 GPU and 32GB RAM. For Transformer, the 'Close' column of a dataset using MinMaxScaler, splits it into training and testing sets, and creates input-output sequences of length 30 for time series forecasting.

We employed an LSTM model with 4 input layers of hidden nodes of size 50, 60, 80, and 120 respectively, which had dropout values of 0.2, 0.3, 0.4, and 0.5 respectively. We conducted experiments on Reliance stock, the results obtained for the MAPE metric were 0.10, 0.20, 12.63 for 1 min, 2 min, and 1 day time skips. During the training phase, epochs were set to 50. In the case of GAN with a generator and discriminator, each consisting of two fully connected layers with 128 hidden nodes and ReLU activation. The generator transforms 100-dimensional noise into sequences of length 100, while the discriminator classifies sequences as real or fake using a sigmoid output. Experiments were conducted on time series data, with training using Adam optimizers ($\text{lr} = 0.0002$) and binary cross-entropy loss. In the Transformer model with a single input layer of hidden dimension 64, 1 encoder-decoder layer, and 2 attention heads. Experiments were conducted on stock price data, with the model predicting the next value in the sequence. During training, the learning rate and dropout were set to default values, and the model was optimized using a regression loss function. While the LSTM model developed a relatively modest MAPE of 0.1% for 1-minutely RIL forecasts, this good performance may be partially attributable to decreased volatility in short-term intervals and dataset-specific patterns, which might restrict generalizability to different stocks or market situations without additional validation.

Tables 4 and 5 conveys High volatility and quick price changes can hurt the performance of GAN and Transformer models if not handled with good pre-processing or strong loss functions. Prediction accuracy also depends on the type of data. Daily data often has more noise, while short-term data usually has less volatility. These differences in the data can affect how well the models can predict stock prices. the evaluation measures for different models, but a deeper study helps explain these results and system behaviors. One reason for the poor performance of the GAN model, with 84.35% MAPE for 1-day RIL predictions, is its low ability to catch long-term trends in volatile stock data. This often leads to mode breakdown and unstable results. GANs can build realistic data distributions but struggle with accurate sequence predictions in noisy financial data. In comparison, LSTM models can track patterns over time, helping them adjust to quick changes in market trends and instability. The Transformer model catches short-term trends well but has problems with long-term forecasts. This is due to its fixed location encodings and limited receptive fields when using small datasets. The lack of seasonality-specific models also limits the Transformer's ability to catch repeating market trends over long periods. High volatility and quick price changes can hurt the performance of GAN and Transformer models if not handled with good pre-processing or strong loss functions. Prediction accuracy also depends on the type of data. Daily data often has more noise, while short-term data usually has less volatility. These differences in the data can affect how well the models can predict stock prices. Hyperparameter choices like learning rates and sequence lengths also impact how well each model generalizes in volatile situations. Analyzing mistake trends across different stocks and time intervals would give better insights into each model's strengths and flaws.

As illustrated in Fig. 2, the residual plots demonstrate significant error patterns among models. GAN has substantial residual variance and outliers, suggesting instability under turbulent settings. The Transformer reveals systematic biases during trend reversals, whereas the LSTM has reduced residual variance, implying more consistent predicting performance (Fig. 3).

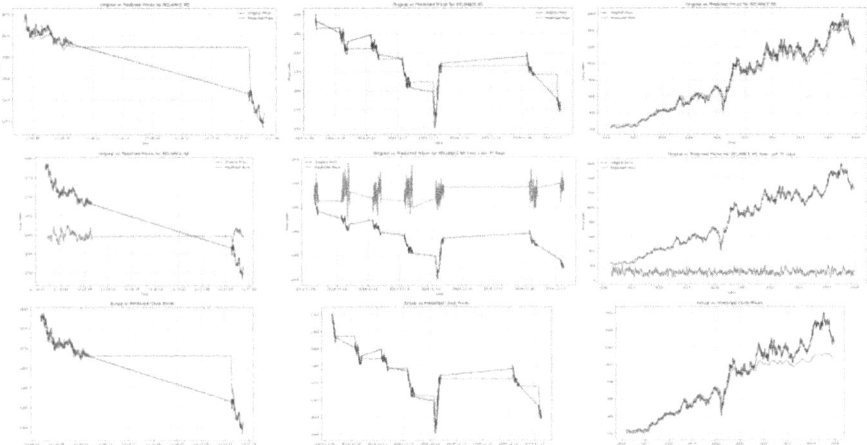

Fig. 1. Provides a clear visual comparison of performance by displaying time series plots of anticipated vs actual closing prices for all models and time skip options.

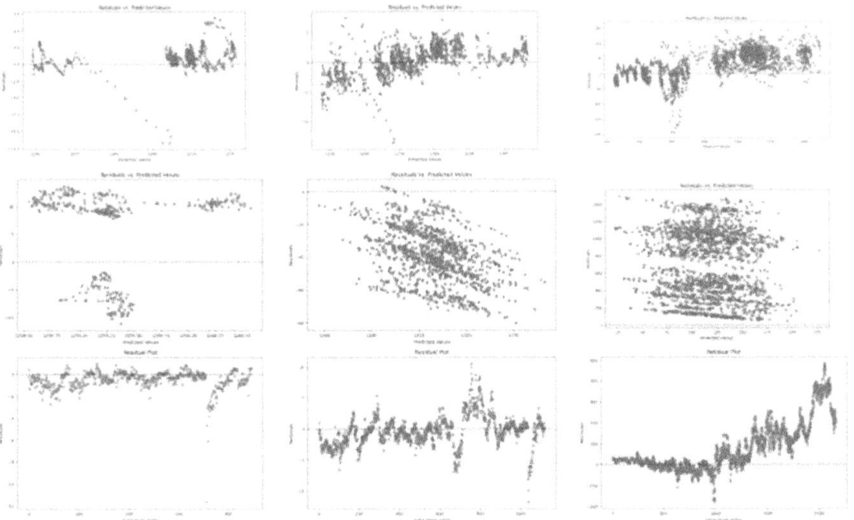

Fig. 2. Residual plots displaying the patterns and distribution of prediction errors for GAN, Transformer, and LSTM models over various time periods. The charts demonstrate the spread, variation, and systematic biases in residuals, with GAN displaying significant variance and outliers, Transformer showing systematic under- and over-predictions, and LSTM having reduced variance and stability across predictions.

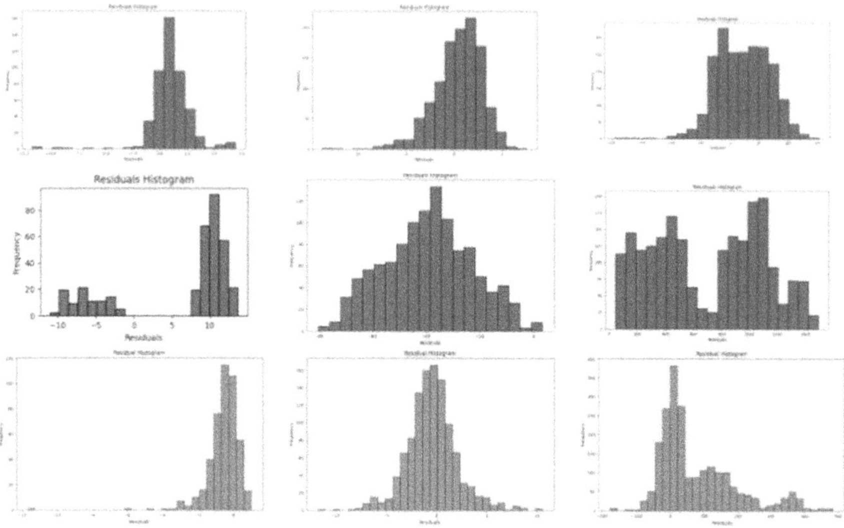

Fig. 3. Residual histograms to aid in the analysis of the model errors' normalcy and distribution properties.

4.4   Discussion

The experimental results in Tables 4 and 5 compare the performance of LSTM, GAN, and Transformer models for stock price prediction of Reliance Industries Limited (RIL) and Tata Consultancy Services (TCS) across different time horizons (1 min, 2 min, and 1 day). The LSTM model consistently demonstrates strong performance, achieving the lowest MAPE, RMSE, and MAE values for both stocks, particularly for short-term predictions (1 and 2 min). The Transformer model shows competitive results, outperforming LSTM in some cases for 1-min predictions but struggling with longer-term forecasts (1 day). In contrast, the GAN model performs poorly across all metrics and time horizons, with significantly higher errors, especially for 1-day predictions. This suggests that while GANs have potential for generative tasks, they are less effective for precise stock price forecasting compared to LSTM and Transformer models. Overall, LSTM remains the most reliable method for stock prediction, while Transformers show promise for short-term forecasting.

Table 4. Comparison of experimental results for Reliance Industries Limited stocks.

Metrics	Methods	1 min	2 min	1 day
MAPE(%) ↓	LSTM	0.10	0.20	12.63
	GAN	1.81	0.40	84.35
	Transformer	0.14	0.09	15.42
RMSE(e-2) ↓	LSTM	1.72	3.70	77.60
	GAN	23.41	5.72	825.08
	Transformer	2.09	1.58	196.53
MAE(e-2) ↓	LSTM	1.30	2.47	68.59
	GAN	22.79	4.94	722.87
	Transformer	1.73	1.18	152.27

Table 5. Comparison of experimental results for Tata Consultancy Services stocks.

Metrics	Methods	1 min	2 min	1 day
MAPE(%) ↓	LSTM	0.18	0.40	3.77
	GAN	0.79	3.37	83.65
	Transformer	0.10	1.23	23.35
RMSE(e-2) ↓	LSTM	9.56	25.72	120.30
	GAN	39.58	158.07	2588.58
	Transformer	5.16	60.61	879.08
MAE(e-2) ↓	LSTM	7.31	16.63	94.68
	GAN	32.27	143.34	2452.97
	Transformer	3.93	52.23	748.59

5   Conclusion

Predicting stock market prices with deep learning models has become a significant focus for researchers and investors due to the market's inherent complexity and nonlinear behavior. This study conducted a comprehensive analysis of three advanced deep learning frameworks: LSTM, Transformer, and GAN for stock closing price predictions using Yahoo Finance data. LSTM, with its ability to capture long-term dependencies, emerged as the most effective model, achieving the lowest prediction errors for stocks such as Reliance and TCS across all time horizons. In contrast, the Transformer, leveraging its encoder-decoder architecture and multi-head attention mechanism, performed admirably for short-term forecasts but showed limitations in handling longer-term market dynamics. GANs, while innovative, underperformed significantly compared to the other models.

The outcomes of this research emphasize the capabilities of LSTM in managing the intricacies of stock market prediction owing to its power in modeling temporal sequences. However, the Transformer framework exhibited promise in capturing sophisticated stock market dynamics in shorter periods, showing possibilities for improvement. GANs, despite their limited success here, could still contribute to future hybrid approaches when combined with other models.

Although this study demonstrates that the models are capable of capturing price and volume patterns, it excludes external elements that may impact stock prices, such as economic data or news mood. This restricts the algorithms' capacity to manage the intricacy of actual markets. These outside variables will be included in the future to increase forecast precision and usefulness. This research employed raw OHLCV data without technical indicators and lacked XAI algorithms, which will be introduced in future work for improved inputs and interpretability. We also want to investigate latency for real-time application and study hybrid LSTM-Transformer models to boost forecasting performance. This research employed just two Indian equities, therefore future research will test additional stocks to increase generalizability. This study does not examine deep learning models with common techniques like ARIMA and SVM, and future work will integrate these evaluations to illustrate the practical benefits of deep learning for stock prediction. This research examined only two Indian equities, limiting generalizability, and future work will test other stocks to boost robustness. Future study should strive to increase long-term forecasting by applying sophisticated training methods such as transfer learning and hybrid modeling techniques. Integrating the robust sequence modeling of LSTMs with the complex attention mechanisms of Transformers may give a method to leverage the capabilities of both designs. This approach could better address the unpredictable nature of financial markets and further improve the accuracy of stock price prediction.

References

1. Ariyo, A.A., Adewumi, A.O., Ayo, C.K.: Stock price prediction using the Arima model. In: 2014 UKSim-AMSS 16th International Conference on Computer Modelling and Simulation, pp. 106–112 (2014)
2. Armano, G., Marchesi, M., Murru, A.: A hybrid genetic-neural architecture for stock indexes forecasting. Inf. Sci. **170**(1), 3–33 (2005)
3. Bollerslev, T.: Generalized autoregressive conditional heteroskedasticity. J. Econometrics **31**(3), 307–327 (1986)
4. Chandar, K.S., Punjabi, H.: Cat swarm optimization algorithm tuned multilayer perceptron for stock price prediction. Int. J. Web-Based Learn. Teach. Technol. **17**(1), 1–15 (2022)
5. Choudhry, R., Garg, K.: A hybrid machine learning system for stock market forecasting. Int. J. Comput. Inf. Eng. **2**(4), 689–692 (2008)
6. Engle, R.F.: Autoregressive conditional heteroscedasticity with estimates of the variance of united kingdom inflation. Econometrica **50**(4), 987–1007 (1982)
7. Fu, J., Lum, K.S., Nguyen, M.N., Shi, J.: Stock prediction using FCMAC-BYY. In: Liu, D., Fei, S., Hou, Z., Zhang, H., Sun, C. (eds.) ISNN 2007. LNCS, vol. 4492, pp. 346–351. Springer, Heidelberg (2007). https://doi.org/10.1007/978-3-540-72393-6_42

8. Gudelek, M.U., Boluk, S.A., Ozbayoglu, A.M.: A deep learning based stock trading model with 2-D CNN trend detection. In: 2017 IEEE Symposium Series on Computational Intelligence (SSCI), pp. 1–8 (2017)
9. Jain, A.K., Mao, J., Mohiuddin, K.M.: Artificial neural networks: a tutorial. IEEE Comput. **29**(3), 31–44 (1996)
10. Lai, S., Wang, M., Zhao, S., Arce, G.R.: Predicting high-frequency stock movement with differential transformer neural network. Electronics **12**(13), 2943 (2023)
11. Lu, W., Li, J., Li, Y., Sun, A., Wang, J.: A CNN-LSTM-based model to forecast stock prices. Complexity **1–10**, 2020 (2020)
12. Ngo, D.: Predicting stocks with LSTM-based DRNN and GAN. Master's Projects, 1046 (2021)
13. Oyewola, D.O., Akinwunmi, S.A., Omotehinwa, T.O.: Deep LSTM and LSTM-attention q-learning based reinforcement learning in oil and gas sector prediction. Knowl.-Based Syst. **284**, 111290 (2024)
14. Romero, R.A.C.: Generative adversarial network for stock market price prediction (2019). https://cs230.stanford.edu/projects_fall_2019/reports/26259829.pdf
15. Roondiwala, M., Patel, H., Varma, S.: Predicting stock prices using LSTM. Int. J. Sci. Res. **6**(4), 1754–1756 (2017)
16. Samarawickrama, A.J.P., Fernando, T.G.I.: A recurrent neural network approach in predicting daily stock prices an application to the Sri Lankan stock market. In: 2017 IEEE International Conference on Industrial and Information Systems (ICIIS), pp. 1–6 (2017)
17. Suykens, J.A.K., Vandewalle, J.: Least squares support vector machine classifiers. Neural Process. Lett. **9**(3), 293–300 (1999)
18. Tao, Z., Wu, W., Wang, J.: Series decomposition transformer with period-correlation for stock market index prediction. Expert Syst. Appl. **237**, 121424 (2024)
19. Tsantekidis, A., Passalis, N., Tefas, A., Kanniainen, J., Gabbouj, M., Iosifidis, A.: Forecasting stock prices from the limit order book using convolutional neural networks. In: 2017 IEEE 19th Conference on Business Informatics (CBI), pp. 7–12 (2017)
20. Vijh, M., Chandola, D., Tikkiwal, V.A., Kumar, A.: Stock closing price prediction using machine learning techniques. Procedia Comput. Sci. **167**, 599–606 (2020)
21. Wang, J., Chen, Z.: Factor-GAN: enhancing stock price prediction and factor investment with generative adversarial networks. PLoS ONE **19**(6), e0306094 (2024)
22. Wanjawa, B.W., Muchemi, L.: ANN model to predict stock prices at stock exchange markets. arXiv preprint arXiv:1502.06434 (2015)
23. Wen, X., Li, W.: Time series prediction based on LSTM-attention-LSTM model. IEEE Access **11**, 48322–48331 (2023)

A Deep Learning-Driven Approach to Automated Dragon Fruit Quality Grading

Sarasij Majee[1], Ayan Das[2], Pritoma Saha[3], Subhadip Das[4], Shruti Pandey[4], Suptasish Sarkar[5], and Kousik Roy[4(✉)]

[1] Department of Computer Science Engineering, Swami Vivekananda Institute of Science & Technology (SVIST), Dakshin Gobindapur, Sonarpur, Kolkata 700145, India
[2] Department of Computer Science and Technology, Institute of Engineering and Management (IEM) Newtown, University of Engineering and Management (UEM), Kolkata 700160, India
[3] Department of Computer Application, Techno India University, Kolkata 700091, India
[4] Department of Computer Science and Engineering, Bengal College of Engineering and Technology, Durgapur 713212, West Bengal, India
kousikroy002@gmail.com
[5] Department of Electrical Engineering, Brainware University, Kolkata 700125, West Bengal, India

Abstract. Pitaya or dragon fruit is a tropical fruit prized for its unusual look and several health advantages including a high vitamin and antioxidant content. Dragon fruit is becoming more and more popular worldwide which benefits emerging countries like Bangladesh, Vietnam, China, Thailand, Indonesia, Israel and India economically. The present study offers a very large collection of high resolution dragon fruit photos that will help the machine learning models in their determination of the ripeness and quality of the fruit. The dataset was created with the utmost care and guidance from specialists over a period of four months from three different locations in Bangladesh. The collection is of great importance in facilitating the operations of dragon fruit production by giving resources for robotic harvesting, quality evaluation, and packing systems etc. We performed quality assessment using the Nasnet Mobile, DenseNet121 and MobileNetV2 models which yielded test accuracies of 94.89%, 96.06% and 97% respectively. MobileNetV2 model got the maximum accuracy of 97.00%. It showed a recall of 0.97, F1-score of 0.97 and precision of 0.97 which means very trustworthy and even performance. The data of this study along with the outcomes of the deep learning models besides being a valuable asset for researchers and practitioners in the industry also lead to the establishment of automated systems for the dragon fruit production.

Keywords: Dragon fruit · Deep learning Model and Quality grading

K. Chandra Mondal et al. (Eds.): CICBA 2025, CCIS 2862, pp. 314–326, 2026.
https://doi.org/10.1007/978-3-032-17187-0_24

1   Introduction

The development of this dataset was primarily driven by the difficulties associated with recognizing the various growth phases of dragon fruit making it a widespread problem in agriculture that needed solving. It contributes to precision agriculture goals which aim to modernize crop management practices and therefore improve output. Moreover, the lack of comprehensive datasets pertaining to dragon fruit development and diseases proved to be an additional reason for the project as such datasets are indispensable for creating accurate detection models. The collection comprises exceptionally picked photographs that depict all different aspects of growth and conditions making it an effective instrument for the training and testing of deep learning algorithms. It also accelerates and enhances the accuracy of recognizing the different growth stages and quality grades of dragon fruit. The dataset that is made public is supportive of the continuous research work since it provides raw data for scientists and researchers in the agricultural sector, thus keeping the process transparent and also pushing the modernity of the farming methods even further. One of the issues caused by uneven harvesting is that some dragon fruits are picked too early or too late which results in less sweet, less tasty, and lower-quality fruit. Such issues can cause customers dissatisfaction and market demand can decline resulting in financial losses, increased labor and farmers' reduced profits. Traditional methods like weight, texture and peel color assessment are noninvasive methods to determine dragon fruit ripenes [1]. The capacity to identify freshness as well as detect flaws in dragon fruit is of paramount significance in maintaining product quality, reducing wastage, avoiding economic consequences and supporting international trade. As an added bonus, it encourages the manufacture of high-quality commodities that adhere to global market standards [2]. The main goal of this study is to leverage a comprehensive dataset of dragon fruit image to develop and test automated systems using machine learning, deep learning techniques and computer vision.

2   Related Work

Current studies on dragon fruit classification and ripeness detection have utilized more and more deep learning and computer vision methods to enhance efficiency and accuracy. Ensemble models,e.g., the use of VGG19 and locally designed convolutional neural networks(CNNs) have reported high accuracy in classifying dragon fruit by identifying minute variations in color, texture and shape with reported test accuracies above 95 at optimal learning rates [3]. Other research has center detecting ripening stages employing neural networks enabling smart agriculture applications through the automation of fruit maturity assessment [4]. Fast recognition and counting algorithms from video streams have also been established which allow real-time tracking of dragon fruit flowers and fruits in agricultural environments [5]. Quality classification with CNNs has also been found to be effective in sorting fruits according to external appearance allowing quality control in post harvest operations [6]. Conventional machine learning methods, e.g., Naive Bayes classifiers using HSV color space features have also been investigated for detecting maturity, although deep learning methods tend to provide better accuracy and flexibility [8]. All these advancement spool together to provide more robust, scalable and automated solutions to dragon fruit classification and maturity detection, benefiting both producers and supply chain players. Deep learning-based methods for automatic dragon fruit quality grading have been investigated with diverse neural network structures and machine learning algorithms and some studies have achieved accuracies less than 97%. Mohapatra et al.attained more than 94% grading accuracy with a VGG19 model for fruit quality prediction showing the applicability of deep learning in this application [10]. Ismail and Malik created areal-time visual quality inspection system, claiming 96.7% accuracy for apples and 93.8%for bananas in field trials revealing the difficulty of sustaining high accuracy in non-laboratory settings [11]. Knott et al. employed Vision Transformers for fruit quality estimation with results competing with top-performing CNNs at within 1%, yet with reduced training samples, thus applicable in data-constrained environments [13]. Other research has implemented deep learning for fruit grading and freshness inspection with models such as ResNet, AlexNet and Google Net with validation accuracies sometimes being lower than 97% depending on the complexity of the dataset as well as environmental variation [9, 12]. These studies collectively indicate that deep learning models work well for robotic fruit grading, yet real-world implementation shaves lightly decreased accuracies due to issues including dataset diversity, illumination, and the complexity of fruit properties. This highlights the necessity for more studies to enhance robustness and generalizability in real-world implementations.

3   Data Description

The Dragon Fruit Quality Grading Dataset has been carefully selected to facilitate the creation of automated systems that use image based analysis to access the quality of dragon fruits. The primary exterior characteristics that aid in assessing the overall quality of the fruit are the subject of this dataset including surface color consistency, flaws and textural characteristics. With the goal of supporting binary classification jobs for sorting product according to quality requirements, it is separated into two primary categories: Fresh Dragon Fruit and Defect Dragon Fruit. Photographs were collected from May to August 2023 from three farms in Bangladesh: Gazipur, Jhenaidah, and Munshigonj, with the assistance of agricultural experts [14]. High-resolution mobile devices such as the Samsung S22 and Redmi Note 11 Pro Plus which both have sophisticated photography sensors were used to snap pictures. The dataset used in this study comprises images resized to 224×224 pixels and saved in JPG format. In total, 1,980 defective fruit images and 1,320 fresh fruit images were used for training. During the validation and testing phases, 425 defective and 275 fresh fruit images were applied, which made it possible to have a balanced and representative evaluation of the model performance. The dataset was diversified by using augmentation techniques such as rotation, scaling and contrast modifications to add more photographs. The dataset has original and enhanced folders available. Each category is marked according to visual cues assessed by experts in order to assist the development of effective, consistent and trustworthy fruit grading systems.

4 Methodology

A deep learning framework that was able to customize according to the needs of the project was developed to produce a consistent and trustworthy model for the quality and ripeness of dragon fruits evaluation. The whole process was divided into five main parts: data preprocessing, image segmentation, model training, validation and testing. One of the objectives of the method was to increase the overall system and model's performance, reliability and impressiveness in variety of image inputs. The first step in the process was performing a comprehensive data preprocessing activity. The expertise of a professional was the source of complete and error-free labels for each image, thereby guaranteeing precise classifications. Then image size was made uniform across the board so that there would be no difference in the amount of computational load being handled and the performance of deep learning models would be equally improved by it. Different approaches for image segmentation were implemented in order to cut out and get rid of extra backgrounds, thus drawing out and making clearer the specific features of the fruit. In order to make the dataset more diverse, augmentation techniques such as flipping, rotating and changing brightness and contrast were applied. These methods helped the model to spot subtle visual characteristics, reduced overfitting, and made the training data larger. After preprocessing, the dataset was divided into training and testing sets. A random division was done whereby 80% of the images were used for training while 20% were set aside for testing. This method avoided any overlap between the sets and guaranteed an unbiased assessment of the model's performance. This carefully selected dataset was used for model training and performance was tracked via continuous validation. The accuracy of the trained model in differentiating fruit ripeness stages and identifying flaws was then assessed using unseen data. This approach guaranteed accurate results that matched actual agricultural grading applications. In Fig. 1, we have described the preprocessing procedures of the proposed deep learning model.

5 Mobile Net V2 Deep Learning Model [15]

The MobileNetV2 model is specially well suited for image classification tasks on mobile and edge devices with constrained processing resources because of its lightweight design. In order to take use of previously learned features, the model is initialized using pre-trained weights from the ImageNet dataset. It is modified for a binary classification job by adding custom classification head with thick layers and global average pooling. In order to preserve the pretrained capabilities

Fig. 1. The actual dragon fruit specimens sourced directly from the fields where we gathered the dataset images.

of MobileNetV2, the first layers are frozen. The model is properly equipped for binary predictions as it is constructed with the Adam optimizer alongside the categorical cross-entropy loss. To increase the model's ability to generalize over the whole input data, data augmentation techniques like rotation, flipping and scaling are employed during training. The performance of the model is assessed on a different test set after training. This configuration shows how MobileNetV2 can provide precise categorization while preserving computational performance.

6 Densenet 121 Deep Learning Model [16]

An advanced deep learning technique that makes use of DenseNet121 architecture pretrained on ImageNet dataset has been applied for the purpose of binary classification of dragon fruit images into two categories namely immature and mature. In order to conserve the essential knowledge obtained through pre-training, the entire layers of the base DenseNet121 model were made non-trainable. After that, a custom classification head was built which consisted of a flattening layer followed by fully connected deep layers and a final layer with a softmax activation function to give the probabilities of classes as an output. The model adopted categorical cross entropy as the loss function, which is suitable for multiclass tasks and the Adam optimizer for learning. Image rescaling was done for both training and validation datasets. Besides, the training set was augmented with a variety of data augmentation techniques which were employed to make the model more capable of generalization. After training for a hundred epochs, the model's accuracy was checked on a separate test dataset and also estimated through visual metrics such as ROC curves and confusion matrices.

7 NasNet Mobile Deep Learning Model [17]

In this project, we utilized the NASNet Mobile architecture to classify images of dragon fruits into two datasets one is immature and mature and another is fresh and defect dataset. The model architecture employed a pretrained NASNet

Mobile as the backbone. The classification head included a Global Average Pooling layer, a fully connected layer with 128 neurons and a final fully connected layer using softmax activation. In order to prevent overfitting and to make the most of the features, the backbone layers were slowly fine-tuned during training with the new head layers. Massive data augmentation methods like rotation, width and height shifts, shear, zoom and horizontal flips were applied to make the model robust. The training process was split into training and validation sets. The performance of the model was monitored by drawing the graphs of accuracy and loss. A conclusive assessment on a different test set verified the high classification accuracy, which was further supported by a confusion matrix and comprehensive classification reports.

MobileNetV2, DenseNet121 and NasNet Mobile are the deep learning models employed in this investigation and their architectural structures are shown in Figs. 2, 3 and 4 respectively. A thorough illustration of the model layers is shown in each figure, which high lights the specially designed classification heads created for effective binary classification of dragon fruit photos.

8   Experimental Results and Discussion

Deep learning and classification tasks require a thorough evaluation matrix which consists of metrics like Accuracy, F1-Score, Precision and Recall. These metrics are very important and serve as the key benchmarks for the performance evaluation of Accuracy, Precision, Recall, F1-score and Confusion Matrix. To assess the performance of the deep learning model, the evaluator relied on two augmented datasets. For the quality detection, three models were used DenseNet 121, NasNet Mobile and MobileNetV2. The MobileNetV2 model reached a remarkable accuracy of 97% which was the highest among the evaluated models.

8.1   Experimental Result Using Densenet121 Model

In identifying the quality of dragon fruit, the deep learning model based on DenseNet121 showed excellent results by effectively distinguishing between fresh and defective samples. The model's performance was assessed by overall accuracy of 96.06%, which indicated a strong control over the classification process. The confusion matrix affirmed that the model successfully detected 397 defective and 285 fresh samples, also that it mistakenly classified as fresh only 28 defective samples and did not mislabel any fresh samples. The model's ability to tell the freshness of the fruit with great accuracy is thus established. Consistency and reliability are also mentioned in the classification report, which has an F1 score of 0.97 and recall value of 0.93 for the defective class, thus confirming the model's quality in predictin. The model obtained an F1-score of 0.95 and an accuracy of 0.91 for the fresh class. Both the weighted and macro-averaged F1-scores were 0.96 indicating that performance was consistently balanced across classes. Furthermore, early in training, the model training curve demonstrated almost perfect convergence, and the validation accuracy remained high and steady suggesting no discernible overfitting.

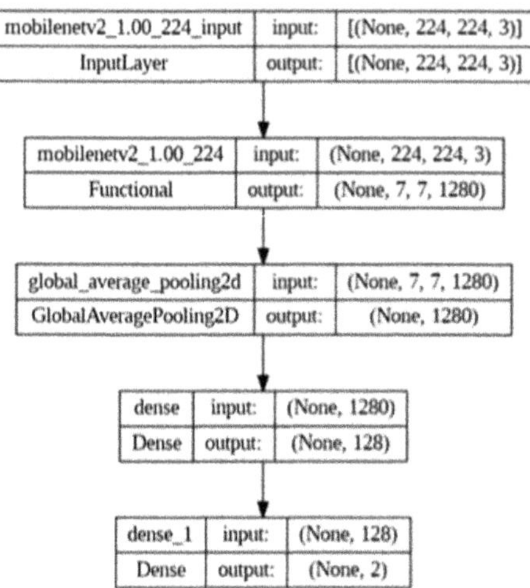

Fig. 2. Architecture of Mobilenet V2

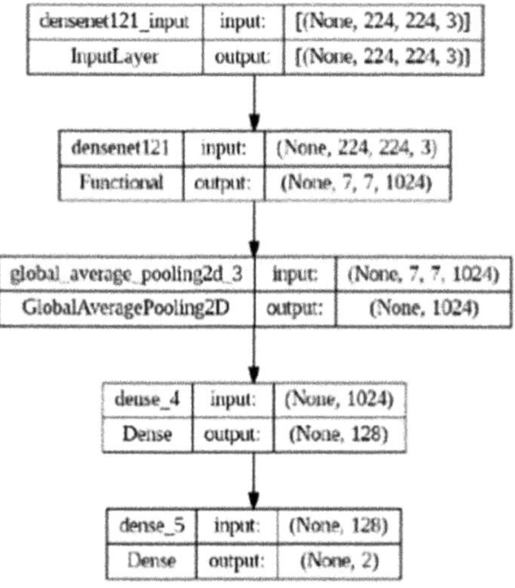

Fig. 3. Architecture of Densenet 121

8.2   Experimental Result Using NasNetMobile Model

The implemented code utilizes a NasNetMobile based model for quality grading detection of dragon fruits. The pre-trained deep learning model based on ImageNet weights and with the input shape of (224, 224, 3) was adjusted for binary classification. The structure was changed by adding a Global Average Pooling layer, a fully connected layer with 128 neurons and ReLU activation and a final softmax layer with two neurons. The original pre-trained layers were frozen to keep the learned features. The new layers were specifically trained for

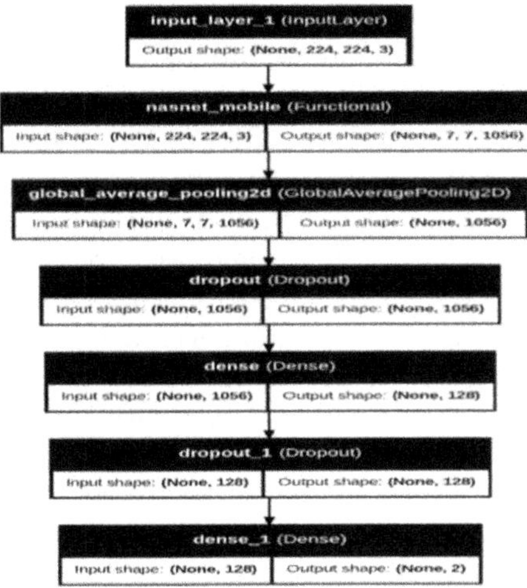

Fig. 4. Architecture of NasNetMobile

the quality grading task. The model was compiled with the Adam optimizer and categorical cross entropy loss. Different data augmentation methods were used on the training dataset to improve generalization. When the training epochs were done, the model's ability to correctly classify dragon fruit quality grades was tested on a separate test dataset. This approach under scores the efficiency of NASNetMobile in quality grading detection tasks, show casing its potential for accurately identifying various quality at tributes of dragon fruits. With an overall classification accuracy of 95%, the model demonstrated its efficiency in managing the classification job.

8.3   Experimental Result Using MobileNetV2 Model

The experimental evaluation of the MobileNetV2 model for dragon fruit quality classification yielded test accuracy of 97% indicating highly positive results. The training and validation accuracy improved rapidly in the first epochs and quickly leveled off near perfect accuracy indicating that the model learned the important patterns in the data. The loss values also decreased quickly and plateaued near zero indicating that the model learned well without any indications of overlearning or overfitting. When looking at the classification metrics, the model's strong classification can be seen more clearly. The model classified all fresh samples correctly with zero wrong classifications. Some defective fruits were categorized as fresh so the precision for the defective class was 0.91 reflecting a slight over-classification. The overall weighted F1 score of 0.97 indicates balanced and accurate predictions across both groups supported by F1 scores of 0.97 for defective fruits and 0.95 for fresh fruits. Furthermore, the ROC curve showed an AUC of 0.97, indicating that the model is highly effective at distinguishing between classes. Overall, MobileNetV2 proved to be a strong and dependable architecture for determining the quality of dragon fruit, providing excellent accuracy and generalization suitable for real-world implementation in agricultural inspection systems.

Figures 5(a) and 5(b) show the training and validation loss and accuracy curves respectively for the DenseNet121 model. These plots demonstrate the model's strong generalization capability, as it quickly converged with consistent accuracy and minimal loss. Figures 5(c) and 5(d) present the training and validation loss and accuracy curves for the NasNet Mobile model. These plots show erratic loss patterns and varying validation accuracy in comparison to the other two models, which may indicate difficulties with generalisation and a propensity for overfitting. Figures 5(e) and 5(f) illustrate the training and validation loss and accuracy trends for the MobileNetV2 architecture, which demonstrate stable convergence and strong performance throughout training and validation.

These graphs demonstrate the model's effective performance on both visible and invisible data, as well as its consistently high accuracy and quickly decreasing loss values throughout epochs.

The confusion matrix for the test set prediction is shown in Fig. 6(a), Fig. 6(b) and Fig. 7 below. Both the absolute values and percentages are provided for a clear understanding of model performance.

Table 1 displays the classification reports for DenseNet121, NasNet Mobile, and MobileNetV2 respectively. DenseNet121 and MobileNetV2 achieved balanced and high performance across both classes, while NasNet Mobile showed a significant imbalance, performing well on defective samples but poorly on fresh ones indicating limited generalization.

Table 1. Comparison of classification reports for DenseNet121, NasNet Mobile and MobileNetV2 models.

Class	DenseNet121			NasNet Mobile			MobileNetV2		
	Precision	Recall	F1	Precision	Recall	F1	Precision	Recall	F1
Defect	1.00	0.93	0.97	1.00	0.93	0.97	1.00	0.93	0.97
Fresh	0.91	1.00	0.95	0.91	1.00	0.95	0.91	1.00	0.95
Accuracy	0.96			0.95			**0.97**		
Macro Avg	0.96	0.97	0.96	0.95	0.97	0.95	0.96	0.97	0.97
Weighted Avg	0.96	0.96	0.96	0.95	0.95	0.95	0.97	0.97	0.97

The ROC curve graph given below shows the performance of the MobileNetV2 model over the various classes, thus giving a complete assessment of its classification capabilities which is presented below in Fig. 8

The MobileNetV2 network was capable of conducting the quality grading detection process for dragon fruits and came out with a superior performance. The model scored a total test accuracy of 97%.

In Table 2, we compare the performance of three advanced deep learning models—DenseNet121, NasNet Mobile, and MobileNetV2 for the task of quality

(a) Training and validation loss for DenseNet121   (b) Training and validation accuracy for DenseNet121

(c) Training and validation loss for NasNet Mobile (d) Training and validation accuracy for NasNet Mobile

(e) Training and validation loss for MobileNetV2   (f) Training and validation accuracy for MobileNetV2

Fig. 5. Comparison of training and validation performance for different model architectures: DenseNet121, NasNet Mobile, and MobileNetV2.

grading detection of dragon fruit. MobileNetV2 not only showed its exceptional feature extraction and classification abilities but also scored the highest accuracy (97%) and a strong AUC score. The impeccable performance, which came from its training on a well-structured dataset along with the use of extensive image augmentation for strength, marks MobileNetV2 as the best model for dragon fruit's quality grading that is automated in this research.

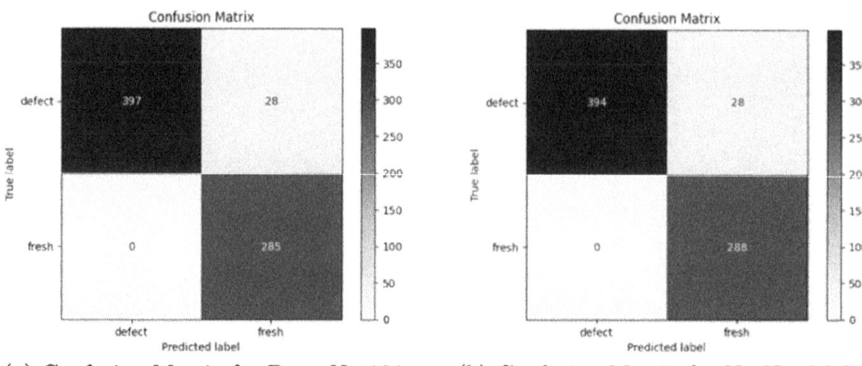

(a) Confusion Matrix for DenseNet121   (b) Confusion Matrix for NasNet Mobile

Fig. 6. Comparison of confusion matrices for DenseNet121 and NasNet Mobile models.

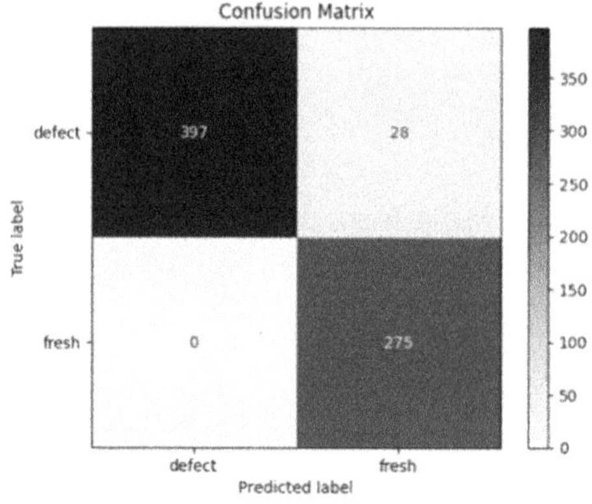

Fig. 7. Confusion Matrix for the MobileNetV2

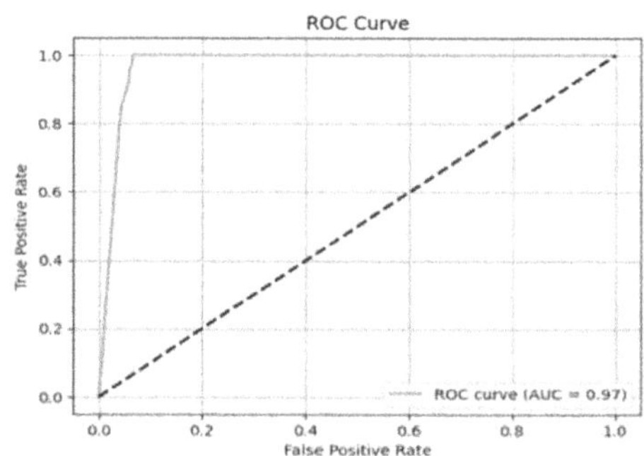

Fig. 8. ROC curve of Mobile NetV2 model

Table 2. Model Performance on Dragon Fruit Quality Grading Dataset

Model	Test Accuracy (%)
NasNet Mobile	94.89%
DenseNet-121	96.06%
MobileNetV2	97.00%

9 Conclusion

This research examined the latest deep learning methods for automated quality grading of dragon fruit, which is a economically and nutritionally, rapidly growing global tropical commodity. We developed strong AI models based on a very selective dataset consisting of high-quality images. These images were collected from three different spots in Bangladesh over a span of four months and were checked by experts to make sure the data quality and diversity were good.

Three advanced convolutional neural network models, DenseNet121, NasNet Mobile and MobileNetV2 were applied and compared. Among the models, MobileNetV2 performed the best achieving a test accuracy of 97% and equally high precision, recall and F1-score of 0.97, thus showing its supreme capability to classify correctly dragon fruit ripeness and quality. MobileNetV2's performance can be attributed to its light structure, featurization success and the model's capability to maintain high accuracy even on low resource usage.

The outcomes of this research substantiate the power of deep learning in assessing agricultural best quality and also offer a very important dataset that can be publicly accessed to support the research in computer vision and intelligent farming. To sum up, the work provides a highly scalable and robust framework for dragon fruit automated quality grading, thus opening up new technologically advanced islands in precision agriculture especially in those developing countries where the need for fruit production efficiency is more acute. Besides, the question of real-time model deployment, IoT device integration and other horticultural crops' expansion as a smart agriculture support would be worth asking in the course of future investigations.

References

1. Deep, L., Narayana, C.K., Karunakaran, G., Rao, D.S., Anuradha, S.: Maturity determination of red and white pulp dragon fruit. J. Horticult. Sci. **17**(1), 157–165 (2022)
2. Shameena, S., Geetha Lekshmi, P.R., Gopinath, P.P., Gidagiri, P., Kanagarajan, S.: Dynamic transformations in fruit color, bioactive compounds, and textural characteristics of purple-fleshed dragon fruit (Hylocereus costaricensis) across fruit developmental stages under humid tropical climate. Horticulturae **10**(12), 1280 (2024)

3. Kaur, A., Kukreja, V., Tiwari, P., Manwal, M., Sharma, R.: Fruitful fusion: an accuracy-boosting ensemble of VGG19 and convolutional neural networks for dragon fruit classification. In: Proceedings of the IEEE International Conference on Interdisciplinary Approaches Technology and Management for Social Innovation (IATMSI), pp. 1–5. IEEE, Gwalior (2024)

4. Abhishek, G., Prabhu, A., Rani, N.S.: Identification of stages of ripening of dragon fruit using neural networks for smart agriculture. In: Proceedings of the 2nd International Conference on Edge Computing Application (ICECAA) (2023)

5. Li, X., Wang, X., Ong, P., Yi, Z., Ding, L., Han, C.: Fast recognition and counting method of dragon fruit flowers and fruits based on video stream. Sensors **23**, 8444 (2023)

6. Trieu, N.M., Thinh, N.T.: Quality classification of dragon fruits based on external performance using a convolutional neural network. Appl. Sci. **11**(22), 10558 (2021)

7. Yusamran, N., Hiransakolwong, N.: DIPDEEP: classification for Thai dragon fruit. Eng. Appl. Sci. Res. **49**(4), 521–530 (2022)

8. Khisanudin, I.S., Murinto: Dragon fruit maturity detection based on HSV space color using Naive Bayes classifier method. In: IOP Conference Series: Materials Science and Engineering, vol. 852, p. 012045 (2020)

9. Vijayakumar, T., Vinothkanna, M.R.: Mellowness detection of dragon fruit using deep learning strategy. J. Innov. Image Process. (2020). https://doi.org/10.36548/jiip.2020.1.004

10. Mohapatra, D., Das, N., Mohanty, K.K., Shresth, J.: Automated visual inspecting system for fruit quality estimation using deep learning. In: Mishra, M., Sharma, R., Kumar Rathore, A., Nayak, J., Naik, B. (eds.) Innovation in Electrical Power Engineering, Communication, and Computing Technology. LNEE, vol. 814, pp. 379–389. Springer, Singapore (2022). https://doi.org/10.1007/978-981-16-7076-3_33

11. Malik, O., Ismail, N.: Real-time visual inspection system for grading fruits using computer vision and deep learning techniques. Inf. Process. Agric. (2021). https://doi.org/10.1016/j.inpa.2021.01.005

12. Fu, Y., Nguyen, M., Yan, W.: Grading methods for fruit freshness based on deep learning. SN Comput. Sci. **3** (2022). https://doi.org/10.1007/s42979-022-01152-7

13. Knott, M., Pérez-Cruz, F., Defraeye, T.: Facilitated machine learning for image-based fruit quality assessment. J. Food Eng. (2022)

14. Khatun, T., Nirob, M.A.S., Bishshash, P., Akter, M., Uddin, M.S.: A comprehensive dragon fruit image dataset for detecting the maturity and quality grading of dragon fruit. Data Brief **52**, 109936 (2024)

15. Al-Huqail, A., et al.: Deep learning-based ensemble model for accurate tomato leaf disease classification by leveraging ResNet50 and MobileNetV2 architectures. Sci. Rep. **15** (2025)

16. Albelwi, S.: Deep architecture based on DenseNet-121 model for weather image recognition. Int. J. Adv. Comput. Sci. Appl. (2022)

17. Adedoja, A., Owolawi, P., Mapayi, T.: Intelligent mobile plant disease diagnostic system using NASNet-Mobile deep learning (2021)

An Autonomous Roadside Parking System Based on Kinematic Modelling and Trajectory Planning

Tathagata Banerjee[1], Anumoy Majhi[1], Arnab Biswas[1], and Sumit Gupta[2]([✉])

[1] Department of Computer Science and Engineering, University Institute of Technology, The University of Burdwan, Golapbag (North), Burdwan 713104, West Bengal, India
[2] Department of Computer Science & Engineering, Academy of Technology, Adisaptagram, Aedconagar, Hooghly 712121, West Bengal, India
`sumit1.gupta@aot.edu.in`

Abstract. Driver drowsiness is a major reason for road accidents, especially on unstructured or under-marked roads, where conventional Advanced Driver-Assistance Systems (ADAS) generally fail to work. The paper proposes a vision-based real-time autonomous parking system triggered by driver drowsiness detection. The system integrates SegFormer-B0 for efficient road segmentation, Sobel edge detection for boundary amplification, and YOLOv8x-seg for real-time object segmentation and recognition. When drowsiness is identified, the pipeline computes the distances to neighboring obstacles and road boundaries in pixel-space Euclidean units. When a safe parking spot is identified in accordance with deterministic logic rules, the car carries out an autonomous parking procedure along a smooth cubic Bézier curve path, with the addition of a simple kinematic motion model to make maneuvering realistic and stable. The Bézier curve dynamically adapts its control points to respond to real-time movement of obstacles. Extensive testing on structured and unstructured road datasets demonstrates the system provides stable perception, safe decision-making, and uninterrupted autonomous parking execution with mid-range GPU hardware real-time performance (~15–20 FPS). This integrated approach proves the feasibility of combining advanced perception, kinematic modeling, and trajectory planning for enhanced autonomous emergency parking in real-world driving conditions.

Keywords: Drowsiness Detection · Road Segmentation · Object Detection · Autonomous Parking · Bézier Curve Trajectory · Path Planning · Kinematic Modeling · Emergency Vehicle Control · Computer Vision · Deep Learning

1 Introduction

Driver drowsiness is among the major causes of road accidents, responsible for approximately 20% of all accidents and a quarter of fatal and severe crashes. Even though Advanced Driver-Assistance Systems (ADAS) have contributed to safer roads over the last few years [1, 2], the majority of available solutions are based on structured environments with distinct lane markings and boundaries. In such well-defined environments,

K. Chandra Mondal et al. (Eds.): CICBA 2025, CCIS 2862, pp. 327–339, 2026.
https://doi.org/10.1007/978-3-032-17187-0_25

computer vision techniques such as Haar cascade classifiers [3] and YOLOv5-based detectors [4] hold potential in identifying formal parking spots. But these strategies are usually ineffective on unstructured or unmarked roads, where lighting, occlusion, and surface irregularity render detection uncertain, particularly when the driver is sleepy or loses control. To overcome this, a novel system integrating real-time monitoring of the driver with autonomous decision-making to stop or park the vehicle safely without depending on infrastructure has been proposed.

The proposed system is triggered upon detecting driver fatigue such as drowsiness, yawning etc. and applies semantic segmentation, edge detection, and object detection to scan the road ahead and around the vehicle. It computes safe parking spaces and computes a smooth parking trajectory through a cubic Bézier curve, enriched with kinematic modelling to provide stable and realistic vehicular motion. Thus, this paper proposes a comprehensive end-to-end system that couples perception and motion planning for emergency roadside parking.

The key contributions of this research work are:

a. A lightweight segmentation and edge detection pipeline applicable for unmarked and unstructured roads.
b. Real-time object detection for real-time dynamic obstacle avoidance.
c. Kinematic-based Bézier trajectory planning for secure and smooth parking under emergency situations.

The remaining part of the paper is structured as follows: Sect. 2 discusses about the pros and cons of the related works. Section 3 describes the suggested architecture and dynamic parking logic. Section 4 outlines implementation and experimental setup. Section 5 presents the results and finally Sect. 6 concludes the paper with future work.

2 Related Works

A number of works have focused on road edge detection, obstacle detection, and autonomous parking primarily individually.

Chand et al. [1] proposed an edge-based allocation of parking space to enhance traffic flow in city environments. Feng et al. [2] and Jain & Nair [3] utilized Sobel and Canny edge detection under structured environments, while Trivedi et al. [4] generalized Canny method for real-time parking detection under well-labeled scenarios.

To improve perception, deep learning techniques have been proposed as well. Amato et al. [6, 15] and Musabini et al. [5] utilized smart cameras and transformer networks for parking occupancy detection. These approaches, however, are highly dependent on centralized infrastructure. Ordóñez et al. [7] and Li et al. [8] suggested vision-based detection for dedicated parking lots, but not roadside environments.

Trajectory planning approaches have also been explored by few researchers. Zeng et al. [10] and Li et al. [11] employed the use of Bézier curves for motion planning in a safe manner, while other research works [9, 12, 13] investigated mathematical modeling for parking evaluation. Shen et al. [14] employed genetic algorithms for the optimization of parking space utilization in formal areas.

Even with the aforementioned developments, most parking systems make the ide-alistic assumptions of well-marked lanes and external assistance. Emergency situation such as abrupt driver drowsiness on unstructured roads is still a less explored avenue. In addition, kinematic motion modeling for realistic and stable path generation is seldom implemented. This paper fills these gaps by introducing an integrated system consisting of drowsiness detection, real-time perception, and kinematic-aware Bézier trajectory planning for secure roadside parking.

3 Proposed Methodology

To tackle driver fatigue and support autonomous parking on both structured and unstructured roads, a kinematics-aware, multi-stage computer vision pipeline has been proposed. The framework (Figs. 1 and 2) runs in real time, implementing the following prominent steps:

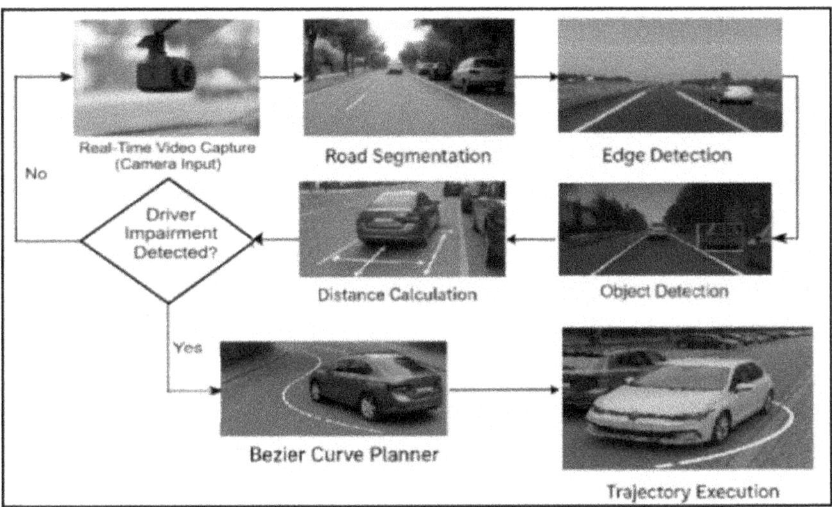

Fig. 1. Architecture of the Proposed System.

a. *Input Preprocessing*

   Incoming frames are first resized to 512×512 pixels for consistency in computation and are fed in parallel to segmentation, edge detection, and object detection modules.

b. *Road Segmentation*

   A SegFormer-B0 model, which is pretrained on Cityscapes, does semantic segmentation. The 'road' class is separated to create a binary mask, utilized in further edge and distance calculations.

c. *Edge Detection*

A Sobel operator is used on the binary mask to extract edge gradients, highlighting strong horizontal and vertical transitions. Contour detection isolates the closest road edge of interest to the ego-vehicle (system's autonomous vehicle).

d. *Object Detection*

YOLOv8x-seg is employed to detect and segment forward obstacles like vehicles, pedestrians, and barriers. Bounding boxes are filtered to give more importance to dynamic threats that are closer in the vehicle's immediate path.

e. *Distance Estimation*

In the kinematic frame of reference (ego-vehicle at bottom center), Euclidean distances are calculated with respect to the road edges as well as the detected obstacles. These spatial measurements guide safety decisions.

f. *Safety Logic*

The system designates a space as "Safe to Park" if Road edge $\geq$ 80 px ($\approx$ 1–1.5 m) and no obstacle is within 100 px vertically from center-bottom. Otherwise, the spot is considered unsafe. A reinforcement learning based logic can extend this rule-based system in future versions.

These thresholds are determined using constant rules currently, which might not be very flexible with respect to different road widths or vehicle sizes.

g. *Dynamic Parking with Bézier Curve*

Apart from autonomous parking detection, the system conducts a dynamic parking maneuver based on a real-time trajectory adjustment strategy. If direct parking is hindered, the ego-vehicle performs a controlled lane change under the guidance of a cubic Bézier curve, taking into consideration moving obstacles and kinematic feasibility.

The workflow of the proposed autonomous parking system can be summarized in the following steps:

a. *Simulation Setup*

A simulation was created specifically using Python, NumPy, and Matplotlib to visualize the ego-vehicle parking in a structured lane with dynamic obstacles. Objects are placed in front of and behind the target parking slot to simulate real-world constraints.

b. *Dynamic Obstacle Handling*

Obstacles travel at different speeds compared to the ego-vehicle. Constant recalculation of the trajectory is needed to prevent collisions and ensure accurate parking. The Bézier curve has four control points: the ego-vehicle's current position, front and rear positions of obstacles, and the destination parking lane center.

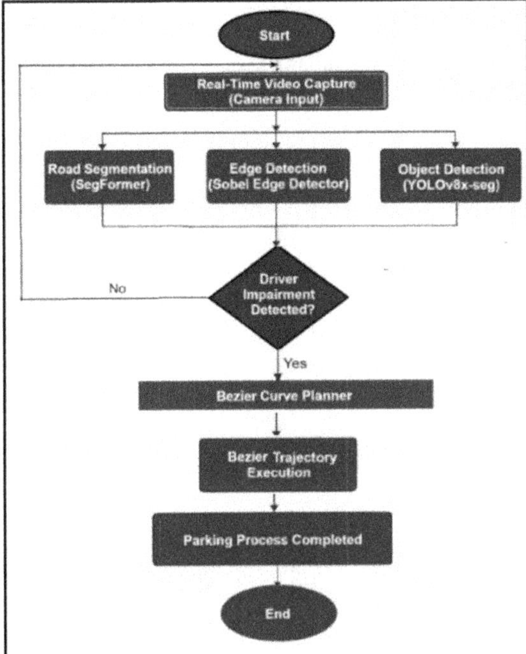

Fig. 2. Workflow Diagram of the Proposed System.

c. *Real-Time Trajectory Recalculation*

At every step, the system re-computes the Bézier path based on the latest obstacle positions. This guarantees the planned trajectory to be smooth, continuous, and collision-free. The maneuver is controlled by a simple kinematic model to ensure motion stability and avoid sudden steering acts during lane changing.

4   Implementation and Result

4.1   Dataset and Testing Conditions

For this work, a dataset created from manual compilation of 500 images of both structured and unstructured roadside environments is used. The intricacy and unpredictability of real-world driving conditions are reflected in these images, which included situations without structured parking lines or appropriate lane markings.

To assess system's performance under various road conditions, a number of video sequences have been tested in addition to still images. These sequences show both the well-defined & structured environments, with clearly defined lanes and markings, and the unstructured & unmarked ones.

While the existing dataset is made up of 500 manually gathered images, its diversity and size are still constrained. Subsequent releases will be to develop a larger, more diverse dataset with multiple weather conditions, light variations, and urban/rural road classes to provide wider generalization.

4.2 Experimental Study and Observations

In this section, various results in the form of figures, formulae & graph have been demonstrated explaining the different phases along with outputs as per the proposed system's pipeline.

a. *Feature Detection Using Edge Segmentation*
   I. Initially, edge features were extracted using a SegFormer-based semantic segmentation model to broadly detect the drivable surface (Fig. 3).
   II. Sobel edge detection was then used to further enhance boundary details such as roadside edges (Fig. 4). Sobel was selected for its effectiveness in detecting horizontal and vertical gradients with a suitable compromise between accuracy and computation for real-time performance (Fig. 5).

Observation: After combining SegFormer and Sobel, the system significantly improved in detecting complex unstructured roadside features like broken kerbs, grass edges, and muddy boundaries.

Fig. 3. Road Segmentation using SegFormer

Fig. 4. Road Segmentation after applying SegFormer + Sobel Edge Detection

b. *Object Detection Using YOLOv8x-Seg*
   I. YOLOv8x-seg was used to identify obstacles such as cars, pedestrians, animals, and other road objects (Fig. 6). Custom object classes were implemented to enable context-aware decision-making during parking.

Observations: YOLOv8x-seg showed strong segmentation even in cluttered backgrounds, and the system successfully categorized objects with high confidence scores.

Fig. 5. Highlighting the Road with Sobel Edge Detection.

Fig. 6. Object Detection on road using YOLOv8x-Seg.

c. *Integration and Real-time Video Testing*

I. The full pipeline was tested on video sequences comprising both structured and unstructured roads.

II. In the video output (Figs. 7, 8 and 9):

[i] Visual overlays displayed the road in blue and detected edges in green. Object distances were continuously presented in pixels, with real-time updates for front, side proximity (distance to road boundary) and object (like a vehicle, human, etc.).

[ii] If there was no object found in the front zone, the system displays a default high value (e.g., float('inf')), and showed it as "INF" to represent no near obstacle.

d. *Mathematical Calculations*

I. *Front Distance Calculation:* Find the minimum Euclidean distance from the ego vehicle's center to any detected obstacle in front.

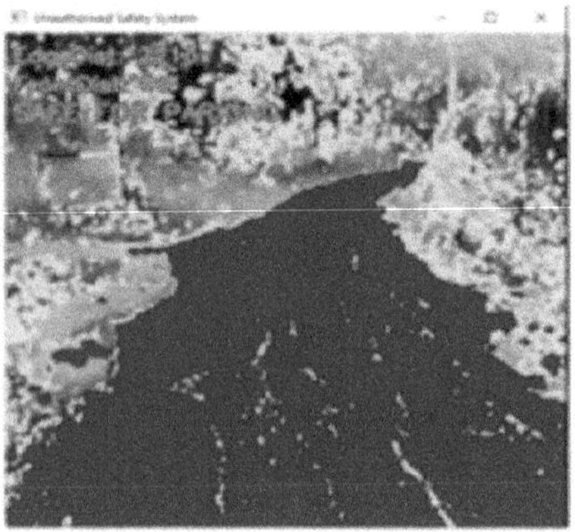

Fig. 7. Edge detection of Unstructured Road

Fig. 8. Edge & Object Detection of Unstructured Road.

[i] Mathematical Formula:

$$d = \sqrt{\left(x_{ego} - x_{object}\right)^2 + \left(y_{ego} - y_{object}\right)^2}$$

[ii] Implementation:

  During object segmentation, for each detected object pixel, the Euclidean distance to the ego center (bottom-center of the frame) was calculated. The

Fig. 9. Object Detection of Structured Road.

minimum distance was taken as the front distance. If no object is detected, a large placeholder value is used, indicating no immediate obstacle.

II. *Edge Distance Calculation:* Find the minimum distance from the ego to edge detected on the left.

   [i] Mathematical Formula:

$$d = \sqrt{(x_{ego} - x_{edge})^2 + (y_{ego} - y_{edge})^2}$$

   [ii] Implementation:

      Every point on the contour (output from Sobel edge detection) is compared, and the shortest distance is selected.

   [iii] Threshold Decision:

- A threshold was defined (based on the pixel-to-meter mapping) to decide if the vehicle is sufficiently away from the edge (typically equivalent to 1–1.5 m).
- If the distance is less than the threshold, it is deemed unsafe to park.
- If the distance is greater than the threshold and no front object is within a dangerous proximity, it is safe to initiate emergency parking.

e. *Dynamic Parking using Bézier Curve Path Planning* (Figs. 10, 11 and 12)

   I. *Smooth Transitions between Path Segments:* Cubic Bézier curves, under control of a kinematic motion model, provided for continuous curvature path segments with reduced acceleration ($\leq$0.3 m/s^2) and restricted steering divergence ($<$5°per time step), maintaining stable maneuverability.

II. *Real-Time Dynamic Control Point Tuning:* Every 200–300 ms, control points were adjusted based on LiDAR and vision sensing inputs, such that positional tracking remained within 15 cm in relation to surrounding moving obstacles.

III. *Collision Avoidance:* Dynamic safety envelopes (2.5 m buffer) maintained obstacle-free lane changes, including at speeds as high as 40 km/h, by regulating the path along kinematic feasibility.

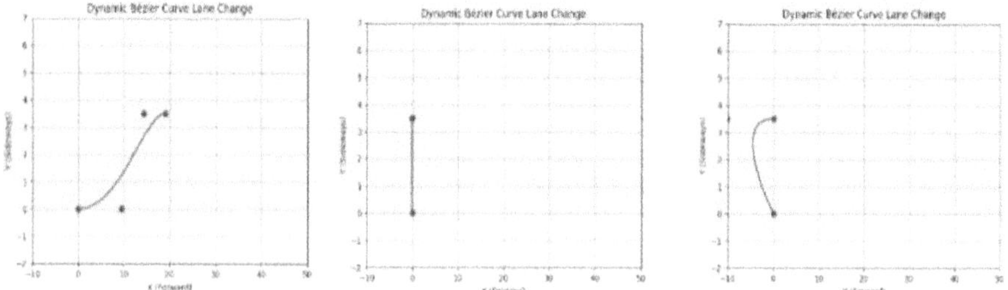

Fig. 10. Dynamic lane changing path using Bézier curve.

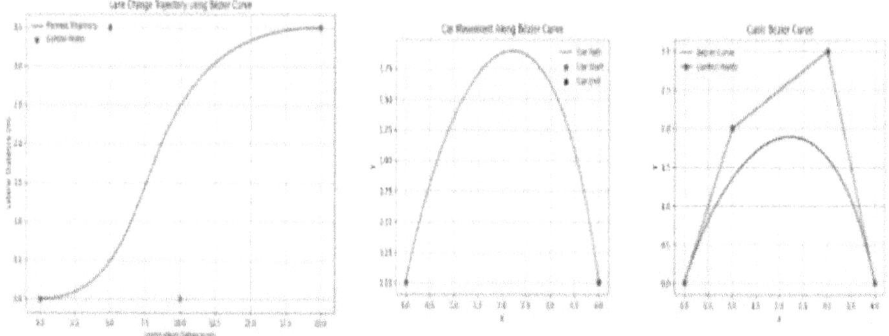

Fig. 11. Lane Change Trajectory of car along Bézier curve and cubic Bézier curve.

4.3 Discussion and Analysis

The system tested was assessed on both structured and unstructured environments like countryside roads with blurry or broken kerbs.

a. The model reliably located road borders in unstructured environments because of the synergy between Sobel-based edge enhancement and semantic segmentation, which increased its sensitivity to subtle boundary signs like broken kerbs, grassy roadside shoulders or faded lane markings.

Fig. 12. Detection of Safe parking using Bézier curve.

b. The system achieved real-time performance of 15–20 FPS on mid-range GPU hardware, showcasing its computational efficiency and real world deployability on embedded systems.

c. The system has not been compared with conventional ADAS or other autonomous parking systems yet. Future activities will involve performance comparisons with the current state-of-the-art systems to assess detection accuracy improvement, responsiveness, and safety outcomes quantitatively.

d. While simulation and image-based tests have been successful, deployment in the real world is the next priority step. The system will be implemented into hardware-in-the-loop simulations and experimented with using platforms like ROS or CARLA to understand practical feasibility.

e. The Bézier path provided smooth parking maneuvers through continuous curvature and was controlled with a kinematic model that allowed it to reduce sudden steering or acceleration transitions.

f. The system repetitively placed the car near the target lane centerline within ~ 15 s, which verifies the precision of the distance estimates and the efficiency of the safety logic for successful completion of the maneuvers.

5   Conclusion and Future Scope

The proposed work proves that the hybrid method using SegFormer and Sobel for road edge detection, YOLOv8x-Seg for segmentation of obstacles, and a kinematic model for motion planning can be efficiently used in autonomous vehicles. The system successfully detects road edges and obstacles in structured and unstructured scenarios, employing Euclidean distance to determine obstacle positions and contour analysis to detect proximity to edges, while providing smooth, stable parking maneuvers through the generation of dynamic Bézier curves.

The major findings of this work include:

a. The integration of SegFormer and Sobel effectively identified road edges in structured and unstructured settings.

b. Future research will investigate adaptive thresholding based on reinforcement learning or environment-based heuristics to enhance flexibility and generality.

c. YOLOv8x-Seg effectively detected dynamic obstacles, which was critical for making safe parking decisions.
d. The end-to-end pipeline delivered real-time performance and proved practical viability for deployment on autonomous vehicles.
e. For more accuracy in curved and high-speed cases, higher vehicle dynamics models (e.g., Ackermann steering) will be taken into account in future releases.
f. The Bézier curve-based lane-change maneuver, combined with a kinematic motion model, provided smooth, stable, and collision-free trajectory generation under dynamic conditions.

As for future scope of improvements, the following avenues are worth exploration:

a. Investigate adaptive algorithms for improved detection in low-contrast or adverse lighting conditions.
b. Implement speed modulation in addition to lateral control for full vehicle autonomy.
c. Increase object classes to enhance decision-making (e.g., dynamic road signs).
d. Test further in diverse real-world environments such as various weather or challenging urban environments.
e. Add more sophisticated vehicle motion models (e.g., kinematics) to enhance control and stability when changing lanes, as well as taking into consideration environmental variables like road curvature, weather conditions, and surface friction.
f. Machine Learning algorithms can be incorporated to predict obstacle behavior and optimize path planning in dynamic and complex traffic conditions.

References

1. Chand, V., Sabharwal, S., Carie, A., Kumar, S.A.: A study on parking space allocation and road edge detection for optimizing road traffic. In: Intelligent Cyber Physical Systems and Internet of Things, ICoICI 2022. Springer, pp. 393–403 (2023)
2. Feng, S., Chen, X., Chen, S., Lu, X.: Obstacle edge extraction technology in the parking assistant system. Int. J. Comput. Intell. Syst. **4**, 1342–1349 (2011)
3. Jain, R., Nair, J.S.: Intelligent parking space detection system using Sobel edge detection in OpenCV. Int. J. Sci. Res. (IJSR) **7**(12) (2018)
4. Trivedi, J., Devi, M.S., Dave, D.: Canny edge detection based real-time intelligent parking system. Sci. J. Silesian Univ. Technol. Ser. Transport **106**, 197–208 (2020)
5. Musabini, A., et al.: Enhanced parking perception by multi-task fisheye cross-view transformers. In: IET Conference Proceedings CP887, vol. 2024, no. 10, pp. 31–38. The Institution of Engineering and Technology, Stevenage, UK (2024)
6. Amato, G., Carrara, F., Falchi, F., Gennaro, C.: Car parking occupancy detection using smart camera networks and deep learning. In: Proc. IEEE Symp. Comput. Commun. (ISCC) (2016)
7. Ordóñez, D., Gomez, E., Avalos, H.: An architectural proposal for an automatic vacant parking detection system. In: Proc. Int. Conf. Inf. Syst. Comput. Sci. (INCISCOS) (2018)
8. Li, W., Zhou, S., Tang, Y., Zhang, X.: Where should I park?: Real-time detection of parking space occupancy. Camb. Explor. Arts Sci. 1(2) (2023)
9. Toommakorn, P., Kamsa-ard, W., Tippayawong, K.Y., Kanjanawanishkul, K., Tipdecho, T.: Mathematical modeling of the efficiency of car parking spaces along the roadside. Suranaree J. Sci. Technol. **30**(3), 1–8 (2023), Art. no. 030108

10. Zeng, D., Yu, Z., Xiong, L., Zhang, P., Fu, Z.: A unified optimal planner for autonomous parking vehicle. Control Theory Technol. **17**(4), 346–356 (2019)
11. Li, H., Pang, H., Xia, H., Huang, Y., Zeng, X.: Research on trajectory planning method based on Bézier curves for dynamic scenarios. Electronics **14**(3), 494 (2025)
12. Mahadevan, A.P.G., Annamalai, M., Ramya, S., Baskar, S., Srinivasan, K., Chandrasekaran, M.: Mathematical modeling of the efficiency of car parking spaces along the roadside. Math. Model. Eng. Probl. **11**(9), 2319–2326 (2024)
13. Shi, Z., Ou, Q., Zheng, W., Liao, R.: A driver-side parking evaluation model for roadside spaces. IEEE Sens. J. **24**(16), 26248–26259 (2024)
14. Shen, T., Hua, K., Liu, J.: Optimized public parking location modelling for green intelligent transportation system using genetic algorithms. IEEE Access **7**, 176870–176882 (2019)
15. Amato, G., Carrara, F., Falchi, F., Gennaro, C., Vairo, C.: Deep learning for decentralized parking lot occupancy detection. Expert Syst. Appl. **72**, 327–334 (2017)

Enhancing Intrusion Detection Systems with Conditional Adversarial Autoencoders for Class Imbalance Mitigation

Soumyajit Datta[(✉)] [iD], Jaysmito Mukherjee [iD], and Kousik DasGupta [iD]

Kalyani Government Engineering College, Nadia 741235, West Bengal, India
soumyajitdatta123@gmail.com

Abstract. Class imbalance is a critical challenge in intrusion detection systems, often limiting the effectiveness of classifiers in low-occurrence classes on datasets like CICIDS 2017. We propose a novel framework leveraging Conditional Adversarial Autoencoders (CAAEs) to generate synthetic features for underrepresented attack classes. This augmentation improves dataset balance, leading to better classification performance in intrusion detection systems. By formulating binary classification tasks, we evaluated the impact of CAAE-generated data using Artificial Neural Networks (ANNs). Compared to traditional feature generation techniques like SMOTE, CAAEs achieved superior performance even for minority classes with an average F1-Score of 99.38%.

Keywords: Intrusion Detection Systems · Feature Generation · Conditional Adversarial Autoencoders · CICIDS-2017

1   Introduction

Cybersecurity is an ever-evolving field, and intrusion detection systems (IDSs) play a vital role in monitoring and analyzing network traffic for malicious activities. With the increasing sophistication of cyber threats such as Distributed Denial of Service (DDoS) attacks, ransomware, and botnets, IDSs have become an essential layer of defense for modern networks. These systems can be broadly categorized into signature-based and anomaly-based detection methods. Signature-based IDSs detect known attack patterns but struggle against novel threats, while anomaly-based IDSs identify deviations from normal behavior but may suffer from high false positives.

Despite their importance, IDSs face several challenges. The growing volume and complexity of network traffic make real-time processing difficult. Additionally, distinguishing between normal and malicious activity is challenging due to encrypted traffic, evasion techniques used by attackers, and the presence of benign anomalies. Machine learning (ML) has emerged as a powerful tool to

K. Chandra Mondal et al. (Eds.): CICBA 2025, CCIS 2862, pp. 340–351, 2026.
https://doi.org/10.1007/978-3-032-17187-0_26

enhance IDS capabilities, enabling automated threat detection. However, ML-based IDS models face their own set of issues, including adversarial attacks, high computational costs, and class imbalance in training data.

Class imbalance is a well-documented problem in machine learning, affecting various domains such as cybersecurity, fraud detection, and medical diagnosis. In IDS datasets, certain types of attacks occur far less frequently than others, leading to skewed model performance where frequent attack classes are detected with high accuracy while minority classes remain underrepresented. This imbalance can result in biased models that fail to detect rare but critical threats. In other fields, class imbalance can lead to misclassification in fraud detection, where fraudulent transactions are overlooked, or in healthcare, where diseases with fewer cases remain undiagnosed. Addressing class imbalance is crucial to ensuring that ML models are robust, fair, and capable of generalizing to real-world scenarios.

The rest of the paper is structured as follows:

- Section 2 gives a background of previous work done in this field.
- Section 3 provides an overview of the dataset and the feature selection process.
- Section 4 describes our proposed CAAE-based approach for class imbalance mitigation.
- Section 5 outlines the experimental setup and evaluation strategy.
- Section 6 presents the results and performance comparisons.
- Section 7 discusses the potential limitations of our paper.
- Section 8 concludes the paper with a discussion of future directions.

2 Related Work

Several studies have utilized artificial neural networks (ANNs) and deep learning techniques for intrusion detection. In [17], a shallow network coupled with an autoencoder was proposed to improve anomaly detection, showing promising results. Similarly, a two-stage deep stacked autoencoder combined with shallow learning techniques was employed in [18], achieving high detection accuracy and zero false positives. Another work [19] proposed a rule-based deep neural network for detecting novel attacks, emphasizing its applicability in modern IoT systems.

Autoencoders have also been leveraged for improving IDS performance. A recent study [20] explored variational autoencoders to generate synthetic data resembling unknown attacks, demonstrating the potential of generative models in enhancing detection rates. Additionally, methods like the Conditional Variational Autoencoder (CVAE) have been applied in other domains but remain underexplored in the context of class-specific data generation for intrusion detection.

Beyond autoencoders, generative models such as GANs and adversarial training techniques have been explored for network intrusion detection. A study by [21] applied Wasserstein GANs to generate synthetic intrusion data, significantly improving detection accuracy for minority classes. Similarly, [22] proposed a hybrid approach combining reinforcement learning with generative models to enhance IDS robustness against adversarial attacks.

Another key challenge in IDS is feature selection and dimensionality reduction. A study in [23] utilized evolutionary algorithms to optimize feature selection, improving model efficiency while maintaining high detection accuracy. Additionally, [24] introduced a graph neural network-based feature extraction method that captures complex network behaviors more effectively than traditional approaches.

Despite these advancements, most existing works have not adequately addressed the issue of class imbalance in the CICIDS 2017 dataset. The underrepresentation of certain attack types limits the effectiveness of machine-learning models in detecting minority-class intrusions. Moreover, while synthetic data generation techniques have been applied to other datasets, their application in producing targeted, high-quality synthetic data for CICIDS 2017 remains a relatively unexplored area.

3 Proposed Work

3.1 Dataset

The CICIDS 2017 dataset [1], developed by the Canadian Institute for Cybersecurity, is a comprehensive benchmark for evaluating intrusion detection systems. It replicates real-world network traffic by incorporating both normal and malicious activities across various scenarios, such as Distributed Denial of Service (DDoS), Brute Force, and Botnet attacks. The dataset contains over 2.8 million records with 80 network flow features, including packet size, duration, and flow-based attributes. However, a significant challenge lies in its class imbalance. Figure 1, as certain attack types like Heartbleed, SQL Injection are severely underrepresented, which can hinder the performance of machine learning models. This imbalance makes the dataset ideal for exploring advanced feature generation techniques to improve classification performance, particularly for minority classes.

3.2 Feature Selection

To ensure the most discriminative attributes are utilized, we employed Mutual Information Classification (MIC) [2] to rank features based on their relevance to intrusion detection. We selected the top 70 features as a trade-off between model complexity and predictive power. Choosing too few features (e.g., 10 or 20) would lead to information loss, reducing the model's ability to capture complex attack patterns, as observed in prior studies [26]. Conversely, using all available features (80) resulted in overfitting and increased computational cost without significant accuracy improvements. Empirical evaluation showed that after selecting the top 70 features, additional features contributed less than a 0.5% improvement in F1-score but increased training time by 15%. Thus, 70 features provide an optimal balance, ensuring robust classification while maintaining computational efficiency.

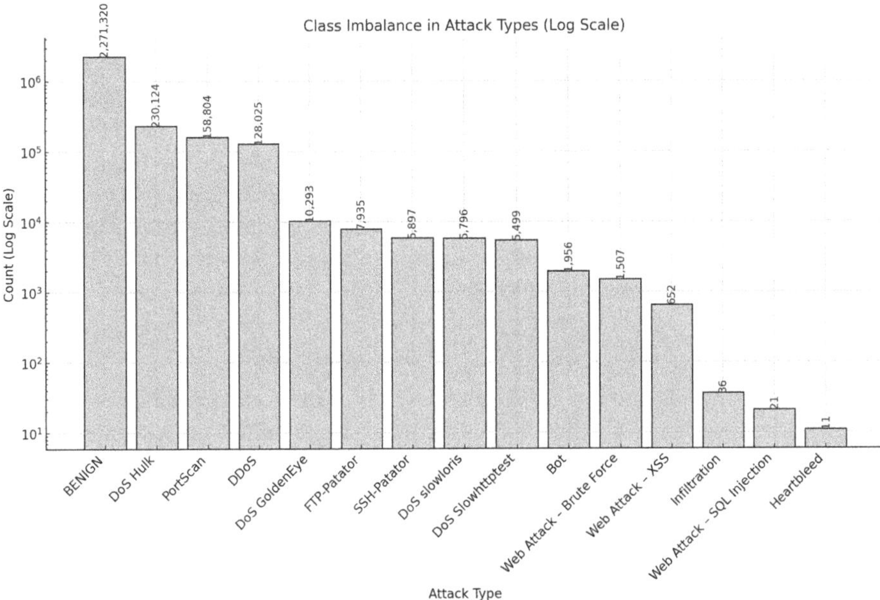

Fig. 1. A visualization of the distribution of attack types in the CICIDS 2017 dataset, highlighting the significant class imbalance where certain attack types are underrepresented

3.3   Task Formulation

We designed multiple binary classification tasks, each targeting a specific attack type versus all other classes like in [3]. This approach allowed us to evaluate the effectiveness of our feature-generation technique across diverse attack scenarios.

3.4   Baseline Model

As previous studies for classification discussed in the related work section have highlighted the strong performance of Artificial Neural Networks(ANNs) or simply neural network [4] on the CICIDS 2017 dataset, we adopted ANNs as our baseline classifier. Each ANN comprised:

- Input Layer: Accepting 70 features.
- Hidden Layers: Four fully connected layers with 128, 256, 128, and 64 neurons, respectively, utilizing ReLU activation.
- Output Layer: A single neuron with a sigmoid activation for binary classification.

The models were trained using the original dataset to establish baseline metrics.

3.5 SMOTE (Synthetic Minority Oversampling Technique)

SMOTE [5] is a popular oversampling technique designed to address the issue of class imbalance by generating synthetic samples for the minority class. Unlike random oversampling, which simply duplicates existing samples, SMOTE creates new data points by interpolating between existing samples in the feature space. This approach helps reduce overfitting and improves the diversity of the dataset.

The generation process begins by identifying a sample x_i from the minority class and one of its k -nearest neighbors x_{neighbor}. A new synthetic sample $x_{\text{synthetic}}$ is then generated as follows:

$$x_{\text{synthetic}} = x_i + \delta \cdot (x_{\text{neighbor}} - x_i) \tag{1}$$

where δ is a random number in the range $[0, 1]$. This equation ensures that the synthetic sample lies on the line segment connecting x_i and x_{neighbor}, introducing variability while maintaining consistency with the original data distribution.

The SMOTE algorithm repeats this process for each sample in the minority class until the desired class balance is achieved. The resulting augmented dataset can then be used to train machine learning models, leading to improved classification performance, particularly in detecting minority class instances. However, while SMOTE is effective in many cases, it assumes linearity between data points and does not explicitly account for the underlying data distribution, which may limit its performance in complex, nonlinear datasets. This limitation is addressed by advanced generative methods such as Conditional Adversarial Autoencoders (CAAEs).

3.6 Conditional Adversarial AutoEncoder:

The Conditional Adversarial Autoencoder (CAAE) [6] is a generative model that combines the principles of adversarial learning and autoencoders to generate high-quality synthetic data conditioned on specific labels. It extends the standard autoencoder architecture by integrating a discriminator, similar to Generative Adversarial Networks (GANs) [7], to ensure that the generated samples closely mimic real data distribution.

The architecture of a CAAE comprises three principal components: the encoder, the generator, and the discriminator. Together, they optimize a dual-objective function that ensures both data fidelity and adversarial realism.

Encoder. The encoder transforms input data $\mathbf{x} \in \mathbb{R}^n$ and its corresponding class label y into a latent space representation

$$\mathbf{z} : \mathbf{z} = E(\mathbf{x}, y) \tag{2}$$

Here, $\mathbf{z} \in \mathbb{R}^k$ is the latent representation, and $E(\cdot)$ denotes the encoding function. The explicit inclusion of y in the encoding process ensures that the latent space is class-conditional, thereby enabling the subsequent generation of class-specific features.

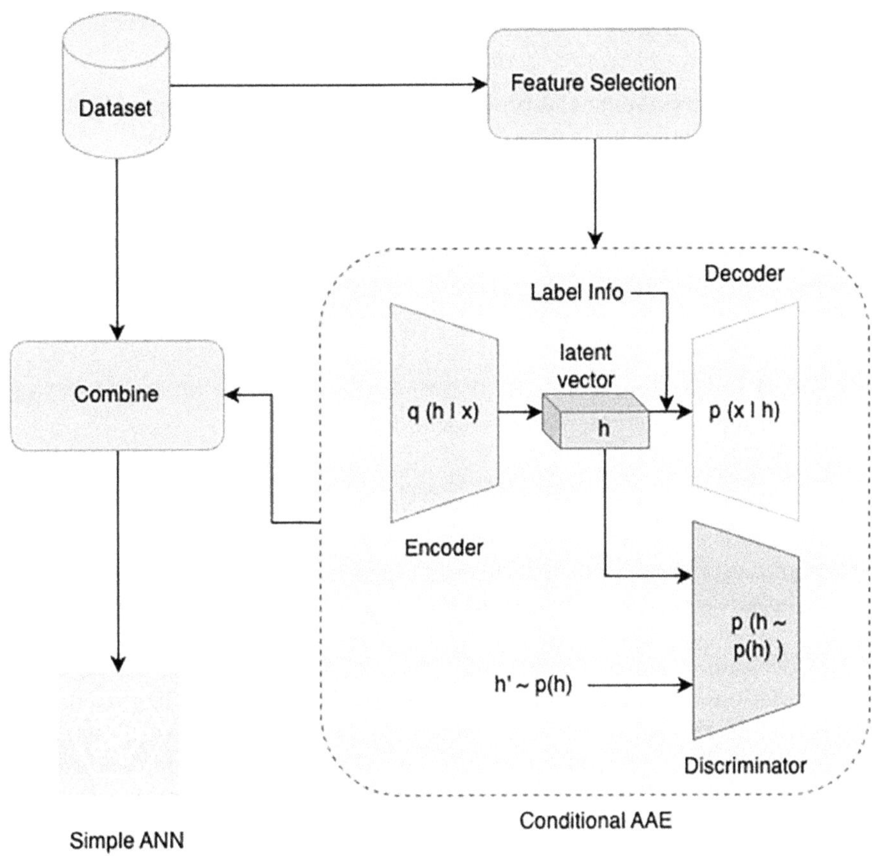

Fig. 2. Design of our synthetic generation pipeline: The proposed CAAE model consists of an encoder, generator, and discriminator, designed to generate realistic synthetic features for minority attack classes to mitigate class imbalance in intrusion detection

Generator. The generator maps the latent representation back into the data space, conditioned on the class label:

$$\hat{\mathbf{x}} = G(\mathbf{z}, y) \tag{3}$$

where $G(\cdot)$ is the generative function, and $\hat{\mathbf{x}}$ represents the reconstructed or synthesized data. The generator aims to minimize a reconstruction loss:

$$\mathcal{L}_{\text{recon}} = \|\mathbf{x} - \hat{\mathbf{x}}\|_2^2 \tag{4}$$

This loss ensures that the generated data accurately captures the intrinsic structure of the input data.

Discriminator. The discriminator distinguishes between real data samples $\mathbf{x}$ and synthetic samples $\hat{\mathbf{x}}$ by learning a probabilistic mapping:

$$p = D(\mathbf{x}, y) \tag{5}$$

where $p \in [0, 1]$ represents the probability that $\mathbf{x}$ is real (as opposed to generated). The discriminator is trained to minimize an adversarial loss:

$$\mathcal{L}_{\mathrm{adv}} = -\mathbb{E}_{\mathbf{x}, y}[\log D(\mathbf{x}, y)] - \mathbb{E}_{\hat{\mathbf{x}}, y}[\log(1 - D(\hat{\mathbf{x}}, y))] \tag{6}$$

This adversarial training compels the generator to produce samples that are indistinguishable from real data, thereby enhancing the realism of the synthetic features.

Combined Objective. The overall optimization objective of the CAAE integrates both reconstruction and adversarial losses:

$$\mathcal{L}_{\mathrm{CAAE}} = \mathcal{L}_{\mathrm{recon}} + \lambda \mathcal{L}_{\mathrm{adv}} \tag{7}$$

Here, λ in Eq. 7 is a tunable hyperparameter that balances the reconstruction fidelity and adversarial realism. This combined loss ensures that the generated data maintains structural integrity while being indistinguishable from real samples.

Our decision to adopt Conditional Adversarial Autoencoders (CAAEs) over other variations of Adversarial Autoencoders (AAEs), including Generative Adversarial Networks (GANs), is motivated by the unique requirements of class-specific data augmentation for imbalanced intrusion detection datasets like CICIDS 2017. While GANs have demonstrated impressive generative capabilities [7], they are prone to issues like mode collapse, where the generator fails to capture the diversity of the data distribution, resulting in limited variations in the generated samples [8]. This limitation is particularly problematic when addressing class imbalance, as it risks exacerbating the underrepresentation of minority classes. Other AAEs, while addressing some of GANs' limitations, often lack the explicit conditioning mechanism needed for generating class-specific features.

CAAEs, by contrast, are explicitly designed to condition both the encoding and generation processes on class labels, ensuring that the synthetic data aligns with the distinct characteristics of each class [9]. Moreover, the integration of a reconstruction objective in CAAEs provides an additional layer of supervision, preserving the structural fidelity of the generated features, a property that GANs and other AAEs often lack [10]. This dual-objective framework makes CAAEs particularly well-suited for generating diverse, realistic, and class-specific samples, enabling more balanced and effective training of machine learning models. These attributes make CAAEs an ideal choice for addressing the challenges of class imbalance in intrusion detection task

Our CAAE was trained on up to 10,000 samples from the majority class, supplemented by all available samples from the minority class (Fig. 2). This targeted approach enriched the feature space of underrepresented classes, making the data more suitable for classification.

Table 1. Performance Comparison Across Different Attacks (Accuracy and F1-score)

Attack Name	A_{Base}	A_{SMOTE}	A_{CAAE}	$F1_{\text{Base}}$	$F1_{\text{SMOTE}}$	$F1_{\text{CAAE}}$
BENIGN	0.9802	0.9840	**0.9909**	0.9876	0.9783	**0.9877**
Bot	0.9996	0.9957	**0.9998**	0.5330	0.9469	**0.9973**
DDoS	0.9991	0.9989	**0.9996**	0.9903	0.9910	**0.9969**
DoS GoldenEye	0.9998	0.9996	**0.9999**	0.9716	0.9946	**0.9982**
DoS Hulk	0.9926	0.9977	**0.9978**	0.9529	0.9849	**0.9858**
DoS Slowhttptest	0.9997	0.9994	**0.9998**	0.9232	0.9917	**0.9971**
DoS Slowloris	0.9998	0.9993	**0.9998**	0.9495	0.9905	**0.9977**
FTP-Patator	0.9999	0.9998	**1.0000**	0.9885	0.9972	**0.9996**
Heartbleed	**1.0000**	**1.0000**	**1.0000**	0.8000	**1.0000**	**1.0000**
Infiltration	**1.0000**	0.9997	**1.0000**	0.0000	0.9955	**1.0000**
PortScan	0.9883	0.9944	**0.9945**	0.9057	0.9586	**0.9587**
SSH-Patator	**0.9996**	0.9740	**0.9996**	0.8973	0.7474	**0.9943**
Web Attack Brute Force	0.9995	0.9710	**0.9998**	0.0919	0.6044	**0.9969**
Web Attack SQL Injection	**1.0000**	0.9832	**1.0000**	0.0000	0.7183	**0.9999**
Web Attack XSS	0.9998	0.9725	**1.0000**	0.0000	0.6569	**0.9985**

4 Results and Discussion

We trained 14 separate ANNs (1 for each class) using datasets augmented with:

- Original data (baseline).
- Original data + SMOTE generated data for minority classes
- Original data + CAAE generated data for minority classes

The classification results for the binary tasks are summarized in Table 1 and Table 2. Performance was measured using standard metrics, including Accuracy(8), Precision(9), Recall(10), and F1-Score(11).[1]

---

[1] Note: We round off the figures to up to 4 decimal places. So for values like 0.9999976, the rounded value would be 1.

Table 2. Performance Comparison Across Different Attacks (Precision and Recall)

Attack	R_{Base}	R_{SMOTE}	R_{CAAE}	P_{Base}	P_{SMOTE}	P_{CAAE}
BENIGN	**0.9808**	0.9628	0.9785	0.9944	0.9944	**0.9971**
Bot	0.3652	**0.9993**	**0.9947**	0.9856	0.8997	**0.9999**
DDoS	0.9809	**0.9987**	0.9950	**0.9998**	0.9834	0.9988
DoS GoldenEye	0.9671	0.9969	**0.9971**	0.9761	0.9922	**0.9993**
DoS Hulk	0.9118	0.9982	**0.9994**	**0.9979**	0.9720	0.9726
DoS Slowhttptest	0.9674	0.9918	**0.9968**	0.8828	0.9915	**0.9973**
DoS slowloris	0.9835	0.9885	**0.9965**	0.9177	0.9926	**0.9990**
FTP-Patator	0.9789	0.9967	**0.9998**	0.9982	0.9976	**0.9994**
Heartbleed	0.6667	**1.0000**	**1.0000**	**1.0000**	**1.0000**	1.0000
Infiltration	0.0000	0.9917	**0.9991**	0.0000	0.9994	**1.0000**
PortScan	**0.9986**	0.9973	0.9958	0.8287	0.9227	**0.9242**
SSH-Patator	0.8611	**0.9910**	0.9904	0.9367	0.5999	**0.9983**
Web Attack – Brute Force	0.0483	0.5766	**0.9938**	0.9545	0.6350	**1.0000**
Web Attack – Sql Injection	0.0000	0.5625	**0.9999**	0.0000	0.9935	**1.0000**
Web Attack – XSS	0.0000	0.6888	**0.9971**	0.0000	0.6278	**0.9999**

$$\text{Accuracy} = \frac{\text{TP} + \text{TN}}{\text{TP} + \text{TN} + \text{FP} + \text{FN}} \tag{8}$$

$$\text{Precision} = \frac{\text{TP}}{\text{TP} + \text{FP}} \tag{9}$$

$$\text{Recall} = \frac{\text{TP}}{\text{TP} + \text{FN}} \tag{10}$$

$$\text{F1-Score} = 2 \cdot \frac{\text{Precision} \cdot \text{Recall}}{\text{Precision} + \text{Recall}} \tag{11}$$

In a few baseline tasks, especially with severely underrepresented classes like SQL Injection and XSS, the classifier defaulted to predicting only the majority class, leading to a reported F1-score of zero despite accuracy being close to 100%. This behavior stems from the extreme imbalance in the evaluation set (ratios as high as 80,000:1), where minority-class examples were present but too scarce to allow meaningful precision and recall computation.

CAAE outperformed SMOTE and the baseline across all metrics consistently. The enhanced F1 score demonstrates the CAAE's ability to generate diverse and realistic samples for minority classes, leading to improved detection rates.

5   Limitations

The λ, which was a tunable hyperparameter, was fixed at 1 to balance the reconstruction and adversarial objectives. We recognize that tuning this parameter could further enhance performance and will explore this and add ablation studies in future work.

This study focused exclusively on Artificial Neural Networks (ANNs) for evaluation, following their proven effectiveness on the CICIDS-2017 dataset in existing literature. The computational cost of training CAAEs, especially on large datasets, was not profiled and remains to be done as future work. Our formulation addressed binary classification tasks; extending this approach to multi-class intrusion detection remains an important direction for future work.

While our results show consistently high F1-scores, particularly after CAAE augmentation, we did not conduct statistical significance testing to validate improvements across multiple runs, and our future work will incorporate methods such as bootstrapped confidence intervals or t-tests.

6   Conclusion

In this study, we introduced Conditional Adversarial Autoencoders (CAAEs) as a novel approach to addressing class imbalance in intrusion detection tasks, with a focus on the CICIDS 2017 dataset. By leveraging a conditioned latent space, CAAEs generated realistic and diverse synthetic features, significantly improving classification performance compared to traditional oversampling techniques.

Future work will extend this approach to other intrusion detection datasets, such as NSL-KDD [12], UNSW-NB15 [13], TON-IoT [14], and BoT-IoT [15], to evaluate the generalizability of CAAEs across diverse network environments. Real-time integration into network intrusion detection systems and computational optimization for large-scale applications will also be a focus. Furthermore, applying explainability techniques, such as SHAP [11] or LIME [16], can help uncover how generated features influence model decisions, thereby improving transparency and trust. This study lays the groundwork for leveraging generative models to address class imbalance and advance intrusion detection in real-world cybersecurity scenarios.

References

1. Sharafaldin, M., Lashkari, A.H., Ghorbani, A.A.: Toward generating a new intrusion detection dataset and intrusion traffic characterization. In: 2018 4th International Conference on Information Systems Security and Privacy (ICISSP), pp. 108–116 (2018). https://doi.org/10.5220/0006639801080116.
2. Beraha, M., Comminiello, E.F., Uncini, A., Mandic, D.: Feature selection via mutual information: new theoretical insights. arXiv preprint, arXiv:1907.07384 (2019)
3. Zhang, M.-L., Li, Y.-K., Liu, X.-Y., Geng, X.: Binary relevance for multi-label learning: an overview. Front. Comp. Sci. **12**(2), 191–202 (2018). https://doi.org/10.1007/s11704-017-7031-7
4. Rumelhart, D.E., Hinton, G.E., Williams, R.J.: Learning representations by back-propagating errors. Nature **323**, 533–536 (1986). https://doi.org/10.1038/323533a0

5. Chawla, N.V., Bowyer, K.W., Hall, L.O., Kegelmeyer, W.P.: SMOTE: synthetic minority over-sampling technique. J. Artif. Intell. Res. **16**, 321–357 (2002). https://doi.org/10.1613/jair.953

6. Zhang, Z., Song, Y., Qi, H.: Age progression/regression by conditional adversarial autoencoder. In: Proceedings of the IEEE Conference on Computer Vision and Pattern Recognition (CVPR), pp. 5810–5818 (2017)

7. Goodfellow, I., et al.: Generative adversarial networks. In: Advances in Neural Information Processing Systems (NeurIPS) (2014)

8. Salimans, T., et al.: Improved techniques for training GANs. In: Advances in Neural Information Processing Systems (NeurIPS) (2016)

9. Makhzani, A., et al.: Adversarial autoencoders. In: International Conference on Learning Representations (ICLR) (2016)

10. Mirza, M., Osindero, S.: Conditional Generative Adversarial Nets. arXiv preprint arXiv:1411.1784 (2014)

11. Lundberg, S.M., Lee, S.I.: A unified approach to interpreting model predictions. Adv. Neural. Inf. Process. Syst. **30**, 4765–4774 (2017)

12. Tavallaee, M., Bagheri, E., Lu, W., Ghorbani, A.A.: A detailed analysis of the KDD CUP 99 data set. In: 2009 IEEE Symposium on Computational Intelligence for Security and Defense Applications, pp. 1–6 (2009)

13. Moustafa, N., Slay, J.: UNSW-NB15: a comprehensive data set for network intrusion detection systems (UNSW-NB15 network data set). In: 2015 Military Communications and Information Systems Conference (MilCIS), pp. 1–6 (2015)

14. Ferrag, M.A., Shu, L., Derhab, A., Mukherjee, M.: TON_IoT telemetry datasets for the research of heterogeneous IoT attacks. Electronics **9**(2), 1–23 (2020)

15. Koroniotis, N., Moustafa, N., Sitnikova, E., Slay, J.: Towards the development of realistic botnet dataset in the Internet of Things for network forensic analytics: Bot-IoT dataset. Futur. Gener. Comput. Syst. **100**, 779–796 (2019)

16. Ribeiro, M.T., Singh, S., Guestrin, C.: Why should I trust you? Explaining the predictions of any classifier. In: Proceedings of the 22nd ACM SIGKDD International Conference on Knowledge Discovery and Data Mining, pp. 1135–1144 (2016)

17. Patel, T., Sharma, A., Kumar, R.: An intrusion detection model for CICIDS-2017 dataset using machine learning algorithms. In: Proceedings of International Conference on Machine Learning Big Data, Cloud Parallel Computing, pp. 1–8. IEEE Xplore (2023)

18. Chawla, A.: Two-stage deep stacked autoencoder with shallow learning for network intrusion detection system. In: Proceedings of IEEE Conference on Secure Computing Applications, pp. 88–95. Springer, Heidelberg (2022)

19. Arafah, M., et al.: Anomaly-based network intrusion detection using AE-WGAN hybrid model. Appl. Soft Comput. (2025)

20. Yu, L., Xu, L., Jiang, X.: An effective method for detecting unknown types of attacks based on log-cosh variational autoencoder. Appl. Sci. **13**(22), 12492 (2023)

21. Shahriar, M.H., Haque, N.I., Rahman, M.A., Alonso Jr, M.: G-IDS: generative adversarial networks assisted intrusion detection system (2020). arXiv preprint arXiv:2006.00676

22. Park, C., Lee, J., Kim, Y., Hong, D.: An enhanced AI-based network intrusion detection system using generative adversarial networks. IEEE Access (2022)

23. Kamalov, F., Moussa, S., Zgheib, R., Mashaal, O.: Feature selection for intrusion detection systems (2021). arXiv preprint arXiv:2106.14941

24. Lo, W.W., Layeghy, S., Sarhan, M., Gallagher, M., Portmann, M.: E-GraphSAGE: a graph neural network based intrusion detection system for IoT. IEEE/IFIP NOMS (2022)

25. Sharafaldin, M., Lashkari, A.H., Ghorbani, A.A.: Toward generating a new intrusion detection dataset and intrusion traffic characterization. In: Proceedings of 4th International Conference on Information Systems Security and Privacy (ICISSP) (2018)
26. Arreche, O., Guntur, T., Abdallah, M.: XAI-based feature selection for improved network intrusion detection systems. arXiv preprint (2024)

A Data Hiding Method to Secure and Authenticate Large Bengali Text by Concealing English Secret Text

Sakhi Bandyopadhyay, Subhadip Mukherjee, Sunita Sarkar[✉],
and Somnath Mukhopadhyay

Department of Computer Science and Engineering, Assam University, Silchar 788011,
India
sarkarsunita2601@gmail.com

Abstract. Data hiding is the science and art of securing multimedia files such as audio, text, video, etc., which cannot be predicted by human eyes. However, because a text file lacks redundant data, using text as a cover medium is much more challenging than using other available multimedia files. In order to avoid detection and ensure secret communication, text steganography is essential for discretely conveying information by enclosing it in harmless language. Situations requiring privacy, security through obscurity, and evading censorship without drawing suspicion give rise to this exigency. In this paper, a data hiding method is proposed to secure and authenticate by hiding English secret text within a large Bengali text. The Bengali transliteration and reflexive nature of English alphabets are used to hide the secret information. This data hiding approach is lossless, i.e., it can extract 100% of concealed secret information. With the cover text selected from various sources, like Bengali novels, daily newspapers, and stories, our suggested approach shows satisfactory experimental outcomes.

Keywords: Text Steganography · Large Text Authentication · Data Hiding · Text Summarization · Bengali Transliteration

1 Introduction

Large volumes of textual material, from historical records and literary masterpieces to modern digital content, are produced by the Bengali language's rich literary and cultural legacy. As of 2025, Bengali is the fifth most spoken native language and the seventh most spoken language globally, with approximately 242 million native speakers and an additional 43 million second language speakers. Advanced natural language processing (NLP) techniques that can manage the intricacies of the Bengali script and grammar are needed for processing and evaluating this material [4]. Layers of complexity are added by elements such as compound characters, different dialects, and the language's historical development [1]. Ensuring the authenticity and integrity of huge Bengali text documents is essential when it comes to Bengali text authentication, particularly in

K. Chandra Mondal et al. (Eds.): CICBA 2025, CCIS 2862, pp. 352–361, 2026.
https://doi.org/10.1007/978-3-032-17187-0_27

settings like digital archives, academic papers, and legal documents. Bengali and English are commonly used and of great importance as a means of communication among people who use it for their daily lives. It has not only been commonly used as a form of communication language but also recognized by many people across the globe [6]. So, when someone uses it for knowledge sharing, it comes in a position to make it accessible only to the right people. Following the rapid development of the Internet and the proliferation of electronic services, digital publishing has become an important subject, and offices (e.g. agencies and publishers) tend to be paperless in the next generation of organizations. There are currently numerous studies underway to implement and coordinate ideas such as ecommerce, e-government, and online libraries [10, 11, 17]. Digital publishing has many advantages, but it does have some fundamental challenges, such as the unauthorized use of any content, the manipulation of data and the dissemination of such information [5, 13].

Data hiding is a strategy that makes it difficult for unauthorized parties to find or access sensitive information by hiding it in a non-sensitive multimedia [2, 12]. This technique is employed to prevent sensitive data from being stolen or intercepted. Data hiding using text as cover media or text steganographyis required to shield text from online dangers and illegal access. By hiding sensitive information inside non-secret text, it guarantees secure communication. In the current digital era, where data security and privacy are top priorities, this method is essential. It preserves the privacy of important data and aids in preventing data breaches [14]. In this research, we are developing a new algorithm to hide English secret text inside large Bengali text to secure and authenticate large Bengali writings.

In this research, we have developed a new algorithm to hide English secret text inside large Bengali text to secure and authenticate large Bengali writings. This research will help in maintaining integrity of information in such a way that information transmitted in a secret manner would indeed be indistinguishable from white noise and there will be no signs of its presence, even though the message is suspected by the potential intruder. Our objective is to develop data hiding method for authentication and copyright protection of large Bengali texts.

Section organization: literature review is illustrated in Sect. 2. Text hiding and extraction methods are explained in Sect. 3. Results and conclusions are in Sect. 4 and Sect. 5, respectively.

2   Literature Review

Both plain texts and Web page texts can be encrypted using text-based steganography techniques. It is equally possible to broadcast messages with and without concealed information on the Web (for example, HTML codes and hashtags in social networks). It indicates that the steganography method in place is very secure and that the reader of a webpage is unable to decipher the hidden information that has been sent. One can use a variety of techniques, including blank space, feature repetition, and element order on Web pages, to conceal content.

These techniques use the features of Web pages in the code or content to conceal the secret message [20]. To investigate the viability of cross-modal steganography, [15] suggest a unique text steganography. The language model, message extractor, image encoder, and message encoder networks that make up the suggested system produce stego texts that are semantically coherent with the input reference image. Additionally, because these heuristic methods hide information by creating a mapping between candidate tokens and secret text, existing generative data hiding, where text is used as cover media, techniques are susceptible to text attacks by substituting the corresponding synonyms. In [19], the authors investigated LLM-Stega, a black-box generative text steganographic technique based on massive language model user interfaces. LLM-Stega's primary objective is to leverage LLM user interfaces to provide safe, secret communication between Alice (sender) and Bob (receiver). In particular, in order to implant secret messages, firstly create a set of keywords and a new encrypted steganographic mapping. Additionally, to ensure precise secret message extraction and rich semantics of generated stego texts, reject sampling by an optimization algorithm. In order to address the issues of low capacity and invisibility in text steganography, [18] suggests the Color and Spacing Normalization stego (CSNTSteg) paradigm. Regardless text color, CSNTSteg resolves the problem of color differences between the stego and cover texts. CSNTSteg works by standardizing the RGB coding as well as the spacing of characters in cover and stego texts. In [3], a unique text steganography based on extended readable text generation to address the aforementioned problems. It first chooses the stego-text subject based on the communication circumstances between both parties. In order to produce a lengthy, readable stego-text that adheres to the topic with semantic coherency, the plug and play language model (PPLM) is then investigated. Some other important research works are illustrated in [7–9,16].

3   Proposed Methodology

A data hiding method is proposed to secure and authenticate large Bengali text by hiding English secret text. The Bengali transliteration and reflection symmetry of English alphabets are used to embed the secret information. In the embedding, the secret text S_{text} is hidden within a cover Bengali text C_{Ben} and produces a stego Bengali text S_{Ben}. In extraction, the secret text S_{text} is retrieved from the stego Bengali text S_{Ben}. In Subsect. 3.1 and Subsect. 3.2, the hiding and extraction methods are described, respectively. The fundamental concept of the proposed text steganographic approach is depicted in Fig. 1. Some examples of vertical and horizontal reflections are shown in Fig. 2.

In Table 1 and Table 2, the characters of the cover text are categorized in to groups based on bisection of the letters along horizontal and vertical axes. In Table 3, which is composed of Table 1 and Table 2, four final groups VH1, VH2, VH3 and VH4 are constructed with corresponding 2 bits encoding for hiding 2 bits of S_{text} within the cover text. The S_{text} is converted to binary using the 6 bits encoding rules illustrated in Table 4. In Table 4, the key 27 represents the space character whose corresponding binary coding is 011011.

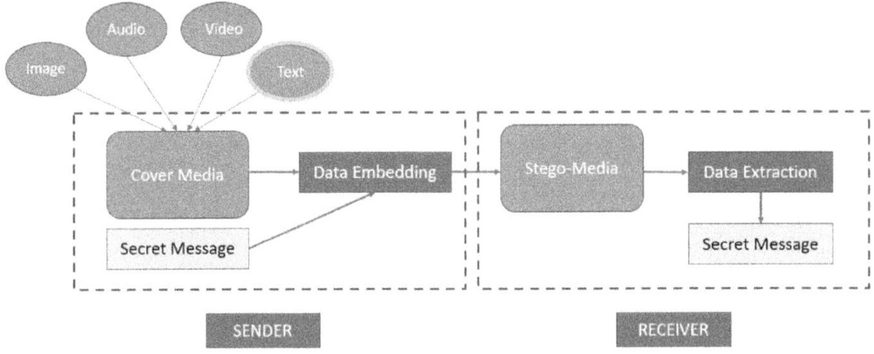

Fig. 1. Block diagram of data hiding where text is used as cover media.

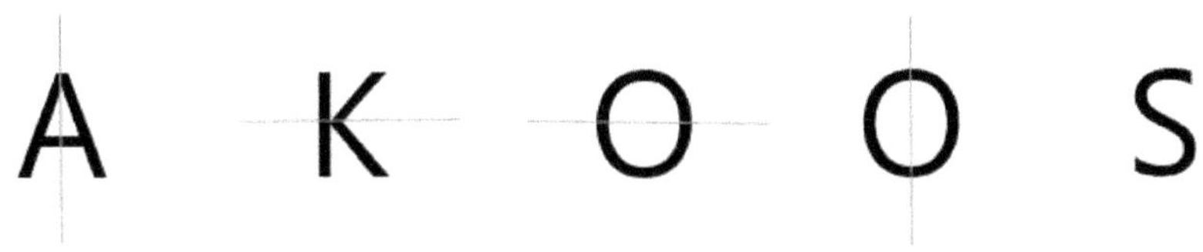

Fig. 2. Example of vertical and horizontal reflections.

3.1 Text Hiding Procedure

The secret information hiding strategy is described below.

Step 1: Input the cover text C_{Ben} and secret text S_{text}.

Step 2: Convert the cover Bengali text C_{Ben} in equivalent English text C_{Eng} by Bengali transliteration to English.

Step 3: Convert the secret data S_{text} in upper case and generate equivalent secret bitstream M_B using Table 4.

Step 4: Now, divide the total bitstream M_B in the groups of two bits, where g_i represents the ith group.

Step 5: For the first group g_1, select the K of the first sentence and convert it to binary according to Table 3 as K_b, where K is the first character of the first word of that sentence. Now check, if $K_b = g_1$ then keep the entire sentence and goto step 5. If $K_b \neq g_1$, then select the K of the next sentence and check for K_b is equal to g_1 or not. Do this until a match found and whenever $K_b = g_1$, keep that sentence and goto the next step.

Step 6: Now select the second secret group g_2 and find the K of the next sentence. Perform the same logic $K_b = g_2$ to decide whether a sentence is to be kept or deleted. Whenever a sentence satisfies the condition $K_b = g_2$, keep the sentence and goto the next step, otherwise delete the current sentence and select the next sentence until $K_b = g_2$.

Table 1. Alphabet grouping according to reflexive nature by performing bisection of the alphabets along horizontal axis.

Group	Description	Group Alphabets
h1	*reflexive nature on horizontal axis* not followed	Z, A, U, G, J, L, M, Y, P, Q, S, R, T, F, V, W, N
h2	*reflexive nature on horizontal axis* followed	E, C, X, B, O, I, K, H, D

Table 2. Alphabet grouping according to reflexive nature by performing bisection of the alphabets along vertical axis.

Group	Description	Group Alphabets
v1	*reflexive nature on vertical axis* not followed	S, C, D, Q, F, G, P, L, K, N, J, E, R, Z, B
v2	*reflexive nature on vertical axis* followed	T, H, O, M, I, A, V, U, Y, X, W

Table 3. Alphabet grouping according to reflexive nature on both vertical and horizontal axes.

Group ID	Group name	Letters in Group	Bits to be hidden
VH1	reflexive nature on neither axis	J, G, R, L, N, Z, Q, F, S, P	00
VH2	reflexive nature on vertical axis	T, M, A, Y, W, V, U	01
VH3	reflexive nature on horizontal axis	C, B, D, K, E	10
VH4	reflexive nature on both axes	O, X, H, I	11

Table 4. 6 bits binary encoding and decoding of each character of the secret text.

Key	Value	Binary Bit	Key	Value	Binary Bit	Key	Value	Binary Bit
1	A	000001	10	K	001010	19	O	010011
2	B	000010	11	L	001011	20	T	010100
3	C	000011	12	M	001100	21	V	010101
4	D	000100	13	I	001101	22	W	010110
5	F	000101	14	N	001110	23	X	010111
6	G	000110	15	P	001111	24	Y	011000
7	E	000111	16	Q	010000	25	U	011001
8	H	001000	17	R	010001	26	Z	011010
9	J	001001	18	S	010010	27		011011

Step 7: For rest of the groups perform step 4 and step 5 repeatedly until all the secret groups are hidden.

Step 8: When the set of the secret groups becomes empty i.e., all the secret bits successfully hidden, generate the summarized English text with Bengali pronunciation as the stego English text S_{Eng}.

Step 9: Now convert S_{Eng} into equivalent stego Bengali text with Bengali pronunciation S_{Ben}.

Step 10: Stego Bengali text S_{Ben} generated.

3.2   Text Extraction Procedure

The secret extraction is described below:

Step 1: Input the Stego Bengali text S_{Ben}.
Step 2: Generate the equivalent stego text in English S_{Eng} by Bengali transliteration.
Step 3: Fetch the first letter of the first word of each sentence and generate a string of characters E.
Step 4: Convert the strings E into equivalent bitstream E_b according to Table 3.
Step 5: Convert the bitstream E_b to equivalent text E_{text} using Table 4.
Step 6: The E_{text} is the extracted secret text at receiver end.

4   Experimental Results

We have used python 3.13 and Jupyter Notebook 7.2.2 to implement our proposed English text inside large Bengali text data hiding method. With the cover text selected from various sources, like Bengali novels, daily newspapers, and stories, and our suggested approach shows a satisfactory experimental outcomes. This data hiding approach is lossless i.e., it can extract 100% of concealed secret information. The Bengali text shown in Fig. 3 is used as a cover text[1]. Using the Bengali transliteration the English cover text is generated which is shown in Fig. 4. After that, the stego English text is produced in the form of summarized English text by hiding the secret English text "SB" (see Fig. 5). The distribution of alphabets in each group of VH1, VH2, VH3 and VH4 of Table 4 are displayed in Fig. 7. Finally, the stego English text is converted to stego Bengali text shown in Fig. 6.

The secret text "SB" is converted to binary stream 010010000010 using Table 4. Now, the groups of two bits are $g_1 = 01$, $g_2 = 00$, $g_3 = 10$, $g_4 = 00$, $g_5 = 00$, $g_6 = 10$ to be hidden within the C_{Eng}. Now, $g_1 = 01$ is to be hidden first. For the first sentence, the value of $K =' P'$ i.e., $K_b = 00$ according to Table 3 and $K_b \neq g_1$. So, this sentence is deleted. For the second sentence, $K =' A'$ i.e., $K_b = 01$ according to Table 3 and $g_1 = K_b$. So, this sentence is kept. Now, $g_2 = 00$ is to be hidden next. For the third sentence, $K =' P'$ i.e., $K_b = 00$ and $g_2 = K_b$. So, this sentence is kept. In this way, all the secret groups are hidden within the secret text and produce the stego English text as shown in Fig. 5. Finally, stego Bengali text is generated as shown in Fig. 6. At the extraction end, stego Bengali text converted to stego English text and then from each sentence, the first letter of the first word is extracted. This forms the string "$APERNB$" which give the bitstream 010010000010 using Table 3. By grouping this bitstream of 6 bits and utilizing Table 4, the secret text "SB" is extracted.

---

[1] https://tagoreweb.in/Stories/galpoguchchho-84/denapaona-464(accessed   on   14 February, 2025).

পাঁচ ছেলের পর যখন এক কন্যা জন্মিল তখন বাপমায়ে অনেক আদর করিয়া তাহার নাম রাখিল নিরুপমা। এ গোষ্ঠীতে এমন শৌখিন নাম ইতিপূর্বে কখনো শোনা যায় নাই। প্রায় ঠাকুরদেবতার নামই প্রচলিত ছিল, গণেশ, কার্তিক, পার্বতী, তাহার উদাহরণ। এখন নিরুপমার বিবাহের প্রস্তাব চলিতেছে। তাহার পিতা রামসুন্দর মিত্র অনেক খোঁজ করেন কিন্তু পাত্র কিছুতেই মনের মতন হয় না। অবশেষে মস্ত এক রায়বাহাদুরের ঘরের একমাত্র ছেলেকে সন্ধান করিয়া বাহির করিয়াছেন। উক্ত রায়বাহাদুরের পৈতৃক বিষয়-আশয় যদিও অনেক হ্রাস হইয়া আসিয়াছে কিন্তু বনেদি ঘর বটে। বরপক্ষ হইতে দশ হাজার টাকা পণ এবং বহুল দানসামগ্রী চাহিয়া বসিল। রামসুন্দর কিছুমাত্র বিবেচনা না করিয়া তাহাতেই সম্মত হইলেন; এমন পাত্র কোনোমতে হাতছাড়া করা যায় না। কিছুতেই টাকার জোগাড় আর হয় না। বাঁধা দিয়া, বিক্রয় করিয়া, অনেক চেষ্টাতেও হাজার ছয়-সাত বাকি রহিল। এ দিকে বিবাহের দিন নিকট হইয়া আসিয়াছে। অবশেষে বিবাহের দিন উপস্থিত হইল। নিতান্ত অতিরিক্ত সুদে একজন বাকি টাকাটা ধার দিতে স্বীকার করিয়াছিল কিন্তু সময়কালে সে উপস্থিত হইল না। বিবাহসভায় একটা তুমুল গোলযোগ বাধিয়া গেল। রামসুন্দর আমাদের রায়বাহাদুরের হাতে-পায়ে ধরিয়া বলিলেন, "শুভকার্য সম্পন্ন হইয়া যাক, আমি নিশ্চয়ই টাকাটা শোধ করিয়া দিব।" রায়বাহাদুর বলিলেন, "টাকা হাতে না পাইলে বর সভাস্থ করা যাইবে না।"

Fig. 3. Block diagram of data hiding where text is used as cover media.

PANCH CHELE AR POR JOKHON EK KONNYA JONMILO TOKHN BAP MAYE ONEK ADOR KORIYA NAM RAKHILO NIRUPOMA. A GOSTHI TE EMON SOUKHIN NAM ITIPURBE KOKHONO SHONA JAINAI. PRAI THAKUR DEBOTAR NAM E PROCHOLITO CHILO. GANESH. KARTIK, PARBATI, TAHAR UDHARAN. EKHON NIRUPOMAR BIBHA ER PROSTAB CHOLITECHE. TAHAR PITA RAMSUNDAR MITRA ONEK KHONJ KOREN KINTU PATRA KICHUTAI MONER MOTON HOI NA. OBOSESHE MOSTO EK RAIBAHADURAR GHORAR EKMATRA CHELE KE SONDHAN KORIYA BAHIR KORIYACHEN. UKTO RAIBAHADUR AR POITIK BISOI-ASOI JODIO ONEK HRASH HOIYA ASIYACHE KINTU BONADI GHOR BOTE. BORPOKHO HOITE DOS HAZAR TAKA PONE EBONG BOHUL DANSAMOGRI CHAHIYA BOSILO. RAMSUNDOR KICHUMATRO BIBECHONA NA KORIYA TAHATAI SOMMOTO HOILEN; EMON PATRA KONOMOTE HATCHARA KORA JAI NA. KICHUTAI TAKAR JOGAR R HOY NA. BANDHA DIYA. BIKROINKORIYA, ONEK CHESTATAO HAZAR CHHOI-SAAT BAKI ROHILO. E DIKE BIBHAHAR DIN NIKOT HOIYA ASIYACHE. ABOSESE BIBAHER DIN UPOSTHIT HOILO. NITANTO ATIRIKTO SUDHE AKJON BAKI TAKA TA DHAR DITE SHIKAR KORIYACHILO KINTU SOMOY KALE SHE UPOSTHIT HOILO NA. BIBAHOSHOVAY AKTA TUMUL GOLJOG BADHIYA GELO. RAMSUNDOR AMADER RAYBAHADUR AR HATE-PAYE DHORIYA BOLILEN," SUDHOKARJO SOMPONNO HOIYA JAK .AMI NISCHOI TAKA TA SODH KORIYA DIBO". RAYBAHADUR BOLILEN, "TAKA HATE NA PAILE BOR SHOBHOSTHO KORA JAIBE NA".

Fig. 4. Block diagram of data hiding where text is used as cover media.

A GOSTHI TE EMON SOUKHIN NAM ITIPURBE KOKHONO SHONA JAINAI. PRAI THAKUR DEBOTAR NAM E PROCHOLITO CHILO, GANESH, KARTIK, PARBATI, TAHAR UDHARAN. EKHON NIRUPOMAR BIBHA ER PROSTAB CHOLITECHE. RAMSUNDOR KICHUMATRO BIBECHONA NA KORIYA TAHATAI SOMMOTO HOILEN; EMON PATRA KONOMOTE HATCHARA KORA JAI NA. NITANTO ATIRIKTO SUDHE AKJON BAKI TAKA TA DHAR DITE SHIKAR KORIYACHILO KINTU SOMOY KALE SHE UPOSTHIT HOILO NA. BIBAHOSHOVAY AKTA TUMUL GOLJOG BADHIYA GELO.

Fig. 5. Block diagram of data hiding where text is used as cover media.

এ গোষ্ঠীতে এমন শৌখিন নাম ইতিপূর্বে কখনো শোনা যায় নাই। প্রায় ঠাকুরদেবতার নামই প্রচলিত ছিল, গণেশ, কার্তিক, পার্বতী, তাহার উদাহরণ। এখন নিরুপমার বিবাহের প্রস্তাব চলিতেছে। রামসুন্দর কিছুমাত্র বিবেচনা না করিয়া তাহাতেই সম্মত হইলেন; এমন পাত্র কোনোমতে হাতছাড়া করা যায় না। নিতান্ত অতিরিক্ত সুদে একজন বাকি টাকাটা ধার দিতে স্বীকার করিয়াছিল কিন্তু সময়কালে সে উপস্থিত হইল না। বিবাহসভায় একটা তুমুল গোলযোগ বাধিয়া গেল।

Fig. 6. Block diagram of data hiding where text is used as cover media.

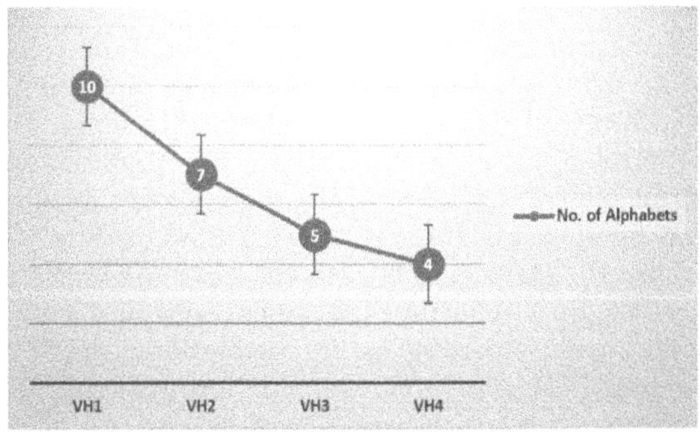

Fig. 7. The distribution of alphabets in each group of VH1, VH2, VH3 and VH4.

5 Conclusion

A data hiding method is proposed using Bengali transliteration and reflection symmetry of English alphabets to secure and authenticate large Bengali text. Here, we have used large Bengali text as cover media and small English text as secret information. This data hiding approach is lossless i.e., it can extract 100% of concealed secret information. Firstly, the large Bengali text is transliterated and the cover English text generated. Then, based on the horizontal or vertical reflexive categorization, encoding rule and proposed hiding procedure, the setgo Bengali text is generated. At the receiving end, the secret information is extracted using the proposed extraction steps. This method is useful to authenticate novels or reports by hiding the name of the writer(s). Our method can also be applied in areas such as, secure messaging with large text, digital rights management, web content protection, protection of sensitive information in industries like finance and healthcare, and research and development. One of the future challenge of the proposed research is to increase the hiding capacity. The security can also be improved in future by employing cryptographic algorithms.

References

1. Akhter, A., Acharjee, U.K., Talukder, M.A., Islam, M.M., Uddin, M.A.: A robust hybrid machine learning model for Bengali cyber bullying detection in social media. Nat. Lang. Process. J. **4**, 100027 (2023)
2. Bandyopadhyay, S., Mukherjee, S., Mukhopadhyay, S., Sarkar, S.: Parallel BFS through pennant data structure with reducer hyper-object based data hiding for 3D mesh images. Secur. Priv. **7**(5), e390 (2024)
3. Cao, Y., et al.: Generative steganography based on long readable text generation. IEEE Trans. Comput. Soc. Syst. (2022)
4. Chakraborty, S., Nayeem, M.T., Ahmad, W.U.: Simple or complex? Learning to predict readability of Bengali texts. In: Proceedings of the AAAI Conference on Artificial Intelligence, vol. 35, pp. 12621–12629 (2021)
5. Chowdhury, P., Sarkar, N., Nath, S., Sharma, U.: Analyzing the effects of transcription errors on summary generation of Bengali spoken documents. ACM Trans. Asian Low-Resour. Lang. Inf. Process. **23**(9), 1–28 (2024)
6. Dash, S.R., Guha, P., Mallick, D.K., Parida, S.: Summarizing Bengali text: an extractive approach. In: Intelligent Data Engineering and Analytics: Proceedings of the 9th International Conference on Frontiers in Intelligent Computing: Theory and Applications (FICTA 2021), pp. 133–140. Springer (2022)
7. Knöchel, M., Karius, S.: Text steganography methods and their influence in malware: A comprehensive overview and evaluation. In: Proceedings of the 2024 ACM Workshop on Information Hiding and Multimedia Security, pp. 113–124 (2024)
8. Li, Y., Zhang, R., Liu, J., Lei, Q.: A semantic controllable long text steganography framework based on LLM prompt engineering and knowledge graph. IEEE Signal Process. Lett. (2024)
9. Majeed, M.A., Sulaiman, R., Shukur, Z., Hasan, M.K.: A review on text steganography techniques. Mathematics **9**(21), 2829 (2021)
10. Mukherjee, S., Mukhopadhyay, S., Sarkar, S.: ChatGPT based image steganography (CGIS): a novel intelligent information hiding approach to achieve secure covert communication. In: 2023 First International Conference on Advances in Electrical, Electronics and Computational Intelligence (ICAEECI), pp. 1–5. IEEE (2023)
11. Mukherjee, S., Mukhopadhyay, S., Sarkar, S.: Personal social network profile authentication through image steganography. Eng. Proc. **56**(1), 129 (2023)
12. Mukherjee, S., Mukhopadhyay, S., Sarkar, S.: IoTSLE: securing IoT systems in low-light environments through finite automata, deep learning and DNA computing based image steganographic model. Internet of Things **28**, 101358 (2024)
13. Mukherjee, S., Mukhopadhyay, S., Sarkar, S.: A shell-matrix-based image steganography technique for multimedia security and covert communication. Innov. Syst. Softw. Eng. **20**(4), 653–668 (2024)
14. Mukherjee, S., Sarkar, S., Mukhopadhyay, S.: Pencil shell matrix based image steganography with elevated embedding capacity. J. Inf. Secur. Appl. **62**, 102955 (2021)
15. Peng, W., Wang, T., Qian, Z., Li, S., Zhang, X.: Cross-modal text steganography against synonym substitution-based text attack. IEEE Signal Process. Lett. **30**, 299–303 (2023)
16. Roslan, N.A., Udzir, N.I., Mahmod, R., Gutub, A.: Systematic literature review and analysis for Arabic text steganography method practically. Egypt. Inform. J. **23**(4), 177–191 (2022)

17. Roy, A., Sarkar, K., Mandal, C.K.: Bengali text classification: a new multi-class dataset and performance evaluation of machine learning and deep learning models (2023)
18. Thabit, R., Udzir, N.I., Yasin, S.M., Asmawi, A., Gutub, A.A.A.: CSNTSteg: color spacing normalization text steganography model to improve capacity and invisibility of hidden data. IEEE Access **10**, 65439–65458 (2022)
19. Wu, J., Wu, Z., Xue, Y., Wen, J., Peng, W.: Generative text steganography with large language model. In: Proceedings of the 32nd ACM International Conference on Multimedia, pp. 10345–10353 (2024)
20. Yaghobi, S.R., Sajedi, H.: Text steganography in webometrics. Int. J. Inf. Technol. **13**(2), 621–635 (2021). https://doi.org/10.1007/s41870-020-00572-z

Analysis of Lung CT Images Using VGG16 and VGG 19 Algorithms

Susmita Das[1]([⊠]) [iD], Susanta Das[2] [iD], Saurabh Pal[3] [iD], and Swanirbhar Majumder[1] [iD]

[1] Tripura University, Agartala, Tripura, India
susmitadasre@gmail.com
[2] NIT Agartala, Agartala, Tripura, India
[3] Calcutta University, Kolkata, West Bengal, India

Abstract. Lungs serve as the key organs of the human respiratory system, and any abnormalities can significantly disrupt respiratory functions. Lung cancer, known as the most lethal form of cancer, poses a serious threat to human health [1]. However, early detection greatly enhances the chances of successful treatment and improved prognosis. Deep learning techniques, have become instrumental in assisting medical professionals by automating Lung cancer detection and classification [2]. Although we have multiple medical imaging techniques—such as X-rays, Whole Slide Imaging (WSI), CT scans, and MRI—in our study, we have utilized lung CT images to comprehensively examine the efficiency of deep learning systems in the diagnosis and classification of pulmonary cancer. We have implemented VGG16 and VGG19 algorithms on IQ-OTH/NCCD Database for detection of lung cancer and obtained accuracy of 94.66 and 95.14 which are better than Simple CNN and Inception V3 earlier implemented on the same dataset in our previous research work [2].

Keywords: Deep learning algorithms · CT image · lung dataset · lung cancer

1 Introduction

Lung is the vibrant organ which performs air exchange amid the exterior atmosphere and blood. Therefore, lung diseases may lead to death if left untreated. Lung abnormalities in human beings can be further categorized as a) Infectious diseases b) Pneumonia c) Tuberculosis d) Lung cancer. Lung Cancer is a deadly disease and proper treatment is required to cure this disease. Worldwide, cancer is considered as one of the primary causes of mortality, according to WHO approximately 10 million people died in the year 2020 [1]. In Lung cancer there are unregulated divisions of abnormal cells in lungs of human body. After enlargement, the abnormal cells grow in tumours and therefore affect with the natural functioning of lungs. In studies, we have found that there are several reasons for lung cancer, smoking is considered as one of the common causes, as because the patients breath in harmful substances from cigarettes, etc. In pulmonary cancer, patients may have lung nodules or masses, and these lung masses may be benign or malignant. In occasions of benign cases, lung masses may noy not grow rapidly and are not life

K. Chandra Mondal et al. (Eds.): CICBA 2025, CCIS 2862, pp. 362–373, 2026.
https://doi.org/10.1007/978-3-032-17187-0_28

threatening. But, in cases of malignant masses, cells grow aggressively and spread to other organs of human body. Supervision and detection of pulmonary cancer is mainly thought-provoking. In recent studies, we have seen that 10-year comparative survival rate may increase by 20% through yearly screening with low dose computed tomography during initial phases of cancer. In other words, we can say that early detection can reduce mortality rate and therefore, increase rate of existence [3]. Hence, in order to support radiologists, recently several computer-aided diagnostic structures are developed for the detection of malignant lung cancer. One of the widely used non-invasive imaging technology in radiology is Computed Tomography (CT) and with this technology detailed images of vital organs, Muscular tissues, Arteries and veins and bones. CT scans are the most common modality used for lung cancer screening. Accurate identification and clarification of lung nodules are essential for diagnosing lung cancer. However, radiologists face significant challenges in this task due to the vast number of pulmonary voxels in each CT scan and the typically small size of lung nodules. Often, the early signs of cancer—a tiny lesion no bigger than a dime—go unnoticed, and by the time it is revealed, it may already be too late for real treatment. Two categories of CAD systems for classification of lung cancer are there, one is traditional handcraft model and other one is advanced deep learning-based model. Traditional feature-based CAD models depended on intensity, texture and shape descriptors like HOG, Wavelet features and LBP after that TRAIN classifiers which are designed as SVM, Combined classifier for categorization of lung cancer. But, from studies we have found that, deep learning algorithms perform better than traditional CAD systems. With deep learning algorithms, CAD systems use CNN architectures for the classification of lung CT images. In our research work, we have applied Deep learning architectures of VGG 16 and VGG 19 models, and compared the results with our previous research works. In our previous research work we have implemented lung cancer classification with Deep learning algorithms Simple CNN, Inception V3 models [2]. We have compared the results of VGG 16 and VGG 19 deep learning algorithms with the results of Simple CNN and Inception V3 model. We have found that the accuracy of Simple CNN, Inception V3 model, VGG 16 and VGG 19 models are 93.44%, 88.83%, 94.66% and 95.14% respectively (Fig. 1).

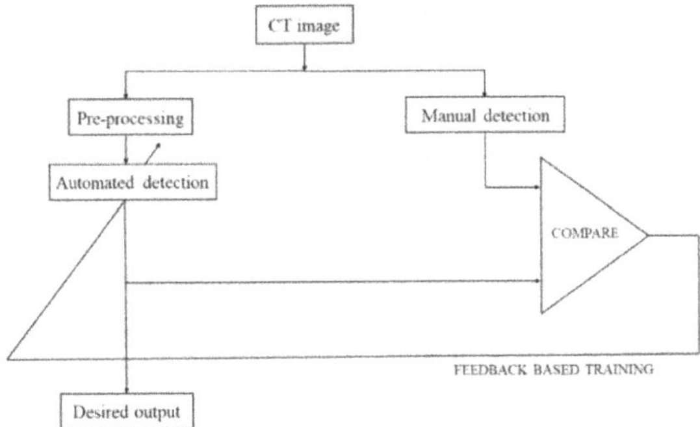

Fig. 1. Flowchart of the CNN Model

In the research paper, our contributions are as written below:

- In our research work, we have provided the architectures of Deep learning algorithms like VGG 16 and VGG 19.
- We have implemented VGG 16 and VGG 19 on IQ-OTH/NCCD dataset and obtained results.
- At last, we have compared the results with results obtained from our previous research work with deep learning models Simple CNN and Inception v3 model.

2 Literature Review

In 2025, Mohammad Q. Shatnawi et al. [4] proposed a deep learning-based system to automatically diagnose lung cancer using Chest CT-Scan Images Dataset from Kaggle. They have utilized the dataset consisting of 1000 CT scans obtained from Kaggle with several types of cancer. Their adapted (CNN) system accomplished extraordinary testing accuracy of 100%, beating prevailing systems, making an important improvement for detection, mainly concluded pioneering enrichment methods and execution of ConvNet.

In 2024, Rabia Javed et al. [5] conducted a comprehensive Systematic Literature Review (SLR) on lung cancer research, focusing on the application of deep learning techniques. The review provides an in-depth overview of methodologies, recent advancements, quality assessment criteria, and tailored deep learning approaches for improved diagnostic and prognostic outcomes of deep learning systems.

In 2023, Asghar Ali Shah et al. [6] developed Deep Ensemble 2D CNN model for detection and prediction of lung cancer with Luna 16 dataset. They have implemented three CNN models in their study CNN1, CNN2 and CNN3 and achieved accuracy of 95%.

In 2023, Abdul Rahaman Wahab Sait [7] constructed CNN model using the DenseNet-121 model for feature extraction for detection and diagnosis of lung cancer. They have tested their model on Lung-PET-CT-Dx dataset collected from healthcare centers across China. With fewer parameters Their projected model attained 98.6% accuracy and 95.8Cohen's Kappa value.

In 2023, Shalini Wankhade et al. [8] proposed a novel method for an early and accurate diagnosis called Cancer cell Detection using Hybrid Neural Network (CcDC-HNN). In order to improve accurateness of analysis of cancerous and non-cancerous tumours in LIDC-IDRI dataset is classified with 3D CNN and RNN groupings. They have achieved 90% selectivity, 87% sensitivities, and 95% accuracy by their projected advanced model.

IN 2022, Sharmila Nageswaran et al. [9] proposed a system for Lung Cancer Classification and Prediction using like ANN, KNN, and RF Machine Learning algorithms. LIDC-IDRI dataset is used classification. They have used K-means and fuzzy C-means clustering.

In 2022, Akitoshi Shimazaki et al. [10] developed a model for detecting lung cancer on chest radiographs and evaluated its performance. In addition, they have presented pixel-level sorting of nodules in test dataset with deep learning system which led to sensitivity of 0.73 and 0.13 mFPI.

In 2021, Spoorthi Rakesh et al. [11] proposed a cuckoo search optimization technique for optimization of the initial segmentation of the lung portion, and Active Contour (AC) technique has been applied to segment the nodules from the segmented lung image. Lastly, they have applied Markov Random Field (MRF) to fine tune the post processing operation. Their model achieved the best coefficient of resemblance and overlap section of the model with 0.914 and 0.584 and 0.074 and 0.089 are worst.

In 2018, Yiran Lei et. al [12] proposed lung tumour segmentation and three-dimensional reconstruction methods and tested them on lung CT images using region growing and correlation algorithms. After implementing the system, they have found that region growing algorithm construct tumours in a better way as they work with grey scale image in order to shape the tumour and on average has F-measure of 95.8%.

In 2015, Senthilkumar Krishnamurthy et al. [13] presented the three-dimensional analysis on lung CT images in their study for the detection of malignant lung nodules. They have implemented an automatic 3 D segmentation algorithm for segmentation of well-circumscribed lesion within the lung using an automated morphological region-grow segmentation. The algorithms proposed in this article achieved a sensitivity of 88%.

In 2021, Zhang X et al. [14] implemented an improved U-Net network to segment different types of lung nodules, they have applied Otsu thresholding and alpha-hull algorithm for correction of lung contours. They have used LIDC/IDRI database including 358 lung nodules and after comparing with MSE in addition to Binary cross entropy loss and estimated that Dice loss remains better for the procedure of segmentation and DSC is 0.8623.

In 2023, Hongfeng Wang et al. [15] developed lung nodule classification using novel deep learning approach known as multiple -scale residual network (MResNet) based on the ResNet architecture. They have obtained accuracy of 99.12%, sensitivity of 98.64%, specificity 97.87%, (PPV) of 99.92%, and a negative predictive value (NPV) of 97.87% on implementation of their system on LIDC-IDRI dataset.

In 2020, Xinying Zhang et al. [16] implemented an improved method of U net segmentation to solve the problem of low segmentation accuracy of lung nodule from CT images LIDC-IDRI dataset. They have combined residual structure and dense network with U-net structure in order to obtain higher performance as in comparison to architectures like FCN, SegNet, U-Net, ResNet, U-Net++. Applying their model on test dataset, they have got Dice coefficient and accuracy 92.37% and 97.68%.

In 2018, Isa Ali et al. [17] proposed and validated a reinforcement learning model based on deep artificial networks inspired by AlphaGo system. They have utilised LUNA Dataset and achieved outcomes as accuracy of 99.1% PPV 99.1%, NPV 99.2% on training dataset., But on applying test dataset the outcomes obtained are of 64.4% accuracy, 58.9% sensitivity, specificity 55.3%, PPV 54.2%, and NPV 60.0%.

In 2018, Brahim AIT SKOURT [18] proposed a lung CT image segmentation using the U-net architecture, for detection of lung cancer using LIDC/IDRI dataset. They have used U-net architecture model for segmentation of Pulmonary parenchyma and obtained Dice-coefficient index of 0.9502. Their Segmentation model can be used in vast area of medical image application as because the system is uniform.

In 2021, Hamdalla F.Kareem et al. [19] proposed a computer system for detection and classification of lung cancer in three classes normal, benign and malignant lung cancer with IQ-OTH/NCCD lung cancer dataset. After applying image enrichment, they have segmented and extracted features and classified the images with support vector machine (SVM) and achieved accuracy of 89.8876%.

In 2021, Meraj Begum et al. [20] developed a system for lung cancer detection and classification of using U-Net Convolutional Neural Network for nodule segmentation. They have employed three datasets containing annotated nodules for the purpose of segmentation of CT images and classification of cancer/non-cancer labels. The sensitivity achieved by the nodule detection system was 65% with the two stage neural networks vs 51–81.3% with performance of radiologists. Despite the false positive rate is much higher than the neural networks which is at 6.78 false positives per case with the neural networks vs 0.33–1.39 false positives per case with radiologists. Despite the large number of false positives rate, the research provided improved cancer prediction system.

3 Methodology

3.1 Dataset Used: The IQ-OTH/NCCD Database

In the dataset IQ-OTH/NCCD, there are 2056 pulmonary CT images which are categorized open-source pulmonary CT images obtained Kaggle. Helped us a lot in training our CNN model. The cases are categorised into three classes: normal, benign, and malignant. There are CT images of 1425 benign and malignant lung masses and 631 normal lungs.

Artificial Intelligence developed by learning from training database can take decisions similar to humans. The flow of the process that takes place in the model is shown in Fig. 2. The initial phase in this flow chart is of the CT images that can involve enhancement of the image and its smoothening.

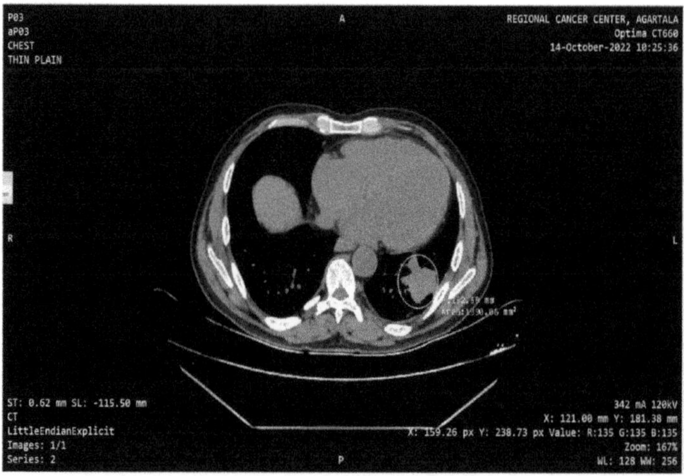

Fig. 2. Lung CT image (Abnormal)

The pre-processing step also identifies the region of interest or ROI in the images though a process of passing the images through multiple filters which is shown in Fig. 2.

so, we have used raw dicom images converted into png format to train and test the model. The process followed inside the later stages of the model is shown in Fig. 3.

Before training the model, the image dataset is split into training and testing sets. In our model 80% of the database images are chosen for training the model and 20% of them are used for testing. The selection of the images is done in random manner. Once the model is trained, the tumor is classified as either cancerous or non-cancerous.

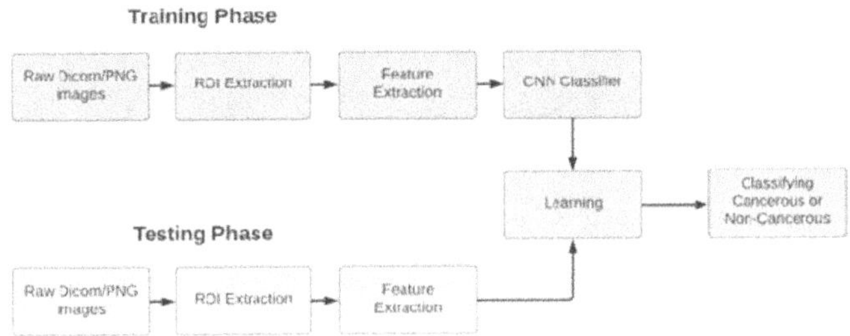

Fig. 3. Process of training and testing a CNN model

Figure 3 shows the process that is done while training and testing the CNN model. In the figure it mentions the step of ROI extraction but in our model the dataset was not preprocessed so there was no step of ROI extraction, still the model made prediction with quite high accuracy. If the model was provided with prepossessed dataset the accuracy of the model could have been much better in all architectures tried in our research work.

4 The CNN Architectures

The Convolutional Neural Network Architectures that were used in the research work are VGG16, VGG19.

4.1 VGG 16 CNN Architecture (16 Weight Layers)

VGG 16 architecture consists of 16 weight layers, thirteen convolutional layers and 3 fully connected dense layers. The complete architecture has five MaxPooling layers, totaling 21 layers. The model has an input image size of 224*244 with 3 color channels. The first block contains 64 filters, the second block contains 128, the third block contains 256, the fourth and fifth each contain 512 filters (Fig. 4).

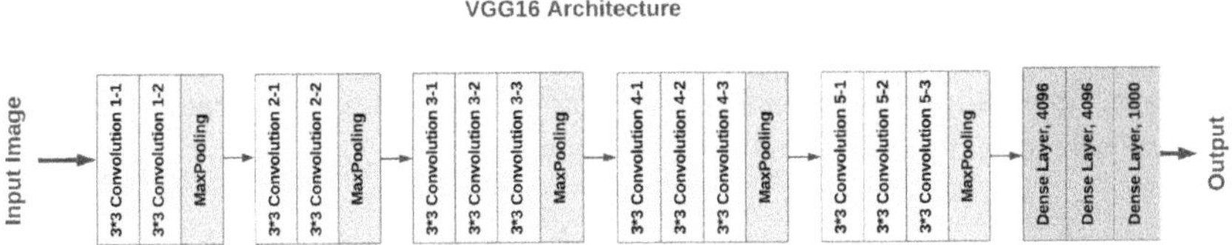

Fig. 4. VGG16 Architecture

4.2 VGG19 CNN Architecture (19 Layers)

The VGG19 Architecture is a variant of VGG 16 model consisting of 19 weights layers. Sixteen convolution layers, and three are fully connected dense layers, five are MaxPool layers and lastly one SoftMax layer.

The model takes an input image of fixed size of 224*224 with 3 color channels which means the image matrix is of shape (224,224,3). Its kernel is of size 3*3 (Fig. 5).

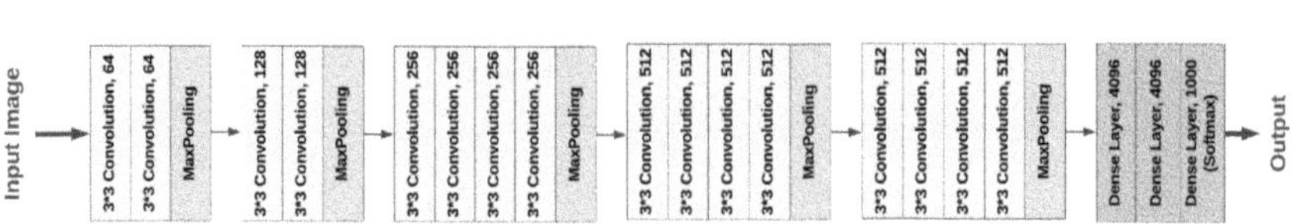

Fig. 5. VGG19 Architecture

4.3 Implementation of the Architectures Using Python

Python is an interpreted, interactive, object-oriented programming language. It includes modules, exceptions, dynamic typing, very high dynamic data types and classes. It supports multiple programming paradigms beyond object-oriented programming, such as procedural and functional programming. Python combines remarkable power with a very clear syntax. It interfaces to many system calls and libraries, as well as to various windowing systems, and is extensible in C or C++. It can also be used as an extension language for applications that require programmable interface. Finally, Python is portable as it runs on various Unix variants including Linux, macOS, and Windows.

It is widely used in data science and for producing deep learning algorithms. Advantages that make Python a perfect solution for machine learning and AI-driven projects include simplicity and consistency, flexibility, access to powerful AI and machine learning (ML) libraries and frameworks, platform independence, and large communities. These things increase the popularity of the language.

4.4 Splitting and Normalizing the Dataset

After reading the image database and storing the image data in the array **dataset** and the labels 0 and 1 in the array **label**. To train and test the model with the same image database we need to split the database into two parts with a ratio. In this case it is 4:1, where 4 parts goes for training the model and 1 part goes for testing the knowledge of models. Normalization is a Scale transformation technique that helps to improve the performance as well as the accuracy of the model. It is an optional step that can be performed if the training does not converge and its done.

After normalization of the data is done, the CNN models are created then trained and tested using the normalized data.

4.5 Training and Testing the Models

After any of the model is built, the **model fit** function is used to adjust the **weights** according to the data values so that better accuracy can be achieved.

Weights are the parameters which decide where the input data will go within the hidden layers from one neuron in a layer to another neuron in another layer.

The cycles it will take to achieve its accuracy is given as number of **epochs** in the argument. **Batch size** defines the maximum number of batch size of training images within each epoch. **Xtest** is validation or testing data and **Ytest** is the output that the model gives after looking at the corresponding test data. The **shuffle** attribute randomizes the test and train data while splitting so that the model does not train from only the images from a single class in case of ordered labeling. The **verbose** attribute is the mode of logging the data while the model is getting trained and tested.

5 Results and Analysis

The CNN models were run on various devices with different configurations and how those different configurations effected the model's output is tabulated. The configuration used for the above output was GPU: Nvidia GTX 1650Ti, GPU Memory: 4GB, RAM: 8 GB DDR4 and Train-Test ratio 4:1.

5.1 Graphical Analysis of the Results

Difference in Performance in Different Configurations
The model was run on a **Local device** with configuration GPU: Nvidia GTX 1050, GPU Memory: 4GB and RAM: 8 GB DDR4, Google Collab with GPU: Nvidia Tesla K80, GPU Memory: 12GB and RAM: 16 GB DDR4 and Kaggle with GPU: Nvidia Tesla P100, GPU Memory: 16GB and RAM: 16 GB DDR4 (Fig. 6).

Confusion matrix of VGG16 and VGG19

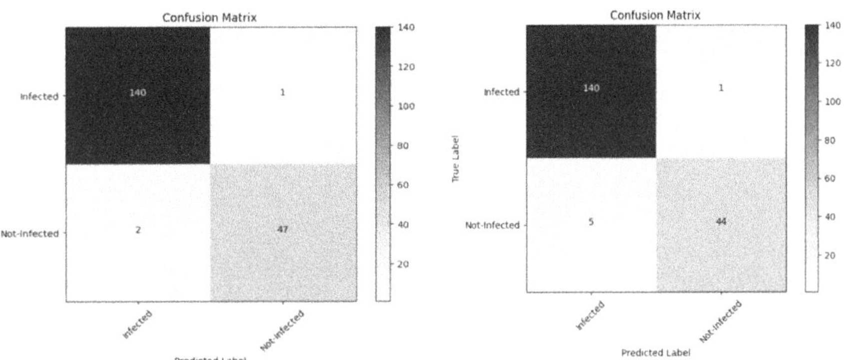

Fig. 6. (a): Confusion Matrix of VGG16 and VGG19 models

5.2   Graphical Analysis of the Results

From the results produced by the VGG 16 and VGG19 model we can analyze the model's training and testing accuracy; training and testing loss and we can also compare the model's accuracy and loss at the same time for both the training and testing data. The graphs generated by the analysis are shown below (Figs. 7, 8 and 9):

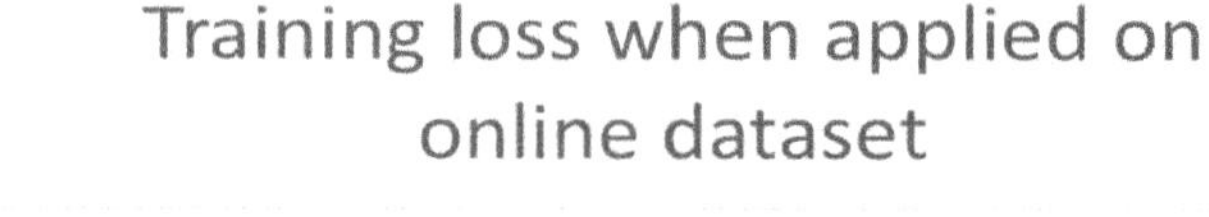
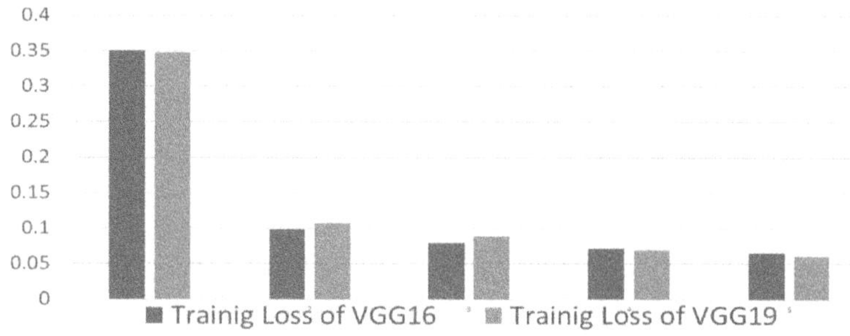

Fig. 7. Training loss of VGG 16 AND VGG19 models.

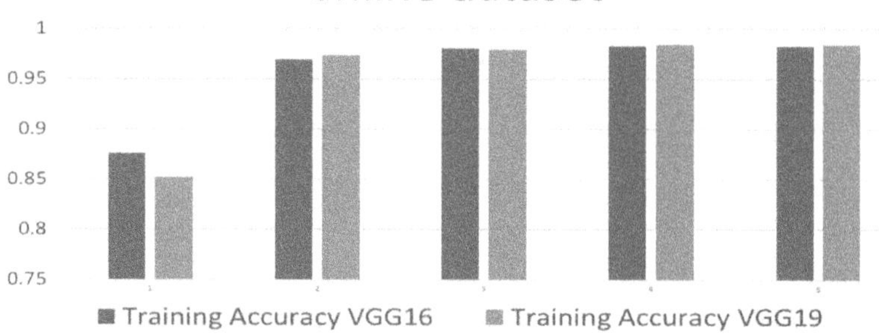

Fig. 8. Training accuracy of VGG 16 AND VGG19 models

Fig. 9. Validation loss of VGG 16 AND VGG19 models

5.3   Comparison Table Between the Different Models.

Based on GPU: Nvidia GTX 1650Ti, GPU Memory: 4GB, RAM: 8 GB DDR4 and Train-Test ratio 4:1 for 10 epochs (Table 1).

Table 1. Comparison table of results of different CNN architectures

CNN Architecture	Accuracy (%)	Precision (%)	Specificity (%)	Sensitivity (%)	Run Time (mm:ss.ms)
Simple CNN	93.44	93.18	82.35	94.23	01:16.66
InceptionV3	88.83	90.75	76.47	83.48	11:42.65
VGG16	94.66	94.13	84.87	96.19	06:04.81
VGG19	95.14	95.04	87.39	95.41	09:31.61

6   Conclusion and Future Plan

We have implemented VGG16 and VGG 19 deep learning in our research work, earlier we have implemented Simple CNN and Inception V3 algorithms. We have found that, accuracy and precision of VGG 16 and VGG 19 model are better than Simple CNN and Inception V3 algorithms. We hope that our research work will be beneficial for the radiologists in their lung cancer prediction for lung cancer patients. In future, we will implement these algorithms in local dataset from Tripura and compare the results with the results obtained in our research work. We shall implement new updated deep learning models like ResNet50, DenseNet and EfficientNet to evaluate their performances on other widely accessible Lung Datasets like LIDC-IDRI, NSCLC Radiomics in our future research works.

Acknowledgments. This study was not funded by any agency.

Disclosure of Interests. The authors have no competing interests to declare that are relevant to the content of this article.

References

1. Das, S., Majumder, S.: Lung cancer detection using deep learning network: a comparative analysis. In: 2020 Fifth International Conference on Research in Computational Intelligence and Communication Networks (ICRCICN), Bangalore, India, pp. 30–35 (2020). https://doi.org/10.1109/ICRCICN50933.2020.9296197
2. Das, S., Kumar, P., Pal, S., Majumder, S.: Automated prediction of lung cancer using deep learning algorithms. Appl. Artif. Intell., 93–120 (2023)
3. Das, S., Chawngsangpuii, R., Sengupta, P., Pal, S., Majumder, S.: Detection of lung cancer using deep learning algorithms. Sci. Technol. J. **12**(1), 1–6 (2024). https://doi.org/10.22232/stj.2024.12.01.02
4. Shatnawi, M.Q., Abuein, Q., Al-Quraan, R.: Deep learning-based approach to diagnose lung cancer using CT-scan images. Intell.-Based Med. **11**, 100188 (2025). https://doi.org/10.1016/j.ibmed.2024.100188
5. Javed, R., Abbas, T., Khan, A.H., et al.: Deep learning for lungs cancer detection: a review. Artif. Intell. Rev. **57**, 197 (2024). https://doi.org/10.1007/s10462-024-10807-1
6. Shah, A., Malik, H.A.M., Muhammad, A., et al.: Deep learning ensemble 2D CNN approach towards the detection of lung cancer. Sci. Rep. **13**, 2987 (2023). https://doi.org/10.1038/s41598-023-29656-z
7. Wahab Sait, S.: Lung cancer detection model using deep learning technique. Appl. Sci. **13**(22), 12510 (2023). https://doi.org/10.3390/app132212510
8. Wankhade, S., Vigneshwari, S.: A novel hybrid deep learning method for early detection of lung cancer using neural networks. Healthc. Anal. **3**, 100195 (2023). https://doi.org/10.1016/j.health.2023.100195
9. Nageswaran, S., et al.: Lung cancer classification and prediction using machine learning and image processing. Biomed. Res. Int. **2022**, 1755460 (2022). https://doi.org/10.1155/2022/1755460
10. Shimazaki, D., et al.: Deep learning-based algorithm for lung cancer detection on chest radiographs using the segmentation method. Sci. Rep. **12**, 727 (2022). https://doi.org/10.1038/s41598-022-02903-x
11. Spoorthi, R., Mahesh, S.: Nodule segmentation of lung CT image for medical applications. Glob. Transit. Proc. **2** (2021). https://doi.org/10.1016/j.gltp.2021.01.011
12. Lei, Y., Zheng, L., Lyu, Z.: Lung tumor segmentation and 3D reconstruction based on region growing and correlation. J. Phys. Conf. Ser. **1168**, 062018 (2019). https://doi.org/10.1088/1742-6596/1168/6/062018
13. Krishnamurthy, S., Ganesh, E.N., Rengasamy, U.: Three-dimensional lung nodule segmentation and shape variance analysis to detect lung cancer with reduced false positives. Proc. Inst. Mech. Eng. H **230**(1), 58–70 (2016). https://doi.org/10.1177/0954411915619951
14. Zhang, X., et al.: Accurate segmentation for different types of lung nodules on CT images using improved U-Net convolutional network. Medicine **100**(40), e27491 (2021). https://doi.org/10.1097/MD.0000000000027491
15. Wang, H., Zhu, H., Ding, L., Yang, K.: A diagnostic classification of lung nodules using multiple-scale residual network. Sci. Rep. **13**, 11322 (2023). https://doi.org/10.1038/s41598-023-38350-z
16. Zhang, X., Kong, S., Han, Y., Xie, B., Liu, C.: Lung nodule CT image segmentation model based on multiscale dense residual neural network. Mathematics **11**, 1363 (2023)
17. Skourt, B.A., Hassani, A.E., Majda, A.: Lung CT image segmentation using deep neural networks. Procedia Comput. Sci. **127**, 109–113 (2018). https://doi.org/10.1016/j.procs.2018.01.104

18. Kareem, H.F., AL-Husieny, M.S., Mohsen, F.Y., Khalil, E.A., Hassan, Z.S.: Evaluation of SVM performance in the detection of lung cancer in marked CT scan dataset. Indones. J. Electr. Eng. Comput. Sci. **21**(3), 1731–1738 (2021). https://doi.org/10.11591/ijeecs.v21.i3. pp1731-1738
19. Shaikh Ismail, M.B.: Lung cancer detection and classification using machine learning algorithm. Turk. J. Comput. Math. Educ. **12**(13), 7048–7054 (2021). https://doi.org/10.17762/tur comat.v12i13.10122
20. Begum M, Ismail S (2021) Lung cancer detection and classification using machine learning algorithm. Turk. J. Comput. Math. Educ. 12(13), 7048-7054. https://doi.org/10.17762/tur comat.v12i13.10122

Evaluating the Impact of Pruning on Transformer Models: A Comparative Study

Sourabh Sathe[(✉)] [iD], Purvaja Kale[iD], and Ashish Tiwari[iD]

Visvesvaraya National Institute of Technology, Nagpur, Maharashtra, India
{mt23mcs003,mt23mcs005}@students.vnit.ac.in, at@cse.vnit.ac.in

Abstract. Self-Attention plays a crucial role in machine learning. At the heart of a transformer, the attention mechanism is used to build complex relationships between words in sentences. A transformer uses a sequence of layers with multiple attention heads. Studies have shown that not all attention heads contribute useful information. Some heads can be pruned with little to no effect on the accuracy of the model. However, pruning can have a huge impact on the computational performance such as reduction in inference time and memory usage. Many existing optimization techniques employ pruning with a focus on attention heads while little to no optimization in the Feed Forward Network (FFN) layers. The key challenge is identifying which heads and neurons should be pruned. In this paper, we employ a hybrid dual-step pruning algorithm that optimizes both attention heads and FFN neurons by pruning them to evaluate the impact of pruning. Through experimentation, we assess the performance of multiple transformers with multiple datasets. We further conclude if pruning is really beneficial and explain its real-life implications.

Keywords: Transformer · Pruning · Optimization · Attention Mechanism · Large Language models · Self-Attention · Multi-Head Attention

1 Introduction

The transformer architecture was first proposed by Vaswani et al. [8] in the paper *"Attention Is All You Need"*, which has, in turn, greatly shaped deep learning and Natural Language Processing (NLP). Self-attention as a mechanism enables transformers to establish sophisticated dependencies between words in a sequence regardless of their relative position in the sentence. But the problem is, these attentions add significantly to the memory footprint and inference latency of the model. A study by Michel et al. [4] has shown that all attention heads are not equally important for the performance of the models. Some heads encode redundant or less useful information, leading to excessive consumption

K. Chandra Mondal et al. (Eds.): CICBA 2025, CCIS 2862, pp. 374–388, 2026.
https://doi.org/10.1007/978-3-032-17187-0_29

of memory and computation with no benefit at all. It led to studies in model pruning where redundant components are targeted to be removed for more efficiency without much loss in accuracy. But, another problem is many researchers have written model pruning algorithms with a primary focus on pruning attention heads as discussed further in the related work. However, FFN layers, which constitute a large portion of the model parameters, also introduce redundant computations. Furthermore, whether pruning is really beneficial in optimizing the memory and inference time of the transformer model remains a question to be answered. To address these problems, we use a hybrid **Dual-step pruning algorithm** that jointly optimizes both attention layers and FFN layers. We perform rigorous experimentation on multiple transformer models with multiple datasets to analyze its impact on accuracy, inference time, and memory usage. Our research aims to answer the following key questions:

- Which attention heads can be pruned without affecting model accuracy?
- How does pruning attention heads and FFN layer neurons impact the overall performance of transformers?
- What are the trade-offs between inference time, memory, and accuracy?
- How does pruning affect different transformer models across various NLP tasks and datasets?
- Does pruning affect the output on real-life question-answering task?

2   Related Work

2.1   The Lottery Ticket Hypothesis

[2] Neural network pruning techniques can reduce the total no. of parameters of a trained model by over 90% and improve storage and performance without compromising accuracy. Standard pruning techniques naturally uncover subnetworks. Actual experiments show that such subnetworks can be as small as 10–20% of the original network's size yet still achieve the same or even better performance than the full model. Following the core ideas of the Lottery Ticket Hypothesis (LTH), recent works have begun to consider its implications for Large Language Models (LLMs), especially pruning. For instance, Chen et al. [1] demonstrated that within pre-trained models like Bidirectional Encoder Representations from Transformers (BERT), it is possible to identify sparse subnetworks–termed "winning tickets"–that, when trained in isolation, can achieve performance comparable to the full model across various downstream tasks. These findings suggest that significant portions of the attention parameters in LLMs may be redundant, and that pruning can lead to more efficient models without substantial loss in accuracy. Our research stems from this fact.

2.2   Existing Optimization Techniques

Voita et al. [9] focused on analyzing multi-head attention and its importance for translation task to find whether we can significantly reduce the number of attention heads while preserving translation quality. Their key findings conclude that only a small subset of heads are important for translation, and rest of which heads can be pruned.

Sun et al. [7] introduced a novel, straightforward yet effective pruning method, termed Wanda (Pruning by Weights and activations), designed to induce sparsity in pretrained LLMs. Motivated by the recent observation of emergent large magnitude features in LLMs, their approach prunes weights with the smallest magnitudes multiplied by the corresponding input activations, on a per-output basis. This technique successfully prunes LLMs to high degrees of sparsity without any need for modifying the remaining weights.

Jaiswal el at. [3] comprehensively studies induced sparse patterns across multiple large pre-trained vision and language transformers. With exploding parameter counts, LTH and its variants, have lost their pragmatism in sparsifying them due to high computation and memory bottleneck of repetitive train-prune-retrain routine of Iterative Magnitude Pruning (IMP) which worsens with increasing model size.

Rogers at al. [6] focused on the current proposals to improve BERT's architecture, pre-training and fine-tuning. They also discussed approaches to compress BERT model and the area of pruning as a model analysis technique. They proved that BERT can be efficiently compressed with minimal accuracy loss, which would be highly desirable for real-world applications.

2.3   Limitations

A common limitation among existing optimization techniques is often focusing exclusively on either attention heads or FFN layers. These methods treat the components in isolation, potentially missing out on optimization opportunities arising from their interdependencies. The techniques are, however, complex when it comes to implementation which is why we choose iterative pruning as the optimization algorithm. Furthermore, they give only a rough idea of the model's real world performance and benefits. Our research addresses this limitation by performing rigorous experimentation, analysis by comparisons, thus proving the Lottery Ticket Hypothesis.

3   Methodology

3.1   Preliminary Study

Michel et al. [4] in his paper *"Are Sixteen Heads Really Better than One?"* made a surprising observation that even if models have been trained using multiple heads, in practice, a large percentage of attention heads can be removed without significantly impacting performance. In fact, some layers can even be reduced to a single head. We verified this fact by examining heat maps of the attention heads as shown in Fig. 1. For this we built a basic custom transformer as given in original paper by Vaswani et al. [8]. This transformer has 6 encoder-decoder layers and 8 attention heads. We used English sentences from "English to Marathi machine translation" dataset from Kaggle. After training using a Word level tokenizer, visualization was performed using the source text *"However, malls, market complexes and big shops will remain closed."*. It was found that layer 5 head 1 contains less useful information and can be pruned without loss of accuracy. Similarly other heads were also found to be redundant and were candidates for pruning.

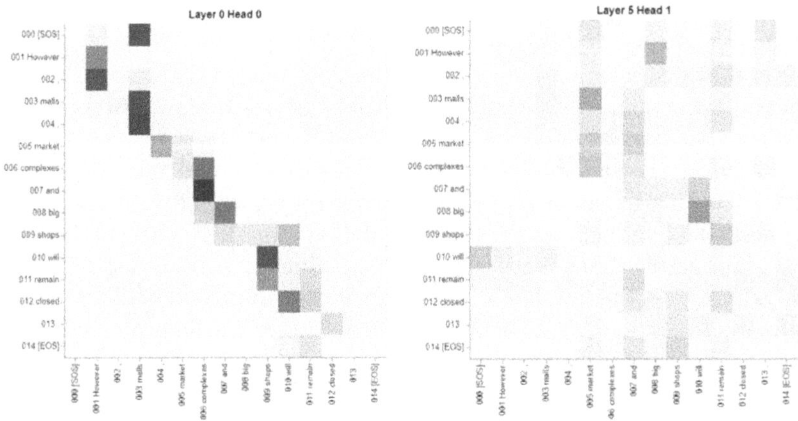

Fig. 1. Heat maps of attention heads extracted from the transformer

Just like attention heads in transformer models often exhibit redundancy where multiple heads learn similar patterns or contribute marginally to the model's output, the FFN layers also contain redundant neurons or channels. In many cases, different neurons in the FFN layers learn overlapping representations or remain inactive for most inputs, leading to inefficiencies in computation and memory usage. Studies have shown that a significant fraction of FFN activations contribute minimally to the final output, suggesting that these layers are over-parameterized. This redundancy forms a strong motivation for pruning, which can reduce model size and inference cost without significantly affecting performance.

3.2   Proposed Work

To evaluate the impact of pruning on transformer models, we employ a systematic approach:

1. **Head Importance Analysis in Attention Layers:** We use an importance score and analyze the contribution of each attention head using gradient-based and information-theoretic methods.

2. **Neuron Importance Analysis in FFN Layers:** We use an importance score to analyze which neurons are redundant and need to be pruned using saliency-based, structured pruning methods.

3. **Dual-step Pruning:** We employ a pruning strategy that jointly optimizes attention heads and FFN neurons to achieve a better trade-off between efficiency and accuracy. Figure 2 summarizes an overall view of steps 1 to 3.

4. **Evaluation of Multiple Transformer Models and Tasks:** We conduct experiments on various Transformers and NLP benchmark tasks, comparing pruned models against baseline transformers. We use pre-trained transformers from the Hugging Face Library [11] which have state-of-the-art Transformer architectures under a unified API. Initial experimentation prunes the `bert-base-uncased` model which is 12-layer, 768-hidden, 12-heads, 110M parameter model, trained on lower-cased English text. We then extend the use of this algorithm on different transformers against different General Language Understanding Evaluation (GLUE) tasks. After training, to perform comparisons, the baseline and pruned transformer undergo a benchmark to find accuracy scores, inference time, memory usage and total no of parameters. For this we use `PyTorchBenchmark` from hugging face library which allows to flexibly benchmark the Transformers models. Then we benchmark the pruned `bert-base-uncased` model on different GLUE tasks to compare the accuracy of the baseline model against the pruned model.

5. **Inference on a Question-Answering Task:** We fine-tune the baseline and the pruned `bert-base-uncased` model on Stanford Question Answering Dataset (SQuAD) [5] which is a reading comprehension dataset built from Wikipedia articles, where crowdworkers generate questions. Each answer is either a text span directly taken from the related passage or, in some cases, no answer is possible at all. We then use a custom context and ask a question to the model. Further, we assess and compare the outputs of the fine-tuned baseline model and the fine-tuned pruned model.

6. **Analysis and Comparison:** We compare the impact of pruning transformer models by evaluating major performance indicators such as accuracy, inference time, memory usage, and total number of parameters between the baseline and pruned models. On the basis of this comparative study, we obtain insights and make conclusions about the trade-offs and advantages brought in by the pruning process. We then answer the major questions our research sought to answer.

3.3   GLUE Benchmark

The General Language Understanding Evaluation (GLUE) benchmark is a large collection of diverse natural language understanding tasks designed to assess the generalization, robustness, and linguistic capabilities of machine learning models, in particular transformer-based models. [10] It encompasses a broad variety of tasks like sentiment analysis (SST-2), linguistic acceptability (CoLA), natural language inference (MNLI, RTE, and QNLI), paraphrase identification (MRPC

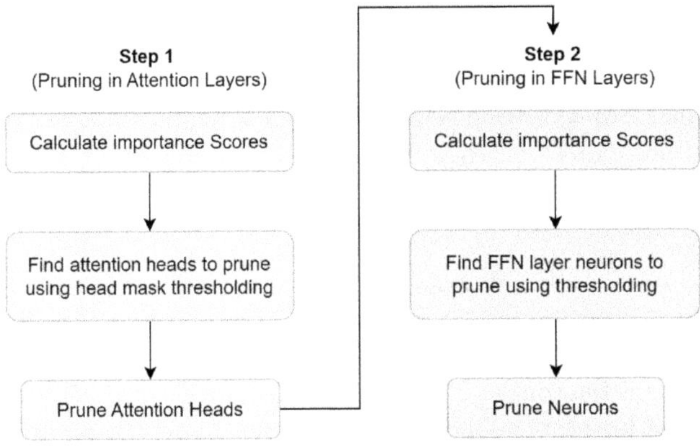

Fig. 2. Flowchart of steps used in our dual-step pruning algorithm

and QQP), and so on, providing a highly balanced evaluation framework. The following Fig. 3 shows all the tasks that GLUE supports:

Name	Download	More Info	Metric
The Corpus of Linguistic Acceptability			Matthew's Corr
The Stanford Sentiment Treebank			Accuracy
Microsoft Research Paraphrase Corpus			F1 / Accuracy
Semantic Textual Similarity Benchmark			Pearson-Spearman Corr
Quora Question Pairs			F1 / Accuracy
MultiNLI Matched			Accuracy
MultiNLI Mismatched			Accuracy
Question NLI			Accuracy
Recognizing Textual Entailment			Accuracy
Winograd NLI			Accuracy
Diagnostics Main			Matthew's Corr

Fig. 3. A list of tasks in GLUE benchmark

Due to its broad coverage of tasks and popularity throughout the NLP community, GLUE is used as a standard measure for the comparison of model performance. For our work, we utilize the GLUE benchmark to evaluate the effectiveness of our pruning techniques against transformer models. This evaluation will serve to attest to the actual-world practicality of our pruning framework when efficiency and scalability are critical. We use Semantic Textual Similarity Benchmark (SST-2) for the first experimentation and then generalize to other tasks of the list.

3.4 Importance Scores

We calculate importance score to find out the contribution of each attention head or FFN neurons. For attention heads we use a weighted sum of the normalized gradients and normalized entropy.

$$importance\_score_{head} = \alpha \times norm\_grad + (1 - \alpha) \times (1 - norm\_ent) \tag{1}$$

Gradients measure how much changing the head's output would affect the loss. Higher gradient norms generally indicate the head is more significant since its output has a bigger influence on the loss. Entropy indicates how sharp or confident the head's attention is. Lower entropy (more peaked attention) typically indicates the head is more confident and more useful. α lets us balance between gradient-based (sensitivity) and entropy-based (confidence) signals. Hence, the formula suggests that the attention heads with a low score are potential candidates for pruning.

Similarly, for FFN neurons we use an absolute product of the normalized activations and the normalized gradients.

$$importance\_score_{neuron} = |norm\_act \times norm\_grad| \tag{2}$$

Activations tell us how active a neuron is throughout the data. If a neuron never activates (always close to zero), it's probably useless. Gradients tell us how much effect changing the neuron's output has on the loss. High gradient means that neuron's output is important. By taking the product of the two, we want to identify neurons that are both active and influential. Therefore, the formula implies that the neurons with a low score are good candidates for pruning.

3.5 Algorithm

We use an iterative head masking and pruning method. A binary head mask $H \in {0, 1}^{L \times N}$ is initialized along with zeroed importance (I) and entropy (E) matrices. For each mini-batch from dataset $\mathcal{D}$, model outputs and gradients of the loss $\mathcal{L}$ w.r.t. H are computed. I accumulates absolute gradients, and E captures attention entropy. Entropy is computed as

$$E_\ell = -\sum_{i=1}^{N} A_{\ell,i} \log(A_{\ell,i}) \tag{3}$$

where $A_{\ell,i}$ is the attention distribution for head i in layer ℓ

After processing $\mathcal{D}$, both I and E are normalized. Each head's score S is computed as a weighted combination of normalized importance $\tilde{I}$ and $1 - \tilde{E}$, controlled by hyperparameter α. Heads are ranked, and the bottom μ fraction is masked iteratively. After each masking, performance $M(H)$ is re-evaluated, stopping when it drops below τM_0, where τ controls the allowed degradation. Finally, masked heads are pruned using native functionality. Hyperparameters α, μ, and τ

respectively is alpha that control the importance-entropy trade-off, masking fraction that control masking aggressiveness per iteration, and the masking threshold which is maximum allowed accuracy drop. This method is summarized in Algorithm 1.

Algorithm 1. Head Masking and Pruning in Attention Layers

Require: Dataset $\mathcal{D}$, model with L layers and N heads, metric M, original score M_0, threshold τ, masking fraction μ, weight α

1: Initialize head mask $H \leftarrow \mathbf{1}_{L \times N}$
2: Initialize importance I, entropy E to zero matrices
3: **for** each mini-batch (x, y) in $\mathcal{D}$ **do**
4:     Compute outputs with mask H
5:     Backpropagate loss to get $\nabla_H \mathcal{L}$
6:     Update importance: $I \leftarrow I + |\nabla_H \mathcal{L}|$
7:     Update entropy E using attention distributions
8: **end for**
9: Normalize I, E by token count
10: (Optional) Normalize per-layer or globally
11: **while** $M(H) \geq \tau M_0$ **and** unmasked heads exist **do**
12:     Compute score: $S = \alpha \tilde{I} + (1 - \alpha)(1 - \tilde{E})$
13:     Rank heads by S, mask bottom μ fraction
14:     Update H, recompute $M(H)$
15: **end while**
16: Prune heads where $H_{\ell,i} = 0$ for each layer

Ensure: Pruned model

After attention head pruning, we apply neuron-level pruning to FFN modules of the Transformer model to further reduce its size and computational cost. First, for each linear FFN layer m, we initialize a neuron mask $mask_m$ set to ones. The model's original performance M_0 is evaluated on the dataset D. Then, for each mini-batch, a forward pass is performed using the current neuron masks, followed by backward propagation to compute the loss gradients. For each FFN module, the cached activations and gradients are used to estimate neuron importance: specifically, by averaging the absolute elementwise product of activations and gradients across all tokens and batches. This provides an importance score $I_m \in \mathbb{R}^{d_o}$ for each output neuron. After processing all batches, the importance scores are averaged, and a pruning threshold τ_m is determined using the μ-th quantile, where $\mu \in (0, 1)$ is a hyperparameter that controls the fraction of neurons to retain (higher μ keeps more neurons). Neurons with significance scores lower than τ_m are masked out by zeroing the corresponding rows in the weight matrix and, if applicable, the bias vector. The pruned model M is then re-evaluated to measure performance loss using the new metric M_{pruned}. The hyperparameter μ is the neuron quantile threshold which controls the sparsity of the FFN layers: smaller μ results in more aggressive pruning and higher compression, at the risk of greater performance degradation. This method is summarized in Algorithm 2.

Algorithm 2. Neuron Pruning in FFN Layers

Require: Model M, dataset $\mathcal{D}$, device $\mathcal{D}ev$, pruning quantile μ, metric $M(\cdot)$, loss $\mathcal{L}$
1: Initialize $\mathbf{mask}_m \leftarrow \mathbf{1}$ for each FFN module m
2: $M_0 \leftarrow \text{Evaluate}(M, \mathcal{D})$
3: **for** each batch $(x, y_{\text{true}}) \in \mathcal{D}$ **do**
4:     $y = M(x; \{\mathbf{mask}_m\})$, compute $\mathcal{L}(y, y_{\text{true}})$, backward pass
5:     **for** each FFN m **do**
6:         Cache activations A_m, gradients G_m
7:         $I_m \leftarrow I_m + |A_m \odot G_m|$ (sum over batch/tokens)
8:     **end for**
9: **end for**
10: **for** each m **do**
11:     Normalize I_m; threshold $\tau_m = \text{Quantile}(I_m, \mu)$
12:     $\widetilde{I}_m[i] = \mathbb{1}(I_m[i] \geq \tau_m)$
13:     $W_m[i, :] \leftarrow W_m[i, :] \cdot \widetilde{I}_m[i], \quad b_m[i] \leftarrow b_m[i] \cdot \widetilde{I}_m[i]$
14: **end for**
15: $M_{\text{pruned}} \leftarrow \text{Evaluate}(M, \mathcal{D})$
Ensure: Pruned model M, metric M_{pruned}

Figure 4 shows an implementation workflow of the above algorithms for the BERT model. The path in green is for the baseline model. The blue path is for the pruned model.

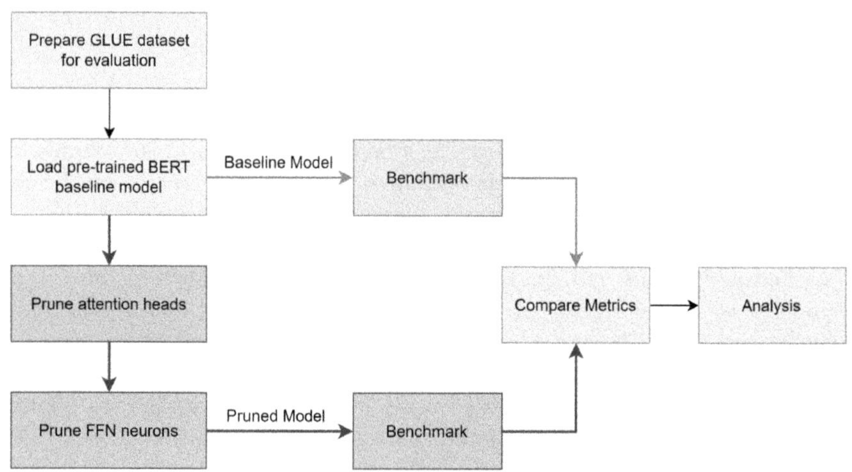

Fig. 4. Algorithm Implementation Workflow for BERT model

4   Experimentation

Implementation consisted of a series of 4 experiments.

1. Experiment 1 began with the standard `bert-base-uncased` model. The dual-step pruning algorithm was applied to this model using the SST-2 task from the GLUE benchmark. The resulting output was a pruned BERT model whose metrics such as GLUE score, total number of parameters, etc. were compared. This experiment was conducted on a local workstation.
2. Experiment 2 extended the analysis by applying the same pruning algorithm to multiple transformer models from the BERT family, including `roberta-base`, `bert-large-uncased` and `distilbert-base-uncased`, all evaluated on the SST-2 task. In this case, inference time and memory usage across models were compared. This experiment was also executed on the local workstation.
3. Experiment 3 involved fine-tuning the BERT model on multiple GLUE tasks, specifically SST-2, MRPC, RTE, and WNLI after pruning. Given the higher memory requirements, this experiment was run on Kaggle Notebooks.
4. Finally, in Experiment 4, the pruned model was fine-tuned for a real-world application: a question answering task using the SQuAD dataset. Inference was then performed on a context to evaluate performance. This final experiment was also carried out on Kaggle Notebooks.

5   Results and Observations

5.1   Metric Comparison

To evaluate the performance of multiple transformers on our algorithm, we conducted rigorous experiments. Running our algorithm on a transformer yield a table displaying the attention heads ranked by their importance scores. The rows indicate the layers while the columns indicate the attention heads. These values are visualized in Fig. 5.

```
INFO:__main__:layer 12: 0.54995 0.15767 0.91759 0.69265 0.16049 0.07857 0.55749 0.01579 0.00925 0.14551 0.20258 0.1769.
INFO:__main__:Head ranked by importance scores
INFO:__main__:lv, h >   1      2      3      4      5      6      7      8      9      10     11     12
INFO:__main__:layer 1:  54     91     83     129    64     0      87     140    62     79     113    92
INFO:__main__:layer 2:  7      118    33     134    126    51     30     55     103    17     128    32
INFO:__main__:layer 3:  110    86     135    59     26     25     11     72     116    84     12     89
INFO:__main__:layer 4:  37     20     56     35     43     102    15     31     49     42     125    90
INFO:__main__:layer 5:  97     61     3      10     80     82     111    107    85     53     100    136
INFO:__main__:layer 6:  45     130    41     60     6      14     114    78     115    71     44     69
INFO:__main__:layer 7:  29     8      73     117    48     23     58     104    68     50     88     28
INFO:__main__:layer 8:  46     106    52     94     66     16     131    9      19     122    101    27
INFO:__main__:layer 9:  95     39     109    38     75     121    22     24     47     5      120    63
INFO:__main__:layer 10: 93     124    142    138    123    99     96     139    2      65     133    13
INFO:__main__:layer 11: 18     112    57     4      108    132    127    21     34     143    76     119
INFO:__main__:layer 12: 36     81     1      98     74     105    40     137    141    77     67     70
INFO:__main__:Masking: current score: 0.491972, remaining heads 60 (41.7 percents)
```

Fig. 5. Heads ranked by importance scores

After computing the importance scores, the algorithm generates a dictionary of key values pairs that tell which attention head need to be pruned from which layer. The following example shows a sample output of the algorithm.

```
Heads to prune:
{0: [0, 1, 4, 5, 6, 7, 8, 9, 11],
 1: [0, 2, 3, 5, 7, 8, 9, 10, 11],
 2: [3, 4, 5, 6, 7, 8, 10, 11],
 3: [1, 2, 3, 4, 6, 7, 8, 10, 11],
 4: [0, 1, 4, 6, 8, 9, 10],
 5: [2, 4, 8],
 6: [7],
 7: [0, 5, 8],
 8: [1, 3, 7, 8, 9, 11],
 9: [2, 5, 8, 10, 11],
 10: [0, 3, 7, 8, 11],
 11: [2, 5, 6, 8, 9]}
```

This says that head 0,1,4,5,6,7,8,9,11 need to be pruned from layer 0 and so on.

Table 1 compares the glue score, total no of parameters, inference time and the memory usage of the baseline and pruned `bert-base-uncased` model on SST-2 task. For this experiment we used `masking threshold = 0.92` and `alpha = 0.5` giving equal importance to entropy and gradients and a `neuron fraction = 0.1`. The model was trained on a single NVIDIA RTX 4050 6GB GPU with a `batch size = 4` and `max sequence length = 128`. The pruned model saw a massive 30.14% decrease in inference time and a 14.01% reduction in memory usage with only a 3.64% drop in the GLUE score.

Table 1. Comparing Baseline vs. Pruned `bert-base-uncased` model on SST-2

Metric	Baseline	Pruned	% Change
GLUE Score	0.5355	0.5160	−3.64%
Total no. of Parameters	109483778	92952578	−15.09%
Inference Time (s)	0.0647	0.0452	−30.14%
Memory Usage (MB)	771	663	−14.01%

Table 2 and Table 3 compares inference time in seconds and memory usage in MB respectively for different transformer models evaluated on SST-2 task. Same configuration of hyperparameter was used in this experiment compared to the previous experiment with only change in the transformer model. `roberta-base` and `distilbert-base-uncased` showed little to no drop in GLUE score while showing a huge improvement in inference. The `distilbert-base-uncased` model showed only a 4.06% drop in memory usage indicating how efficiently the model is already optimized that further reduction is negligible.

The above two experiments use GLUE benchmark in evaluation mode. However, this does not give the true picture of the actual tradeoff between accuracy and performance unless it is fine-tuned on a specific task. Hence, we performed

Table 2. Inference Time Comparison of Baseline vs. Pruned model on SST-2

Transformer model	GLUE	Inference Time (s)		
	% Change	Baseline	Pruned	% Change
bert-base-uncased	–3.64%	0.0647	0.0452	–30.14%
bert-large-uncased	–4.41%	0.1950	0.1150	–41.02%
roberta-base	–0.01%	0.0712	0.0393	–44.80%
distilbert-base-uncased	0.00%	0.0734	0.0629	–14.31%

Table 3. Memory Usage Comparison of Baseline vs. Pruned model on SST-2

Transformer model	GLUE	Memory Usage (MB)		
	% Change	Baseline	Pruned	% Change
bert-base-uncased	–3.64%	771	663	–14.01%
bert-large-uncased	–4.41%	1617	1165	–27.95%
roberta-base	–0.01%	875	673	–23.08%
distilbert-base-uncased	0.00%	812	779	–4.06%

fine-tuning on various GLUE tasks and compared the accuracies between baseline and pruned `bert-base-uncased` model. The findings have been summarized in Table 4. These models were trained on Kaggle using two NVIDIA Tesla T4 15GB GPU using `max sequence length = 128, per device batch size = 32, learning rate = 2e-5` and `number of epochs = 3` (except for MRPC and WNLI where we used 5 epochs instead of 3 due to its tiny size).

Table 4. Comparison of accuracies between baseline and pruned `bert-base-uncased` model after fine-tuning on various GLUE tasks

GLUE Task	Accuracy (Baseline)	Accuracy (Pruned)	% Change
SST-2	92.32	91.97	–0.38%
MRPC	84.07	81.71	–2.81%
RTE	65.70	59.57	–9.33%
WNLI	56.34	26.78	–52.46%

5.2   Question Answering

Finally, we experimented on a real-life use case by fine-tuning the `bert-base-uncased` model on SQuAD dataset to perform a question answering task. This was trained on Kaggle using a single NVIDIA P100 16GB GPU with `learning`

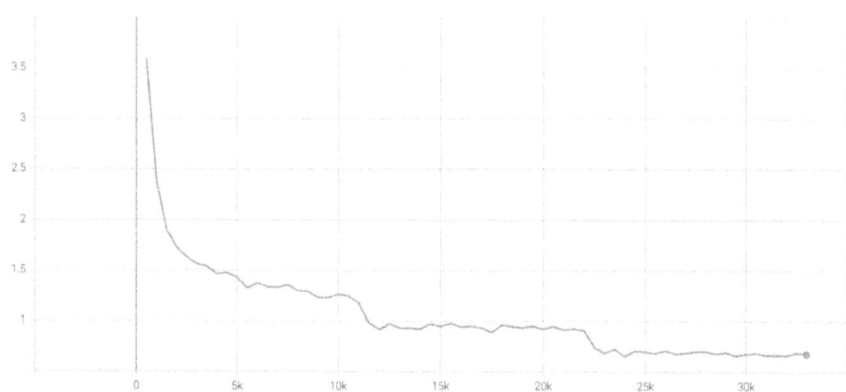

Fig. 6. Training Loss vs No. of Training Steps

rate = 2e-5, number of training epochs = 3 and weight decay = 0.01. The training graph is shown in Fig. 6

An inference on the fine-tuned model yields an interesting output where the answer given by both models were exactly the same with a very small change in the accuracy scores. These findings are shown below.

```
Context: "Transformers is backed by the three most popular deep learning
    libraries - Jax, PyTorch and TensorFlow - with a smooth integration
    between them. You can easily train a model using one framework and
    switch to another for inference without hassle."

Question: "Which deep learning libraries back Transformers?"

Ground Truth: "Jax, PyTorch and TensorFlow"

Output (Baseline): {'score': 0.9979003071784973, 'start': 78, 'end': 105,
    'answer': 'Jax, PyTorch and TensorFlow'}

Output (Pruned): {'score': 0.9623586535453796, 'start': 76, 'end': 103, '
    answer': 'Jax, PyTorch and TensorFlow'}
```

Both the models gave the exact same answer "Jax, PyTorch and TensorFlow" with only 3.51% decrease in the accuracy score of pruned model.

As part of this experiment, we uploaded the above pretrained, pruned, and fine-tuned BERT model on Hugging Face's Model Hub, available under the model name: 22sourabh/bert-pruned-finetuned-squad.

6   Conclusion and Discussion

While there is a small drop in the GLUE score, there is a significant improvement in the inference time, memory usage and total number of parameters indicating that pruning is beneficial if the model needs to be compressed to be deployed on hardware where memory and computational power is a constraint. Instead of relying on servers, this compressed model could run locally on our existing smartphones, smartwatches, and other smart gadgets.

The experiments indicates that there is a tradeoff between the accuracy and other performance metrics. Certain use cases where accuracy need not be a big issue can benefit largely from pruning the model. However, models like RoBERTa and DistilBERT have seen to be robust when it comes to the tradeoff with only little to no change in the accuracy. This indicates that there is always a scope for building robust architectures that can tackle the problem of high computational cost.

The Hugging Face library contains hundreds of transformers whose performance can be improved by pruning. This could be a scope for future research.

Pruning may not always seem beneficial e.g. The pruned BERT model failed miserably on WNLI task while it saw a very slight decrease in accuracy on SST-2. This says that which transformer to prune for with task is use case dependent.

Our experiments show that pruning attention heads significantly impacts the benchmark as compared to pruning neurons. This shows that attention mechanism contributes majorly in making decisions in the transformer.

Removing neurons without any subsequent fine-tuning can sometimes lead to little/no change in accuracy, as the network might be robust to these changes. Hence fine tuning is necessary after every successful model pruning.

The pruned model performed very well during inference on a real-life task of question answering with only a little drop in accuracy without affecting the output indicating its practicality in several use cases.

As future research, our pruning algorithm can be further tested on multiple transformers to perform NLP tasks like Token classification, Text summarization, language translation, etc.

References

1. Chen, T., et al.: The lottery ticket hypothesis for pre-trained BERT networks. CoRR arxiv:2007.12223 (2020)
2. Frankle, J., Carbin, M.: The lottery ticket hypothesis: training pruned neural networks. CoRR arxiv:1803.03635 (2018)
3. Jaiswal, A., Liu, S., Chen, T., Wang, Z.: The emergence of essential sparsity in large pre-trained models: the weights that matter (2023). https://arxiv.org/abs/2306.03805
4. Michel, P., Levy, O., Neubig, G.: Are sixteen heads really better than one? CoRR arxiv:1905.10650 (2019)
5. Rajpurkar, P., Jia, R., Liang, P.: Know what you don't know: unanswerable questions for squad. CoRR arxiv:1806.03822 (2018)
6. Rogers, A., Kovaleva, O., Rumshisky, A.: A primer in bertology: what we know about how BERT works. CoRR arxiv:2002.12327 (2020)
7. Sun, M., Liu, Z., Bair, A., Kolter, J.Z.: A simple and effective pruning approach for large language models (2024). https://arxiv.org/abs/2306.11695

8. Vaswani, A., et al.: Attention is all you need. CoRR arxiv:1706.03762 (2017)
9. Voita, E., Talbot, D., Moiseev, F., Sennrich, R., Titov, I.: Analyzing multi-head self-attention: specialized heads do the heavy lifting, the rest can be pruned. In: Korhonen, A., Traum, D., Màrquez, L. (eds.) Proceedings of the 57th Annual Meeting of the Association for Computational Linguistics, pp. 5797–5808. Association for Computational Linguistics, Florence (2019). https://doi.org/10.18653/v1/P19-1580. https://aclanthology.org/P19-1580/
10. Wang, A., Singh, A., Michael, J., Hill, F., Levy, O., Bowman, S.R.: GLUE: a multitask benchmark and analysis platform for natural language understanding. CoRR arxiv:1804.07461 (2018)
11. Wolf, T., et al.: Huggingface's transformers: state-of-the-art natural language processing. CoRR arxiv:1910.03771 (2019)

Automating Research Paper Analysis and Citation Retrieval Using Generative AI

Anurag De[1(✉)], Gyanada Chowdary Myneni[1], Akshitha Gopu[1], Bindusree Yella[1], and Gautam Pal[2]

[1] School of Computer Science and Engineering, VIT-AP University, Inavolu, Amaravati 522237, Andhra Pradesh, India
anurag.de111@gmail.com
[2] Computer Science and Engineering Department, Tripura Institute of Technology, Narsingarh, Agartala 799009, Tripura, India

Abstract. In recent years, many scientific publications have emerged, so the ability to automatically summarize content, extract important topics, and obtain relevant citations is increasingly needed. This article introduces AI research assistants. It supports the literature with an interactive platform for integrating NLP algorithms (Natural Language Processing) for the creation of overviews and citations. The assistant is designed based on Python using Gradio for the interface, consisting of an option for uploading a PDF file and URL. The input is then processed through PyPDF2 and BeautifulSoup, but the core features are achieved by using Google AI Model. The model is used to access semantic reviews and scientific citations via Springer - API and Semantic Scholar. Results are categorized and deduced by title, source, and year of publication metadata. Using the same underlying AI model integrated into the system, users can ask context-related questions to improve understanding and interaction. Users can view the accuracy of the results to ensure transparency and reliability of their academic work processes. Therefore, it can be said that this research assistant model provides quality and speed that is associated with automating work for research. The architecture of our proposed model is practical and time-efficient while working on various literature from different domains. The proposed model successfully attained a citation accuracy of 95%, showing its efficiency in fetching references that are both highly relevant and accurate. This would further establish the platform as suitable for academic and scientific reviews.

Keywords: Research Tools · Citation Extraction and Analysis · Scientific Literature Summarization · Citation Ranking · Similarity check

© The Author(s), under exclusive license to Springer Nature Switzerland AG 2026
K. Chandra Mondal et al. (Eds.): CICBA 2025, CCIS 2862, pp. 389–400, 2026.
https://doi.org/10.1007/978-3-032-17187-0_30

1   Introduction

In research publications, traditional time-saving methods use sensitive manual search queries and rely on incompatible goals that are not justified. Recent progress in NLP and Generative-AI automatically extracts important results, allowing researchers to spend more on analysis than queries. Kökver et al. [1] have studied the application of language processing techniques to explore misconceptions. Although such a study has focused on educational applications of NLP, it failed to provide solutions to dynamic citation retrieval. To extend this work, we applied NLP to continuous citation refinement. So, our approach on the research assistant is operated with AI and uses NLP models to summarise papers, extract important topics, and record semantic scalars and related citations. It includes seamless PDF uploads, URL-based text extraction the proposed model was developed to easily edit PDF and Web-URL extraction. We deal with gaps in previous research such in Liu et al. [2] as an adaptive citation link after extraction, it was not supported. Furthermore, the error handling mechanism ensured that issues such as invalid URL issues, data shortages, and API errors are treated with improved robustness for the core area focused in contrast to previous research.

The propsed system summarizes loaded documents or web sources without static citation context under the Gemini 2.0 Flash model providing real-time summarization of queries unlike static citation approaches of previous research of Maheshwari et al. [3] the research used the context of static citations and was missing in real-time summary of real-time queries. Furthermore, Topic Extraction via AI dynamically identifies the top two keywords in our model, in contrast to what was performed by Zhang et al. [4]. It was marked only for manual topic tagging. The propsed method integrated Multi-Source Citation Fetching that combines the results of Semantic Scholars and Springer's APIs to attain a much in-depth citation retrieval. This is very different from previous research efforts which were only sourced from a single citation retrieval. To keep it relevant, our system also holds Citation Ranking by using the concepts of TF-IDF and Cosine Similarity rather than static keyword matching, where citations that would be most similar to the extracted topics would get higher priority. The Real-Time AI Chatbot Integration allows researchers to ask questions and receive topic specific answers through Gemini-2.0-Flash, because this creates a real-time feedback loop that was not incorporated in earlier applications or systems such as the ones explored by Yang et al. [5], thus it greatly improves interactivity and research productivity. Another important aspect of our design is the responsive user interface created using gradio made CSS. Our architecture uses parallel system components with dedicated modules for overviews, summaries, text extraction, query processing and chatbot interactions. Our architecture uses parallel system components to parallel system architecture explained in Yin et al. [6].

The proposed study develops a Gradio-based Research Assistant Platform that enhances automated research text extraction, summarization, and citation retrieval.

- Text from PDF documents and web URLs can be extracted in PyPDF2 or BeautifulSoup.
- The Google Gemini large language model is integrated to summarize the input papers and extract valuable keywords to improve the relevance of research queries.
- The paper's reference citation mechanism brings citations from different scholarly databases, i.e., Semantic Scholar and Springer are ranked based on TF-IDF vectorization and Cosine Similarity.
- An adaptive re-ranking based on semantic similarity to the original query is processed which refines citation accuracy and relevance.
- Development of a user-friendly Gradio-based interface that allows researchers to upload PDFs, input URLs, view AI-generated summaries, retrieve citations, and chat with the AI chatbot for additional insights in real time.

The remainder of the paper is structured as follows. Section 2 gives a brief background survey. Section 3 is literature review which provides an overview of Citation Retrieval and Automation of Research. Section 4 discusses the methodology that briefs the Text extraction preprocessing, Word Processing, UI, and Citation ranking model. Section 5 discusses the results and evaluation of the model's citation accuracy and processing time, along with a comparative study. Section 6 presents the Conclusion and Future Scope, summarizing the findings and emphasizing the model's potential in automating research.

2 Background Study

2.1 PyPDF2

Extracting research work from PDF using PyPDF2 library and extracting one web- based paper can be done through BeautifulSoup and requirements. It gives the flexibility of input and helps researchers to understand the core content quickly without reading the entire document. The extracted keywords allow researchers to improve the process of literature research.

2.2 Gradio Interface

The tool is integrated into a Gradio interface that allows users to easily interact with the system. In previous research Abid et al. [7] developed a model using Gradio as a user-centric interface framework. Though comprising a plethora of user-friendly interaction, Gradio does not feature an integrated citation retrieval ranking system. In our case, this feature Gradio, which will allow users to upload PDFs, provide URLs, extract keywords, receive summary.

3 Related Work

The previous research related to the context of citations has dramatically changed the equipment that has been used primarily in recent academic research.

This study was primarily based on previous studies that relied heavily on processing all forms of natural language for citation analysis. Building on the foundational models, Li and colleagues [8] have revisited traditional retrieval models like TF-IDF and cosine similarity, which serve as the core mechanism for ranking citations. Our effort brings in custom re-ranking using the same metrics TF-IDF and Cosine but combining it with Gemini-2.0-Flash model.

Zhang et al. [4] proposed a hierarchical integration of knowledge graphs for cross-vector call tasks to improve context-based recommendations. In Maheshwari et al. [3] Scibert was used to automate citation tasks in academic work by categorizing citation contexts. This was an efficient process, but lacked multi source citation rankings and dynamic user feedback that influenced different applicability across research areas.

In Ogundepo et al. [9] Set afrimatrix for information transfer in African languages was mentioned. Although, AI-controlled personalized interactions were not optimized for queries. As discussed in Huang et al. [10] Advanced distillation techniques for transferring knowledge from English models to other languages were used. Although, their research did not include domain-specific AI tuning. In-text citation: Bengesi et al. [11] developed Advances in Generative AI by laying foundations for AI-based re-ranking and summarization of content. However, this did not address the incorporation of real-time feedback from users.

Later Liu et al. [2] not only highlighted improvements in speech models with multilingual knowledge variations, but also the continuous learning mechanism of users and the total extraction of document sources, such as PDF and URL text extraction. Yang et al. [5] extended the translation distillation framework to improve regular information. Despite its efficiency, the frame does not have a comprehensive feedback loop that adapts to user-specific requirements and continuously optimizes citation rankings. Zhang et al. [4] and Maheshwari et al. [3] Focus on classifying citation contexts implement AI Control Chatbots to support real-time research and dynamically optimize query results based on user interaction. This function allows for an adaptive approach to ranking and distinguishing previous models and systems with quotes based solely on predefined algorithms.

Keyword and topic extraction for effective citation systems have been highlighted by Azam et al. [12] as their effective and successful method has not been able to draw upon fine-grained topic adaptation across academic disciplines. To add to this, incorporation of Gemini-2.0-Flash in our project will result in improved topic extraction. Ofori Boateng et al. [13] considered the role of AI on automated systematic checks and had valuable entries in automated citation extraction. The previous approach was not feasible for real-time user interaction and focused more on the extraction tools which are static. Our model inspired by the previous study is based on dynamic user interactions which includes an AI chatbot parallel to the research assistant. This improvisation allowed the users to interact with the system to understand topic specific queries and document contexts giving access to relevant citations.

The Ogundepo et al. [9] and Huang et al. [10] continued AI-powered questions help you continuously improve your search results. By pulling the system to content from a variety of sources and attracting content, we ensure that citation recommendations are relevant, continuous updates, and dealing with limited or manually curated data records with previous restrictions on support.

Bolaños et al. [14] and de la Torre-López et al. [15] have placed AI-assisted systematic literature review methodologies in the forefront of discussion citing the necessity for automated citation workflows. Hagos et al. [16], Sengar et al. [17] have reviewed trends in generative AI that have affected our continuous learning framework for citation ranking. While their research concepts mainly on automation, our research assistant further allows interactive citation refinement and ranking loops to facilitate a more responsive and personalized literature review process. Jiang and S. M. Goetz [18] remarked on the application of NLP in specialized areas like patent analysis, thus laying down the broader applicability of domain-centered citation tools. In contrast, our work integrates a multi-domain citation retrieval mechanism, facilitating a smarter and more efficient approach.

4   Methodology and Implementation

The specific approach to this methodology is to use a modular methodology that allows efficient processing of text and extraction of keywords. Every module will handle a different task, thus it would have clear, scalable and easy debugging.

4.1   Modules

The system is embedded in specific modules as shown in Fig. 1 and is explained below.

Text Extraction and Preprocessing. The system extracts text from the given online sources using BeautifulSoup and research work in PDF using PyPDF2. The extracted text is created using standard NLP techniques such as tokenization, stopword removal, and rearrangement to improve the accuracy of keyword extraction. Key entities for research units and concepts are identified by a NER-based method of specified entity recognition (NER) according to the study by Nadeau and S. Sekine [19]. The preprocessing module also includes documentary segmentation on large scale research that allows access to efficient analysis in small logically structured sections.

Word Processing. The text extracted from PDFs and URLs in real time is used to generate a summary and access relevant words. AI dynamically adapts based on context-related meanings, ensuring a more targeted search of queries. Word processing is integrated into the summary module, allowing researchers to analyze their work in several languages. This module also includes semantic similarity analysis that connects coherent research topics and keywords to improve access accuracy. In contrast to existing citation call systems based solely on the most important cooperation, our method improves summarization by expanding AI-controlled queries. This increases relevance and accuracy.

User Interface. The Gradio-based interactive interface allows users to upload PDFs, extract text from URLs, check AI-generated summaries, refine queries, and interact with AI-powered chatbots. A chatbot created using Gradio allows dynamic reinterpretation and real-time research results.

Citation Ranking Model. The system includes citation adjustments to ensure extensive research calls in several languages. Additionally, the system provides real-time research trend analysis, identifies new topics and proposes relevant citations from the latest publications. We integrated the similarities between TF-IDF and COSINE as mentioned in C.D Manning [20] to measure the relationship between queries and existing papers or extracted content. Using TF-IDF, the citation titles and queries were converted to vectors to understand the meaning and importance of terms within the paper. The cosine similarity was then checked by the system between each query vector which was created earlier and citation's title to establish the extent of similarity to the given query. The similarity score is further used to rank the citations accordingly.

$$TF - IDF(t,d) = TF(t,d) \times IDF(t) \tag{1}$$

$$\text{Cosine Similarity}(A, B) = \frac{A \cdot B}{\|A\| \times \|B\|} \tag{2}$$

Equation (1) denotes TF-IDF. Here t = TF is Term Frequency. IDF, t, and d denote Inverse Document Frequency, term, and document respectively. Equation (2) denotes Cosine similarity. Here, A and B refers to TF-IDF vectors.

The citation-ranking model is used as the main evaluation metric to assess how relevant and accurate the suggested citations are. The developed algorithm estimates the similarity between the title or abstract of user searches and citations retrieved from several sources using the TF-IDF and cosine similarity metrics. The similarity scores are employed in ranking the citations wherein a higher similarity score means more relevance to the query. This ranking scheme validates whether the retrieval model is working correctly impactful citations are put forth for each context. Therefore, the TF-IDF and cosine similarity framework serves not only as a retrieval scheme but also as a quantitative basis to evaluate the performance and precision of the model.

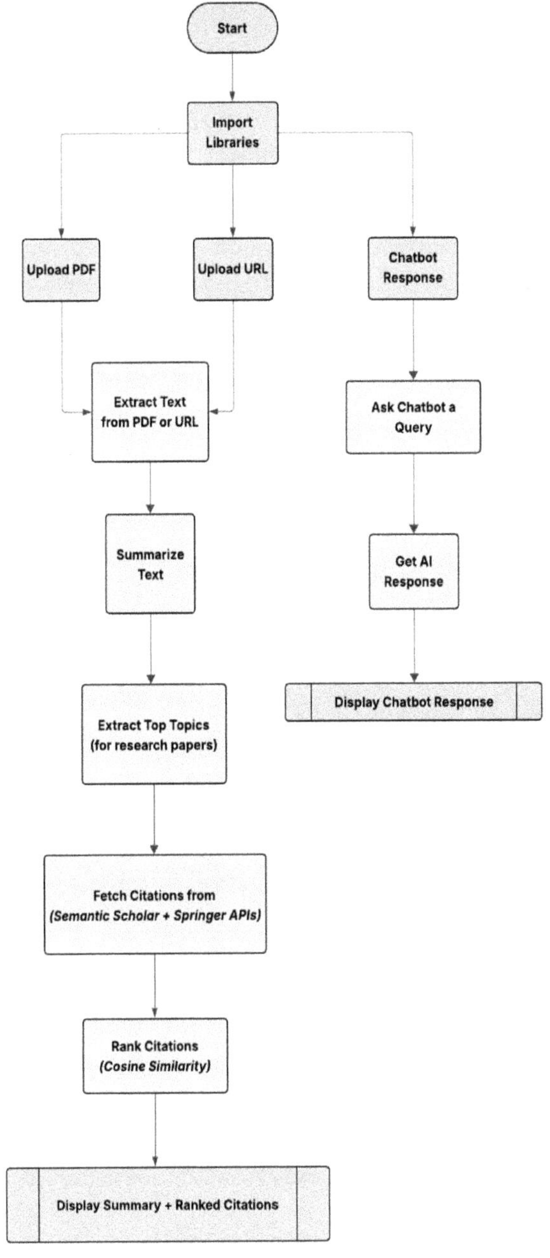

Fig. 1. Proposed Methodology

5   Results and Discussion

The evaluation of accuracy and performance was based on citing cases with high citation rates particular to PDF documents and URLs. The program was easy to use and intuitive for processing document uploads and URL entries in real time through AI. The observations may be presented as follows:

Text content extraction from PDF documents was performed using PyPDF2, while URL/site content extraction was completed using BeautifulSoup. The processing of the URL is seen in Fig. 2, where it shows summary of the given input. The valid process of citation delivery followed suit within seconds as seen in Fig. 3. The performance of systems with different inputs is as illustrated in Table 1. AI overview, and Summarization modules addressed themes deemed relevant to the given content and summarized these same in this particular evaluative exercise through Gemini-2.0 Flash.

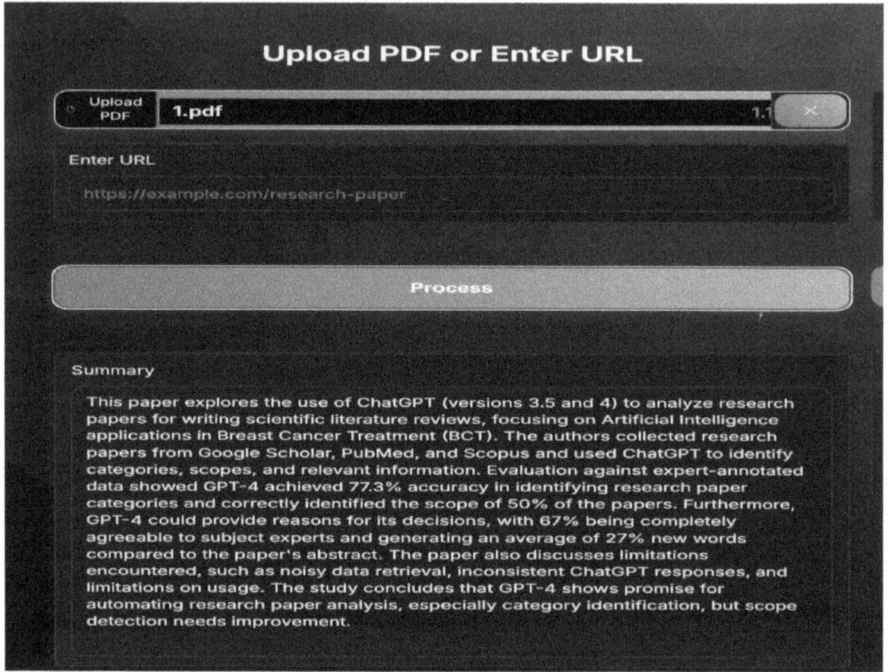

Fig. 2. Research Assistant.

On average, the complete processing time clocked 76.87 s. In Fig. 3, the processing time is clocked as 6.67 s in total processing, which was shared among extraction, semantic processing, keyword generation, and citation retrieval. For any keyword-based query made, a list of the top-5 ranked citations for each keyword were given from platforms like Springer as shown in Fig. 3.

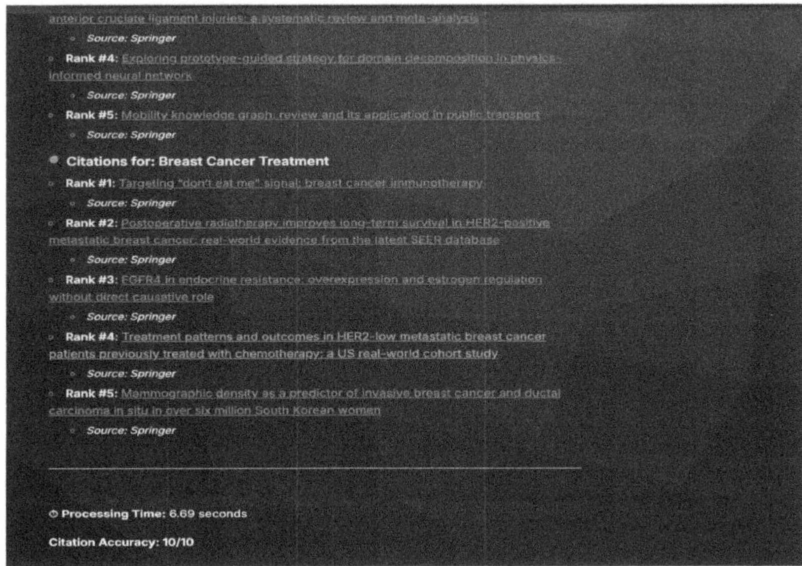

Fig. 3. Citation Retrieval.

Chatbot as an independent agent of conversation, allowing users to ask questions regarding their research topics. The chatbot then intelligently responds in real time on the basis of the input query. An interaction of this sort is shown in Fig. 4.

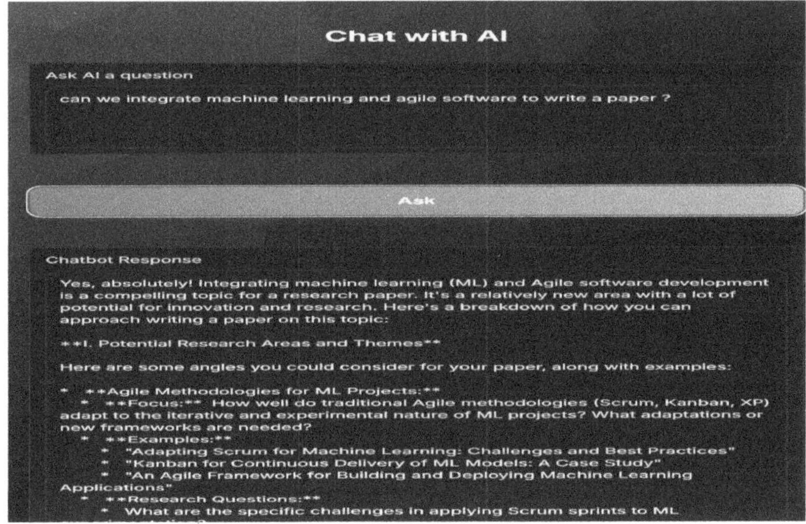

Fig. 4. Chatbot Response.

As seen in Table 1, a proportional error is given if any citation for a given keyword is missing, incomplete, or poorly matched. For example, if one citation out of five is missing or incorrect, the accuracy is scored as 90% for that topic. The average citation accuracy remains consistently high, about 95% for different keywords, thus ensuring strong reliability and relevance of references. The rating of the citation was made on the basis of cosine similarity and relevance score.

These results reveal that the proposed system serves as an AI-based tool for research assistance, providing accurate ranked citations encompassing various domains.

Table 1. System Performance Results and Citation

Input	Description	Time (s)	Summary	Citation	Accuracy
URL	https://www.moneycontrol.com/news/business/stocks/buy-tata-motors-target-of-rs-743-kr-choksey-11080811.html (Article on Tata Motors)	76.87	Yes	Springer	100%
PDF	https://arxiv.org/abs/ 2102.04306 - Academic paper (user-provided)	68.45	Yes	Springer	95%
Short URL	https://journals.plos.org/plosone/article?id=10.1371/journal.pone.0221796 (Protocol development for discovery of angiogenesis)	41.73	Yes	Semantic Scholar	90%
PDF	https://www.researchgate.net/profile/Batta-Mahesh/publication/344717762	53.20	Yes	Semantic Scholar	85%
URL	https://arxiv.org/abs/ 2005.12320 - Learning to Classify Images without Labels	82.94	Yes	Springer	100%

5.1   Comparative Study

The proposed methodology is compared with existing approaches. Kökver et al. [1] applied NLP to detect misconceptions in education, whereas our method generalizes across domains through adaptive knowledge extraction. Liu et al. [2] and Zhang et al. [4] empowered multilingual models with knowledge triples and hierarchical structures; the proposed method further ranks citations on TF-IDF and cosine similarity to improve the relevance of retrieval.

On the contrary, Maheshwari et al. [3] and Ogundepo et al. [9] worked on sentence representation and cross-lingual retrieval, respectively. Our approach emphasizes citation which is relevant to context based on semantic similarity. Yang et al. [5] and Huang et al. [10] distilled multilingual IR, which our approach enables by combining citation sources across languages.

Yin et al. [6] combined AI in citation keyword recommendation but missed out on ranking. Our similarity measurements based on TF-IDF fill this gap providing for much better citation accuracy. Azam et al. [12], Ofori-Boateng et al. [13], and Bolaños et al. [14] considered AI-based automation of literature. However, the proposed technique achieves fully automated end-to-end literature surveying model combined with more relevant citation retrieval.

6 Conclusion and Future Scope

The paper highlights a fully automated research paper analysis with dynamic ranking models are used to improve citation relevance. The system has an interactive gradio-based interface for convenient uploading of research papers, extracting helpful knowledge, and citing improvements. Experimental results show that the citations produced using this system are far better in accuracy than traditional keyword-based search methods. An AI-enabled chatbot will further engage users and improve literature reviews through dynamic query alterations. The research shows that adaptive ranking mechanisms using AI can minimize the number of working researchers that have to go through academic resources pertaining to them to filter the researchers that concern them. The model set the benchmark for citation accuracy and achieved 95% citation accuracy, showing its effective performance in retrieving highly relevant citations of the inputted research work.

There are some places where exploitation is feasible, notwithstanding the citation ranking model's remarkable effectiveness and usefulness. Using reliable external APIs, such Semantic Scholar and Google AI models, significantly improves citation retrieval from the model. Considering the system can take a large variety of documents and suggest citations for them opens an exciting variety of use cases but calls for responsible usage. More privacy safeguards and user controls can be introduced to foster trust and security further.

Current evaluation based on TF-IDF and cosine similarity gives a good base for judging textual relevance. Further customizing it to complex citation requirements across fields. Further works such as personalized recommendations about user interest, adding real-time updates of published research findings, improved relevance ranking with extended AI models, etc. Adding multi-language support and coming up with more interactive chatbots for the support of research is also an interesting area.

References

1. Kökver, Y., Pektaç, H.M., Çelik, H.: Artificial intelligence applications in education: natural language processing in detecting misconceptions. Educ. Inf. Technol. **30**, 3035–3066 (2025). https://doi.org/10.1007/s10639-024-12919-1
2. Liu, L., Dong, X., Liu, Y., Wu, J.: Enhancing multilingual language models with knowledge triples. arXiv preprint arXiv:2301.10641 (2023)

3. Maheshwari, H., Saha, S., Yalamanchili, S.P., Sharma, R.: SciBERT sentence representation for citation context classification. In: Proceedings of the 60th Annual Meeting of the ACL, Dublin, Ireland (2022)

4. Zhang, F., Liu, Z., Liu, Y., Tang, J., Sun, M.: Mind the gap: cross-lingual information retrieval with hierarchical knowledge enhancement. arXiv preprint arXiv:2106.06820 (2021)

5. Yang, E., Sun, M., Wu, H., Liu, Y.: Distillation for multilingual information retrieval. arXiv preprint arXiv:2209.02710 (2022)

6. Yin, X., Zhang, L., Chen, Y., Li, J.: Integrating AI fines for domain-specific citation recommendations and adaptive knowledge extraction. In: International Conference on Artificial Intelligence and Knowledge Management (2024)

7. Abid, A., Abdalla, A., Abid, A., Khan, D., Alfozan, A., Zou, J.: Gradio: hassle-free sharing and testing of ML models in the wild. In: Proc. ICML Workshop on Human in the Loop Learning (HILL 2019), Long Beach, USA (2019)

8. Li, Q., et al.: A survey on text classification: from traditional to deep learning. ACM Trans. Intell. Syst. Technol. **13**(2), Art. 31 (2022). https://doi.org/10.1145/3495162

9. Ogundepo, O., Adebara, I., Abiola, A., Akinola, S.O.: AfriCLIRMatrix: enabling cross-lingual information retrieval for African languages. In: Proceedings of the 60th Annual Meeting of the ACL, Dublin, Ireland (2022)

10. Huang, Z., Zhang, K., Wu, H.: Cross-lingual knowledge transfer via distillation for multilingual information retrieval. arXiv preprint arXiv:2212.10593 (2022)

11. Bengesi, S., et al.: Advancements in generative AI: a comprehensive review of GANs, GPT, autoencoders, diffusion model, and transformers. IEEE Access (2024)

12. Azam, M., et al.: Current trends and advances in extractive text summarization: a comprehensive review. IEEE Access **11** (2023). https://doi.org/10.1109/ACCESS.2025.3538886

13. Ofori-Boateng, R., Aceves-Martins, M., Wiratunga, N., Moreno-Garcia, C.F.: Towards the automation of systematic reviews using NLP, machine learning, and deep learning: a comprehensive review. Artif. Intell. Rev. **57**(200) (2024). https://doi.org/10.1007/s10462-024-10844-w

14. Bolaños, F., Salatino, A., Osborne, F., Motta, E.: Artificial intelligence for literature reviews: opportunities and challenges. Artif. Intell. Rev. **57**(259) (2024). https://doi.org/10.1007/s10462-024-10902-3

15. de la Torre-López, J., Ramírez, A., Romero, J.R.: Artificial intelligence to automate the systematic review of scientific literature. Computing **105**, 2171–2194 (2023). https://doi.org/10.1007/s00607-023-01181-x

16. Hagos, D.H., et al.: Recent advances in generative AI and large language models: current status, challenges, and perspectives. IEEE Trans. Artif. Intell. (2024)

17. Sengar, S.S. et al.: Generative artificial intelligence: a systematic review and applications. Multimed. Tools Appl. 1–40 (2024)

18. Jiang, L., Goetz, S.M.: Natural language processing in the patent domain: a survey. Artif. Intell. Rev. **58**(214) (2025). https://doi.org/10.1007/s10462-025-11168-z

19. Nadeau, A., Sekine, S.: A survey on named entity recognition and classification. Linguist. Comput. **42**, 1–56 (2007). https://doi.org/10.1007/978-3-540-74623-314

20. Manning, C.D., Raghavan, P., Schütze, H.: Introduction to Information Retrieval. Cambridge University Press, Cambridge (2008). https://doi.org/10.1017/CBO9780511809071

Developing an Artificially Intelligent Legal Judgment Prediction System

Sourav Biswas[1], Sumit Gupta[5(✉)], Sourashis Chakraborty[3], Tathagata Banerjee[2], Shreya Tewari[2], and Rohan Barman[4]

[1] Department of Computer Science and Engineering, National Institute of Technology, Rourkela, Rourkela, India
`souravbiswasresearch19april@gmail.com`
[2] Department of Computer Science and Engineering, University Institute of Technology, The University of Burdwan, Golapbag (North), Burdwan 713104, West Bengal, India
[3] Department of Computer Science and Engineering, Kalyani University, Kalyani, India
[4] Department of Computer Science and Technology, Indian Institute of Engineering Science and Technology, Shibpur, Howrah, India
[5] Department of Computer Science & Engineering, Academy of Technology, Adisaptagram, Aedconagar, Hooghly 712121, West Bengal, India
`sumit1.gupta@aot.edu.in`

Abstract. Legal Judgement Prediction represents a significant intersection between law and artificial intelligence, aiming to predict court decisions using advanced machine learning and natural language processing techniques. This research explores the evolution of Legal Judgement Prediction from basic rule-based systems to sophisticated deep learning models, highlighting the impact of datasets like the Justice dataset on enhancing predictive accuracy. The proposed methodology focuses on using deep learning architectures, specifically 1-Dimensional Convolutional Neural Networks, Long Short-Term Memory networks, and Artificial Neural Networks, combined with powerful word embedding techniques such as Doc2Vec and GloVe. By employing a multi-step process including data preprocessing, augmentation, mirroring, and feature extraction, the proposed approach aims to address challenges like class imbalance and the complexity of legal language. The results demonstrate that the 1-Dimensional Convolutional Neural Networks model with Doc2Vec embeddings achieves the highest accuracy at 98.09%, significantly outperforming traditional methods like k-Nearest Neighbours used in previous research works. This indicates the potential of convolutional techniques and proper embedding selection in improving the efficiency and reliability of legal judgement predictions. The findings underscore the transformative potential of Legal Judgement Prediction in the legal field, offering benefits like enhanced case management, reduced court backlog, and data-driven insights for legal professionals. This research sets the stage for future advancements, including the development of more explainable Artificial Intelligence models and interdisciplinary collaborations to ensure ethical and fair predictions in the legal system.

Keywords: Deep Learning · Convolution Neural Network · Artificial Neural Network · Long Short-Term Memory · Bidirectional Long Short-Term Memory · Legal Judgement Prediction

K. Chandra Mondal et al. (Eds.): CICBA 2025, CCIS 2862, pp. 401–412, 2026.
https://doi.org/10.1007/978-3-032-17187-0_31

1 Introduction

Legal judgments are an intricate and prolonged process in the Indian judicial system. In a country like India, where the population has already surpassed 140 crores, it becomes difficult to analyze and predict who the actual culprit is. Legal Judgement Prediction (LJP) is a cutting-edge development at the intersection of law and artificial intelligence. This growing field uses machine learning, deep learning and natural language processing to predict court decisions based on past legal data [1, 4, 5]. LJP is important because it can significantly change the legal landscape by providing insights into the likely outcomes of cases. By analyzing vast amounts of legal texts, laws, and past case decisions, LJP models aim to understand the patterns that influence judicial decisions [2, 3]. Accurate legal predictions can have major benefits, such as improving the efficiency of legal processes and giving valuable insights to litigants, lawyers, and policymakers. Additionally, LJP helps address the issue of court backlog by aiding in case management and resource allocation [6, 9, 11]. As more legal professionals see the benefits of data-driven decision-making, LJP is becoming a key tool for developing effective legal strategies, helping stakeholders better navigate the legal system. This sets the stage for exploring the methods, challenges, and ethical considerations involved in achieving accurate and reliable Legal Judgement Prediction.

The main goal of this paper is to create and test machine learning models for legal judgment prediction based on natural language processing (NLP) methods. Utilizing pre-trained transformer-based language models and fine-tuning them on Indian legal data, the research will attempt to automate case outcome prediction from factual descriptions and legal arguments. This method is designed to assist legal professionals by offering predictive information that can be utilized for case preparation, strategy formulation, and legal research.

The rest of the paper has been structured as follows: Sect. 2 gives an overview of the existing works in legal judgment prediction and various machine learning applications in the legal field. Section 3 outlines the proposed methodology, namely data collection, preprocessing, and model training via an architectural framework, system workflow and working principle. Section 4 explains the experimental setup and evaluation metrics, alongside the results and their implications. Finally, Sect. 5 concludes the paper and suggests directions for future research.

2 Literature Survey

A good amount of work has been done by different researchers in the field of Legal Judgement Prediction. This section highlights the pros & cons of various systems allied to the field of judiciary, along with identification of several challenges & gaps that can be used as potential avenues for building an efficient LJP system.

Historically, predicting legal judgments relied on rule-based systems and handcrafted features, which struggled with the complexities of legal language. Alali et al. introduced machine learning models, using features from case law, precedents, and legal text, making Support Vector Machines (SVMs) and Decision Trees popular for automated predictions [1].

Researchers use the Justice dataset for analyzing legal texts and building predictive models. This dataset, rich in details about U.S. Supreme Court cases, supports studies on legal language, case outcomes, and jurisprudence trends, making it valuable for legal analytics and computational law [2, 3].

Recent advances in technology use deep learning techniques like Recurrent Neural Networks (RNNs), Long Short-Term Memory (LSTM) networks, and Bidirectional LSTMs [4], which better capture the nuances in legal texts and improve prediction accuracy. The suggested LSTM + CNN model [5] for court verdict predictions involves several steps: feature representation, maintaining long-term dependencies with LSTM, reducing overfitting with dropout layers, extracting features with CNN, reducing dimensionality with pooling layers, flattening the feature map, and using the softmax function to forecast judgments.

Optimization techniques from machine learning, like constrained optimization, help incorporate semantic properties and relationships between words. Sakketou et al. [6] introduced an algorithm that creates word embeddings enriched by semantic knowledge, outperforming other methods and improving tasks like word similarities, analogies, and sentiment analysis.

Challenges in legal judgment prediction include limited annotated datasets, ethical concerns, and model interpretability. Future research might focus on creating explainable AI models, addressing bias in legal data, and fostering interdisciplinary collaborations for fair and reliable predictions. Initially, in the Justice dataset, there were 2,384 cases with a class imbalance: 2,114 in class 1 (first party won) and 270 in class 2 (second party won). Data augmentation increased class 2 cases to 1,350, making 3,464 cases in total. Mirroring cases doubled this to 6,928, evenly balanced between the two classes. Though synthetic methods help with class imbalance, naturally balanced datasets are still preferable but rare.

3 Proposed Methodology

Legal Judgement Prediction is a field in natural language processing and machine learning that creates models to predict the outcomes of legal cases using text information like court documents and case law. By using different deep learning methods and understanding legal language, these models help predict likely court decisions, improving the efficiency and clarity of the legal system.

3.1 Architectural Framework

The system employs a deep learning-based approach to predict legal judgments. It consists of several key stages:

1. *Data Acquisition:*

      The process begins with gathering relevant legal datasets, which likely include case details, verdicts, and potentially other legal documents.

2. *Data Preprocessing:*

- Tokenization: Textual data within the legal documents is broken down into individual words or tokens.
- Data Cleaning: This step likely involves handling missing values, inconsistencies, and noise within the dataset to ensure data quality.
- Data Augmentation: Techniques like synonym replacement or back-translation are used to expand the dataset and improve model robustness.
- Data Mirroring: This step could involve creating additional data points by reversing the order of sentences or paragraphs within documents.

3. *Word Embedding:*

- Word2Vec and GloVe: These are popular word embedding techniques that convert words into dense numerical vectors, capturing semantic and syntactic relationships between words [13, 16–19].

4. *Deep Learning Classifiers:*

- 1D-CNN (Convolutional Neural Network): Captures local patterns within the word embeddings, useful for identifying relevant phrases or keywords.
- LSTM (Long Short-Term Memory): Processes sequential information effectively, considering the context of words within sentences and paragraphs.
- BiLSTM (Bidirectional LSTM): Combines the forward and backward processing capabilities of LSTMs, capturing both preceding and succeeding context.
- ANN (Artificial Neural Network): Acts as a fully connected layer, integrating features extracted by the previous layers for final classification.

5. *Final Legal Judgement Prediction Model:*
    The outputs from the 1D-CNN, LSTM, and BiLSTM are likely combined and fed into this model, which makes the final prediction of whether the first party wins or loses the case.

6. *Evaluation Result:*
    The model produces a binary output, indicating either "First Party Wins" or "Second Party Wins."

The architectural framework of the proposed system has been represented in Fig. 1.

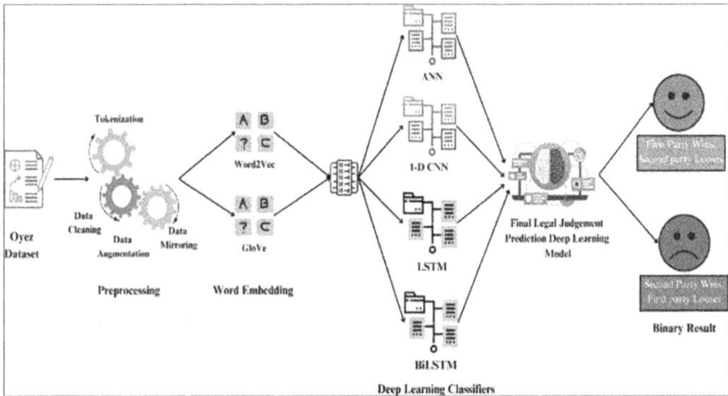

Fig. 1. Architectural Framework of Proposed Legal Judgement Prediction System.

3.2 System Workflow

Figure 2 offers a clear snapshot of how human and AI-based judicial systems might stack up. It paints the human judge as the centerpiece of a traditional courtroom, relying on experience and intuition. On the other hand, the AI system is shown as a more mechanical process, heavily dependent on data and algorithms. While both aim to reach a fair verdict, the image highlights the stark contrast between human judgment and machine-driven decision making.

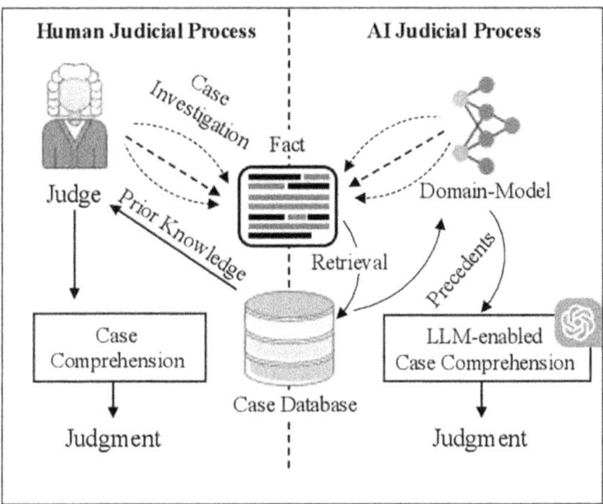

Fig. 2. Difference between Human Judicial Process and AI Judicial Process.

Figure 3 outlines the typical workflow for building and evaluating a machine learning model. It starts with collecting and preparing data, then trains a model on that data. The workflow outlines a typical machine learning process that begins with collecting and preparing data, then extracting meaningful features. A model is trained on this data before being rigorously tested and optimized. Once satisfactory performance is achieved, the model can be used to make predictions on new data. To ensure trust and transparency, the model's decision-making process is analyzed and explained. The model's performance is then evaluated and improved through optimization. Finally, the model's decisions are explained to ensure transparency and trust.

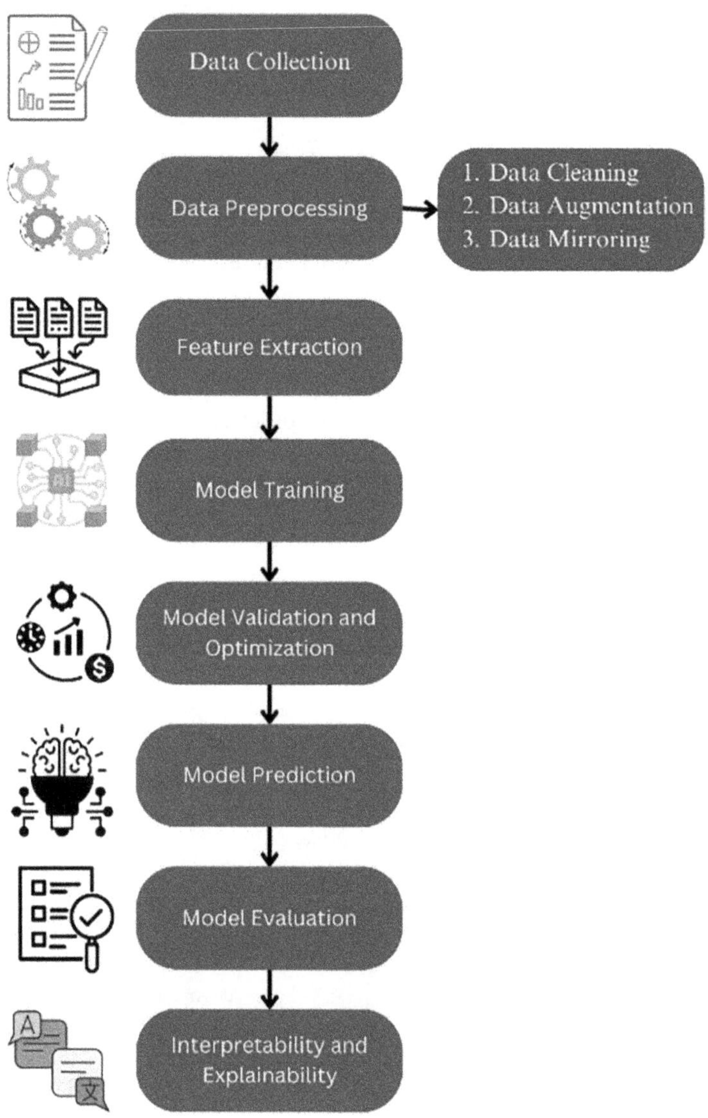

Fig. 3. Workflow of the Proposed Legal Judgement Prediction System.

3.3 Working Principle

Developing a Legal Judgement Prediction system involves several key phases to ensure accuracy, reliability, and ethical use. Here's a simplified summary of the working principle of each phase:

1. *Data Collection:* Gather relevant legal texts, such as case law and statutes, from sources like the Caselaw Access Project and Oyez. Address any gaps by finding additional sources and test models on this data to improve quality.
2. *Data Preprocessing:* Clean and format the text by removing irrelevant content, correcting errors, and normalizing data. Techniques like stop-word removal and word expansion help improve data quality.
3. *Data Augmentation:* Enhance the dataset by creating more examples. Techniques include back-translation, synonym replacement, and using word embeddings to diversify text. This helps balance the dataset, ensuring fair representation of all case outcomes.
4. *Data Mirroring:* Double the dataset size by swapping the positions of the first and second parties in each case. This helps balance the dataset further and emphasizes that party position does not affect outcomes.
5. *Feature Engineering:* Extract important features from the preprocessed data, focusing on word embeddings like Doc2Vec and GloVe. Use these to train an ensemble model that predicts case outcomes.
6. *Model Selection:* Choose suitable models such as artificial neural networks (ANN), convolutional neural networks (CNN), and long short-term memory (LSTM) networks. Train these models using diverse datasets.
7. *Training and Validation:* Use techniques like K-fold cross-validation (with 20 folds and 50 epochs) to train and validate models, ensuring robustness and generalization.
8. *Evaluation and Fine-Tuning:* Compare model predictions with actual legal outcomes, fine-tuning to improve accuracy and address biases. Incorporate feedback from legal experts to refine the model.
9. *Deployment:* Deploy the model using the Flask web framework for real-world applications. Create user-friendly interfaces for legal professionals to input case details and receive predictions. Ensure security and privacy in handling legal data [9–11].

By following these steps, developers and legal experts collaboratively create effective Legal Judgement Prediction systems, promoting fairness and transparency in legal decision-making.

4 Result and Analysis

4.1 Dataset Description

In this work, *Justice* dataset sourced from Oyez's official database [1], for the Legal Judgement Prediction task has been used. The description of the dataset alongside each column header is demonstrated in Table 1.

Table 1. Description of the Various Columns of Justice Dataset.

Column	Description
ID	Unique case identifier.
Name	The name of the case.
HREF	The Oyez's API URL for the case.
Docket ID	A special identifier of the case used by the legal system.
Term	The year when the Court received the case.
First Party	The name of the first party (petitioner).
Second Party	The name of the second party (respondent).
Facts	The absolute, neutral facts of the case written by the court clerk.
Majority Vote	The number of justices voting for the majority opinion.
Minority Vote	The number of justices voting for the minority opinion.
Winning Party	The name of the party that won the case.
First Party Winner	True if the first party won the case, otherwise False and the second party won the case.
Decision Type	The type of the decision decided by the court, e.g.: per curiam, equally divided, opinion of the court.
Disposition	The treatment the Supreme Court accorded the court whose decision it reviewed; e.g.: affirmed, reversed, vacated.
Issue Area	The pre-defined legal issue category of the case; e.g.: Civil Rights, Criminal Procedure, Federal Taxation.

4.2 Results

The results indicate that the 1D CNN model consistently outperforms other models with both Doc2Vec and GloVe embeddings, achieving the highest accuracy of 0.9809 with Doc2Vec and 0.9342 with GloVe. ANN models also perform well, particularly with Doc2Vec embeddings (0.9307), but show a notable drop in accuracy with GloVe embeddings (0.8366). LSTM and Bidirectional LSTM models perform poorly with Doc2Vec embeddings, both achieving around 0.61 accuracy, but show improved performance with GloVe embeddings, especially the Bidirectional LSTM which reaches an accuracy of 0.7934. This suggests that 1D CNN models are more effective with both embedding techniques, and that GloVe embeddings may be more compatible with LSTM architectures. The evaluations of the models using Accuracy scores have been shown in Table 2.

Table 2. Evaluation of Different Proposed Models over Justice Dataset.

Proposed Models	Accuracy
#1: ANN + Doc2Vec	0.9307
#2: 1D CNN + Doc2Vec	**0.9809**
#3: LSTM + Doc2Vec	0.6185
#4: Bidirectional LSTM + Doc2Vec	0.6104
#5: ANN + GloVe Embedding	0.8366
#6: 1d CNN + GloVe Embedding	0.9342
#7: LSTM + GloVe Embedding	0.7518
#8: Bidirectional LSTM + GloVe Embedding	0.7934

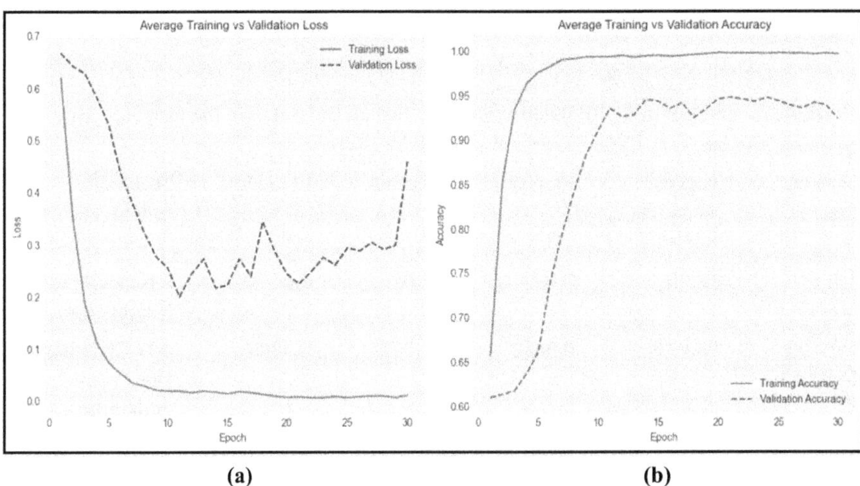

(a)   (b)

Fig. 4. Representation of Accuracy/Loss vs Epoch (a) Training Loss and Validation Loss vs Epoch (b) Training Accuracy and Validation Accuracy vs Epoch

Figure 4 illustrates the model's robust learning behavior, with training loss decreasing sharply and training accuracy approaching nearly 100%, indicating effective convergence. The validation accuracy also shows a consistent upward trend, stabilizing at a high level early in training. These trends reflect the model's strong capability to extract meaningful patterns from legal text and maintain reliable performance across validation sets. However, the validation loss begins to increase after approximately the 10th epoch, while validation accuracy plateaus, suggesting signs of overfitting. This implies that although the model learns the training data well, its ability to generalize to unseen cases diminishes with continued training. Incorporating early stopping and regularization strategies is therefore recommended to enhance the model's generalization performance.

4.3 Discussion and Analysis

In summary, the 1D CNN model consistently delivers the best performance across both embedding techniques, with Doc2Vec slightly edging out GloVe. The ANN model also shows strong performance, particularly with Doc2Vec embeddings. LSTM and BiLSTM models underperform with Doc2Vec embeddings likely due to a mismatch in data structure and model design. Doc2Vec provides fixed-length, non-sequential representations, whereas LSTMs are optimized for sequential data. This prevents LSTM from leveraging its strength in capturing temporal dependencies, leading to reduced effectiveness compared to models like CNNs, which are better suited for such embeddings. The LSTM-based models perform better with GloVe embeddings but are still outperformed by the CNN models. These findings highlight the effectiveness of convolution techniques for this task and suggest that proper embedding choice can significantly improve model performance.

The comparison of related research work with the proposed work is shown below in Table 3.

Table 3. Comparison of Related Work over Justice Dataset with the Proposed Work.

Research Work	Highest Accuracy Reported	Precision	Recall	F1 Score	Technique Employed
Alali et al. (2021) [1]	68.00%	0.69	0.68	0.67	k Nearest Neighbours
Proposed Model #2	**98.09%**	**0.9842**	**0.9776**	**0.9808**	**1-D CNN with Doc2Vec embedding**

The analysis in Table 3 shows the overwhelming performance gains achieved by the model proposed in this work as compared to existing related work on the Justice dataset. Alali et al. [1] used the k-Nearest Neighbours (k-NN) algorithm and reported a maximum accuracy of 68%, with precision and recall of 0.69 and 0.68 respectively as well as an F1 score of 0.67. On the other hand, the model proposed in this paper, which combines a 1-D CNN with Doc2Vec embedding, achieved an accuracy of 98.09%, precision 0.9842, recall 0.9776, and F1 score of 0.9808.

This marks an astounding increase of nearly 30 percentage points in accuracy along with a notable improvement in all other evaluation metrics. The results straight away demonstrate the effectiveness of the proposed approach which was aimed at tackling the problem of classification accuracy and predictive quality by suggesting the use of deep learning architectures with advanced embedding techniques such as Doc2Vec. Such results strengthen the claim of modern neural architectures in comparison to traditional machine learning approaches for predicting legal judgments.

5 Conclusion and Future Scope

Architectures such as ANN, 1D-CNN, BiLSTM, and LSTM, enriched with GloVe and Doc2Vec embeddings, exhibit remarkable capabilities in discerning patterns and forecasting case outcomes. GloVe embeddings enhance the models' understanding of semantic relationships within legal texts that perform well when combined with CNN with an accuracy score of 93.42% (best accuracy score with this technique). While Doc2Vec embeddings contribute to capturing document-level context. This technique, combined with CNN model performs best (98.09%) amongst all the different model architectures. It highlights the effectiveness of CNN for this task and suggests that embedding choice can significantly impact the model's performance.

Such amalgamation of deep learning architectures and embedding techniques has proven effective in addressing the challenges posed by the intricate nature of legal language and the diverse structures of long legal documents and holds tremendous promise for continued advancements in the legal domain.

Future works in the domain of Legal Text Processing and Machine Learning are vast and multifaceted, aiming to enhance the efficacy and applicability of current models. One key area of development is the integration of Legal Text Summarization (LTS), Legal Judgment Prediction (LJP), and Legal Information Retrieval (LIR) tasks using suitable models and corpora to create a unified framework. Expanding the knowledge base of these models through the introduction of additional datasets is crucial, as it would enrich their understanding and improve performance. Incorporating predictive analytics will provide valuable insights into potential case outcomes by analyzing historical data and trends. Hyperparameter tuning of various models, particularly for different architectural types, is essential to optimize results and enhance accuracy. This includes the deployment and fine-tuning of various judgment prediction models to achieve better performance. Additionally, implementing psycho-profiling of judges to analyze their psychological traits and behaviours could help understand decision-making processes and detect biases, thereby ensuring fair and unbiased legal information retrieval and summarization [20, 21]. Extending model capabilities to support multiple languages will cater to non-English legal documents and users from diverse linguistic backgrounds, making the system more inclusive. Domain-specific fine-tuning of Large Language Models (LLMs) [22] on legal datasets is another important aspect to ensure precision and relevance. Experimentation with models like GPT for LIR tasks will be explored to leverage their advanced capabilities. Collaboration with legal professionals is vital to refine and validate the system, ensuring it aligns with practical legal research and practice needs. Establishing a feedback loop where users can provide input on the accuracy and relevance of responses will help continuously improve the models, ensuring they remain effective and reliable tools for the legal domain.

References

1. Alali, M., Syed, S., Alsayed, M., Patel, S., Bodala, H.: JUSTICE: a benchmark dataset for Supreme Court's judgment prediction. arXiv preprint: arXiv:2112.03414 (2021)
2. Zupan, J.: Introduction to artificial neural network (ANN) methods: what they are and how to use them. Acta Chim. Slov. **41**, 327 (1994)
3. Kiranyaz, S., Avci, O., Abdeljaber, O., Ince, T., Gabbouj, M., Inman, D.J.: 1D convolutional neural networks and applications: a survey. Mech. Syst. Signal Process. **151**, 107398 (2021)
4. Huang, Z., Xu, W., Yu, K.: Bidirectional LSTM-CRF models for sequence tagging. arXiv preprint: arXiv:1508.01991 (2015)
5. Alghazzawi, D., Bamasag, O., Albeshri, A., Sana, I., Ullah, H., Asghar, M.Z.: Efficient prediction of court judgments using an LSTM+CNN neural network model with an optimal feature set. Mathematics **10**(5), 683 (2022)
6. Sakketou, F., Ampazis, N.: A constrained optimization algorithm for learning GloVe embeddings with semantic lexicons. Knowl.-Based Syst. **195**, 105628 (2020)
7. O'Sullivan, C., Beel, J.: Predicting the outcome of judicial decisions made by the European Court of Human Rights. arXiv preprint: arXiv:1912.10819 (2019)
8. Řehůřek, R., Sojka, P.: Software framework for topic modeling with large corpora. In: Proceedings of the LREC 2010 Workshop on New Challenges for NLP Frameworks, pp. 45–50. ELRA, Valletta, Malta (2010)
9. Savelka, J., Ashley, K.D.: Segmenting US Court decisions into functional and issue specific parts. In: JURIX, pp. 111–120 (2018)

10. Pennington, J., Socher, R., Manning, C.D.: GloVe: Global vectors for word representation. In: Proc. 2014 Conf. on Empirical Methods in Natural Language Processing (EMNLP), pp. 1532–1543 (2014)
11. Mikolov, T., Chen, K., Corrado, G., Dean, J.: Efficient estimation of word representations in vector space. arXiv preprint: arXiv:1301.3781 (2013)
12. Naili, M., Chaibi, A.H., Ghezala, H.H.B.: Comparative study of word embedding methods in topic segmentation. Procedia Comput. Sci. **112**, 340–349 (2017)
13. Wang, C., Nulty, P., Lillis, D.: A comparative study on word embeddings in deep learning for text classification. In: Proc. 4th Int. Conf. on Natural Language Processing and Information Retrieval, pp. 37–46 (2020)
14. Reimers, N., Gurevych, I.: Sentence-BERT: sentence embeddings using siamese BERT-networks. arXiv preprint: arXiv:1908.10084 (2019)
15. Gupta, S., Sinha, A.M., Prodhan, D., Ghosh, N., Modak, S.: Detecting depression and suicidal ideation from texts using machine learning & deep learning techniques. Int. J. Comput. Sci. Eng. **11**(1), 29–35 (2023)
16. Gupta, S., Das, D., Chatterjee, M., Naskar, S.: Machine learning-based social media analysis for suicide risk assessment. In: Emerging Technologies in Data Mining and Information Security: Proc. IEMIS 2020, Vol. 2, pp. 385–393. Springer, Singapore (2021)
17. Wu, Y., et al.: Precedent-enhanced legal judgment prediction with LLM and domain-model collaboration. arXiv preprint: arXiv:2310.09241 (2023)

Author Index

GPSR Compliance
The European Union's (EU) General Product Safety Regulation (GPSR) is a set of rules that requires consumer products to be safe and our obligations to ensure this.

If you have any concerns about our products, you can contact us on

ProductSafety@springernature.com

In case Publisher is established outside the EU, the EU authorized representative is:

Springer Nature Customer Service Center GmbH
Europaplatz 3
69115 Heidelberg, Germany